# INDEPENDENT SCHOOLS –
# LAW, CUSTOM AND PRACTICE

# INDEPENDENT SCHOOLS –
# LAW, CUSTOM AND PRACTICE

**Robert Boyd**

JORDANS
1998

Published by
Jordan Publishing Limited
21 St Thomas Street
Bristol BS1 6JS

**British Cataloguing-in-Publication Data**

A catalogue record for this book is available
from the British Library.

ISBN 0 85308 523 4

The publishers would like to thank Shrewsbury School for allowing them to use
photographs from its prospectus in the cover design for this book.

Photoset by Mendip Communications Ltd, Frome, Somerset
Printed by MPG Books Ltd, Bodmin, Cornwall.

# Dedication

To my wife Marilyn, and my children James, Alexander and Eleanor, for their education.

# Preface

This book, the first of its kind, sets out to explain the law and the related custom and practice applicable to independent schools, their staff, parents and pupils, and those who are concerned with the schools' governance and management.

The key differences between an independent school and one that is State-funded are to do with its method of regulation and its funding. Independent schools are not, for the most part, affected by the Education Acts or by DfEE circulars. Instead, they are regulated by their governing instrument, the policies of the governors, their procedures and practices, their contracts with parents and by the general law of the land, including compliance legislation and the Charities Act 1993, where applicable.

The net effect is that the head of an independent school has *genuine* – and not merely residual – authority to make and enforce rules about such matters as admissions, the curriculum, behaviour and discipline, expulsion or the requirement to leave, disciplinary appeals, and teachers' pay and conditions. The contract for educational services between an independent school and parents is an *enforceable* contract, unlike home/school agreements that are sometimes used in the State-funded sector.

As to funding, most independent schools have little expendable endowment. In financial terms, their very existence depends on the goodwill and confidence of the parents who pay the fees, and of the pupils. Quite simply, an independent school must satisfy its customers or it will soon close.

Thus, the right to self-regulation and the ability to make enforceable contracts with parents and collect fees are fundamental to the acknowledged success of the schools in this sector. Those rights have been challenged in a number of ways during the 1990s, a decade that has been marked by an unprecedented increase in education-related litigation, new statutes and regulations and political intervention, all now to be overlaid by the Human Rights Act 1998. 'Education law' has become a legal classification in its own right, with two new sets of dedicated law reports, a number of new textbooks, mainly covering the State-funded sector, and several new periodicals; but until now, little has been written for independent schools alone.

I hope, therefore, that this book will be of use – both for general information about the law and also as a practical reference guide – to governors, heads, bursars, directors of finance and members of senior management teams; and also to their professional bodies, and all who work or have an interest in independent schools. The book recognises that every independent school has its own unique culture, although many areas of custom and practice are common throughout the sector.

I have tried to avoid over-detailed legal analysis, preferring in many instances to deal with the practical aspects of the case-law. Cases referred to as 'advisory' or 'anecdotal' are usually those in which my firm has advised but which have not necessarily gone to litigation. To reduce the need for cross-references, I have on occasions repeated quotations from statute and case-law. I have steered clear of certain matters that are strictly heads' or bursars' business such as the curriculum and inspections. I have not dealt with the detailed law of employment, which is fully covered in other recent text books, nor have I always identified differences in the legislation governing Scotland and Wales. References to charitable law will not apply to non-charitable private schools. Much of the book will be relevant also to special schools that are independent or non-maintained, but the detail of their compliance legislation is a separate specialty, and not covered.

Finally, any mistakes are my own and will be corrected in future editions. I have not consciously acceded to the demands of political correctness and have aimed for syntax that is gender-neutral.

The law is stated as at 1 November 1998.

Robert Boyd
*Bristol*
*November 1998*

# Acknowledgements

I am grateful to the many governors, heads and bursars who have encouraged me to persevere through the summer evenings and weekends of the last 2 years in between a busy legal practice and our seminar programme at Veale Wasbrough, and to my family for their forbearance.

Particular thanks for material contributions are due to Peter Anwyl, District Judge Gordon Ashton, Mike Davies, Susan Hampton, Beverley Morgan, Sister Frances Orchard, and Bob Repper.

For their information, comments and encouragement I should like also to thank Bob Acheson, Vivian Anthony, David Banwell, Nick Bawtree, Ian Beer, Brian Bissell, Audrey Butler, Crispin Champion, David Collyer, Alistair Cooke, Jim Corbett, Mike Coward, David Crawford, Madeleine Evans, Judith Franklin, Tim Ham, David Hanson, John Hawkins, Arthur Hearndon, Tim Hoult, Danice Iles, David Jewell, Barry Lane, Jackie Lang, James Macpherson, Helen Madaras, Hugh Monro, Frank Morgan, Jeremy Nichols, Penelope Penney, Mike Sant, Tony Smith, Murray Smythe, Andrew Thornhill, Vicky Tuck, Stephen Winkley, and many others.

I must acknowledge the immense value of Neville Harris's book *The Law Relating to Schools* (Tolley, 1995) as a source of information about the law applicable to the State sector, and also the book by Richard Gold and Stephen Szemerenyi *Running a School 1998* (Jordans, 1997); and the Education section in the Central Library in Bristol, which provided everything I could have asked for; and the advice of John Friel and Tanya Callman, both of counsel, in the cases we have dealt with together.

I am also grateful to HarperCollins for granting permission to publish extracts from Dr John Rae's books, *Delusions of Grandeur* (1993) and *Letters to Parents* (1998).

I should like to thank Martin West of Jordans for seeing the project through and Jo Morton, Senior Editor, for her improvements and for dealing with last-minute changes occasioned by new legislation and case-law.

My colleagues in the Schools Unit at Veale Wasbrough have been magnificent and, in particular, Alison Castrey, but thanks above all go to my secretary Karen Usher who has processed almost every word of the book and has done so with unfailing patience and good humour.

Robert Boyd
*Bristol*
*November 1998*

# Contents

DEDICATION                                                    v
PREFACE                                                      vii
ACKNOWLEDGEMENTS                                              ix
TABLE OF CASES                                              xxix
TABLE OF STATUTES                                         xxxvii
TABLE OF STATUTORY INSTRUMENTS                             xliii
TABLE OF EC MATERIAL                                         xlv
TABLE OF ABBREVIATIONS                                     xlvii

**Part 1   THE DEVELOPMENT OF INDEPENDENT SCHOOLS**

Chapter 1      HISTORICAL CONTEXT                              3

1.1    The early schools                                      3
       1.1.1    The Middle Ages                               3
       1.1.2    The Renaissance                               4
1.2    The boys' public school system from 1600              5
1.3    The girls' public schools from 1650                   8
1.4    The 'progressive schools'                            12

Chapter 2      THE CHARACTERISTICS OF THE PUBLIC SCHOOLS     13

2.1    'Public schools' and related terminology             13
       2.1.1    Meaning of 'school'                          13
       2.1.2    Meaning of 'independent school'              13
       2.1.3    Meaning of 'public school'                   14
       2.1.4    Meaning of 'college', 'collegiate', 'academy' and
                'foundation'                                 15
       2.1.5    Closed communities                           16
2.2    The characteristics                                   17
       2.2.1    Cost                                         17
       2.2.2    Predominantly boarding                       17
       2.2.3    Location                                     17
       2.2.4    All boys                                     18
       2.2.5    The type of education                        18
       2.2.6.   House system                                 18
       2.2.7    Prefectorial system                          18
       2.2.8    The importance of games                      19
       2.2.9    Pre-service military training                19
       2.2.10   Training in community life                   19

2.2.11     Religious training                                    19

Chapter 3     DEVELOPMENTS IN EDUCATION 1860–1944          21

3.1     Elementary education                                     21
3.2     The national secondary system                            21
3.3     Two World Wars                                           23
        3.3.1     World War I (1914–18)                          23
        3.3.2     Between the Wars (1919–39)                     23
        3.3.3     World War II (1939–45)                         25

Chapter 4     EDUCATION FROM 1945 TO THE PRESENT          29

4.1     The post-war years                                       29
        4.1.1     Aftermath                                      29
        4.1.2     Independent schools                            29
        4.1.3     State secondary schooling                      30
4.2     Independent schools                                      31
        4.2.1     The 1960s and 1970s                            31
        4.2.2     The 1980s onwards                              32
        4.2.3     The rise of day-schools                        33
        4.2.4     The future                                     34

**Part 2   THE CONTRACT FOR EDUCATIONAL SERVICES**

Chapter 5     INTRODUCTION TO THE PARENT CONTRACT         39

5.1     Overview                                                 39
        5.1.1     Main features                                  39
        5.1.2     Opportunity                                    39
5.2     What is a contract?                                      40
5.3     The terms of a contract                                  41
        5.3.1     Express and implied terms                      41
        5.3.2     Unfair contract terms                          43
5.4     Some other aspects of contracts                          44
        5.4.1     Exclusion clauses                              44
        5.4.2     Misrepresentation                              44
        5.4.3     Contracts induced by mistake                   45
        5.4.4     Duress and undue influence                     45
        5.4.5     Illegal and void contracts                     45
        5.4.6     The capacity of children to enter contracts    46
5.5     Privity of contract                                      46
        5.5.1     Suing on a cheque                              46
        5.5.2     Agency                                         47
        5.5.3     Collateral contract                            47
5.6     Performance and the time for performance of a contract   48
        5.6.1     The contractual obligations                    48
        5.6.2     Substantial performance                        48
        5.6.3     The time for performance                       49
5.7     Termination of contract                                  49
5.8     Frustration of contract                                  49

| | | | |
|---|---|---|---|
| | 5.8.1 | Frustrating events | 50 |
| | 5.8.2 | Events that will not frustrate a contract | 51 |
| | 5.8.3 | The Law Reform (Frustrated Contracts) Act 1943 | 52 |
| 5.9 | | Breach of contract | 53 |
| 5.10 | | Unilateral variation of a contract | 54 |
| 5.11 | | Contractual remedies | 55 |
| | 5.11.1 | Action by the school for an agreed sum | 55 |
| | 5.11.2 | Action by the school for liquidated damages | 55 |
| | 5.11.3 | Claim by school or parent on a *quantum meruit* | 56 |
| | 5.11.4 | Claim for unliquidated damages | 57 |
| | 5.11.5 | Specific performance and injunction | 58 |

**Chapter 6    FORMATION OF THE CONTRACT    59**

| | | | |
|---|---|---|---|
| 6.1 | | Introduction | 59 |
| 6.2 | | Overview | 59 |
| 6.3 | | The parties to the contract | 60 |
| | 6.3.1 | Scope | 60 |
| | 6.3.2 | The school as a party | 60 |
| | 6.3.3 | The parents | 61 |
| | 6.3.4 | The pupil | 61 |
| | 6.3.5 | Third parties | 62 |
| 6.4 | | Formalities and documents | 63 |
| | 6.4.1 | Formation | 63 |
| | 6.4.2 | The prospectus | 63 |
| | 6.4.3 | The contractual offer | 65 |
| | 6.4.4 | The offer letter | 65 |
| | 6.4.5 | The acceptance form | 69 |
| | 6.4.6 | The standard terms and conditions | 70 |
| | 6.4.7 | Fees forms | 72 |
| | 6.4.8 | Policies | 73 |
| | 6.4.9 | Custom and practice | 74 |

**Chapter 7    ADMISSION, ENTRY AND ATTENDANCE    75**

| | | | |
|---|---|---|---|
| 7.1 | | Introduction | 75 |
| 7.2 | | Overview | 75 |
| 7.3 | | Selection of pupils | 76 |
| 7.4 | | Discrimination on grounds of race, sex or disability | 76 |
| | 7.4.1 | The main legislation | 76 |
| | 7.4.2 | Some relevant cases | 78 |
| | 7.4.3 | Access to sporting activities | 78 |
| 7.5 | | Admissions policy | 78 |
| | 7.5.1 | Criteria for admission | 78 |
| | 7.5.2 | Matters that should not be included in the admission criteria | 80 |
| | 7.5.3 | HIV, AIDS, hepatitis and haemophilia | 80 |
| 7.6 | | Admission and entry procedures | 82 |
| 7.7 | | Some problems encountered over admissions | 84 |
| 7.8 | | Legal compliance | 84 |

| | | |
|---|---|---|
| 7.8.1 | Compulsory school age | 84 |
| 7.8.2 | Parents' duty to educate | 85 |
| 7.8.3 | Registered pupils | 85 |
| 7.8.4 | Admission register | 85 |
| 7.8.5 | Deletions from the admission register | 86 |
| 7.8.6 | Attendance register | 86 |
| 7.8.7 | Absences | 86 |
| 7.8.8 | Inspection and use | 87 |

| | | | |
|---|---|---|---|
| Chapter 8 | | THE SCHOOL COMMUNITY | 89 |
| 8.1 | Introduction | | 89 |
| 8.2 | Aspects of community | | 89 |
| | 8.2.1 | Background | 89 |
| | 8.2.2 | Characteristics | 90 |
| | 8.2.3 | Authority of the head | 93 |
| | 8.2.4 | Limitations to authority | 94 |
| | 8.2.5 | Undermining the head's authority | 95 |
| 8.3 | Aspects of the head's duty and authority | | 95 |
| | 8.3.1 | Sources | 95 |
| | 8.3.2 | Powers and duties under the Children Act 1989 | 95 |
| | 8.3.3 | Duties under the Health and Safety at Work etc Act 1974 | 95 |
| | 8.3.4 | Admissions | 96 |
| | 8.3.5 | Setting the curriculum | 96 |
| | 8.3.6 | Setting regulations and sanctions | 97 |
| | 8.3.7 | Ethos and culture | 97 |
| | 8.3.8 | School security | 97 |
| | 8.3.9 | *In loco parentis* | 98 |
| | 8.3.10 | Requiring a medical examination | 98 |
| | 8.3.11 | Reports, references and confidence | 99 |
| | 8.3.12 | Engaging and dismissing staff | 99 |
| | 8.3.13 | Delegation of tasks | 99 |
| | 8.3.14 | Collective worship and religious education | 100 |
| | 8.3.15 | School fees | 100 |
| | 8.3.16 | Pupil's records | 100 |
| 8.4 | Rights and duties of parents and pupils | | 101 |
| | 8.4.1 | Satisfactory standards | 101 |
| | 8.4.2 | Acting reasonably | 102 |
| | 8.4.3 | Supporting the head's authority | 102 |
| | 8.4.4 | Consultation and communication | 103 |
| | 8.4.5 | Community aspects | 103 |
| | 8.4.6 | Compliance with rules and policies | 104 |
| | 8.4.7 | Financial obligations | 104 |
| | 8.4.8 | Notice of withdrawal | 104 |
| | 8.4.9 | Reasonable expectations | 105 |
| | 8.4.10 | Intellectual property rights | 105 |
| | 8.4.11 | Domestic circumstances | 105 |
| | 8.4.12 | Withholding property and information | 106 |

8.4.13   Child's rights v parents' rights            106
8.4.14   Complaints                                   107

Chapter 9      SCHOOL FEES                            109

9.1    Introduction                                   109
9.2    Meaning of 'fee' and 'deposit'                 109
9.3    Registration fee                               109
9.4    The acceptance deposit                         110
       9.4.1    Cancellation on a term's notice       110
       9.4.2    Cancellation on less than a term's notice   111
9.5    Additional deposit                             111
9.6    Deposits for overseas pupils                   111
9.7    Discounted places                              112
9.8    School fees                                    112
       9.8.1    The fees list                         112
       9.8.2    Extras, charges and disbursements     113
       9.8.3    Damage done by the pupil              113
       9.8.4    Boarding and tuition fees             113
       9.8.5    Do the rules of *quantum meruit* apply to school fees?   113
       9.8.6    The time for payment of fees          114
       9.8.7    Exclusion for non-payment of fees     114
       9.8.8    Refund and waiver of fees             115
       9.8.9    Walking out                           115
       9.8.10   Fees increases                        116
       9.8.11   Responsibility for payment of fees    117
       9.8.12   Parents who are divorced              117
       9.8.13   Other third parties                   118
       9.8.14   Guarantors of the fees                119
       9.8.15   Interest, administration and legal costs following late
                payment                               119
       9.8.16   Short payment and payments on account 120
       9.8.17   Scholarships, bursaries and assisted places   121
       9.8.18   Lump-sum prepayments and composition of fees   121
       9.8.19   Payment of fees by instalments        121

Chapter 10     NOTICE AND FEES IN LIEU OF NOTICE      123

10.1   Introduction                                   123
10.2   The notice rule                                123
10.3   The reasons for the rule                       123
       10.3.1   The governors                         123
       10.3.2   The parents                           124
       10.3.3   The authorities                       125
10.4   Unfair Terms in Consumer Contracts Regulations 1994   127
10.5   The rate of fees in lieu of notice             128
10.6   When are fees in lieu of notice payable?       129
10.7   The period of notice                           130
10.8   The notice period for extra tuition            131
10.9   The form of notice                             131

10.10   Timing                                                         132
10.11   Provisional notice                                             132
10.12   Cancelling acceptance of a place                               133
10.13   When the pupil decides to leave                                134
10.14   Common disputes over fees in lieu of notice                    134
        10.14.1   Cancellation of acceptance of a place                134
        10.14.2   Counting weeks                                       134
        10.14.3   The rate of fees in lieu                             134
        10.14.4   Complaints about change                              134
        10.14.5   The family leaving the area                          134
        10.14.6   Alleged defective teaching                           134
        10.14.7   Complete breakdown of education at the school        135
        10.14.8   The pupil was unhappy and/or became ill              135
        10.14.9   Alleged defect in formation of contract              135
        10.14.10  The place has been filled                            135
        10.14.11  Discounting extra tuition                            135
        10.14.12  Parental contribution                                135
        10.14.13  Disputes over the notice given                       136
        10.14.14  Provisional notice                                   136
        10.14.15  League tables                                        136
        10.14.16  Allegations of discrimination                        136
        10.14.17  Bussing in                                           136
        10.14.18  Alleged defamation                                   136
        10.14.19  Bogus qualifications of teacher                      136
        10.14.20  Scholarship withdrawn without justification          137
        10.14.21  Notice of fees increase                              137
        10.14.22  Preserving confidentiality                           137
        10.14.23  School-leaving age                                   137

Chapter 11    CARE AND SUPERVISION OF CHILDREN AT
              SCHOOL                                                   139

11.1    Introduction                                                   139
11.2    The law of negligence                                          139
        11.2.1    Overview                                             139
        11.2.2    Proving negligence                                   140
11.3    The existence of a duty of care                                141
        11.3.1    Reasonable foreseeability of harm                    141
        11.3.2    Legal proximity or neighbourhood                     143
        11.3.3    Whether it is just and reasonable to impose a duty of
                  care                                                 144
11.4    The standard of care                                           145
        11.4.1    The careful parent                                   145
        11.4.2    The teacher as a professional                        146
        11.4.3    Some relevant cases                                  147
        11.4.4    Objective standard                                   148
11.5    Negligence in practice                                         150
        11.5.1    Balancing and minimising risk                        150
        11.5.2    Negligence and contributory negligence of children   153

| | | |
|---|---|---|
| 11.6 | Breach of the duty of care | 154 |
| | 11.6.1 Vicarious liability | 155 |
| | 11.6.2 Necessity | 156 |
| | 11.6.3 Warnings, exemption clauses and disclaimers | 155 |
| | 11.6.4 *Volenti non fit injuria* | 155 |
| | 11.6.5 Statutory authority | 155 |
| | 11.6.6 Contributory negligence | 157 |
| | 11.6.7 Other defences | 157 |
| 11.7 | Causation and damage | 157 |
| | 11.7.1 Causation generally | 157 |
| | 11.7.2 Damage suffered by a pupil | 159 |
| 11.8 | Measure of damages | 161 |
| | 11.8.1 The purpose of damages | 161 |
| | 11.8.2 Damages for personal injuries | 162 |
| 11.9 | Particular situations | 163 |
| | 11.9.1 Children wandering | 163 |
| | 11.9.2 Supervision before the start of the school day | 163 |
| | 11.9.3 Responsibility during break times and lunch times | 164 |
| | 11.9.4 Responsibility after school hours | 166 |
| | 11.9.5 Out-of-school activities | 166 |
| | 11.9.6 Supervision on school transport | 167 |
| | 11.9.7 Some particular circumstances | 167 |
| | 11.9.8 Supervision ratios | 169 |
| | 11.9.9 Sports and games injuries | 169 |
| 11.10 | Safety of school premises | 174 |
| | 11.10.1 Negligence and breach of statutory duty | 174 |
| | 11.10.2 Occupier's liability | 175 |
| Chapter 12 | TEACHERS AND PROFESSIONAL LIABILITY | 179 |
| 12.1 | Introduction | 179 |
| 12.2 | Nature of professional liability | 179 |
| | 12.2.1 The professional standard | 179 |
| | 12.2.2 Teachers | 180 |
| 12.3 | Contract and tort | 181 |
| | 12.3.1 Overview | 181 |
| | 12.3.2 Professional negligence in contract | 182 |
| | 12.3.3 Professional negligence in tort | 183 |
| 12.4 | Learning difficulties | 184 |
| | 12.4.1 Special needs legislation | 184 |
| | 12.4.2 The case-law | 185 |
| | 12.4.3 Social aspects of learning difficulties | 192 |
| | 12.4.4 Policy on learning difficulties | 193 |
| 12.5 | Teaching standards | 194 |
| | 12.5.1 National Curriculum | 194 |
| | 12.5.2 Curriculum policies | 195 |
| | 12.5.3 Substandard teaching | 196 |
| | 12.5.4 Examination disappointment | 196 |
| | 12.5.5 Changes of teacher | 196 |

|        | 12.5.6 | Inability to keep order | 197 |
| 12.6   | Withholding examination results | | 197 |
| 12.7   | Wrongful expulsion | | 198 |
| 12.8   | Parents' claims | | 198 |
| 12.9   | Sports | | 199 |
| 12.10  | Psychological injury | | 199 |
| 12.11  | Negligent reference | | 200 |
| 12.12  | Limitation periods | | 200 |
| 12.13  | Professionalism | | 201 |
|        | 12.13.1 | Meaning of 'professional person' | 201 |
|        | 12.13.2 | Case-law | 202 |
|        | 12.13.3 | Implications for teachers | 202 |

| Chapter 13 | PASTORAL CARE | | 205 |

| 13.1   | Introduction | | 205 |
| 13.2   | Legal aspects | | 205 |
|        | 13.2.1 | Statute and regulation | 205 |
|        | 13.2.2 | Contract | 206 |
|        | 13.2.3 | Tort | 206 |
|        | 13.2.4 | Case-law | 207 |
|        | 13.2.5 | Guidance | 207 |
|        | 13.2.6 | Fair procedures | 207 |
| 13.3   | Community aspects | | 207 |
| 13.4   | Health and medication | | 208 |
|        | 13.4.1 | Legal duties | 208 |
|        | 13.4.2 | Practical approach | 209 |
|        | 13.4.3 | Information and records | 210 |
|        | 13.4.4 | Medication | 210 |
|        | 13.4.5 | Emergency treatment | 211 |
|        | 13.4.6 | Late X-ray | 211 |
| 13.5   | Boarders | | 212 |
|        | 13.5.1 | Nature of boarding | 212 |
|        | 13.5.2 | Structure | 213 |
|        | 13.5.3 | Conduct of boarding house | 213 |
|        | 13.5.4 | Legal compliance | 213 |
|        | 13.5.5 | Contracts made by pupils | 214 |
|        | 13.5.6 | Change from boarding | 215 |
|        | 13.5.7 | Boarders from overseas | 215 |
| 13.6   | Child protection | | 215 |
|        | 13.6.1 | Rehabilitation of offenders | 216 |
|        | 13.6.2 | Barring for misconduct | 216 |
|        | 13.6.3 | Checking background | 217 |
|        | 13.6.4 | Misconduct reports | 217 |
|        | 13.6.5 | Guidance for staff | 218 |
|        | 13.6.6 | Social services | 218 |
|        | 13.6.7 | Worries and complaints procedure | 221 |
| 13.7   | Counselling | | 221 |
|        | 13.7.1 | The 'Blue Book' | 221 |

| 13.7.2 | Legal compliance | 222 |
| 13.7.3 | Confidentiality | 223 |
| 13.7.4 | Practical considerations | 225 |
| 13.7.5 | Credentials | 225 |
| 13.7.6 | Records | 225 |

| Chapter 14 | CARE OF PUPILS FROM OVERSEAS | 227 |

| 14.1 | Introduction | 227 |
| 14.2 | Overview | 227 |
| 14.3 | Role of the UK guardian | 228 |
| 14.4 | Contractual aspects | 229 |
| | 14.4.1 Generally | 229 |
| | 14.4.2 The school | 229 |
| | 14.4.3 The pupil/student | 230 |
| | 14.4.4 The overseas parents | 230 |
| | 14.4.5 The guardianship practice | 231 |
| | 14.4.6 The guardian family | 231 |
| 14.5 | Private fostering | 231 |
| 14.6 | Duty of care in tort | 232 |
| | 14.6.1 The holiday guardian | 233 |
| | 14.6.2 The school | 233 |
| | 14.6.3 Guardianship practice | 235 |
| 14.7 | Delegated parental responsibility | 235 |
| 14.8 | Privacy and confidentiality | 236 |
| 14.9 | Child protection | 236 |
| 14.10 | Race relations | 236 |
| 14.11 | Jurisdiction | 237 |
| 14.12 | Scope of holiday guardianship | 237 |
| | 14.12.1 Periods of care and accommodation | 237 |
| | 14.12.2 Consent of the overseas parents | 237 |
| | 14.12.3 Insurance | 238 |
| | 14.12.4 Information and confidentiality | 238 |
| | 14.12.5 Vetting | 238 |
| 14.13 | The main obligations of a holiday guardian | 239 |
| | 14.13.1 Responsibility and welfare | 239 |
| | 14.13.2 Passing information | 239 |
| | 14.13.3 General discipline and good order | 239 |
| | 14.13.4 Supervision of the child | 239 |
| | 14.13.5 Absence and delegation of duties | 239 |
| | 14.13.6 Accommodation and privacy | 240 |
| | 14.13.7 Contact with the parent and the school | 240 |
| | 14.13.8 Dangerous sports and activities | 240 |
| | 14.13.9 Emergencies | 240 |
| | 14.13.10 General approach | 240 |
| | 14.13.11 Termination of the arrangement | 240 |
| | 14.13.12 Payment of the holiday guardian | 241 |
| | 14.13.13 Legal liability and insurances | 241 |
| | 14.13.14 Jurisdiction | 241 |

14.14   Some practical problems                                    241
14.15   Forms of legal agreement                                   242

Chapter 15      BEHAVIOUR AND DISCIPLINE                            243

15.1    Introduction                                               243
15.2    Policy                                                     243
15.3    Bullying                                                   244
        15.3.1   Meaning of 'bullying'                             244
        15.3.2   Reported cases                                    245
        15.3.3   Approaches to bullying                            246
        15.3.4   Alternative approach                              247
        15.3.5   School's duty                                     248
        15.3.6   Legal proceedings                                 249
        15.3.7   Settlement of claims                              249
        15.3.8   Records                                           250
15.4    Discipline and sanctions                                   250
        15.4.1   Background                                        250
        15.4.2   Teacher's authority                               250
        15.4.3   Statutory provisions                              251
        15.4.4   Corporal punishment                               252
        15.4.5   Rough handling and physical abuse                254
        15.4.6   Lawful restraint                                  254
        15.4.7   Investigations                                    256
        15.4.8   Suspension and expulsion                          257
        15.4.9   Detention                                         258
        15.4.10  Search                                            259
        15.4.11  Confiscation of property                          259
        15.4.12  Punishments generally                             260
        15.4.13  Extent of jurisdiction                            260
        15.4.14  Appeals against disciplinary sanctions            260
15.5    Drugs and substances                                       260
        15.5.1   Education issue                                   261
        15.5.2   Criminal law                                      261
        15.5.3   Independent schools                               261
        15.5.4   Policy on drugs                                   262

Chapter 16      EXPULSION AND REVIEW                                265

16.1    Introduction                                               265
16.2    Legal aspects                                              265
        16.2.1   Overview                                          265
        16.2.2   Contract                                          266
        16.2.3   Tort                                              267
        16.2.4   Fair procedures                                   267
        16.2.5   Human rights                                      269
        16.2.6   Proportionality of sanction                       269
        16.2.7   Conduct of parents                                269
        16.2.8   Reinstatement of the pupil                        270
        16.2.9   Guidance from DfEE                                270

| | | |
|---|---|---|
| | 16.2.10 Exclusion from State-funded schools | 271 |
| 16.3 | Custom and practice | 272 |
| | 16.3.1 Meaning of 'expulsion' | 272 |
| | 16.3.2 Changing mores | 273 |
| | 16.3.3 Expulsion | 274 |
| | 16.3.4 Asking the parents to withdraw the pupil | 274 |
| | 16.3.5 Required removal | 274 |
| | 16.3.6 Leaving status | 275 |
| 16.4 | Governors' review | 276 |
| | 16.4.1 Head's authority | 276 |
| | 16.4.2 Appeals – rehearing and review | 277 |
| | 16.4.3 Formalities | 277 |
| | 16.4.4 Procedures | 277 |
| 16.5 | Conclusion | 280 |

**Part 3  ASPECTS OF GOVERNANCE AND MANAGEMENT**

| | | |
|---|---|---|
| Chapter 17 | CHARITABLE TRUSTS AND EDUCATIONAL CHARITIES | 283 |
| 17.1 | Introduction | 283 |
| 17.2 | Private trusts | 283 |
| | 17.2.1 Meaning of 'trust' | 283 |
| | 17.2.2 Development of trusts | 283 |
| | 17.2.3 Trustees generally | 284 |
| | 17.2.4 Duties of trustees | 285 |
| | 17.2.5 Breach of trust | 285 |
| | 17.2.6 Consequences of breach | 285 |
| | 17.2.7 Exemptions and reliefs for trustees | 286 |
| 17.3 | Charitable trusts | 287 |
| | 17.3.1 Development of charitable trusts | 287 |
| | 17.3.2 The 1601 preamble | 288 |
| | 17.3.3 Meaning of 'charitable status' | 289 |
| | 17.3.4 Objects of a charitable trust | 289 |
| | 17.3.5 *Cy-près* doctrine | 289 |
| | 17.3.6 The Charity Commissioners | 290 |
| | 17.3.7 Registration of charities | 291 |
| | 17.3.8 Permanent endowment | 292 |
| | 17.3.9 Charity trustees | 294 |
| | 17.3.10 Directors of a charitable company | 294 |
| 17.4 | Duties of charity trustees | 295 |
| | 17.4.1 Immediately on appointment | 295 |
| | 17.4.2 Comply with the terms of the trust | 295 |
| | 17.4.3 Fidelity and prudence | 296 |
| | 17.4.4 Act personally | 296 |
| | 17.4.5 Impartiality between beneficiaries | 296 |
| | 17.4.6 Keep accounts and give information | 296 |
| | 17.4.7 Investment | 296 |
| | 17.4.8 Compliance with the Charities Act 1993 | 297 |

| | | |
|---|---|---|
| 17.4.9 | Apply for a scheme | 297 |
| 17.4.10 | Act gratuitously | 297 |
| 17.4.11 | Not to make a personal profit from the trust | 298 |
| 17.5 | The powers of charity trustees | 299 |
| 17.5.1 | Power to sell etc | 300 |
| 17.5.2 | Power to borrow money | 301 |
| 17.5.3 | Power to insure | 301 |
| 17.5.4 | Power to make ex gratia payments | 302 |
| 17.5.5 | Power to waive entitlement to property | 302 |
| 17.6 | Educational charities | 302 |
| 17.6.1 | Education as a charitable purpose | 302 |
| 17.6.2 | Trading activities of charitable schools | 303 |
| 17.6.3 | Discrimination provisions | 303 |
| 17.7 | Taxation of educational charities | 304 |
| 17.7.1 | Income tax | 304 |
| 17.7.2 | Corporation tax | 305 |
| 17.7.3 | Capital gains tax | 305 |
| 17.7.4 | Value Added Tax | 306 |
| 17.7.5 | Stamp duty | 308 |
| 17.7.6 | Rates | 308 |
| 17.8 | Taxation of charitable gifts | 308 |
| 17.8.1 | Income tax | 309 |
| 17.8.2 | Corporation tax | 309 |
| 17.8.3 | Capital gains tax | 309 |
| 17.8.4 | Inheritance tax | 310 |

| | | |
|---|---|---|
| Chapter 18 | LEGAL STRUCTURES | 311 |
| 18.1 | Introduction | 311 |
| 18.2 | Public corporations | 311 |
| 18.2.1 | Meaning of 'corporation' | 311 |
| 18.2.2 | Different kinds of corporation | 312 |
| 18.2.3 | Corporations sole and aggregate | 312 |
| 18.2.4 | Establishing a corporation | 312 |
| 18.2.5 | Part VII of the Charities Act 1993 | 313 |
| 18.2.6 | Schools established by Royal Charter | 313 |
| 18.2.7 | Livery companies | 315 |
| 18.2.8 | Schools established by special Act of Parliament | 315 |
| 18.2.9 | Schools incorporated under the Companies Acts | 316 |
| 18.2.10 | Friendly societies and industrial and provident societies | 317 |
| 18.3 | Incorporation of the trustees | 318 |
| 18.4 | Corporate trustee | 319 |
| 18.5 | Unincorporated charitable schools | 320 |
| 18.5.1 | Unincorporated trusts generally | 320 |
| 18.5.2 | Personal liability | 321 |
| 18.5.3 | Other practical considerations | 325 |
| 18.5.4 | Remaining unincorporated | 325 |
| 18.6 | Unincorporated associations | 326 |
| 18.7 | Proprietary schools | 327 |

Chapter 19    THE GOVERNING BODY                                         329

19.1    Introduction                                                     329
19.2    Classes of governor                                              329
        19.2.1    Life governors                                         329
        19.2.2    Ex-officio governors                                   330
        19.2.3    Representative governors                               331
        19.2.4    Nominative governors                                   331
        19.2.5    Co-optative governors                                  332
19.3    Governance structures                                           332
        19.3.1    Three-tier                                             332
        19.3.2    Two-tier                                               333
        19.3.3    Single-tier: large governing body                      334
        19.3.4    Single-tier: small governing body                      334
19.4    Chairman and officers                                           335
        19.4.1    Chairman                                               335
        19.4.2    Officers                                               335
19.5    New governors                                                   336
        19.5.1    Prior to appointment                                   336
        19.5.2    On appointment                                         337
19.6    Composition of governing body                                   337
        19.6.1    Requirements of scheme                                 337
        19.6.2    The head                                               338
        19.6.3    The bursar                                             338
        19.6.4    Current parents                                        338
        19.6.5    Teachers                                               339
        19.6.6    Solicitors                                             339
        19.6.7    Suppliers                                              340
        19.6.8    Skills                                                 340
        19.6.9    Relevance                                              340
        19.6.10   Communication                                         340
19.7    Functions of the governing body                                 341
        19.7.1    Committee structure                                    341
        19.7.2    General functions                                      342
        19.6.3    Relationships                                          342
19.8    Accountability                                                  343
        19.8.1    Governors' position                                    344
        19.8.2    Parents' position                                      344
        19.8.3    Confidence in the head                                 345
        19.8.4    Accountability generally                               345
19.9    Retirement and disqualification                                 346
        19.9.1    Retirement                                             346
        19.9.2    Disqualification                                       347
        19.9.3    Removal                                                347
19.10   The governor as member of a company                             348
19.11   The governor as company director                                349
        19.11.1   Fiduciary duties                                       349
        19.11.2   Breach of fiduciary duty                               350
        19.11.3   Contracts with third parties                           350

|   |   |   |
|---|---|---|
| 19.11.4 | Vicarious liability | 350 |
| 19.11.5 | Statutory liability | 350 |
| 19.11.6 | Criminal liability | 350 |
| 19.11.7 | Liability for the acts of co-directors | 350 |
| 19.11.8 | Insolvency | 351 |
| 19.11.9 | Wrongful trading | 351 |
| 19.11.10 | Environmental issues | 351 |
| 19.11.11 | Shadow directors | 351 |

| Chapter 20 | HEADSHIP | 353 |
|---|---|---|
| 20.1 | Overview | 353 |
| 20.2 | The head's job | 354 |
| 20.2.1 | Survival | 354 |
| 20.2.2 | Early dealings | 354 |
| 20.2.3 | Winning the confidence of others | 354 |
| 20.2.4 | Effecting change | 354 |
| 20.2.5 | The 'old guard' | 355 |
| 20.2.6 | Relations with the governors | 355 |
| 20.3 | The aspiring head | 356 |
| 20.3.1 | Model of school | 356 |
| 20.3.2 | Preparation for headship | 356 |
| 20.3.3 | Personal objectives | 357 |
| 20.3.4 | Interview | 357 |
| 20.3.5 | Information required to make an informed decision | 357 |
| 20.4 | Appointment of a head | 359 |
| 20.4.1 | Search committee | 359 |
| 20.4.2 | The 'person specification' | 360 |
| 20.4.3 | Job description | 361 |
| 20.4.4 | Dealing with applications | 362 |
| 20.4.5 | Interview | 362 |
| 20.4.6 | References | 362 |
| 20.4.7 | Salary | 363 |
| 20.4.8 | Pension provision | 363 |
| 20.4.9 | Expenses | 363 |
| 20.4.10 | Benefits in kind | 364 |
| 20.4.11 | Professional subscriptions | 364 |
| 20.4.12 | Private medical insurance | 364 |
| 20.4.13 | Education of the head's children | 364 |
| 20.4.14 | Provision of a car | 364 |
| 20.4.15 | Mobile telephone | 365 |
| 20.4.16 | Relocation costs | 365 |
| 20.4.17 | Staff accommodation | 366 |
| 20.4.18 | Employment contract | 367 |
| 20.5 | Confidence issues | 368 |
| 20.5.1 | Confidence generally | 368 |
| 20.5.2 | Basis of confidence | 369 |
| 20.5.3 | The governing instrument | 370 |
| 20.5.4 | Practical aspects | 370 |

20.5.5  'Without prejudice' meeting 371
20.5.6  Suspension etc 372
20.5.7  Staff and parents 373
20.5.8  Dismissal 373
20.5.9  Confidentiality 373
20.5.10 Compromise agreement 374
20.6  Headship generally 374
*Table 1* – Specimen 'person specification' for a head 376
*Table 2* – Specimen job description for a head 377
*Table 3* – Outline of the main terms of employment for a head 381
*Table 4* – Specimen interview questionnaire for headship candidates 383

Chapter 21  THE BURSAR 387

21.1  Introduction 387
21.2  Role of the bursar 387
21.2.1  Bursars generally 387
21.2.2  Division of responsibilities 388
21.2.3  Preparatory schools 388
21.2.4  Clerk to the governors 389
21.2.5  Secretary 389
21.2.6  Fees disputes 390
21.3  Legal compliance 390
21.3.1  Companies 391
21.3.2  Consumer credit 392
21.3.3  Contract for educational services 392
21.3.4  Copyright 392
21.3.5  Data protection 392
21.3.6  Educational charities 392
21.3.7  Employment contracts and procedures 393
21.3.8  Health and safety 393
21.3.9  Liability insurance 394
21.3.10 Licensing 395
21.3.11 Money laundering 395
21.3.12 Registration of independent schools 395
21.3.13 School transport 396
21.3.14 Town and country planning 396
21.4  Community law 396
*Table 1* – Specimen job description for a bursar 398

Chapter 22  PRIVACY AND CONFIDENTIAL INFORMATION 401

22.1  Introduction 401
22.2  Interests to be protected 401
22.2.1  Pupils 401
22.2.2  Parents 401
22.2.3  Staff 401
22.2.4  Governors 402
22.2.5  The school 402
22.3  Confidential information 402

| | | |
|---|---|---|
| 22.4 | Privacy | 403 |
| | 22.4.1 Civil liberties | 403 |
| | 22.4.2 Common law rights | 404 |
| | 22.4.3 Statute | 405 |
| | 22.4.4 Where the law does not give protection | 405 |
| 22.5 | Intellectual property | 406 |
| | 22.5.1 Obligation of confidence | 406 |
| | 22.5.2 Copyright | 407 |
| | 22.5.3 Registered designs | 407 |
| | 22.5.4 Patent | 408 |
| 22.6 | Privacy rights of teachers | 408 |
| | 22.6.1 Intellectual property rights | 408 |
| | 22.6.2 Waiver of privacy | 409 |
| | 22.6.3 Statutory provisions | 410 |
| 22.7 | Privacy rights of pupils | 411 |
| | 22.7.1 Photographs | 411 |
| | 22.7.2 Personal space | 412 |
| | 22.7.3 Search and detention | 412 |
| | 22.7.4 Correspondence | 412 |
| | 22.7.5 Sexual orientation | 413 |
| | 22.7.6 Progress reports | 413 |
| | 22.7.7 Counselling | 414 |
| | 22.7.8 Secrets | 414 |
| | 22.7.9 The *Gillick* principle | 414 |
| | 22.7.10 HIV, AIDS, and hepatitis | 415 |
| | 22.7.11 Pupils' health generally | 415 |
| | 22.7.12 Data protection | 415 |
| | 22.7.13 School medical officer | 415 |
| | 22.7.14 Medical records | 416 |
| | 22.7.15 Special educational needs | 416 |
| | 22.7.16 Confidential references | 416 |
| | 22.7.17 Waiver of privacy | 417 |
| 22.8 | Privacy rights of parents | 417 |
| | 22.8.1 Unpaid fees | 417 |
| | 22.8.2 School file | 418 |
| 22.9 | Reporting restrictions | 419 |
| | 22.9.1 Family proceedings | 420 |
| | 22.9.2 Sexual crime | 420 |
| | 22.9.3 Any proceedings – any court | 420 |
| | 22.9.4 Youth courts | 421 |
| | 22.9.5 Committal proceedings | 422 |
| | 22.9.6 The course of justice | 422 |
| | 22.9.7 Hearings in chambers | 422 |
| | 22.9.8 Press Complaints Commission | 422 |
| | 22.9.9 Employment tribunals | 423 |
| | 22.9.10 Duty of counsel | 424 |
| 22.10 | Other protections | 424 |

Chapter 23    DATA PROTECTION                                    425

23.1    Introduction                                             425
23.2    Overview                                                 425
        23.2.1    Main points                                    425
        23.2.2    Terminology                                    426
        23.2.3    The data protection principles                 427
        23.2.4    Relevance to independent schools               427
        23.2.5    Exemptions                                     428
23.3    Registration                                             428
23.4    The First Data Protection Principle                      428
        23.4.1    The Principle                                  428
        23.4.2    Schedule 2                                     429
        23.4.3    Schedule 3                                     429
        23.4.4    Interpretation                                 430
23.5    The other Principles                                     430
        23.5.1    The Second Principle                           430
        23.5.2    The Third Principle                            431
        23.5.3    The Fourth Principle                           431
        23.5.4    The Fifth Principle                            431
        23.5.5    The Sixth Principle                            431
        23.5.6    The Seventh Principle                          431
        23.5.7    The Eighth Principle                           431
23.6    Rights of data subjects                                  432
        23.6.1    Making an enquiry                              432
        23.6.2    Subject access rights                          432
        23.6.3    Automatic processing                           432
        23.6.4    Direct marketing                               433
        23.6.5    Injunction                                     433
        23.6.6    Compensation                                   433
        23.6.7    Correction                                     434
23.7    Transitional provisions                                  434
        23.7.1    Commencement                                   434
        23.7.2    Exemptions                                     434
        23.7.3    Manual data                                    435
23.8    Compliance summary                                       435

Chapter 24    MARKETING AND QUALITY                              437

24.1    Introduction                                             437
24.2    Overview                                                 437
24.3    Internal culture                                         438
24.4    External culture                                         439
24.5    The product                                              440
        24.5.1    The buyer                                      441
        24.5.2    Product analysis                               441
        24.5.3    Branding                                       443
24.6    Marketing strategy                                       444
        24.6.1    Explanation of strategy                        444
        24.6.2    Assessment of present position                 445

|         | 24.6.3   | The quality markers and product | 446 |
|         | 24.6.4   | Market segments | 446 |
|         | 24.6.5   | Vision, objective, aim and market focus | 446 |
|         | 24.6.6   | Financial review | 446 |
|         | 24.6.7   | Short-term needs and options | 446 |
| 24.7    | Drawing up a plan | | 447 |
| 24.8    | Implementation | | 447 |
|         | 24.8.1   | Marketing budget | 447 |
|         | 24.8.2   | Management | 447 |
|         | 24.8.3   | Segmenting the market | 448 |
|         | 24.8.4   | Database | 448 |
|         | 24.8.5   | Management of fund-raising groups | 448 |
|         | 24.8.6   | 'Front of mind' | 448 |
|         | 24.8.7   | Direct mailing | 449 |
|         | 24.8.8   | Communications audit | 449 |
|         | 24.8.9   | Use of school premises | 450 |
|         | 24.8.10  | Overseas visits by head | 451 |
|         | 24.8.11  | Promotional material | 451 |
|         | 24.8.12  | Kerb appeal | 451 |
|         | 24.8.13  | Changes to the curriculum and school hours | 451 |
|         | 24.8.14  | Fees | 452 |
|         | 24.8.15  | New scholarships and bursaries | 452 |
| 24.9    | Times of adversity | | 452 |
|         | 24.9.1   | Complaints | 452 |
|         | 24.9.2   | Adverse publicity | 453 |
|         | 24.9.3   | Falling pupil rolls | 453 |
| 24.10   | Fund-raising and appeals | | 453 |
|         | 24.10.1  | Legal aspects | 454 |
|         | 24.10.2  | Preparation | 454 |
| 24.11   | Suggested reading | | 455 |
| *Table 1* – Abbreviated example of a 'what' and 'how' model | | | 456 |

| Chapter 25    | HUMAN RIGHTS | | 459 |

| 25.1 | Introduction | | 459 |
| 25.2 | Scope of the Act | | 460 |
| 25.3 | The Articles | | 462 |
| 25.4 | Operation and interpretation | | 462 |
| 25.5 | Practical application of the Act | | 463 |
|      | 25.5.1 | Public authorities exercising a public function | 463 |
|      | 25.5.2 | Private authorities exercising a public function | 464 |
|      | 25.5.3 | Employment disputes | 464 |
| 25.6 | Maintaining a balance | | 465 |
| 25.7 | Independent schools | | 465 |

| BIBLIOGRAPHY | 467 |

| INDEX | 469 |

# Table of Cases

**All references are to paragraph numbers.**

Adams v Cape Industries [1990] Ch 433, [1990] 2 WLR 657, [1991] 1 All ER 129,
 CA     19.11.4
Affutu-Nartoy v Clarke and ILEA (1984) *The Times*, 9 February     11.9.9
Alcock v Chief Constable of South Yorkshire, *sub nom* Jones v Wright [1992] 1
 AC 310, [1991] 3 WLR 1057, [1991] 4 All ER 907, HL; *affirming* [1991] 3
 All ER 88, CA     11.7.2
Alliance Perpetual Building Society v Belrum Investments [1957] 1 WLR 720,
 [1957] 1 All ER 635, (1957) 101 SJ 406     22.9.7
Attorney-General v Dean and Canons of Christ Church (1821) Jac 474     18.5.1
Attorney-General v Guardian Newspapers Ltd (No 2) [1988] 3 WLR 776, [1988] 3
 All ER 545, (1988) 132 SJ 1496, HL; *affirming* [1988] 2 WLR 805, (1988)
 132 SJ 566, CA     22.4.1

B (Minors), Re (1994) *The Times*, 12 May, CA     8.3.8, 13.2.4
Barfoot v East Sussex County Council (unreported), 1939     11.9.9
Barnes v Bromley London Borough Council (1983) *The Times*, 16 November, DC     11.5.1,
     11.5.2
Barnes v Hampshire County Council, *sub nom* Barnes (An Infant) v Hampshire
 County Council [1969] 1 WLR 1563, [1969] 3 All ER 746, (1969) 113 SJ 834,
 HL *reversing sub nom* Barnes (An Infant) v Hampshire County Council (1968)
 112 SJ 599, [1968] CLY 2725, CA     11.9.4
Barr-Lindsay v Barr-Lindsay and Another (unreported) January 1996, CA     11.4.1, 11.5.1
Bates v Parker [1953] 2 QB 231, [1953] 2 WLR 642, [1953] 1 All ER 768, CA     11.10.1
Beaumont v Surrey County Council (1968) 112 SJ 704, (1968) 66 LGR 580     11.4.3, 11.9.3
Berridge v Isle of Wight County Council (unreported), 1955     11.9.9
Black v Kent County Council [1984] LGR 39, CA; *affirming* (1983) *The Times*,
 23 May     11.3.1, 11.5.1
Blasdale v Coventry City Council (1981) TES, 13 November     11.9.3
Bolam v Friern Hospital Management Committee [1957] 1 WLR 582, [1957] 2 All
 ER 118, (1957) 101 SJ 357     8.4.1, 11.4.4, 12.2.1
Bolton v Stone [1951] AC 850, [1951] All ER 1078, [1951] 1 TLR 977, HL     11.3.1
Bradfield House Ltd v Walsall Metropolitan Borough Council (1997) 4 EPLI 68,
 Walsall County Court     5.11.3, 9.8.5, 9.8.8
Butt v Cambridgeshire and Isle of Ely County Council (1970) 68 LGR 81, (1969)
 119 New LJ 1118     11.3.1, 11.5.1

Camkin v Bishop [1941] 2 All ER 713, 165 LT 246, CA     11.5.1
Campbell and Cosans v United Kingdom [1982] 4 EHRR 293     15.4.3
Caparo Industries plc v Dickman [1990] 2 AC 605, [1990] 2 WLR 358, [1989] 1
 All ER 568, HL; *reversing* [1989] QB 653, [1989] 2 WLR 316, [1989] 1 All
 ER 798, CA     11.3, 12.3.2

Carmarthenshire County Council v Lewis [1955] AC 549, [1955] 2 WLR 517,
    [1955] 1 All ER 565, HL; *affirming sub nom* Lewis v Carmarthenshire County
    Council [1953] 1 WLR 1439, [1953] 2 All ER 1403, CA                    11.9.1
Carr v Inland Revenue Commissioners [1994] 2 All ER 163                    12.13.2
Ching v Surrey County Council [1910] 1 KB 736, 79 LJK 481, 102 LT 414, 74 JP
    187                                                                    11.10.1
Christmas v Hampshire County Council [1998] ELR 1, QBD, *see also* E (A Minor)
    v Dorset County Council                                                12.4.2
Church Education Corporation v McCoig & McCoig (unreported), 8 December
    1995                                                                   6.4.4
City Equitable Fire Insurance Co Ltd, Re [1925] Ch 407, [1924] All ER Rep 485,
    94 LJ Ch 445, 133 LT 520                                               17.3.10
Clark v Monmouthshire County Council (1954) 118 JP 244, (1954) 52 LGR 246,
    CA                                                                     11.9.3
Clarke v Bethnal Green Borough Council [1939] 3 All ER 54, 160 LT 292, 103 JP
    160, 55 TLR 519                                                        11.3.1
Cleary v Booth [1893] 1 QB 465, 62 LJMC 87, 68 LT 349, 57 JP 375          15.4.2
Collins v Price (1828) 6 LJOSCP 244, (1828) 5 Bing 132, 2 MOO&P 233, 130 ER
    1011                                                                   9.8.1, 9.8.8
Commissioners of Inland Revenue v Maxse [1919] 1 KB 647                    12.13.2
Condon v Basi [1985] 1 WLR 866, [1985] 2 All ER 453, CA                    11.9.9
Conrad v ILEA (1967) 65 LGR 543, (1967) 111 SJ 684, CA; *reversing* (1966) 116
    New LJ 1630, [1966] CLY 8179                                    11.4.4, 11.9.9
Costello-Roberts v United Kingdom (1995) 19 EHRR 112, [1994] ELR 1, [1994] 1
    FCR 65                                                                 15.4.4
Cranston, Re, Webb v Oldfield [1898] 1 IrR 431                             17.3.1
Crouch v Essex County Council (1966) 64 LGR 240                            11.5.1


Daborn v Bath Tramways Motor Co Ltd [1946] 2 All ER 33, CA                 11.5.1
Davis Contractors Ltd v Fareham UDC [1956] AC 696, [1956] 3 WLR 37, [1956] 2
    All ER 145, HL; *affirming* [1955] 1 QB 302, [1955] 2 WLR 388, [1955] 1 All
    ER 275                                                                 5.8.1
Debell v Bromley LEC (1994) *The Guardian*, 13 November                    7.4.2
Denman v Winstanley (1887) 4 TLR 127                                       9.8.5
Donoghue v Stevenson [1932] AC 562, 101 LJPC 119, 48 TLR 494   11.2.1, 11.3.2, 11.10.1
Donovan v Landy's Ltd [1963] IR 441                                        11.5.2
DPP v G (Duty to Investigate) (1997) *The Times*, 24 November, (1997)
    *Independent*, 20 October, QBD                                         15.4.7
Duffy v Fahy [1960] Ir Jur Rep 69                                          11.5.2


E (A Minor) v Dorset County Council, Christmas v Hampshire County Council,
    Keating v Bromley London Borough Council [1995] 2 AC 685, [1994] WLR
    853, [1994] 4 All ER 640, [1994] ELR 416 , CA        8.4.1, 12.2.2, 12.4.2, 12.5.4
Edwards v Hall (1855) 6 De GM&G 74, 25 LJ Ch 82, 26 LTOS 170, 20 JP 38    17.3.8
English v Mill Hill School Foundation [1997] reported in EPLI             10.7, 10.10
Equal Opportunities Commission v Birmingham City Council, *see* R v Birmingham
    City Council, ex parte Equal Opportunities Commission


Felgate v Middlesex County Council (unreported), 1954                      11.9.9
Fitzgerald v Northcote (1865) 4 F&F 656                                    16.2.2
French Protestant Hospital, Re [1951] 1 Ch 567, [1951] 1 All ER 938, (1951) 95 SJ
    426                                                                    17.3.10

Fryer v Salford Corporation [1937] 1 All ER 617, 101 JP 263, 81 Sol 177, 35 LGR
    254, CA             11.4.4, 11.5.1

Gibbs v Barking Corporation [1936] 1 All ER 115, CA   11.9.9
Gibbs v McDonnell [1990] Ch 1, [1989] 2 WLR 1094, [1989] 2 All ER 129   17.3.2
Gillick v West Norfolk and Wisbech Area Health Authority and the DHSS [1986]
    AC 112, [1985] 3 WLR 830, [1985] 3 All ER 402, [1986] 1 FLR 224, HL   13.7.2,
          22.7.9
Gillmore v London County Council [1938] All ER 31, 159 LT 615, 103 JP 1, 55
    TLR 95, DC     11.10.1
Gilmour v Coats [1949] AC 427, [1949] LJR 1034, [1949] 1 All ER 848, HL;
    *affirming sub nom* Re Coats Trusts, Coats v Gilmour [1949] Ch 340, [1948]
    LJR 1178, [1948] 1 All ER 521   17.3.2
Glasgow Corporation v Muir [1943] AC 448, [1943] 2 All ER 44, [1943] ACT 448,
    112 LJPC 1   11.4.3
Gleave v Lancashire County Council (unreported), 1951   11.9.9
Good v ILEA (1980) 10 Fam Law 213, CA   11.9.4
Gorely v Codd [1967] 1 WLR 19, [1966] 3 All ER 891, (1966) 110 SJ 965   11.5.2
Gough v Thorne [1966] 1 WLR 1387, [1966] 3 All ER 398, (1966) 110 SJ 529, CA
         11.5.2
Governors of E. Ivor Hughes Education Foundation v Denfield [1992] CL
    September 58, Willesden County Court   5.11.3, 9.8.5, 9.8.8
Grant v South West Trains [1998] 1 FCR 377, GC   22.7.5
Greaves & Co (Contractors) Ltd v Baynham Meikle & Partners [1975] 1 WLR
    1095, [1975] 3 All ER 99, (1975) 119 SJ 372, CA   12.2.1
Gregory v Frensham Heights Educational Trust Ltd (1997) EPLI 66, Chichester
    County Court   8.3.15, 10.11
Grenar v The Royal School, Hindhead (unreported), 1997   5.11.5, 8.4.12, 11.3.3, 12.6,
         12.10
Gwillym v Monmouthshire County Council, unreported   11.9.9

Hamad v Dame Allen's School (1997) *Daily Telegraph*, 14 May   15.3.2
Harris v Church Commissioner for England [1992] 2 All ER 300   17.4.7
Harris v Evans and Another [1998] 1 WLR 1285, (1998) *The Times*, 5 May, CA   12.3.2
Hedley Byrne & Co Ltd v Heller & Partners Ltd [1964] AC 465, [1963] 3 WLR
    101, [1963] 2 All ER 575, HL   12.3.2, 12.3.3, 16.2.3, 20.4.6
Hellewell v Chief Constable of Derbyshire [1995] 1 WLR 804, [1995] 4 All ER
    473, (1995) 92(07) LS Gaz 35   22.4.4
Henderson v Merrett Syndicates, Hallam-Eames v Same, Hughes v Same,
    Arbuthnott v Feltrim Underwriting Agencies, Deeny v Gooda Walker (In
    Liquidation) [1995] 2 AC 145, [1994] 3 WLR 761, [1994] 3 All ER 506, HL   12.3.2
Herne Bay Steam Boat Co v Hutton [1903] 2 KB 683, [1900–3] All ER Rep 627,
    72 LJKB 879, 89 LT 422, CA   5.8.1
Hippolyte v London Borough of Bexley [1995] PIQR 309, CA   12.3.2, 12.3.3, 12.4.2
Holmes v Mather (1875) LR 10 Ex 261, 44 LJ Ex 176, 33 LT 3612, 39 JP 567   11.6.4
Hotson v East Berkshire Area Health Authority [1987] AC 750, [1987] 3 WLR
    232, [1987] 2 All ER 909, HL   11.9.9
Hudson v Governors of Rotherham Grammar School [1938] LCT 303   11.5.1
Hunt v Damon (1930) 46 TLR 575   16.2.3
Hunter and Others v Canary Wharf Ltd [1997] AC 655, [1997] 2 WLR 684, [1997]
    2 FLR 342, HL   22.4.2

Income Tax Special Purposes Commissioners v Pemsel [1891] AC 531, [1891–4]
    All ER Rep 28, 61 LJQB 265, 65 LT 621                                                                                17.3.2
IRC v Educational Grants Association [1967] Ch 993, [1967] 3 WLR 41, [1967] 2
    All ER 893, CA; *affirming* [1967] Ch 123, [1966] 3 WLR 724, [1966] 3 All
    ER 708                                                                                                                                    17.7.1


Jacques v Oxfordshire County Council (1967) 66 LGR 440                                                                11.9.6
Jarvis v Swans Tours [1973] 1 QB 233, [1972] 3 WLR 954, [1973] 1 All ER 71,
    CA                                                                                                                                          5.11.4
Jeffery v London County Council (1954) 52 LGR 521, *sub nom* Jefferey v London
    County Council (1954) 119 JP 45                                                                                    11.5.1, 11.9.4


Keating v London Borough of Bromley, *see* E (A Minor) v Dorset County Council
Kershaw v Hampshire County Council (unreported), 1982                                                              11.9.9
Kershaw v Whelan [1996] 1 WLR 358, [1996] 2 All ER 404, (1995) *The Times*, 20
    December, QBD                                                                                                                    22.7.17
Krell v Henry [1903] 2 KB 740, [1900–3] All ER Rep 20, 72 LJKB 794, 89 LT
    328, CA                                                                                                                                   5.8.1


Lancaster v County Council of Lancashire (unreported), 1952                                                     11.9.9
Langham v Wellingborough School Governors and Fryer (1932) 30 LGR 276,
    (1932) 101 LJKB 513, 147 LT 91, 96 LJ 236, CA                                                    11.5.1, 11.9.3
Lyes v Middlesex County Council (1962) 61 LGR 443                                                          11.4.3, 11.10.1


M (A Minor) v Newham London Borough Council, *see* X (Minors) v Bedfordshire
    County Council
McCord v Swansea City AFC (1997) *The Times*, 11 February                                                      11.9.9
Malik v BCCI [1997] 3 WLR 95, [1997] 3 All ER 1, [1997] ICR 606                                         20.5.9
Mandla v Lee, Dowell [1983] 2 AC 548, [1983] 2 WLR 620, [1983] 1 All ER
    1062, HL                                                                                                                                  7.4.2
Mansell v Griffin [1908] 1 KB 947, 77 LJKB 676, 99 LT 132, 72 JP 179                                 15.4.5
Martin v Middlesborough Corporation (1965) 109 SJ 576, (1965) 63 LGR 385                           11.4.3
Mays v Essex County Council (1975) *The Times*, 11 October                                                     11.9.2
Meeham v Derbyshire County Council (unreported), 1965                                                          11.9.9
Mills v Winchester Diocesan Board of Finance [1989] Ch 428, [1989] 2 WLR 976,
    [1989] 2 All ER 317                                                                                                              17.3.6
Moore v Hampshire County Council (1982) 80 LGR 481, CA                                                      11.9.9
Morales v Eccleston [1991] RTR 151, CA                                                                                       11.5.2
Morris v Carnarvon County Council [1910] 1 KB 840, 79 LJKB 670, 102 LT 524,
    74 JP 201                                                                                                                                11.10.1
Mount v Oldham Corporation [1973] 1 QB 309, [1973] 2 WLR 22, [1973] 1 All
    ER 26, CA        5.3.1, 5.8.1, 5.11.2, 6.4.4, 8.4.8, 9.8.5, 9.8.12, 10.2, 10.3.3, 10.5, 10.7,
                                        10.9, 10.14.10, 12.5.5, 13.2.2
Murphy v Bradford Metropolitan Council [1991] ICR 80, (1991) *The Times*, 11
    February, (1991) *Daily Telegraph*, 15 February, CA                                     11.4.3, 11.9.2, 11.10.1


Nettleship v Weston [1971] 2 QB 691, [1971] 3 WLR 370, [1971] 3 All ER 581            11.4.4,
                                                   12.2.1
Noah v Shuba [1991] FSR 14                                                                                                           22.6.1
Noonan v ILEA (1974) *The Times*, 14 December                                                                      11.5.1
Norman v Theodore Goddard [1991] VCLC 1028                                                                        17.4.4

Nwabudike v The Mayor and Burgesses of the London Borough of Southwark
 [1997] ELR 35   11.9.1

Pearson v Lightning (1998) *The Times*, 30 April   11.3.1
Pepper (Inspector of Taxes) v Hart [1993] AC 593, [1992] 3 WLR 1032, [1993] 1
 All ER 42   20.4.13
Pettican v Enfield London Borough Council (1970) *The Times*, 22 October   11.9.3
Phelps v Hillingdon London Borough Council (1998) *The Times*, 9 November, CA   12.3.2,
   12.4.2

Pollard v Photographic Co (1888) 40 ChD 345, 58 LJ Ch 251, 60 LT 418, 37 WR
 266   22.7.1
Porter v Barking and Dagenham London Borough Council (1990) *The Times*, 9
 April   11.5.1, 11.9.3, 11.9.9
Porter v City of Bradford Metropolitan Council [1985] LEXIS, 14 January, CA   11.9.5
Pott v Stevens (1948) 99 LJ 164   9.8.10, 10.7, 10.14.21
Practice Direction (Periodical Payments: Ancillary Relief: Payment of School Fees)
 (1983) 4 FLR 513   9.8.12
Price v Caernarvonshire County Council (1960) *The Times*, 11 February   11.9.9
Price v Dennis [1988] LEXIS, CA   5.1.1, 5.9, 6.4.2, 6.4.3, 6.4.6, 8.3.12, 8.4.2, 8.4.8,
   10.3.3, 10.9, 10.14.7, 19.8.2, 20.5.7
Price v Wilkins (1888) 58 LT 680, 4 TLR 231   16.2.2, 16.2.4

R v Birmingham City Council, ex parte Equal Opportunities Commission [1989]
 AC 1155, [1989] 2 WLR 520, [1989] 1 All ER 769, HL   7.4.2
R v Board of Governors of Stoke Newington School and Others, ex parte M [1994]
 ELR 131   16.2.4, 16.2.8
R v Board of Governors of the London Oratory School, ex parte R (1988) *The
 Times*, 17 February   16.2.4
R v Central Independent Television plc [1994] 3 WLR 20, [1994] 3 All ER 641,
 CA   22.4.2
R v Cobham Hall School, ex parte S [1998] ELR 389, QBD   5.11.5, 6.3.4, 6.4.4, 12.4.2,
   12.7, 16.2.2, 16.2.4, 16.2.8, 25.2
R v East Sussex County Council, ex parte Tandy, *sub nom* R v East Sussex County
 Council, ex parte T [1998] 2 WLR 884, [1998] ELR 251, (1998) *The Times*,
 21 May, HL   12.3.2, 12.4.2
R v Fernhill Manor School, ex parte A [1994] ELR 67, [1993] 1 FLR 620   5.3.1, 8.2.2,
   8.2.5, 8.4.1, 13.2.6, 15.4.7, 16.2.2, 16.2.4
R v Governors of Haberdashers' Aske's Hatcham College Trust, ex parte T [1995]
 ELR 350   16.2.4, 25.2, 25.5.2
R v Governors of St Gregory's RC Aided High School and Appeals Committee, ex
 parte M [1995] ELR 290, (1995) *The Times*, 27 January, QBD   16.2.4, 16.4.4
R v Hopley [1860] F&F 202   15.4.5, 15.4.9
R v Hove Justices, ex parte Gibbons (1981) *The Times*, 19 June   22.10
R v Income Tax Special Commissioners (1909) 78 LJKB 576, 100 LT 585, 25 TLR
 368, 53 Sol Jo 320, CA   17.6.1
R v Leicester Crown Court, ex parte S (1991) 155 JPN 139, [1991] COD 231,
 [1991] Crim LR 365   22.9.3
R v London Borough of Camden and The Governors of Hampstead School, ex
 parte H [1996] ELR 360, CA   15.4.7, 16.2.8
R v London Borough of Islington, ex parte Rixon [1997] ELR 66, QBD   16.2.9
R v London Borough of Newham, ex parte X [1995] ELR 303   16.2.6
R v McBratney and Murray (1997) *Daily Telegraph*, 28 May   15.3.2
R v Neale and Another, ex parte S [1995] ELR 198   16.2.7

R v Newport (Salop) Justices, ex parte Wright [1929] 2 KB 416, 98 LJKB 555, 141
    LT 563, 93 JB 179                                                          15.4.13
R v Roman Catholic Schools, ex parte S [1998] ELR 304, QBD                     15.4.7
R v Socialist Worker Printers and Publishers Ltd, ex parte Att-Gen [1975] QB 637,
    [1974] 3 WLR 801, [1975] 1 All ER 142, DC                                  22.10
R v Staffordshire County Council, ex parte A (1996) *The Times*, 18 October    16.2.6
R v Surrey County Council Education Committee, ex parte H (1984) 83 LGR 219     8.4.1,
                                                                               12.2.2
Ralph v London County Council (1947) 63 TLR 546, (1947) 111 JP 548, CA;
    *affirming* (1947) 63 TLR 239                                              11.10.1
Rawsthorne v Ottley [1937] 3 All ER 902                                        11.9.3
Reffell v Surrey County Council [1964] 1 WLR 358, [1964] 1 All ER 743, (1964)
    128 JP 261                                                                 11.10.1
Registrar's Direction (Periodical Payments: Children) [1987] 2 FLR 255         9.8.12
Rich v London County Council [1953] 1 WLR 895, [1953] 2 All ER 376, (1947)
    117 JP 353; *reversing* [1952] CLY 2398                                    11.4.3
Ricketts v Erith Borough Council [1943] 2 All ER 629, [1943] 42 LGR 71, 113
    LJKB 269, 108 JP 22                                                11.4.3, 11.9.1


School Fees: Maintenance: Enforcement [1997] 2 FLR 252, CA                     9.8.12
Scorgie v Lawrie (1883) 10 RCSR 610, 20 Sc LR 397                              15.4.5
Scott v Scott [1913] AC 417, [1911–13] All ER Rep 1, 82 LJP 74, 109 LT 1       22.9.7,
                                                                        22.9.9, 22.10
Scottish Power plc v Britoil (Exploration) Ltd and Ors (1997) 94(47) LSG 30,
    (1997) 141 JJLB 246, (1997) *The Times*, 2 December                        6.2
Seager v Copydex Ltd [1967] 1 WLR 923, [1967] 2 All ER 415, (1967) 111 SJ
    335                                                                        22.3
Secretary of State for Education and Science v Tameside Metropolitan Borough
    Council [1977] AC 1014, [1976] 3 WLR 641, [1976] 3 All ER 665, HL          15.4.7
Shanklin Pier Ltd v Detel Products Ltd [1951] 2 KB 845, [1951] 2 All ER 471,
    (1951) 95 SJ 563                                                           5.5.3
Sharp, Sebastian (unreported)                                                  15.3.2
Shrimpton v Hertfordshire County Council [1911–13] All ER Rep 359, 104 LT
    145, 75 JP 201, [1911] 104 LT                                             11.9.6
Simkiss v Rhondda Borough Council (1983) 81 LGR 460, CA                        11.5.1
Smart v Gwent County Council [1991] LEXIS                                      11.4.3
Smerkinich v Newport Corporation (1912) 76 JP 454, 10 LGR 959, DC             11.5.1
Smith and Another, Re (1998) *The Times*, 14 January                           22.9.7
Smith v Bush (Eric S) Harris v Wyre Forest District Council [1990] 1 AC 831,
    [1989] 2 WLR 790, [1989] 2 All ER 514, HL                                  12.3.2
Smith v Safeway plc [1995] ICR 472, [1995] 1 IRLR 132, (1994) *The Times*, 16
    December                                                                   7.4.2
Smoldon v Whitworth [1997] ELR 249, [1997] PIQR P133, (1996) *The Times*,
    18 December, CA; *affirming* [1997] ELR 115, (1996) *The Times*, 23 April,
    QBD                                                            7.4.3, 11.4.4, 11.9.9
Société Commerciale de Reassurance v Eras (International) Ltd [1992] 2 All ER
    82, [1992] 1 Lloyd's Rep 570, CA                                           12.12
Spring v Guardian Assurance plc [1995] 2 AC 296, [1994] 3 WLR 354, [1994] 3
    All ER 129, HL                          8.3.11, 12.3.2, 12.11, 16.3.6, 20.4.6
Staley v Suffolk County Council and Dean Mason (unreported), 26 November 1986
                                                                               11.5.2
Starkey, Tony (1992) *Daily Telegraph*, 20 November                    5.11.4, 12.4.2

Steel v Union of Post Office Workers [1978] 1 WLR 64, [1978] 2 All ER 504,
    [1977] ICR 181      7.4.2
Steel v Wellcome Custodian Trustees Ltd [1988] 1 WLR 167, (1987) 131 SJ 1589   17.4.10
Stovin v Wise and Norfolk County Council [1996] 1 AC 923, [1996] 3 WLR 388,
    [1996] 3 All ER 801      12.3.2
Suckling v Essex County Council (1955) *The Times*, 27 January      11.5.1
Surtees v Kingston-upon-Thames, Same v Hughes [1991] 2 FLR 559, (1991)
    *Independent* 27 March, CA; *affirming* [1990] 1 FLR 103, [1990] Fam Law 62    11.3.3,
     11.4.1

T v North Yorkshire County Council (1998) *The Times*, 10 September, CA      11.6.1
T v Surrey County Council [1994] 4 All ER 577      12.3.2
Taunton School v Wright (1997) 4 EPLI 67, Yeovil County Court      8.3.13, 13.2.4
Terrington v Lancashire County Council (unreported), 1986      15.4.9
Thompson v Stanhope (1774) AMb 737, 27 ER 476, LC      22.7.4
Tillotson v Harrow Borough Council (unreported), 1981      11.9.9

Van Oppen v Bedford Charity Trustees [1990] 1 WLR 235, [1989] 3 All ER 389,
    (1989) 139 NLG 900, CA; *affirming* [1989] 1 All ER 273    11.5.1, 11.9.9, 12.4.2
Vickery, Re [1931] 1 Ch 572      17.2.5

Wagon Mound, The, The Wagon Mound and Overseas Tankship (UK), The v
    Miller Steamship Co Pty, Wagon Mound (No 2) [1967] 1 AC 617, PC      11.7.1
Wallersteiner v Moir, Moir v Wallersteiner [1974] 1 WLR 991, [1974] 3 All ER
    217, (1974) 118 SJ 464      19.11.4
Ward v Hertfordshire County Council (1969) 114 SJ 87, (1969) *The Times*, 19
    December, CA; *reversing* [1969] 1 WLR 790, [1969] 2 All ER 807, (1969)
    113 SJ 343      11.5.1, 11.9.2
White v Jones [1995] 2 AC 207, [1995] 2 WLR 189, [1995] 1 All ER 691, HL      12.3.2
Williams v Cardiff Corporation [1950] 1 KB 514, [1950] 1 All ER 250, (1950) 94
    SJ 161      11.10.1
Williams v Eady [1893] 10 TLR 41, CA      11.4.3
Williams v Natural Life Foods Ltd [1998] 1 WLR 830, HL      12.4.2
Woodward v Mayor of Hastings [1945] KB 174, [1944] 2 All ER 565, 114 LJKB
    211      11.9.2, 11.10.1
Wright v Cheshire County Council [1952] 2 All ER 789, [1952] 2 TLR 641, (1952)
    96 SJ 747, CA      11.4.4, 11.9.9

X (Minors) v Bedfordshire County Council; M (A Minor) v Newham London
    Borough Council; E (A Minor) v Dorset County Council; Christmas v
    Hampshire County Council; Keating v Bromley London Borough Council
    [1995] 2 AC 633, [1995] 2 WLR 152, [1995] 3 All ER 353, [1995] ELR 404,
    HL; *reversing sub nom* M (A Minor) v Newham London Borough Council; X
    (Minors) v Bedfordshire County Council [1995] 2 AC 648, [1994] 2 WLR
    554, [1994] 4 All ER 602, CA      7.5.1, 8.2.2, 8.4.1, 12.2.2, 12.3.2, 12.3.3, 12.4.2,
     12.4.4, 15.3.5, 16.2.3
X v Z Ltd (1997) *The Times*, 18 April, CA      22.9.9

Yachuk v Oliver Blaise Co Ltd [1949] AC 386, [1949] 2 All ER 150, [1949] 65
    TLR 300, PC      11.5.2

# Table of Statutes

**All references are to paragraph numbers.**

| | |
|---|---|
| Access to Health Records Act 1990 | 13.4.3, 22.7.14 |
| Access to Medical Reports Act 1988 | 22.6.3, 22.7.14 |
| s 7(1) | 22.6.3 |
| Administration of Justice Act 1960 | 22.9.7 |
| Administration of Justice Act 1970 | |
| s 11 | 9.8.12 |
| | |
| Banking Act 1987 | 21.3.1 |
| s 5 | 9.2 |
| s 6(2)(a) | 9.2 |
| Business Names Act 1985 | 18.7, 21.3.1 |
| | |
| Charitable Trustees Incorporation Act 1872 | 18.3 |
| Charitable Trusts Act 1858 | 17.3.6 |
| Charities Act 1958 | 17.3.1 |
| Charities Act 1960 | 17.3.5 |
| Charities Act 1992 | 18.5.4 |
| Pt II | 24.10.1 |
| Charities Act 1993 | 6.3.2, 17.3.6, 17.4.7, 17.5, 18.5.4, 18.7, 19.8.4, 21.2.5, 21.3.6, 2.1.5 |
| s 1(3) | 17.3.6 |
| (4) | 17.3.6, 17.4.9 |
| s 3 | 17.3.3, 17.4.8, 18.6 |
| (6) | 21.3.6 |
| (7) | 17.3.7, 21.3.6, 24.8.5 |
| s 5 | 21.3.6 |
| s 16 | 17.3.6 |
| s 26 | 17.3.6, 17.4.7 |
| s 29 | 17.3.6, 17.49 |
| s 33 | 17.3.6, 17.3.8 |
| s 35 | 18.4 |
| ss 36–38 | 19.7.2 |
| ss 36–40 | 17.5, 17.5.1 |
| s 36 | 17.5.1, 21.3.6 |
| s 37 | 17.4.8 |

| | |
|---|---|
| s 38 | 17.5.2, 21.3.6 |
| Pt IV | 17.3.5 |
| ss 41, 42, 43, 45 | 17.4.8 |
| s 45(6) | 18.5.4 |
| s 46 | 17.4.8 |
| s 47 | 18.5.4 |
| Pt VII | 18.2.5, 18.5.1, 20.4.18 |
| ss 50–62 | 18.2.5, 18.3 |
| s 50 | 18.2.5, 18.3, 17.3.7, 18.4, 18.5.2 |
| s 54 | 18.3 |
| s 67 | 18.2.9 |
| s 68(3) | 18.2.9 |
| s 70 | 17.4.7 |
| s 72 | 19.9.2, 19.9.3 |
| s 73 | 19.9.2 |
| s 80 | 17.3.7 |
| s 83 | 17.3.9 |
| s 96(2) | 18.2.2 |
| (3) | 17.3.8 |
| s 97(1) | 17.3.9, 18.2.9, 18.4, 19.3.1, 19.3.2, 19.6 |
| Sch 2 | 6.3.2, 17.3.7, 18.2.10 |
| Sch 5 | 17.5.1 |
| Children Act 1989 | 5.3.1, 8.2.2, 8.3.2, 8.4.13, 13.2.3, 13.4.1, 13.5.4, 13.6.6, 13.6.7, 13.7, 15.4.3, 16.3.2, 21.3.2 |
| s 2 | 6.3.1, 6.3.3 |
| (9) | 6.3.1, 8.3.2, 13.2.1, 13.4.1, 13.4.4, 13.7.2, 14.2, 14.4.3, 14.7, 15.4.3 |
| s 3(1) | 15.4.3 |
| (5) | 8.3.1, 8.3.9, 8.3.10, 8.3.11, 8.3.16, 11. 9.4, 13.2.1, 13.4.5, 13.6.6, 13.7.2, 15.3.5, 15.4.3, 15.4.10, 22.7.4 |
| s 5 | 6.3.1, 6.3.5, 14.2 |
| s 39 | 7.8.2 |
| Pt VIII | 21.3.12 |
| s 63 | 13.5.2 |
| Pt IX | 14.5 |

Children Act 1989 – *cont*

s 66                                                    14.2

(2)                                                    14.5

s 67                                                    14.5

s 69                                                    14.2

s 70

s 87          8.4.14, 13.5.4, 13.7.2, 15.4.3,
                                                     21.3.12

(1)          8.3.1, 10.12, 15.3.5

s 97(2)                                             22.9.1

Sch 6                                             21.3.12

Sch 8, para 9                                     14.2

Children and Young Persons Act
1933

s 39          22.9.3, 22.9.4, 22.10

s 68                                                22.9.3

s 70(1)                                             22.9.3

Companies Act 1862    18.2.4, 18.2.9, 18.5.1

Companies Act 1985          17.3.10, 18.2.1,
                18.2.4, 18.2.10, 18.5.2, 18.5.4,
                19.10, 19.11, 21.2.5, 21.3.1

s 2(4)                                               18.2.9

s 4                                                   19.10

s 9(1)                                               19.10

s 17(1)                                              19.10

s 28(1)                                              19.10

s 30              18.2.9, 18.7, 21.3.1

s 303       17.3.10, 18.2.9, 19.9.3, 19.10

s 304                                              17.3.10

s 307(1)                                            19.10

s 308                                               19.10

ss 348–351                             18.7, 21.3.1

s 349(1), (2)–(4)                         18.2.9

(4)                                               19.11.3

s 727                                              19.11.7

s 741(2)                                          19.11.11

Sch 24                                             21.3.1

Companies Act 1989

s 16                                                 19.10

s 137                                             19.11.1

Company Directors Disqualification
Act 1986      17.3.10, 19.9.2, 19.11.8,
                                                     21.3.1

Consumer Credit Act 1974      6.4.7, 9.8.19

s 8(3)                                              9.8.19

s 22                                               9.8.19

Pt V                                               9.8.19

Contempt of Court Act 1981                22.9.6

s 2(2)          22.9.4, 22.9.6, 22.10

s 4(2)                                              22.9.6

Copyright Designs and Patents Act
1988                                                21.3.4

s 1                                                   22.5.2

s 11(2)                                             22.6.1

Credit Consumer Act 1974     9.8.19, 21.3.2

Criminal Justice Act 1988               21.3.11

Criminal Justice Act 1991

s 70                                                22.9.4

Data Protection Act 1984          7.5.1, 8.3.11,
                8.3.16, 13.4.3, 20.4.1, 21.3.5,
                21.3.12, 22.4.3, 22.7.12,
                22.7.14, 22.7.16, 22.8, 22.8.1,
                22.8.2, 23.1, 23.2.1, 23.2.5,
                23.3, 23.4.4, 23.6.5, 23.6.6,
                                                      24.8.4

Data Protection Act 1998          7.5.1, 8.3.16,
                8.3.11, 13.4.3, 20.4.1, 21.3.5,
                21.3.1, 22.2.5, 22.4.3, 22.7.12,
                22.7.16, 22.8, 22.8.1, 22.8.2,
                23.1, 23.3, 23.6.1, 23.8, 24.8.4

s 4(3)                                              23.5.7

s 7(1)(b)                                           23.7.2

(c)(ii)                                            23.7.2

(d)                                  23.6.3, 23.7.2

ss 9–11                                             23.7.2

s 9                                      23.2.1, 23.6.5

s 10                                                23.6.4

s 11                                    23.2.1, 23.6.6

s 12                                    23.6.7, 23.7.3

s 13                                    23.6.3, 23.7.2

ss 26–38                                            23.2.5

s 31                                                23.2.5

s 32                                                23.2.5

s 69                                    23.1, 23.7.1

Sch 1, Pt II, para 2              23.7.2, 23.7.3

para 13                                  23.7.2

Sch 2          22.8.2, 23.2.1, 23.4, 23.4.2,
                                23.4.3, 23.7.2, 23.8

paras 1–4                                23.6.5

Sch 3          22.8.2, 23.2.1, 23.4.2, 23.4.3,
                                            23.7.2, 23.8

Sch 4                                              23.5.7

Sch 7                                              23.2.5

para 1                          22.7.16, 23.2.5

paras 7 and 8                           23.2.5

Sch 8                                                23.1

Debtors Act 1869

s 5                                                 9.8.12

Disability Discrimination Act 1995       7.4.1

Drug Trafficking Act 1994               21.3.11

Drug Trafficking Offences Act
1986                                               21.3.11

Education Act 1870                                    3.1

Education Act 1902                3.1, 3.2
Education Act 1918                3.3.2
Education Act 1921                3.3.2
Education Act 1944   3.1, 3.3.3, 4.1.3, 4.2.1,
                                  12.4.1
    s 70                          4.1.2
Education Act 1977                8.2.3
Education Act 1980                4.2.2
Education Act 1981           12.4.1, 22.7.15
Education (No 2) Act 1986   15.4.1, 15.4.4,
                                  15.4.5
    s 47                     15.4.1, 15.4.4
        (1)(a), (b)               15.4.4
        (4)                       15.4.4
Education Act 1993
    s 293(2), (4)                 15.4.4
    s 298                    12.4.2, 15.4.4
Education Act 1996   4.471, 7.9.6, 8.4.14,
                         10.14.23, 12.4.1, 15.4.3,
                              15.4.4, 22.7.15
    s 4(1)                        2.1.1
    s 7            5.1.1, 6.3.4, 7.8, 7.8.2
    s 8                           7.8.1
    s 9                           15.4.3
    s 19                          12.4.2
    ss 154–160                    16.2.10
    s 156(2)                      16.2.10
    s 312(1), (2), (3)            12.4.1
    ss 375–399                    8.3.14
    ss 437–448                    7.8.2
    s 444(1)                      7.8.3
    Pt VII                        21.3.12
    s 463                         2.1.1
    ss 469–471                    8.4.14
    s 469                    8.4.14, 19.8.4
    s 470                         8.4.14
    s 473(2)                      13.6.2
    ss 479–481                    6.4.4
    s 479(6)                      2.1.2
    s 546                         15.4.4
    s 549(1), (2)                 15.4.4
    s 550                         15.4.4
    s 550A                   15.4.5, 15.4.6
    s 551                         8.3.16
    Sch 38, Pt I                  2.1.1
Education Act 1997                7.9.6
    s 4                           15.4.6
    ss 6, 7                       16.2.10
    s 51                          2.1.1
    s 52(4)                       7.8.1
Education Reform Act 1988         12.5.1
Education (Schools) Act 1997  4.2.2, 6.4.4,
                              8.2.1, 18.5.2

Employers' Liability (Compulsory
    Insurance) Act 1969
    s 1(1)                        21.3.9
Employment Rights Act 1996        20.4.6,
                                  21.3.7
    s 203                         20.5.10
Endowed Schools Act 1869          3.2
Endowed Schools Acts 1869–1873    19.3.3
Environmental Protection Act 1990  21.3.14
    s 157                         19.11.10


Finance Act 1982
    s 129(2)                      17.7.5
Finance Act 1986                  17.7.3
Finance Act 1993
    s 76                          20.4.16
    Sch 5                         20.4.16
Fire Precautions Act 1971         13.5.4
Food Safety Act 1990              13.5.4
Friendly Societies Act 1992       18.2.10
Further and Higher Education Act
    1992
    s 14(5)                       2.1.1


Health and Safety at Work etc Act
    1974                    8.3.3, 21.3.8
    s 3                           8.3.3
        (1)                  13.2.1, 13.7.2
    s 7                           8.3.3
    ss 34–42                      21.3.8
Human Rights Act 1998      8.2.2, 13.2.1,
                15.4.3, 15.5.2, 16.2.1, 16.2.5,
                        22.1, 22.4.1, 22.7.5,
                                  25.1 et seq
    s 1(2)                        25.3
        (3)                       25.3
    s 4                           25.4
    s 6(1)                        25.2
        (3)                       25.2
            (b)                   25.2
        (5)                       25.2
    ss 14, 15                     25.3
    Sch 1                         25.3


Income and Corporation Taxes Act
    1988
    s 505                         17.3.7
        (1)(a)                    17.7.1
    s 832(1)                      17.7.2

Income and Corporation Taxes Act
  1988 – *cont*
  Schedules A–C                          17.7.1
  Schedule C6                            17.7.1
  Schedule D              17.7.1, 17.8.1
    Case I                17.7.1, 17.8.1
    Case II                              17.8.1
  Schedule E               17.7, 17.8.1
  Schedule F                             17.7.1
Industrial and Provident Act 1965    18.2.10
Inheritance Tax Act 1984
  s 23(1)                                17.8.4
Insolvency Act 1986       19.11.8, 21.3.1
  s 84(1)                                 19.10
  s 122(1)(a)                             19.10
  s 123                                  19.11.8
  s 213                                  21.3.1
  s 214           19.11, 19.11.9, 21.3.1
  s 217                                  21.3.1
  s 310                                  19.11.1
  ss 366, 366A                            19.10
  s 368                                   19.10
  s 376                                   19.10
  s 382                                   19.10
  s 393                                   19.10
  s 429(2)(b)                            19.9.2
Interception of Communications
  Act 1985
  s 1                                    22.7.4

Latent Damage Act 1986                   12.12
Law Reform (Contributory
  Negligence) Act 1945                   11.6.6
  s 1(1)                                 11.5.2
Law Reform (Frustrated Contracts)
  Act 1943                                5.8.3
  s 1(2), (3)                             5.8.3
Law Reform (Miscellaneous
  Provisions) (Scotland) Act
  1990
  Pt I                                   17.3.7
  s 7                                    19.9.2
Limitation Act 1980                      12.12
  ss 11–14                               12.12
  s 14A                                  12.12
    (5)                                  12.12
  s 33                                   12.12
Local Authority and Social Services
  Act 1970                               13.2.5
  s 7                           13.2, 13.7.1
Local Government Act 1889                  3.2

Local Government Finance Act
  1988
  s 43(6)                                17.7.6
Local Taxation (Customs and
  Excise) Act 1890                         3.2

Magistrates' Courts Act 1980
  s 8(1)                                 22.9.5
Matrimonial Causes Act 1973             9.8.12
Minors Contracts Act 1987      5.4.6, 5.5.2,
                             6.3.1, 6.3.3, 13.5.4
Misrepresentation Act 1967
  s 2(1)                                  5.4.2
Misuse of Drugs Act 1971
  s 8              13.7.2, 15.4.10, 15.5.3

Occupiers' Liability Act 1957
  s 2(1)                                 11.10.2
Occupiers' Liability Act 1984           11.10.2
  s 1(3)                                 11.10.2
    (4)                                  11.10.2
    (8)                                  11.10.2

Patents Act 1977
  s 1(2)                                 22.5.4
  s 3                                    22.5.4
Police and Criminal Evidence Act
  1984                                   15.4.7
Post Office Act 1953
  s 58(1)                                22.7.4
Proceeds of Crime Act 1985             21.3.11
Protection From Harassment Act
  1997                                   22.4.4
Public Interest Disclosure Act 1998     25.5.3
Public Schools Act 1868          2.1.3, 3.2
Public Schools Act 1869                  2.1.3
Public Schools Act 1871                  2.1.3
Public Schools (Shrewsbury and
  Harrow Schools Property) Act
  1873                                   2.1.3

Race Relations Act 1976          7.2, 7.4.1
  Pt II                                   14.10
  s 17                        7.4.1, 7.5.2, 9.6
  Pt IV                                   14.10
  s 34                                    7.4.1
  s 35                                    7.4.1
  s 36                                    14.10

| | |
|---|---|
| Recreational Charities Act 1958 | 17.3.2 |
| Registered Designs Act 1949 | 22.5.3 |
| Rehabilitation of Offenders Act | |
| 1974 | 13.6, 13.6.1, 22.6.3 |
| s 8 | 22.4.3 |
| | |
| Settled Land Act 1925 | 18.4 |
| s 29 | 17.5.1 |
| s 117(xxx) | 18.4 |
| Sex Discrimination Act 1975 | 7.2, 7.4.1, |
| | 22.7.5 |
| s 22 | 7.4.1 |
| (b) | 7.4.1 |
| s 26(1), (2) | 7.4.1 |
| s 27 | 7.4.1 |
| s 43 | 7.4.1 |
| s 46 | 7.4.1 |
| s 78 | 7.4.1 |
| (2) | 17.6.3 |
| Sch 2 | 7.4.1 |
| art 5 | 7.4.1 |
| Solicitors Act 1974 | 18.5.2 |
| Statute of Charitable Uses 1535 | 17.3.1, |
| | 18.5.1 |
| Statute of Charitable Uses 1601 | 17.3.1, |
| | 17.3.2, 17.6.1 |
| Supply of Goods and Services Act | |
| 1982 | 12.3.2 |
| s 13 | 5.3.1, 8.4.1, 13.2.1 |
| | |
| Taxation of Chargeable Gains Act | |
| 1992 | |
| s 256(1) | 17.7.3 |
| Technical Instruction Act 1889 | 3.2 |
| Technical Instruction Act 1891 | 3.2 |
| Theft Act 1968 | |
| s 1(1) | 17.2.6 |

| | |
|---|---|
| Torts (Interference with Goods) Act | |
| 1977 | |
| s 1 | 11.7.1 |
| ss 12–13 | 8.4.12 |
| Sch 1 | 8.4.12 |
| Town and Country Planning Act | |
| 1990 | 21.3.14 |
| Trade Descriptions Act 1968 | |
| s 14 | 6.4.2 |
| Transport Act 1962 | 21.3.13 |
| Transport Act 1985 | 21.3.13 |
| Trustee Act 1925 | 17.2.3, 17.5.3 |
| s 3 | 17.3.3 |
| s 16 | 17.5 |
| s 23(1) | 17.5, 24.10.1 |
| s 30(1) | 17.2.6 |
| s 34(3)(a) | 17.5 |
| ss 36, 37, 40–56 | 17.3.9 |
| s 61 | 17.2.6, 17.2.7 |
| Trustee Investments Act 1961 | 17.4.7 |
| Trusts of Land and Appointment of | |
| Trustees Act 1996 | 17.2.3, 17.4.7, |
| | 17.5.1 |
| s 9 | 17.5 |
| ss 41, 42 | 17.5.1 |
| s 51 | 17.5.1 |
| s 71 | 17.5.1 |
| | |
| Unfair Contract Terms Act 1977 | 5.3.2 |
| s 2 | 11.6.3, 11.10.2 |
| (2), (4)(b) | 11.10.2 |
| | |
| Value Added Tax Act 1994 | |
| Sch 9 | 17.7.4 |
| Group 6, Items 1, 4, 5 | 17.7.4 |

# Table of Statutory Instruments

**All references are to paragraph numbers.**

Access to Health Records (Control of Access) Regulations 1993, SI 1993/746     22.7.14

Charities (Accounts and Reports) Regulations 1995, SI 1995/2724     21.3.6
Children (Private Arrangements for Fostering) Regulations 1991, SI 1991/2050     14.5
Companies (Tables A–F) Regulations 1995, SI 1995/ 805
    18.2.9, 18.4
Construction, Design and Management Regulations 1994, SI 1994/3140     11.10.2, 21.3.8
Consumer Credit (Agreements) Regulations 1983, SI 1983/1553     9.8.19, 21.3.1
Consumer Credit (Exempt Agreements) Order 1989, SI 1989/869     21.3.1
    art 3     9.8.19
Control of Substances Hazardous to Health Regulations 1994, SI 1994/3246     21.3.8
County Court Rules 1981, SI 1981/1687
    Ord 19, r 4     9.8.15

Data Protection (Miscellaneous Subject Access Exemptions) Order 1987, SI 1987/
    1906     22.7.15
Data Protection (Subject Access Modification) (Health) Order 1987, SI 1987/1903     22.7.14
Disqualification for Caring for Children Regulations 1991, SI 1991/2094     14.9

Education (Assisted Places) Regulations 1995, SI 1995/2016     6.4.4
Education (Particulars of Independent Schools) Regulations 1982, SI 1982/1730     5.4.5,
    13.6.4, 21.3.12
Education (Particulars of Independent Schools) Regulations 1994, SI 1994/537     13.6.4,
    21.3.12
Education (Particulars of Independent Schools) Regulations 1997, SI 1997/2918     5.4.5, 18.7
    Pt II     13.6.4
    reg 7     12.13.3, 13.6.4, 15.4.5, 20.5.6, 21.3.12
    reg 8     13.6.4
       (2), (3)     13.6.4
Education (Pupil Registration) Regulations 1995, SI 1995/2089     7.8.1, 7.8.4
    reg 5     7.8.6
    reg 6     7.8.4
    reg 7     7.8.7
       (1), (2)     7.8.1
       (3)(a)     7.8.7
       (4)     7.8.7
    reg 8     7.8.7
       (2)     7.8.7

Education (Pupil Registration) Regulations 1995, SI 1995/2089 – *cont.*
  reg 8(4) ............................................................................................... 7.8.7
  reg 9 ................................................................................................... 7.8.5
  reg 10 ................................................................................................. 7.8.7
  regs 11, 12 .......................................................................................... 7.8.8
  reg 14 ................................................................................................. 7.8.4
  reg 15 ........................................................................................ 7.8.4, 7.8.6
  reg 16 ................................................................................................. 7.8.4
    (3) ................................................................................................. 7.8.4
Education (School Premises) Regulations 1996, SI 1996/360 ....... 13.4.1, 13.5.4
Education (School Records) Regulations 1989, SI 1989/1261 ............... 8.3.16
Education (Teachers) (Amendment) (No 2) Regulations 1995, SI 1995/259 ... 13.6.2
Education (Teachers) Regulations 1993, SI 1993/543 ........................ 13.6.2
Employment Tribunals (Constitution and Rules Procedure) Regulations 1993, SI
  1993/2687
  Sch 1, r 14(1) .................................................................................... 22.9.9


Food Hygiene (Amendment) Regulations 1990, SI 1990/2486 .............. 13.5.4
Food Hygiene Regulations 1970, SI 1970/1172 .............................. 13.5.4


Health and Safety (Safety Signs and Signals) Regulations 1996, SI 1996/341 ... 8.3.6


Rehabilitation of Offenders Act 1974 (Exceptions) Order 1975, SI 1975/1023
  art 14 ....................................................................... 13.6.1, 22.6.3
Road Vehicles (Construction and Use) (Amendment) (No 2) Regulations 1996, SI
  1996/163 ....................................................................... 21.3.13


Transfer of Undertakings (Protection of Employment) Regulations 1981, SI 1981/
  1794 .................................................................................... 18.4


Unfair Terms in Consumer Contracts Regulations 1994, SI 1994/3159 ... 5.3.2, 6.4.6, 10.4,
    10.12
  reg 4(1), (2) ........................................................................... 5.3.2
  reg 5(1) ................................................................................. 5.3.2
  reg 6 ..................................................................................... 5.3.2
  Schs 2, 3 ................................................................................ 5.3.2
Upholstered Furniture (Safety) Regulations 1980 ............................ 13.5.4


Working Time Regulations 1998, SI 1998/1833 ....................... 21.3.7, 25.5.3

# Table of EC Material

**All references are to paragraph numbers.**

## Directives

| | |
|---|---|
| Council Directive 92/57/EC | 21.3.8 |
| Council Directive 93/104/EC | 21.3.7 |
| | |
| EC Directive 91/1308/EEC | 21.3.11 |

## Treaties

| | |
|---|---|
| Euratom Treaty 1958 | 21.4 |
| European Economic Area Agreement 1994 | 21.4 |
| | |
| Treaty of European Union 1993 | 21.4 |
| Treaty of Paris 1951 | 21.4 |
| Treaty of Rome 1957 | 21.4 |

## Conventions

| | |
|---|---|
| European Convention on Human Rights 1950 | 13.2.1, 15.4.3, 21.4, 25.1 et seq |
| Art 2 | 25.3 |
| Art 3 | 15.4.4, 25.3 |
| Art 4 | 25.3 |
| Art 5 | 25.3 |
| Art 6 | 25.3, 25.5.2 |
| Art 7 | 25.3 |
| Art 8 | 15.4.3, 15.4.4, 25.3, 25.5.1, 25.5.2, 25.5.3, 25.6 |
| Art 9 | 25.3, 25.5.2, 25.6 |
| Art 10 | 25.3, 25.5.2, 25.5.3, 25.6 |
| Art 11 | 25.3, 25.6 |
| Art 12 | 25.3, 25.5.1 |
| Art 13 | 15.4.4 |
| Art 14 | 25.3, 25.5.1, 25.5.2, 25.5.3 |
| Art 16 | 25.3 |
| Art 17 | 25.3 |
| Art 18 | 25.3 |
| Art 177 | 21.4 |
| First Protocol | |
| Art 1 | 25.3, 25.5.2 |
| Art 2 | 25.3, 25.5.1, 25.5.2 |
| Art 3 | 25.3 |

European Convention on Human Rights 1950 – *cont.*
  Sixth Protocol
    Art 1                                                            25.3
    Art 2                                                            25.3

United Nations Convention on Human Rights 1950            15.4.3
  Art 2                                                            15.4.3
United Nations on the Rights of the Child 1989               15.4.3
  Arts 2, 28                                                    15.4.3

# Table of Abbreviations

CFI Court of First Instance
CONDAM Construction (Design and Management) Regulations 1994
COSHH Control of Substances Hazardous to Health Regulations 1994
CYPA Children and Young Persons Act
DES Department of Education and Science
DFE Department for Education
DfEE Department for Education and Employment
DoH Department of Health
ECHR European Convention on Human Rights 1950
ECJ European Court of Justice
EEA European Economic Area
GBA Association of Governing Bodies of Public Schools
GBGSA Association of Governing Bodies of Girls' Public Schools
GCE General Certificate of Education
GCSE General Certificate of Secondary Legislation
GSA Girls' Schools Association
HMC Headmasters' [and Headmistresses'] Conference
IAPS Independent Association of Preparatory Schools
ICFM Institute of Charity Fund-raising Managers
IPS Industrial and Provident Society
ISA Independent Schools Association
ISBA Independent Schools Bursars' Association
ISC Independent Schools Council
ISIS Independent Schools Information Service
ISJC Independent Schools Joint Council
LEA local education authority
OFT Office of Fair Trading
RRA 1976 Race Relations Act 1976
SDA 1975 Sex Discrimination Act 1975
SHMIS Society of Headmasters and Headmistresses of Independent Schools
SORP Statement of Recommended Practice
TUPE Transfer of Undertakings (Protection of Employment) Regulations 1981
UNCRC United Nations Convention on the Rights of the Child 1989
UNHCR United Nations Convention on Human Rights 1950

# PART 1

# THE DEVELOPMENT OF INDEPENDENT SCHOOLS

# Chapter 1

## HISTORICAL CONTEXT

### 1.1 THE EARLY SCHOOLS

#### 1.1.1 The Middle Ages

Independent schools today have their origins in the grammar schools of the Middle Ages (which, for these purposes, means before 1485AD) and, later, in the public schools. In 1382, when William of Wykeham founded Winchester College, there were already some 400 grammar schools, most of them under the control of monasteries, cathedrals, guilds or chantries. Many of the poor boys who attended them were destined to become clerks or priests, since the Church was the career most easily open to them. Daughters of the gentry would receive a short training in their own homes in religion, reading and writing from a governess or from their own mother.

Famous schools that predate Winchester in their original form include The King's School, Canterbury (c 600AD), St Peter's York (627), St Alban's (948), Westminster and Christ's Hospital and, in Scotland, the High School of Glasgow (1124). After Winchester came Eton College, founded in 1440 by Henry VI and modelled almost entirely on Winchester.

The earliest recorded reference to a public school (*publicae scolae*) was written probably by Abbot Samson of Bury, who in 1180 wrote of King Canute (1017–1035): '... he established public schools in the cities and towns, appointing masters to them and sending to them to be taught well-born boys of good promise and also freed the sons of slaves meeting the expense from the royal purse'.

The expression *publicae scolae* was also used in a letter of 1364 written by the Bishop of Winchester and later in 1437 in a document referring to the Cathedral Grammar School at Lincoln. It seems that *publicae scolae* as used at that time denoted schools in contrast to private establishments or private tuition. But, as time went on, it came to mean a school with certain characteristics including:

- an ancient foundation often designed for the poor who, unlike the nobility and later the rising class of merchants and traders, were unable to educate their children at home;
- a boarding establishment – boys governing boys under the prefectorial system – with a continuous history and a continuity of tradition;
- an establishment with its own system of rituals, custom, tradition, terminology and prejudices, and an ethos that favoured the strong and was designed to equip a man for the highest offices in Church and State.

## 1.1.2   The Renaissance

The Middle Ages gave way to the Renaissance which, in England, was marked by the accession of Henry VII in 1485, and gathered pace throughout the Tudor period reaching its height under Elizabeth I, who died in 1603. The Renaissance was a time when ideas and beliefs that had been unquestioned in Medieval times were openly examined and criticised. There was a revival of learning throughout central Europe led by scholars and artists and financed by princes, noblemen and rich merchants.

The time was ripe for the development of schools. In 1476, William Caxton set up the first printing press in England. Copernicus (1473–1543) revealed that the earth revolved round the sun. The period from 1486 to 1553 saw the voyages of discovery in which Diaz rounded the Cape of Good Hope (1488), Columbus reached the West Indies (1492), Cabot discovered Newfoundland (1497), Vasco da Gama reached India (1498), Cortez conquered Mexico (1519), Magellan circumnavigated the world (1522), Willoughby and Chancellor attempted to find the North East Passage (1553) and Hudson discovered Hudson Bay (1610).

It was also the time of the Oxford Reformers Thomas Linacre and William Grocyn and, later, John Colet, who was to found St Paul's School in 1510; of the great scholars Erasmus and More, and artists Da Vinci, Raphael and Michelangelo; and of the poets and dramatists William Shakespeare (1564–1616), Ben Jonson, Marlowe and Spenser. The reformation in England was pushed forward by Thomas Cranmer, in Germany by Martin Luther (1483–1546) and in France and Scotland by John Calvin (1509–1564).

The Renaissance in England was led by undergraduates and teachers, mainly at Oxford and Cambridge. The Oxford Colleges, Baliol and Merton, had been founded in the 1260s, and Peterhouse College Cambridge in 1284. Winchester, Eton and Westminster were closely associated with New College Oxford, and King's College and Trinity College Cambridge, respectively. Under the Tudors (1485–1603), the sons of merchants and country gentlemen began to fill the schools and universities where Renaissance ideas were already well entrenched. School children and university students were taught a wider range of subjects and did not necessarily plan a career in the Church.

Such was the political and social climate which fostered the development of the boys' public schools, there being no similar provision for girls at that time. The earliest of the public schools founded or re-founded on the lines of Winchester included Eton (1440), St Paul's (1510), Shrewsbury (1552), Christ's Hospital (re-founded 1553), Westminster (re-founded 1559), Merchant Taylors (1562), Harrow (1571), Rugby (1567), and Charterhouse (1611).

In Wales, 18 collegiate and independent grammar schools were founded, including Brecon (1531), Abergavenny (1543), Bangor Friars (1560), Ruthin (1574) and Carmarthen (Queen Elizabeth's) (1576).

Among the earliest independent schools in Scotland were The High School of Glasgow (1124), Dundee High School (1239), George Heriot's School (1628), Hutchesons' Grammar School (1641), Mary Erskine School (1694) and George Watson's College (1723).

The earliest surviving schools in Northern Ireland are Portora Royal School (1608) and Belfast Royal Academy (1785), and in the Republic of Ireland, Kings Hospital (1669).

There was a great variety in the aims and organisation of these schools. William of Wykeham's aim for Winchester was to provide capable recruits for the priesthood from the poorer classes. John Colet's aim for St Paul's, whose textbooks were written by Erasmus, was to educate 'children of all nations and countries indifferently'. Shrewsbury was a municipal undertaking and attracted the children of town burghers and the neighbouring nobility. Harrow was designed as a grammar school for the local poor. Christ's Hospital had a long history as an institution for 'fatherless children and other poor men's children'. Stonyhurst had a different history: it was founded in 1592 at St Omer in order to escape the effect of the persecution of Catholics in England under Elizabeth I; the school moved to England in 1794.

Many more schools were founded during the Renaissance period, among them Bristol Grammar School (1532), The King's School Canterbury (1541), Oundle (1556), Sedburgh (1525), Bristol Cathedral School (1542), Uppingham (1584), Oakham (1584) and Queen Elizabeth's Hospital School (1590) also in Bristol.

## 1.2   THE BOYS' PUBLIC SCHOOL SYSTEM FROM 1600

The population of England at the time of Henry Tudor's accession in 1485 was under 5 million. There were few towns of any size. London was the largest, with a population of about 100,000. Norwich, Gloucester, Hull, Bristol and Liverpool were growing in size and importance. The Tudor monarchy was strongly supported by a new class of capitalist merchants and industrialists together with lawyers and professional men. This was the new middle class of landed gentry who sought a good education for their sons at the developing public schools and universities. The old grammar schools such as Wisbech (1371) continued to thrive, and schools for rich and poor alike were founded between 1600 and 1825, but little is known about daily life at those schools before about 1700.

In 1659, a pamphlet written by English followers of the Czech thinker, John Comenius, visualised an 'English' elementary school in every parish, with a grammar school in each town. No child should be neglected 'for hereby hath it come to pass that many are now holding the plough, which might have been fit to steer the state'. At about that time, a teacher, George Snell, protested that 'slavish correction with the whip breedeth in the corrected ... a very hatred against the school, the teacher and against learning'. This movement was, however, stifled after the restoration of Charles II in 1660 when the aristocracy and the Anglican Church establishment saw education as partly responsible for the Puritan Revolution of Oliver Cromwell. The grammar schools were seen as having been educating boys out of their proper social station. Claimed the Earl of Newcastle, 'those whom nature or fortune had determined to the plough, the oar, or other handicrafts, were being diverted to the study of Liberal Arts'. For the next hundred years until about 1750, the grammar schools went into decline with fewer foundations and fewer pupils.

A large and respectable body of opinion thought in terms of abolishing the public school system. But there were also some vociferous supporters, among them:

– Lord Clarendon, who declared in 1670: 'I must rather recommend the education in public schools and communities than under governors and preceptors in the private families of their parents ...';
– *The Spectator*, in which an essay appeared in 1711 referring to certain of the larger and more famous grammar schools as 'great schools'; and
– Oliver Goldsmith, who wrote in 1759: 'a boy will learn more true wisdom in a public school in a year than by private education in five'.

James Boswell was more sceptical. He wrote in 1775:

'There is now less flogging in our great schools than formerly, but then less is learned there; so that what the boys get at one end they lose at the other',

and in 1791:

'More is learned in public than in private schools from emulation; there is the collision of mind with mind, or the radiation of many minds pointing to one centre.'

Later, he also wrote:

'At a great school there is all the splendour and illumination of many minds; the radiance of all is concentrated in each, or at least reflected upon each. But we must own that neither a dull boy, nor an idle boy, will do so well at a great school as at a private one.'

For the public schools, the period 1700–1825 was often marked by savagery and intolerance between boys and also between masters and their pupils. It was a time when learning of a sort was more often beaten into a boy by blows than willingly acquired. Flogging was the norm. The greatest flogger of all was the notorious Dr John Keate, Headmaster of Eton (1809–1834), of whom his pupil AW Kingslake wrote: 'He was little more than five feet in height, but within this space was concentrated the pluck of ten battalions'. After a cheating incident, he beat 72 boys. Kingslake wrote: 'It was a grand scene in the Library. The floor was covered with victims; the benches and tables with spectators ... jeers and laughter accompanied the execution'.

Masters were paid their fees in accordance with how many pupils were in their class and so class sizes were sometimes enormous. Kingslake reported that Dr Keate, for example, tried to teach 200 boys at once.

From the 1750s onwards, an unwritten system of 'boy rule' evolved with the acquiescence of the masters who saw it as a means through which a boy could fight for status among his fellows and evolve 'superior manliness, generosity and self-control'. Various forms of bullying were the result of this regime, including being tossed in blankets, boys being forced to toast bread with their bare hands, a boy being branded, and the system of 'fagging' (bearers of faggots for the fire).

The failure by masters to supervise the free time of boys resulted in Eton boys gambling on cock fighting, going to the races and drinking in taverns. Westminster boys were notorious for terrorising local people with their violence, and boys at country schools went poaching.

In the 1790s, some attempts were made by masters to curtail these excesses, but that only resulted in rebellions on the part of boys whose imaginations were no doubt fired by the events of the French Revolution (1789).

Winchester had its 'Great Rebellion' in 1793 when some boys had pistols and hurled stones from a tower; and another in 1818 when pupils, objecting to the headmaster's 'spying', were only quelled by soldiers with bayonets. Rugby had a revolt in 1797 when boys blew up the headmaster's door. At Harrow, in 1808, senior boys paraded banners inscribed 'Liberty and Rebellion', as a protest against curtailment of their flogging powers.

Official concern about the public (endowed) schools was recorded in Parliament in 1820 when Lord Brougham unsuccessfully sponsored a parliamentary bill whose object was to bring about some exercise of control over them. In 1858, the Newcastle Commission was set up to investigate popular education.

In 1861, the Clarendon Commission was appointed to inquire into the revenues and management of nine colleges and schools, namely: Eton, Winchester, Westminster, Charterhouse, St Paul's, Merchant Taylors', Harrow, Rugby and Shrewsbury. The Clarendon Commission reported in 1864, following which the Taunton Commission was appointed to inquire into 782 grammar, proprietary and private schools which had not been comprised within the Clarendon Commission.

The Taunton Commission reported in 1868 and recommended the setting up of a system of State education with local control. The Endowed Schools Act 1869 embodied some of the recommendations of the Taunton Commission and set up an Endowed Schools Commission to approve new schemes for the schools. Its powers were later transferred to the Charity Commission, and later again in 1899 transferred to the then newly formed Board of Education.

From about 1825, against the background of growing official concern over institutionalised cruelty and the lack of control over the public schools, Dr Thomas Arnold, Headmaster of Rugby School from 1828 to 1842, began to tackle the problems. He was concerned by the aimless brutality of school life and his stated intention was to create 'a place of Christian education, to form Christian men'. His list of priorities was: 'First, religious and moral principle; second, gentlemanly conduct; thirdly, intellectual ability'.

His ideas were taken up by other leaders in education, most notably Thring of Uppingham (appointed 1853), who did much to humanise boarding schools; Sanderson of Oundle (appointed 1892), who saw the need to adapt education to an industrial society; and Vaughan of Harrow, who saw the value of organised games as a means of channelling excess energy. These leaders set ideals in the place of mere conventions and enabled the public school system to increase its numbers greatly.

Arnold's great legacy was to give education a religious foundation and in his wake came compulsory games, the ideas of team spirit, 'good form', tremendous changes in the curriculum and a series of distinguished headmasters. Arnold's method had been one of conscious and earnest leadership, and the moral ascendancy of the teacher over his pupils in pursuit of some ideal. By 1864, the report of the Public School

Commission stood as evidence of the complete acceptance of the public school system as the best possible means of education for those who were to be leaders of the country in peace or war.

The rehabilitation of the public schools brought about by Arnold and his successors enabled the rise of the proprietary schools. The demand for proprietary schools came from newly rich parents who had made fortunes in the Industrial Revolution and wanted their sons to rise socially. They wanted value for money from new and cheaper boarding schools. A proprietary school would be set up as a company with wealthy local people investing in it by buying shares, so receiving the right to nominate pupils. Their investors were often unashamedly biased in favour of wealthy parents, although some, such as Marlborough (1843), were intended for clergymen's sons, and Epsom (1853) was intended for doctors' sons.

The proprietary schools included University College School (1830), the City of London School (1837), Liverpool College (1840), Cheltenham College (1841), Marlborough College (1843), Rossall School (1844), Radley College (1847), Bradfield College (1850), Wellington College (1852), Epsom College (1855), Clifton College (1862), Malvern College (1862) and Haileybury (1862). In all, 31 public schools were started between 1840 and 1869.

In 1869, Thring, the Headmaster of Uppingham, founded the Headmasters' Conference. The headmasters attending the first meeting came from Uppingham, Repton, Sherborne, Tonbridge, Liverpool College, Bury St Edmunds, Richmond (Yorks), Bromsgrove, Oakham, King's School (Canterbury), Felsted, Lancing and Norwich.

Lancing College (1848) became the flagship of the Woodard Schools, founded by Nathaniel Woodard, a minister of the Church who became the greatest founder of public schools. He saw a need to provide boarding schools for the new commercial class created by the Industrial Revolution, which would be imbued with the spirit of Anglican Christianity and would be run on the pattern of Arnold's Rugby.

He began at Lancing and Hurstpierpoint (1849). In 1870, he established Ardingly College for poorer parents and, in 1873, he founded Denstone on a donated site. In 1879, he founded Ellesmere and, in 1890, Worksop. He died in 1891. The Woodard Corporation lived on and continued to acquire new schools. In 1985, there were some 32 schools in the five regional divisions of the Woodard Corporation.

## 1.3   THE GIRLS' PUBLIC SCHOOLS FROM 1650

From about 1100AD or earlier, monasteries and nunneries provided schooling for both boys and girls. At about the age of 10, some girls (especially those not expected to marry) would be sent to a nunnery where they might continue with their education. Others would be sent to board with a family of a higher social status than their own until marriage at the age of 13 or 14.

For girls from the upper class, the nunnery school provided the only type of organised schooling, but the dissolution of the monasteries from 1536 onwards meant that these nunnery schools were also closed. Upper-class boys still had the chance to attend a grammar school but their sisters had practically no chance of any organised schooling.

The great teachers of the Renaissance, Erasmus, More and Vives all advocated the education of women but in a very narrow sense. However noble in rank, however learned, 'let those books be taken in hand that may teach good manners'. In addition to their Latin and Greek, girls should be taught to be 'sober-minded, to love their husbands, to be discreet, chaste, housewifely, good, obedient to their husbands'.

Wives of merchants needed to be able to read and write so that they could run the business and their large households when their husbands were away, possibly overseas. Many widows remained in trade.

Martin Luther (1483–1546) thought every town should have a girls' school in which 'little maids might hear the gospel for an hour daily, whether in German or in Latin' and John Comenius saw no reason why the 'weaker sex' should be excluded from 'the pursuit of knowledge'. Mulcaster agreed, but advised that, after attending the petty-school where they learned to read, boys and girls should go to separate schools, where the girls might learn to read and write, sing and play an instrument and possibly learn languages as the boys did. Thomas Becon thought that schools should be set up for girls 'in every Christian commonweal and honest, sage, wise, discreet, sober, grave and learned matrons made rulers and mistresses of the same'. In practice, few girls went beyond the petty-school.

For centuries, marriage and domestic life had been considered the only roles suitable for women of upper and middle classes. Any education they received had been to fit them for these roles. Although the Royal tutor to Henry VIII (1509–1547) thought that 'Women should study wisdom, which doth instruct their manners and inform their living', female learning was broadly out of fashion between 1550 and 1700.

Even so, a number of boarding schools for girls were opened from the early 1600s onwards. In the major towns such as Manchester, Oxford, Leicester and, in particular, near London, in Hackney, Chelsea and Putney, there were private boarding schools designed to teach girls the 'accomplishments'. Girls were required to learn what was thought to be necessary for 'ladies of leisure'. The curriculum included reading, writing and religion, but also a great deal of needlework, music, dancing, household management and French.

The restoration of the monarchy with the accession of Charles II in 1660 emphasised the dichotomy between academic learning and 'accomplishments' for girls. It was thought unladylike to display any interest in academic matters, but the boarding schools that taught the accomplishments thrived and by about 1700 there were many of them.

A smaller number of charitable boarding schools for girls existed before 1700. The oldest of these, independent of the Church, is probably the Red Maids' School at Bristol, founded by a local merchant, John Whitson, in 1632 as a hospital school. 'Hospital' at that time had a wider meaning than today and included a charitable institution for reception and education of the needy young. To begin with, there were 12 girls, but only six beds. This was regarded at the time as the best way of keeping the girls warm at night. New Hall School was founded in 1642.

During the 1700s, Brighton had a number of little 'Academies' – boarding schools where girls learned some reading, writing and scripture, but concentrated on music, dancing, domestic skills and 'curious works of the needle'. In 1759, a *London Chronicle* writer noted how, in villages near London, 'There are one or two little boarding schools with an inscription over the door, "Young ladies boarded and educated" ... Hither the blacksmith, ale-housekeeper, the shoemaker etc sends his daughter, who, from the moment she enters these walls, becomes a young lady'.

By about 1800, most girls were still destined for domestic service, although women from the upper and middle classes were expected not to work and only did so if they were unable or unwilling to marry or became widowed. Although often poorly educated themselves, teaching was the only respectable occupation open to these women.

The period 1800 to 1850 in England was one of changing social attitudes and demand for reform. One aspect of this was a realisation by the early Victorians that education was a means of wider social reform and that female teachers had a key part to play in this. If they were to teach effectively they must themselves receive a proper education.

Queens College (1848) and Bedford College (1849) both opened in London to provide lectures for teenage girls and some more mature women to provide a supply of well-educated female teachers.

Among the first pupils at Queens were Frances Buss (1826–94) and Dorothea Beale (1831–1906), two great pioneers of girls' education. The third pioneer, who did not attend Queens, was Emily Davies (1830–1921), a determined reformer who linked girls' schooling to the rising feminist movement. Dorothea Beale became Principal of The Ladies' College Cheltenham in 1858 where she remained for about 50 years. The curriculum was widened to include science, Latin and Greek. There were no physical punishments and, in 1864, the first boarding house opened.

In 1850, Frances Mary Buss started the school later to be known as the North London Collegiate School for Girls, which became the model for girls' day schools throughout the country. This was followed by the foundation of the Girls' Public Day School Company (now the Girls' Day School Trust) in 1872 which opened its first high school in 1873, and by 1903 had established no fewer than 34 girls' schools in different parts of the country.

The Taunton Commission (1864) reported in 1868 that there were 820 endowed schools for boys but only about 20 comparable schools for girls. The final report officially recognised the general deficiency in girls' education and pointed to the problems of lack and misuse of school endowments. Even where the original endowment of a school specified that only boys were to benefit, the Taunton Commission often decided that it should be extended to support girls as well.

Girls' boarding schools founded on the lines of the boys' public schools, with houses and a prefect system, included St Leonard's School, St Andrew's (1877), Roedean (1885), the Godolphin School (1886), Queen Anne's, Caversham (1894), Wycombe Abbey (1896), St Felix, Southwold (1897), Sherborne (1899), Benenden (1923) and Westonbirt (1928).

In Wales, the three main girls' schools in 1881 were Howells Llandaff, Howells Denbigh, and Dolgelley. In 1894, Liverpool College for Girls was founded as a boarding and day school.

The Association of Headmistresses was founded by Miss Buss and Miss Beale in 1874. Out of that Association came two special-interest groups: the Association of Heads of Girls' Boarding Schools (1922) and a later group called the Association of Independent and Direct Grant Schools. These later amalgamated to form the Girls' Schools Association (GSA) in 1974. In the meantime, it had been noted in 1944 that the Association of Governing Bodies of Girls' Public Schools (GBGSA) represented 80 independent and 59 direct grant girls' schools.

The Association of Headmistresses had combined the heads of the girls' public schools with the other secondary school headmistresses in a single body, but the Association was not perceived as an organisation to define and confirm the status of the girls' schools in the way that the Headmasters' Conference (HMC) did for boys' schools. The Association of Governing Bodies of Public Schools (GBA) (1941) allowed the occasional co-educational school of the right type into membership, and accepted Bedales, for example, but drew the line at girls' schools.

The GBA did not regard the role of a girls' school as the same as that of a school for boys. Girls' schools were also far fewer in number, they placed less emphasis on boarding and they were not so distinct from the national system as were the boys' schools. Nor were they part of a complete system. They did not recruit so exclusively from preparatory schools nor send such a high proportion of pupils to Oxford and Cambridge. The girls' schools did not have the same influence as the boys' schools over the general education system or over national life as a whole. Nor by 1940 were they regarded as a problem in quite the same way as the boys' schools.

The Bryce Commission of 1894 commended the spread of girls' schooling: 'The idea that a girl, like a boy, may be fitted by education to earn a livelihood, or . . . be a more useful member of society, has become more widely diffused'.

In the post-war years from 1945 under strong leadership from within, coupled with support from their professional associations, the girls' public schools have forged ahead, making up much of the leeway caused by the legal disadvantage and institutional neglect of earlier decades. Whilst acknowledging the potential benefits of co-education for some children, they have successfully maintained cogent and persuasive arguments for all-girl secondary education to A-level.

The success of all-girl schools, both maintained and independent, can be measured superficially by reference to performance tables in which, without making any allowance for smaller numbers or size, they frequently occupy more than half of the top ten places and also perform consistently as well further down the tables.

A more reliable measure of their success, however, is the increase during the last 20 years in the number of girls from these schools taking up university education and moving into the professions, business and industry and entering public life.

## 1.4  THE 'PROGRESSIVE SCHOOLS'

From the 1880s onwards, a new type of private school started to emerge, with the object of keeping the best traditions of the public school system, whilst giving pupils a wider and more balanced education than had been customary and with the emphasis on encouraging the growth of each individual in sympathy, spontaneity and leadership.

The originator of this movement was Dr Cecil Reddie who founded Abbotsholme in Staffordshire in 1889. Dr Reddie was the originator of a movement which embraced the *Leitz Schule* in Germany and led to the foundation of Bedales, Gordonstoun and many others.

These were the so-called progressive schools that were viewed with some suspicion by the establishment. They offered a positive alternative to the public school model and appealed to the same social class. They took as their starting-point a criticism of traditional educational methods as established in the public schools and largely imitated in the emerging State schools. In the words of WAC Stewart (*The Educational Innovators*, Vol 2 (1968), p 343) they rebelled 'against certain procedures in schools, against condescension to children in any society, against academic emphases in the curriculum, against formality and lack of spontaneity in personal relationships, and against authoritarianism in all its forms'.

Those that were regarded as less radical included Bedales (1893), Clayesmore (1896), Rendcomb (1920), and Bryanston (1928). They were all seen as fully respectable by 1941 when the GBA was formed. But others, like Dartington Hall and Summerhill, remained isolated as radical alternatives to the existing provision.

# Chapter 2

## THE CHARACTERISTICS OF THE PUBLIC SCHOOLS

### 2.1 'PUBLIC SCHOOLS' AND RELATED TERMINOLOGY

#### 2.1.1 Meaning of 'school'

The statutory definition of 'school' given at s 14(5) of the Further and Higher Education Act 1992 was repealed by Education Act 1996, Sch 38, Part I and replaced by the Education Act 1996, s 4(1). Section 4(1) has in turn been substituted by the Education Act 1997, s 51 which applies from 1 September 1997.

'School' is now defined as meaning:

> '... an educational institution which is outside the further education sector and the higher education sector and is an institution for providing – (a) primary education, (b) secondary education, or (c) both primary and secondary education, whether or not the institution also provides part-time education suitable to the requirements of junior pupils or further education.'

The effect of these changes in the legislation is to remove institutions from the definition of 'school' if they do not provide full-time education for pupils of compulsory school age.

#### 2.1.2 Meaning of 'independent school'

Section 463 of the Education Act 1996 defines an independent school as one at which full-time education is provided for five or more pupils of compulsory school age (whether or not such education is also provided for pupils under or over that age), not being a school maintained by a local education authority, a grant-maintained school or a special school not maintained by a local education authority. The awkward double negative in relation to special schools causes some problems of interpretation.

For the purposes of the assisted places scheme, s 479(6) of the same Act defined an 'independent school' as a registered school that is conducted for charitable purposes only. Proprietor-owned schools are thus excluded from that definition but are otherwise to be treated as independent schools.

For most regulatory purposes, therefore, there is no legal distinction in principle between a major public school, college or academy, a proprietor-owned school or a small private school of five pupils operating from the front room of a house. The legal classification of each is that of an independent school.

### 2.1.3   Meaning of 'public school'

The term 'public school' has no statutory, or generally accepted, definition.

– The Clarendon Commission Report of 1864 listed nine schools only as public schools. They were Eton, Winchester, Westminster, Charterhouse, St Paul's, Merchant Taylors', Harrow, Rugby and Shrewsbury.

– The Taunton Commission 1868 had considerable difficulty in deciding what the term 'public school' was intended to convey. They excluded the 'charitable foundations where a limited number of boys selected as objects of charity were clothed, fed and instructed such as Colston's and Queen Elizabeth's at Bristol and many others [on the grounds that] they cannot be considered as instances, for from their nature they are confined to a favoured few'. The Taunton Commission used the term 'public schools' to comprise both endowed and proprietory schools but stated later that it is freedom of admission which gives endowed schools a special claim to the title 'public schools'.

– The Public Schools Acts 1868–73 omitted St Paul's and Merchant Taylors' from the list of nine given by the Clarendon Commission.

– The Fleming Committee, which reported in 1944, considered public schools to be those independent schools which were (or whose heads were) members of Headmasters' Conference (HMC), the Association of Governing Bodies of Public Schools (GBA) or the Association of Governing Bodies of Girls' Public Schools (GBGSA). There were 288 such schools when the Fleming Committee was appointed, including 11 in Scotland. At p 121 of the Committee's report it was stated: '... it is clear that the term [public school] has no precise significance in the public mind'.

– In 1810, Sidney Smith wrote: 'By a public school, we mean an endowed place of education of old standing, to which the sons of gentlemen resort in considerable numbers and where they continue to reside from 8 or 9 to 18 years of age ... the characteristic features of these schools are their antiquity, their numbers, the ages of the young people who are educated at them ...'.

– In 1821, Samuel Butler, Headmaster of Shrewsbury, wrote to Henry Brougham laying down the following criteria to distinguish the public school, as follows:

   (1)   a school open to the public, ie a school to which persons from all parts of the kingdom are in the habit of sending their children for education;
   (2)   one at which boys are educated in the higher departments of literature, with a view to their entrance into public life;
   (3)   one of ample foundation, endowed with valuable exhibits.

Many would argue nowadays that the expression 'public school' has no value in terms that are modern or forward-looking. It is a throwback to 600 years or more of history.

Others in contemporary life are content to use the expression to mean quite simply an independent secondary school – a school not receiving a grant from public funds.

In practice, the term 'public school' will normally be applied to one which is old-established, often with provision for boarding, and with fine buildings, land and, perhaps, endowments; which is open to boarders and also to day-pupils six days per week and until 8 pm or later from Monday to Friday, providing optional meals; which has extensive facilities and aspires to excellence not only in academic matters but in a wide range of other activities; and which groups its pupils under a house system for boarding and/or social and pastoral purposes. At present rates, the fees for these schools are often £1,000 or more per term greater than the fees of a five-day 8.30 am–4 pm day-school without most of these other attributes. The point may be of importance not only to explain a substantial difference in the fees for a day-pupil between two neighbouring schools, but also to indicate differences of ethos and the range of opportunities being offered.

The expression 'public school' is used in the Income and Corporation Taxes Act 1988, s 505 in the context of income tax exemption for charities. Whether or not a school is a public school for these purposes depends on the facts of the case. The following decisions have been noted in *Halsbury's Laws of England* (4th edn, reissue) Vol 15, para 204:

–   'public school' is not a term of art (1931);

–   the City of London School is a public school (1807);

–   a school reserved primarily for members of the Society of Friends, substantially self-supporting, was not exempt from income tax as a public school (1915);

–   a Roman Catholic secondary day-school was exempt from tax as a public school (1920);

–   Free Church College, Edinburgh, intended for the training of candidates for the ministry of the Free Church of Scotland, was not a public school (1897);

–   a technical college providing day-time instruction wholly related to the principles and practice of woollen manufacture was not a public school (1926);

–   a secondary school of 450 boys and 40 boarders with almost all of its income coming from fees and in which parents frequently purchased shares but which charged additional fees for the sons of non-shareholders was not a public school (1926).

### 2.1.4   Meaning of 'college', 'collegiate', 'academy' and 'foundation'

'College'denotes a self-maintained and independent organisation subject, from its constitution, to no dictatorship either of Church or of State. A college was often founded with royal or ecclesiastical patronage and more often than not is constituted under an Act of Parliament or Royal Charter. Many of the proprietary schools (later charitable) that were founded from 1830 onwards are described as a 'college' but others, such as the City of London School (1837) and Rossall (1834), are designated as schools. Thus, the expression 'college' is a description of constitution rather than function. The function of a college is to be a school.

'Collegiate' denotes some attachment to an ecclesiastical or other institution, and so not entirely independent, although independent of State control. Many of the early grammar schools, particularly those in Wales, were 'collegiate' grammar schools.

An 'academy' was defined by Samuel Johnson in his Dictionary of 1755 as 'a place of education, in contra distinction to the universities or public schools. The thing, and therefore the name, is modern'. However, in Scotland, 'academy' means a place of study.

'Foundation' denotes the establishment of an endowed institution, such as a monastery, college or hospital, entitled to benefit by its funds and its revenues. The expression is therefore more appropriate to a college or school with endowments than an unendowed school. It can equally be applied to a scholarship or bursary fund if sufficiently substantial.

### 2.1.5   Closed communities

An independent school, whether boarding or day, is often described as a closed community. This is not a legal expression or a term of art but it none the less has an important significance in the way schools have developed.

A closed community is a private, self-regulating community whose conduct is not specifically regulated by law and which to that extent is unaccountable and free to regulate its own affairs within the general framework of the law. In this sense, a school is less 'closed' than a monastery because there is greater accountability in education than in a religious community.

Traditionally, an important characteristic of a closed community, such as a monastery, convent or independent school, was that those who joined the community waived a number of their civil liberties and legal rights. They submitted to the jurisdiction of the community but, unlike a cult, the members were free to withdraw at any time, subject, in the case of a school, to giving one term's notice or paying one term's fees in lieu of notice. Those who by their conduct made it clear they would not conform to the rules of the community could be expelled or asked to leave and were not entitled to the procedures of natural justice unless the rules of the community so provided.

Another characteristic of closed communities was that they tended to develop their own system of ethics, rituals, terminology, rules, sanctions and mode of dress.

These characteristics were both a strength and a weakness. They enabled abuses of the kind described in *Tom Brown's School Days*. On the other hand, they generally created an environment that produced the nation's leaders.

The concept of a closed community is a theme that has continued throughout the history of independent schools and was still very strong in the 1970s. Particularly in boys' schools, the headmaster, rightly or wrongly, was customarily regarded as the sole authority in matters relating to pupils and parents, without any right of appeal or review, other than in a handful of cases, when the law could intervene.

Even now, independent schools remain private, self-regulating communities, still with their own system of ethics, rituals, terminology, rules, sanctions and dress. They deal internally with offences such as theft, assault and minor possession of drugs if they occur. They are not bound by the National Curriculum nor by most of the provisions of the Education Acts, but they are more accountable in a number of respects, particularly under the Charities Act 1993 (where applicable).

Since the 1970s, they have also become increasingly affected by the new social and consumer legislation in such areas as employment, health and safety, children, discrimination and unfair contract terms. The law of negligence and the procedures of natural justice have also become more accessible to those who use independent schools. To a large extent, the authority of the head remains intact provided he (or she) acts and can be seen to act in a way that is fair – fairness being of greater legal importance than being right or wrong.

Subject to these matters, an independent school remains self-regulating and is entitled and often legally bound to keep private its own affairs and those of its parents and pupils – a position not always understood or treated fairly by the media.

## 2.2   THE CHARACTERISTICS

In his book *English Public Schools* (Norton, 1985), James McConnell described the public schools in this way:

> 'The reputation of the public schools conferred a certain cachet for life on their pupils. What set them apart was that they had shared an experience only available to a minority; they had left home and family to live in an enclosed society under Spartan conditions, where regimes and rituals of almost tribal severity prevailed. There were many unhappy boys but those who came through had one great asset; they had learned early in life to be a member of a community.'

Several features were particularly characteristic in the schools that were regarded as public schools. Taken individually, each feature was almost always shared by some schools which were not public, and not shared by some schools which were. But taken together, they sum up what was generally meant by a public school. Dr Michael Davies, in his thesis entitled *The Public Schools 1939 to 1945*, identified the following characteristics.

### 2.2.1   Cost

Public schools were expensive. Independence had to be paid for and outstanding success and prestige could not be bought cheaply. Many of the public schools were housed in magnificent buildings of great architectural and historic value with an estate to match. The money to pay for this came from fees contributed by parents.

Some schools had endowments, some had special interests behind them, such as the City livery companies or the religious denominations. A few, such as Winchester and Eton, had very large resources, such as collections of plate and valuable libraries. In the main, they were middle-class schools, but there were exceptions, such as Christ's Hospital School.

### 2.2.2   Predominantly boarding

Although most public schools were for boarders, there were exceptions. St Paul's, Westminster, Merchant Taylors' and the City of London, for example, were exclusively, or primarily, day-schools. Boarding was a feature which clearly separated public schools from the general education system where boarding was reserved for the delinquent, the defective, and in some cases those who lived in remote areas.

### 2.2.3   Location

With some exceptions, the public schools were non-local. Even some of the day-schools like St Paul's and Westminster drew day-boys from an area covered by a number of local authorities, and their prestige extended much further. The minority denominational schools such as Stonyhurst (Catholic) and Kingswood (Methodist) attracted pupils from all over the country.

### 2.2.4   All boys

There were girls' public schools but their role was not regarded as the same as that of the boys' public schools. Girls' education had been neglected in the past and by 1940 there were far fewer girls' schools in number. They placed less emphasis on boarding and they were not so distinct from the national system.

### 2.2.5   The type of education

The public schools were characterised by the type of education they provided. From Arnold's time onwards, they were concerned with all aspects of the growth and development of their pupils. Their aim was to educate the whole man, intellectually, physically, socially and spiritually. It was an ambitious aim, but one for which they could not avoid responsibility since, as residential schools, they had the whole lives of their pupils in their hands for a large part of the year during a crucial stage in their development.

The public schools specialised in an academic, grammar school education and placed the greatest emphasis for all their pupils on this intellectual training. Classics were still the most important subjects at the time of the Second World War. There were high staffing ratios and masters with high academic qualifications. The prospects for entering Oxbridge with or without a scholarship were greater for those in public schools than in other secondary schools.

### 2.2.6   House system

The house system was, and remains, a feature common to public schools and has, in various forms, been copied by other schools of all kinds. The house meant much more than a building which accommodated 50–90 boys or girls. It was, and remains, the means of dividing a large school into manageable units by age and/or gender for purposes of pastoral care, social activity and competition. It was Arnold of Rugby who first gave the housemaster a pastoral role, so that he came to be the most important influence in a boy's school life. In the most traditional schools, loyalty to house often surpassed loyalty to school, and parents regarded the choice of a house as no less important than the choice of school.

### 2.2.7   Prefectorial system

The prefectorial system was an early feature of the public schools when seniors were placed in charge of junior boys, and prefects had authority to beat other boys even until the mid-1960s at some of the more traditional public schools such as Stonyhurst. Fagging (said to teach humility) was another feature of the power of senior boys over juniors, but the system had largely disappeared by the 1950s.

### 2.2.8 The importance of games

Physical activities were a prominent part of the work at the public schools, although by the end of the 1930s the cult of athletics was less dominant than it had been earlier in the century. None the less, the public schools fostered a spirit of competition stimulated by the house system and inter-school rivalries and they had the land and other facilities and the quality of coaching necessary to excel.

### 2.2.9 Pre-service military training

A strong public school tradition, facilitated by boarding, was to prepare boys for a military career. Schools such as Rossall (1844) and Wellington (1853) had particularly close links with the services.

### 2.2.10 Training in community life

A boy progressed through a public school from being an insignificant and often abused fag in the first place to a position of responsibility as a prefect later on. A boy was said to learn valuable social lessons from the community life, which taught him to extend loyalty to his house at first and then to the wider world of the school, and finally to the nation as a whole.

### 2.2.11 Religious training

Most public schools attached the greatest importance to the religious training they provided. A strong Christian tradition ran throughout the whole system and the majority had clear links with particular denominations. Most of the public schools incorporate a magnificent chapel which became, and remains, the centre of the school's spiritual life.

These were the main features that combined to characterise the public schools system as a whole and to separate it from the other schools catering for children of the same age.

# Chapter 3

## DEVELOPMENTS IN EDUCATION 1860–1944

### 3.1 ELEMENTARY EDUCATION

The General Election of 1868 returned a Liberal Government that was ardent for reform. Gladstone appointed WE Forster (1819–86) to supervise a considered measure for the education of the people.

Forster's Education Act 1870 created a dual system of elementary schools run by the School Board in each area or by the Church (voluntary schools) so as to bring some schooling within reach of every English child. There were one million pupils in inspected schools in 1870 and six million by 1900, approximately half of them in Board schools and the other half in Church schools or private or public schools.

School Boards contained from five to 15 members, elected by local ratepayers to hold office for three years. A Board had to raise rates, buy land and borrow money to build its schools. The idea of compulsory schooling spread only gradually. The 1870 Act empowered Boards to make by-laws that children must attend school. London and other large cities compelled attendance for 5- to 10-year-olds and this regime was gradually taken up in other areas, although attendance was difficult to enforce in the countryside, where child labour was still useful and powerful squires or farmers could override the law.

The school staff at a Board school might consist of a certificated head, an assistant or two, and some teenage apprentice pupil-teachers. School life for the pupils was grim and discipline was harsh. The cane was in constant use.

The voluntary (Church) schools remained under-resourced and found it difficult to keep pace with the Board schools. The declining condition of voluntary schools became a political issue. Liberals favoured the Boards, Conservatives the Church schools. Demands for general reform grew. The Education Act 1902 dissolved the Boards and replaced them with local education authorities.

### 3.2 THE NATIONAL SECONDARY SYSTEM

The system of national secondary schools has its origins in the decade from 1860 to 1870, although the system as such did not emerge until after 1902, and it only became a national system under the Butler Education Act 1944. Until then, most children went to elementary schools only and left at 14.

From 1860 onwards, the government showed a determination to exercise some measure of control over the governance of the endowed schools as well as addressing the secondary education of girls. There was concern about the social divisions in the country and the need for greater technical and manual skills. The decade 1860–70 saw the report of the Clarendon Commission in 1864, the report of the Schools Inquiry Commission in 1868 and the report of the Taunton Commission, also in 1868. The latter included recommendations for the setting up of a system of State education under local control.

Parliament also took a hand in the passing of the Public Schools Act 1868 and the Endowed Schools Act 1869.

The development chronology for the remainder of the period may be summarised as follows:

(a)  The Technical Instruction Acts 1889 and 1891 empowered county and borough councils and urban sanitary authorities in England and Wales to levy a rate not exceeding one penny in the pound to supply or add the supply of technical or manual instruction.

(b)  The Local Government Act 1889 set up county councils.

(c)  The Local Taxation (Customs and Excise) Act 1890 made provision from beer and spirit duties known as 'whiskey money' for developing technical education, including instruction in science and art, as a result of which, by 1894, there were 240 endowed secondary schools receiving some grant from the Department of Science and Art.

(d)  In 1895, the Bryce Commission reported a great improvement in the condition of the endowed grammar schools since 1868 and found that the Endowed Schools Act 1869 had already done something 'to open schools which lead directly to the universities to the sons of men who fall into the categories neither of the rich nor of the educated'. Also in 1895, the report of the Secondary Education Commission recorded the fact that many county councils were already spending large sums of money on the direct or indirect assistance of education.

(e)  In 1899, the Board of Education was instituted and, among other things, introduced a new system of inspections.

In 1902, the new Education Act laid the basis for grants ('Direct Grant') to be paid to secondary schools by the Board of Education on a capitation basis. From this time onwards, the public schools and others that remained privately funded were increasingly affected by developments in the evolving national secondary system.

The national secondary system that evolved identifiably from 1902 onwards was composed of old grammar schools which were ready to receive public grants from the central or local authorities in return for taking pupils from the elementary schools. New grammar schools were built and maintained by the authorities to supplement this provision.

A hierarchy began to appear which seemed to depend on how close each type of school came to the public school model. The nearer the top of the hierarchy, the smaller was the proportion of free pupils, the higher the cost of the fees and the greater the degree of independence. The direct grant schools came at the top, followed by the aided schools, and finally came the local authority maintained schools.

The national secondary system began to affect the public schools particularly in the following ways:

## *Salaries*

Salary levels and pension rights were laid down from 1918 onwards by regulation in the national sector, and the public schools were obliged to make parallel arrangements for their own staff.

## *Career opportunities*

An increasing number of assistant masters in public schools sought promotion by accepting headships in the new secondary schools.

## *Scholarships*

Between 1920 and 1936, the public schools were excluded from the system of State scholarships which would take pupils from grant-aided schools to universities. From 1936 onwards, the public schools were allowed to compete in this respect.

## *Inspections*

Between 1899 and 1936, the pressure grew for public schools to submit to inspection. In 1936, Eton was inspected and recognised as efficient. By 1939, virtually all public schools had been inspected.

## 3.3   TWO WORLD WARS

### 3.3.1   World War I (1914–18)

Empire Day (24 May) was celebrated each year from 1906 onwards with the aim of instilling into the minds of children the privileges, responsibilities and duties of citizenship of the Empire. During the pre-war years, children were encouraged to 'think imperially' and when war came they were expected 'to do their bit'.

School buildings were taken by the military authorities or turned into hospitals or refugee centres. Male teachers were eventually taken by conscription. A report of 1917 noted an increase in juvenile delinquency and crime in large cities. Another report of 1917 commented 'excessive hours of strenuous labour have overtaxed the powers of young people while many have taken advantage of the extraordinary demand for juvenile labour to change from one blind alley employment to another'.

During the First World War, the casualties from the public schools were catastrophically high in proportion to their numbers and, understandably, public schools pointed to their war record as an indisputable justification of their value to the country.

### 3.3.2   Between the Wars (1919–39)

The Fisher Act (Education Act 1918) set out to repair the war's intellectual wastage and to limit the industrial pressure on the child life of the nation. School life was to be extended to the age of 14. Part-time education to 18 was provided, and also nursery schools. Employment of school-age children, except on part-time delivery rounds was forbidden. Elementary schools would be completely free of charge, and new 'percentage grants' would help to finance secondary schooling. The aspirations of the 1918 Act were overtaken by the depression of 1921. The 'Geddes axe' (1922) reduced education expenditure by a third. Teacher–pupil ratios increased and, in 1922, a quarter of all elementary classes still had more than 60 pupils.

In 1919, three types of secondary school came into existence: maintained, aided and direct grant. In the same year, three leading public school headmasters suggested to the President of the Board of Education that they would take a proportion of elementary school boys whose fees would be paid from public money. HAL Fisher, the President, turned down this offer on the grounds that there was no demand and suggested instead that the public schools should take boys from other schools at a later age, perhaps 15 or over. The dialogue ceased.

The Education Act 1921 gave power to local education authorities '... to pay or assist in paying the fees of students at schools or colleges or hostels within or without their areas'.

Britain's first Labour Government (headed by Ramsay Macdonald) took office in 1924. The new men of influence included Ernest Bevin, JH Thomas and Ben Turner who were ready to support increased opportunity in education. The Labour slogan of the '20s was 'Secondary education for all'. The Hadow Report, published in 1926, suggested a complete reorganisation of schooling, which was to be conceived as 'primary' up to 11 years and 'secondary' up to 15 years, with 'modern schools' to be developed for the average child alongside grammar schools.

However, the massive economic depression of the early 1930s crippled educational progress. Resources were not available for the Hadow reforms. By 1938, only 72% of pupils had some secondary schooling.

A second Hadow Report (1931) stated that school was to teach children how to live. Learning was best based on 'the experience, the curiosity and interests of children themselves'. This report became the basis of modern primary education and was heavily influenced by the ideas of Maria Montessori who had pioneered the Montessori method in 1912 in Rome. Educational developments during this period included sponsored educational films and radio lessons to schools. Educational psychology became influential at this time. Intelligence tests, devised in Europe before the Great War, were adapted for English use by the psychologist Cyril Burt after 1922.

During the 1920s, the public schools entered a period of unprecedented prosperity and popularity. The system was expanded with a wave of new foundations and the enlarging of many existing schools. In 1929, Cyril Norwood, Headmaster of Harrow, seemed certain that the public schools were poised for a period of confident growth and undisturbed success. It was not to be.

During the 1930s, the outlook for many of the public schools was transformed for the worse. It became clear that the demand for places was declining, and with it the income derived from fees. The whole basis of their position was threatened. In 1939, *Whittaker's Almanac* suggested that 45% of independent HMC schools were in decline, while about 30% were expanding and about 25% were stable. *The Times* for 3 April 1939 declared: 'Nothing can be more certain than the imminent and hastening decline in the numbers of what is sometimes called the public school class'. Even so, there were new foundations such as Canford (1923), Stowe (1923) and Bryanston (1928).

### 3.3.3 World War II (1939–45)

The war years for education were characterised by fear of air bombing and mass evacuation of people from threatened areas, mainly to the countryside. The effects of war on children included air-raid disruptions, changes of staff and restless family movement. Average retardation of one year was reported from tests on war pupils.

There were, however, some benefits. The expansion of medical services led to diphtheria vaccination of nearly seven million children, which reduced deaths, and the modest pre-war meals and milk services were massively expanded.

The Second World War was a test for the public schools (here meaning those that were not part of the national system). According to their response, their future position in the State was likely to be determined. To survive, they would have to demonstrate an ability to adapt and a readiness to become more outward-looking and to relate to the needs of the wider community in a number of ways.

The most severe test faced those schools which were forced to move from their own premises. Some, such as Haileybury and Wellington, were saved from requisitioning by old boys in high places, but many had to move. Nearly all managed to find alternative accommodation, but Wycombe Abbey, a girls' school, was forced to close. Malvern was moved twice. Kingswood was moved to Uppingham. Wherever they found themselves, the schools generally settled down to derive what advantages they could from their new situation, and also contribute to the war effort. One natural advantage was that most were situated in rural and relatively safe places. They could offer a stability and safety which the national system, in many areas, could not rival.

Almost all public schools had formed branches of the Junior Training Corps, Air Training Corps and, for masters and older boys, the Home Guard. There were fire-watching rotas and definite assigned duties to be carried out in the event of air raids. It was felt by officials that most headmasters were eager to help the war effort and, for those situated in rural areas, an obvious form of war work was in food production.

Sherborne's farming programme started in May 1940, while Felsted organised lumber camps in the Forest of Dean during its wartime summer holidays. At Tonbridge, a football field was given over to agriculture and Wellington managed to make itself almost self-sufficient in vegetables as well as sending boys to harvest camps during the summer. At Merchant Taylors', parts of the playing fields were ploughed up and sown with wheat, and harvest camps were held during the holidays. At Oundle and Radley, 'boys became their own domestic servants'. The Abbot of Downside pressed forward with his plan for the boys at his own school to help move coal from the local collieries, while boys at Eton helped in the local munitions factories. These and other contributions to the war effort were replicated in schools all over the country.

The shortage of teaching staff was a common difficulty. Masters were kept on beyond retirement age and women teachers were employed to a greater extent, breaking down the monastic tradition of some of the public schools. There was a sense of a greater mutual understanding between the public schools and the Board of Education.

Even so, by 1942, the pre-war difficulties over finance and numbers and the question about the part (if any) that the public schools should play in the reconstructed post-war world continued to exercise the authorities and politicians of the day.

In July 1942, the Fleming Committee was appointed to do something about the public schools and reduce the importance of the question as a live political issue. At that time, it was noted that there were 793 maintained schools, 381 aided schools and 232 direct grant schools, and a further 288 schools (including 11 in Scotland) that were comprised within membership of HMC, GBA and GBGSA, in addition to an unknown number of schools fitting none of these categories.

The Fleming Committee was in fact appointed in response to a request by the public schools for an inquiry to consider how they might be more closely related to the national system. That request was, however, seen by some radical socialist politicians at the time, notably Sir Richard Acland, as a deft piece of footwork which would ensure that the public schools could not be included in the government's then current proposals for educational reform.

The Fleming Committee reported in 1944, expressing enthusiasm for boarding school education and the desire that more and more boarding schools should be built so that more children from various backgrounds could enjoy the benefits of the education provided by the public schools. It preferred the expression 'endowed schools' to 'public schools' stating, at p 121, '... it is clear that the term [public school] has no precise significance in the public mind'.

The government's response to the Fleming Report was the appointment of a further committee to consider some of the report's recommendations in detail. That committee produced its own report which was presented to the new Minister of Education, Ellen Wilkinson, in August 1945.

The outcome of these events was that Ellen Wilkinson and her successor in February 1947, George Tomlinson, both expressed themselves, in different ways, to be quite reconciled to the idea of public schools continuing in their existing form. A detailed account of the recommendations of the Fleming Committee is outside the scope of this chapter. Suffice it to say, the Committee gave a firm vote of confidence to the actual work done by the public schools. Members of the Committee had no difficulty in agreeing that they were dealing with a valuable institution which should be preserved. The report went on to outline Scheme A and Scheme B as follows:

–   Scheme A was to extend the association already existing between some public schools (mainly direct grant) and the general system;

–   Scheme B made detailed proposals for implementing one of the general aims in the report that places at public schools should be available to children capable of profiting without regard to the income of their parents. It was proposed that participating schools which were accepted by the Board, recognised as efficient and not conducted for private profit should offer a minimum of 25% of their annual admissions to State-funded pupils.

In the event, the recommendations in the Fleming Report were not implemented, and the public schools then embarked on a period of renewed popularity and prosperity brought about by a new wave of enthusiasm for education and optimism for the future.

In the meantime, Butler's Education Act 1944 came into force. It was a landmark in the restructuring of State-maintained education. It raised the school leaving age to 15 (eventually to be 16); it provided for secondary education for all children according to ability and aptitude in secondary, grammar, technical, or modern schools; it provided for the eventual establishment of county colleges for compulsory part-time education to the age of 18; it abolished school fees in schools assisted by local authority grants; and it established a Ministry of Education. Schools that were not maintained by local authorities were 'independent'. The Act made no reference to 'public schools'.

# Chapter 4

## EDUCATION FROM 1945 TO THE PRESENT

### 4.1  THE POST-WAR YEARS

#### 4.1.1  Aftermath

Enemy action during the war had destroyed or damaged thousands of schools – all but 50 London schools had suffered. Teachers were in short supply and an emergency training scheme launched in 1943 succeeded in producing 35,000 teachers by 1951.

The Conservative Governments of 1951 (Churchill), 1955 (Eden/Macmillan), and 1959 (Macmillan/Home) poured resources into the State secondary schools. There were new buildings, libraries, kitchens, dining rooms, laboratories and other specialist rooms and games facilities. They were provided with books, film and film-strip projectors, radio, television, record-players, duplicators, games equipment, materials for art, craft, needlework and domestic science, and posters, slides and classroom aids of all kinds. The Emergency Training Scheme and the expansion of the training colleges and university training departments provided an increasing supply of teachers.

Successive governments became concerned about the number of secondary school pupils who left school without entering the sixth form. A report on early leaving in 1954 showed the close correlation of this with the father's occupation: 43.7% of sixth-form pupils were the children of professional and managerial workers; 12%, the children of clerical staff; 37%, the children of skilled manual workers; 5.8%, of semi-skilled; and only 1.5%, of unskilled workers.

The Crowther Report of 1959 stressed the importance of sixth-form work and advocated a programme to ensure that by 1980 half of the boys and girls in the country would stay in full-time education to the age of 18.

#### 4.1.2  Independent schools

Section 70 of the Education Act 1944 established the expression 'independent school' as meaning, broadly, a school that was entitled to charge fees and would be independent of State control. Although the post-war years saw an almost un-precedented rate of demand for places at independent schools, those years were also characterised by uncertainty and shortages of every kind, especially of books and even pens and pencils. Materials were very scarce and only the most essential repairs and redecoration could be carried out. There was a serious shortage of teachers. New pupils were less well trained after the deprivations of the war years and many were less stable and less able to concentrate on their work. Some schools had suffered war damage. There was little help for the independent schools, but they prospered none the less. In 1950, the School Certificate was replaced by the General Certificate of Education (GCE), with O levels and A levels.

John Wakeford, in his study of the English public boarding school at this time, pointed out that these schools made a virtue of necessity, building on a long tradition of austerity and claimed that the 'relative deprivation' in which their pupils lived was a necessary element in the building of character. Wakeford was to some extent critical of the restrictions of boarding school life and the very small opportunity afforded by most boarding schools for contact with the opposite sex. Wakeford also noted that, in the schools he visited early in the 1960s, about two-thirds of the staff had no formal qualifications in teaching.

### 4.1.3   State secondary schooling

The 1944 Act did not specify any particular scheme of organisation of State secondary schooling. There were broadly two schemes in view:

(a)  the tripartite structure of grammar, technical and modern schools originally proposed by Hadow; and
(b)  the multilateral school discussed by Spens in a report of 1938, under which all secondary-age pupils would attend a single (comprehensive) school where they would be divided into appropriate streams.

The Labour Government of 1945 supported the tripartite structure, the Ministry noting in 1947 that 'different types of school would be needed to meet the differences that exist between children'.

Local education authorities (LEAs) were required to submit their plans. Only five LEAs intended to try the multilateral or comprehensive model. Twenty-five others proposed to carry out 'experiments', the most ambitious of which was London's 'school plan' of 1947 which decided on partial comprehensive reorganisation.

Selection at '11-plus' resulted, on average, in one child out of five attending a grammar school, the remainder attending secondary modern schools, or technical schools which were never widely established. The 11-plus examination fell into disrepute because public opinion came to think of it as 'the scholarship' which a child passed or failed, notwithstanding the official Ministry line that the test enabled every child successfully to find the right school for his or her abilities.

In the 1950s, disquiet about the fairness of the '11-plus' grew. There was concern about late developers being deprived of an appropriate education and the 11-plus became seen as a social divider rather than a fair assessment of intellectual ability. The Conservative Government adhered to the tripartite system, but public opinion, supported by the Labour Party in opposition, began to support the comprehensive principle. When Labour took power in 1964 under Harold Wilson, the Ministry of Education became the Department of Education and Science (DES), and issued Circular 10/65 requesting LEAs to submit plans for comprehensive reorganisation within 12 months, even though there was inadequate evidence about the merits of comprehensive schools. Most LEAs complied with the circular and, with few exceptions, the State secondary system became comprehensive.

## 4.2 INDEPENDENT SCHOOLS

### 4.2.1 The 1960s and 1970s

During the 1960s, the rising standard of living led to an increase in the demand for boarding education generally, particularly among parents posted overseas for their employment with the Armed Forces or otherwise and for children from broken homes. There followed a period of boom for the independent sector when school buildings and facilities were modernised and new buildings put up. Every aspect of the curriculum was expanded; more teachers with better qualifications became available.

Direct grant schools had, since 1902, received State financial aid direct from the Board of Education, by-passing the local authority. By 1958, it had become clear that local education authorities would soon stop using places in direct grant schools and that all schools would have to become either State schools or independent. Selection by means of the 11-plus examination would be abolished, and all State schools would become comprehensive. There would be no place for smaller schools in the State system, which would typically envisage mixed comprehensives, catering for 11–18-year-olds, with sixth-form entry, each with its own neighbourhood catchment area. With some exceptions, there would be no boarding schools, mixed or single-sexed, in the State system.

Successive Labour Governments reduced and then abolished the State subsidies to direct grant schools. The direct grant sector rose to the challenge and about 100 of them accepted independence. That meant preparing for and satisfying the registration criteria under the Education Act 1944 and obtaining the approval of the Charity Commissioners to a new scheme. In most cases, the move to independence was successful, helped by the economic conditions at the time and the growing demand for places at good independent schools.

The recession during the mid-1970s led to a reversal of fortunes for independent schools and a reduction in the demand for places. John Dancy at Marlborough was the first headmaster of a traditional public school to admit girls, but only into the sixth form. This was regarded as revolutionary, even though Bedales had been educating boys and girls together since its foundation by JH Badley in 1893. From the mid-1970s onwards, many single-sex independent schools moved into co-education, often starting with the sixth form and moving downwards by age. In a few cases, this was in response to changing social attitudes and demands in the market place for co-education. In most cases, however, it was a defensive strategy which added edge to the debate about the respective merits of single-sex and co-education, particularly from the girls' schools who felt their numbers to be under threat. During the 1990s, this became the only context in which independent schools acknowledged any value in the annual performance tables.

### 4.2.2 The 1980s onwards

The next major development was the Assisted Places Scheme introduced by the first Thatcher Government in the Education Act 1980 but always disliked on doctrinaire grounds by the Labour Party, which pledged to abolish the scheme. As many as 30–40% of pupils at some schools held assisted places. The Scheme enabled those children to develop their talents in a way that might not or would not be achieved in the comprehensive system. It also ensured a wider social mix at those schools to the benefit of all. Thus, the scheme helped to fulfil the ancient charitable objects of the many schools that were established centuries earlier for the free education of children of the neighbourhood. However, the Education (Schools) Act 1997, which came into force on 1 September 1997, prevented new intakes to the schools from September 1998 and phased out the scheme altogether over seven years.

The National Curriculum introduced for State schools after the Education Reform Act 1988 did not apply to the independent sector, although notice was customarily taken of it.

Performance tables (often referred to as 'league tables') introduced in the 1990s have caused very great frustration in parts of the independent sector. League tables are essentially a process of comparison; yet it is difficult to compare a highly selective 'hot-house' on the one hand with a school that admits mixed ability pupils and offers them a wide range of opportunity to a high standard. Even so, it is noticeable that the official league tables show most independent schools regularly out-performing most maintained schools on a region-by-region basis.

The recession years from 1988 to 1995 were a time of great anxiety and hardship for independent schools and those who used them, but also provided an opportunity for reform, many schools shedding poor staff, becoming leaner and fitter and eschewing the complacency of the boom years.

Fee levels became more competitive and negotiable, and a further by-product was that far greater attention was paid to the modern principles of 'quality of service'. Some schools closed, others merged and many expanded their age-range by opening a nursery and pre-prep school or else moved into co-education. The trend in the UK away from boarding enabled many schools to admit a greater number of overseas pupils and to operate weekly and casual boarding arrangements. The Nursery Voucher Scheme made a brief appearance in 1996 only to be abolished by the new Labour government in 1998.

The 1990s also saw huge advances in the use of computer technology, bringing corresponding demands for greater expertise and costly equipment. The decade also saw the development of 'the outcomes society' with parents demanding the best facilities and the highest results and being encouraged by the media to resort to litigation or the threat of litigation when disappointed.

### 4.2.3   The rise of day-schools

British boarding schools continue to be in strong demand and are famous world-wide for the quality of their education and pastoral care, and training in community life. Boarding is an ideal arrangement for many children and their parents. There are, however, fewer all-boarding schools than 20 years ago.

There were 587,453 pupils in independent education in the academic year 1996/97, an increase of 28,280 on the 559,173 of a decade earlier. During that period, however, boarding numbers had fallen by about 36,000 to 89,668. These statistics indicate that independent education remained accessible to, broadly, the same percentage of the population, but greater numbers entered at the lower end of the age range, where fees were less, more pupils came from outside the UK, and day education became increasingly preferred. Part of the reason was the effect of the so-called 'peace dividend', with fewer members of the armed forces serving abroad or requiring a subsidised boarding education for their children, but this is only a small part of the explanation.

Nowadays, there tends to be less difference between the opportunities provided by day schools and those provided at boarding school. Many of the former boarding schools now offer day-pupils an extended day with a programme of cultural activities and a reasonable sports and games curriculum, which can be more attractive to parents – and also to pupils, who often make the final decision about the school they will attend. This, together with the lower up-front cost of a day-school, may be a significant consideration. There are other factors also.

### (a)  Parent factors

Many of today's parents were, themselves, at boarding schools in the 1960s and 1970s when the schools were very different from now. Their recollection may be of long periods of separation from their parents, difficult travelling conditions, harsh discipline, unchecked bullying and a 'stiff upper lip' ethos that inhibited discussion of worries. Parents who were not themselves in boarding schools may to some extent be influenced by what they know of that reputation without realising the extent of the changes that have taken place in boarding schools.

A major, and possibly deciding, reason for choosing day schools (not always borne out by market research) may be cost, particularly where there are two or more children to educate. Cost impacts in a number of ways. First, with the passing of 'jobs for life' there is a greater sense of insecurity and risk in making what is seen as a long-term commitment to high fees. There is also much greater expenditure on holidays and other leisure activities.

Many parents are concerned about reports in the media about the effect of bullying when it occurs and of the availability of drugs and Internet pornography at schools. They want the opportunity to check their children's welfare on a day-to-day basis. Moreover, the stakes are now so high when it comes to a successful performance in GCSEs and A levels that some parents feel the need to see their children daily and be satisfied that nothing untoward is inhibiting their progress. There is also a sense among some social groups that sending children into boarding will be seen as 'politically incorrect', although this is by no means a widespread attitude.

### (b)  Pupil factors

Leisure has assumed much greater importance in the lives of adolescents and adults during the last ten years. Many families belong to leisure clubs which provide facilities that are, in many respects, as good as those available at school. Weekends are, in practice, the main opportunity for family activities. Less importance is attached to compulsory team sports and more to individual sports such as badminton and tennis and also to fitness. Those who want to play organised sports can often do so at club level. The world outside school is ever more informal, with fewer demands being made of pupils in matters of dress, manners and speech. Adolescents have greater sexual and other social freedom outside boarding school. Moreover, most families in this market place have a powerful home computer from which the Internet can be accessed and project work completed without necessarily needing school facilities over the weekend.

### (c)   School factors

Independent schools have made parents very much more welcome at school premises compared to 10 or 20 years ago when they were sometimes discouraged from appearing other than on formal occasions. This may have contributed to the strong day-to-day interest that many parents take in their children's progress. Moreover, there is often a choice of day-school provision to suit every family ranging from the short to the extended five-day week and the six-day week, with the opportunity of day boarding and casual boarding and sometimes Sunday chapel; also the opportunity to share many of the activities that boarders enjoy. In other words, there need be little apparent difference between day and boarding provision, except the up-front cost.

Overall, there is a strong inference that, in many areas of the country, families can obtain from a day school a service whose flexibility will only be reduced by a boarding regime, and pupils increasingly see benefit in that flexibility.

There are undoubtedly a number of brand-name schools and 'boarding magnets' which are unaffected by these trends and which are among the first choice of parents who have decided on boarding in any event. But for schools that are not in this category, if the social trends indicated above are correct, it seems that boarding numbers in the future are more likely to be maintained by increasing the intake of overseas pupils than from selling into the domestic market. None the less, for the present, boarding remains popular. Parents often live within a 30-mile radius of the school, and sometimes even in the same city.

### 4.2.4   The future

Every age brings its own threats and concerns. Those of the current age include violence, dysfunction in the family and the widespread acceptance and availability of drugs and pornography. Independent schools have been spared most of the regulation and restriction of the maintained sector and are able to call on parental support in taking a robust approach to combating many, but by no means all, of these problems.

Independent schools in the UK are known and respected world-wide, not only for their academic standards and other achievements but also for their insistence on discipline and good order, and the upholding of some more traditional community values and manners that have all but disappeared from many parts of modern society. Even so, they face strong competition in cost and quality from some of the best of the maintained and grant-maintained schools and from some sixth-form colleges.

The independent schools of today are very different places from those of 20 or 600 years ago. But, despite the body of legislation that entrenches their right of existence and their right to charitable status, they remain under constant threat of political interference. Even so, they continue to thrive and out-perform most competitors.

Statistics published by the Department for Education (as it was then known) in August 1993 showed that there were 2,432 independent schools in England, Scotland and Wales educating 594,107 pupils, of whom 102,302 were boarders. There were some 30,000 State-aided pupils, and average fees were £9,700 pa for boarders and £4,200 pa for day pupils.

A survey in *The Sunday Times* of 21 August 1994 analysed parents' reasons for choosing independent education: 80% identified good discipline; 79% said they were influenced by the school's reputation; 77% thought the attitude towards school work was most important; 68% were swayed by the rightness of the school for the individual child; and 67% felt small classes were important.

At the time of writing, the pupil rolls of many schools are building back up to or have exceeded levels before the onset of the recession in 1988. The *Daily Telegraph* of 13 May 1997 reported that for the academic year 1996/97 there were 587,453 pupils in independent education. Nurseries showed an increase of 6.3% and preparatory education showed a 3.3% increase. Sixth-forms pupil numbers increased by 2.4%. But the number of boarders in 1996/97 was 89,668 compared to 125,920 in 1985/86. It was also reported that a MORI poll had found that 49% of the population said they would use independent schools if they could afford to do so.

The *Daily Telegraph* report added that no fewer than 19% of pupils (that is, about 111,500) at independent schools received financial assistance through scholarships, bursaries and other allowances, including 37,183 assisted places. The schools themselves estimate that up to 10% (and sometimes as much as 15%) of their revenue from all sources, including endowments, is distributed in different forms of financial assistance to families who use these schools. The majority also make provision for the local community to use their land and facilities.

Notwithstanding the loss of government-assisted places, the savings from which have not, at the time of writing, yielded any discernible benefit to the State sector, the independent sector appears to be in good heart as it approaches the millennium and begins to prepare its response to the government's request for greater partnership with the State-funded sector.

# PART 2

# THE CONTRACT FOR EDUCATIONAL SERVICES

# Chapter 5

# INTRODUCTION TO THE PARENT CONTRACT

## 5.1 OVERVIEW

This chapter sets out to explain the contract for educational services in the context of the general law of contract.

There is probably no contract which is wider in its scope, potentially longer in its duration, more complex in its elements, less specific in what is promised and less quantifiable in what is delivered – and about which less has been written – than the contract for educational services.

### 5.1.1 Main features

The 'parent contract' is the name given by independent schools and their legal advisers to the form of legal contract known as 'the contract for educational services'. There is no equivalent contract with a State-funded school, where the relationship is created and regulated mainly by statute law and secondary legislation.

When an independent school admits a child as a pupil, a legally binding contract is formed or arises by implication of law. The most basic terms of the contract are that the school will use reasonable skill and care to educate the child and safeguard and promote the child's welfare, and the parents will arrange for the pupil to attend the school, will pay the fees and will act reasonably in relation to the school. The requirement that parents act reasonably was established by the Court of Appeal in *Price v Dennis* [1988] LEXIS.

The contract continues until it expires when the child has reached the end of the school's provision, or until it is brought to an end by notice, by frustration or by breach. The contract may last for any period from one term up to 15 years or more. It can cover almost every aspect of the life and development of a child or young person.

Parts of the education service fall within the scope of the compulsory education that is required by s 7 of the Education Act 1996. Other parts are covered by express or implied agreement. The remainder of the service is 'value added', for which there is no contractual basis.

### 5.1.2 Opportunity

Education is a complex service. The essence of education at an independent school is the intangible concept of opportunity. More specifically, it is the environment provided and the opportunities that arise from life as a day pupil, day boarder, weekly boarder or full boarder, in a school that is properly resourced and driven by a clear vision, objective, aim and ethos. These together make up the culture of the school.

Opportunity and environment alone are not enough. They must be made accessible to the pupil and converted for each pupil to the reasonable satisfaction of each parent and in accordance with the child's abilities and aptitudes.

Life in a community seldom stands still, nor should it. Staff and children will come and go. There will be good and less good times, ups and downs, success and failure. Children develop at different rates. Each child will be exposed to the influences of many hundreds of different people during his or her time at school. Some influences will be positive and others less so.

Moreover, the scope of education itself is immense. In addition to the academic and sports curriculum and all the extra-curricular activities, is the development of the child's intellectual, moral, physical and manipulative skills and powers in many areas, and also the child's spiritual, social and cultural dimensions. The school is also concerned with the health, safety, pastoral care and general welfare of the child. Boarding schools have the additional aspect of providing full board and lodging, travel arrangements and, sometimes, arrangements for holiday guardianship.

Education is above all a 'people business'. It depends on relationships and, in particular, on there being mutual trust and confidence between the governors, the staff, the parents and the children, and, to some extent, between parents themselves. Very little of this can be measured by examination certificates and performance tables alone. Equally, matters have to go very far wrong before a school is to be held in fundamental breach of the contract for so complex a product.

## 5.2   WHAT IS A CONTRACT?

Contracts are the most frequent legal dealing between people. Most lawful transactions involving goods or services in exchange for money are legally binding contracts, whether written or unwritten. There are also other kinds of contract, such as those relating to employment and land.

A legal contract is an agreement of a kind that the law recognises and will enforce. The basic elements in its formation are that:

(a)   an offer has been made by one party;
(b)   it has been accepted by another party;
(c)   some consideration or value has been given by one or both parties; and
(d)   both parties intend to be bound by the agreement they have reached.

Once these elements are present, the contract has been formed, whether or not anything has been put in writing. The contract will be enforceable unless its subject matter is contrary to public policy or illegal. In general, a contract can only be enforced by a person who has given *some* value or consideration. This is the rule known as privity of contract, which will be referred to later.

Contracts are a creature of common law. By 'common law' is meant the law that has arisen since 1189AD (being the fictional date of time immemorial) from the way people deal with each other and decisions of the court about those dealings. The tradition of English law is that people must be held to their contracts. During a civil trial in 1982, Bingham J (as he then was) reminded the parties that 'an agreement is an agreement, is an agreement'.

As commercial life became more complex during the twentieth century, Parliament intervened by means of legislation – statutes and regulations – to limit the effect of certain kinds of contractual term that were operating unfairly. Gradually, through the growth of consumerism, the law is developing an ethic of 'fairness of contract' rather than 'freedom of contract'. As a result, many contractual terms no longer carry the legal significance that their simple wording suggests. An example of this is that an attempt by contract to exclude a person's liability for negligence causing death or personal injury is wholly ineffective as a contractual term.

The reminder from Bingham J remains valid, but has to be interpreted. It means that agreed contractual terms will be enforced in accordance with the intentions of the parties, but only if those intentions are lawful and capable of being enforced.

## 5.3   THE TERMS OF A CONTRACT

The various conditions, statements, representations, promises, stipulations and warranties in a contract are known collectively as contractual terms or simply as terms or terms and conditions. It is unnecessary here to give a full account of the different meanings of these expressions but in a general sense the major terms which are the basis of the contract are known as *conditions* and those which are less important but may attract damages if broken are known as *warranties*.

The following aspects of contractual terms are of importance in the context of 'the parent contract'.

### 5.3.1   Express and implied terms

'Express terms' are those that have been expressly agreed orally or in writing. They include a school's standard terms and conditions if they have been incorporated into the contract.

'Implied terms' are, broadly, those which may not have been expressly discussed or negotiated but are none the less necessary if the contract is to be carried out as the parties intend. There are three ways in which terms may be implied into the contract:

(a)  *By the court* – if the point in question is so obvious that it goes without saying or if it is necessary as a matter of law to imply the term. Examples of this are the implied term that the school will safeguard and promote the welfare of the child, as contemplated by the Children Act 1989, and the implied term that there will be procedural rules designed to ensure that pupils receive fair treatment in accordance with natural justice in the case of an expulsion or requirement to leave (see *R v Fernhill Manor School ex parte B* [1993] 1 FLR 620).

(b)  *By custom and usage* – where a lawful practice or custom is very common in a particular business or activity. There will then be an implied term in the contract giving effect to that practice or custom unless there is an express term in the contract to the contrary. An example in the case of independent schools is the rule about fees in lieu of notice. In *Mount v Oldham Corporation* [1973] 1 QB 309, CA, Lord Denning MR said of the rule that it is:

'... a usage well known throughout the education world. So well known that we can take notice of it ourselves. If the parent wishes to avoid this liability, he must show that the school has been guilty of a breach going to the root of the contract, such as to entitle the parent to treat himself as discharged from any further obligation ...'

(c) *By statute* – an increasing number of statutes imply terms into a contract that cannot be excluded. An example of relevance to those who supply services is s 13 of the Supply of Goods and Services Act 1982 which provides:

'in a contract for the supply of a service where the supplier is acting in the course of a business [which includes an independent school], there is an implied term that the supplier will carry out the service with reasonable care and skill.'

The formation of a contract and of its express and implied terms can be described by reference to the following example of buying a bar of chocolate in a shop. The shop display showing goods with their price labels is known as the *invitation to treat*, that is, an invitation to a customer to make an offer to buy. The customer picks up a bar of chocolate and places it on the counter. He has made a *contractual offer* even though no words have been spoken. The customer offers the price in money. This is the *consideration* or *value*, because the chocolate bar is a thing of value. The shopkeeper takes the money, which is an indication that the customer may take the bar of chocolate away. That is the *contractual acceptance* by the shopkeeper. Both parties have shown by their conduct that they *intend to be bound* by their transaction. A contract has been formed.

Even though nothing has been said, a number of *express and implied terms* have come into operation. The express terms include the price written on the bar of chocolate and the promises made on the wrapping, unless they are 'mere puff'.

The implied terms include a promise that there really is chocolate inside the wrapper, that it is of satisfactory quality and will not poison the customer, that it contains the ingredients reasonably to be expected, that the shopkeeper will not try and change the price once the offer has been accepted, and so on. All of this has arisen without a word being said.

Different kinds of goods will give rise to different express and implied terms. If the same customer goes on to buy a packet of cigarettes there will be an express term that the cigarettes *will* seriously damage his health and *may* kill him if he smokes them. It is an express term because it is written on the packet. But, equally, there is an implied term that death will not happen instantly from that cause. The cigarettes will not blow up if lit. Of course, an opposite implied term applies to a sale of fireworks.

It is possible that a person who buys 100 different items at one time in a supermarket has made 100 different contracts, many of them with different express and implied terms and all without a word spoken, other than the normal courtesies. Or, depending on the circumstances, he or she may have made one contract with 100 different parts. This point is a students' examination question in its own right.

## 5.3.2 Unfair contract terms

The contract for educational services is a *consumer contract* to which (with certain exceptions not relevant here) the Unfair Contract Terms Act 1977 does not apply. However, there are some important regulations, entitled the Unfair Terms in Consumer Contracts Regulations 1994, which will apply if the contract contains unfair terms.

These regulations affect contracts made after January 1995. They introduce a general requirement that all terms *which have not been individually negotiated* in consumer contracts shall be *fair.*

Regulation 4(1) provides:

'In these Regulations, subject to paragraphs (2) and (3) below, "unfair term" means any term which contrary to the requirement of good faith causes a significant imbalance in parties' rights and obligations under the contract to the detriment of the consumer.'

Regulation 4(2) provides:

'An assessment of the unfair nature of a term shall be made taking into account the nature of the goods or services for which the contract was concluded and referring, as at the time of the conclusion of the contract, to all circumstances attending the conclusion of the contract and to all the other terms of the contract or of another contract on which it is dependent.'

Schedule 2 to the Regulations sets out four matters to which regard shall be had in particular in making an assessment of good faith, namely:

(1) the strength of the bargaining positions of the parties;
(2) whether the consumer had an inducement to agree to the term;
(3) whether the goods or services were sold or supplied to the special order of the consumer; and
(4) the extent to which the seller or supplier has dealt fairly or equitably with the consumer.

Schedule 3 of the Regulations provides what has become known as a *grey list* of 17 examples of contract terms that may be unfair. The list is indicative and illustrative, but is far from being exhaustive.

Regulation 5(1) provides that an unfair term in a consumer contract shall not be binding on the consumer although the remainder of the contract remains in force if it is capable of being performed without that term.

Regulation 6 requires the seller or supplier to ensure that any written terms of the contract are expressed 'in plain intelligible language'. It leaves unanswered the question of whether the English language is plain and intelligible to a person who cannot read English.

The Regulations do not apply to a contractual term which has been individually negotiated, but that expression would be construed restrictively.

Individual consumers can seek to have unfair terms held to be non-binding, whilst the Regulations give the Director General of Fair Trading new powers to seek injunctions against the use of unfair terms.

Following the introduction of these Regulations, the Office of Fair Trading (OFT) set up an Unfair Contract Terms Unit. Experience of the approach taken by the unit to date is that they are likely to consider the effect of a contract term not only at the time when the contract is formed but also at the time when an allegation is made that it has been operated unfairly. It is submitted here that this approach may be in excess of the OFT's jurisdiction under the Regulations.

## 5.4  SOME OTHER ASPECTS OF CONTRACTS

### 5.4.1  Exclusion clauses

An exclusion clause is one which is intended to exclude or financially limit a party's liability for breach of contract or for misrepresentation or negligence. These clauses are disliked by the courts and are also addressed to some extent in the unfair contract terms legislation described above. Ambiguous wording is construed as narrowly as possible against the party who wants to rely on an exclusion clause, and the clause cannot protect a party from liability for a serious breach of the contract. As noted earlier, a clause which seeks to exclude liability for negligence causing death and personal injury is wholly ineffective.

To have any chance of being effective, the exclusion clause must be incorporated into the contract. In the case of a document which is unsigned and merely delivered to the other party, reasonable and sufficient notice of the existence of an exclusion clause must be given. However, this rule is less strict where there has been a previous and consistent course of dealing between the parties on the same terms. It should be noted also that an exclusion clause may be rendered wholly or partly ineffective by an inconsistent oral promise.

### 5.4.2  Misrepresentation

A misrepresentation is a *false statement of existing or past fact* made by one party to the other which induces the other party to enter the contract. An hypothetical example is a parent being told that all staff have formal qualifications when it turns out that one has not. Depending on the circumstances, the legal character of such a misrepresentation may be:

–   A statement that did not help to induce the contract: this is not an operative misrepresentation in the legal sense and probably has no legal consequence.
–   A mere representation that did help to induce the contract: if it proves false the parent can rescind the contract (ie set it aside) and/or claim damages for misrepresentation. That means in practice that the pupil can be withdrawn without liability to pay fees in lieu of notice.
–   A representation that not only helped to induce the contract but became a contractual term because the parties intended that it should. The remedy for non-compliance is an action for breach of contract.
–   A representation that amounted to a collateral contract in its own right if all the elements of a separate valid contract were present. The remedy for non-compliance would be an action for breach of the collateral contract.

A false representation is also actionable in its own right. The remedies depend on whether it was fraudulent, negligent or wholly innocent, as follows:

– *For fraudulent misrepresentation* – the injured party may elect to rescind the contract with effect from the outset and may also claim damages for deceit which can include aggravated damages for distress.
– *For negligent misrepresentation* – the injured party can again claim rescission, and either damages for negligent misstatement (*Hedley Byrne v Heller* [1963] 3 WLR 101) or damages for negligent misrepresentation under s 2(1) of the Misrepresentation Act 1967. However, for negligent misrepresentation the court can refuse rescission and award damages in lieu.
– *For wholly innocent misrepresentation* – the only remedy is rescission which may be accompanied by an indemnity.

A statement of future conduct or intention is not a misrepresentation unless it is a wilful lie, in which case it may amount to a misrepresentation of fact. The same is true of statements of belief or opinion where the opinion is not honestly held. 'Mere puff' cannot amount to misrepresentation. A false statement as to what the law is, is not actionable misrepresentation. Remaining silent or not disclosing some fact does not normally amount to a misrepresentation but may render the contract void for mistake.

### 5.4.3  Contracts induced by mistake

Occasionally, a mistake may be made over the offer of an assisted place or scholarship. Equally, a parent might accept a place believing a subject such as Latin is in the curriculum when it is not. The legal position is broadly as follows:

– If it is a case of *mutual mistake of fact*, ie the parties are at cross-purposes over a matter that is sufficiently important to be a condition of the contract, then the contract is likely to be void at law. This rule applies where both parties were unaware of the mistake.
– If the mistake is *unilateral*, ie one party only is fundamentally mistaken concerning the contract and the other party did or must have realised the mistake, the contract will be void. This rule fills the lacuna that arises out of the rule that silence does not amount to a misrepresentation.

### 5.4.4  Duress and undue influence

It seems inherently unlikely that questions of duress and undue influence would ever arise over the formation of a contract between school and parents, and further discussion of such issues is unnecessary here.

### 5.4.5  Illegal and void contracts

The courts will not enforce a contract whose purpose is illegal. Contracts may be rendered illegal by statute; or they may be illegal or unenforceable at common law on the grounds of public policy. Plainly, education as the subject matter of a contract is both lawful and desirable. However, there is anecdotal evidence of an attempt being made to argue illegality as a defence to a claim for fees or fees in lieu of notice in cases where the school has been in breach of a compliance obligation.

In one case, a long-established school had opened a new nursery and pre-prep department. In error, the school had failed to give particulars to the Department for Education and Employment as required by the Education (Particulars of Independent Schools) Regulations 1982, as amended (now the 1997 Regulations, SI 1997/2918). Whether or not those regulations gave rise to an implied condition or warranty in the contract, it is submitted that the breach complained of would not be capable of rendering the contract itself illegal when the subject matter, education, was in itself lawful.

### 5.4.6   The capacity of children to enter contracts

By virtue of the Minors Contracts Act 1987, which in effect restated the common law, children can bind themselves to a contract for instruction and education if the subject matter or circumstances of the contract make it *necessary* or *of benefit to the child*, having regard to the status and position of the particular child.

There is no doubt that education is both necessary and of benefit to a child. It is less clear as a matter of law whether education at an independent school is either necessary or of benefit in every case. Leaving aside any argument of this nature, there is no reason in principle why a pupil of sufficient maturity and understanding should not contract directly with the school for his own education. In one case, the discussion arose in relation to a 16-year-old pupil with trust funds and sympathetic trustees, whose parents had divorced and could not agree over the pupil's schooling.

## 5.5   PRIVITY OF CONTRACT

It is a general rule of contract law that only a party to a contract who has given consideration can sue or be sued in respect of that contract. This is the rule known as privity of contract. The rule is of particular significance to independent schools, parents and pupils because, as the law stands at present, a pupil is not *privy* to the contract between the school and parents.

Parents cannot sue in respect of a personal injury caused to the pupil by the negligence of the school. The right of action is that of the pupil acting by a next friend who will usually be a parent. Conversely, the pupil cannot sue the school for a return of fees following a wrongful expulsion because the pupil is not a contracting party. It follows for the same reason that a school sues the parents and not the pupil for unpaid fees and fees in lieu of notice unless a specific and enforceable agreement exists under which the pupil has agreed to pay the fees.

The rule about privity of contract has proved inconvenient in many cases, and some exceptions have been made to it. The following might be relevant to an independent school.

### 5.5.1   Suing on a cheque

If fees are paid by means of a cheque signed by a third party and payable to the parent, and the cheque is endorsed in favour of the school and then dishonoured, the school may none the less be entitled to sue the third party.

### 5.5.2 Agency

When P (the principal) appoints A (the agent) to make a contract with T (a third party) there is a contract of agency. The mechanism is that the agent brings about the contract between the principal and the third party but is not himself liable on the contract.

Considerations of agency can arise in the parent contract if a pupil orders goods or services on the parents' account. Whether or not those goods or services are necessary or of benefit to the pupil in accordance with the Minors Contracts Act 1987, the parent is probably bound by the agency of the child unless the school has plainly acted irresponsibly.

Express terms and conditions can provide for agency in a number of circumstances, for example if the school stipulates that it acts as agent when sending the pupil's laundry or dry cleaning to an external contractor or when arranging music tuition with a visiting teacher. Sometimes, the school acts as an agent when introducing overseas parents to a holiday guardian in the UK. The school may wish expressly to exclude any question of agency when introducing parents to certain forms of insurance.

It has been argued that the pupil is the agent of the parents as respects his or her progress and conduct at the school. The consequence of this agency is that the pupil's serious breach of school discipline is a breach of contract by the parent as the principal. A more satisfactory legal analysis of this problem, however, is that there is an implied if not express condition in the parent contract that the parents assure the attendance and good behaviour of the pupil.

### 5.5.3 Collateral contract

If the school were to make a promise which induced the parents to enter a contract, that promise could itself give rise to a secondary or *collateral* contract based upon that promise.

In one instance (anecdotal), the school arranged for a party of its pupils to go on a one-week skiing trip to Italy at a cost of £500 per pupil. A particular pupil who wanted to join the party had been bullied by another pupil (X) in the past but was promised that X would not be allowed to join the party. In reliance on that promise, the parents contracted with the school on the pupil's behalf and paid the full cost in advance. A day before departure, the pupil discovered that X had been allowed to join the party.

It is submitted that in these circumstances a collateral contract arose between the school and the pupil based on the school's oral assurance. The consideration for the agreement was the pupil agreeing to join the skiing party. The inclusion of X in the skiing party was a breach by the school of the collateral contract. It is further submitted that damages might lie for holiday disappointment in such a case. Although the main contract was between school and parent to which the pupil was not privy, the pupil could sue on the collateral contract.

A commercial case concerning collateral contracts was that of *Shanklin Pier Ltd v Detel Products Ltd* [1951] 2 KB 845, in which a paint manufacturer represented to the pier owner that its paint would last 7–10 years. In reliance on that promise, the pier owner instructed its contractors to buy the paint. The contract for the paint was thus between the contractor and the manufacturer. The pier company was not privy to it. When the paint lasted only 3 months, it was held that the pier owner was entitled to sue the manufacturer under a collateral contract.

It is possible to envisage circumstances under which a certain state of affairs is promised by a school to a pupil, particularly an older pupil about to enter the sixth form. As a result of that promise, the pupil persuades his parents to contract with the school. The promises are not fulfilled. It is submitted that in those circumstances there may be a collateral contract which the pupil can enforce against the school even though the pupil is not privy to the main contract for educational services.

## 5.6   PERFORMANCE AND THE TIME FOR PERFORMANCE OF A CONTRACT

It was noted earlier that the essential terms of the contract for educational services are that the school will use reasonable skill and care to educate the child and will safeguard and promote the child's welfare, and that the parents will arrange for the pupil to attend the school, will pay fees for that service and act reasonably in relation to the school. Once the contract has been formed, both parties must perform their obligations.

### 5.6.1   The contractual obligations

It is convenient to consider contractual obligations in two layers as follows.

(1)  *The primary layer* consists of the mutual obligations to perform the contract in the way that has been agreed or is implied.

(2)  *The secondary layer* consists of what happens following a breach of contract. Although lawyers tend to talk in terms of the contract being terminated or brought to an end by breach that, in reality, means only that the primary layer of obligations has come to an end. The secondary layer is the obligation to compensate or provide such other remedy as the court may order.

### 5.6.2   Substantial performance

In theory, performance of a contract must be precise and exact. That may be a practical rule in relation to a contract for the supply of commodity products such as baked beans, but it can be highly impractical in relation to the supply over many years of a complex service such as education. There are therefore two rules that operate in practice:

(1)  The standard of performance of the service must at least fall within the bracket of what is acceptable in the circumstances of the particular case.

(2)  If there is *substantial performance* within that bracket but also a part that falls outside the bracket (without being so fundamental as to destroy the root of the contract) there may be a liability in damages in respect of partial performance, if damage has been suffered by a party who is entitled to bring a claim.

It is submitted that the traditional analysis between *entire* or non-divisible contracts and *severable* or divisible contracts is probably too difficult to apply in the case of the contract for education.

### 5.6.3   The time for performance

The general rule is that each party must perform its obligations within a reasonable time, whatever that may mean in the particular circumstances. Time is of the essence of the contract only in the following circumstances:

- where the contract expressly provides that time is of the essence;
- where time is made of the essence by a party who is subjected to unreasonable delay;
- where it must be inferred from the circumstances that time is of the essence – as in some kinds of commercial agreement.

Where time is of the essence and is not complied with, the innocent party may treat himself as discharged from performing his primary layer of obligations. Where time is not of the essence but there is a failure to perform by the stipulated time there is still a breach of contract, but the innocent party is entitled only to damages. The right to damages depends on damage having been suffered by a party who is entitled to bring a claim.

## 5.7   TERMINATION OF CONTRACT

A contract may come to an end in one of the following ways:

- *By performance*, for example by expiry of the school's provision for pupils, such as at the end of the sixth form.

- *By agreement*, either the express or implied agreement for termination of the contract by a term's notice given by either party to the other; or some other agreement between the parties for bringing the contract to an end earlier than expected without the need for notice to be given or fees to be paid in lieu.

- *By frustration*, which automatically discharges the contract. This topic is considered in more detail below.

- *By breach*, where one party has failed to fulfil, or makes it clear he does not intend to fulfil, his obligations under the contract. This topic is also considered in more detail below.

## 5.8   FRUSTRATION OF CONTRACT

A contract is said to be frustrated if, without the fault of either party, something *fundamental* has happened which has either *radically changed the obligations* to be performed; or has made it physically, commercially or legally *impossible to perform* the contractual obligations. This is 'the doctrine of frustration', not to be confused with the looser expression 'frustration by breach' referred to in **5.9**(c) below, which deals with breach of contract.

In the theory of English law, contracts that are genuinely consensual and lawful must be performed and will be rigorously enforced by the courts. Therefore, a frustrating event would have to be one that is fundamental and beyond the control of both parties if it is to bring the contract to an immediate end. For these reasons, it will be rare to establish frustration, particularly so in the context of educational services.

### 5.8.1   Frustrating events

There are broadly three kinds of frustrating event.

### (a)   The contract has become impossible to perform

Cases from the 1860s have established that if the subject matter of the contract between A and B in effect 'disappears' through a cause outside the control of A and B, the contract will be held frustrated. One example was of a concert hall that burnt down, making it impossible for concerts to be held on the specified dates. Another example was of a ship which became stranded and was unavailable to complete the purposes of the contracting parties. However, the contract will not necessarily be held frustrated if a different method of performance could be found.

In the context of educational services, the death of the pupil would plainly frustrate the contract. Long-term illness would also frustrate the contract if it was so long-running, serious or incapacitating that the pupil could not receive most, at least, of the benefits contracted for by his parents. It is difficult to suggest hard and fast rules about illness as a frustrating cause because the contract for educational services may last for anything from one term to 15 years and the matter has to be looked at partly in the context of duration.

An example would be of a pupil who had been entered into the sixth form for a two-year A-level course. If the pupil fell seriously ill in the fourth term, the point might come at which it was plain he would be insufficiently prepared to sit the A-level examinations that year as contemplated by the parties. At that point, it is submitted, the contract would be discharged. As will be seen, the exact moment of frustration may be relevant to the financial and other consequences.

Frustration would be less clear in the case of a 5-year-old pupil entering pre-prep school and then being away for many months because of illness. It might be argued that time is far less critical at that stage of education and that if neither party had taken steps to terminate the contract by notice, it would remain in force and would not be held frustrated.

During the 1990s, there were examples of school buildings being substantially destroyed by fire. However, with the aid of temporary buildings, the schools continued to function normally. Although some of the facilities contracted for were not available during the rebuilding period, the contracts for education were not frustrated.

## (b) Radical change in the circumstances

When a contract is formed, each of the parties will normally have a clear idea of its fundamental purpose. Perhaps some additional benefits will be contemplated but not of themselves sufficient to induce the contract. If an extraneous event occurs that removes the main purpose and turns the obligations into something radically different than that contracted for, the contract will be frustrated.

The classic case on this point is *Krell v Henry* [1903] 2 KB 740, CA, which concerned the hiring of a room by the plaintiff from which he would view the coronation procession of King Edward VII. The coronation was cancelled and it was held that the contract was thereby frustrated because the main purpose and foundation of the contract had been removed.

The position will be different, however, if there is more than one main purpose, and one is lost but the other is fulfilled. In *Herne Bay Steam Boat Co v Hutton* [1903] 2 KB 683, CA, the plaintiff hired a steamboat for two purposes: to see the King's Naval Review and also for a cruise around the fleet. The Naval Review was cancelled but the cruise could continue. The contract was held not to be frustrated.

Nor will the contract be held frustrated where the extraneous event or change in circumstances makes the contract more difficult to perform or causes it to take much longer than envisaged, provided it is still capable of being performed in accordance with its main purpose (*Davis Contractors Ltd v Fareham UDC* [1956] AC 696, HL).

In *Mount v Oldham Corporation* [1973] 1 QB 309, CA, the proprietor, who was also the headmaster of a private special school, was charged with indecency. He was away from the school for six months, but was cleared of the charges and his character was vindicated. In the meantime, local authorities had withdrawn pupils without giving notice. The detail of this case is discussed in a later chapter, but on the issue of frustration, Lord Denning MR in the leading judgment said:

> 'I can well understand that in some special schools the services of the headmaster may be so personal and his presence so important that if he were to die or have a prolonged illness, or any other misfortune causing prolonged absence, the contract might be frustrated. But this school is not in that category. First, the position of the headmaster was not so very personal. Everything would not come to an end if he had died or had a long illness or was absent for a term or two. The staff here could and did carry on the school. Secondly, he was not likely to be absent for very long. It was only as if he had been taken ill with a serious illness from which he should recover in 6 months. I do not think this contract was frustrated by what happened.'

## (c) Illegality

A contract will be frustrated if its subject matter is rendered illegal by a change in the law happening after the contract has been formed in good faith. There would be no frustration if the illegality did not relate to the core subject matter of the contract. An example of this would be a contract for educational services in which it was agreed between the school and the parent that corporal punishment might be used. If there were supervening legislation rendering the use of corporal punishment unlawful, that would not frustrate the contract. It would be impossible to argue that the use of corporal punishment rather than education in the wider sense was the subject matter of the contract.

### 5.8.2   Events that will not frustrate a contract

Events that are expressly provided for in the contract will not frustrate the contract. An example is a contractual term to the effect that the contract between school and parents will not be frustrated if the pupil, without sufficient fault on the part of the school, walks out and/or refuses to attend. In those circumstances, it is submitted that the parents' liability for fees continues until the expiry of a term's notice, failing which, fees in lieu of notice would be payable.

It is submitted, however, that in the absence of an express contractual provision to this effect, a pupil's refusal to attend school probably would frustrate the contract unless the parents had warranted that the pupil would attend or the contract provided that for these (and other) purposes the pupil was agent of the parents. The parents would then be fixed by the pupil's act of 'self-induced frustration' which is, of its nature, a breach of contract rather than a frustrating event.

### 5.8.3   The Law Reform (Frustrated Contracts) Act 1943

Frustration has the effect of discharging the contract automatically from that point onwards but does not render the contract void from the start. Until the 1943 Act the common law provided that following frustration, the loss would lie where it fell. That meant that money paid before the frustrating event could not be recovered and that tended to cause injustice.

Section 1(2) of the 1943 Act provides (in paraphrase) to the effect that:

- money *paid* before the frustrating event is recoverable;
- money *payable* before the frustrating event ceases to be payable;
- certain of the expenses incurred in performing the contract prior to the frustrating event may be recoverable.

A party who has received a valuable benefit before the frustrating event may be ordered to pay a just sum in respect of it (s 1(3)).

The 1943 Act applies to consumer contracts although it does not apply to contracts of insurance or contracts for the sale of specific goods where the goods have perished, nor to contracts for the carriage of goods by sea and certain kinds of charter.

There appear to be no reported cases on the application of the 1943 Act to frustration of a contract for educational services. However, the following guidelines are suggested here:

(a)   The registration fee would not be repayable by the school since it is a fee and not a deposit and of its nature is not refunded.

(b)   A deposit paid by the parents would be repayable or credited by the school.

(c)   Arrears of fees for previous terms would cease to be payable under s 1(2) of the Act, but under s 1(3) the court could order payment of part or all of those arrears in exchange for the valuable benefit obtained by the parents having regard to all the circumstances and all the expenditure incurred by both parties. Thus, in practice, arrears would probably be payable.

(d) Arrears of fees for the current term would follow the same principles as arrears for previous terms.

(e) Fees that have been paid for the current term would, on the face of it, be repayable to the parents, but the school should be entitled to pro rata payment for the valuable benefit obtained by the parents and pupil.

(f) A composition fee (for example 3 years' fees paid in advance at a discounted rate) would be repayable pro rata the unused portion, again subject to the valuable benefit rule.

## 5.9   BREACH OF CONTRACT

There is a breach of contract if one party:

–   makes it clear by act or default that he does not intend to fulfil his contractual obligations; or
–   actually fails to fulfil his contractual obligations.

The real meaning of a breach of contract is that there has been a breach of one or more terms of the contract. Some breaches will be minor in nature, entitling the innocent party to damages but leaving both parties under a continuing obligation to perform. Other breaches will be far more serious, entitling the innocent party both to claim damages and to treat himself as discharged from the contract.

An example of a minor breach of contract by a school would be substandard teaching in a particular subject which was not of an order that would be likely to affect the pupil's future education or job prospects. That kind of breach might or might not be quantifiable in damages, but would not bring the contract to an end.

An example of a minor breach of contract by a parent would be conduct which is unreasonable in relation to the school or members of its staff but which does not constitute serious misconduct. It was held in *Price v Dennis* [1988] LEXIS, CA, that it is an implied term of the contract that parents will act reasonably. Moreover, a parent may be fixed with liability for breach of contract if a pupil is in serious breach of school discipline although it can be argued that a minor breach, although it justifies a proportionate sanction, falls within the range of conduct contemplated by the contracting parties and is not capable of amounting to a breach of contract.

The language of breach of contract is sometimes contradictory and confusing. Lawyers frequently use the expressions *anticipatory breach, repudiatory breach, fundamental breach, frustration by breach, renunciation* and *rescission* to describe various aspects of a breach of contract. These expressions are not always used consistently. For the purposes of this book, they are used in the following way:

(a) *Anticipatory breach* means an expression of intention to break or end a contract before the time for performance has arrived. An example is the parent who accepts an offer of a place and then changes his or her mind before the entry date and cancels the place, or where the pupil is a 'no show' at the start of his first term. That is an anticipatory breach of contract. It is correct also to call it a *renunciation*. The school can accept the renunciation and treat itself as discharged from its contractual duties. It can fill the place, and still sue for a term's fees, giving credit for the deposit if that is what the contract provides. The essence of an anticipatory breach is that it goes to the root of the contract and is not just a minor matter.

(b) *Repudiatory breach*: this is a serious breach by one party, that is to say, a breach of a contractual condition which affects the substance and foundation of the contract once the time for performance has arrived. An example is where a parent withdraws a pupil in the middle of a term when the school is substantially performing its obligations.

(c) *Frustration by breach* is an unhelpful expression denoting that a failure of performance by one party is due to the act or default of the other party. This is quite different from the doctrine of frustration (referred to at **5.8** above) where a change of circumstances after formation of the contract has rendered it impossible to fulfil the contract as originally envisaged.

(d) *Fundamental breach*: it is necessary to distinguish between breach of a contractual term which is *not* fundamental to the contract and breach of a term that *is* so fundamental that it goes to the root of the contract. 'Breach going to the root of the contract' is an expression that is more in favour than 'fundamental breach'. Alternative ways of describing breaches which go to the root of the contract are breaches which:

  – affect the very substance of the contract;
  – provide the innocent party with something different in substance from that for which he contracted;
  – deprive the innocent party of substantially the whole benefit which the parties intended he or she should obtain;
  – or frustrate the purpose of the contract.

(e) *Rescission* means setting aside the contract. Where a contract is rescinded, it is terminated as if from the outset. The object of rescission is to put the parties back in the position they would have been in had the contract never been made. In some cases, the injured party may elect to rescind. In other cases, the court may order rescission. The expression is used mainly in cases of misrepresentation, mistake, duress and undue influence, and is often misused so as to mean a simple termination of the contract following a breach.

## 5.10   UNILATERAL VARIATION OF A CONTRACT

A unilateral variation of a contract occurs when one party decides unilaterally that he is going to change one of the terms of the contract. Quite a number of unilateral variations are built into the parent contract, expressly or by custom and practice, in any event, for example, that there will be reasonable increases in the fees from time to time and other reasonable changes in many aspects of the school.

A unilateral variation that has not been provided for in the contract is not of itself a breach of contract. The innocent party has given no consideration for it so he is not bound by it. However, he has to decide whether:

– to accept the variation and continue with the contract on the new terms; or
– to reject the variation and insist on performance on the old terms.

An example would be a greater than reasonable increase in the school fees without a term's notice being given. If the parent communicates a rejection of that increase but the school insists on it as a condition before the pupil can return, the school would be in repudiatory breach at that stage.

This rule emphasises the importance of a school giving a term's notice to parents of significant changes of any kind at the school, that is, changes which are outside those normally to be expected from an educational environment. Thus, at least a term's notice should be given of a merger or relocation of the school or of a greater than normal increase in the fees or of an intention to drop a major subject or sport from the curriculum or to discontinue the sixth form.

## 5.11 CONTRACTUAL REMEDIES

The general contractual remedies are an action for damages, an action for *quantum meruit*, an action for an agreed sum, and the equitable remedies of specific performance, injunction and rescission. Remedies in the employment tribunal for breach of employment contracts are differently named and structured, and are not considered here.

The remedies of most relevance in the contract for educational services are the following.

### 5.11.1 Action by the school for an agreed sum

School fees for a current or past term are an agreed sum and a debt. By custom and practice, fees are payable on or before the first day of term. Express contractual terms may provide that they are payable *before* the first day of term or by instalments or there may be an agreement for lump sum prepayment, known as *composition*. In the absence of frustration or breach of contract, the parents' failure to pay fees is a breach of a contract to pay an agreed sum and gives rise to an action in debt. The school needs only to prove the existence of the contract. It need not prove that it has suffered loss or has mitigated its loss.

The school's claim for the previous term's extras, disbursements, late payment charges and damage repairs (if the latter are expressly provided for in the contract) will also be a debt.

### 5.11.2 Action by the school for liquidated damages

It was held in *Mount v Oldham Corporation* [1973] 1 All ER 29, CA, that fees in lieu of notice are liquidated damages which follow similar rules to those which apply to debts. It is submitted that there are two distinct situations in relation to fees in lieu of notice:

(a) The pupil is a 'no show' at the start of a term or is withdrawn summarily during a term without any form of notice. This is a repudiatory breach if it is clear that the parent has evinced an intention no longer to fulfil his part of the contract. The school may then treat itself as discharged from the contract and sue immediately for debt and/or liquidated damages, namely current fees or fees in lieu of notice at the rate that would have applied to the pupil during the term in question.

(b) The parent gives short notice, ie less than a term's notice, of his intention to withdraw the pupil, but wishes to leave the pupil at school for the remainder of the current term. In this case, the school must continue to perform its obligations and provide the full education service contracted for and may only treat itself as discharged from the contract as at the end of the current term. It is submitted that the cause of action for fees in lieu of notice arises at the start of the following term, ie the term of notice, although the point is not free from doubt.

### 5.11.3 Claim by school or parent on a *quantum meruit*

*Quantum meruit* means 'as much as he deserves'. It is a claim for reasonable remuneration or for repayment of a pro rata sum. In general, the remedy does not arise under the contract for educational services because school fees are a fixed amount payable on or before the first day of term for the whole term as an entity unless otherwise agreed.

In *Governors of E. Ivor Hughes Education Foundation v Denfield* [1992] *Current Law* September 58, a parent informed the school that he intended only paying for the GCSE term in respect of weeks before the examinations when tuition was provided. His Honour Judge Sich held that there was no express or implied agreement that less than the full fees were payable in the GCSE term. A parent could only seek to vary the contract in this respect before the final term's fees were due. If he ascertained that a lesser sum was due he would have to tender that sum by the due date. Otherwise, the school took the pupil back for the summer term on the basis of the existing contract.

A similar point received wide attention and comment in the national press during April 1998. It was reported that the Headmaster of Charterhouse had written to the parents of A-level candidates before the start of the summer term to the effect that: 'Pupils should leave school after their final examination, if only for 48 hours or so'. The reported response from some parents was that they intended to withhold or seek repayment of fees for the remaining three weeks or so of the term. Heads of other leading schools were quoted as saying that they 'did not expect their sixth formers to stay on if they did not want to' and 'We do not force them home. However, if they stay they have to be purposeful ... if the 18-year-olds are celebrating the end of exams it is difficult to keep the rest of the school stable'. Another headmaster said: 'If our A-level students wish to go home for a few days they are quite entitled to do so, but we always require them back here for the last week of term'.

The issue is really one of custom and practice which, it is submitted, informs much of the law that applies between independent schools and parents. The practicalities are that pupils often regard their final A-level paper as the end of their school career and are ready to begin their summer holiday or a summer job. Many are exhausted and fit for nothing without a rest. GCSE candidates who have finished their examinations will often begin some form of work experience. The staff likewise have been working at a feverish pitch for seven or eight weeks providing additional support, often late into the evening, and providing pastoral care to stressed and anxious candidates. Moreover, the remainder of the school has to function normally. Against this background it might be thought entirely reasonable to expect A-level candidates to return home for a few days at least, but if they elect then to return to school, it would be an express or implied term of the contract that the school will make suitable provision for them.

In *Bradfield House Ltd v Walsall Metropolitan Borough Council* (1997) 4 EPLI 68, a local authority placed a boy at a special school. The boy absconded after 4 days and was expelled. Both parties accepted that the expulsion was justified. The placing authority argued for a *quantum meruit*, ie that it was only bound to pay for the time the pupil had attended. It was held that this was an entire misconception of the law. If a parent or local authority sends a child to a school and the child has to be expelled, the school should not bear the loss.

### 5.11.4    Claim for unliquidated damages

The expression *unliquidated damages* means damages whose amount is not known until they have been assessed. There are no specific rules for the quantification of damages in contract. Damages are normally awarded on the basis of placing the injured party in the same financial position as if the contract had been properly performed. Damages are *compensation for loss of bargain* or *compensation for loss of expectations under the contract.* In exceptional cases, there may also be damages for *expenses incurred in reliance on the contract* which have been wasted by the defendant's breach.

An example of the latter point was an unreported case where parents had accepted a place and ordered a school uniform. The pupil attended for a preview weekend during which he was bullied, and he was unwilling thereafter to attend the school. It is submitted that the parents would probably have been entitled to compensation for the cost of the school uniform.

The general rule in contract is that damages cannot be recovered in a contract action for mental distress and injury to feelings. There is an exception to that rule in certain types of case about race and sex discrimination and harassment in the workplace, although no such damages are awarded in straightforward cases of wrongful dismissal.

There is a further exception where the contract is for a holiday, recreation or entertainment. Substantial damages may be recovered for disappointment, vexation and mental distress (*Jarvis v Swann Tours* (1973) 1 QB 233, CA).

It is open to doubt whether a claim for damages for disappointment, vexation and mental distress might lie in a case of wrongful expulsion. Although the contract for education is not a contract for a holiday, recreation, entertainment or peace of mind as such, it may be argued that it has as much in common with that genre as with life in the workplace.

In the case of *Tony Starkey* (1992) *Daily Telegraph*, 20 November, a complaint of maladministration was made to the Local Government Ombudsman after a State school had refused to recognise a boy's dyslexia for four years. An award of £5,000 was made to the pupil, £250 to the parents for their time and trouble in pursuing the matter and £850 for one year's remedial teaching. Apparently, there was no element of award for the parents' disappointment, vexation or mental distress.

Following a wrongful expulsion or a sustainable claim based on teaching standards or the failure to detect a learning difficulty, parents may incur the cost of additional school fees and extra tuition, the cost of a new uniform and certain other expenses. These are special damages.

## 5.11.5   Specific performance and injunction

In general, specific performance will not be granted when the contract involves personal services such as a contract of employment and, by analogy, the contract for educational services is similar in this respect.

However, if expulsion, requirement to leave or withdrawal of a pupil's assisted place is found to be wrongful, the parents may apply for a mandatory injunction under the contract and/or if there is a public law element, such as in the case of an assisted place, the pupil may seek an order of mandamus on judicial review.

In *R v Cobham Hall School ex parte S* [1998] ELR 389, QBD, the school had re-allocated a pupil's assisted place. The court found that this was done because of the pupil's poor academic performance, although the head had explained her decision to the effect that it was only a way of requiring the pupil to leave without having the stigma of explusion. The pupil obtained legal aid and applied for judicial review, which would not normally be available against an independent school, but was available in this case because of the element of public funding. Dyson J held that the court had jurisdiction to require the school to reinstate the pupil on a non-paying basis if the assisted place was withdrawn unlawfully or a pupil was wrongfully expelled and funds were no longer available. In the event, reinstatement was not ordered.

An instance in which a mandatory injunction was granted by a district judge, but later discharged by a circuit judge who struck out the pupil's action, occurred in *Grenar v The Royal School, Hindhead* (1997) (unreported). There, a former pupil's action was for damages following the school's withholding her GCSE results because fees were unpaid, and it was held that injunctions granted earlier ordering the release of the results and other documents should not have been granted.

In a different context, there have been cases in which a school has obtained an injunction against parents to restrain them from approaching the school, its staff and pupils. An injunction is generally an interlocutory step which can only be granted if there is a substantive cause of action, such as a breach of contract or a tort, for example, negligence or trespass.

# Chapter 6

## FORMATION OF THE CONTRACT

### 6.1  INTRODUCTION

This chapter is concerned with the parties to the contract for education, the events that may lead to formation of the contract and the documents in which the main terms of the contract are recorded and described.

### 6.2  OVERVIEW

Traditionally, independent schools did not reduce the contractual term into writing except to state the main rules concerning payment of fees. However, 'a gentlemen's agreement is not worth the paper it's written on' and with the ever-present risk of litigation over disputes about goods and services of all kinds, the more that can be clarified in writing, the less will be the scope for litigation, and the school and parents will have a greater understanding of the product.

The days have gone when the supplier of a complex service could get away with not telling the customer what the terms of the contract would be. It is no longer acceptable to say to a customer: 'You are buying a high quality service from me. I know the terms on which I am selling it to you but I am going to leave you to guess what they are'.

Some support for this view may be found from the decision of the Court of Appeal in *Scottish Power plc v Britoil (Exploration) Ltd and Ors* (1997) *The Times*, 2 December. In that case, which did not concern a school, the court held that the circumstances surrounding the formation of a contract should be confined to what the parties had in mind and what was going on around them at the time when they were making the contract. An important inference from this decision is the desirability of ensuring that contractual terms are written out clearly because the court will construe the circumstances at the time of the contract and not their background.

### 6.3  THE PARTIES TO THE CONTRACT

#### 6.3.1  Scope

The usual parties to the contract for educational services ('parent contract') will be the school or its governors on the one hand and the parents or a guardian appointed under s 5 of the Children Act 1989 on the other.

Sometimes, a third party, such as a grandparent, step-parent, sibling, trustee, family company, employer, High Commission, Embassy or holiday guardian, may acquire rights or duties under the contract. It is quite possible for certain of these to become contracting parties in their own right if they have parental responsibility under s 2 of the Children Act 1989 or delegated parental responsibility under s 2(9) of that Act.

It is also possible, but very rare, for the pupil to be a fully contracting party subject to the provisions of the Minors Contracts Act 1987.

Care should be taken to identify those who are the contracting parties as distinct from those who are properly to be regarded as third parties with limited rights and obligations, usually relating to the payment of fees or the care of overseas pupils.

### 6.3.2   The school as a party

Most independent schools are registered as educational charities. Being a charity is a matter of legal status rather than constitution. In general terms, charitable status denotes that the organisation will be regulated by the Charity Commissioners for England and Wales under the Charities Act 1993, although the colleges of Winchester and Eton are exempt charities by virtue of Sch 2 of the Act. Charitable status also denotes certain differences in the powers and duties of charity trustees from those of ordinary trustees and it is a status that confers certain exemptions from tax.

Leaving charitable status to one side, an independent school may be constituted in a number of different ways:

(a)   as an unincorporated trust under which the school has no legal personality separate from that of its trustees;

(b)   as an unincorporated association, again without a legal personality separate from its committee members;

(c)   as an incorporated body of trustees by certificate of the Charity Commissioners under Part VII of the Charities Act 1993;

(d)   as a corporation sole, such as Winchester or Eton, or as a corporation aggregate created by Royal Charter;

(e)   as a statutory corporation created under a special Act of Parliament;

(f)   as a sole proprietor, a partnership of proprietors, a private trust or a limited company, in each case being a business for profit without charitable status. A few such schools do not, however, distribute their profits.

An incorporated school has the choice of contracting in its corporate name or its business name, if different. For example, Bedstone Educational Trust Limited is also known as Bedstone College. A school that is constituted as an unincorporated trust must contract in the name of its governors or trustees, for example: 'The Trustees of the Wisbech Grammar School Foundation'. Some variations of these rules apply when schools are suing or being sued as to which see Ord 15 of the Rules of the Supreme Court.

### 6.3.3   The parents

Even after separation or divorce, parents have joint parental responsibility under s 2 of the Children Act 1989. That implies joint decision-making in such matters as schooling and in turn it implies that both parents should be express contracting parties, ie signatories. Frequently, however, only one parent signs the admission forms. There is then a question as to whether the other parent is equally bound by implied contract. That will depend on a number of circumstances considered in more detail later and, in particular, it will depend on whether the parents live together and whether they have both consented to the child attending the school on the understanding it is a school which charges fees.

### 6.3.4 The pupil

The custom and practice of independent schools is not to treat the pupil as a contracting party, since the statutory obligation under the Education Act 1996, s 7 to educate a child under school-leaving age is that of the persons with parental responsibility. There is also the practical aspect that the pupil will not normally have the means to pay the fees which represent consideration for the contract.

It is legally possible for a person under 18, who is the beneficiary of a discretionary trust under which the trustees are prepared to exercise discretion, to make his (or her) own contract for education and pay the fees accordingly. However, the school's position under the Minors' Contracts Act 1987 would be unsatisfactory. The effect of the Act is that a contract made by a person under 18 is voidable and can be repudiated by the child when he reaches 18 unless it was a contract for necessaries or a contract that was clearly for the child's benefit. Education is clearly both of these, but there can be debate about whether education at an independent school necessarily falls into either or both of these categories for a particular child in particular circumstances.

The disadvantage to the pupil in not being a contracting party is that it appears his only legal remedy against the school is in tort or, in very restricted circumstances, judicial review (see *R v Cobham Hall School ex parte S* [1998] ELR 389). If he wishes to establish a case of negligence he must under the present law establish that he has suffered physical or psychological injury or damage to property or damage to his educational welfare. Even though 'property' can include intellectual property rights, the pupil will not always be able to establish one of these heads of damage.

The only other possibility would appear to be an action for professional negligence based on tort instead of the more usual action in contract. Unlike a simple negligence claim, professional negligence can be a claim for economic loss alone, without personal injury or damage to property. Moreover, the limitation period in such claims will be 6 years from when the pupil reaches 18, and not 3 years, which is the primary period in tort.

### 6.3.5 Third parties

Examples have been given above of those who may acquire rights and obligations as third parties to the contract for educational services. It is quite possible also for them to become full contracting parties expressly or by implication in their own right or at the least as guarantor of the fees, provided the guarantee is in writing.

A step-parent who takes the place of an estranged or deceased natural parent may become bound to the school by implied contract although the detailed terms and conditions of the contract may not apply in full unless they have been expressly drawn to his attention and incorporated into the contract.

Frequently in the case of a pupil from overseas, the fees are paid in sterling by a High Commission. The school should not be lulled into thinking that the High Commission necessarily becomes legally liable to pay fees for the current term or fees in lieu of notice. The role accepted in these cases is normally that of agent trying to obtain payment from the diplomat abroad and, if successful, remitting the money to the school. If the school wishes to fix the High Commission with a legal obligation to pay fees in lieu of notice it will need an express agreement to that effect which is unlikely to be forthcoming. None the less, there is experience of High Commissions being helpful in exerting pressure on a diplomat who has failed to meet his obligations to the school.

Particular care is needed when the fees are to be paid by the trustees of a family trust. The parents or a guardian appointed under s 5 of the Children Act 1989 should remain the contracting parties, and the school should enter a separate agreement in writing with the trustees that fees and extras will be paid promptly, that a term's notice of withdrawal will be given or a term's fees paid in lieu, and that the trustees will be bound by the school's standard terms so far as they relate to financial matters. There is much anecdotal evidence of schools having difficulty obtaining money from a so-called 'family trust', which sometimes does not exist at all.

Sometimes, a parent (employee) will ask the school to contract direct with his employer for the benefit of the specified children of the employee. The reason for this request is to characterise school fees as a *payment in kind* which will be exempt from Class 1 National Insurance Contributions, instead of as *remuneration* which attracts Class 1 contributions. For the parent, the saving may be anything from £300 per year for one child at an inexpensive day school to £3,000 or more per year for several children at a top boarding school.

For this arrangement to work, the Contributions Agency will require clear evidence of a contract between the employer and the school. However, the school will be exposed if the employer ceases business or refuses to pay fees in lieu of notice, or if the employee is summarily dismissed. Moreoever, the school would expect the employer to pay the deposit and to waive his contractual rights to give authorities in relation to the pupil, to receive progress reports on the pupil and to terminate the contract. The school would also expect parents to guarantee fees and extras in the event of non-payment by the employer for any reason. Such complications understandably make these arrangements unattractive to independent schools and, in any event, it is not yet certain that they will be accepted by the Contributions Agency.

## 6.4  FORMALITIES AND DOCUMENTS

### 6.4.1  Formation

A legally binding contract arises as soon as the parents accept the offer of a place for entry at some future date. Invariably, the school requires one or both parents to complete an entry form, but there is no express requirement of law for any written formalities.

If a dispute arises over a contract whose terms have not been set out in writing, there is likely to be litigation unless one or other party concedes the position or some other compromise is found. It has been noted earlier that trends in the development of the law relating to consumer contracts are towards written terms and conditions and also towards fairness rather than freedom of contract.

Thus, a school which relies on its prospectus, or on poorly drafted contractual documents, or on no documents at all, is handing the control of its contracts to the court. In such cases, the court will only imply those contractual terms that are obvious or necessary and in all other respects a solution will be at large.

For these reasons, we explore below the scope of the contractual documents that are available to an independent school, observing in passing that the privilege of self-regulation is confined to the independent sector and not available to the State-funded sector.

### 6.4.2   The prospectus

#### (a)   The purpose of a prospectus

Most independent schools prepare a brochure known as a prospectus. The dictionary meaning of that expression is a descriptive circular announcing the main objects and plans of a commercial scheme. However, the prospectus of an independent school is more than that.

At one level, the prospectus is a sales document designed to appeal to parents and in particular to children who, as they grow older, will strongly influence, or even take, the 'which school' decision. Prospectus documents vary between expensive and glossy on the one hand and entirely plain, without pictures, on the other. Some are bound booklets and have a back pocket for further documents to be inserted. Others are a glossy cover only, with inserts.

At a different level, the prospectus should convey something of the vision, objective, aim, ethos and culture of the school, showing, for example, whether it is a school for high-fliers only, or whether it is for children of mixed ability or with particular needs.

At a third level, the prospectus may be a legal document which sets out the contractual terms and conditions. That is to be avoided for a number of reasons. It can have the effect of converting statements in the prospectus into contractual representations. That situation is litigation-prone. Moreover, changing the terms and conditions may not be possible without the considerable costs of reprinting and issuing the expensive new prospectus to all current parents. It is far better for a school to use standard terms and conditions which are separate from the prospectus, and to ensure that the prospectus contains a prominent disclaimer drafted in terms that are effective at law.

#### (b)   The contractual status of the prospectus

This was one of the issues that arose in *Price v Dennis* [1988] LEXIS, CA. In that case, the prospectus was held to be non-contractual in effect, therefore the contractual terms were implied and had to be found by the court. Lord Justice Glidewell said:

'In my view the prospectus was an invitation to the prospective parents to apply for admission to the school; in other words, it was an invitation to make an offer. I agree with the judge . . . that the broad terms of the prospectus, but not each detail, were incorporated into each contract between parents and Mrs Price [the proprietor of the school]. For instance: what type of school it was; the nature of the education offered; the nature of the facilities to be expected; and broadly the standard of education to be expected.'

Glidewell LJ then held that express, or alternatively necessarily implied, conditions of the contracts with parents were that:

(a)  the plaintiff should conduct the school in a fit, proper and responsible manner; and

(b)  the functions of the school should be carried out with all reasonable care and skill; and

(c)  the proprietor was required to take reasonable steps to retain the confidence of parents who themselves acted reasonably.

The fact that this case went to the Court of Appeal is a good illustration of the difficulty a court may have in finding the terms of a contract when those terms have not been set out expressly. An incidental point that arises relates to offer and acceptance. The school relied on its prospectus alone and Glidewell LJ found that the prospectus amounted to an invitation to treat. The contractual offer was made by the parents and accepted by the school. Matters are normally the other way round when standard terms and conditions are used. Then, the school offers a place on its own terms so that it can adequately manage the relationship with the parents and child. The parents accept the offer on those terms or as otherwise agreed.

## (c)  Misleading statements in the prospectus

In 1994, a determined attempt was made by a parent to have an independent school prosecuted by the Trading Standards Department because its prospectus and school sign board contained a misleading statement. The school had been for children aged 3–18 and therefore included a sixth form. This was advertised in the prospectus and on the school's sign board. However, in one year there were insufficient A-level pupils to justify running a sixth form. The school overlooked the fact that its prospectus and sign board were therefore out-of-date and omitted to send out a notice with the prospectus correcting the error in terms that were at least as prominent as the prospectus description of the sixth form and the courses it offered.

The report to the Trading Standards Office under s 14 of the Trade Descriptions Act 1968 was made by a parent who had contracted to send his 3-year-old daughter to the school and had paid a deposit of £200. He changed his mind about the school, allegedly (but barely credibly) because there was no longer a sixth form. The school did not consider he was entitled to a return of the deposit. Although there was, in the event, no prosecution, considerable cost was occasioned and the case illustrates the need to ensure that the prospectus is kept up-to-date, that corrective information is sent with it when necessary and that the prospectus contains an appropriate disclaimer.

## (d)   The contents of a prospectus

Typically, the printed matter in the prospectus of an independent school contains:

- a summary of the school's foundation and history and the scope of the education offered;
- a statement about the vision for the school and the school's objective and culture;
- separate sections about the way the school is organised, the academic and sports curriculum and other activities, clubs and societies, boarding (if applicable) and the school's place in the local community;
- a page of general information covering admission, scholarships, exhibitions, bursaries and assisted places, fees and extras and school uniform. There may be a number of personal endorsements from current and former pupils, or parents.

There is likely to be a back-pocket containing additional sheets about the governors, staff, recent examination results and a number of other aspects. The back-pocket is likely also to contain a registration form, fees list, a copy of the school's standard terms and conditions, and details about scholarships and other awards and, if appropriate, recent examination results and pupil destinations.

The prospectus should be marked with a date code and should contain a prominent disclaimer to the effect that it is not intended to be a contractual document and that parents wishing to place specific reliance on a matter stated in the prospectus should first enquire further about it.

### 6.4.3   The contractual offer

The legal technicalities of offer and acceptance of a place at an independent school do not often come under scrutiny and detailed analysis is unnecessary here. As we saw in Chapter 5, for a binding contract to be formed there must be *offer* from one party and *acceptance* from the other. A person who seeks to enforce a contract must have given *some* value for it. Usually it is the school which is the *supplier* which offers a place on the basis of its terms, conditions and admission procedures. The parents are the *consumers* who accept the place. It will be noticed that this is the opposite way round from the situation in *Price v Dennis* (above).

### 6.4.4   The offer letter

The letter containing a contractual offer should contain or incorporate all the express terms of the contract so that there is no doubt in the minds of parents exactly what they will be accepting. This does not mean that the offer letter needs to be full of legalese. On the contrary, it can be quite short and welcoming, provided it incorporates a properly drafted set of standard terms and conditions and the current fees list. Four distinct models of offer letter are considered below.

### (a)   An offer of a place at full fees

The suggested elements of the offer letter are these:

- The letter should be expressed as an offer of a place at full fees, and the entry date should be stated.

- An acceptance form should be enclosed with a copy of the current edition of the school's standard terms and conditions. They should be marked with a date code. The letter should make clear that the standard terms and conditions form part of the contract. The parents should be directed to read and retain the standard terms and conditions and to complete and return the acceptance form with a cheque for the deposit.
- A date should be given by which the acceptance form must be received at the school office and after which the place may be offered to another family.

The terminology of the letter should be consistent with that used in the acceptance form and the standard terms and conditions so as to avoid ambiguity.

## *(b)   The award of a scholarship or exhibition*

The charitable scheme or trust deed under which the school is constituted may contain express provision for scholarships, exhibitions, bursaries, maintenance and other awards and prizes and, in addition, leaving exhibitions, together with conditions of award and other provisions including discretion and the right to withdraw awards under certain circumstances. The governors, in their capacity as charity trustees, are required as a matter of law to carry out the trust in accordance with its terms.

*An academic scholarship* is normally awarded following a competitive examination. Many schools offer other kinds of scholarship to children who show promise in a non-academic area. A scholarship may be endowed or not. Most scholarships are for tuition fees only and do not cover the costs of boarding, but in appropriate cases there may be a bursary or some other discretionary arrangement and, very rarely, the scholarship will cover both. A top scholarship may cover all of the fees but usually its value will be between 30% and 50% of the fees tenable for the child's time at the school or a particular part of it. The award of a scholarship will normally be announced in the school magazine and perhaps elsewhere. At some schools, a scholarship confers additional privileges.

*An exhibition* is a minor award, sometimes to a candidate who has done particularly well in one or two areas of scholarship examinations but has narrowly missed winning a scholarship overall. The value of an exhibition is often expressed as an annual sum, such as £1,000 per year.

A scholarship or exhibition should be awarded solely on the basis of merit, not financial need. The latter can be catered for by bursaries. This is important because parents are likely to value an award as much for their perception that it has been earned on merit as for the financial benefit. Moreover, any suspicion that other than objective criteria have been applied can be a cause of ill-feeling which tends to undermine the school's culture.

A school's ability to make these awards is of immense benefit to the school as well as the parents and child. Talent tends to attract other talent, including good teachers. Awards that are well publicised may add a significant contribution to driving standards upwards. This makes it all the more important that there is careful control and that awards are made on proper criteria and are subject to suitable conditions.

The school is entitled to provide for clawback of all or part of the financial benefits received by the parents if the award is abused. If a pupil is withdrawn without notice, the financial benefit should cease forthwith so that fees in lieu of notice are payable at the full rate and are not limited to the parental contribution. The conditions need careful drafting in a form that is consistent with the school's standard terms and conditions and may include, for example:

- that the pupil is required to work hard and contribute positively to the life of the school;
- that the parents are expected to support and encourage the pupil to achieve the purposes of the award and comply promptly with their other financial obligations to the school;
- that the award may be withdrawn, following consultation, if the pupil falls below the required standards of conduct and progress or if the parents default in payment of the balance of the account.

The letter offering a place with an award of a scholarship (or exhibition) should contain the matters that apply to a place at full fees (where consistent) but should also deal with: the reasons why the scholarship has been awarded; the value of the scholarship; the additional privileges (if any); the period for which the scholarship is tenable; and the way in which the benefits will be credited to the account. The award should also be made subject to conditions of the sort outlined above.

One case about scholarship clawback was *Church Education Corporation v McCoig & McCoig* (unreported), 8 December 1995, in which the terms of a scholarship award at an independent school included a provision for clawback of scholarship benefits in the event of the pupil being withdrawn before she completed her A-levels. That condition was upheld by the court subject to the caveat that there needs to be an express term clearly drafted so that no misunderstanding arises. A clawback provision would not operate if the reason for withdrawal of the pupil was a fundamental breach of contract by the school or an equivalent tort in respect of the child.

As a matter of good practice and natural justice, there should be full consultation with parents and pupil and clear warnings given before any question arises of withdrawing an award or enforcing a right to claw back benefits (see *R v Cobham Hall School ex parte S* [1998] ELR 389).

### (c)  The award of a bursary

A bursary may be endowed or funded out of income. It is awarded on a basis of financial need rather than academic merit, although a school is likely to require a degree of merit so that scarce resource is not wasted. The value of the bursary is unlikely to exceed 50% of the fees – often it will be less than that – the remainder being the 'parental contribution'. Sometimes, a way will be found to fund the parental contribution in cases of genuine need and merit. It is reasonable for schools to means-test parents before granting bursaries and annually thereafter in some cases. Bursaries should not be used as a means of poaching pupils from other schools. There is a clearly understood protocol in this respect.

The letter of offer will follow lines similar to those used for a scholarship or exhibition and the conditions will also be similar. The provision for clawback may be of less practical value in the case of a low-income family and most schools would not in any event wish to act oppressively against parents in cases of genuine hardship. There have, however, been instances when the very existence of clawback provision has provided a salutary reminder to parents who were not treating the school reasonably within their financial capabilities.

### (d) The award of a government-assisted place

It is no longer relevant to consider the terms of offer of an assisted place. The Education (Schools) Act 1997 provided for the phasing out of the assisted places scheme with effect from September 1998. The intention of the Labour Government is to phase out the scheme over seven years, releasing £100 million by the millennium and over £100 million per year thereafter. At its height, the scheme benefited some 38,000 children.

The Assisted Places Scheme was governed by ss 479–481 of the Education Act 1996 and the Education (Assisted Places) Regulations 1995. The Act and the Regulations provided that independent schools could enter into 'participation agreements' with the Secretary of State for Education and Employment for the purpose of enabling pupils, who might otherwise not be able to do so, to benefit from education at independent schools. The payment system under such agreements was:

–   that the participating school would remit fees that would otherwise be chargeable in respect of pupils selected for assisted places under the scheme; and
–   that the Secretary of State would reimburse the school for the fees that were remitted.

The school was not entitled to charge parents the difference between the full fees according to the school's fees list and the maximum sum the Secretary of State was authorised to reimburse. The scheme was means-tested using forms AP1 and AP2.

In *R v Cobham Hall School ex parte S* [1998] ELR 389, QBD, Dyson J questioned whether there was a contract at all between the school and the parents of a pupil with an assisted place. The points to which Dyson J had regard in that case were:

–   that the parents could not afford to pay the fees and so, as S had failed in her bid for a bursary, the only basis upon which she could be admitted to the school would be as an assisted pupil;
–   that in these circumstances the standard form of agreement, which was designed for use in the case of private fee-paying pupils, was not apt; and
–   that there were powerful arguments in support of the view that no consideration moved from the parents to the school and/or that there was no intention to enter into contractual relations.

In fact, in many assisted place cases including the *Cobham Hall School* case, there is a parental contribution to pay and payment is enforceable in a contract action. Parents are invariably required to agree that they will give a term's notice to withdraw the pupil or pay a term's fees in lieu of notice, again enforceable in a contract action. Notice, or fees in lieu, is in any event an implied term between the school and parents (see *Mount v Oldham Corporation* [1973] 1 QB 309, CA). Usually, the parents will have been asked for a deposit repayable in circumstances dictated by contract.

Moreover, there are many other aspects of the relationship which can give rise to contractual disputes, such as: the basis on which the school will initiate and respond to change; the authorities that will be provided by parents; the rules as to conduct on the part of the pupil and the parents and as to the attendance of the pupil; the school's requirements over insurance; and the curriculum that will be delivered, since independent schools are not bound to deliver the National Curriculum.

Furthermore, in the case of a boarder, there will inevitably be contractual terms governing the basis on which boarding provision is made and may be withdrawn. There have been numerous unreported cases in county courts up and down the country in which the school has successfully enforced one or another contractual right in assisted place cases. Finally, there is the established custom and practice of independent schools described at **6.4.9** below which, it is submitted, was not replaced by the 1995 Regulations.

The *Cobham Hall School* case therefore gives rise to a number of difficulties. If its reasoning is followed, there appears to be no legal relationship between an independent school and the parents of a pupil who has an assisted place. That, it is submitted, could produce absurd results if the parent or school were in breach of the duties owed to each other. Moreover, the school must follow quite separate regimes for those pupils whose fees are paid privately and those who are paid for partly or wholly by the State. It is, with respect, difficult to see any logical or practical basis for either proposition.

### 6.4.5  The acceptance form

The acceptance form should be designed to elicit the information that the school will require for the proper management of the relationship with the parents and pupil. Quite possibly, the family situation will have changed since registration. The parents may have separated or divorced. Perhaps the fees will now be paid by a third party. The family may have moved house or moved overseas. Names may have changed and, in rare cases, the court may have appointed a guardian or removed parental responsibility from one or both parents.

In addition to formal details of this nature, questions need to be asked about whether those with parental responsibility are agreed that the child should attend the school; whether there is anyone else whose consent to the child coming to the school is required; and whether it is proposed that anyone other than the parents will pay or guarantee payment of the fees. The form normally asks for information about certain kinds of court order, and about learning difficulties, allergies and other health problems.

Whenever possible there should be at least two signatures to the acceptance form even if, because of a death, there is only one person with parental responsibility. Perhaps a grandparent will offer a guarantee which should be contained in a separate form of agreement.

The signatures should subscribe to a declaration at the foot of the form that those with parental responsibility intend the pupil to come to the school; that they have read, understood and agree the terms of the offer letter and the standard terms and conditions. The declaration should also set out the payments that will be due if, for any reason, the child does not enter the school. It may be that a term's fees will be payable, the deposit being credited or that there will be no charge to fees in lieu if the place can be filled but the deposit will not be refunded. The declaration should leave parents in no doubt that they are entering into a legally binding contract which, in the absence of breach or frustration, can only be brought to an end during its currency by a term's notice being given or a term's fees paid in lieu of notice. The declaration often asks parents to certify that fees at the previous school have been or will be paid before the pupil enters the new school.

Care is needed to ensure that the standard terms and conditions are incorporated into the acceptance. The usual way of doing that is to print the acceptance form with a copy of the standard terms and conditions attached, the latter to be read, detached and retained by the parents before the acceptance form is returned to the school with the deposit.

Parents should be informed that, in addition to the standard terms and conditions, the current fees list and school rules are incorporated into the contract and that reasonable changes may be made to all these matters from time to time as circumstances require and in the discretion of the governors.

### 6.4.6   The standard terms and conditions

#### *(a)   Generally*

The standard terms and conditions will be glossed by a number of policies drawn up by the governors. Policies are addressed in more detail in a later chapter but a short explanation is needed here.

An effective set of standard terms and conditions is likely to comprise not less than 50 separate clauses each covering one or a number of aspects of the parent contract. Unless set out in writing, there will often be doubt as to which matters have been expressly agreed, which matters are properly to be treated as implied terms and which matters are not terms of the contract at all. The only way of resolving doubt is by agreement or litigation; it is, of course, far better to reach express agreement in advance.

Consumerism has added great complexity to contractual dealings. As noted earlier, the trend in the law of consumer contract is towards fairness of contract rather than freedom of contract.

#### *(b)   Explanation of the school's ethos*

The standard terms and conditions should be drafted and explained in terms of the ethos of the school if they are to satisfy the requirements of the Unfair Terms in Consumer Contracts Regulations 1994, as explained in Chapter 5.

Reference may be made to the prospectus for an account of the objectives and aims of the school. However, the standard terms and conditions should go further and explain the school's commitment to high standards of teaching and pastoral care and the fact that parental contact is welcomed. It should also be explained that the school is an environment in which pupils are encouraged and expected to make their individual contributions; to participate in work and leisure activities with enthusiasm and commitment; and to behave with tolerance and understanding, respecting the needs of others.

It is widely recognised that education is an organic process and a successful school must both initiate and respond to change. Indeed, a failure to change will lead to stagnation, which is the antithesis of education. The standard terms and conditions should therefore explain in a general way what is meant by change. This is so that both parties may contemplate the nature of the changes that can occur at any school which is well and thoughtfully managed.

These will include reasonable changes from time to time to the standard terms and conditions, to the size and location of the school, to its premises and facilities, to the academic and games curriculum and the structure and composition of classes. There may also be changes to the way in which the school is run, to the rules and disciplinary framework, to the length of school terms and the school day, and to any other aspect of the school. Moreover, fee levels will be reviewed each year and there will be reasonable increases from time to time. The ownership or legal status of the school may change, for example because of incorporation of an unincorporated school, or there may be a merger of schools, an enlargement of the age range, a de-merger of departments or any other structural development.

In order to ensure a fair balance, the terms and conditions should provide that parents will be consulted and/or given adequate notice of any significant proposals or changes of policy likely to affect the school community as a whole.

It should also be explained that the head is responsible for the care and good discipline of pupils while they are in the charge of the school or its staff and for the day-to-day running of the school and the curriculum; also that the standard terms and conditions reflect the custom and practice of independent schools for many generations and that the rules about change and about notice and fees in lieu of notice and the other matters in the standard terms and conditions are provided in good faith. They promote stability, forward-planning and the proper resourcing and development of the school. They help also to protect parents from increases in fees caused by the defaults of others.

The terms and conditions should give a clear indication that the school must be viewed as a community composed of the governors, staff, pupils and parents. A community depends on an ethos of mutual trust and confidence that each party will treat the other reasonably and comply with their legal obligations for the benefit of the community as a whole.

It is submitted that terms and conditions which are provided in good faith and serve these principles will not be found unfair under the 1994 Regulations or at common law.

### (c) *Explanation of what is required of the parents and pupil*

The standard terms and conditions should explain that the school attaches importance to such matters as integrity, good discipline, courtesy and manners; that the pupil is expected to take a full part in the activities of the school, to attend punctually on each school day, to work hard, to be well behaved and to comply with the school rules about the wearing of uniform.

Parents will be expected to give their support and encouragement to the aims and objectives of the school, to uphold and promote its good name, to continue the pupil's education at home and to ensure the pupil's attendance and that the pupil maintains appropriate standards of punctuality, behaviour, diligence, language, discipline, appearance and dress. Parents should be expected to read the school rules through with a pupil of sufficient age and understanding.

### (d)    Reasonableness generally

None of the requirements and expectations described above should cause concern to any parent who expects to treat the school reasonably, in the sense meant by Glidewell LJ in *Price v Dennis* [1988] LEXIS, CA, referred to above. On the contrary, it is to be expected that parents who join a school community will embrace these principles for themselves and welcome the mutual obligations they impose on all parents and pupils.

### 6.4.7    Fees forms

There are various forms that describe the amount and payment method of deposits, fees, extras, interest and other late payment and administration charges. These are likely to have contractual significance. The main forms are listed below.

### (a)    Fees list

The fees list is normally published to parents before the summer term in each school year so as to give at least a term's notice of increases or any other changes in the fee structure.

Sometimes, because of illness or other reason, governors are unable to meet and fix the fees in time to give a full term's notice to parents. There is a certain amount of litigation each year on the part of parents who may have a different reason for wanting to withdraw the pupil. The parents seek to rely on the governors' failure to give a term's notice of the fee increase and say that this amounts to a repudiatory breach of the contract. This stance by parents is difficult to justify. It will be apparent to all parents that fees are normally increased each year to take account of teachers' pay and other economic conditions at the time. This is probably so obvious that it is an implied term of the contract.

If, however, the school insists on an increase of more than a reasonable amount without giving a term's notice and the parent demurs immediately, the school's continued insistence may amount to a breach of contract entitling the parent to treat himself as discharged. The point is not free from doubt, since it may be argued with equal force that the issue is the amount of the increase and not the contract as a whole.

### (b)    Fees payable by instalments

Instalment arrangements are likely to be subject to the provisions of the Consumer Credit Act 1974 unless the agreement complies with art 3 of the Consumer Credit

(Exempt Agreements) Order 1989 discussed at **9.8.19**. Care should be taken over preparation of the documents supporting an instalment arrangement.

### (c)   Fees payable by third parties

Reference has been made earlier to the various kinds of third party who may acquire rights or duties under the contract for educational services. The particular points of difficulty are discussed at Chapter 9.

### (d)   Composition of fees

Schools will often agree a discounted figure for fees paid as a lump sum in advance. The level of discount given by a charitable school must not be such as to place the assets of the charity at risk or to give parents the benefit of tax exemptions enjoyed by a school which is a charity – that would be an abuse of charitable status.

A lump-sum prepayment can be of advantage to a school if the money forms part of the general funds of the school and assists with cash flow or in reducing borrowings or in the funding of a building project. Some of the larger schools receiving substantial sums by way of prepayment have established an advance fees trust which has its own objects, often to provide a scholarship or bursary fund but tax exemptions have now been withdrawn from these schemes.

Making a *composition* – ie granting a discount in exchange for accelerated receipt of funds – can be of value to parents or grandparents who are engaged in estate planning or who have access now to funds which may not be available in the future.

Agreements for composition are of their nature complex and schools should take specialist advice. The level of discount will have regard to the benefit to the school, current interest and inflation rates and the likely increases in fees during the composition period. It will also have reference to whether the composition covers boarding as well as tuition fees. Usually, termly increases and extras will be left out of account and will be payable separately throughout the composition period.

The agreement form will need to take account of who is paying the lump sum. If the payer is a third party such as a grandparent, there needs to be a clear understanding of what will happen upon certain contingency events, for example, family disagreement or the pupil being unable to remain at the school, or being required to leave, or dying.

### 6.4.8   Policies

The policies under which the school is governed may have contractual implications and need to be considered. There are in excess of 60 different policies governing the curriculum; sports, games and other activities; pastoral care; boarding; legal compliance and general administration. By no means all of these will be written out in full or necessarily at all and it is fair to say that policy is sometimes a matter of ethos or developed ad hoc.

The enforceability of a policy depends on a combination of its underlying intention, the way in which it is expressed and the extent to which it is published, known and understood by those to whom it applies. These points should be borne in mind by those who are responsible for drafting and promulgating matters of policy.

An example is in relation to class sizes. An oral statement at a parents' meeting or a note in a newsletter to parents that the governors are aiming to restrict classes in a certain year group to no more than 18 pupils may be taken by one parent as a firm promise amounting to a contractual obligation on which he relies and so does not give notice of withdrawal. It may be taken by another parent as a welcome statement of aspiration but no more. Its legal effect in each case will depend on fine nuances. The conclusion is that care should always be taken to define the legal status of a policy statement.

The core policies that may have contractual implications between school and parents include those relating to admissions; equal opportunities; class sizes; anti-bullying; learning difficulties; access to sports, games and cultural activities; drugs and substances; discipline; expulsion and the requirement to leave; and review procedures.

The legal status of such policies should be identified as 'contractual' or 'non-contractual'.

The school may maintain a policy on illegal drugs which states that pupils found to have been involved with drugs will be expelled or required to leave. Perhaps the intention of the school is to enforce that policy rigorously in the most serious cases bringing drugs on to school premises but to be more flexible in minor cases having regard to all the circumstances. Perhaps, for example, a group of pupils are caught in possession of cannabis at the start of the A-level term and suspended for a week but not required to leave permanently.

If the policy has contractual effect, it might be open to a parent who wishes on other grounds to withdraw a pupil, to say that the failure to expel or require a pupil found in possession of drugs to leave is a breach of his contract with the school and that he is not willing for his child to continue at a school which tolerates the use of drugs. It is submitted that making the policy 'non-contractual' would make it difficult to maintain this argument.

Because the core policies have contractual implications, schools undertaking a revision of their contractual documents should ensure that the policies are written clearly and are consistent with their standard terms and conditions, and that the policies are published by means of the school handbook or newsletter to parents and pupils.

### 6.4.9   Custom and practice

It is custom and practice at independent schools that the offer of a place and its acceptance by parents creates mutual obligations:

–   that the school will reserve a place for the pupil and deliver educational services to a reasonable standard; and
–   that the parents will pay the first term's fees, assure the attendance and good behaviour of the pupil, and thereafter will give a term's notice of intention to withdraw the pupil before the end of the school's provision for that pupil.

Unless varied in the contractual document or by oral agreement, these rules form the basis of the contract for educational services.

# Chapter 7

## ADMISSION, ENTRY AND ATTENDANCE

### 7.1  INTRODUCTION

This chapter is concerned primarily with the policies and procedures at an independent school relating to admission and entry. Consideration is also given to the new statutory provisions regulating the admission register and attendance register.

'Admission' is the process up to the time when the parent accepts the school's offer of a place and the contract is formed. 'Entry' is the time at which the pupil enters the school, usually at the start of the autumn term in September.

### 7.2  OVERVIEW

The tradition of independent schools is that a pupil is admitted at the sole discretion of the head. Thus, the head may refuse admission for any reason and without stating reasons. This discretion is, however, circumscribed by:

–   the school's charitable objects or scheme of administration under those objects which may require certain categories of applicant to be given preference;
–   the school admissions policy or the agreed admissions or selection procedure operated by a group of schools;
–   the equal opportunities legislation, namely the Sex Discrimination Act 1975, which applies in varying degrees to co-educational schools, and the Race Relations Act 1976, which applies to all schools.

A State-funded school is required to state its admissions policy in accordance with Circular 6/96, *Admissions to Maintained Schools*. There is an obligation to publish particulars regarding the annual intake, who exercises the admission function, the criteria that will be followed in deciding admissions, arrangements for pupils outside the area, other information required by regulations and such other information as the local education authority or governors think fit. Local education authorities also have an obligation to give parents the opportunity to express a *preference* as to the school they wish their child to attend and to give reasons for that preference. This is not the same thing as a right of *choice*.

Admissions to an independent school may be regulated by its governing instrument. Otherwise, there is no legal obligation to maintain a formal admissions policy of the kind described above. Even so, an independent school, particularly one that is oversubscribed and serves a mixed ethnic area, is well advised to operate a transparent admissions policy and also to keep a written record of the selection criteria for each child, in case it becomes necessary to justify a decision under the equal opportunities legislation. Professional help may be needed to draft the policy.

## 7.3   SELECTION OF PUPILS

Independent schools commonly select by ability, aptitude and family commitment. There are a number of family-related aspects. Perhaps preference is given to the children of former pupils or children who have current or past siblings at the school. Judgements may also have to be made about the ability and willingness of a family to give the necessary level of support over such matters as homework, moral values and a general sharing of the objectives and aims of the school. The ability to pay fees is also a factor. Care must be taken, however, to avoid selection criteria that are directly or indirectly discriminatory on grounds of sex or race.

Independent schools sometimes co-operate with each other to provide a fresh start for a pupil who has been required to leave his previous school, perhaps because of general misconduct or an involvement with drugs, or perhaps where there was no requirement to leave but the child was unhappy at the previous school. Offering a fresh start to a child in these circumstances is wholly consistent with the aims of an educational charity and gets away from the often misguided notion that requiring a pupil to leave simply passes the problem on to someone else.

A question is sometimes raised, however, about a school which maintains a strict policy of requiring pupils to leave if they are found to have had an involvement with drugs at school premises or elsewhere. The question is how the school can then justify accepting a 'fresh-start' pupil who has just been required to leave his previous school for an involvement with drugs that was more serious on the facts than a breach of discipline for which another pupil has just been required to leave. There are schools that would not offer a fresh start in these circumstances but many that think it is right to do so. The head in those cases will no doubt require assurances from the parent and pupil as to good behaviour and lay down strict conditions, the breach of which will result in expulsion or a requirement to leave. Considerations of this nature should be borne in mind when the selection policy and admission criteria are formulated.

## 7.4   DISCRIMINATION ON GROUNDS OF RACE, SEX OR DISABILITY

### 7.4.1   The main legislation

The Sex Discrimination Act 1975 (SDA) and Race Relations Act 1976 (RRA) deal with issues of direct and indirect discrimination in similar terms.

Both Acts define *direct* discrimination in terms of treating a person less favourably than another person would be treated, and doing so on the ground of that person's sex or race.

Both Acts define *indirect* discrimination in terms of applying a requirement or condition which is such that the proportion of one sex or race who can comply with it is considerably smaller than the proportion of the other sex or another race who can comply with it where that requirement or condition cannot be shown to be justifiable, irrespective of sex or race, and when it is to a person's detriment because he or she cannot comply with it.

Both Acts contain similar provisions about discrimination by bodies in charge of educational establishments (s 22 of SDA and s 17 of RRA). For independent schools, the provisions are, in essence, that it is unlawful for the proprietor (ie governors or school company) of the establishment to discriminate against a person:

(a) in the terms on which it offers to admit him (or her) to the establishment as a pupil; or
(b) by refusing or deliberately omitting to accept an application for his admission to the establishment as a pupil; or
(c) where he is a pupil of the establishment:
  (i) in the way it affords him access to any benefits, facilities or services, or by refusing or deliberately omitting to afford him access to them; or
  (ii) by excluding him from the establishment or subjecting him to any other detriment.

Both Acts have provisions regarding charities. SDA, s 43 allows charitable provision conferring benefits on persons of one sex only. RRA, s 34 provides (without retrospective effect) that a charitable instrument which excludes persons of a certain colour shall be taken as including those persons. The section does not address racial grounds other than colour.

SDA, s 26(1) contains an exception for single-sex establishments which are defined as those which restrict admission to pupils of one sex, disregarding any pupils of the opposite sex whose admission is exceptional or whose numbers are comparatively small and who are confined to particular courses or classes. Section 26(2) applies the same exception to schools which, although not single-sex establishments, admit boarders of one sex only. An extension is given to cover the provision of boarding facilities.

SDA, s 27 deals with single-sex establishments turning co-educational. The proprietor (including governors) may apply in accordance with Sch 2 of the Act for a *transitional exemption order* authorising discriminatory admissions during the transitional period specified in the order. Schedule 2, art 5 deals with schools in the private sector in England and Wales. The governors may submit an application to the Equal Opportunities Commission. An application shall specify the transitional period proposed, the stages by which the school proposes to move into compliance with s 22(b) of the Act and any other matters relevant to the terms and operation of the order applied for.

SDA, s 46 contains a general exemption from all the provisions of the Act for discrimination in the provision of communal accommodation provided that males and females are treated fairly and equitably in the circumstances.

SDA, s 78 (discussed at **17.6.3**) allows the Secretary of State, by order, to make such modifications to the governing instrument of a school as appear to him to be expedient and to conduce to the advancement of education without sex discrimination.

RRA, s 35 contemplates and allows for, in effect, positive discrimination in relation to education, training or welfare: for example, special language training for groups whose first language is not English will be permissible.

These are the main provisions regarding discrimination on grounds of sex and race in relation to admissions but the Acts have far wider scope, particularly in the field of employment.

The Disability Discrimination Act 1995 does not directly apply to the admission of pupils but the point may arise in a different context when the Human Rights Bill passes into law in the UK.

### 7.4.2   Some relevant cases

*Equal Opportunities Commission v Birmingham City Council* [1989] 1 All ER 617, HL
In its single-sex grammar schools, the LEA had five schools (540 places) available to boys and three schools (360 places) available to girls. This meant that girls would have to achieve higher marks than boys to gain a place. This was held to be discrimination.

*Smith v Safeway plc* [1995] ICR 472
It was held that employers are entitled to lay down reasonable requirements as to the way employees present themselves at work having regard to convention. What is conventional for men will often be different from what is conventional for women. Provided requirements for men and women can reasonably be related to current perceptions of convention, such requirements do not treat one sex less favourably than the other. Such rules as exist must receive equal enforcement as between men and women.

*Debell v Bromley LEC* (1984) *The Guardian*, 13 November
A primary school in Bromley was short of space for a fourth-year class. It sent only boys up to this class. Three girls affected by the authority's decision were each awarded compensation of £500 by the county court.

*Mandla v Dowell Lee* [1983] 1 All ER 1062, HL
The head of a private school was found to have discriminated against a Sikh child by refusing to admit him unless he went without his turban and had his hair cut. It was held that this was discrimination which could not be justified on grounds of the school's policy on uniform and its policy of reducing religious and cultural differences.

*Steel v Union of Post Office Workers* [1977] ICR 181
It was held that justification of a discriminatory condition or requirement must involve a need of the business or enterprise and not merely convenience.

### 7.4.3   Access to sports activities

There are a number of unresolved problems over girls playing what were traditionally regarded as boys' sports and vice versa. Now, it should be taken as a general rule that all sports and games at a co-educational school should be open to boys and girls subject to considerations of safety and welfare.

Whether there should be mixed-gender teams depends on whether the physical demands of the activity would place one sex at an undue disadvantage as against the other. For example, a school would be justified in not allowing mixed-gender teams to play rugby and football against each other. This is particularly so since the decision in *Smoldon v Whitworth and Another* [1997] ELR 249, CA, when it was held that a referee had been negligent in the way he conducted a game of colts rugby and had thereby caused the plaintiff's injury. Although that case was about collapsing scrums at rugby and the Court of Appeal stated that that case turned on its own facts, it served to emphasise the duty of referees, among other things, to separate players into groups of comparable ability and physical development. Health and safety must never be compromised in the pursuit of non-discriminatory practices.

Up to a certain age, when the physical powers of boys and girls are similar, there may be no justification for refusing mixed-team activities, but over the age when boys may be faster or stronger than girls there is an objective justification for single-sex teams so that proper competition can take place.

## 7.5   ADMISSIONS POLICY

### 7.5.1   Criteria for admission

The school's admission criteria ought to be relevant to the school's aims, objectives, ethos and culture as they are described in the prospectus. The criteria used cannot be entirely objective but should be as objective as possible so that it can be demonstrated that they were not discriminatory. Examples of objective criteria are:

(a) *Entrance examination* – including common entrance, scholarship examinations and other normal tests and assessments.

(b) *Connections with the school* – for example that a parent is a former pupil of the school or there are relevant siblings.

(c) *Age and maturity of the pupil* – age is entirely objective. Maturity can be a little more difficult if the sheltered environment of some ethnic communities is the reason for the immaturity.

(d) *Feeder school* – it is customary to accord preference to children from certain feeder schools where there is confidence in the curriculum, quality and reports from those schools.

(e) *General health* – health should not be confused with disability. Special problems arise over children who are HIV positive.

(f) *Special aptitudes* – a school may wish to give preference to children with a particular aptitude for sport, dancing, music and singing, art, information technology, chess or other skill.

(g) *Religion* – religion will only be a relevant consideration if the charitable objects of the school make it so. Where this is the case, factors such as baptism, church attendance and a recommendation from the parish priest or other religious leader become relevant. The school will wish to be satisfied that the individual child is likely to benefit from the school's religious environment and it is entitled to take into account the willingness of the parent and child to take part in the religious aspects of the school.

(h) *Special needs* – in *X (Minors) v Bedfordshire County Council* [1995] ELR 404, the House of Lords held among other things that a school which accepts a pupil assumes responsibility not only for his physical well-being but also for his education needs. A school which has no provision for coping with children who have special needs is entitled to refuse admission on that ground.

(i) *Interview* – the interview is likely to have subjective and objective elements. The attitudes and lifestyle of parents and children may emerge during interview but, again, matters connected with race are not relevant. Matters of gender may be relevant depending on the extent to which the school is co-educational and whether it has obtained a transitional exemption order (referred to at **7.4.1**).

(j) *Report and recommendation* – a written report and recommendation is desirable and will no doubt cover matters of attitude, attendance, ability and record of payment of fees. The Data Protection Act 1984 (soon to be amended by the 1998 Act) may have a bearing on this latter point but parents should have been asked to authorise disclosure of the payment record at an earlier stage in the admission procedures.

(k) *Financial considerations* – an independent school is entitled to take into account a parent's ability to pay the fees. It is of little benefit to the child if he (or she) is admitted but then excluded one or two terms later for non-payment. However, there are certain considerations that must not be taken into account in assessing a parent's ability to pay. They include the matters listed in the next section.

(l) *The child's ability to benefit from the school* – the head is entitled to take into account any particular attribute of the child that suggests he (or she) might be more likely to benefit from a school with a gentler or tougher ethos as the case may be. However, matters of race and gender may not be any part of this judgement.

(m) *The date of registration* – earliest first, as the tie breaker.

### 7.5.2   Matters that should not be included in the admission criteria

The following criteria should not appear in or form any part of a school's admission policy.

(a) *Gender of the pupil* – unless the school is a single-sex school or is proceeding towards co-education under a transitional exemption order, gender is legally irrelevant.

(b) *Ethnic origin* – this would be a direct contravention of s 17 of the Race Relations Act 1976.

(c) *Country of origin* – there may be genuine concerns about the lifestyle of families from certain countries that are known to have a high incidence of HIV, AIDS and hepatitis. Even so, these are not a factor that may be taken into account.

(d)  *Religion* – if not prescribed in the charitable objects, to use religion as one of the admission criteria is capable of amounting to indirect racial discrimination. An example of the way this works is to argue that it is statistically more likely in the UK that a white person will follow the Christian religion than a person belonging to an ethnic minority community, and for a non-denominational school to prefer Christian applicants is discriminatory.

(e)  *Area of residence* – stating a criterion that prefers applicants from an area of a city that is predominately white or predominately black is indirect discrimination on grounds of race.

(f)  *Socio-economic group* – selection on this ground can, with other factors, give rise to a claim of discrimination on grounds of race.

### 7.5.3   HIV, AIDS, hepatitis and haemophilia

There is anecdotal evidence of parents withholding information that a child is HIV-positive until after a place has been offered and accepted. The contractual implications are considered elsewhere in this book.

Schools have coped well with haemophiliac children for decades but the first known case of AIDS in a pupil at school was not until 1985. A discovery that has heightened concern is that some 35% of haemophiliac children have been found to be carriers of HTLV–III LAV.

Hepatitis B is also of great concern. It is thought to transmit more easily than HIV by contact with infected blood or body fluids such as saliva or in the course of sexual activity. However, the disease can be treated if caught early, and vaccination is available as a precautionary measure.

The present state of knowledge about HIV and AIDS suggests that in normal social and occupational contact, the risk of transmission is not high. The main risks arise from sexual intercourse with an infected person and direct contact with contaminated blood, blood products and needles. The DFE has issued guidelines for infection control in its document entitled *Children at School and Problems Related to AIDS*. Moreover, there is plainly a public interest in ensuring that an infected child must not become an outcast and be deprived of education in a mainstream school unless genuinely necessary for the protection of the community as a whole. As yet, AIDS is not a notifiable disease.

The genuine concerns of parents and of some independent schools should not be ignored. Children, particularly very young children, are tactile. They regularly fall over and cut or graze themselves and they are less careful over personal hygiene. Qualified staff, however carefully they are supervising, cannot be expected to be aware of every occasion when two children with open wounds might be at risk of direct contact. The problem is greater in the case of parent helpers who may not have received the same level of training as teachers.

Whether from ignorance or understandable concern, it is the view of many parents that they do not wish their child to attend school in a year group where it is known that there is a child with HIV or AIDS. Those concerns are known to influence some schools into refusing admission to an infected child for fear that a significant number of parents will withdraw pupils, possibly even leading to closure of the school. A further consideration is members of staff who would then lose their livelihood and the governors of an unincorporated school who may be personally liable for the debts on an insolvent closure of a school.

Some governors and heads maintain a policy that they will follow the DFE guidelines for infection control for every pupil but they do not want to know if a particular pupil is infected with AIDS or HIV. Nor are parents under a duty to disclose the condition but they are not entitled to lie if asked a direct question. Other heads may be directed by the chairman of governors or may themselves take the decision not to admit. Perhaps they are genuinely of the view that another larger school with experience of this problem will be happy to admit the child and has better resources for coping. Perhaps it is a case that the parents of the infected child are known to have a high profile in the media on the topic of educating children infected with HIV and AIDS, and it will be impossible to operate the 'need-to-know' confidentiality procedures in that particular case. There is then a risk of the infected child being ostracised by his peer group if his condition becomes known by everybody.

The Secretary of State expressed the belief in 1987 that education about AIDS is an important element in the teaching programme offered to pupils in the later years of compulsory schooling. However, this is of no help over the education of younger children.

The problem is immensely difficult. Decisions must not be based on ignorance or prejudice but on a clear understanding and evaluation of all the implications in a particular case. It is suggested here that in a limited number of cases for some schools it is right to refuse admission but in most cases it would be wrong to do so. In a case in 1997/98, the DfEE and the Charity Commission accepted representations made on behalf of an independent school which had been criticised for withdrawing an offer of a place to a 5-year-old child when the parents disclosed the child was HIV positive.

## 7.6   ADMISSION AND ENTRY PROCEDURES

The detail of the procedure and the order of events differs between nursery, junior preparatory and senior school, and also between individual schools. However, the procedures are likely to include some or all of the following.

### (a)   A visit to the school

This may take place at an open day or by arrangement, when the parents and/or the child are shown round without any obligation on either part. The parents will take a copy of the prospectus away with them unless they have already received one. The prospectus will often include a registration form.

### (b)   Registration form

Under modern 'parent contract' procedures, the parents complete a registration form and pay a non-returnable registration fee, commonly between £5 and £50. The status of registration varies between schools. Registration ought not to be seen as a contractual step. It is more in the nature of a serious indication of interest and a request by the parent that the child's name is placed on the waiting list of the school. The parent will then be contacted, perhaps in November for next September entry. The school will enter the family's details on its database and keep in touch in various ways. A number of schools, however, still treat registration as a contractual step, in effect, as the school's acceptance of the parents' offer. This is not, however, a modern contractual procedure.

### (c)  Call-up letter

In about November for next September entry, or a year or more earlier in some cases, the school will contact the parents and explain the timetable of the admissions procedure: for example, a formal interview, a day spent at the school or preview weekend, entrance examination which may include common entrance, scholarship papers, the school's own entry examination and other tests and assessments, and a recommendation from the head of the child's present school.

### (d)  Admission lists

At some point, a list of families to whom an offer will be made is drawn up in categories as appropriate: for example, places at full fees, awards of a scholarship or exhibition, awards of a bursary, and any other form of assistance. Usually, there will be a reserve list in each category. At a medium-sized or large school the admission and reserve list will probably be assembled by a committee composed of governors and senior staff. The committee will need to work from objective criteria so far as possible.

### (e)  The offer of a place

Under modern 'parent contract' procedures this will be the first contractual step in the admission process. The school writes to the parents setting out the offer of the place and the terms of the offer. If the offer is subject to an award such as a scholarship, exhibition or bursary, the terms of the award should be clearly described. Normally, the letter of offer is accompanied by an acceptance form attached to a copy of the school's standard terms and conditions.

### (f)  Acceptance of a place

The usual means by which a parent accepts a place is by completing the acceptance form and returning it to the school with a cheque for the deposit. Often, the acceptance form will direct the parent to detach and retain the standard terms and conditions. The form will explain that the standard terms and conditions are subject to change from time to time. Returning the acceptance form with the deposit completes the formation of the contract for educational services and, where applicable, for boarding provisions.

### (g)  The deposit

The deposit may be a single sum, such as £400, which will be credited to the pupil's final account on leaving. Sometimes, however, the deposit is for a larger sum, say

£1,000, comprising two elements: a part payment of fees for the first term and a security or caution deposit which will be retained until the pupil leaves. There may be a third element known as an entrance fee which is a non-returnable administration charge. A few schools use a more complex system of a staged deposit.

### *(h)   Entry procedures*

The admission procedures will normally be complete by March or April for the following September. Thereafter, the entry procedures will be described in a 'joining pack' dealing with such matters as the pupil's house, a health declaration form, a parental consent form, matters of uniform and clothing generally, the school rules, extra tuition required and other practical matters.

## 7.7   SOME PROBLEMS ENCOUNTERED OVER ADMISSIONS

The following is an anecdotal list of problems that have caused concern to schools and anxiety to families.

(a)   There was perception by a family that a child of one race has been selected on grounds of race in preference to another child of a different race, and a similar perception on grounds of gender.

(b)   An offer has been made in error and the school has withdrawn it either before or after the offer was accepted, giving rise to great disappointment and threats of legal proceedings.

(c)   An offer was sent by post but not received by the family or not dealt with in sufficient time and has been withdrawn.

(d)   There has been a significant unexpected event during or after the admission procedures, for example redundancy or insolvency of the main fee-payer, a serious blot on the child's record at the present school or a discovery that the child is HIV positive or has AIDS or hepatitis B in circumstances where the school does not feel it has sufficient experience or resources to satisfy its pastoral and legal obligations both to that child and for the protection of other children.

(e)   The child is not, after all, eligible for the assisted place or bursary award because the necessary forms have not been completed or material information or documents have been withheld.

## 7.8   LEGAL COMPLIANCE

Parents have a statutory obligation under s 7 of the Education Act 1996 (set out at **7.8.2** below) to ensure that children of compulsory school age receive efficient full-time education either by regular attendance at school or otherwise.

In general, truancy and other absences of school-aged children are not a cause for major concern in the independent sector. None the less, independent schools have been included in recent legislation aimed at enforcing attendance and monitoring absence. The main provisions are set out below.

### 7.8.1 Compulsory school age

Section 8 of the Education Act 1996 defines 'compulsory school age' broadly as:

–   beginning at the age of 5;
–   ceasing at the age of 16 if the pupil attains 16 before, or after the end of the school leaving date prescribed by the Secretary of State and before the start of the next school year.

These provisions were amended by s 52 of the Education Act 1997. At the time of writing, however, only s 52(4) has been brought into force (with effect from 1 September 1997). That section gives the Secretary of State power to make an order specifying certain days in the year that will fix compulsory school age in the case of pupils who attain 5 or 16 years of age during the course of a school term.

In the Education (Pupil Registration) Regulations 1995, 'compulsory school age' is defined as over 5 years of age before the start of that term and under 16 on 1 September of that school year (reg 7(1) and (2)).

### 7.8.2 Parents' duty to educate

The Education Act 1996, s 7 provides:

'The parent of every child of compulsory school age shall cause him to receive efficient full-time education suitable (a) to his age, ability and aptitude, and (b) to any special educational needs he may have, either by regular attendance at school or otherwise.'

If a child is not at school full-time and the local education authority considers that he should be, it must serve a school attendance order and consider applying for an education supervision order (Education Act 1996, ss 437–448). See also the Children Act 1989, s 39. A parent's failure to comply with the order without reasonable excuse is a criminal offence.

### 7.8.3 Registered pupils

The Education Act 1996, s 444(1) provides:

'If a child of compulsory school age who is a registered pupil at a school fails to attend regularly at the school, his parent is guilty of an offence.'

For day-pupils, 'failure to attend regularly' does *not* include absence in the following circumstances:

–   with leave (from the school);
–   due to sickness 'or any unavoidable cause';
–   for religious observance;
–   where the school is beyond walking distance from the child's home and the local authority has failed to make suitable arrangements for transport or boarding or registration at a school nearer home.

For boarding pupils, the only justification for absence is sickness 'or any unavoidable cause'. A parent convicted under s 444 is liable to a fine not exceeding level 3.

### 7.8.4 Admission register

The Education (Pupil Registration) Regulations 1995 require the proprietor of every school to keep an admission register. The admission register must have an index listing the pupils at the school in alphabetical order. Then, for each pupil, the following information must be recorded in the register: full name, sex, date of birth, date of admission, whether day or boarding (if the school takes boarders), the name of the last school attended, and details of all parents (reg 6).

Regulation 16 allows the register to be kept on computer. However, the admission register must be printed out at least once each year. Manual registers must be completed in ink, and any corrections clearly shown as such. Corrections made to computerised registers must also distinguish between the original entry and any correction (regs 14 and 16(3)). Admission registers must be kept for 3 years (reg 15).

### 7.8.5 Deletions from the admission register

A pupil of compulsory school age may only be deleted from the admission register in accordance with reg 9.

The prescribed reasons include:

– registration at another school;
– notification of education 'otherwise than at school';
– absence for more than 10 days following an authorised holiday absence of more than 10 days *and* the school does not believe the pupil is sick or the subject of 'any unavoidable cause';
– 4 weeks' absence *and* the pupil cannot be located;
– the death of the pupil;
– the pupil has ceased to be a pupil at the school (eg because of expulsion or withdrawal by parents).

Every school must also give to its local education authority, within ten school days, the name and address of any pupil whose name has been deleted from the admission register.

### 7.8.6 Attendance register

The same Regulations, namely the Education (Pupil Registration) Regulations 1995, require the proprietor of any school taking day-pupils to keep an *attendance register* (reg 5). For day-pupils, the attendance register must be marked morning and afternoon, noting the presence or absence of each pupil. If absent, and the pupil is of compulsory school age, the register must also show whether the absence is authorised or unauthorised. As explained above, 'compulsory school age' is defined differently in these Regulations than in the Education Acts 1996 and 1997.

Regulation 16 allows for the attendance register to be kept on computer but it must be printed out at least once each month. The rules about manual registers are as described above. The attendance register must be kept for 3 years (reg 15).

### 7.8.7 Absences

Absence is either authorised or unauthorised. DFE guidance, *School Attendance – Policy and Practice on the Categorisation of Absence* (May 1994) suggests 11 different codes for authorised absences which must be interpreted in conjunction with regs 7 and 8 of the Education (Pupil Registration) Regulations 1995 and the Amendment Regulations 1997. There is, however, no requirement to categorise absences for boarders and there are no codes to categorise their unauthorised absences.

General leave of absence (reg 7(3)(a)) covers the following sub-categories:

B    receiving part-time education elsewhere/off-site. This could also include those situations where the pupil is registered at and attending more than one school (reg 10);
C    other circumstances: these must be specified;
H    annual family holiday (with permission) (reg 8(4));
I    attending interview;
M    medical/dental – whole sessions only, not for when children arrive late or have to leave early for a hospital/doctor's/dentist's appointment;
P    approved sporting activity;
S    study leave;
V    educational visit.

The regulations also provide for absence through sickness or any unavoidable cause, religious observance, work experience and pupils who have been 'excluded' (ie suspended, rusticated, required to leave or expelled).

Leave of absence may *not* generally be granted to enable a pupil to undertake employment (whether paid or unpaid) in school hours (reg 8(2)).

Where the reason for the absence was not known at the time the register was marked, the person with responsibility for completing the register must establish the reason and then, as soon as possible, correct the register (reg 7(4)).

### 7.8.8 Inspection and use

The admission register and attendance register may be inspected during school hours by HM Inspector and the local authority (including social services). Any such inspector may make extracts from the registers (regs 11 and 12).

Every school must tell its local education authority (at intervals to be agreed), the name and address of any pupil who fails to attend the school regularly or who has been absent for a continuous period of 10 days or more. This does not however apply to sickness, authorised leave of absence or dual attendance.

# Chapter 8

## THE SCHOOL COMMUNITY

### 8.1   INTRODUCTION

This chapter is concerned with the private, self-regulating community and culture of an independent school and the duties and responsibilities of the head, staff, parents and pupils.

References to 'head' equally include headmistresses and headmasters, by whatever title they are known. The expression 'headteacher', although becoming more common in the independent sector, is not used here.

### 8.2   ASPECTS OF COMMUNITY

#### 8.2.1   Background

'Community' is a theme that runs throughout education and describes an organised body of individuals having an identity of nature or character and having common purposes, rights and interests. Although the success of the Open University may argue otherwise, the most successful education has generally been carried out in a community environment where, as James Boswell with characteristic cynicism put it: '... there is all the splendour and illumination of many minds; the radiance of all is concentrated in each, or at least reflected upon each'.

Education and its advancement has been recognised from earliest times as a charitable or public purpose. Almost all who are involved in education receive some degree of public funding. In the case of independent charitable schools, it is mainly through the system of tax reliefs given to charities and, until the Education (Schools) Act 1997, the assisted places scheme. Proprietor-owned schools receive least benefit.

The erosion of citizenship, family values, care of the young, religious observance and respect for the law have in turn eroded a sense of community in the nation at large and threatened the very existence of community in many of the State-funded schools. There, the law progressively forbade the conventional means of maintaining good order and discipline which independent schools and parents who use them recognise as being the very basis of a viable educational environment.

The independent sector, which is organised in private, self-regulating communities, tended to fare better. Independent schools are not free from political interference or from the effects of dysfunction in society but their independence gives them a means of maintaining a community ethos firmly rooted in traditions, standards, values and rules that can be enforced. The key legal mechanisms underlying this are the contract between the school and parents, the authority given to the head and the policies of the governors.

Those who send their children to an independent school are required to recognise that they and their children are joining a body of people with common purposes, where rights are balanced by obligations and where the community interest is paramount and will be strictly enforced if necessary.

### 8.2.2   Characteristics

Independent schools are closed communities in the sense that they are private and self-regulating, although accountable in a number of ways. The concept of a 'closed community' is more philosophical than legal, but has legal implications. A private or 'closed' community may have the following characteristics:

–   it has a shared history of which the community is conscious as distinguishing it from other communities, and the memory of which helps to keep it alive;
–   it has a cultural tradition of its own, including its own social customs and manners;
–   it has an organisation which is not specifically regulated by statute but is free to regulate itself and its membership by means of some or all of the following: aims; objectives; custom and tradition; standards and values; rules and regulations; attitudes and behaviour; contract and policy – but always subject to the general law of the land;
–   its funding is independent of the State.

Some other characteristics of a private or closed community, although not essential, may include:

–   a tendency to develop its own system of ethics, rituals, terminology, rules, sanctions and mode of dress;
–   a common religion or religious ethos, a means of pursuing common interests, religious beliefs or social or cultural identity with an emphasis on community life;
–   a common response to external oppression or interference.

Boarding schools following the traditional public school model tend to acquire more of these characteristics than day-schools. Independent schools tend to acquire the characteristics more than maintained schools.

Another feature of the private or closed community is that of inter-dependence of its members. Most independent schools are constituted as charitable trusts, although a number are proprietor-owned and usually run for profit. Charitable schools that are unincorporated have no legal personality separate from their governors, who are generally the charity trustees. The governors in these cases run the personal risk that if the school were to close in deficit, certain shortfalls would have to be paid by them personally. Thus, the governors have a personal interest as well as an obligation as trustees to ensure that parents pay the fees contracted for.

Equally, parents need to know that the school they have chosen for their children is stable and will be properly staffed and resourced. Thus, parents depend on each other to meet the contractual obligations that apply to all parents. Members of staff depend on parents to meet their contractual obligations, and parents and pupils rely on staff to safeguard and promote the welfare of the children entrusted to the school.

These mutual expectations create the basic framework of the community. Within the framework is a considerable degree of cross-subsidy. Not all of the parents will have contracted to pay full fees. Independent schools give away as much as 15% of their annual income in assistance to poorer families or in the provision of scholarships, exhibitions, bursaries and other awards and prizes, and in sibling, staff and other discounts, all properly planned and budgeted.

Schools will often invest in improving their facilities. The cost will be paid out of fees or out of borrowings serviced by fees or from appeals to which many parents contribute or assist in other ways. Some of the more costly facilities such as playing fields, sports hall and swimming pool will be used more by some pupils than others. In some cases, fees for day-pupils may subsidise the cost of boarding, or vice versa, but that in turn provides an opportunity for sports and other activities that benefit all pupils.

Thus, an independent school is a community quite independent of the State and which has a culture based on the mutual dependence of all its elements. Its integrity depends on everyone working towards the common aims and objectives, as described in the governing instrument and expressed by the policies of the governors and in the prospectus. Those who do not subscribe to the culture may have to leave the community.

Another feature of closed communities is that, like families, they are entitled in general to deal internally with breaches of their rules and customs, even where, in the outside world, these matters might be investigated and prosecuted as criminal offences. The community and its members are none the less entitled to have recourse to the civil and criminal process provided by the law of the land.

Social legislation since the 1960s has increased the range of legal rights of individuals and their enforceability. To some extent, these have exposed closed communities to greater external control. Examples are the legislation relating to consumer matters, direct and indirect discrimination on grounds of disability, race and sex and the Children Act 1989. There is also a far greater emphasis on the requirement to use procedures that are fair, and often fairness of procedures will matter more to a court or review body than whether or not the original decision was right on the merits.

Whilst the expression 'closed community' is apt to describe the internal organisation of an independent school and its system of self-regulation, it does not describe the place of the school in the community at large. Independent schools are – and, by virtue of their charitable status, must be – a part of their local communities. They are often a significant employer in the locality and they share sports, cultural and other activities with other schools of all kinds in the region. They make their facilities available to the wider community and pupils frequently go out on voluntary service, work experience and a host of other activities.

The closed community concept circumscribes the organisation and all the activities of an independent school and is of particular importance in the following respects.

## (a)   Civil liberties and human rights

Those who join the community do so on the basis that they waive certain of their civil liberties. Whether aged 2 or 19 years they will be under varying restrictions as to where they spend their time, when they can be visited or travel, what they may consume, what physical activities they will undertake and what punishments, sanctions and other rules they must accept. Personal privacy is respected far more these days than used to be the case but is still necessarily subject to limitations in a closed community. Those who do not accept these curtailments, provided they are lawful, may be required to leave the community.

The proviso about being lawful opens up a number of questions particularly in the context of the Human Rights Act 1998. Some leading lawyers have suggested that almost every settled principle of English law will be open to review in the context of human rights. Independent schools will not be immune from this, in the areas of *legitimate expectation* and *proportionality* which are mentioned at (d) below.

## (b)   Admission and expulsion

Much of the head's authority and responsibility derives from headship of the closed community as distinct from headship of the school. The contrast with the State-funded sector is seen in a number of ways, but most clearly in relation to admissions, the curriculum, discipline and expulsions. Traditionally, and to some extent still maintained today, the head is given sole discretion in these areas with very limited rights of appeal.

The custom and practice in this area is being eroded almost imperceptibly by some of the case-law relating to admissions and expulsions (known as 'exclusion' in the State-funded sector). For example, in *R v Head of Fernhill Manor School ex parte B* [1993] 1 FLR 620, which concerned the expulsion of a girl for alleged bullying, Mr Justice Brooke expressed the hope that those responsible for governing independent schools would have procedural rules designed to ensure that parents received fair treatment in accordance with the principles of natural justice in the case of an expulsion.

Another example relates to learning difficulties. In the case known as *X (Minors) v Bedfordshire County Council* [1995] ELR 404, the House of Lords, and earlier the Court of Appeal, made it clear that there is no difference between an independent school and a State school in the obligation to detect and deal appropriately with learning difficulties. The concepts of 'legitimate expectation' and 'proportionality' lead to further erosion of the authority. These are trends that can be marked year by year.

## (c)   Policies

The authority given to the headteacher of a State-funded school is heavily circumscribed by statute, regulation and circulars issued by the Department for Education and Employment and the Department of Health, which, for the most part, are for guidance, but, like the Highway Code, are none the less intended to be followed unless there are very good reasons why they should not be.

Independent schools are much less affected by statute, regulation and circular. Much of their regulation is by way of policy issued by the governors. There may be some contractual aspects of policies of the governors. Their purpose is to serve the aims and objectives of the school and to inform the remainder of the culture. Unless made contractual, they can be adapted as circumstances require and introduced to parents on reasonable notice or sometimes on no notice at all.

This ability to govern and manage by means of policies and in general without interference from the law is, it is suggested here, a factor which underpins much of the success of the independent sector.

### (d)    Independence from the State

Reference has been made above to the relative freedom of independent schools from the statutory framework that applies to State-funded schools. There is, however, another very important aspect, namely that the governors and head of an independent school are accountable to fee-paying parents who, according to surveys carried out by MORI for the Independent Schools Information Service, are buying into a disciplined environment as much or more than into high academic standards. Other than for assisted places and a handful of rare instances in which local education authorities buy places at independent schools, there is no State funding, although charitable schools enjoy certain tax exemptions. The school must perform in accordance with the wishes of the community of governors, staff, parents and pupils or it is likely to fail for lack of pupils and funding.

This raises the issue of *proportionality*. Perhaps the governors' policy is to expect or require a pupil to leave if found to have been involved with illegal drugs. However, if the case involves possession of a small quantity of cannabis for personal use only and the find is made one week before A-levels begin there may be arguments that requiring the pupil to leave is a disproportionate response and an infringement of the parents' and pupil's legitimate expectations.

Whatever may be the merits of arguments such as these, the law on human rights will surely come into conflict with the rights and privileges of a closed community, particularly in cases where an independent school is exercising a public function, for example in relation to a child with an assisted place. (For further discussion on the impact of the Human Rights Act 1998, see Chapter 25.)

### 8.2.3    Authority of the head

One of the decisive factors in the nature and strength of a closed community is the authority that is vested in its head and the head's freedom to exercise that authority. An independent school head generally has the freedom to serve both the school community and the individual pupil in the balance that appears right at the time.

The head's authority is not circumscribed by the system of statutory appeals, codes of practice and department circulars that applies in the State sector. Maintained schools are subject to guidance, sometimes having the effect of law, such as DfEE Circular 10/94 *Exclusions From School*, which sets out, at para 21, ten preliminary factors that a State school headteacher is expected to consider before imposing a fixed period exclusion for up to 15 days in a term (suspension) or permanent exclusion (expulsion). Only two of those factors can be described as community-focused. Nor have other sanctions or means of maintaining order been made easy for teachers, although the Education Act 1997 has held out some prospect of a relaxation in the restrictions on detention and restraint.

The contract between school and parents enables the head of an independent school to exercise an element of authority over parents as well as pupils, if parents act in a way that is contrary to the objectives and aims of the school community. Ultimately, the head has authority to require parents to remove a pupil on grounds of the parents' conduct as much as the pupil's conduct. That is often an express stipulation in the school's standard terms and conditions. To a more limited extent that option is now available in State schools, but it is also subject to the very cumbersome appeals procedures.

For some years, the maintained sector has gone as far as the law permits in replicating the contractual position by means of a *home/school agreement*. Such agreements are unenforceable at law and, unless certain new provisions of the Education Act 1997 are brought into force, they may not be used as a condition of admission or, generally, re-admission following exclusion from a State school.

## 8.2.4   Limitations to authority

Traditionally, the extent of the head's authority in relation to an independent school community was almost absolute. Conventional wording on the registration form which was often treated as a contractual document was to the effect that admission to the school and the pupil's right to remain there was at the sole discretion of the head. The effect of such a condition is now subject to the social legislation even in a closed community, but it continues to have some force.

The limitations to the head's authority at an independent school relate generally to:

–   acts which are outside the powers conferred on the head by the governing instrument or by the governors' policies and instructions, or outside the express and implied terms of the school's contract with parents; or
–   acts or omissions which constitute a breach of the legal duties owed to the pupil; or
–   those acts that would be considered irrational or 'unfair' in the legal sense; or
–   criminal acts.

Authority will extend to certain acts that will be lawful within the closed community but would not necessarily be lawful in the outside world. Examples are:

–   corporal punishment, where still used, other than in respect of a pupil holding an assisted place or one who is otherwise funded by the State (at the time of writing, corporal punishment in independent schools is set for final abolition);
–   reasonable detention;
–   appropriate restrictions over the pupil's movements, property and use of time;
–   the requirement to wear school uniform and comply with the prescribed code of dress and appearance;
–   other rules, so far as not inherently unlawful, which curtail the pupil's civil liberties.

Pupils at school, whether or not they have attained the age of 18, must abide by the lawful rules of the community whether or not those rules seem objectively sensible. If they do not comply with the rules they can be required in appropriate circumstances to leave and, of course, if over school-leaving age, they are free to leave voluntarily at any time subject to appropriate notice or the payment of fees in lieu of notice and subject in the case of overseas pupils to visa conditions.

### 8.2.5 Undermining the head's authority

A closed community such as a school depends on there being a consensus that the authority of the head will be upheld and obeyed both in the spirit and letter to the extent that his (or her) acts are within the lawful rules of the community and the law of the land.

The head is none the less accountable to the governors and, in certain circumstances, the staff, parents and pupils, but 'accountability' is often misunderstood. It is not a licence to second-guess every decision of the head or constantly to carp and criticise unconstructively. That only undermines the culture of the community and the authority of the head.

One of the mechanisms of accountability is a review procedure following expulsion or the requirement to leave. Following the dicta of Brooke J in *R v Head of Fernhill Manor School ex parte B* [1993] 1 FLR 620, it is to be taken as an implied term of the parent contract that there will be procedural rules designed to ensure that pupils receive fair treatment in accordance with the principles of natural justice.

## 8.3 ASPECTS OF THE HEAD'S DUTY AND AUTHORITY

### 8.3.1 Sources

The sources of the head's authority are:

- the governing instrument;
- the powers conferred on the head by the governors under a contract of employment (whether written or unwritten) and comprised in the governors' policies;
- s 3(5) of the Children Act 1989, which provides, subject to the other provisions of the Act, that a person who has care of a child may do what is reasonable in all the circumstances for the purpose of safeguarding or promoting the child's welfare. This to a large extent describes the *in loco parentis* principle;
- any other powers and duties conferred by statute;
- his (or her) position as the head of a closed community.

### 8.3.2 Powers and duties under the Children Act 1989

The duty to *safeguard and promote the child's welfare* is imposed by s 87(1) of the Children Act 1989 on both the governors and the head of a school which provides accommodation for a child. By s 3(5) of the Act, which has been referred to above, the head, when he (or she) has care of a child, may do what is reasonable in all the circumstances for the purpose of safeguarding or promoting the child's welfare. By s 2(9) of the Act, a head may take authorisation from a parent to carry out lawful acts in relation to a child in his care. That is otherwise known as 'delegated parental responsibility'.

### 8.3.3    Duties under the Health and Safety at Work etc Act 1974

Section 3 of the Health and Safety at Work etc Act 1974 imposes a duty on governors (who will delegate related tasks to the head) to conduct the school in such a way as to ensure, so far as is reasonably practicable, that non-employees are not exposed to risks to their health or safety.

By s 7 of the Act, every employee (including the head) while at work must take reasonable care for his (or her) own health and safety and that of other persons who may be affected by his acts or omissions at work, and the governors or school (if corporate) may be vicariously liable in these respects.

The more detailed provisions about legal compliance are contained in a separate chapter.

### 8.3.4    Admissions

The selection of candidates for admission to the school as pupils rests with the head, acting in accordance with the policy approved by the governors. That policy must be lawful and may not discriminate directly or indirectly on grounds of race and sex. Discrimination on grounds of disability is lawful at present within these constraints. The head is entitled to select individuals or families whom he (or she) considers most likely to contribute to the community and support its aims and objectives and also those who would benefit from its opportunities.

If a place is offered in error, it may be withdrawn at any time before the parents' acceptance of the offer has been communicated. If withdrawal of the offer is too late and the parents have given consideration, a legally binding contract will have come into existence. Then, the school is entitled to rely on an implied, if not express, condition that the contract may be brought to an end by a term's notice given by either party. The matter may not, however, be so straightforward if, in consequence of the error, parents refused an award or assisted place at another school for a pupil who might have expected 5 or more years of education up to and including A-levels.

### 8.3.5    Setting the curriculum

For these purposes, 'curriculum' means academic work, games and sports, extra-curricular activities and out-of-school visits.

The head is responsible and has authority to set the curriculum and ensure that it is carried out to a satisfactory standard. An independent school is not bound to comply with the National Curriculum.

Alterations to the academic curriculum policies which have been communicated to parents may amount to a unilateral variation of the contract, unless the right to make changes has been expressly provided in the parent contract in a way that is fair at law. Broadly the same rules apply to the games and sports curriculum.

Clubs, activities and out-of-school visits may or may not be matters of contract and can be subject to greater variation. The head has authority to decide on reasonable grounds who will or will not be entitled to take part in extra-curricular activities. He (or she) must act in good faith but is entitled to take community factors such as personal relationships into account.

## 8.3.6 Setting regulations and sanctions

The head is responsible for the care and good discipline of pupils while they are in the charge of the school or its staff and for the day-to-day running of the school. The setting of regulations is nominally the responsibility of governors but, in practice, they are set by the head with the authority of the governors.

The rules and regulations of an independent school vary greatly in their form and ethos. Some are negative and injunctive in nature. A more modern concept, however, is that of a behaviour protocol which describes matters of principle and helps to form the culture of the school.

Invariably, one of the underlying principles is that acceptance by parents and pupil of the school's regime and the rules, insofar as they are lawful, is a condition of a pupil's remaining at the school. The modern purpose of school rules should be to help every pupil to know what is expected and to encourage courtesy and consideration for others. Rules relating to hazardous areas such as the swimming pool, gymnasium, workshops and laboratories or areas under construction will normally be posted in accordance with the Health and Safety (Safety Signs and Signals) Regulations 1996, among others.

## 8.3.7 Ethos and culture

An important aspect of the head's duty and authority is leadership in the formation of the attitudes of staff and pupils which in turn dictate the ethos and wider culture. These are crucial aspects of a closed community. The head's success will depend on his (or her) qualities of leadership and the support of governors, staff and parents. Mutual trust and confidence that must exist depends on the general acceptance of the head's authority and, in turn, on the head using that authority responsibly and persuasively.

## 8.3.8 School security

The head is responsible for controlling the use of school premises and security arrangements and deciding who is or is not entitled to be there.

School security became a major issue after Dunblane in 1996. In general, it will be impossible for many schools to prevent intruders coming on to school premises but security procedures have been strengthened. Fewer gates have been left open. There is much greater vigilance and, in some cases, surveillance and more access to mobile telephones. These improvements have often been achieved without appearing to turn schools into fortresses.

There have been cases of threatened and actual abduction of a child by an estranged parent, sometimes accompanied by demands and threats even of physical violence against heads or teachers. These incidents vary in gravity between very serious and merely of concern.

The authority of the head in every such case is to place first the interests of the school community, including those of any pupil who is threatened. The head is entitled to require a person, including a fee-paying parent, to leave school premises forthwith in the event of that person behaving improperly, making threats, causing unnecessary anxieties or in any other way disrupting the peace and proper conduct of the school

community. The most eloquent account of this right was given by Butler-Sloss LJ in
*Re B (Minors)* (1994) *The Times*, 12 May, CA, when in another context she said:

> '... children are suffering if they are not given the space and peace that they require to get
> on with their own affairs at school. And their affairs at school are more important than
> either of their parents. School has to be a haven. School has to be a place where children
> get on and do their work in order that they may be successful grown ups ...'

A person who has been required to leave school premises but has failed to do so
having been given a reasonable time in which to comply becomes a trespasser. It is
good practice to telephone the police and, if possible, to obtain a still photograph of an
intruder but the head is entitled to use or authorise the use of reasonable force to eject a
trespasser from school premises including the grounds.

A head has authority to close school premises if to do so is in the interests of the school
community, for example because of a sufficient concern over security, an epidemic or
dangerous conditions such as ice, snow, or defective premises, if the premises cannot
be made reasonably safe.

### 8.3.9   *In loco parentis*

As noted above, s 3(5) of the Children Act 1989 permits a person who has care of a
child to do what is reasonable in all the circumstances for the purpose of safeguarding
or promoting the child's welfare. This is a statutory expression of the *in loco parentis*
rule and supersedes much of the discussion that has taken place about the meaning of
*in loco parentis*.

The limits to the operation of the *in loco parentis* rule will be plain enough in the given
circumstances of most cases. For example, it is quite usual and necessary for nursery
staff to cuddle small children in circumstances that are appropriate. The same conduct
in relation to older children would rarely, if ever, be considered appropriate, other
than to give comfort to an injured or distressed child, always observing normal
propriety.

Sanctions and related measures must equally have regard to the pupil's age and
physical and emotional needs. For example, a pupil should not in general be detained
unaccompanied or in a state of fear. If it is necessary to detain a pupil pending an
investigation or the arrival of police, parents or others, the detention should take place
in a suitable room. The pupil should be accompanied, by a female teacher in the case
of a girl, and given access to a telephone, toilet, drink and, as necessary, food and
prescribed medication. The pupil's privacy and dignity must be observed.

### 8.3.10   Requiring a medical examination

The head may decide on proper grounds that it is necessary for the safety and welfare
of the pupil to require the pupil to be seen by a general practitioner or psychiatrist or
some other specialist. That is within the head's authority by virtue of s 3(5) of the
Children Act 1989.

A pupil of sufficient age and understanding from, say, 13 upwards, may express a
wish that his parents are not told of the circumstances. Then it is a matter within the
authority of the head to decide that the medical examination will be carried out at the

expense of the school, the cost not being added to the pupil's account. Under the *Gillick* principle (discussed at **22.7.9**), the pupil is entitled to have his (or her) wishes respected in these circumstances. However, a head will want to encourage full parental involvement if at all possible.

### 8.3.11 Reports, references and confidence

*Spring v Guardian Assurance plc* [1995] 2 AC 296, HL, is authority for saying that a person is under a legal duty to use reasonable skill and care in the giving of a reference. Where the person giving a reference has insufficient specific knowledge of the subject of the reference, he (or she) is under a legal duty to find out from those who do know and to take reasonable care to verify that information before imparting it. A failure to comply with this duty may give rise to an action for damages.

When a pupil is transferring from one school to another, it is custom and practice for the receiving head to request a recommendation of the pupil. That is in effect a reference and will normally, in the interests of the school and the pupil, include discussion of whether parents can meet and have met their financial obligations. It is clearly not in a pupil's interests to be admitted if exclusion for non-payment of fees is likely to follow directly. However, it is a moot point whether s 3(5) of the Children Act 1989 takes precedence over the obligations of confidence that may arise under the Data Protection Acts 1984 and 1998.

The head is entitled to override duties of confidence owed to the parent and pupil when to do so is reasonable in all the circumstances for the purpose of safeguarding or promoting the child's welfare (s 3(5) of the Children Act 1989).

A head who gives a misleading or incomplete reference in respect of a pupil and thereby causes financial loss to another school may render his school liable to pay compensation under the *Hedley Byrne* principle, referred to at **12.3.3**. An example would be where the head knows that a pupil has moderate or severe learning difficulties, or an emotional or behavioural disorder, or some other special need, but makes a careless misstatement or gives an untruthful answer to the receiving head. If the new school cannot then cope and has to require the pupil to leave, there is a fee loss which, depending on the more detailed circumstances, may fall to be compensated for, partly or in full, by the transferring school.

### 8.3.12 Engaging and dismissing staff

The head will normally have authority to engage and dismiss staff. It was held in *Price v Dennis* [1988] LEXIS, CA, that the proprietor of a school is not accountable to parents as to the circumstances under which staff are dismissed.

### 8.3.13 Delegation of tasks

The head has the authority given to him by the governors to delegate tasks to his staff. It was held in *Taunton School v Wright* (1997) EPLI 67 that it is a feature of certain independent schools in the UK that house masters are the first point of contact with parents. Only if the house master fails to satisfy the parents' enquiries would direct access to the headmaster be expected. It would be impossible for the headmaster to run the school properly if he dealt with every enquiry from the parents. The headmaster's refusal to deal with the parents' complaint in these circumstances was held not to be a fundamental breach of contract.

### 8.3.14   Collective worship and religious education

The statutory provisions contained in ss 375–399 of the Education Act 1996 in relation to religious education and worship apply to maintained schools and are not binding on independent schools. For a variety of reasons, the statutory provisions about collective worship have not worked successfully in the State sector. Parents have a right to withdraw pupils from acts of collective worship without having to give reasons and it was reported in *The Independent*, 1 June 1994, that seven out of ten headteachers in the State sector were unable to comply with the statutory requirements.

Religious education is not part of the National Curriculum and the Secretary of State has no power to prescribe attainment targets or programmes of study in relation to it. Moreover, as with collective worship, parents are entitled to exclude their children from religious education at a school and have their children receive a particular form of such education away from the school premises but during school hours.

The usual practice at independent schools is to hold an assembly at the start of each day, the form and content of which is decided by the head acting in accordance with the authority given to him by the governors and or the governing instrument of the school.

### 8.3.15   School fees

It is a matter for the governors to decide the extent to which the head or bursar will have authority to make payment schemes or arrangements with parents over fees. In *Gregory v Frensham Heights Educational Trust Ltd* (1997) EPLI 66, the parent claimed that the headmaster had accepted provisional notice on an open-ended basis. It was held on the facts of that case that such an agreement would have been wholly unusual. The headmaster would have had no authority to make it, and the parent had not proved her case and was required to pay the disputed fees.

### 8.3.16   Pupil's records

The Education (School Records) Regulations 1989 and s 551 of the Education Act 1996, as amended, apply to maintained and grant-maintained schools but not to independent schools, although the governors are entitled to obtain disclosure under the Regulations of the educational records of a pupil who has applied for admission or has transferred to an independent school.

An independent school head, therefore, has authority to decide, in accordance with the governors' policy, what kinds of records will be kept in relation to pupils, for how long, and the nature, form and content of those records.

The duty to safeguard and promote the child's welfare implies a requirement to keep adequate records. Section 3(5) of the Children Act 1989 (referred to above) forms the basis of the head's authority in relation to disclosure of the records, but this may be subject to the provisions of the Data Protection Acts 1984 and 1998 in relation to computerised records and some manual records and is also circumscribed by the terms of the school's contract with parents and the general law of confidence. Generally, an independent school will retain its educational and disciplinary records of a pupil who is transferring to another school, but there will need to be a high degree of co-operation between heads in ensuring that relevant information is communicated (see **8.3.11** above).

## 8.4 RIGHTS AND DUTIES OF PARENTS AND PUPILS

### 8.4.1 Satisfactory standards

Parents are entitled to expect that there will be satisfactory standards of teaching and pastoral care but, by analogy to *Bolam v Friern Hospital Management Committee* [1957] 2 All ER 118, a case about medical negligence, they are not entitled to expect the highest expert skill from every teacher but only the ordinary skill of an ordinary competent teacher.

A teacher owes a duty of care to a pupil to recognise learning difficulties and take appropriate action and, indeed, the Court of Appeal, in *Keating v London Borough of Bromley* [1994] 4 All ER 640, held to the effect that a teacher owes a duty to detect and react appropriately to gross deviations from normality in a pupil's learning performance or behaviour in circumstances where an ordinarily competent teacher would do so. The matter was put differently by Lord Browne-Wilkinson when the case went to the House of Lords (at which stage it was known as *X (Minors) v Bedfordshire County Council* [1995] ELR 404) when he said:

'A school which accepts a pupil assumes responsibility not only for his physical well-being but also for his educational needs . . .'

It was, however, pointed out by Sir Thomas Bingham MR in the Court of Appeal that:

'. . . teachers, however dedicated and gifted, cannot rectify inequalities of endowment between one pupil and another.'

And in an earlier case, *R v Surrey County Council Education Committee ex parte H* (1984) 83 LGR 219, Slade J said, in effect, that there is no question of an obligation to provide a child with the best possible education. There is no duty to provide such a utopian system or to educate a child to his (or her) maximum potential.

Educational services come within s 13 of the Supply of Goods and Services Act 1982, which provides that a contract for the supply of a service where the supplier is acting in the course of a business contains an implied term that the supplier will carry out the service '*with reasonable care and skill*'. That in general applies both to teaching and pastoral care, but by no means every breach of this implied term is to be treated as a fundamental breach. It is submitted that the education service must be viewed as a whole. Minor breaches may not be quantifiable in damages.

Reference has been made earlier to the dicta of Brooke J, in *R v Head of Fernhill Manor School ex parte B* [1993] 1 FLR 620, who made clear that it is to be taken as an implied term of the contract between school and parents that there will be procedural rules designed to ensure that pupils receive fair treatment in accordance with the principles of natural justice.

These statements of law help to define and circumscribe the rights of parents and pupils at an independent school. They provide little certainty on matters of standard and degree. Instead, they set the standard as one of reasonableness on the facts of each particular case. As will be seen below, there is legal authority for saying that the requirement for reasonableness applies in equal measure to the school and the parents.

### 8.4.2 Acting reasonably

In *Price v Dennis* [1988] LEXIS, CA, it was held that the duty of the school was to take reasonable steps to preserve the confidence of parents who themselves acted reasonably. In that case, parents were held to have acted unreasonably in orchestrating a mass withdrawal from a private school after the principal summarily dismissed the headmaster.

The viability of a school community depends on there being mutual trust and confidence between parents and pupils, and the school, its governors, head and staff. It also depends on the confidence that exists between the parents themselves. Each member of the parent body is entitled to expect the others to treat the school community reasonably and to satisfy their moral and legal obligations and, particularly, to pay fees on time and to give a term's notice of intention of the early withdrawal of a pupil. These obligations are also of importance to governors, who often serve a school at their own personal risk. If an unincorporated school closes in deficit, it will be the governors personally who must satisfy the liabilities.

More positive aspects of the duty to treat the school reasonably are that the success of the community will depend on the general acceptance and contribution of every person to the standards of education and behaviour, the values and the general ethos and culture which the school sets out to build. It is the nature of a closed community that it cannot for long withstand its culture being undermined, and it is both entitled and sometimes under a legal duty to require removal of undermining influences. The paragraphs below serve to illustrate the scope of the duty of parents and pupils to act reasonably in relation to the school.

### 8.4.3 Supporting the head's authority

It will often be an express condition of the school's contract with parents that parents authorise the head (and, by extension, the staff) while *in loco parentis* or acting on behalf of a pupil who has reached the age of 16, to take and/or authorise in good faith all decisions that safeguard and promote the pupil's welfare. Parents are often required to understand that the school attaches importance to such matters as courtesy, integrity, manners and good discipline, and that the pupil is expected to take a full part in the activities of the school, to attend punctually on each school day, to work hard, to be well behaved and to comply with the school rules about the wearing of uniform.

Parents are also expected to give their support and encouragement to the objectives and aims of the school and to uphold its good name, to continue the pupil's education at home and to ensure that the pupil maintains appropriate standards of punctuality, behaviour, diligence, language, discipline and dress.

### 8.4.4 Consultation and communication

Parents are not, in general, entitled to govern or manage the school save to the extent (if at all) that there is provision for parent governors. Nor are they entitled to information about the discussions of governors behind closed doors, or minutes of their meetings. None the less, and to a greater or lesser extent, schools will normally consult with parents about important changes to the school and its curriculum. It is clearly important to the integrity of the community that there should be consultation, but also that a clear line be preserved between the management duties of the governors and the expression of views by the parents.

Communication is vital to the health of a school community. Litigation between school and parents is very often occasioned by a failure on the part of parents to communicate concerns or criticisms early enough or by a school's failure to respond in an appropriate way.

An important aspect of communication is informing the school of matters which the head, or the housemaster or teachers, should know of, especially in relation to a pupil's health, allergies and learning difficulties, and any family history or circumstances relevant to these.

### 8.4.5 Community aspects

It is very important that parents are helped to understand that they are an integral part of the school community and that every parent makes a contribution to its success and can equally cause it damage. The latter is sometimes seen at social events and at the school gates when ill-judged criticisms or misinformation pass into rumour and gossip which not only undermine the community but can cause unjustified personal distress and damage to staff. Nor can that kind of behaviour ever benefit the families who are responsible for it.

It is not uncommon for parents who find themselves in dispute with a school to say that they intend to enlist the help of the press in resolving the problem. That approach seems calculated to cause damage not only to the community but also to individuals. Moreover, it can be seen as a gesture of no confidence in the court system and is unlikely to find favour with judges who may later be asked to decide the issues in dispute.

If there is occasion for concern or criticism, parents owe a responsibility to the community to raise the matter early on and in an appropriate way, privately to the head or chairman of governors in the first place. In particular instances, parents may find it necessary to exercise a measure of persistence, but again these matters should be regarded as essentially private. In a serious case, parents are entitled to seek the help of the association to which the school or its head belongs, for example, the Headmasters' [and Headmistresses'] Conference (HMC), the Girls' Schools Association (GSA), the Independent Association of Preparatory Schools (IAPS), the Independent Schools Association (ISA) or the Society of Headmasters and Headmistresses of Independent Schools (SHMIS), or of the DfEE.

Other community aspects arise: for example, the obligation to ensure children are not sent to school if unwell and are not sent to school with casual medication or objects that could cause injury to other children.

### 8.4.6   Compliance with rules and policies

Consistent with duties to the community, each pupil and, to the extent relevant, each parent is expected to know and comply with the spirit and letter of the school rules and regulations and the known policies of the governors. The rules and their observance are a mainstay of the ethos and culture of any community. They serve the welfare of all and help to promote stability.

### 8.4.7   Financial obligations

The majority of independent schools have little, if any, endowment and depend almost entirely on fees for their income. Some may be asset-rich but cash flow will generally be the decisive factor in the school's viability. Governors and the parent body as a whole are therefore entitled to expect that fees will be paid in full and on time unless an instalment arrangement has been agreed in advance and budgeted.

It is often not understood that the annual surplus or deficit made by a school can depend on the fees paid for the last 3% or 5% of pupils, and the school community as a whole is entitled to expect stern measures to be taken, including exclusion of the pupil, when fees are left unpaid without a satisfactory explanation.

Charity trustees owe a legal duty to manage the assets of the trust with the prudence of a business person managing his or her own affairs but they are not entitled to take commercial risks in the same way. Nor with the ever present risk of personal liability in many schools should they be expected to do so. Moreover, it is the fees which fund staff salaries and the facilities by which standards are improved and the school is developed for the benefit of all. Accordingly, parents who pay late or who default are invariably expected to pay interest or a surcharge at a rate equivalent to the commercial rates which would be applied by a financial institution in a case of unauthorised and unsecured borrowing.

### 8.4.8   Notice of withdrawal

It is an implied, if not express, term that either the school or the parents may bring the contract to an end on a term's notice. A failure to give a term's notice can in some circumstances be a breach of contract and, in the absence of a breach by the school going to the root of the contract, will entitle the school to a term's fees in lieu of notice (*Mount v Oldham Corporation* [1973] 1 QB 309, CA).

The rule about notice, discussed in more detail later, is the bedrock of the contractual relationship between school and parents. It protects governors, who often risk personal liability if the school were to close in deficit. It protects parents from having to pay increases in fees that are occasioned by the defaults of others. It also protects the stability of schools and enables a proper process of resource, staffing and curriculum planning. These are matters in the community interest but also in the wider public interest which, it may be argued, requires that efficient schools should not be destroyed by small minorities.

If there were no adverse consequences of withdrawing a pupil without a term's notice, parents in temporary disagreement with the school could make their point by withdrawal or even by orchestrating a mass withdrawal, as happened in *Price v Dennis* [1988] LEXIS, and the school would collapse. Equally, parents in temporary financial embarrassment would not be deterred from simply not sending their children to the school at the start of a term. Many independent schools could not withstand these levels of volatility.

### 8.4.9 Reasonable expectations

It is for the school to make clear the contribution it expects from each parent and child. This is a part of the school's obligation to manage the parents' expectations and the relationship generally. Parents are not, in general, expert in matters concerning the education and development of children, and a certain amount of litigation results from a perceived mismatch between expectation and delivery.

A common example is the case of a bright child whose technical ability in reading or another activity exceeds his or her maturity of understanding. Other examples are where a difference exists between the school's and the parents' perceptions of a child's abilities and aptitudes or of what can or should be fitted into the timetable for a particular child; and over the control that a school is entitled to exercise in respect of pupils aged 16 or above when they are not in the care of the school.

### 8.4.10 Intellectual property rights

An independent school will normally seek to reserve sole copyright in any literary, musical, dramatic or artistic work created by the school or by a pupil for a purpose associated with the cultural life of the school, but will otherwise acknowledge the right of pupils to assert their intellectual property rights in respect of work of which the pupil is author or inventor.

The matter is rarely as straightforward as this. An example might be the case of a pupil who has an idea for an invention. He (or she) shares it with an employed teacher and a group of other pupils. They develop the idea together using school facilities and perhaps equipment supplied by a third party sponsor. The invention is then entered in and wins a national competition which was open only to schools and not to individuals. In a case like this, the nature and apportionment of the intellectual property rights will be a complex legal matter turning on the facts of the individual case. Each party will require independent legal advice.

### 8.4.11 Domestic circumstances

The success and welfare of a child at school, whether as a boarder or day-pupil, will depend to a significant extent on circumstances at home. It has become common for independent school heads, alarmed at the many signs of breakdown in society, to try and enlist the co-operation of parents over such matters as homework support, vigilance out of school hours, unrestricted access to television and the Internet, and other potentially adverse influences that may lead adolescents into drugs and other damaging influences.

These warnings are given for good reason, since a child's performance at school will often be a direct reflection of circumstances at home, and, increasingly, independent schools which can do so will select children by reference to the integrity, not the wealth, of their family unit, and their confidence that the family will give adequate support to the child and also to the objectives and aims of the school.

The underlying point here is that membership of a school community assumes that parents will, to the extent necessary and appropriate, accept the advice if not the authority of the head in relation to certain aspects of the child's upbringing at home.

On a related matter, it is frequently an express term of the contract between school and parents that if both parents are to be absent from the pupil's home for 24 hours or longer, the school must be told the name, address and telephone number for 24-hour contact of the adult to whom parental responsibility has been delegated. This matters not only in the event of an emergency but also because there have been instances when children have got into difficulties through being allowed by absentee parents to stay in unsuitable accommodation.

### 8.4.12   Withholding property and information

An express term of the parent contract will normally provide that the school is entitled to withhold information or property while fees are unpaid, and this right is capable of extending to examination results, certificates, national record of achievement, artwork portfolio and other property (*Grenar v The Royal School, Hindhead* (1997) unreported).

The issues over withholding examination results are complicated by the fact that the examination contract is made between the school and the examining board. Neither the parent nor the pupil is a party to that contract. It is further complicated if the pupil has left school by the time public examination results are announced. In those cases, there is no longer a contractual relationship between school and parents, and so there is no duty to the pupil *in loco parentis*.

Further, it was held in the *Grenar* case that it is usual custom and practice at independent schools to reserve a right to withhold information and property. It would not be just and reasonable to impose a duty of care in favour of the pupil which rendered a valid contractual term worthless.

There have been examples of schools withholding a pupil's clothing, sports equipment, stereo, musical instruments, computer and, in one case, a horse and tack because of unpaid fees. In the absence of an express agreement for the return or disposal of such property, the procedures set out at ss 12 and 13 of and Sch 1 to the Torts (Interference With Goods) Act 1977 would have to be used. There may, however, be issues as between the pupil and his parents over the legal ownership of certain equipment.

### 8.4.13   Child's rights v parents' rights

The focus of the Education Acts under which the maintained sector is regulated, is directed mainly towards parental rights and far less towards the rights of children.

The focus of an independent school is quite different. The rights and obligations of parents are defined by the contractual terms and conditions, whether express or implied, but the child's rights provided under the Children Act 1989 and in the law of tort will, in general, take precedence when necessary in the interests of the child's safety and welfare. An example is the operation of the *Gillick* principle (discussed at **22.7.9**) in respect of confidential information relating to the child.

### 8.4.14   Complaints

The contract between school and parents will normally provide some form of complaints mechanism designed to ensure that concerns or complaints are resolved swiftly and effectively for the benefit of individuals and the community as a whole.

Sections 469–471 of the Education Act 1996, however, contain provisions under which a person may complain to the Secretary of State on one or more of the following grounds:

- that the school premises or any parts of them are unsuitable for a school;
- that the accommodation provided at the school premises is inadequate or unsuitable, having regard to the number, ages and sex of the pupils attending the school;
- that efficient and suitable instruction is not being provided at the school, having regard to the ages and sex of the pupils attending it;
- that the proprietor of the school or any teacher or other employee employed in the school is not a proper person to be the proprietor of an independent school or (as the case may be) to be a teacher or other employee in any school;
- that there has been a failure in relation to a child provided with accommodation by the school, to comply with the duty imposed by s 87 of the Children Act 1989 (welfare of children accommodated in independent schools).

If the Secretary of State receives a complaint he is required to serve a notice of complaint on the proprietor of the school stating the grounds of complaint which apply, together with full particulars of the matters complained of. Further, and insofar as the matters can be remedied, the notice shall specify:

- the measures necessary in the opinion of the Secretary of State to remedy those matters; and
- the time, not being less than six months after the service of the notice, within which those measures are required to be taken.

Any person on whom a notice of complaint is served under s 469 may, within certain time limits, appeal against the notice by referring the complaint to an Independent Schools Tribunal, and s 470 of the Act describes the procedures that will apply. Under s 471 of the Act, if the proprietor of the school has not referred the complaint to an Independent Schools Tribunal under s 470 within the time limited by the notice, the Secretary of State may make any order which such a tribunal would have had power to make if the complaint had been referred.

# Chapter 9

## SCHOOL FEES

### 9.1   INTRODUCTION

This chapter aims to explain the law, custom and practice of independent schools in relation to deposits, fees, extras and other charges. A number of common situations are considered. Fees in lieu of notice are covered at Chapter 10.

### 9.2   MEANING OF 'FEE' AND 'DEPOSIT'

*A fee* is a payment for the performance of a professional service, such as education, or a charge paid for a privilege, such as admission to an examination or to the entry list of a school. Of its nature, a fee is not repayable.

*A deposit* is defined in s 5 of the Banking Act 1987 as a sum of money paid on terms under which it will be repaid, with or without interest or premium, and either on demand or at a time or in circumstances agreed between the parties.

Schools which take a deposit are not necessarily in a 'deposit-taking business' as defined at s 6 of the Act. If they were, they would need authorisation from the Bank of England. The Act is directed towards those who, in the course of business lend money received by way of deposit. Section 6(2)(a) specifically excludes deposits not accepted on a day-to-day basis or deposits which are accepted only on particular occasions.

A school comes within this exclusion because deposits are normally taken only when parents accept the offer of a place or as a payment on account of a school trip. Whilst the deposit monies contribute to working capital, they do not finance the school to any material extent and they are normally credited to the final term's fees on leaving. In its more general sense used by independent schools, a deposit means a security, pledge or expression of good faith.

### 9.3   REGISTRATION FEE

It is custom and practice at many independent schools that parents wishing to register their child complete a registration form and pay a fee, often between £5 and £50, known as a registration fee. That fee is in the nature of an administration charge in exchange for which the family details are added to the school's database and the child's name is placed on the waiting list, sometimes (misleadingly) called an 'entry list'. Registration does not of itself amount to an offer or a promise to offer the child a place. Depending on the custom and practice of an individual school and what is said in the prospectus, it may imply a promise that the school will take reasonable steps to contact the family in time for them to confirm their interest or otherwise before proceeding to the admission stage at the right time.

There are still some schools whose admission procedures operate with a registration form alone (as discussed at **6.4.3**). These will normally be schools in which there is only a short period between the parents' visit and the child entering the school. Then, the parent completes a registration form and pays the fee as a contractual offer by the parent to have a place at the school.

## 9.4   THE ACCEPTANCE DEPOSIT

The amount of an acceptance deposit varies between nothing at all and a full term's fees. The deposit may (but does not always) consist of three elements:

– a part prepayment of the first term's fees which will be credited to the account for the first term; and/or
– an entrance fee which is a fee, not a deposit, and will be retained by the school; and/or
– a security or caution deposit which will be retained while the child is at school and normally credited without interest to the pupil's final account on leaving.

The custom and practice of independent schools is that deposits form part of the general funds of the school and contribute to the school's working capital. Thus, they help to reduce overheads and this in turn may be reflected in fee levels.

Often a deposit will not be required when a child enters the school at nursery level. It may be hoped that the child will proceed through reception and join the pre-prep school, moving on to the junior, preparatory and middle and senior schools if applicable. In these cases, the school has to decide at what stage, if at all, to charge a deposit. That should be made clear in the contractual documents and, in particular, the fees list.

A deposit paid at the time of acceptance is an expression of good faith and intention on the part of the parents to send their child to the school. In consideration of that, the school sets aside a place for that child. What, therefore, is the position if parents change their minds and wish to break their contract by cancelling acceptance? It is best for this matter to be expressly contemplated in advance and set out in the acceptance form and the standard terms and conditions, but sometimes it is not.

### 9.4.1   Cancellation on a term's notice

In some schools, the standard terms and conditions provide that a term's fees in lieu of notice will be payable following cancellation at any time after acceptance and whether or not the cancelled place has been filled. This is based on the rule of custom and practice explained at **6.4.9** above. It is probably implied also from custom and practice that the full amount of the deposit will be credited without interest in these cases.

Other schools provide that there will be no charge to fees in lieu of notice if a term's notice of cancellation has been given, but that the deposit will not be refunded on the basis that it is a genuine pre-estimate of the damage suffered by the school consequent on the breach of contract.

The position is more complex with a two or three-element deposit, of which a portion was a prepayment of the first term's fees and a further portion was an entrance fee. In the absence of an express condition, the entrance fee element must be returned. It is probably implied that the school will retain the part prepayment and security elements.

### 9.4.2   Cancellation on less than a term's notice

There is normally an express agreement in the offer and acceptance documents that cancellation on less than a term's notice will result in a charge to a term's fees in lieu of notice, the deposit to be credited without interest, whether or not the place is subsequently filled.

Even if not written, it is by custom and practice an implied term that the first term's fees will be paid and the whole deposit credited. The fact that the pupil has not yet entered the school is irrelevant, since it must be assumed that the school has already embarked on its planning of resource for the year and in so doing has relied on acceptances as firm evidence of minimum numbers.

## 9.5   ADDITIONAL DEPOSIT

The standard terms and conditions of some schools include a condition that parents who are persistently in arrears with their fees may be required to top up the deposit to the amount of a full term's fees at the rate applicable to the pupil for day or boarding as the case may be. This provides a measure of security. It is a term which needs to be expressly provided as it will not be implied. If expressly provided, a parent who refuses on request to pay the additional deposit in the circumstances contemplated by the contractual term will be in breach of contract and the pupil can be excluded. Alternatively, if the parent wishes to withdraw the pupil without giving a term's notice, he (or she) will be liable to pay a term's fees in lieu of notice. These clauses need careful drafting. Interest is not payable to parents on the additional element of the deposit unless expressly provided.

## 9.6   DEPOSITS FOR OVERSEAS PUPILS

The cost of debt recovery proceedings in the European Community or other parts of the world tends to be prohibitive in relation to the amounts of money involved in these cases. Understandably, therefore, schools that admit pupils from overseas may want a full term's fees as a deposit or possibly the normal deposit and a full term's fees in addition.

A question arises over whether this infringes s 17 of the Race Relations Act 1976. Section 17 makes it unlawful for an independent school (among other educational establishments) to discriminate against a person on racial grounds in the terms on which it offers to admit him as a pupil.

The grounds for requiring a larger deposit in respect of overseas pupils should have nothing to do with the colour, race, nationality or ethnic or national origins of the person concerned. The sole and simple ground is the cost and difficulty of recovering unpaid fees from defendants who live out of the jurisdiction. Nor is it indirect discrimination if the rule is applied equally as between persons of all racial groups living abroad where the cost of default would be significantly higher than normal.

Whilst parents have no entitlement to interest on an overseas deposit unless so provided by the contract, interest should be paid at a discretionary rate on any amount held in excess of the normal acceptance deposit, as not to do so would amount to a difference of treatment between one kind of deposit-payer and another.

## 9.7   DISCOUNTED PLACES

The practice varies for pupils who have been awarded a scholarship, exhibition, bursary or assisted place. Some schools require a full deposit. Others require no deposit. Others again charge a deposit as a proportion of the parental contribution to fees. Staff receiving a staff discount are often not asked for a deposit. Sibling allowances are usually ignored when calculating the deposit.

## 9.8   SCHOOL FEES

### 9.8.1   The fees list

The fees list for the school year should be published before the start of the preceding summer term if possible. A copy should be sent to each parent and the prospectus updated.

The fees list and/or the standard terms and conditions should specify which items are or are not covered by the fees. Normally covered will be the ordinary curriculum together with most books and stationery, but not extra tuition, outings, fees for public examinations and benefits insurance, such as personal accident cover or healthcare insurance. By custom and practice, fees are payable each term in advance unless otherwise agreed.

The ancient case of *Collins v Price* (1828) 6 LJCP (OS) 244 is the first known reported case about school fees. Four days after the start of a term and before the term's fees had been paid, the pupil was sent home because of illness. He did not return. No satisfactory explanation was given by the parents. It was held that the school was entitled to payment of the term's fees in full.

### 9.8.2   Extras, charges and disbursements

These expressions have broadly the same meaning and refer to items that will be charged in addition to the fees for each term. Extras are normally charged one term in arrear, although the school is entitled to ask for advance payment of extras and would normally do so in a case such as a school skiing trip. Fees in lieu of notice in relation to extra tuition are dealt with in Chapter 10.

### 9.8.3   Damage done by the pupil

Damage done by children at school may be anything from wear and tear to accidental damage, deliberate vandalism ('trashing') or damage to monuments. Irrespective of strict legal rights and obligations, it is the custom and practice of independent schools to charge certain accidental and all deliberate damage to the account. Disputes can arise as to the amount of the charge. It must be confined to a reasonable sum, taking into account the cost of repair, wear and tear and betterment. Broadly, the indemnity basis rather than 'new for old' applies unless the contract makes some other provision. Rather than leaving the matter as an implied term or open to dispute, it is preferable to establish in the standard terms and conditions a contractual right of the school to charge the full replacement cost of damage, recoverable as a debt.

In an advisory case in 1998, a group of pupils painted part of a tarmac surface at school. The only cosmetically acceptable repair was to resurface the whole area, including parts that had not been painted. The parents of the pupils concerned were required to pay the whole cost of repair.

### 9.8.4   Boarding and tuition fees

The nature of the contract for educational services is that of an 'entire' contract, although the harsher effects of that doctrine are mitigated by the doctrine of substantial performance. The contract continues from the date when it is formed until the date the pupil leaves. The price of the contract is payable by termly instalments in advance unless otherwise agreed, for example in the case of a lump sum prepayment or an arrangement for payment by instalments.

A contract that is not *entire* is known as *severable*. That means it is made up of a number of elements that can be viewed quite separately from each other. The inherent complexity of the education product was considered in Chapter 5. It will be plain that in relation to tuition fees there is no part that can be treated as severable from any other part, although tuition may be severable from boarding if the pupil's home is near enough to allow him or her to attend as a day-pupil.

### 9.8.5   Do the rules of *quantum meruit* apply to school fees?

*Quantum meruit* means payment for value received or 'what it is worth'. An example is that if 10,000 cans of baked beans are ordered and only 5,000 are delivered and accepted, only the lower number need be paid for.

It was decided in *Governors of E. Ivor Hughes Education Foundation v Denfield* [1992] *Current Law* September, 58, mentioned at **9.8.8**, that the *quantum meruit* basis does not apply to school fees. The point was also covered in *Bradfield House Ltd v*

*Walsall Metropolitan Borough Council* (1997) 4 EPLI 68, Walsall County Court, also mentioned at **9.8.8**.

The issue sometimes arises in the different context of *consumables not consumed* when a pupil is withdrawn early in a term. The school is under no obligation to give credit in those circumstances. It is already committed to catering and other contracts. The Court of Appeal touched obliquely on *quantum meruit* in *Mount v Oldham Corporation* [1973] 1 QB 309, in disapproving an earlier decision in *Denman v Winstanley* (1887) 4 TLR 127. In the latter case, it was held that fees in lieu of notice meant the profit element of fees only and the court held that only 50% of fees in lieu of notice could be recovered. That case is no longer good law, if it ever was. Moreover, unless an independent school is very heavily endowed, it is inconceivable that its surplus could be anywhere near 50% of its fees if it is properly resourced and operating in the market place.

### 9.8.6   The time for payment of fees

Custom and practice require that fees are payable in advance unless otherwise agreed. In essence that means *before* the first day of term. Some schools use the expression 'on or before' the first day of term, which can give rise to an ambiguity. In one anecdotal case, a number of pupils were expelled on the first day of a term because of a serious event occurring during the holidays. A question arose over the expression 'on or before' as to whether the obligation to pay the term's fees had accrued. Of course, a contractual requirement that fees will be paid *before* the first day of term does not mean that the school will want to take action to enforce payment during the first week of arrears but the right to do so is established for use if necessary. It might be necessary, for example, if the fee-payer is on the point of relocating abroad or is known to be facing bankruptcy.

### 9.8.7   Exclusion for non-payment of fees

The school is a supplier of a service. If it is clear that fees must be paid in advance or in a certain way and, since the wording is such as to make time of the essence, the school is entitled to withhold service when fees are in arrears. This rule permits exclusion of the pupil from school premises while fees are unpaid. Exclusion is an expression used in the maintained sector to cover suspension and expulsion but the traditional use of that word in the independent sector has been in relation to unpaid fees only.

Exclusion for non-payment without some other clear repudiation of the contract does not bring the primary layers of obligation under the contract to an end. It is open to the parents to tender payment and then the school must allow the pupil to return. However, not infrequently after an exclusion, the parents stay out of communication and one or 2 months pass by. The status of the pupil's place becomes uncertain. The school can clarify the position by suing the parent for the term's fees but there is no certainty that a school could recover fees in lieu of notice in addition. The position is plainly unsatisfactory, but there is a solution.

The standard terms and conditions can provide to the effect that a pupil may be excluded from the school at any time when fees are unpaid and will be *deemed withdrawn* without notice 28 days after exclusion, giving rise to a term's fees in lieu of notice in addition to current term's fees. This is plainly consistent with the rule discussed in Chapter 10 about fees in lieu of notice and is a sensible approach for a school to adopt. As a matter of good practice, parents should be told that they are running the risk of the contract being terminated and fees in lieu of notice being charged in addition to fees for the current term if they do not pay for the current term.

### 9.8.8   Refund and waiver of fees

The term 'fee' implies that there will be no refund, but it is as well to make the position clear in the standard terms and conditions. Common situations arise where the child is absent through sickness or where a term has to be shortened because of epidemic or some other reason, or where days are lost because of bad weather, or a vacation is extended or for some other reason before the normal end of term. It should be made clear that fees will not be refunded or waived in any of these circumstances or for any other cause except at the sole discretion of the head. Reported cases in which disputes over this issue have arisen are:

– *Collins v Price* (1828) 6 LJCP (OS) 244 – referred to at **9.8.1** above.

– *Governors of E. Ivor Hughes Education Foundation v Denfield* [1992] *Current Law* September, 58 – in March 1990, the school sent a circular to parents to the effect that there would be no lessons after the GCSE examinations but optional quasi-educational courses would be offered for the remainder of the term. A parent responded by saying that his son would not return to school after examinations and that the contract was to provide tuition only up to the exams, and therefore that fees were payable only on a *quantum meruit* basis in the final term. It was held that the parent had agreed to pay fees on a term-in-advance basis. There was no express or implied term that less than the full fees were payable in the GCSE term. A parent could only seek to vary the contract in this respect before the final term's fees were due. If he ascertained that a lesser sum was due he would have to tender that sum by the due date. Otherwise, the school took the pupil back for the full term.

– *Bradfield House Ltd v Walsall Metropolitan Borough Council* [1997] 4 EPLI 68, Walsall County Court – a local authority placed a boy at a special school. The boy absconded after 4 days and was expelled. Both parties accepted that the expulsion was justified. The placing authority argued that it was only bound to pay for the time the pupil had attended, ie a *quantum meruit*. It was held that this was an entire misconception of the law. If a parent or local authority sends a child to school and the child has to be expelled, the school should not bear the loss. The judge recognised that in this case the local authority would have to pay twice for the same term but said that this is a matter which is entirely foreign to the school. The school still has to pay its expenses in any event.

### 9.8.9   Walking out

Children aged 16 and over are at school voluntarily. They cannot be prevented from walking out. In the absence of a breach going to the root of the contract on the part of the school, no fees should be repayable in these circumstances. It can, however, be argued that the pupil's decision to leave is outside the control of the contracting parties, and the contract is therefore frustrated. It is suggested here that there may be an implied agency between the pupil and his parents, to the effect that the acts of the pupil are to be treated as those of the parent for these purposes and, further, an implied warranty from the parents that the pupil will attend school. An express condition to this effect can place the position beyond doubt and defeat a claim of frustration.

## 9.8.10   Fees increases

It will be apparent and obvious to every reasonable parent that fees at an independent school must be reviewed by the governors every year, or more frequently, if they are managing the organisation properly, and that fees will be increased from time to time, and probably every year, to take account of increases in teachers' salaries, other rising costs and inflation. It must follow from this that there should be no legal consequences of a school's failure to give a term's notice of a reasonable increase in the fees.

However, in *Pott v Stevens* (1948) 99 LJ 164, his Honour Judge Carey Evans held that, where a school required a half-term's notice of withdrawal, they had to give a half-term's notice of a fees increase or the child could be withdrawn without notice. This may have been appropriate to the economic conditions of the time but, it is submitted, would not be the right conclusion today. If it is clear that fees will increase by a reasonable amount from time to time, this must be an implied term of the contract. In any event, the area of dispute is over the amount of the increase and not the contract itself. Thus, it is difficult to see how the failure to notify could amount to a repudiation of the contract by the school.

The more difficult question relates to what is a 'reasonable' increase. 'Reasonable' must have regard to the prevailing economic conditions, the increase being charged by comparable schools in comparable areas and also the purposes of the increase. For example, where, following consultation with the parent body, it has been decided as a matter of policy to improve certain facilities and to service the cost of borrowing through current fees, a small group of parents would not be entitled to defeat the views of the majority by saying that a 10% increase levied for these purposes with the agreement of the community was unreasonable in the context of a 3% increase at comparable schools. It is submitted that an increase which the majority of the community considers reasonable is to be treated as reasonable.

The legal effect of an increase that is unreasonably high may be to entitle a parent to withdraw without notice ('acceptance of the school's repudiation') or to pay the increase none the less ('affirmation of the contract'). It is submitted that this is the effect of *Potts v Stevens* in its proper context.

An alternative, and possibly more practical, view of an unreasonable increase in the level of fees is that the unreasonable element should be disallowed for one term and the remainder should be allowed. That would have been an option open to the judge in *Pott v Stevens* but it is not known whether this point was raised in legal argument.

It is none the less good practice and a matter of courtesy to give a term's notice of every fees increase, although sometimes not possible. The whole of this legal analysis can be avoided by a well-drafted express contractual term contained in the standard terms and conditions.

## 9.8.11  Responsibility for payment of fees

The primary responsibility for payment of school fees, extras and damage rests with those who have contracted with the school, normally the parents. The clearest evidence of responsibility is signatures to a well-drafted acceptance form which incorporates the school's standard terms and conditions.

## 9.8.12  Parents who are divorced

Disputes sometimes arise between parents who are separated or divorced where the absent parent has made a payment to the other which he (or she) has specified is for school fees and the other parent has not passed on the money to the school. The position here is that both remain liable for the fees, even if the payment was made pursuant to an order of the court in matrimonial proceedings, unless the school has agreed otherwise.

It was held in *L v L (School Fees: Maintenance: Enforcement)* [1997] 2 FLR 252, CA, that a father can be committed to prison for contempt of court for failing to comply with an order made in matrimonial proceedings to pay school fees. The case concerned a 16-year-old pupil at an independent school. Her father was ordered to make direct payment to the school of an amount equal to the termly school fees for as long as his daughter was being educated there, or until some further order was made. He was also ordered to pay arrears of £6,000. He did not comply with the order and was committed to prison.

On appeal, Ward LJ explained that s 11 of the Administration of Justice Act 1970 provides that a person may be committed to prison under s 5 of the Debtors Act 1869 for non-payment of a debt where that debt arises in respect of a High Court or county court maintenance order. In his Lordship's view, orders made 'for periodical or other payments . . .' under Part II of the Matrimonial Causes Act 1973 were clearly within the scope of s 11 of the 1970 Act and s 5 of the 1869 Act. Lord Justice Ward went on to explain that an order to pay school fees direct to the relevant school had been recognised as a form of order since *Practice Direction (Periodical Payments: Ancillary Relief: Payment of School Fees)* (1983) 4 FLR 513, as amended by *Registrar's Direction (Periodical Payments: Children)* [1987] 2 FLR 255. That Direction has the approval of the Inland Revenue.

More difficult is the case in which a parent, say the mother, remarries and is dependent on her new husband, a stepfather who has not entered into any formal contractual arrangements with the school. Perhaps the stepfather signs cheques for the fees and sends them, with or without a covering letter, to the school. Perhaps he is a regular visitor to the school and attends parents' evenings and meetings with teachers. Later, when the child is withdrawn without notice, the stepfather denies that any contractual relationship has arisen between himself and the school. Moreover, if the child's natural father has disappeared or is insolvent and the mother is financially dependent, the stepfather may be the only person from whom payment could be obtained. This problem and variations of it arise quite frequently.

The legal position will depend on the facts of each case, but it is suggested here that a stepfather may be fixed with liability for fees in many of these cases. If it is apparent to the stepfather that the child would not be at this school but for his funding and where, in the sense understood in family law, he is treating the child as his own, he should be regarded as fixed at the very least by an obligation to pay fees and, by virtue of *Mount v Oldham Corporation* [1973] 1 QB 309, CA, an obligation to give a term's notice or pay a term's fees in lieu of notice.

A stepfather cannot be fixed with standard terms and conditions that he has not seen, but some schools operate the sound practice of sending out a copy of the standard terms and conditions periodically with bills. Moreover, an appropriate condition will establish joint and several liability for payment of fees and will also establish that the mother in a case such as this cannot claim to have been released from the contract by virtue of the fees being paid by the stepfather.

### 9.8.13   Other third parties

There are also cases of fees being paid by grandparents, family syndicates, family trusts, a family company, an employer or a High Commission or foreign embassy.

The acceptance form should be drafted so as to reveal any third party arrangement which is intended to apply from the outset of the contract, but sometimes a third party comes into the picture later on. In this case, a formal agreement should be prepared and signed.

The nature of an agreement with a third party who is paying the fees is that the third party will not acquire any rights, obligations or capacity in relation to the substance of the main contract. Such rights, etc, will remain with those who have parental responsibility. Thus, the third party cannot bring the main contract to an end. The agreement should, however, provide that the third party must give a term's notice of intention to cease paying the fees or pay a term's fees in lieu of notice.

A High Commission or foreign embassy is likely to be only an agent of the parent diplomat. The school is not entitled to know the terms of the parent's employment contract with his government but it is likely to include provision for part or all of the fees to be paid by the employer. Using the High Commission or foreign embassy as intermediary is helpful in ensuring prompt payment in sterling but there will almost always be a problem over fees in lieu of notice, which can be enforced only against the parent diplomat. If the contractual obligation to pay a term's fees in lieu of notice is in writing and sufficiently clear, a measure of co-operation may be expected from most of these intermediaries but it cannot be guaranteed and an overseas deposit of one term's fees is recommended.

A family syndicate is usually composed of a number of members of the family who contribute by monthly standing order to a school fees account from which the fees are paid. A school is well advised to obtain a signed third-party agreement with one or two members of the syndicate who will be personally liable for the obligations and will collect internally from other members of the family should the arrangement break down.

A different set of problems arises over family trusts. Often the fees are paid by a firm of solicitors who say that they act for the trustees, or one of the partners in the firm is a trustee. A family trust may have no corporate entity, and care should be taken to identify the names and addresses of all the trustees and to request that they enter into a third-party agreement. Anecdotal evidence is that a number of so-called trusts have turned out to be non-existent. There was no trust deed and the solicitor intermediary withdrew from the picture without having identified the trustees, saying that he had no further instructions. Unless the parties concerned are prepared to make full disclosure and written commitments, family trusts should be treated with caution.

A family company may be a small limited company with the parent as the only director. Under the present rules there is an exemption from National Insurance contributions if, as a result of a contractual liability between the company and the school, the company is legally liable to pay the fees. It happens from time to time that the school, at the request of the parent, addresses invoices to the company which then denies liability to pay fees, or fees in lieu of notice, or goes into liquidation. There is then an issue as to whether the parent was released from payment of fees.

The answer in all of these cases is to operate third-party arrangements by means of an appropriate form of agreement to which a copy of the standard terms and conditions is attached and in which the material conditions that are intended to bind the third party are incorporated.

### 9.8.14 Guarantors of the fees

The school may reasonably require a guarantor of the fees when the only contracting party is a single parent who is financially dependent or who has no visible means of support. Guarantees must be obtained in writing and again careful drafting is needed to avoid the usual pitfalls and escapes often associated with guaranteed contracts. The essence of the protections that the school will need is a clause providing that delay, waiver or release of the principal debtor or any change in the terms of payment of the debt will not affect the liability of the guarantor. Further, it should be provided that the school shall not be bound to exercise or exhaust all its remedies against the principal debtor before requiring payment from the guarantor. An obligation to pay interest must be provided specifically in the agreement. There are other issues to be covered as well. Once again, a copy of the school's standard terms and conditions should be annexed to the form of guarantee.

### 9.8.15 Interest, administration and legal costs

A school, as any other organisation, is entitled if the contract so provides to charge interest and other charges if fees are paid late. In the absence of a contractual rate of interest, the judgment rate, which has stood at 8% since 1 April 1993, will be allowed. The rate of interest charged by contract should not be so high as to amount to a fine, penalty or unfair contract term, which would be unenforceable. A simple interest rate of 2% per month has been common in the custom and practice of independent schools for some years. Schools who have not drawn up standard terms and conditions often state their rules about late payment on the invoice. That will be ineffective for the first invoice but may become effective over time.

Anecdotal evidence is that a high rate of interest has on occasions been disallowed by district judges in the small claims courts but it is submitted that the contractual rate should be allowed if it can be justified. Account may be taken of the fact that the charity trustees (where applicable) owe duties in relation to the trust assets, that they contract with parents on a basis of trust and normally without making the credit checks that are common among commercial organisations. It may also be said that the amount of all late payment charges will reflect the commercial rates that would be applied by a financial institution in the case of unauthorised and unsecured borrowing. That is a fair reflection of the position of a school when credit is stolen and not given. It is apt to recall the words of a wise bursar who said 'I want parents to understand that it is cheaper for them to bank with a bank than to bank with this school'.

The standard terms and conditions may also provide for payment in full of the school's legal and administration costs in relation to time spent by the school and its legal advisers in relation to arrears of fees. There is no reason in principle why the time of bursar or accounts staff should not be charged and recovered. Nor is there any reason why solicitors' costs prior to litigation should not be recovered as a matter of contract, provided the sum is reasonable and does not operate as a fine or penalty. Once litigation begins, costs are in the discretion of the court. A claim for less than £3,000 (the current threshold since January 1996) is known as a 'small claim' and nominal costs only can be recovered unless the district judge, exercising his discretion under Ord 19, r 4 of the County Court Rules 1981, finds that one party has acted unreasonably.

### 9.8.16 Short payment and payments on account

Parents who are in dispute with a school have on occasions sent a cheque for short payment (ie less than the full amount due) with or without a written justification for doing so. The school has to decide whether to return the cheque, retain it unpresented or present it on account and claim the balance that is owing. The legal principles that arise over this issue are known as *accord and satisfaction*. This expression means that if there is a genuine agreement between parties that less than the full sum will be paid and accepted in settlement of a dispute, a new contract arises ('accord') and the matter is settled ('satisfaction').

There have been a number of reported cases from commerce about the various problems that can arise over short payment when the court has made it clear that there must be evidence of a genuine agreement to accept a short payment before the recipient will be bound by it. These are some examples:

- The parent sends a cheque for £2,000 instead of £3,000, expressing it to be in full and final settlement. The school presents the cheque to the bank and on the same day sends a letter of demur to the parent making it clear that the money is accepted as a part-payment only. On the authorities, the school would, in these circumstances, be entitled to claim the balance.

- The facts are as above, but the parent denies having received a letter of demur from the school. In such a case, no agreement has been reached because the school did not intend to accept the short payment in satisfaction and the school is probably entitled to claim the balance.

- The facts are as in the first example, but the school omits to send a letter of demur and 2 or 3 months pass before the parent is notified of the demur. In this case, the school's conduct is more consistent with agreement than with demur and it is unlikely that the school would succeed in claiming the balance.

– Again, the facts are the same as in the first example but the parent's covering letter contains a sentence: 'This cheque is sent on the condition that it is accepted in full and final settlement. Only present it if you are in agreement with this otherwise the cheque must be returned to me unpresented'. That is a condition superimposed on the course of dealing with the cheque and if the school presents the cheque in those circumstances it will be bound by accord and satisfaction and unable to recover the balance.

These examples are a rough and ready guideline only. A more detailed analysis of the authorities is outside the scope of this chapter, and legal advice should be sought when in doubt. In any event, the whole issue can be covered by a well-drafted clause in the standard terms and conditions which makes further legal analysis unnecessary.

### 9.8.17 Scholarships, bursaries and assisted places

The rules about parental contribution, conditions of award and breach of those conditions are covered in Chapter 6 and not repeated here.

### 9.8.18 Lump-sum prepayments and composition of fees

Many schools offer a discount to a person who pays fees in advance for one to 5 years. There is an important rule about the discount. Charitable status is both a right and a privilege. One of the privileges is the tax-exempt status of a charity. This must not be abused. It would be an abuse to offer parents a discount which gives parents the benefit of the school's tax-exempt status. There is however sufficient scope for a discount to be given which reflects the accelerated payment that has been made.

### 9.8.19 Payment of fees by instalments

The normal express term which is also implied from custom and usage is that fees are payable each term in advance and extras are payable each term in arrears. Increasingly, schools have recognised that parents tend to have 12 pay days per year, not three, and that some find it easier to pay school fees by monthly direct debit or standing order. Arrangements are made accordingly, usually by means of a separate written agreement, with or without a surcharge. Instalment arrangements are a concession and the agreement should provide that the concession can be withdrawn at any time; also that the concession will cease automatically in the event of a default for 30 days or more. The agreement should provide that, on the instalment arrangement ceasing, the full amount of fees and extras then due shall be payable forthwith as a debt and that interest will start to accrue.

These arrangements are, however, complicated by the Consumer Credit Act 1974. An important point to make clear about the Act is that it regulates agreements to *provide* credit. It does not regulate agreements over credit that has been *stolen*. 'Credit' includes any form of financial accommodation with or without an interest or administration charge or surcharge.

Article 3 of the Consumer Credit (Exempt Agreements) Order 1989 provides (where relevant) that an agreement for fixed-sum credit under which the total number of payments to be made by the debtor does not exceed four payments within a period not exceeding 12 months is not regulated by the Act. This exemption is useful, provided it is understood that the agreement must allow for no more than four instalments per term or per year. The exemption will not apply to agreements that are expressed as 10 instalments per year, even though that is fewer than four per term. This anomaly is the result of poor drafting but important for the reasons given below.

If the agreement is regulated under s 8(3) of the Act the school needs a credit licence under s 22 of the Act and the detailed rules in Part V of the Act about form and execution of the agreement also apply. There are two distinct points here:

(1) *The need for a credit licence* – If a school other than occasionally (for example, two or three times per year) is entering into credit agreements it must obtain a credit licence under s 22 or a compliance offence is committed. Moreover, the agreement will not be enforceable without a validation order from the Director General of Fair Trading.

(2) *Part V execution provisions* – The point about the Part V formalities is that an agreement which is regulated by the Act because it is not exempt must be drawn up and executed in accordance with the Act and the Consumer Credit (Agreements) Regulations 1983 or it will be unenforceable by the school and the Director General will not grant a validation order.

Non-compliance with these rules does not release the school from its contract. On the contrary, the consumer is entitled to apply to the Director General for an order that the agreement can be enforced. In theory at least, this could mean that a school has in good faith granted the concession of an instalment arrangement to a parent, the parent has defaulted, the school cannot enforce the instalments, and the agreement does not contain adequate provisions for termination of the instalment arrangement. Yet, the school has to continue educating (and accommodating the pupil in the case of boarding) without fees until the expiry of a term's notice bringing the contract to an end.

It is suggested here that, in the face of such consequences, the Director General would be unlikely to grant the parent a validation order. None the less, if the point were taken, the school would be unable to enforce its claim for fees through the courts until the position was resolved with the Office of Fair Trading. It cannot have been the intention of the legislature to give consumers a whip with which to beat charitable suppliers who offer to help parents who are in difficulty but that is the potential effect of this legislation. It is long overdue for amendment. Problems of the kind described above can be avoided by using the 'fewer than four instalments per term' formula and by careful drafting of the instalment agreement so as to provide for termination at any time.

# Chapter 10

## NOTICE AND FEES IN LIEU OF NOTICE

### 10.1 INTRODUCTION

This chapter is concerned with the 'notice rule', the reasons for it and some of the case-law that has arisen out of it. Examples of common disputes are also given. These are all situations that have been identified in fees-related litigation or correspondence preceding such litigation.

### 10.2 THE NOTICE RULE

It has been custom and practice for longer than anyone can remember that parents must give a term's notice to withdraw a pupil or pay a term's fees in lieu of notice.

As will be seen, the only grounds on which this obligation may be avoided are if the school is in fundamental breach of its contractual obligations (that is a breach going to the root of the contract) or if the contract has become frustrated. The fees in lieu of notice rule is an implied, if not express, term of the contract, and judicial notice of the rule was taken by the Court of Appeal in *Mount v Oldham Corporation* [1973] 1 QB 309, CA.

It is equally an implied, if not express, term that parents are entitled to a term's notice should the school wish to bring the contract to an end, although notice is not required in the case of an expulsion or requirement to leave that is justified, or other circumstances caused by parents or the pupil that call for the pupil's immediate and permanent removal.

The rule about fees in lieu of notice gives rise to as much litigation as all other aspects of school life put together. A claim for fees in lieu of notice is always unwelcome to parents, and all the more so if they feel they have a genuine grievance. None the less, the rule, when applied in proper circumstances, is an essential protection to the school community as a whole and is firmly upheld by the courts.

### 10.3 THE REASONS FOR THE RULE

#### 10.3.1 The governors

Most independent schools are not well endowed. Their income depends mainly or entirely on fees paid by parents. The majority are registered charities, which means that they exist for the public good. Their purposes are exclusively charitable and their assets are held for the benefit of the community. Their profit or 'surplus' is not distributable. The governors are unpaid and often serve at risk of personal liability if the school closes in deficit.

Another reason why a term's notice is required to bring the contract to an end is the need for sufficient financial certainty so that the governors can safely employ and retain the services of academic, administrative, maintenance and other staff. The academic and sports curriculum and all the other activities of the school have to be planned well in advance if the school is to function properly. The non-teaching staff, usually headed by a bursar or 'director', are responsible for all aspects of business administration and compliance with regulations. The maintenance staff have an equally vital role in keeping the fabric, plant and equipment safe and in good condition for children, staff, visitors and even, to a limited extent, trespassers.

### 10.3.2    The parents

Contracting for independent education is an act of faith and an important commitment. Parents need to have confidence in the stability of the school. There is an unwritten understanding, amounting to a moral responsibility, between all parents that each will comply with his legal obligations, pay the fees and treat the school and its staff reasonably; otherwise the whole culture and even the survival of the school will be undermined. That is the nature of private education.

The fees in lieu of notice rule underpins all the concerns and interest described above. If there were no adverse consequences of withdrawal without notice, parents who suffer a temporary financial setback might decide to opt for a few terms in the State-maintained sector and give the school no notice at all. Likewise, a disaffected parent could make his point by not returning his (or her) child to school at the start of term; or a group of disaffected parents might withdraw a number of children without any notice at all and cause serious damage to a whole class. Schools that make a very small surplus would be unable to withstand this level of volatility. Disaffected parents often provide a good illustration of the appropriateness of the rule about fees in lieu of notice. Invariably, the vast majority of parents are well satisfied and do not share the complaint of the particular parent, whether it be about a fees increase, a staff change, a merger or any other issue.

Thus, the fees in lieu of notice rule is necessary:

(a)  in the public interest to ensure the strong governance and stability of independent schools for the benefit of parents, children and the wider community;

(b)  to enable schools to operate on a marginal level of surplus (as many do) and to serve the community within the spirit of charitable law;

(c)  to protect parents and pupils from sudden closure of the school and to protect parents from unnecessary fees increases and cost occasioned by the defaults of others;

(d)  to protect volunteer governors who govern schools at their own personal risk.

### 10.3.3    The authorities

The leading cases about the fees in lieu of notice rule are *Mount v Oldham Corporation* and *Price v Dennis* – both decisions of the Court of Appeal. Summaries are given below.

## (a)   *Mount v Oldham Corporation* [1973] 1 QB 309, CA

This case established the right of the school to charge and receive fees in lieu of notice in almost all circumstances other than fundamental breach or frustration of the contract. In this case, the proprietor, who was also the headmaster, of a private special school was charged with indecency. He was away from the school for 6 months but was cleared of the charges and his character was vindicated. In the meantime, local authorities had withdrawn pupils without giving any notice. The leading judgment was given by Lord Denning MR. The following passages from the judgment are of relevance to many cases about fees in lieu of notice:

> 'It is an understood thing in all schools that if a parent wishes to withdraw a boy, he can do so; but if he does so he has either to give a term's notice or to pay a term's fee in lieu of notice. *That is a usage well known throughout the education world. So well known that we can take notice of it ourselves. If the parent wishes to avoid this liability, he must show that the school has been guilty of a breach going to the root of the contract, such as to entitle the parent to treat himself as discharged from any further obligation* [emphasis added]. ... After a boy goes to school, he may be very unhappy. The school may not suit him. Other boys may be unkind to him. The staff may change for the worse, and so forth. The parent may be quite reasonable in withdrawing the boy; but he must still give a term's notice or pay a term's fees in lieu of notice.'

Lord Denning went on to say that had the headmaster been found guilty of the charges it would have been a breach going to the root of the contract and he could not have recovered any fees.

On the issue of frustration of contract, he said:

> 'I can well understand that in some special schools the services of the headmaster may be so personal and his presence so important that if he were to die or have a prolonged illness, or any other misfortune causing prolonged absence, the contract might be frustrated. But this school is not in that category. First, the position of the headmaster was not so very personal. Everything would not come to an end if he died or had a long illness or was absent for a term or two. The staff here could and did carry on the school. Secondly, he was not likely to be absent for very long. It was only as if he had been taken ill with a serious illness from which he should recover in six months. I do not think this contract was frustrated by what happened.'

Lord Denning went on to describe the legal character of a claim for fees in lieu of notice. The issue was whether fees in lieu are a 'debt', liquidated damages, or 'damages for breach of contract', ie unliquidated damages. The distinction is important. If fees in lieu of notice are a debt or liquidated damages, the school need prove nothing more than that it was resourced and ready to perform the contract. The school does not have to prove any actual loss suffered as a result of the parents' failure to pay. The school does not have to mitigate its loss. Accordingly (when applicable), the claim can include laundry services and consumables such as food not consumed if they are included in the fee, and fees in lieu of notice can be claimed even if the place has been filled. On this issue, Lord Denning said:

> 'It was suggested that the claim should lie for damages and not a term's fees [ie debt or liquidated damages] ... but I do not think that is correct. The claim can properly be made for fees in lieu of notice, because that is the understanding in the profession.'

Edmund Davies LJ agreed with Lord Denning, 'that the proper remedy in the circumstances of the case was a claim for a term's fees and not for unliquidated damages'. Stephenson LJ also agreed. He said: 'I agree that at this time of day it is quite clear that if notice is required by such a contract to educate as this, so fees in lieu of notice are also required and payable under the contract'.

### (b)   Price v Dennis (1988) LEXIS, CA

This case concerned a mass withdrawal of pupils from a proprietor-owned school for about 100 boys aged between 3 and 13. Halfway through the summer term of 1983, the proprietor, Mrs Price, summarily dismissed the headmaster, Mr Cassidy. The proprietor was herself a fully qualified teacher. She took over as head. She did her best to keep parents informed. However, 71 families formed a new school nearby to start in the autumn term of 1983. They appointed the dismissed head and five of his staff. Only 28 pupils were left at the original school but it quickly grew again to 100 pupils.

It was held that the terms to be implied in the contract for education included that:

– pupils would be educated in a fit and proper manner;
– the functions of the school would be carried out with all reasonable skill and care; and
– the school would take reasonable steps to retain the confidence of parents who themselves acted reasonably.

It was further held that the proprietor had not been in breach of contract. She had done the best she could in the circumstances. Every parent who withdrew a pupil had to pay fees in lieu of notice. Even a parent who said that he had contracted to send his child to a school for 100 pupils not a school for 28 pupils was unable to establish a breach of contract in respect of 4-year-old boys.

Glidewell LJ said:

> 'I do not consider that any of the events which took place within the school amounted to a failure by Mrs Price to provide education. I do not believe that she was required to provide education in accordance with every word of the prospectus ...'

Glidewell LJ also found that the circumstances of this case fell within the principle in *Mount v Oldham Corporation*. (Note that frustration of contract was not an issue in *Price v Dennis* because the parents had brought the situation on themselves.)

Glidewell LJ also addressed a further argument of the parents when he said:

> 'I do not accept that her power to [dismiss Mr Cassidy] can, as a matter of law, be cut down by requiring her to consider the effect that it would have upon other members of the staff and of the parents ... any intelligent person would realise that dismissal of the headmaster was bound to have repercussions. But that as a matter of contract she could be restrained in some way from dismissing him because of those considerations I do not accept.'

## 10.4 UNFAIR TERMS IN CONSUMER CONTRACTS REGULATIONS 1994

These Regulations (considered at **5.3.2**) should be taken as affecting all consumer contracts including those made after January 1995. They introduce a general requirement that all terms in consumer contracts *which have not been individually negotiated* should be *fair*.

Individual consumers can seek to have unfair terms held to be non-binding. The Director General of Fair Trading was given new powers to seek undertakings and injunctions against the use of unfair terms. In response to these Regulations, the Office of Fair Trading (OFT) formed an Unfair Contract Terms Unit in 1995.

In 1996, the OFT, acting on the report of a disaffected parent, decided to challenge the fees in lieu of notice rule. The circumstances were that in February 1995, halfway through the spring term, a merger between two schools was announced which would take effect in the following September. That allowed parents about 6 weeks in which to give notice to withdraw their children before the merger took effect without incurring liability to pay fees in lieu of notice. During those 6 weeks, the parents would have an opportunity to visit the new site and discuss the proposed arrangements with staff and with each other. The complainant did not give notice during the 6-week period but, after the summer term had started, he gave notice which was expressed to take effect at the end of the summer term. This gave rise to a claim by the school for fees in lieu of notice. The complainant made a complaint to the OFT.

The OFT approached the school on the basis that the merger announcement was later than necessary, that the timing was a breach of the requirement of good faith, and that a claim for fees in lieu of notice in such circumstances was unfair. The OFT sought an undertaking from the school that fees in lieu of notice would not be charged and warned of an injunction if an undertaking was not given. They also questioned the operation of the rule as a general principle.

The Independent Schools Joint Council (as it then was) instructed solicitors to respond to this challenge by means of a detailed explanation of the history, nature and purpose of the fees in lieu of notice rule, the balance that it maintained and the reason why it was necessary. Explanation was also given of the reason why mergers are normally announced in January or February for the following September when it is not feasible to give longer notice, and of the period that allows for proper consultation. The OFT accepted this explanation and withdrew its objection.

The case is mentioned here to illustrate the point that whenever the fees in lieu of notice rule comes under a challenge of principle, the challenge should be defended. Without the protection of this rule, schools could be destabilised by small numbers of parents, and some schools might even have to close.

## 10.5 THE RATE OF FEES IN LIEU OF NOTICE

This is a short point, but it features surprisingly often in disputes over fees in lieu of notice. A school normally publishes its fees list in February or March, before the start of the summer term, for the following September. There will generally, but not always, be an increase in the fee levels, reflecting the annual pay increase for teachers, other rising costs and economic conditions generally. If the pupil is then withdrawn without notice during the summer term, a question sometimes arises about the rate of fees in lieu of notice: whether the liability is to pay at the rate prevailing in the term when the pupil was withdrawn and the contract breached, or at the new published rate for the following term, which is the term of notice. There can be a significant difference, especially if the child was a day-pupil when withdrawn or when short notice was given but the parents had contracted for boarding in the following term.

It is straightforward enough to provide in the standard terms and conditions that fees in lieu of notice will be payable at the full rate ignoring the value of any award or discount that would have applied to the pupil had he attended in the term of notice. However, the position often has to be considered for schools that do not yet use express terms and conditions.

The legal analysis that applies probably differs according to whether the parents have suddenly withdrawn the pupil in the middle of term or given short notice during the term. The first case is certainly a repudiatory breach of the contract by the parents. It is clear the parents do not intend to return the child for the following term, and the school is entitled to accept that position, seek to fill the place and also charge fees in lieu of notice. In the second case, the school is bound to continue supplying the services until the end of term if the fees have been paid. It is submitted, however, that the school is also entitled to treat the notice as a repudiatory breach of the contract with effect from the end of term. It may, therefore, attempt to fill the place and charge fees in lieu of notice. It is the withdrawal or short notice that gives rise to the right to fees in lieu of notice.

A different aspect of the problem arises in a case of a pupil who has a scholarship, exhibition, bursary, assisted place or some other award or discount. It is regularly argued that fees in lieu of notice are limited to the amount of the parental contribution. That is unsound in principle, since the purpose of the award or discount is to facilitate the education of the child and also to enhance the standing of the school. That fundamental purpose fails if the pupil has been withdrawn from attendance. To allow the discount would mean that the school is subsidising the breach, which would be an absurd position.

It has also been argued that the character of fees in lieu of notice is different from that of current term's fees, and that the school is not entitled to payment for consumables not consumed in the term of notice. This argument should normally fail. It was made clear in *Mount v Oldham Corporation* (above) that the cause of action for fees in lieu of notice is 'a term's fees'. Fees invariably include a number of consumables. However, if it is the custom and practice of the school to charge lunch as an extra or tea as an optional extra, those charges might not fall within fees in lieu of notice.

## 10.6   WHEN ARE FEES IN LIEU OF NOTICE PAYABLE?

The question addressed here is whether a term's fees in lieu of notice are payable at the time when notice to withdraw a pupil is given, or whether they are payable at the end of the term in which notice is given, or whether they are only payable at the start of the following term which is the term of notice. No decided case on the point has been reported.

As indicated above, an immediate withdrawal of the pupil without any notice at all is a repudiatory breach of contract by the parent. The school is entitled to accept that breach and would normally do so. The consequences are that the school is entitled to try and fill the place and to charge fees in lieu of notice whether or not the place is filled. The position is similar if parents give short notice during the term and withdraw the pupil at the end of term. Again, the school can accept the breach.

In either case, the breach brings the primary layer of contractual obligations to an end whereupon the secondary layer of obligations comes into effect, namely liability to pay for the consequences of the breach.

When the school accepts a repudiatory breach committed by parents it is entitled to invoice for fees in lieu of notice immediately without having to wait until the start of the following term. This is because the amount of the liability is crystallised at the moment of breach.

The position may be different if the school does not accept the breach but decides to leave the position open in the hope the parent will change his mind. The right to sue for fees in lieu of notice will then arise on the earlier of the school eventually accepting the breach or the first day of the following term.

In a case that was settled, short notice was given during the summer term but the school did not accept the breach or try and fill the place. The pupil then returned for the autumn term and was withdrawn at the end of the autumn term without any further notice having been given. The view taken by the school following advice was that by not having accepted the breach, the school had left the parents the choice of paying for a term of education not received or receiving the term of education, and the parents had chosen the latter. The school was not entitled to further fees in lieu of notice.

It will be seen from the above that, in the absence of an express condition dealing with these circumstances, the school should act decisively once notice has been received. The least controversial practice in the absence of an express term is to invoice when short notice is received, but express the invoice payable on the first day of the term of notice. But a school is entitled to invoice for immediate payment if it so wishes.

The question of whether the school can accept the breach and sue in the term when notice is given or whether it must wait 2 or 3 months in order to sue can be of more than academic interest if there is reason to think the family might be moving abroad or may otherwise be difficult to trace in 3 months' time.

## 10.7  THE PERIOD OF NOTICE

The custom and practice for at least 100 years, and probably much longer, and therefore an implied, if not express, condition of the contract, is that notice will be not less than one school term. For these purposes, a school term is the period between and including the first and last days of the term as advertised by or on behalf of the governors.

The meaning of 'a term's notice' was recently considered in *English v Mill Hill School Foundation* [1997] reported in EPLI. It was held that where the school's terms and conditions defined 'term' and what was meant by a full term's written notice, even a few days less than a full term's notice is inadequate and the school is entitled to fees in lieu of notice with interest.

In earlier days, some schools required only half a term's notice to be given. That was the situation in *Pott v Stevens* (1948) 99 LJ 164. It is assumed that this was an express term of the contract. In the absence of an express term to that effect, the notice period should be taken as being a full term. That was the period contemplated in *Mount v Oldham Corporation* (see **10.3.3** above).

## 10.8   THE NOTICE PERIOD FOR EXTRA TUITION

Extra tuition may be for music lessons, remedial or additional teaching or simply an extra language or activity. Often, extra tuition is provided by visiting teachers known as peripatetics who supply their services to more than one school. The school's contract with a peripatetic may require the school to give that teacher a term's notice. In that case, the school would expect a term's notice from the parents.

This can work harshly. For example, it may be that in the first half of the summer term the pupil finds that extra tuition and associated study and practice is imposing too great a strain and a distraction from preparation for public examinations, or else the demands made by sports teams, school orchestra, choir and other activities are proving too much. If a term's notice has to be given, it will not expire until the end of the next autumn term which is 8 months away. Either there is pressure on the pupil to continue with the tuition when it may not be in that child's best interests to do so or the parents are in effect asked to pay for a term and half of tuition for which no value is received. That can very easily become a source of irritation on which other minor complaints are heaped, and the whole relationship of trust and confidence is undermined.

It is much better practice to settle for half a term's notice or that sum in lieu of notice, whatever the standard terms and conditions may provide.

## 10.9   THE FORM OF NOTICE

Standard terms and conditions invariably require notice of withdrawal to be given in writing, addressed to and actually received by the head. They should also provide that no other notice will suffice and that notices must be hand-delivered to the head or sent by recorded or guaranteed delivery post to the school address.

It is good practice to insist on strict requirements of this nature. One child-centred reason is that withdrawal of a pupil may have a significant effect on the child's education. It is a matter which ought to be discussed between parents and head in any event. As a matter of courtesy and good sense, it should be discussed before notice is given but, if no such discussion has taken place, the head should have an early opportunity to invite the parents at least to discuss the matter over the telephone. Withdrawal of a pupil can seem to the head and staff as a rejection of the school and, if that is the case, a good head wants to know the reason.

A sound management reason for imposing strict requirements as to the form and delivery of the notice is to avoid the many opportunities for misunderstanding. There have been cases in which parents said, truthfully or otherwise, that they had given oral or written notice to the form teacher who had failed to pass it on or who had said that short notice would be acceptable; or they had given oral notice to the head who had forgotten; or that notice sent by post had gone astray. In one case, an undated form of notice was found crumpled up in the school letterbox in August, whereas the parents insisted they had delivered it in an envelope in early April. In a number of instances, there have been good grounds for suspicion that a form of notice has been backdated.

In the absence of an express contractual term, the custom and practice is that notice should be given in writing, but parents will not necessarily know this and the point was not covered in either *Mount v Oldham Corporation* or *Price v Dennis*. It ought to be covered in the standard terms and conditions.

## 10.10  TIMING

Standard terms and conditions should make it clear whether notice must be given *before* the first day of term or if a notice given *on* the first day of term will be sufficient. Parents have been known to argue the *de minimis* principle that the law disregards very small differences. Strictly, however, that argument should not prevail when there is an express condition making it clear that notice must be received before the first day of term. (See *English v Mill Hill School Foundation* discussed at **10.7** above.)

Leaving aside the strict legal position in these cases, the fees in lieu of notice rule should be operated in a manner that is fair and reasonable, having regard to the purposes of the rule. If the school has not been prejudiced by a notice that is a day or so late, the notice should be treated in a manner that is appropriate in all the circumstances.

## 10.11  PROVISIONAL NOTICE

Provisional notice given by a parent to withdraw a pupil is of two kinds: (1) a term's provisional notice; or (2) less than a term's provisional notice.

A term's provisional notice is normally given when a parent would like the pupil to stay on, but other events such as financial problems or a pending divorce or job relocation make it unlikely that he (or she) will be able to do so. In those circumstances, an agreement will normally be reached between the parent and the head so that the risk of incurring fees in lieu of notice will not arise.

Less than a term's provisional notice is most likely to arise when the parent is dissatisfied with one or another aspect of the school. Perhaps the child is not making sufficient progress in the classroom or is unhappy or there is some perceived failure of pastoral care which the head recognises is in the power of the school to improve. In this case, an agreement may be reached which varies the normal terms of the contract so that the pupil may be withdrawn on short notice without the parents having to pay fees in lieu. Another instance may occur if the pupil has been unwell for some time and there is doubt about how soon he (or she) will be able to come back. This latter case can eventually turn into a frustration of the contract.

The essential point about provisional notice is that the head and parent have reached a mutual understanding which both of them recognise as a variation of the normal contractual arrangement. It is also essential that the parties reach a clear understanding as to the duration of the provisional notice and when it ceases to apply. There have been examples of a parent suddenly withdrawing the pupil in the middle of a term and claiming to rely on a provisional notice given a year or more earlier. Invariably, the dispute centres around the nature of the notice given, the reasons for it and the understanding that was reached about the period for which it would be valid.

In *Gregory v Frensham Heights Educational Trust Ltd* (1997) 4 EPLI 66, the parent claimed that the headmaster had accepted an open-ended provisional notice. The headmaster's recollection was that provisional notice given early in the autumn term led to a resolution of the problems by the end of that term. This was confirmed by a Christmas card from the parent with a message to the headmaster saying 'I think we have cracked it – I owe you a bottle of champagne'. The pupil then returned for the start of the spring term but was suddenly withdrawn after the first few days because of an alleged recurrence of the problem. The parent refused to pay fees or fees in lieu of notice and counterclaimed the return of fees paid in earlier terms. It was held that an agreement for open-ended provisional notice would have been wholly unusual. The headmaster would have had no authority from the governors to make such an agreement and the parent had not proved to the contrary. Accordingly, the school's position was upheld and the parent's counterclaim was dismissed.

Because of the scope for misunderstandings over provisional notice, standard terms and conditions should contain a clear description of what is meant by that expression to place the matter beyond doubt.

Provisional notice may also be given by the school to the parents and this follows broadly the same rules. Perhaps the head is of the opinion that the pupil's general conduct is unsatisfactory or else that the pupil is not making sufficient progress. Sometimes, the underlying problem is a learning difficulty and the school has no specialist staff who can give appropriate additional tuition or remedial teaching. In such a case, it would be usual for the head to agree with the parents that, unless there is improvement by the end of term, the parents will withdraw the pupil, without legal consequences for either side. If the parents are unwilling to co-operate, it may become necessary for the head to require the pupil to leave on the grounds that the school cannot adequately discharge its legal duties under the contract with parents and its duties to the pupil in tort.

## 10.12    CANCELLING ACCEPTANCE OF A PLACE

The issues that arise here have been covered in more detail at **6.4.9**. Briefly, once the contract has been formed and there is an agreed date when the child will enter the school as a pupil, the school is entitled to the first term's fees on the due date and one term's notice threafter. Thus, cancellation on less than a term's notice entitles the school to a term's fees against which the deposit must be credited. This is consistent with the structure of the contract for educational services. It cannot be said to be unfair in that context and for clarity it should be made an express term in the standard terms and conditions.

It is unlikely that more than a term's fees in lieu of notice would ever be *implied* but an *express* term can contain that provision. It might, however, be treated as an unfair term within the meaning of the Unfair Terms in Consumer Contracts Regulations 1994. This is suggested because of the relatively long period between contractual commitment and the pupil entering the school, and also because the contract is essentially one of personal services to a child.

In one case under advice, the contract was formed. The pupil then spent an induction weekend at the school where he was miserable. The parents, supported by medical evidence, contended that it was not in the child's best interests to attend the school and that, in those circumstances, the school would be unable to safeguard and promote the welfare of the child as required under s 87(1) of the Children Act 1989. The school did not in the event charge a term's fees. Whether it would have been entitled to do so depends on the facts of the case. Mere unhappiness for a day or two would not be enough to release the parents, but a serious fault on the part of the school would.

## 10.13    WHEN THE PUPIL DECIDES TO LEAVE

A pupil aged 16 and over is at school voluntarily and is free to leave at any time if he is prepared to take the consequences under the school rules. For these reasons, there should be an express contractual term dealing with the financial consequences if the pupil walks out contrary to his parents' wishes and without the consent of the school. In the absence of an express term, it may be argued with some force that there is an implied term that the parents warrant the pupil's attendance and that they are fixed with the pupil's actions accordingly. This is likely to be the result. Since it is plainly necessary for the pupil to attend if education is to be delivered, it cannot be said that the contract is frustrated if one of the parties, or an agent of a party, is at fault. As yet, there are no reported cases on the point.

## 10.14    COMMON DISPUTES OVER FEES IN LIEU OF NOTICE

The following is a summary of the main issues that have arisen over fees in lieu of notice since 1985. They illustrate the wide scope of disputes that have actually occurred and in many instances have been heard at a small claims arbitration.

### 10.14.1    Cancellation of acceptance of a place

This heading covers a variety of cases where a place has been accepted but the parents change their mind about the school, perhaps because of adverse publicity about the school or because the child was unhappy at a preview event. It also covers the case where the fee-payer has been made redundant and will be unable to afford the fees. On occasions there is simply a 'no show' at the start of the autumn term. None of these instances are likely to involve events that frustrate the contract at law. However, schools sometimes waive the term's fees but retain the deposit in a *genuine* case where it is equitable to do so and in the interests of good relations with feeder schools.

### 10.14.2    Counting weeks

Parents sometimes claim that as they withdrew the pupil in, say, the second week of term they need only pay fees in lieu for the first two weeks of the following term. That defence fails. A term's notice means a term's notice for the period between and including the first and last day of the term as published. That is custom and practice, and is normally provided in the standard terms and conditions, in any event.

### 10.14.3    The rate of fees in lieu

The parent who argues that the rate of fees in lieu of notice is the pre-increase rate, or the day rate only in the case of a boarder, ought to fail in that argument if the terms and conditions make the position clear, and by custom and practice in any event.

### 10.14.4    Complaints about change

There are numerous disputes concerning changes to the size and location of the school, its premises and facilities, the academic and games curriculum and the structure and composition of classes, or changes to the way in which the school is run, to the rules and disciplinary framework, to the length of school terms and the school day and to other aspects of the school. Another complaint is about mergers. Parents will normally have to pay fees in lieu of notice in these cases, since a cycle of change is an inherent characteristic of every successful school.

### 10.14.5    The family is leaving the area

The family may be moving out of choice to another part of the country, or a parent's employment may have been relocated or he (or she) may have been posted abroad. The parents' defence may be stronger in the case of a day-pupil than a boarder, but will normally fail. However, a forced move at short notice can give rise to a legal argument that the contract has been frustrated in the case of a day-pupil and even for a boarding pupil if the contract was for day education only. The school should enquire whether a parent's relocation expenses include provision for fees in lieu of notice.

### 10.14.6    Alleged defective teaching

The context is normally a learning difficulty, a failure to notice a change in the syllabus, a poor teacher in a particular year or examination disappointment. In an extreme case there may be a fundamental breach by the school, but in the majority of cases the parents are ordered to pay fees in lieu of notice. An exception would be where the poor teaching was in a subject that was of fundamental importance to the next stage of the pupil's education or career.

### 10.14.7   Complete breakdown of education at the school

There have been cases in which a number of parents have withdrawn pupils alleging that there was a complete breakdown of education and pastoral care. These cases depend on their facts. The most useful authority is *Price v Dennis* (1988) LEXIS, CA, discussed at **10.3.3**.

### 10.14.8   The pupil was unhappy and/or became ill

This is a wide category. In one case, building work started on an adjoining plot exacerbating a pupil's asthma. The heading also covers pupils who do not settle and are withdrawn after the first week, pupils who cannot find a friendship group and cases of bullying. These cases tend to involve legal argument about fundamental breach and frustration of contract and also negligence, and turn on their individual facts.

### 10.14.9   Alleged defect in formation of contract

In one unreported case, a parent had accepted a place and paid a deposit. The place was conditional upon success in entrance examinations. The parent changed his mind about the school and withdrew the pupil from the entrance examinations. He then claimed the return of the deposit on the grounds that a fundamental condition of the contract – success in the entrance examination – had not been satisfied. He claimed the return of his deposit and resisted the claim for a term's fees. He failed. He had to pay a term's fees and the deposit was credited.

### 10.14.10   The place has been filled

Parents often argue that following cancellation or withdrawal of a pupil the place has been filled; or, alternatively, if the school was a successful school it would have been filled. The law under *Mount v Oldham Corporation* [1973] 1 QB 309, CA, is that fees in lieu of notice are their own cause of action. The school does not have to prove its loss or mitigate its loss. It is entitled to fees in lieu of notice whether or not the place has been filled. In any event it is unlikely (although not impossible) that a place will be filled during the course of the school year.

### 10.14.11   Discontinuing extra tuition

Most schools require half a term's notice to discontinue extra tuition such as music. Some schools require a full term's notice because that is their commitment to the peripatetic teacher. Disputes tend to revolve round the quality of tuition, the pupil's interest, aptitude and willingness to work, and the demands made on the pupil's time by the other activities of the school.

### 10.14.12   Parental contribution

The issue here is whether fees in lieu of notice are payable gross or whether parents are liable only for the parental contribution in cases where the pupil had a scholarship, exhibition, bursary or assisted place. It is custom and practice that assistance given to pupils, often out of charitable funds, is intended to enable the pupil to attend school, and not to subsidise a breach of contract.

### 10.14.13   Disputes over the notice given

Parents sometimes claim to have given written notice of withdrawal which was not acknowledged by the school, or they say they gave oral or written notice to a house master or teacher who, they claim, said that was sufficient. On occasions, a letter of notice which has patently been backdated is found in the school letterbox. Efficient terms and conditions will normally overcome these problems.

### 10.14.14   Provisional notice

This is discussed at **10.11**.

### 10.14.15   League tables

Parents sometimes claim that a fall in the school's position in the league tables justifies withdrawal of the pupil without a term's notice. Of itself, it does not.

### 10.14.16   Allegations of discrimination

Pupils have been withdrawn on the pretext that, although there is no physical bullying or harassment, they are being left out of activities because of race, gender or disability. Parents do not normally succeed in making out these claims unless there is concerted misconduct sufficient to amount to bullying in the legal sense. Bullying is discussed at **15.3**.

### 10.14.17   Bussing in

In one case, the school provided transport to and from the child's home each day. The family then moved 5 miles away, outside the range of the school's transport. The parents claimed the school was in fundamental breach for not re-routing the transport. They withdrew the pupil without notice. The parents were ordered to pay fees in lieu.

### 10.14.18   Alleged defamation

In a number of cases, parents have sought to justify withdrawal without notice by alleging that the head or a teacher has breached confidence or made defamatory statements about the pupil or parents. These cases turn on their facts.

### 10.14.19   Bogus qualifications of teacher

There have been a handful of cases in recent years where the academic qualifications of a head or teacher turned out to be bogus. These have been used as a pretext for withdrawing pupils without notice. These cases also turn on their facts. However, a parent relying on this ground would need to show some material connection between withdrawal of the pupil and the reason given. There is no statutory requirement for teachers at independent schools to have formal qualifications, although the school associations do make this a requirement of membership.

### 10.14.20   Scholarship withdrawn without justification

In one case, the governors considered that a pupil had abused his scholarship. The scholarship was withdrawn. The parents withdrew the pupil without notice alleging that the school had acted in breach of contract. These cases will turn on their facts. There is a reasonable expectation that, as a matter of natural justice and, therefore, an implied term of the contract, the head would consult with parents and give a clear warning before fees assistance of any kind is withdrawn. Wrongful withdrawal of an award for which consideration has been given would be a repudiatory breach by the school.

### 10.14.21   Notice of fees increase

In many cases, parents have used short notice of an increase in fees as a pretext for withdrawing a pupil without notice. *Pott v Stevens* (1948) 99 LJ 164 (discussed at **9.8.10**) suggests that they are entitled to take this course. However, the more modern view is that it is an implied term of the contract (which should also be made an express term) that fees will increase from time to time by a reasonable amount, and it is only necessary to give a term's notice of an amount that is higher than would be considered reasonable to take account of increasing costs and the prevailing economic conditions.

### 10.14.22   Preserving confidentiality

A 15-year-old girl pupil had under-age sex with her boyfriend. Fearing she was pregnant and not wanting to tell her parents, she confided in a member of staff. Arrangements were made for her to receive advice from a family planning clinic. The pupil was driven there by members of staff but they took no part in the consultation. The girl was prescribed, and took, a morning-after pill and was unwell for a few days. The parents alleged that the school had acted negligently and in breach of contract and sought to use this as a justification for not paying arrears of fees. The matter was settled when the parents were persuaded that the school had acted properly and in accordance with the principle in *Gillick*. They agreed to pay by instalments.

### 10.14.23   School-leaving age

A person ceases to be of compulsory school age when he (or she) has reached the age of 16 on 1 September of that school year (see **7.9.1**). Cases occasionally come before the courts in which the school claims fees in lieu of notice after a pupil who has been successful at GCSE has been offered a place in the sixth form but has declined it.

In one unreported case in East Anglia in 1997, it was held that the requirement to give notice or pay a term's fees in lieu of notice does not apply in respect of the GCSE term if the pupil will have reached school-leaving age by the start of the following term. It is suggested, with respect, that this decision is a misunderstanding of the contract with a school which provides educational services up to and including A-levels. However, the fact that the misunderstanding has arisen highlights the need to make the contractual position clear in the parent contract documents. The position should normally be that the pupil will be offered a place in the sixth form subject to satisfying the admission requirements at the time. Fees in lieu of notice will be payable if a sixth-form place is offered but not accepted, but will not be payable if a place is not offered.

# Chapter 11

## CARE AND SUPERVISION OF CHILDREN AT SCHOOL

### 11.1  INTRODUCTION

This chapter is mainly about the physical well-being and the care and supervision of children and their property at school and the civil claims that are brought when personal injuries and other loss or damage have been caused by breach of a legal duty. The chapter concerns the acts or omissions of teachers but it also covers the acts or omissions of pupils who cause injury to each other and to adults.

Because there is normally no contractual relationship between an independent school and its pupils, most claims for damages for personal injuries brought by or against a pupil will be based on the tort of negligence which is now considered in more detail.

### 11.2  THE LAW OF NEGLIGENCE

#### 11.2.1  Overview

Negligence was established as an independent tort by the House of Lords in *Donoghue v Stevenson* [1932] AC 562. Since then, the tort of negligence has been developed through the common law, made by judges in their courts with minimal intervention from Parliament.

Running in parallel with the law of negligence is another tort, *breach of statutory duty* The essence of a breach of statutory duty is that an obligation laid down by statute or regulation has been broken and the statute or regulation was of a type that was intended by Parliament to give individuals a right to sue in respect of that breach. Often, liability for a breach of statutory duty is *strict*, ie not dependent on the plaintiff proving fault or blame.

People commit negligent acts every day at home, in the work place and in public areas. Usually no harm is caused, and there is no legal negligence. A person is only negligent at law if he (or she) owed a *legal duty* of care (ie a duty to take reasonable care); and the duty was *breached*; and the breach *caused damage* of a type which the law recognises. Negligent conduct without each of these elements – duty, breach, causation and damage – has no legal consequences in the law of tort, although it may be a compliance offence with criminal sanctions.

Another important feature of the tort of negligence in its present stage of development is that the damage which is recognised by law as sufficient for an action in negligence (as distinct from professional negligence) is restricted to *personal injury* (which includes physical and psychological injuries) and *damage to property*. With some exceptions, considered in Chapter 12, economic, ie financial, loss alone, for example loss of earnings, is not sufficient to found an action in negligence, but a claim for economic loss can be added to an action that is properly founded on personal injury or damage to property.

## 11.2.2 Proving negligence

Proving negligence is an imprecise exercise which depends on the interaction of statements such as the following.

### (a) Foreseeability of risk/harm

There was a *real risk* as distinct from a mere possibility of injury or damage. It was a risk that a reasonable person would anticipate. It was also one that could not be justified on grounds of its social value or utility. It was one that could reasonably have been eliminated or minimised and then the harm would probably not have happened.

### (b) Proximity/neighbourhood

The person who suffered the harm should have been in the defendant's contemplation at the time of the act or omission. There was 'legal proximity' in that sense.

### (c) Just and reasonable

It was just and reasonable to impose a duty of care on the defendant in the particular circumstances. Doing so would not mean imposing restrictions that were impractical or unreasonable in terms of their scope or cost, for example requiring a kitchen environment in a home to be free of hazards or a school to be contained within fortress-style fencing. Imposing a duty of care would not mean curtailing daily activities to an unreasonable extent.

These three headings can be described as the *duty of care matrix*. If a duty of care is thus established the following further headings need to be considered.

### (d) Standard of duty

The duty being imposed was proportionate to the risk. For example, it is not a case of applying different standards between school and home where that is not justified.

### (e) Breach of duty

The defendant failed to use reasonable care, given the level of risk and given the *factual matrix*, ie the circumstances the defendant was presented with.

### (f) Causation

The defendant's act or omission wholly *caused* or else made a *material contribution* to the injury or damage without there being an intervening event that was the real cause.

## (g) Personal injury or damage

The plaintiff has actually suffered personal injury or damage to property. It is of a kind that was reasonably foreseeable even though the risk of it happening was slight and its extent is greater than could have been known at the time.

These variables are examined in more detail in the remainder of this chapter. Usually, liability will turn on perhaps one or two of them, such as foreseeability of risk or the standard of the duty or causation. They give very wide scope to a judge to decide each case on its particular facts without feeling unduly constrained by precedent other than on matters of settled principle. There is good reason to think that judges will on occasions be influenced by sympathy for the plaintiff and the knowledge that damages and costs will be paid by insurers.

## 11.3   THE EXISTENCE OF A DUTY OF CARE

The starting-point for legal negligence is to show that a duty of care existed as a matter of law. As noted above, the law does not impose a duty of care unless there is a harm which is reasonably foreseeable; and the person who might suffer harm is legally proximate or 'in neighbourhood'; and it is considered just and reasonable to impose a duty of care. These principles were restated by the House of Lords in *Caparo Industries v Dickman* [1989] 1 All ER 568. They are now considered in turn.

### 11.3.1   Reasonable foreseeability of harm

'Reasonably foreseeable' has reference to 'risk', ie that there is a foreseeable risk of harm, and is the first hurdle in establishing that a duty of care existed. It means 'real risk' as opposed to a mere possibility. It may be a small risk but it is none the less 'real' if a reasonable person would have anticipated it.

A recent illustration was the decision of the Court of Appeal in *Pearson v Lightning* (1998) *The Times*, 30 April. The defendant was a golfer whose ball bounced off a tree and hit another player, the plaintiff, 80–90 yards away on the next fairway. The defendant had been playing a difficult recovery shot which had to clear a coppiced hazel. It failed to clear the bush and was deflected to the left. The blow was sufficient to fell the plaintiff, causing a substantial injury to his right eye. When the defendant realised the ball was going towards the plaintiff he shouted 'Fore' as a warning, but the plaintiff did not hear him. The areas of dispute in this case centred on *risk* and the *duty of care*, there being no significant dispute over the factual matrix and causation.

In the leading judgment, Simon Brown LJ said that the central issue was whether there was a *real risk* that in playing the shot when he did, the defendant would cause injury to another player. The judge held that there was a real risk of injury as opposed to a mere possibility. Given the difficulty of the shot, which could all too easily go wrong and hit the coppiced hazel ahead, the likelihood of deflection of the ball onto the plaintiff was foreseeable. That was sufficient to establish a duty owed to the plaintiff and breach of it by the defendant. The risk of injury was not so remote that a reasonable person would not have anticipated it. On the facts of the case, the defendant should have called to the other players, asking whether they preferred him to play on or wait until they had safely passed. That would have been courteous and would have alerted them to the need to watch out. The risk the defendant took was small but sufficient to render him liable.

Reasonable foreseeability may be easier to assess in the case of a single act or omission, such as where a motorist overtakes in the face of oncoming traffic. He (or she) is reasonably likely to cause an accident if his overtaking manoeuvre can only be completed by driving too fast or in too short a distance for safety. If he is the cause of injury or damage he will be liable.

More difficult is foreseeability in 'kaleidoscope' situations such as the classroom or workplace if an element of risk is unavoidable and has to be balanced against social utility. In *Butt v Cambridgeshire and Ely County Council* (1970) 68 LGR 81 a class of 37 9- and 10-year-olds were using sharp pointed scissors. One child accidentally poked another child in the eye with his pair. The school authority was held not liable. Clearly there was risk, but it was outweighed by the social purpose and value of children of this age using scissors of that kind.

However, in *Black v Kent County Council* [1984] LGR 39, a child aged 7 was jabbed in the eye by a pair of sharp pointed scissors he was using in an art class of 27 7-year-olds. The school authority was held liable. It was held to be reasonably foreseeable that the use of sharp pointed scissors as compared with blunt-ended ones involved quite a degree of risk to children of this age.

The gymnasium carries high risk. Each exercise that is attended by risk should be treated as a single event rather than as a kaleidoscope situation. Injury is usually reasonably foreseeable. If current good practice is used together with the right level of care in the circumstances, then liability will be avoided.

The position is different in rugby and football, which are contact sports attended by a high level of risk even when that risk has been minimised. Contact sports are considered later at **11.9.9**.

The risks that arise from cricket depend to some extent on the nature and size of the ground being used. Cricket is essentially a set piece rather than a fast-changing scene. If the ground being used is so small that there is a risk of the ball causing personal injury or damage to the property of those not playing or spectating there is a much greater likelihood of liability than if the game is being played on a suitable ground.

In *Bolton v Stone* [1951] 1 All ER 1078, HL, a batsman had scored a 'six' and the ball went out of the ground and hit a passer-by. It was held that similar hits had occurred only about six times in the previous 30 years. The batsman had received the right kind of ball and dealt with it in the right kind of way, and it was a suitable cricket ground.

The risk of injury from that cause was not reasonably foreseeable, ie not necessarily likely to happen. In a later case, Lord Denning held there was no liability for damage to property when a housing estate was erected near the boundary of an established cricket ground. That case probably turned on arguments of social utility rather than foreseeability.

In *Clarke v Bethnal Green Borough Council* [1939] 3 All ER 54, it was held that there was no liability for a sudden accident, which could neither be foreseen nor prevented.

## 11.3.2    Legal proximity or neighbourhood

This is the second hurdle in establishing that a duty of care existed.

### (a)    The principle

Even when harm is likely to happen, a duty of care is owed only to those who are 'neighbours' ie, in legal proximity. No duty is imposed in respect of the world at large. In *Donoghue v Stevenson* [1932] AC 562, HL, Lord Atkin said that neighbours are:

> 'persons who are so closely and directly affected by my act that I ought reasonably to have them in contemplation when I am directing my mind to the acts or omissions that are called in question.'

The concept is one of *legal* proximity which will not always be the same thing as *physical* proximity. The concept also limits the categories of person who can claim that a duty was owed to them. An example might be where a motorist negligently causes an accident in which a teacher is so severely injured he (or she) will never be able to return to work. The school is put to the expense of finding his replacement and employing supply teachers in the interim. The motorist would be held in breach of duty to the teacher but would not be held in breach of duty to the school, there being insufficient legal proximity.

### (b)    Accidents and emergencies

A person who comes upon the scene of an accident or emergency is under no legal obligation to stop and help. He (or she) may have a moral duty to do so, but that is not necessarily the same thing as a legal duty. However, if a rescuer does stop and help he comes into a relationship of 'neighbourhood' or 'proximity' and falls under a legal duty of care. The standard of the duty will depend on the circumstances but will normally be low and sometimes very low. It will usually be difficult for a plaintiff to prove that his rescuer acted negligently.

In some circumstances, there will be an existing relationship of neighbourhood or proximity which compels a rescuer to help. A school is a good example, where teachers who are on duty are already *in loco parentis*. If a teacher in that case comes upon a pupil in the playground who has swallowed his (or her) tongue and may be thought in danger of choking to death, the teacher is under a duty to act.

In *Hippolyte v London Borough of Bexley* [1995] PIQR 309, CA, a 16-year old girl pupil suffered an asthma attack during a Home Economics lesson at a State school in January 1986. She sustained grave brain damage as a result. The court found that the girl started to use her inhaler at 10.15 am. It gave no relief. On three occasions, the teacher suggested she should go home but the pupil refused. On advice from a senior teacher, a note was written to the school secretary to the effect that the pupil should go home. At 10.45 am, the pupil was supported by two class mates and taken to the secretary's office, a distance of 105 paces. The pupil was gasping for breath and resisting. At 11.04 am, another teacher carried the pupil to reception. It was decided to call an ambulance but by coincidence at 11.02 am a call had already been made for an ambulance for another girl in distress. The ambulance arrived at 11.11 am and oxygen was immediately administered, but, the trial judge found, it was about 5 minutes too late.

The trial judge said that had been a developing situation, progressing from one which gave rise to concern, then to anxiety, then to alarm, then to serious alarm and crisis. The judge held that the steps taken at each stage of the escalating sequence from concern to crisis were such as reasonable teachers could reasonably be expected to take in all the circumstances. An important circumstance was that they were lay people and not medically trained. Steyn LJ added that awareness of the dangers of asthma was lower in 1986 than at the date of trial in 1994. Steyn LJ also stated:

> '... the common law has been cautious to recognise duties to take affirmative steps. The distinction between nonfeasance and misfeasance is still relevant. On the other hand, it has long been recognised that there is a special relationship between a teacher and a pupil which may potentially give rise to a duty on a teacher to take positive steps to protect the pupil from physical harm ... such duties to take affirmative action may arise when the requirements of foreseeability and proximity, as well as the requirement that it is reasonable and just to impose a particular duty, as explained in *Caparo Industries plc v Dickman* [1990] 2 AC 605 are satisfied ... It is not difficult to visualise circumstances in which a school may by conduct assume a relevant responsibility on which the parent and pupil then rely. Duties of affirmative action may be generated in such circumstances. In short, school children, whatever their ages, are in principle within the protective pale of a teacher for whom an education authority is responsible. Of course it will depend on all the circumstances of a particular case whether a duty of care is established.'

Less clear is the position of a teacher who is off duty and walking out of the playground on the way home. In terms of strict legal principle, he (or she) is not under a duty to act but if he does so he comes under a duty of care. Perhaps the victim is a pupil who has fallen from a structure or a piece of apparatus and may have suffered a head or neck injury. Perhaps the teacher is young and inexperienced and not a qualified first-aider and is unsure about correct procedures in these circumstances. It may also be that because the teacher is off duty he is no longer acting in the course of his employment, and his acts and omissions are not at that moment covered by the school's liability insurances (a convenient point at which to remember that everyone should obtain public liability insurance which will often be provided as an extension to a home contents policy).

Every such case will turn on its own facts. For example, at a boarding school there will be times when even a teacher who technically is 'off duty' may be regarded as 'on duty' and it becomes artificial to distinguish between a day-pupil and a boarder at the same school in an emergency. At the very least, there is a moral duty to act. Moreover, the negligence principles may be flexible enough to allow a judge to find that the teacher was acting in the course of employment and was insured, and whilst on school premises was in a relationship of proximity or neighbourhood.

Overall, it is not the purpose of the law to deter a teacher or anyone else from acting out of common humanity and offering help in an emergency. For a teacher in the circumstances described, there may be litigation risks either way and it is submitted that, in almost every case, the safe and proper course is for the teacher to have confidence in the law and render assistance.

### 11.3.3   Whether it is just and reasonable to impose a duty of care

This is the third hurdle in establishing that a duty of care existed. Even where harm is likely to happen to a person in legal proximity, it will not always be found just and reasonable to impose a duty of care.

An everyday example from the home is where a busy mother leaves a sharp kitchen knife on a work surface within possible reach of a very young child who is then injured by it. It is submitted that it would not be held just and reasonable to impose a duty of care on the mother to ensure that such a risk could never arise. One recent authority in support of this is the *Surtees* case [1991] 2 FLR 559, discussed at **11.4.1** below.

There can be an element of overlap between 'proximity' and 'just and reasonable'. It is not just and reasonable to impose a duty of care in respect of a person who is not in proximity.

There are signs of reluctance on the part of the court to impose a duty of care in tort when the rights and duties of parties are regulated by contract. This may be of relevance to an independent school where the duties between school and parents arise under the parent contract, and the duties between school and pupil are based on tort.

*Grenar v The Royal School (Hindhead)* (unreported, 1997) is a recent first instance decision in point. The parents owed £8,000 to the school in unpaid fees. Their contract with the school provided that 'the school may withhold any information or property while fees are unpaid'. When the parents refused to reach any agreement at all for payment of fees, the school warned that it would withhold the pupil's GCSE results, certificates, National Record of Achievement and portfolio of artwork. The pupil issued proceedings claiming that the school had negligently caused her to suffer a psychiatric condition known as 'an adjustment disorder' by withholding this information and the documents. On the application of the school, his Honour Judge Sleeman, sitting at Epsom County Court on 23 June 1997, struck out the claim on the ground, among others, that it was not just and reasonable to impose a duty of care in relation to the pupil in these circumstances. To do so would have the effect of defeating the school's contractual right.

The *just and reasonable* principle also arises in the context of activities which necessarily carry risk but are so much a part of daily life that imposing liability in negligence would involve unacceptable levels of curtailment. These are considered later in relation to 'social utility' and 'minimising and balancing risk'.


## 11.4   THE STANDARD OF CARE

Once it has been established that a duty of care exists (because there is a reasonable foreseeability of harm, there is legal proximity or neighbourhood and it is just and reasonable to impose a duty of care), the next question to be considered is the *standard* of the duty, ie the standard of care required having regard to the known risks and the circumstances.

There are two distinct aspects to the standard of duty:

- In any given circumstances, from supervising children in a playground to teaching them rock-climbing, the standard of the duty is the same whether the supervisor is an expert or a novice. In this sense, there is only one standard, and the law does not recognise differing degrees of negligence.
- However, the standard of the duty *does* differ according to the activity. Supervising a playground requires the standard of the careful parent, and no more. Supervising rock-cimbing demands a much higher standard of expertise altogether.

### 11.4.1 The careful parent

A parent at home may have 24-hour care of a small number of children. The attention which a parent can give is punctuated by the demands of running a home, dealing with such matters as cooking, washing up, cleaning, laundry, shopping, answering the telephone and callers to the house. In addition, there may be financial and administrative matters and correspondence before any consideration is given to working and leisure activities and time spent on family matters. The demands are constant, and the courts recognise the impracticability of imposing too high a standard of duty.

An illustration of this was the decision of the Court of Appeal in *Barr-Lindsay v Barr-Lindsay and Another* (unreported), January 1996. A 7-year-old boy, deaf in both ears from infant meningitis, was allowed by his mother to play a game of hide and seek that involved racing across the road outside her house with 'normal' 11- and 12-year-old children. The mother instructed the children to look after the 7-year-old. At one point, a 10-year-old tried to restrain him but he ran into the side of a passing car and suffered brain damage. It was held that 'there is a duty of care but the parent should not be held in breach unless he or she has failed to take reasonable care to take reasonable precautions for the child's safety'. The mother did not actually know about the racing aspect. In other words, what matters is what the mother knew, not what she ought to have known.

Another example of the standard to be expected of a parent was the Court of Appeal decision in *Surtees v Kingston-Upon-Thames Borough Council* [1991] 2 FLR 559. A child living with foster parents was scalded by hot water. It was held that the duty owed by foster parents is exactly the same as that owed by the ordinary parent:

> '... the court should be wary in its approach to holding parents in breach of a duty of care owed to their children ... we should be slow to characterise as negligent the care which *ordinary loving and careful mothers* are able to give to individual children, given the rough-and-tumble of home life' (emphasis added).

### 11.4.2 The teacher as a professional

The working life of a teacher at school is in most respects very different from that of the parent at home. A teacher is normally in charge of many more children. Often the children will be of a similar age to each other but will have very different responses to discipline and authority. The periods of care and supervision will be much shorter.

A teacher is an education professional who will be involved in a greater variety of activities and sometimes in situations that carry much higher risk than at home.

Teachers will normally have had more specialist training and developed greater skills in certain respects than a lay parent.

The main overlap between teachers and parents concerns the practical reality that neither can be expected to watch children all the time. Some risk is inherent in many aspects of child development and the standard of care differs according to events and situations. Not every injury caused to a child will give rise to blame or a right to damages.

### 11.4.3 Some relevant cases

The following cases illustrate the way in which the courts have moved from the approach that said '*A school master is bound to act as a careful father*' to the more modern approach, which is that teachers will be treated as professionals and the scope and standard of their duties will depend on all the circumstances of the case.

#### *Williams v Eady* [1893] 10 TLR 41, CA
In this case, it was held that a schoolmaster is bound to act as a *careful father* in taking notice of the ordinary nature of young boys, their tendency to do mischievous acts and their propensity to meddle with anything that came in their way, and that, having phosphorous in his house, he was bound not to leave it in any place in which they might get at it.

#### *Glasgow Corporation v Muir* [1943] AC 448
Lord Thankerton said: 'the court must be careful to place itself in the position of the person charged with the duty and to consider what he or she should have reasonably anticipated as a natural and probable consequence of neglect, and not to give undue weight to the fact that a distressing incident has happened or that witnesses in the witness box are prone to express regret that they did not take some step which it is now realised would definitely have prevented the accident.'

#### *Ricketts v Erith Borough Council* [1943] 42 LGR 471
It was said that when considering the position of a teacher at a school, 'one has to visualise a parent with a very large family'.

#### *Rich v London County Council* [1953] 1 WLR 895
It was held that the school authority was under no obligation to take measures to keep boys away from an unfenced pile of coal in the school playground because *a careful parent* would not necessarily do so.

#### *Martin v Middlesborough Corporation* (1965) 63 LGR 385
There was a broken milk bottle in the playground. An 11-year-old girl slipped on some ice and cut her hand on the broken glass. It was held that the risk of this injury was foreseeable. A *reasonably prudent parent* would have made better arrangements for disposing of empty milk bottles.

#### *Lyes v Middlesex County Council* (1962) 61 LGR 443
It was held to be important to apply the *careful or prudent parent test* in the context of the school rather than the home. In the school situation, a teacher has the care of far more children than a parent ever has to deal with (although the fact that the risk of injury arising from an activity which is considered safe in the home is no greater in the school when more children are participating will mean that there may not be liability).

*Beaumont v Surrey County Council* (1968) 66 LGR 580

The standard of care expected of a teacher was described as follows: a [Head]teacher is bound to take: 'all reasonable and proper steps to prevent any of the pupils under his care from suffering injury from inanimate objects, the actions of their fellow pupils, or from a combination of the two. That is a high standard' (Jeffrey Lane J).

*Murphy v Bradford Metropolitan Council* [1991] ICR 80, CA

Lord Jauncey said that the scope of the duty depends on all the circumstances of the case. In some situations, the parent's duty to child will be identical to that of another person to the child.

*Smart v Gwent County Council* [1991] LEXIS

A girl aged 3 lost the fleshy tip of her thumb when she trapped her hand in the wooden door of a Wendy house at nursery school. It was held that there had been a reasonably foreseeable risk of injury on the hinged side of the door but the risk was no greater than it would have been in the child's own home. The children were not out of control, nor were all 30 of them playing in the Wendy house at the same time. The class was supervised by a competent teacher. A prudent parent would run the same risk.

### 11.4.4   Objective standard

As noted in the previous section, the law does not recognise differing degrees of negligence. A person is negligent or not according to the standard which should apply in the particular case. It is an objective standard, ie what a reasonable person engaged in that activity *should* do, not what a particular person has done. Examples of this rule are as follows.

### *(a)   Competitive sport*

The standard of care required of a participant in relation to fellow players and spectators is usually low. This must be the case because each player consents to the normal risks inherent in the sport, although there is no consent to deliberate breaches of the rules or misconduct and skulduggery. The Court of Appeal decision in *Smoldon v Whitworth* [1997] ELR 249 explained rather than altered the standard of duty. In that case, the duties under consideration were principally those of the referee.

### *(b)   Motorists*

Motorists are expected to achieve standards approaching perfection. It was decided by the Court of Appeal in *Nettleship v Weston* [1971] 2 QB 691 that a learner driver must exercise the skill of a reasonably competent experienced driver.

This standard reflects the very high risk associated with motor vehicles and the fact that third-party risks must be insured by law. In general, inexperience, lack of intelligence, slow reactions or physical disability provide no excuse for legal negligence. Doing one's 'incompetent best' will not be a defence to negligence if it causes harm when using the appropriate standard of care would not have caused harm.

## (c) Children

Children will be judged objectively in accordance with standards of behaviour reasonably to be expected of a child of the age in question. As a gloss to this principle, a parent or teacher may be liable instead of the child because of a failure to exercise proper supervision and control over a young child.

## (d) Professional persons

A professional person, by which is meant a person who holds himself out as having a particular skill or profession, must attain the standard of the reasonably competent person exercising that skill or profession. A teacher may be such a person. However, the level of skill that is demanded in a particular case will depend on the extent of the risk. For example, the risks of ordinary play in the school playground are very much lower than the risks of rock climbing. The standard of care expected of the professional teacher will vary accordingly. There may be two generally accepted methods of doing things, both supported by a responsible and skilled body of opinion. It is not negligence to choose one method which, in the event, results in an accident instead of another method which, with hindsight, would not have caused injury.

### The case-law

The main authorities from the case-law are set out below. It should be noted, however, that professionals are expected to keep up to date with changes in guidance about good and best practice. The practices that were approved by the court in the case of *Wright* (below) are probably now out of date. It is quite possible the same facts would not be decided in the same way 45 years on.

### Bolam v Friern Hospital Management Committee [1957] 2 All ER 118
A medical negligence case in which McNair J said that if there are two conflicting opinions, the adoption of one practice will be justified if it is accepted as proper by 'a responsible body of medical men skilled in that particular art'. The *Bolam* test is of general application to professions or callings requiring special skill, knowledge or experience.

### Fryer v Salford Corporation [1937] 1 All ER 617
Slesser LJ thought that the fact that it was educational practice at the time not to guard stoves used in domestic science was an insufficient reason for not installing a guard. In other words, a body of opinion which is 'negligent' is not to be taken as 'responsible' for these purposes.

### Wright v Cheshire County Council [1952] 2 All ER 789, CA
A child was injured taking part in gymnastic exercises. The facts were that a 12-year-old boy was injured while vaulting. The boy who was supposed to help him land left on hearing the school bell. The teacher had instructed other pupils to assist in the safety procedure. It was held that this was a general and approved practice and the teacher was therefore not negligent. As noted above, it is unlikely this case would be decided in the same way today.

*Conrad v ILEA* (1967) 65 LGR 543
It was recognised that there were two schools of thought as to appropriate initial instruction in judo. The school authority was not liable for the pupil's injuries when one recognised practice was followed.

## 11.5   NEGLIGENCE IN PRACTICE

Having considered above the three elements that dictate whether a duty of care existed, and the standard of that duty, we now consider questions of balancing risk with social utility, and the negligence and contributory negligence of children.

### 11.5.1   Balancing and minimising risk

One of the greatest areas of risk at school is the ordinary play of children running, jumping, falling, rolling, tree climbing, throwing, wrestling, roller blading, tobogganing, and pursuing a host of other activities. There is ample authority from the case-law that injuries caused by children to themselves or others in the ordinary course of play at school will not of themselves give rise to a finding of negligence against the school authority provided reasonable care has been taken to minimise the risks.

There are many instances when an inflexible application of the negligence principles would mean that the normal activities of daily life would have to be curtailed to an unacceptable extent. This is another aspect of the 'just and reasonable' principle referred to earlier. It also recognises that there are many ordinary activities in daily life that carry inherent risk which cannot be eliminated or even minimised. A number of the issues relating to *risk* are considered below.

### (a)   Social utility – allowing children to develop normally

The courts recognise, in effect, that nature has assigned to children the full-time job of widening their experience, pushing out boundaries and testing limits. A balance has to be struck between protecting them from excessive danger and allowing them to develop normally. There will be bumps and bruises and sometimes serious injuries and even death. Such are the inherent risks of childhood. But social utility considerations include allowing children to develop normally, with the element of risk which that implies.

There is a line of cases from the 1930s onwards which recognises the 'social utility' of an activity and the inevitable trade-off between risk and normal development.

*Hudson v Governors of Rotherham Grammar School* [1938] LCT 303
Boys were using a cricket pitch roller. They accidentally caused it to roll onto one of their number. Hilbery J dismissed an action brought against the governors and a teacher, saying 'if boys were kept in cotton-wool, some of them would choke themselves with it'.

*Camkin v Bishop* [1941] 2 All ER 713, CA
A boy of 14 received injuries when ragging after being struck by a flying clod of earth thrown at him by another boy. Goddard LJ, exonerating the school authority, said:

'If every master is to take precaution to see that there is never ragging or horseplay among his pupils, his school would indeed be too awful a place to contemplate.'

## *Daborn v Bath Tramways Motor Co Ltd* [1946] 2 All ER 33, CA
Lord Asquith gave an example of 'social utility' as follows:

'... if all the trains in this country were restricted to a speed of 5 miles per hour, there would be fewer accidents, but our national life would be intolerably slowed down'.

## *Jeffrey v London County Council* (1954) 52 LGR 521
McNair J said that a balance has to be struck 'between the meticulous supervision of children ... and the very desirable object of encouraging their sturdy independence'.

## *Suckling v Essex County Council* (1955) *The Times*, 27 January
An 11-year-old boy was injured during horseplay involving a scorer knife which another boy had taken from a cupboard while the teacher was out of the room. Vaisey J said:

'It seems to me that if I were to hold that every school with small children was committing an actionable wrong in leaving unlocked such implements as these scorer knives, I would be putting an altogether excessive burden on educational establishments. Not only would it be difficult for them to be conducted in a successful and reasonable manner, but it would run the serious risk of turning these children into votaries of the principle of safety first. *It is better that a boy should break his neck than allow other people to break his spirit.*' (An element of judicial hyperbole not to be taken as a literal statement of the law!)

## *Ward v Hertfordshire County Council* (1969) 114 SJ 87, CA
It was said that it is wrong to try to protect children against minor injuries, such as grazed knees caused by falling down when running in the playground, 'by forbidding them the ordinary pleasures which school children so much enjoy'.

## *Simkiss v Rhondda Borough Council* (1983) 81 LGR 460, CA
Dunn LJ said that one had to balance the robustness which would make children take the world as they found it and the tenderness which would give them nurseries wherever they went. Social utility is relevant.

## *Van Oppen v Clerk to the Bedford Charity Trustees* [1989] 3 All ER 389, CA
Ralph Gibson LJ said:

'It is fundamental to the relationship between school and pupil that the school undertakes to educate him in as wide a sense as it reasonably can. This involves the school having the pupils in its care and it involves the pupils in various activities in the classroom, in the chapel, in the gymnasium, on the sports field and so on. There are risks of injury inherent in many human activities, even of serious injury in some. Because of this, the school, having the pupils in its care, is under a duty to exercise reasonable care for their health and safety. Provided due care is exercised in this sphere, it seems to me that the school's duty is fulfilled.'

## *Barr-Lindsay v Barr-Lindsay and Another* (unreported), January 1996, CA
This case, discussed at **11.4.1**, is a further illustration of the courts' reluctance to find parents negligent when their children are injured in the ordinary course of play.

## *(b)   Minimising risk by warning of dangers*

Perhaps the most dangerous areas of a school are the gymnasium, swimming pool, science laboratories, workshops and transport systems, but there are many other circumstances of potential danger both on school premises and during out-of-school trips. Teachers are expected to warn of dangers in appropriate terms. That depends on the normal 'children factors' given at (c) below, including the ages and understanding of the children. Reported cases on this issue include those discussed at **11.9.5** and the following:

### *Crouch v Essex County Council* (1966) 64 LGR 240

It was held that clear warnings given to a class may absolve the teacher from liability, *depending on the age of the class* and on whether the class might be expected to be well behaved as opposed to being given to horseplay or carelessness.

### *Noonan v ILEA* (1974) *The Times*, 14 December

Warnings of the specific dangers involved in a particular activity should be given. For dangerous substances, 'don't touch' is not sufficient unless the risk is obvious to a child of that age. A more graphic and specific warning is required.

## *(c)   Minimising risk in relation to the use of equipment*

The degree of supervision required when children are using equipment that is potentially dangerous will depend on all the variables of the case, such matters as the age and understanding of the children, their intelligence, disabilities and generally known behaviour, the nature of the equipment and the place where it is used and the duration of the activity. Some examples from the cases are the following:

### *Langham v Governors of Wellingborough School and Fryer* (1932) 30 LGR 276, CA

A boy in the playground hit a golf ball which injured a boy in the school buildings. The school authority was held not liable because it was not proved that the supervising master knew that boys hit golf balls dangerously or that the master failed to exercise proper supervision on this occasion.

### *Smerkinich v Newport Corporation* (1912) 76 JP 454

A 19-year-old was injured when using a circular saw at a technical institute. The institute was held not to be liable, but the decision might have been different had the plaintiff been a child.

### *Fryer v Salford* [1937] 1 All ER 617

The school provided an unguarded cooker which 11-year-old girls crowded round. One girl's apron caught fire. It was held that the school should have anticipated this danger and provided a guard: the school was negligent because it had not done all that was reasonable to guard against a reasonably foreseeable risk.

### *Suckling v Essex County Council* (1955) *The Times*, 27 January

The pupil was an 11-year-old boy and the equipment was a scorer knife. Further details of the case have been given above.

### *Crouch v Essex County Council* (1966) 64 LGR 240

See *(b)* above.

*Butt v Cambridgeshire and Ely County Council* (1970) 68 LGR 81
A class of 37 9- and 10-year-olds were using sharp pointed scissors. One child accidentally poked another child in the eye with his pair. The school authority was held not liable.

*Black v Kent County Council* [1984] LGR 39
A child aged 7 was jabbed in the eye by a pair of sharp pointed scissors he was using in an art class of twenty-seven 7-year-olds. The school authority was held liable. It was held to be reasonably foreseeable that the use of sharp pointed scissors as compared with blunt ended ones involved quite a degree of risk to children of this age.

*Noonan v ILEA* (1974) *The Times*, 14 December
Referred to at (b) above.

*Barnes v Bromley London Borough Council* (1983) *The Times*, 16 November
A teenage pupil in the metal workshop was given an old and brittle riveting tool to use. The boy was working on a bicycle. He hit the bicycle with the tool, it splintered and he was injured. The school was held negligent in view of the condition of the tool. The risks of an activity that carried dangers had not been minimised. The boy was held one-third to blame for his own conduct.

*Porter v Barking and Dagenham London Borough Council* (1990) *The Times*, 9 April
Two 14-year-old boys were practising their shot putting unsupervised. One was injured. It was held there was no liability from the failure to supervise boys of this age in that activity. If, however, the activity had been supervised and it had been found that the teacher could reasonably have prevented the accident happening, the school would probably be held liable.

### 11.5.2 Negligence and contributory negligence of children

This section examines some of the circumstances under which a child may be held negligent for his own acts or omissions which cause injury to other children or third parties. It also looks at the circumstances under which a child may be found guilty of *contributory negligence*. As a matter of legal theory, a child can be capable of negligence and contributory negligence at any age.

In practice, the standard of care expected of a child is set in proportion to the responsibility to be expected of a child of the age in question. This amounts to a departure from the normal rule that negligence is judged by an objective standard of care. Instead, the age and mental development of the particular child is considered in relation to that of the average child of that age (*Duffy v Fahy* [1960] Ir Jur Rep 69, at 74). In practice, however, the courts are not anxious to penalise a child who is unusually intelligent or well informed.

### (a) Contributory negligence

A person whose negligence is in part the cause of his own injuries is said to be guilty of contributory negligence and his damages will be reduced accordingly. This rule is provided by s 1(1) of the Law Reform (Contributory Negligence) Act 1945. The rule also applies to certain torts other than negligence. The main cases concerning the contributory negligence of children are the following.

### *Donovan v Landy's Ltd* [1963] IR 441
A child of 6½ was held capable of contributory negligence.

### *Gough v Thorne* [1966] 1 WLR 1387, CA
A 13-year-old girl stepped past a stationary lorry whose driver had beckoned her to cross. She was then knocked down by a negligent motorist. It was held that she was not guilty of contributory negligence.

### *Morales v Eccleston* [1991] RTR 151, CA
An 11-year-old boy was kicking a ball in the middle of a road with traffic passing in either direction. He was struck by a driver who was found to be negligent. It was held that the boy's damages would be reduced by 75%.

### *Yachuk v Oliver Blaise Co Ltd* [1949] AC 386, PC
A 9-year-old boy was given some petrol. He set fire to it and was injured. Those who supplied it were found liable. It was held that at his age he could not be expected to appreciate the dangerous properties of petrol and he was not therefore guilty of contributory negligence.

### *Barnes v Bromley London Borough Council* (1983) *The Times*, 16 November
See **11.5.1***(c)* above.


### *(b)   Injuries caused to others*

Children of all ages may be the cause of injuries to other children and adults. A child is sued through his *guardian ad litem* who handles the proceedings for him. A child may have public liability insurance by virtue of his parents' home contents policy or the public liability policy maintained by a school. If not, it is unlikely he could pay damages unless he was the beneficiary of a non-discretionary trust fund. Cases in which children have been held legally liable for their torts include the following:

### *Staley v Suffolk County Council and Dean Mason* (unreported) 26 November 1986
A 12-year-old boy threw a tennis ball into a classroom at another boy and hit the dinner lady, causing injury. The boy was held liable.

### *Gorely v Codd* [1967] 1 WLR 19
A boy of 16 was held negligent in the use of an air rifle.


Injuries caused by one pupil to another that have occurred in recent years have included: horseplay between 14-year-olds with a hockey stick which resulted in damage to a child's front teeth; deafness caused to a 14-year-old boy by the negligent throwing of a shot; and injuries sustained in the course of fighting in the playground, on a sports pitch and elsewhere. Many other situations can be envisaged, often which could not reasonably have been prevented by teachers or other supervising adults.

## 11.6 BREACH OF THE DUTY OF CARE

Once a duty of care has been established, a person is in breach of duty if he (or she) has caused personal injury or damage of a kind recognised at law for the particular tort (in this case negligence) because his acts or omissions were below the standard of care required of the 'reasonable person' in the particular circumstances.

As we have seen, the standard of care expected will be very much higher in some cases than in others but it is an *objective standard* and will apply equally to a novice as to an expert acting or omitting to act in those circumstances.

Also, as we have seen, the concept of what is reasonable will depend on various aspects of the risk of harm and in particular:

- the magnitude of the risk;
- the opportunities for minimising or eliminating the risk and the relative cost and difficulty of doing so;
- the social utility or value of the activity or omission giving rise to the risk, for example, allowing cars to travel at 70 miles per hour on a motorway, instead of restricting the speed to 50 miles per hour.

Because the standard of care is an *objective standard* the defendant is always viewed as an hypothetical person. In cases of ordinary negligence, he (or she) used to be described as 'the man on the Clapham omnibus'. In professional negligence, he (or she) is described as 'the reasonably competent man or woman exercising that skill or profession'.

There are a number of defences to an allegation of breach of the duty of care. These are considered briefly below.

### 11.6.1 Vicarious liability

It is a settled principle of law that an employer is vicariously liable for the negligence of an employee who was acting in the course of his (or her) employment. There has been much discussion in the case-law about what is meant by 'in the course of his employment'. In practical terms, it comes down to this:

- If the employee was carrying out an act authorised by his employer but doing it in an unauthorised way, the employer would be vicariously liable.
- If, however, the act was independent of and quite separate from anything that would be expressly or by implication authorised by the employer, the employer would not be held vicariously liable for the employee's act.

*T v North Yorkshire County Council* (1998) *The Times*, 10 September, CA, provided a clear illustration of this rule. The deputy headmaster of a special needs school committed serious sexual assaults on a pupil, who suffered from epilepsy and mental handicap, when on a school trip to Spain. At first instance, the judge held that the deputy headmaster was effectively *in loco parentis* with a duty to care for and supervise the pupil, and therefore his acts were so connected with his authorised responsibilities that they could be regarded as an improper mode of performing his duties. That decision was reversed in the Court of Appeal. Butler-Sloss LJ said that it was difficult to visualise serious sexual misconduct as an unauthorised mode of carrying out an authorised act. Rather, it was an independent act outside the course of employment for which the employer could not be vicariously liable.

It is worth noting that if the employer is not vicariously liable in these circumstances the teacher may be uninsured in respect of such acts and may therefore lack the resources to pay an award of damages, leaving the pupil to claim under the more restricted tariffs of the Criminal Injuries Compensation Scheme. Moreover, it is unclear from the *North Yorkshire* case whether an employer would be vicariously liable if the assault was minor in nature.

### 11.6.2   Necessity

The defence of necessity, if it exists at all, is very limited and contemplates a person who interfered with the person or property of another to prevent greater damage being caused. The defence may be more readily available to a rescuer of life than to a rescuer of property but it can apply in either case.

### 11.6.3   Warnings, exemption clauses and disclaimers

A *warning* given by an occupier of land (such as a school) can be sufficient to discharge the duty of care if it warns visitors of a particular danger, provided that the warning is sufficient to enable the visitor to be reasonably safe. A warning that is sufficient for adults will often be insufficient for young children.

An *exemption clause* or exclusion notice is different from a warning. An exclusion purports to take away the right to recover damages in respect of a breach of duty. A number of statutory provisions including s 2 of the Unfair Contract Terms Act 1977 provide that liability for death or personal injury resulting from negligence cannot be excluded and that an exclusion or restriction of liability for other loss or damage is subject to the test of reasonableness.

A *disclaimer* is in the nature of a notice given to persons generally as distinct from an exclusion which is a contract term. The rules that apply to disclaimers both in negligence and contract situations are similar to those that apply to exclusions and are subject to s 2 of the Unfair Contract Terms Act 1977 as explained above.

### 11.6.4   *Volenti non fit injuria*

This Latin maxim means 'no injury is done to one who consents'. In other words, a person who has expressly or by implication assented to run the risk complained of cannot then blame someone else for the injury or damage he suffers. In general, *volenti* can only be used as a defence if it can be shown that consent to the risk was fully and freely given, and that it was that risk and no other which caused the injury or damage. Mere knowledge of the risk is not enough. An example of the way *volenti* works was the early case of *Holmes v Mather* (1875) LR 10 Ex 261, when it was held that he who uses a highway consents to run the risk of pure accidents, but not the risk of injury due to other persons' carelessness.

*Volenti*, if established, is a complete defence to an allegation of negligence but it is out of favour with the courts and very unlikely to succeed as a defence where young children are concerned.

### 11.6.5 Statutory authority

It is a defence to an allegation of negligence that a person has acted in accordance with a statute or regulation that specifically authorised a certain act to be done by a certain person.

### 11.6.6 Contributory negligence

The Law Reform (Contributory Negligence) Act 1945 provided that a person guilty of contributory negligence would suffer a reduction in his (or her) damages 'to such extent as the court thinks just and equitable having regard to the claimant's share in the responsibility for the damage'.

Examples of contributory negligence include failing to wear a seat belt or a crash helmet, and travelling in a vehicle with a drunk driver. Many other examples can be envisaged. The concept of contributory negligence rests on the requirement that a person must take reasonable precautions for his own safety. The standard of that duty is the familiar standard of the 'reasonable person' having regard to all the circumstances.

Where children are concerned, there is an age up to which a child cannot be expected to take any precautions for his (or her) own safety. Thereafter, it is a question of fact for the trial judge to decide whether the child, having regard to his age and mental development, may properly be expected to take some precautions for his own safety and consequently be capable of being guilty of contributory negligence. It is then for the court to rule on the evidence whether the child has fallen short of the standard which might reasonably be expected from him, having regard to his age and development. This approach seems to depart from the principle that negligence is judged by an objective standard of care to be applied to an hypothetical defendant.

### 11.6.7 Other defences

There are a number of other defences to an allegation of negligence which include consent of the plaintiff, lawful arrest, self-defence, and *ex turpi causa*. These are described in more detail in the standard textbooks on the law of tort (eg *Clerk and Lindsell on Torts* (Sweet & Maxwell, looseleaf), *Salmond and Heuston on the Law of Torts* (Sweet & Maxwell, 1996), Rogers *Winfield and Jolowicz on Torts* (Sweet & Maxwell, 1994)).

## 11.7 CAUSATION AND DAMAGE

Once a duty of care and a breach of that duty have been established, the two final elements of legal negligence are 'causation' and 'damage'. Negligence is then completely founded and the only remaining task is to identify the remedy, which will normally be an assessment of damages on the rules that apply to the tort of negligence.

Another way of saying the same thing is that negligence which causes no personal injury or damage to property (or in the case of professional negligence, no economic loss either) is not negligence at law and will, in general, have no legal consequences under the law of tort.

### 11.7.1   Causation generally

The first principle of causation is that the breach of duty complained of was the *sole* or *principal cause* or else *materially contributed* to the damage suffered by the plaintiff. There are three distinct aspects of causation.

#### (a)   Factual causation

Where there are two or more causes of damage, it is usual to look at the *proximate cause*, that is the cause which is latest in time, to see whether that gives a sensible analysis. For example, A, who is a passenger, negligently opens the door of a moving coach. B stands in the stairwell. C deliberately trips D who is walking towards the stairwell. D loses his balance and accidentally pushes B out of the coach. B is injured. Leaving aside any liability on the part of the driver who might have had an opportunity to slow or stop the coach, it may be said the accident would not have occurred *but for* C tripping D. Thus, the tripping was the proximate and operating cause of the accident.

The '*but for*' analysis is appropriate to a case like this, but not to one which has two simultaneous breaches of duty.

Care must also be taken not to confuse *occasion of damage* with *cause of damage*. In the above example, it may be said that opening the coach door provided the 'occasion' of the damage, ie the conditions without which the injury would not have occurred. However, it is probable there would have been no injury without the additional factor of C tripping D, and therefore opening the door was the occasion of the accident but not its cause.

A different case can be envisaged where A is under a duty of care and negligently advises B to drive his car in one direction when the correct route would have been in the opposite direction. Whilst driving in the wrong direction, B suffers an accident caused by the negligence of D. It is an accident that would not have occurred had the correct directions been given. Here, however, the negligent directions would be held too remote to be a cause of the accident.

#### (b)   Causation of damage

The above examples concerned establishing which acts or omissions caused the damage. It is also necessary to look at the damage itself and ask whether all of the damage or only part of it was caused by the breach of duty.

The leading case in this regard, which still represents the law, was *The Wagon Mound (No 2)* [1967] 1 AC 617, PC. In that case, a huge quantity of fuel oil was negligently discharged into Sydney Harbour. The oil drifted to the plaintiff's wharf where welding was in progress. On the facts, it was reasonably foreseeable that the slipway would be fouled by the oil. A fire broke out and damaged the plaintiff's wharf and two ships. It was held that although the risk of fire was very slight, it was none the less foreseeable and therefore not too remote. The damage caused by fire was within the scope of the damages that could be recovered.

An example of a case where the damage would be held too remote is where D negligently injures P. P's father, whilst driving to visit P in hospital, is involved in an accident. The analysis in this kind of case would be that the need for a hospital visit is reasonably foreseeable but not the likelihood of an accident.

## (c)  Extent of damage

*The Wagon Mound*, discussed above, was concerned with the *nature* of the damage and whether it was reasonably foreseeable. There is an additional principle relating to the *extent* of the damage and this is known as the '*egg-shell skull rule*'. In essence, this states that the defendant takes his plaintiff as he finds him.

An example is where the defendant negligently inflicts a blow which might reasonably be expected to bruise the plaintiff but which, because of the plaintiff's particular predisposition, results in a more serious injury or death. In this case, the defendant is liable for the full extent of the damage. Likewise, it was held in *Page v Smith* [1995] 2 WLR 644 that it matters not whether the injury is psychiatric or physical, provided *some* injury was reasonably foreseeable.

The principle has been held to apply to a burn which triggered cancer, and to a plaintiff who had an '*egg-shell personality*', and in many other cases.

More detailed consideration of causation and damage is outside the scope of this chapter but can be found in the standard textbooks on the law of torts.

## 11.7.2  Damage suffered by a pupil

A pupil at school may suffer the following kinds of damage recognised at law:

## (a)  Physical injury

Most of the cases cited elsewhere in this chapter are concerned with physical injuries sustained by a pupil as a result of negligence or sometimes because of a breach of statutory duty. Physical injuries are proved by means of a report and sometimes oral evidence from a medical expert who has examined the plaintiff and seen his (or her) medical records. The fact and causation of the physical injury have to be proved, together with the circumstances of negligence. If the injury has exacerbated an existing disability, the task of the expert and the court is to identify the extent to which the act or omission complained of has aggravated the disability.

## (b)  Psychological injury

Psychological injury can be caused by *nervous shock*. In the leading case, *Alcock v Chief Constable of South Yorkshire* [1992] 1 AC 310, Lord Ackner said that shock 'involves the sudden appreciation by sight or sound of a horrifying event, which violently agitates the mind.' Lord Ackner stated also that there could be no recovery of damages for psychiatric illness 'caused by the accumulation over a period of time of more gradual assaults on the nervous system.' Those dicta reflected the restrictive approach which the law has adopted over the development of awards in cases of nervous shock.

During the 1990s, however, there has been growing acceptance by the medical profession, followed by the law, of post-traumatic stress disorder and other recognised psychological illnesses where those can be shown to have been caused by a particular event or series of events. Litigation following the Hillsborough Stadium disaster in 1992 and other cases have led to the courts developing a three-point test of whether a particular psychological injury will be recognised at law. The conditions broadly are:

(1) the plaintiff has sustained a recognisable psychiatric illness which has been diagnosed; and

(2) a person of reasonable fortitude would be likely to suffer shock in the circumstances of the case; and

(3) the condition would not have been suffered *but for* the acts or omissions complained of (this is the very important issue of causation).

Psychological illness in children at school may be caused by a number of different factors including family circumstances, undetected, misdiagnosed or neglected learning difficulties or other special needs (discussed further in Chapter 12), bullying, or other forms of shock and distress.

The condition can show itself in a variety and combination of ways, for example: not sleeping; not eating; not washing; general self-neglect and low self-esteem; obsessional thoughts or nightmares; lethargy and lassitude; anxiety and tearfulness; panic attacks; rebellious behaviour; inability to work effectively; complex relationship problems; statements such as 'I wish I wasn't here …'; drug overdoses; attempted suicide; eating disorders (anorexia nervosa or bulimia); or by 'cutting' and other types of self-harm.

None of these is of itself enough to establish psychological injury. That is a matter for expert diagnosis which will have regard to the possible causes – of which there may be a number – and the long-term effects (if any). Proving causation between the act or omission complained of and the injury can be very difficult in cases of psychological injury. The real cause may have more to do with family circumstances and the temperament, lifestyle, general intelligence and application of the pupil than with the act or omission complained of.

### (c)   Loss or damage to property

When pupils hand valuables to a teacher for safe-keeping, the school through the agency of the teacher becomes a *gratuitous bailee* of the property. Bailment is a device of common law, and is independent of tort, contract and trust. Thus, claims against a bailee are based on *breach of bailment*, ie breach of a common law duty of care, and may not fall within the overall category of 'wrongful interference with goods' defined in s 1 of the Torts (Interference with Goods) Act 1977.

A bailee who is negligent will be liable to the bailor, but the accidental loss or destruction of the property without default on the part of the bailee will excuse his (or her) failure to return it. The burden of proof will be on the bailee in each case.

Schools normally deter pupils from bringing valuable items or large sums of money to school, and most losses will relate to items of clothing, sports equipment, personal effects and small sums of money. However, musical instruments, computers and bicycles can have considerable value, and a pupil might on occasions wish to bring in to school items such as a collection of stamps, coins or medals or a rare book or manuscript. A small number of schools allow pupils to keep ponies which, at law, are classified as chattels. Pupils in the upper sixth form may be permitted to park a car on school premises.

It will normally be a contractual term that parents must arrange their own insurance of pupils' property at school. Insurance arrangements apart, the extent to which the school is under a duty of care to the pupil or parents in relation to such property will depend on all the circumstances of the case. However, if a duty of care is established and the school is in breach of that duty, the pupil or parents will be entitled to bring a claim for all loss and damage that falls within the various causation tests discussed above.

Pupils' property handed in for safe-keeping can present a problem, for example when children change into sports kit for games and PE, and have no lockable space in which to keep watches, wallets, cash, etc. One system is for the school to provide a transparent bag in which the pupil puts his (or her) identity card and property before the bag is handed to a member of staff. Consistent with a school rule that valuables should not be brought into school, it is reasonable for the school to limit its liability to £5.00 in cash and £25.00 for property (at today's values) in the event of the bag going missing.

Copyright is a right of 'intellectual property' which confers rights of privacy and protection in respect of the pupil's original work. The main legislation is the Copyright, Designs and Patents Act 1988. The Act protects literary works, dramatic works, musical works, artistic works, sound recordings, films including videos, broadcasts and cable programmes, and published editions. Breach of copyright and of the various other intellectual property rights are independent torts but it is also possible in some circumstances to frame an action in negligence.

### (d)    Economic loss

On the present state of the law, a person who has suffered economic loss without physical or psychological injury or damage to property or breach of the professional duty of care cannot recover that loss in an action for negligence. Financial loss may, however, be claimed in a properly founded action in negligence.


## 11.8   MEASURE OF DAMAGES

### 11.8.1   The purpose of damages

The purpose of damages in negligence is so far as possible to place the plaintiff in the position he (or she) would have been in had the negligence not occurred. In general, therefore, the purpose is to compensate the plaintiff and not to punish the defendant.

The plaintiff can only claim for losses he has actually sustained and he is also required to *mitigate his loss*. In practice, that means he must take such reasonable steps as are open to him to prevent the loss increasing. If the plaintiff's Rolls Royce is damaged by the defendant's negligence, the plaintiff will not necessarily recover all the costs of hiring an alternative Rolls Royce during the period of repair if a different car hired at lower rates would have provided sufficient transport and there was no essential need for a Rolls Royce.

In addition to ordinary damages, an award of *aggravated damages* can be made in any class of action and is common in defamation cases although rare in negligence. The intention of aggravated damages is to compensate the plaintiff for injury to his feelings.

*Exemplary* or *punitive damages* may only be awarded in two specific categories of case in addition to any that have been expressly authorised by statute. These categories are:

(1)   cases of oppressive, arbitrary or unconstitutional action by servants of the government; and

(2)   cases in which the defendant's conduct has been calculated by him to make a profit for himself which may well exceed the compensation payable to the plaintiff.

### 11.8.2   Damages for personal injuries

There are two distinct kinds of damages for personal injuries. They are:

(1)   damages for pain and suffering and loss of amenities or enjoyment of life. These are known as *general damages*; and

(2)   damages for financial loss, including such matters as loss of earnings and expenditure incurred. These are known as *special damages*. Special damages can include the expenses of a third party such as a parent visiting the plaintiff in hospital and providing nursing services at home.

If a plaintiff has suffered disability that will continue long into the future, there may also be an award of general damages to cover future nursing care, aids and equipment, adaptation of a vehicle or of a house, and future medical and travel costs. In addition to damages, the plaintiff may be entitled to interest at variable rates and for varying periods.

The measure of damages in negligence under English law is ungenerous. At the time of writing, damages awarded to a young person rendered tetraplegic or severely brain damaged are unlikely to exceed £120,000, the remainder of the award being for special damages, future loss and interest.

A plaintiff who was guilty of contributory negligence will have his (or her) damages reduced pro rata. He will normally be entitled to his legal costs at a rate to be agreed with the defendant or else to be assessed ('taxed') by the court. Costs of litigation are not reduced for contributory negligence. A plaintiff with legal aid whose action is unsuccessful will normally be ordered to pay the other party's costs but the order will be expressed 'not to be enforced without leave'. This is sometimes referred to as a 'football pools' order signifying that the plaintiff will not be required to pay the costs unless he receives a windfall.

In many cases, it will be some years before the award of damages can be finally assessed. It is quite common for there to be an agreement or else a trial of the liability issues at an earlier stage and then one or more interim payments of damages pending final settlement or order.

An agreement over the damages payable to a minor (ie under 18) does not bind the minor unless the settlement has been approved by the court. This point is of particular relevance to schools and their insurers, especially where psychological injury is in issue.

## 11.9 PARTICULAR SITUATIONS

### 11.9.1 Children wandering

Under normal circumstances, a child under the age of 8 and sometimes older will be in the full-time care of either a parent, the school or some other person entrusted with care. Damage done by a very young child because of a negligent failure of care is likely to be the primary liability of the carer. However, not every escape from care will be the liability of the carer. Some examples from the cases are as follows.

*Carmarthenshire County Council v Lewis* [1955] AC 549, HL
A boy aged 4 and another child at a nursery school were made ready to go for a walk with one of the teachers and another child. The teacher left the room to get herself ready. Whilst she was out of the room she had to attend to an emergency. She was away for 10 minutes. The two children left the classroom and wandered out of an *unlocked school gate* onto a busy road. A lorry driver had to swerve to avoid hitting one of the children. His vehicle collided with a telegraph pole and he was killed. It was held the teacher was not negligent but that the LEA was liable for failing to take adequate precautions to avoid what was a foreseeable accident.

*Ricketts v Erith Borough Council* (1943) 42 LGR 471
A 10-year-old child left school premises during the lunch break and returned with a bow and arrow which he fired causing injury. There was held to have been no failure of supervision.

*Nwabudike v The Mayor and Burgesses of the London Borough of Southwark* [1997] ELR 35
A primary-school child ran out of the playground during the lunch break and into the path of a car. It was held that it was the duty of the school to take all reasonable and adequate steps to prevent a child from leaving the school premises at a time when he should have been in school. However, it was necessary to strike a balance between maintaining security and turning the school into a fortress. Here, the child was determined to break the rules that were designed to protect him. There had only been one similar incident 6 years earlier. This was evidence that all proper and reasonable precautions had been taken. The child's claim failed.

### 11.9.2 Supervision before the start of the school day

The general rule is that the school authority is under no duty to provide supervision before the advertised start of the school day provided it has been made clear that there is no supervision before that time. Some examples from the cases are as follows.

*Ward v Hertfordshire County Council* (1969) 114 SJ 87, CA

This case concerned the school's practice of allowing children into the playground before the start of the school day, but not supervising them. An 8-year-old boy crashed into a jagged wall during a race and injured his skull. The school staff knew that children frequently raced in the playground. It was found that the wall was not dangerous, bearing in mind its nature, typicality and long-standing and the fact that complaints had never been made about it. Lack of supervision is irrelevant where accidents occur in the ordinary course of play. It is impossible so to supervise children that they never fall down and hurt themselves. It was held that there was no negligence. The accident had occurred in the ordinary course of play. Note that the trial judge at first instance had decided that the jagged wall in the playground was inherently dangerous and that there should have been supervision, but, even so, the Court of Appeal decided there was no duty to supervise before the start of the school day.

*Woodward v Mayor of Hastings* [1944] 2 All ER 505

Failure to clear snow from a school step or a path leading to a school, resulting in injury where there was a fall, was held to be negligence; see also the Occupiers Liability Acts 1957 and 1984.

*Mays v Essex County Council* (1975) *The Times*, 11 October

It was held reasonable for 14-year-old children to be allowed to slide on unsalted ice in an orderly fashion whilst unsupervised. It was held that there is a difference between:

– opening the school gates early for the convenience of parents and the safety of pupils, in which case there was no duty to provide supervision. The school must, however, make it clear that no supervision will be provided before a certain time; and
– voluntarily accepting responsibility for children arriving early, in which case there would be a duty to provide supervision.

*Murphy v Bradford Metropolitan Council* [1991] ICR 80, CA

The school was held liable when the plaintiff slipped on a frozen path into school which had not been gritted (this was not a supervision case).

### 11.9.3   Responsibility during break times and lunch times

Nowadays it is to be expected that there will be a degree of supervision during break times and lunch times when children are in the care of the school. However, from the following examples, it may be seen that the cases are not altogether consistent:

*Beaumont v Surrey County Council* (1968) 66 LGR 580

Usually, there were two members of staff assigned to playground supervision. On the day of the accident, they were absent. Some pupils found a heavy-duty piece of elastic discarded from a mini-trampoline in a waste bin. They played about with it and one pupil suffered a serious eye injury. It was held that the school was liable because the *system* was not working properly at the time. It is a schoolmaster's duty, bearing in mind the known propensities of children between the ages of 11 and 18, to take all reasonable and proper steps to prevent any of the pupils under his care from suffering injury from inanimate objects, from the actions of their fellow pupils or from a combination of the two.

*Langham v Wellingborough School Governors and Fryer* (1932) 30 LGR 276, CA

A pupil hit a golf ball with a stick in the playground. The ball flew through an open door to strike the plaintiff, inside the school building, in the eye. There was no express evidence as to supervision in the playground. The plaintiff's claim against the school authority failed.

*Rawsthorne v Ottley* [1937] 3 All ER 902

A tip-up lorry with a single driver delivered coke to the school playground. A pupil aged 13 jumped on to the lorry behind the driver's cab. When the tipping part of the lorry was released it fell and crushed the pupil's leg. It was held that the headmaster was not negligent in leaving boys in the playground without supervision.

*Clark v Monmouthshire County Council* (1954) 52 LGR 246, CA

A boy of 13 was stabbed in the leg by another boy in the playground during morning break. The staff did not know that the other boy was carrying a knife. At the time of the accident there was no prefect on duty in the playground. The master in charge passed through the playground twice during break. It was held that the school was not liable: 'The duty of a school does not extend to constant supervision of all the boys all the time' (per Denning LJ at 247–248).

*Pettican v Enfield London Borough Council* (1970) *The Times*, 22 October

It was held that, during lunch time supervision, staff could not be expected to perform 'as policemen or security guards'. In this case, children were sent indoors on a wet day. In an unsupervised classroom, the plaintiff was struck in the eye by a piece of chalk during horseplay. Neither the school nor the LEA were liable. The judge rejected the idea that a teacher should have been on duty in each classroom when the children were sent indoors on wet days.

*Blasdale v Coventry City Council* (1981) TES, 13 November

This is similar to the *Pettican* case but with a different result. During lunch time, the children were allowed indoors because of rain. A pupil fired a paper clip at another boy, damaging his eye. One dinner lady had been given the task of supervising two classrooms. This was found to have been inadequate.

An inference to be drawn from the *Pettican* and *Blasdale* cases is that there is more likely to be liability if supervision is provided, but carried out negligently, than if there is no supervision. See also *Porter v Barking and Dagenham London Borough Council* in this connection (mentioned at **11.5.1***(c)* above).

### 11.9.4    Responsibility after school hours

The school's responsibility is to ensure that there is an adequate system for handing children over to their parents – especially very young children. The following examples appear from case-law.

*Jefferey v London County Council* (1954) 52 LGR 521

It was held that if parents simply fail to collect or meet the child, the school will not be liable.

It is submitted that this is oversimplification. If a child remains on the premises after school hours and if the parents cannot be contacted, the school ought to ensure that the child is handed over to social services or to the police. A teacher is entitled to do what is reasonable in the circumstances of the case for the purposes of safeguarding or promoting the welfare of the child (Children Act 1989, s 3(5)). If insured, a member of staff would be entitled to drive the child home.

### *Barnes v Hampshire County Council* [1969] 1 WLR 1563, HL

This case concerned children being let out of school 5 minutes before the scheduled time. A 5-year-old wandered out into the street because her mother had not yet arrived at the school gate. The child was injured on the road one minute before the normal leaving time of 3.30 pm. The school authority was held to be negligent. A school is not required to detain small children until their parents collect them, but must adhere to the timetable of which the parents had been informed.

Again, it is submitted that this is an oversimplification. A school is not entitled to release a young child into a situation of danger.

### *Good v ILEA* (1980) 10 Fam Law 213, CA

It was normal for some children to be on the premises after school hours. The children knew they should stay in a play centre across the playground. Two children wandered to a roped off area where a swimming pool was to be constructed. One child threw sand into the eye of another. It was held that there was no breach of duty on the part of the school. There was no duty to watch each child all the time.

The standard is different in the case of a hazardous activity.

## 11.9.5    Out-of-school activities

Most teachers would admit to experiencing relief at the end of a safe and happy out-of-school event. Reasonable care should be taken to acquire the necessary degree of knowledge about the risks that are likely to be encountered on an out-of-school trip. That may involve a reconnoitre in advance. In addition, the sound practice of preparing guidelines and checklists for party leaders and those who will accompany the trip is strongly encouraged. Children engaged on a school trip are under the care of the school, and the teacher in charge is both entitled and expected to enforce order, good discipline and procedures that are reasonably safe. Two cases in particular illustrate these points.

### *The Austrian Alps Disaster 1988*

This disaster, when four children slid to their deaths, led to a report from the Berkshire Education Authority which concluded:

> 'Telling the pupils what to do and trusting them to obey was not enough ...; the teachers should not have allowed the pupils to go unsupervised for some 50 minutes; their presence might have discouraged the pupils from leaving the path.'

### *Porter v City of Bradford Metropolitan Council* [1985] LEXIS, 14 January, CA

A dozen 15–16-year-olds and their geology teacher went on an outing to Shipley Glen. A teacher reprimanded a boy who was rolling large stones down a slope at the bottom of which were five pupils. Later, the same boy was left unsupervised and for 15 minutes he dropped or threw stones from a bridge. One of them injured the head of a girl pupil. Stephenson LJ held that he did not wish to impose on teachers a duty of supervision which went beyond that of a reasonable parent in the context of a trip of this nature, but in this case the teacher failed in his duty to supervise. He should have kept both the willing and unwilling pupils together.

The duty of supervision applies equally during trips and outings as it does on school premises. Hazardous activities or circumstances call for a higher standard of care. The starting-point is the question 'Can reasonable safety be assured?'.

## 11.9.6 Supervision on school transport

The conduct of pupils on transport arranged by the school authority is in general the responsibility of the school and, as may be seen from the dates of the two cases cited below, the problems in this respect are not new.

*Shrimpton v Hertfordshire County Council* [1911] 104 LT 145
Children on school buses must be supervised on the 'careful or prudent parent' standard.

*Jaques v Oxfordshire County Council* (1967) 66 LGR 440
A child was injured by a pellet fired at him by another pupil when they were both travelling on a school bus. Supervision had been left to prefects. The school was held not to have been negligent.

In an emergency, teachers may be tempted to use their own vehicles but they need to make certain they are covered by their own car insurance policies for doing so. It is better to use school transport if possible. The bursar, or those responsible in lieu, should check that every member of staff is covered for these contingencies.

## 11.9.7 Some particular circumstances

### *Leaving school premises during the day*

No child under 8 should be allowed to leave school premises during school time unless accompanied by a parent, teacher or other responsible person. Whether it is safe for a child aged 9 or over to leave school on his (or her) own depends on the usual factors of age and understanding, the nature of the area, the distance, the roads to be crossed and other known risks. If in doubt, supervision by a 'responsible person' – who could be an older pupil – should be arranged.

### *Bus duties*

As soon as the pupil boards a bus that has been arranged by the school, the pupil is under the care of the school. The position is different if the pupil is using public transport. Pupils boarding the school bus at the end of the day should be supervised or there will be a risk of liability on the part of the school.

### *Lunch time supervision*

The head is responsible for ensuring that adequate arrangements are in operation. He (or she) has to balance this with staff entitlement to a break at midday. The alternative of sending pupils home at lunchtime if their reasonable safety cannot be assured is almost always impractical because the head has the residual duty of ensuring that parents have been given notice and that the child can get home safely and gain access.

## Split-site schools

Teachers do not have the authority of law to control traffic and have no sanction against drivers who ignore them. If a road accident occurs as a result of attempts at traffic control by a teacher, the blame at law may fall upon the teacher as well as any other person who causes an accident. There is no satisfactory answer to this problem, since the school has a duty to take reasonable care to ensure the safety of a child moving from one site to another while the child is in the care of the school. Common sense is likely to be a better guide than a strict analysis of legal duties.

## Supervision by helpers

A helper (eg parent or student teacher) undertakes the same responsibility as a teacher for the care he (or she) provides. The teacher, however, remains primarily responsible. As a general rule, helpers should not be left in sole charge of pupils other than for short periods and where the helper has demonstrated competence in dealing with children.

## The use of a private car

As noted at **11.9.6**, insurance cover should always be checked before teachers and helpers carry pupils in their private cars. There is then the normal duty of care owed to all passengers. If a teacher allocates pupils in his (or her) care to a particular driver who has been drinking or whose car is unroadworthy or who is an irresponsible driver, the teacher could be held liable for breach of duty.

## High-risk school departments

The departments that are to be regarded as high risk include physical education, contact sports, swimming, laboratories, art and pottery, and craft design and technology. There are detailed health and safety provisions relating to each of these. The standard of supervision required is higher than for medium- and low-risk areas such as playgrounds and classrooms.

## 11.9.8 Supervision ratios

Legislators have deliberately refrained from prescribing teacher : pupil ratios in most circumstances. Instead, it is the responsibility of the head to organise teaching staff so as to maintain *reasonable* supervision of all children – having regard also to gender – on school premises and in the care of the school at other times.

The factors to be taken into account when deciding supervision ratios are:

- *the children* – their age and understanding, gender, intelligence, handicaps and generally known behaviour, and the number of children involved. Children aged up to 8 are 'younger children' and those from 9 to 16 'older children';
- *the supervisor/instructor* – his (or her) general calibre and ability;
- *the activity* – whether it is low, medium or high risk;

- *the facilities in use* – how safe they are;
- *the location* – for example, whether supervision is on school premises, on a journey or at a distant location;
- *the duration of the activity* – the considerations that apply to a one-hour activity are different from those that arise on a 12-hour or longer trip away from the school.

The Amateur Swimming Association has recommended a ratio of one teacher to 20 children as a general guideline, but fewer children should be supervised if they are young, inexperienced or difficult; more children, perhaps, where they are well behaved, good swimmers, trained in the 'buddy' system and working in a quiet, well-designed pool in the care of a very able teacher.

In the case of mixed gender groups away from the school, there should be at least one teacher of each sex.

It is good practice to be sure that help can be found in an emergency. A mobile 'phone is probably a necessary precaution on trips away from the school.

### 11.9.9   Sports and games injuries

#### (a)   Contact sports

Even after everything reasonable has been done to minimise the risk of injury, contact sports such as rugby and football carry inherent risk. The school will not be held legally liable for injuries resulting from that inherent risk. However, negligence over and above that level of risk can give rise to legal liability. The following are examples from the case-law.

*Affutu-Nartoy v Clarke and ILEA* (1984) *The Times*, 9 February
In a game of rugby, the teacher tackled a teenage boy in a legitimate manner under the rules of the game and caused injury. It was held that even for the purpose of demonstration such conduct was unlawful and dangerous. The risk of injury was unacceptably high. The school was vicariously liable.

*Van Oppen v Clerk to the Bedford Charity Trustees* [1989] 3 All ER 389, CA
This case involved alleged negligent rugby coaching. A 16-year-old pupil was crippled whilst making a rugby tackle. The school and teacher were found not to have been negligent because the staff were aware of the inherent risks in the game and of the need for correct techniques and the correction of errors and lapses; the standard of supervision was high; the refereeing was vigilant and strict; the game was being played correctly.

*Condon v Basi* [1985] 1 WLR 866, CA
In an adult football match, the defendant challenged the plaintiff by sliding in from a distance of about 3–4 yards. The slide tackle came late and was made by the defendant lunging with his boot studs showing about 9 inches from the ground. The plaintiff sustained a broken right leg and the defendant was sent off. Sir John Donaldson MR said that players in competitive sports each owed a duty to the other to take all reasonable care in the particular circumstances in which they were placed. Therefore,

if one player injured another either because he had failed to exercise the degree of care which was appropriate in all the circumstances or because he had acted in a way to which the other player could not be expected to consent, he would be held liable in negligence. Damages of £4,900 were awarded.

It was also suggested in *Condon v Basi* that a higher degree of care is required of a football player in a First Division (now Premier League) football match than of a player in a local league game, but that reasoning seems hard to justify in a case of dangerous fouls.

### *Smoldon v Whitworth* [1997] ELR 249, CA

A 17-year-old was playing Colts rugby during the 1991–92 season. It was a bad-tempered match. More than 20 scrums collapsed. The linesman expressed concern. In the last few minutes of the game, the plaintiff's neck was broken when yet another scrum collapsed. It was held that rugby is 'a tough, highly physical game, not for the timid or the fragile'. Participants expect a fair share of physical injuries. The authorities have responded to the risk by requiring players to conform with a 'crouch, touch, pause, engage' sequence in Colts rugby games. Bingham LJ said that the threshold of liability is a high one. The referee was not to be held liable for human failings, mere errors of judgement, oversights and lapses but he must enforce the approved procedures. Liability arose when the degree of care exercised by the referee fell below that required by the circumstances. The standard of refereeing fell below that which was appropriate in these circumstances and the referee was liable.

### *McCord v Swansea City AFC* (1997) *The Times*, 11 February

It was held that John Cornforth was guilty of a serious mistake or misjudgement when he made a tackle in a football match. There was a foul, and an intentional one in the linesman's interpretation of the rules, in that he took a course which led to his kicking the plaintiff's leg. It did not assist to label the action as reckless or rash. Cornforth's error was inconsistent and unmistakably inconsistent with his taking reasonable care towards the plaintiff and gave rise to liability in negligence.

It is now recognised that there may be negligence if players of grossly unequal weight, strength and skill are selected to play or practise against each other since, consistent with the decision in *Affutu-Nartoy* above, the risk of injury becomes unacceptably high.

## (b)    Cricket and rounders

Cricket probably carries a greater inherent risk than rounders. As with contact sports, there will be a finding of negligence if those responsible for supervising the game or practice fail to perceive and deal with the areas of risk that are avoidable. Key areas of risk including positioning of players and provision of protective equipment. Two cases in point are the following.

### *Barfoot v East Sussex County Council* (unreported) (1939)

A pupil was successful in his claim for damages for injuries received while playing cricket at school. The judge found as a fact that the boy was very considerably less than 10 yards from the wicket and that this was a dangerous position in the circumstances. He said: 'I am satisfied that the master would not have allowed the boy to be there if he had noticed him but, owing to his other duties as umpire, he failed to exercise the care which the law required from a master in charge of pupils in these circumstances'.

### Price v Caernarvonshire County Council (1960) The Times, 11 February

A child was struck by a rounders bat which was being used in a confined playground at midday. The head had warned pupils against using the bat in the confined space. There was a patrol on the school premises during the midday period and, just prior to the accident, the head, who was on duty, had visited the particular playground. It was held that the school authority was not liable.

### (c)    Gymnastics, apparatus and judo

The combination of hazards in a gymnasium – slippery floor, obstacles, apparatus of many kinds and potentially dangerous exercises – often create quite a high risk of injury. That in turn increases the standard of the care and supervision that is expected. Current good practice should be followed and equipment that is not in use should be put away. A number of the older cases summarised below (for example, *Wright* and *Lancaster*) were probably good law under the guidance at the time but would be decided against the school today.

### Conrad v ILEA (1967) 65 LGR 543

It was recognised that there were two schools of thought as to appropriate initial instruction in judo. The school authority was not liable for the pupil's injuries.

### Moore v Hampshire County Council (1981) ATLGR 481, CA

A 12-year-old girl broke her ankle while attempting a handstand in a PE lesson at school. She had a medical history of congenital dislocation of the hips. The teacher knew she was not to take PE but had allowed herself to be persuaded. The teacher was allowing the pupil to perform an activity which was beyond her reasonable capabilities and the teacher should have known this. It was held there had not been adequate supervision of the girl.

### Gibbs v Barking Corporation [1936] 1 All ER 115, CA

In this 'catching' case, a teacher who failed to assist a boy landing from a vault during gymnastics was held not to have taken reasonable care.

### Wright v Cheshire County Council [1952] 2 All ER 789, CA

In another 'catching' case, the facts were that a 12-year-old boy was injured while vaulting. The boy who was supposed to help him land left on hearing the school bell. The teacher had instructed other pupils to assist in the safety procedure. It was held that this was a general and approved practice and the teacher was therefore not negligent.

### Gleave v Lancashire County Council (unreported) (1951)

In this 'catching' case, a girl vaulting over the buck, fell and was injured. It was held that the girl was capable of attempting the jump without physical assistance but not of attempting it safely without a catcher. The PE mistress was not standing close enough to act as catcher. The school was held liable.

### Lancaster v County Council of Lancashire (unreported) (1952)

In this 'catching' case, a secondary school pupil was injured when she vaulted over a buck. There was no one standing by to support or catch her and before making the jump the girl had to run along a wooden platform. The PE teacher provided a framework within which the girls were to choose what they wanted to do but she would not tell the girls what they had to do. The teacher would say 'I want you to do a strong exercise or a light exercise, etc'. The judge found this method of instruction to be perfectly reasonable. The pupil's claim failed.

### *Felgate v Middlesex County Council* (unreported) (1954)
A 6-year-old girl attending infant school was engaged in recreational exercises. There were seven pieces of equipment in the hall including a 'jungle gym'. The girl sat on the lower bar of this apparatus which was 3'6" from the ground. She fell off and broke her arm. Although there was a teacher nearby, she was attending to a small boy who had climbed up the step ladder on the 'jungle gym'. It was held that the school authority was not liable.

### *Berridge v Isle of Wight County Council* (unreported) (1955)
A 5-year-old boy went onto a climbing frame in the playground, fell and was injured having earlier, to the knowledge of the supervising teacher, sustained serious injuries in a road accident. The judge said that he was satisfied that children as a rule at this age 'will not go further than they can manage ...' and the school was held not liable. A reasonable parent would probably have allowed a child to use this apparatus.

### *Kershaw v Hampshire County Council* (unreported) (1982)
A pupil in a class of 12-year-old girls was using a trampette to assist with vaulting and somersaulting over a box. She ran and bounced on the trampette but went too high and too fast and fell. The judge found that it was known, or should have been generally known to responsible organisers in a field, that the use of a trampette was more dangerous than the use of the normal springboard. The trampette did have a greater tendency to lead to an accident. The girl had already completed this exercise successfully. Two girls were acting as catchers when the accident occurred. The teacher left the gymnasium temporarily and so there was no supervising adult when the accident occurred. It was held that if the teacher had to leave the pupils, she should have stopped the activity until her return. The school was held liable.

### *Meehan v Derbyshire County Council* (unreported) (1965)
A pupil fell from an unsupervised agility apparatus in the playground. It was held that accidents can happen in the best regulated families. This case was analogous to tree climbing. The school was not liable.

### *Advisory case*
The parents of a 12-year-old girl at a grant-maintained school, according to their religious beliefs, required the girl to wear a long dress during gym. The school took the view that this would endanger the girl's safety. Accordingly, arrangements were made for the girl to perform exercises during gym sessions.

### *Gwillym v Monmouthshire County Council* (unreported)
A boy fell and injured his arm in the course of a PE lesson whilst in his stockinged feet. It was found that the floor of the gymnasium was 'somewhat slippery' and judgment was given for the parents of the injured boy on the grounds that due precautions should have been taken to see that the class in general and that the boy in particular were correctly shod before going into the gymnasium.

## (d)  Athletics

Athletics involves equipment such as spiked shoes, javelins, shot, discus and hammer that are inherently dangerous when in use. It also involves other equipment such as starting blocks and starting pistols that may become a hazard unless properly supervised. Reasonable care is needed not only in the maintenance and use of equipment but over the selection of those who are sufficiently skilled, healthy and responsible to be permitted to use it. Some examples are:

*Tillotson v Harrow Borough Council* (unreported) (1981)
The school admitted liability when a girl broke her leg while jumping a hurdle. Her weight increased by 50% following the accident. She was awarded £9,000.

*Porter v Barking and Dagenham London Borough Council* (1990) *The Times*, 8 April
Two 14-year-old boys were practising their shot putting unsupervised. One was injured. It was held there was no liability from the failure to supervise boys of this age in that activity.

In a similar case which was settled out of court in 1990, a shot putting activity was being supervised by a teacher. The injury was caused when the boys were messing about. The teacher was in a position to restore order but failed to do so. The school was therefore negligent.

In a case settled during 1998, there was an inter-school athletics match. Starting blocks used for the 4 × 100 metres relay were not removed from the track after the start of the race. The final runner for the winning team tripped over the starting blocks in lane 1 and sustained internal injuries. It was accepted that leaving the starting blocks in place had created an avoidable risk of injury.

## (e)  Swimming

In 1993, there was a case of sudden death syndrome in which a pupil was found dead in the swimming pool some time after the group had left the area. The school in that case was prosecuted and fined a substantial sum.

## (f)  Canoeing

### The Lyme Bay Disaster 1993
This was not a schools' case but is analogous. Eight teenagers and their teacher went on what should have been a 2-mile canoe trip on open sea organised by OLL Ltd (the St Albans Centre) whose director was Peter Kite. Prior to the disaster, two instructors had left the company because they were not satisfied with the safety arrangements. One of the instructors made these concerns known to Mr Kite. The deaths were avoidable. OLL Ltd was the first company in English legal history to be convicted of corporate manslaughter (death resulting from gross negligence), and the company was fined £60,000. Kite became the first director of a company to be given an immediate custodial sentence in that capacity for manslaughter. A sentence of 3 years' imprisonment was reduced to 2 years on appeal. The court accepted that Kite had no knowledge that school children were undertaking trips of this kind.

## (g)    Tree climbing

Tree climbing and tree houses are an area of particular difficulty. Each case will turn on its own facts and take account of circumstances such as the age of the child; and the suitability of the tree as regards its height, strength, the sharpness of its features and so on. Specific consent from parents should be obtained in relation to the use of tree houses and there should be a specific system for checking the safety of construction, the numbers using the tree house at any one time and the degree of responsibility with which they are used. The following cases illustrate these points:

### *Meehan v Derbyshire County Council* (unreported) (1965)

Although this case concerned an injury to a pupil who fell from an unsupervised agility apparatus, the judge drew a parallel with parents who allow their children to climb trees considering that this may have the advantage of developing the sense of adventure and self-confidence of the child, even though it is not an activity without risk.

### *Hotson v East Berkshire Health Authority* [1987] 3 WLR 232, HL

The child was injured as a result of falling out of a tree but then received negligent medical treatment. The court had to consider whether the child's personal disability was caused by injuries sustained in the fall or by the medical treatment or both; in the case of both, the court would have had to make an apportionment. In the event it was held that the permanent disability was entirely caused by the fall from the tree.

## 11.10   SAFETY OF SCHOOL PREMISES

Claims under this head may be founded on the tort of negligence or the separate tort 'breach of statutory duty'. Instances may relate to the premises themselves or equipment used there. A school needs to devise systems that include routine inspection and a readiness to deal quickly with complaints and obvious hazards.

### 11.10.1   Negligence and breach of statutory duty

Several of the reported cases predate *Donoghue v Stevenson* [1932] AC 562 in which negligence was first established as an independent tort. The following cases illustrate some of the more common hazards relating to glass, slippery floors and access ways affected by snow and ice.

### *Ching v Surrey County Council* [1910] 1 KB 736

There was a hole in the school playground surface. A child was injured. Damages were awarded for breach of statutory duty.

### *Morris v Carnarvon County Council* [1910] 1 KB 858

A child caught a hand in a door which was too highly sprung and represented a danger. The school authority was held liable.

### *Woodward v Mayor of Hastings* [1944] 2 All ER 505

The school authority was held liable when a pupil slipped on frozen snow on a step which had not been cleared.

*Murphy v Bradford Metropolitan Council* [1991] ICR 80, CA
The school authority was held liable when a visitor slipped on a frozen path into school which had not been gritted.

*Gillmore v London County Council* [1938] All ER 31, DC
A child slipped on a highly polished school hall floor. The injury was held to have been foreseeable. The floor had been polished to such an extent that there was a serious risk of injury. The school authority was held liable.

*Williams v Cardiff Corporation* [1950] 1 All ER 250
It was held that a child aged 4 might be at risk of injury where there was a grassy slope with broken glass at the bottom.

*Ralph v London County Council* (1947) 111 JP 548, CA
A pupil took part in a game of 'touch' being played in the school assembly hall under the supervision of a teacher. One side of the hall consisted of glass partitions with doors in them, the glass partitions being 3 feet from the ground. During the game the pupil, whilst being chased by another boy, unwittingly put his hand through one of the glass partitions. It was held that a reasonable and prudent father would have contemplated that such an accident might have happened and that the boy was accordingly entitled to damages.

*Bates v Parker* [1954] 1 All ER 768
If a child was unaccompanied by a parent or guardian, the fact that the occupier might reasonably have expected the child to have been accompanied might be taken into account. This might be relevant if a school has a system for the delivery of children to school by their parents which envisages the parents accompanying the child to a certain place on the premises and an injury occurs to a child who is unaccompanied.

*Lyes v Middlesex County Council* (1962) 61 LGR 443
A pupil's prank caused another pupil to break the glass in a door. It was held that the glass was too thin for the rough-and-tumble of school life.

*Refell v Surrey County Council* [1964] 1 All ER 743
A girl was badly cut when her hand went through a glass panel on a swing door in a school corridor – the glass was too thin. The school authority was held liable.

## 11.10.2   Occupier's liability

### *(a)   General principles*

In addition to common law negligence, an occupier of land, for example a school or its governors, is under the statutory duty provided in the Occupier's Liability Act 1957. Section 2(1) of the Act provides:

> 'An occupier owes the same duty, the "common duty of care", to all his visitors, except insofar as he is free to and does extend, restrict, modify or exclude his duty to any visitor or visitors by agreement or otherwise.'

For the purposes of the Act:

–   an occupier is a person who is in control of premises sufficient to place him under a duty of care to visitors;

- 'premises' means any fixed or moveable structure including a vehicle, ladder or scaffolding;
- 'visitors' includes those expressly invited onto the premises; and those such as tradesmen who by implication have the right to enter the premises; those who enter under the terms of a contract, and those who have contracted with the occupier so as to permit a third party to enter the premises.

The Act contemplated that an occupier might be able to exclude or limit his liability by notice, provided that reasonable steps were taken to bring it to the visitor's attention and that it was in clear and unambiguous terms. That right has, however, been severely reduced by s 2 of the Unfair Contract Terms Act 1977 which provides that a person cannot, by reference to a contract term or to a notice, exclude or restrict his liability for death or personal injury caused by negligence; and, in the case of other loss or damage, he cannot exclude or restrict his liability for negligence unless the term or notice satisfies the requirement of reasonableness.

The duty defined in s 2(2) of the Act is known as 'the common duty of care'. It is defined as:

> 'A duty to take such care as in all the circumstances of the case is reasonable to see that the visitor will be reasonably safe in using the premises for the purpose for which he is invited or permitted to be there.'

There is little difference between this and the 'common law' duty of care.

### (b)  Independent contractors

Section 2(4)(b) of the Act provides that the occupier will not be liable if it was reasonable to entrust work to a contractor and the occupier took such steps (if any) as he reasonably ought, to see that the contractor was competent and had done the work properly.

As a general guideline, the following would be expected of an occupier:

- if the independent contractor is engaged in work of a technical nature, the occupier is not necessarily expected to check the work;
- if the work is a complex project, the occupier may be expected to employ a qualified specialist to check;
- if the work is of a routine nature requiring no particular skill or expertise, the occupier may himself be expected to check it and will be liable for failing to do so if injury or damage to property is thereby caused.

These obligations have to some extent been circumscribed by the Construction, Design and Management Regulations, SI 1994/3140.

### (c)  Duty owed to trespassers and others

The expression 'trespasser' can mean anything from a child who has wandered or an adult who takes a short cut across a farmer's field without permission, to a person who is intent on burglary or even murder. Trespassers have acquired quite a measure of protection under the law by virtue of the Occupiers' Liability Act 1984 which also protects persons exercising private rights of way. Different legal provisions protect those who use public rights of way.

Section 1(3) of the 1984 Act provides that the occupier owes a duty if:

– he is aware of the danger or has reasonable grounds to believe that it exists;
– he knows or has reasonable grounds to believe that the 'trespasser' is in or may come into the vicinity of the danger concerned; and
– the risk is one against which, in all the circumstances of the case, the occupier may reasonably be expected to offer the 'trespasser' some protection.

This duty applies only to personal injury or death but liability for loss of or damage to property is expressly excluded by s 1(8) of the 1984 Act.

The duty when it applies is described at s 1(4) in terms of a duty 'to take such care as is reasonable in all the circumstances of the case . . .'.

# Chapter 12

## TEACHERS AND PROFESSIONAL LIABILITY

### 12.1   INTRODUCTION

This chapter is concerned with the professional liability of teachers and the vicarious liability of their employers in relation to the educational well being of pupils. For the purposes of this chapter, 'teacher' is used to include a head, assistant teacher or advisory teacher. Reference is also made to psychiatrists, educational psychologists and social workers.

In general, there is no difference in the duty owed to pupils at an independent school or a State-funded school, but there are important differences in the causes of action and the remedies.

### 12.2   NATURE OF PROFESSIONAL LIABILITY

A teacher is an 'education professional' and owes a duty to each pupil to use the reasonable skill and care of a professional person exercising that particular skill.

#### 12.2.1   The professional standard

The standard of care of a professional person was described by McNair J in *Bolam v Friern Hospital Management Committee* [1957] 2 All ER 118, a case about medical negligence. Now widely known as the 'Bolam test', his statement of the law was approved by the House of Lords in three leading cases of the 1980s. He explained the law in these terms:

> '... where you get a situation which involves the use of some special skill or competence, then the test of whether there has been negligence or not is not the test of the man on the Clapham Omnibus, because he has not got this special skill. The test is the standard of the ordinary skilled man exercising and professing to have that special skill. A man need not possess the highest expert skill at the risk of being found negligent ... it is sufficient if he exercises the ordinary skill of an ordinary competent man exercising that particular art ...'

> 'A doctor is not guilty of negligence if he has acted in accordance with a practice accepted as proper by a responsible body of medical men skilled in that particular art ... Putting it the other way round, a doctor is not negligent, if he is acting in accordance with such a practice, merely because there is a body of opinion that takes a contrary view.'

This is the standard that is applied to all those who exercise professional skills, including teachers. The standard is *reasonable care*; it is not a guarantee against all error. The teacher will not be judged by the standards of the most experienced, the most skilful or the most highly qualified teacher, but by reference to the standards of the ordinarily competent teacher in that particular field.

Moreoever, it will be rare for the courts to condemn a commonly accepted practice as negligence unless it is an inherently bad practice. This implies an obligation on the part of professionals to keep up to date with new developments in their particular field. In the *Bolam* case, McNair J pointed out that a medical practitioner cannot 'obstinately and pigheadedly carry on with some old technique if it has been proved to be contrary to what is really substantially the whole of informed medical opinion'.

The standard of care expected is judged objectively and not subjectively. Thus, it was held in *Nettleship v Weston* [1971] 2 QB 691, a case about a learner driver who caused an accident, that a defendant who is inexperienced or who is just learning a particular task or skill must come up to the standards of the reasonably competent and experienced person. His 'incompetent best' is not good enough. That rule applies to professionals and non-professionals alike.

It has long been recognised by the law that in many spheres of professional activity there can be no guarantee of success although a professional person does guarantee that he will use reasonable skill and care to the professional standard for the particular case. Often, success or failure depend upon factors beyond the professional person's control. The doctor cannot guarantee that a particular medicine or surgical procedure will be successful. The lawyer cannot guarantee that a judge or jury will find in his (or her) client's favour. Nor can the teacher guarantee a pupil's rate of learning and development, success in public examinations or entry to a particular job or university. In most cases, there is bound to be an appreciable failure rate but that is not of itself an indication of negligence.

In *Greaves & Co (Contractors) Ltd v Baynham Meikle & Partners* [1975] 1 WLR 1095, CA, Lord Denning MR said:

> 'The law does not usually imply a warranty that a [professional man] will achieve the desired result, but only a term that he will use reasonable care and skill. The surgeon does not warrant that he will cure the patient. Nor does the solicitor warrant that he will win the case.'

## 12.2.2   Teachers

These principles are also reflected for teachers in the case-law.

In *X (Minors) and Others v Bedfordshire County Council* [1995] 2 AC 633, the House of Lords confirmed that teachers are subject to the professional standard.

In *R v Surrey County Council Education Committee ex parte H* [1985] 83 LGR 219, CA, Slade J said that there is no duty placed upon a school to educate a child to the best possible standards. There is no duty to provide such a Utopian system or to educate him to his maximum potential.

Moreover, in *E (A Minor) v Dorset County Council; Christmas v Hampshire County Council; Keating v Bromley London Borough Council* [1994] 4 All ER 641, CA (known as 'the *Keating* case'), Sir Thomas Bingham MR said at p 657:

'... teachers, however dedicated and gifted, cannot rectify inequalities of endowment between one pupil and another; teachers have no duty to ensure that any pupil achieves his full potential; and they are not liable, as no professional person is liable, for mere errors of judgment.'

Elsewhere, it has been suggested that educating children is not as straightforward as manufacturing products. Every child is unique. There can be no guarantee that tried and tested techniques will benefit every pupil.

## 12.3  CONTRACT AND TORT

### 12.3.1  Overview

A certain amount of the litigation in professional negligence cases has been concerned with whether the claim should be brought in contract, or the tort of negligence or the independent tort known as breach of statutory duty. This distinction is relevant to the way the action is pleaded, the loss and damage that can be claimed and in some instances, the limitation period. In general, contract should be used where there is a contractual relationship.

A *contract* is a legally enforceable agreement between two or more parties. Only a party to the contract can sue in respect of it. He (or she) may sue for breach of a contractual duty. As respects damage suffered, he may sue for economic (ie financial) loss alone and for an unrealised gain and/or loss actually suffered. 'Economic loss' means loss arising independently of personal injury or damage to property.

A *tort*, on the other hand, is non-consensual and arises out of an act done by a person who has caused some form of wrongful harm to another or to his property or reputation. To prove the tort of negligence a person must first establish that he (or she) was owed a duty of care which was breached. Unlike in contract, a person suing in tort can sue only for loss suffered, not for an unrealised gain and he cannot generally sue for economic loss alone. He must establish that he has suffered personal injury (mental or physical) or damage to property. However, in a case of educational needs, it may now be sufficient to establish that there was a negligent failure by a school authority to mitigate the adverse consequences of a congenital defect by early diagnosis and appropriate treatment or educational provision.

A *breach of statutory duty* is a species of tort which is of particular relevance in the context of the educational needs of a pupil at a State-funded school but not, in general, at an independent school. Not every statutory duty imposed on a public authority creates a duty of care to the private citizen. Much depends on whether Parliament intended a specific duty to arise. During the 1990s, the House of Lords has been concerned in a number of cases to evolve principles that maintain a balance between:

– ensuring that individuals have a remedy either under a statutory mechanism or through the courts; without
– opening the floodgates to claims that would cast on public authorities an impossible burden of litigation, and expense in the form of damages and legal costs.

## 12.3.2    Professional negligence in contract

The law of professional negligence developed under the principles of the law of contract because most professional relationships arose out of a contract to provide professional services in return for a reasonable fee. Each contract for services includes an implied, if not express, term that the supplier will exercise reasonable skill and care. This is implied both by common law and by s 13 of the Supply of Goods and Services Act 1982.

As the law developed, the rule, known as 'privity of contract', that only a party to a contract can sue in respect of it gave rise to difficulties when there was professional negligence but no contractual relationship. Some examples were as follows:

–    Where a house-buyer relied on a negligent report prepared by a surveyor on the instructions of a building society – see *Smith v Eric S Bush* [1990] 1 AC 31, HL.

–    Where plaintiffs decided to take over a public limited company having relied on audited accounts negligently prepared by the company's auditors – see *Caparo Industries plc v Dickman* [1990] 2 AC 605, HL.

–    Where beneficiaries under a will lost their inheritance because solicitors delayed in carrying out their client's instructions to draw up the will – see *White v Jones* [1995] 2 AC 209, HL.

–    Where a negligent reference was given in respect of a former self-employed agent – see *Spring v Guardian Assurance plc* [1995] 2 AC 296, HL.

–    Where managing agents caused loss both to direct and indirect names at Lloyds by failing to carry out their functions with reasonable skill and care – see *Henderson v Merrett Syndicates* [1995] 2 AC 145, HL.

–    Where a highway authority failed promptly to rectify a stretch of road which it had determined was dangerous – see *Stovin v Wise* [1996] 1 AC 923.

–    Where negligent advice from a Health and Safety Executive Inspector caused two local councils to impose an *ultra vires* ban on the plaintiff using a crane for the provision of bungee jumping – see *Harris v Evans and Another* [1998] 1 WLR 1285, CA.

–    Where a local authority made a careless misstatement about whether it was safe for a mother to send her son to a particular childminder – see *Harrison v Surrey County Council and Others* [1994] 2 FCR 1306, QBD, and *Hedley Byrne*, which is discussed at **12.3.3** below.

–    Where an educational psychologist employed by a local educational authority gave negligent advice with respect to a pupil – see *Phelps v Hillingdon London Borough Council* (1998) *The Times*, 9 November, CA.

–    Where a local education authority wrongly took account of financial resources when failing to provide suitable education for a sick child – see *R v East Sussex County Council ex parte T* [1998] 2 WLR 884, HL.

– Where local education authorities allegedly failed to detect and/or deal appropriately with children with special educational needs – see *X (Minors) and Others v Bedfordshire County Council* [1995] 2 AC 633, HL: the *Dorset, Hampshire* and *Bromley* cases.

– Where local authorities allegedly failed to protect children from child abuse – see *X (Minors) and Others* (above): the *Bedfordshire* and *Newham* cases.

In the same category will be a case where a pupil at a State-funded or independent school (there being no contractual relationship between the school and the pupil in either case) suffers a negligent failure to detect or appropriately treat his (or her) learning difficulties or where some other negligence causes economic loss alone.

Irrespective of whether the plaintiff could succeed in any of these or similar cases, a rigid rule that professional negligence actions or claims for economic loss alone could be pursued only in contract and not in tort would deprive plaintiffs of the opportunity to seek a remedy.

### 12.3.3   Professional negligence in tort

To fill this lacuna, the courts have allowed a person to sue for professional negligence in tort if he (or she) can show that there was an assumption of personal responsibility to him and/or that a non-contractual professional duty was owed to him and was broken and that he has suffered loss or damage of a kind the law recognises and the cause was not too remote. The senior judges who developed the law of tort have generally declined to allow claims in negligence for purely economic loss because of the large number of potential claimants in certain kinds of case. This rule has, however, been ameliorated so as to give plaintiffs the opportunity of a remedy in certain of the cases of the kind listed at **12.3.2** above.

Moreover, a claim may be brought for economic loss alone if a careless misstatement was made in the context of a 'special relationship' between the parties, for example a relationship that was contractual, fiduciary or 'equivalent to contract'. In other words, the principal mechanism was the nature of the relationship between the parties rather than the nature of the loss. In *Hedley Byrne & Co Ltd v Heller & Partners Ltd* [1964] AC 465, HL, the plaintiffs suffered financial losses when they acted in reliance on favourable references given by a banker 'without responsibility'. The plaintiff's claim failed but the House of Lords outlined some principles on which the courts have subsequently developed this area of the law. *Hedley Byrne* is the leading case on 'careless misstatement'.

In *Hippolyte v London Borough of Bexley* [1995] PIQR 309, CA, Steyn LJ stated:

> '. . . it has long been recognised that there is a special relationship between a teacher and a pupil which may potentially give rise to a duty on a teacher to take positive steps to protect the pupil from physical harm.'

It is submitted, that since *X (Minors) and Others* discussed at **12.4.2** below, the special relationship will now also give rise to a duty to deal appropriately with a pupil's educational needs. This would be no more than an incremental development of the duty that can arise out of a 'special relationship'.

It will be noticed that many of the cases on professional negligence in tort, careless misstatement and special relationships and also breach of statutory duty have finished in the House of Lords. That is a measure of the immense implications these cases have for public authorities as well as for education and the professions. It is a complicated and embryonic area of the law and its future development is difficult to predict.

## 12.4   LEARNING DIFFICULTIES

### 12.4.1   Special needs legislation

The Education Act 1944 contained provisions for the approval of certain schools at which pupils with special educational needs would be placed. In those days the emphasis was on 'handicap' per se, but there was little understanding of the kinds of learning difficulties that are now often classified as dyslexia, dyspraxia, dyscalculia, attention deficit hyperactivity disorder (ADHD), and emotional and behavioural difficulties (EBD).

The Education Act 1981 gave effect to the central recommendations of the Warnock Committee's Report entitled *Special Educational Needs* (Cmnd 7212, 1978). The Warnock Committee set out a new way of identifying children who needed special help under the education system. Special education would be conceived in terms of need and provision rather than defined categories of handicap.

Since 1980, the picture has at times become confused by what have been referred to as 'boutique disorders' reported by educationists from America which may in some cases be little more than a guise for idleness, indiscipline or cheating in public examinations.

The law relating to special needs was consolidated in the Education Act 1996. Section 312(1) of the Act provides:

> 'A child has "special educational needs" for the purposes of this Act if he has a learning difficulty which calls for special educational provision to be made for him.'

Section 312(2) of the Act provides:

> '... a child has a "learning difficulty" for the purposes of this Act if –
>
> (a) he has a significantly greater difficulty in learning than the majority of children of his age
> (b) he has a disability which either prevents or hinders him from making use of educational facilities of a kind generally provided for children of his age in schools within the area of the local education authority, or
> (c) he is under the age of five and is or would be if special educational provision were not made for him, likely to fall within paragraph (a) or (b) when of or over that age.'

Section 312(3) provides:

> 'A child is not to be taken as having a learning difficulty solely because the language (or form of the language) in which he is, or will be, taught is different from a language (or form of language) which has at any time been spoken in his home.'

## 12.4.2   The case-law

The law in this area is being developed rapidly and with great difficulty, a number of the cases ending up in the Court of Appeal or House of Lords. This is because most of the litigation about special needs arises out of State-funded education, and it carries very wide implications for all the services and regulatory functions of a local authority, not merely those that are educational.

There are four main questions being explored in the cases:

(1)   Is dyslexia a personal injury? Or is it a congenital condition and not an injury, and therefore not capable of founding a claim for damages for personal injury?

(2)   If it is not an injury, under what circumstances may a person recover damages in tort for economic loss alone arising out of a failure to detect dyslexia or deal appropriately with some other special educational need?

(3)   When is it fair, just and reasonable for the law to impose a *direct* duty of care on an LEA in favour of a recipient of its services? To what extent does the public interest require that the LEA's immunity from suit should be preserved?

(4)   When is it fair, just or reasonable to impose a duty of care on an *employee* of an LEA, the breach of which would render the LEA *vicariously liable*, thus circumventing the authority's immunity?

The public policy aspects are not, for the most part, directly relevant to independent schools. The questions that are relevant, however, are those relating to: whether dyslexia (and failure to deal appropriately with it) is a matter of personal injury or of congenital condition; the circumstances under which a pupil may be able to sue for economic loss alone; the duty of care and the standard of the duty; and the causation of loss and quantum of damages. All these aspects have been considered in the case-law since 1994, the most recent authority, at the time of writing, being the decision of the Court of Appeal in *Phelps v Hillingdon London Borough Council* (1998) *The Times*, November 9, discussed at **12.4.2(d)** below.

### (a)   The Tony Starkey case (1992)

One of the first dyslexia cases to receive wide coverage in the press was that of *Tony Starkey* in 1992. A complaint of maladministration was made to the Local Government Ombudsman where a maintained school had refused to recognise a boy's dyslexia for 4 years. An award of £5,000 was made to the pupil, £250 to the parents for their time and trouble in pursuing the matter, and £850 for one year's remedial teaching ((1992) *Daily Telegraph*, 20 November).

### (b)   The Keating case; and M v Newham LBC (1994)

The three cases heard together in *E (A Minor) v Dorset County Council; Christmas v Hampshire County Council; Keating v Bromley London Borough Council* [1994] 4 All ER 641, CA, were collectively known as 'the *Keating* case'. These make up three of the five cases heard together in the House of Lords and reported as *X (Minors) and Others v Bedfordshire County Council* [1995] 2 AC 633. The other two cases are

*M and Another v Newham London Borough Council* and *X (Minors) and Others v Bedfordshire County Council*, Court of Appeal judgments of which are reported together at [1994] 4 All ER 602.

The *Keating* case involved consideration of whether a number of claims of undetected, misdiagnosed or neglected special needs of children should be allowed to proceed or should be struck out. The residual value of the *Keating* case and *M v Newham LBC* is to be found in some of the opinions expressed by the senior judges in what was then, and continues to be, a volatile and developing area of the law. The questions addressed in the reports of these cases include:

### (i)   Is a teacher's negligence in detecting and referring special needs capable of causing a pupil damage of a kind recognised by law?

In the *Keating* case at p 669 of the report, Evans LJ said:

> 'In my judgment, for the reasons given at the outset, the failure to treat or the delayed treatment of dyslexia does arguably give rise to a form of injury which can support a claim for damages for negligence in tort. It follows from this that the school teacher's duty to exercise reasonable skill and care to safeguard the pupil from injury includes a duty to be aware of symptoms which a reasonably careful parent or a reasonably skilled and careful teacher would regard as symptoms either of dyslexia or, more generally, of a need for specialist advice ...'

However, in the *Phelps* case discussed at **12.4.2(d)** below, Stuart-Smith LJ held that this was obiter and he disagreed with it, stating that dyslexia is a congenital condition and not an injury.

### (ii)   Is there any difference between the duties owed by a State-funded school and those owed by an independent school?

Evans LJ said at p 669 of the *Keating* case:

> 'This degree of skill and care seems to me to be no less than the parent could reasonably expect from a private school where the duty would be regulated by an implied (or possibly express) term of the contract between the parents and school and in any event, in my judgment, would be owed in tort to the child. If the school failed to notice and report upon specific problems which indicated or might indicate a dyslexic condition, or the child's need for special educational provision, then it seems to me that the parents and the child would have a legitimate cause for complaint.'

Evans LJ then cited with approval a passage from the judgment of O'Connor LJ in *Van Oppen v Bedford Charity Trustees* [1989] 3 All ER 389 at 416 as follows:

> 'When one considers the duty owed by a school to its pupils one finds first of all the duties which the law imposes on all schools because they are schools. These duties are of general application whether the school be provided by the state, or privately, and regardless of whether it be fee-paying or free.'

### (iii)   Is a plaintiff entitled to sue when undetected dyslexia has been caused by a congenital defect?

Sir Thomas Bingham MR said at p 685 of the *Keating* case:

> 'It is also quite clear that none of the plaintiffs can recover damages for a congenital defect. If, however, a plaintiff can show: (1) that the adverse consequences of his congenital defect could have been mitigated by early diagnosis of the defect and appropriate treatment or educational provision; (2) that the adverse consequence of his congenital defect were not mitigated because early diagnosis was not made, or

appropriate treatment not given or provision not made, with resulting detriment to his level of educational attainment and employability; and (3) that this damage is not too remote I do not regard the claim for damage to be necessarily bad.'

### (iv)　Are social workers to be regarded as 'professionals'?

Sir Thomas Bingham MR said at p 662 of the report of the *Keating* case:

'Those who engage professionally in social work bring to their task skill and expertise, the product partly of training and partly of experience, which ordinary uninstructed members of the public are bound to lack. I have no doubt that they should be regarded as members of a skilled profession. Their task is one of immense difficulty, and frequently they are exposed to unjust criticism; but those things may, to a greater or lesser extent, be said of other professionals also.'

### (v)　Is it just and reasonable for the law to allow novel claims in tort of this kind?

Staughton LJ at p 630 of *M v Newham LBC* recognised the difficulties that such claims would cause, in this way:

'... I do not doubt that many claims will be brought, placing further strain on an already stretched system (which will be provided with no more resources). I do not doubt that many claims with little or no prospect of success will be financed by the Legal Aid Fund. Nor that many will be delayed for years, perhaps until the plaintiff is 21. Nor that many claims will be settled, or even decided in favour of a plaintiff whose misfortunes attract sympathy, although there has been no more than an error of judgment.'

### (vi)　What is the extent of a teacher's duty to detect and refer special needs?

Sir Thomas Bingham MR said at p 657 of the *Keating* case:

'... as trained and skilled professionals [teachers] would owe a duty to detect and react appropriately to gross deviations from normality in a pupil's learning performance or behaviour in circumstances where an ordinarily competent teacher would do so. Officials of local education authorities are similarly said to owe the subject of their decisions and actions a duty to exercise reasonable care and skill ... It is hard to say that those who give their advice to parents or know that their advice will be communicated to parents, owe a duty only to their employer and not to those parents and their children ...'

### (c)　X (Minors) and Others v Bedfordshire County Council (1995, HL)

The appeal to the House of Lords in the *Keating* case is reported under the title *X (Minors) and Others v Bedfordshire County Council* [1995] 3 WLR 152. No fewer than 40 previous authorities were considered and referred to in their Lordships' opinions, and a further 89 cases were cited in argument. Three pupils with special educational needs were allowed to continue with their cases. The judicial committee was composed of Lord Jauncey of Tullichettle, Lord Lane, Lord Ackner, Lord Browne-Wilkinson, who gave the leading opinion, and Lord Nolan. The education cases in *X (Minors)* are shortly referred to as the *Bromley* case, the *Dorset* case and the *Hampshire* case, respectively.

Lord Browne-Wilkinson accepted (at p 199 of the report) that the plaintiff in the *Hampshire* case was entitled to amend his claim so as to allege that the failure properly to treat the plaintiff's dyslexia caused psychological damage sufficiently serious to constitute an identifiable mental illness but declined to consider the merits of that claim at that stage.

However, Lord Browne-Wilkinson declined to make a ruling on the local education authority's argument in the *Bromley* case that impairment of the plaintiff's personal and intellectual development was not a form of damage recognised by law.

Perhaps the key passage from the opinion of Lord Browne-Wilkinson is at p 198 of the report where he stated (emphasis added):

> 'The question therefore is whether the headmaster of any school, whether private or public, or a teaching adviser is under a duty to his pupils to exercise skill and care in advising on their educational needs? It is accepted that a school and the teachers at the school are under a duty to safeguard the physical well being of the pupil: *Van Oppen v Clerk to the Bedford Charity Trustees* [1990] 1 WLR 235. *But there is no case where a school or teacher has been held liable for negligent advice relating to the educational needs of a pupil.* The defendant authority maintains that there is no duty of care in relation to such advice.
>
> *In my judgment a school which accepts a pupil assumes responsibility not only for his physical well being but also for his educational needs.* The education of the pupil is the very purpose for which the child goes to school. The head teacher, being responsible for the school, himself comes under a duty of care to exercise the reasonable skills of a headmaster in relation to such educational needs. If it comes to the attention of the headmaster that a pupil is under-performing, he does owe a duty to take such steps as a reasonable teacher would consider appropriate to try to deal with such under-performance. To hold that, in such circumstances, the head teacher could properly ignore the matter and make no attempt to deal with it would fly in the face, not only of society's expectations of what a school will provide, but also the fine traditions of the teaching profession itself. If such head teacher gives advice to the parents, then in my judgment he must exercise the skills and care of a reasonable teacher in giving such advice.
>
> Similarly, in the case of the advisory teacher brought in to advise on the educational needs of a specific pupil, if he knows that his advice will be communicated to the pupil's parents, he must foresee that they will rely on such advice. Therefore in giving that advice he owes a duty to the child to exercise the skill and care of a reasonable advisory teacher ...
>
> The *Bolam* test [1957] 1 WLR 582 will apply and the judge at the trial will have to decide whether or not the advice tendered by the head teacher and advisory teacher was in accord with the views that might have been entertained at the time by reasonable members of the teaching profession.'

The effect of the *Keating* case and *X (Minors)* was to open the way to novel claims for damages arising out of failures by the school to deal adequately with special educational needs including dyslexia, provided that the pupil can prove that proper treatment or referral would have given a more favourable outcome and that the deficit could be quantified in damages. The indication given by the House of Lords was that these claims could be brought in simple negligence on the basis that a failure to detect and treat special needs of itself caused psychological damage sufficient to constitute an identifiable mental illness, although the facts would have to be proved in each case.

Subsequent decisions considered below, however, suggest that successful claims of failure to diagnose a child's dyslexia are likely to be exceptional unless based on something more than a mere failure to perform statutory functions.

## (d)  The Phelps case (1998, CA)

*Phelps v Hillingdon London Borough Council* (1998) *The Times*, November 9, CA, concerned alleged negligence by an educational psychologist employed by a local education authority (LEA). At first instance, Garland J held that the educational psychologist (and the LEA, vicariously) was under a duty of care to a dyslexic plaintiff and was in breach of this duty in failing to discover her dyslexia. The judge also found that, had the LEA known that the plaintiff was dyslexic, it would have adopted a different approach, with the result that her literacy skills would have been improved; and that the failure to mitigate the adverse consequences of a congenital defect, such as dyslexia, sounded in damages and constituted injury.

The Court of Appeal (Stuart-Smith, Otton and Tuckey LJJ) overturned that decision and, in summary, stated, per Stuart-Smith LJ:

(i) For the public policy reasons explained in *X (Minors) and Others*, it was not fair, just or reasonable to impose a direct duty of care on a local education authority to whom a child had been referred for assessment.

(ii) Nor was it fair, just or reasonable to impose such a duty on an educational psychologist employed by the LEA *unless* the employee, in addition to performing her duty to her employers, assumed a personal responsibility to the plaintiff. Imposing such a duty would mean the LEA becoming exposed to vicarious liability through the back door, which would defeat the powerful public policy reasons for granting immunity.

(iii) Dyslexia is a congenital condition and not a personal injury. Failure to ameliorate or mitigate the effects of dyslexia was not a personal injury. Remarks by Evans LJ to the contrary in the *Keating* case were *obiter*.

(iv) However, if the LEA employee had assumed responsibility to protect the plaintiff from the type of loss sustained, then damages for economic loss would be recoverable in tort if that loss was caused by negligence. But there would need to be very clear evidence that the employee had undertaken such a responsibility. Merely because the plaintiff was the object of certain advice, and that parents were told what the advice was, would not amount to such an assumption of responsibility.

(v) An educational psychologist, consulted privately by parents who were concerned at the lack of literacy progress of their child, could be liable in contract for failing to take reasonable care in diagnosing dyslexia, if it was in the reasonable contemplation of the parties that the child would, as a result, be seriously handicapped in achieving literacy. In such a case, the parents could be regarded as acting as agents for the child although there might be serious difficulties in establishing causation.

Stuart-Smith LJ stated that he had derived much assistance from the speech of Lord Steyn in *Williams v Natural Life Foods Ltd* [1998] 1 WLR 830, HL. The court ought to be slow to superimpose on a duty which the employee owed to his employer, a further duty towards the plaintiff, in the absence of very clear evidence that the employee had undertaken such responsibility.

The facts of the *Phelps* case remain relevant to issues of causation and quantum in these cases. The plaintiff had a long history of poor performance at various schools. At the age of 12, she had been referred to an educational psychologist employed by the LEA who attributed the pupil's under-performance to emotional and behavioural problems and reported that, although the plaintiff's verbal skills were below average, she had no specific weaknesses and did not need to be in a special school. Over the next 3 years, the plaintiff had made little or no progress despite remedial teaching provided by the school and she left unable to write down a telephone number correctly or record a simple message. At no time was there a diagnosis of a specific learning difficulty despite the fact that dyslexia was already a well-recognised condition. Further assessments from the age of 17 onwards found her to be severely dyslexic. At first instance, Garland J had awarded the plaintiff general damages of £12,500, together with an award of £25,000 for future loss of earnings and £6,550 for past and future tuition fees plus interest and costs. The plaintiff was aged 23 at trial and was accepted as having been dyslexic from the age of 12.

An inference to be taken from this award, had it survived appeal, is that the courts will be more ready to award special damages, for example the provable cost of private education which meets a child's dyslexic needs, rather than general damages representing the loss incurred in a life blighted by lack of educational provision.

It is submitted that, subject to proving causation, the outcome of the *Phelps* case might have been different had the school itself been negligent by ignoring clear signs of a special educational need. The *Hippolyte* case mentioned at **12.3.3** above seems to be authority for saying that there is a special relationship between a teacher and pupil, and Lord Browne-Wilkinson said in *X (Minors) and Others* that a school which accepts a pupil assumes responsibility not only for his physical well-being but also for his educational needs. (See **12.4.2(c)** above.) After *Phelps*, however, the pupil's action would lie in tort for economic loss, rather than as a personal injury claim.

Against an independent school, the pupil's claim would also lie in tort, for economic loss, and the parents might have a claim in contract for their separate losses (if any), although in the *Cobham Hall* case (see **6.6.4(d)** above), Dyson J doubted whether there was a contract at all between the school and the parents if the pupil had an assisted place.

### (e)   The Christmas case (1998, QBD)

*Christmas v Hampshire County Council* [1998] ELR 1 (QBD), decided before *Phelps* reached the Court of Appeal, was one of the cases which had been considered by the House of Lords in *X (Minors) and Others* and was allowed to proceed. In the event, the plaintiff was unable to prove causation in his case against the LEA.

The facts were that the plaintiff exhibited behavioural problems and reading difficulties at his primary school. It was his headteacher's view that his lack of progress was simply the result of a lack of self-discipline. The plaintiff was transferred to an independent school as a day-pupil at the age of 11 and before long earned himself the reputation of being the 'most disruptive' pupil at the school. He became a boarder for the last 2 years and after leaving school at 16 he obtained low-grade but worthwhile employment. However, his prospects for advancement were placed at nil because of his difficulties in reading, spelling and writing. The plaintiff's case was that if his learning difficulties had been identified at an early age, then appropriate special educational provision would have been made available for him.

It was held by Ian Kennedy J that the evidence suggested the plaintiff had below average attainments, but only to a relatively minor degree, in reading, writing and spelling in his early years at school. Nothing suggested that those deficiencies could not be addressed within the normal school provision, and indeed, the fact that his work improved when he made the necessary effort confirmed this. The headteacher at the primary school had in fact sought out the help of the school's special needs advisory teacher. The evidence pointed to a lack of application on the plaintiff's part and to the need for additional help to be provided for him from within the school's normal resources. A more structured environment at the private secondary school, particularly after he became a boarder in the last 2 years, may well have played a vital part in his subsequent progress. Even so he had continued to under-perform. The evidence suggested that his lack of standard attainment was due to factors other than his specific learning difficulty.

## (f) The Tandy case (1998, HL)

*R v East Sussex County Council ex parte T* [1998] ELR 251, HL (the *Tandy* case), was different from the dyslexic cases because it concerned a duty owed by a local authority directly to a sick child. The plaintiff, since she was 7, had found it very difficult and at times impossible to attend school. In September 1996, her parents were told by the local education authority that provision of home tuition for her would be cut from 5 to 3 hours per week because of a need to achieve a reduction in public spending, ie the decision was related to financial considerations and not the child's illness or educational needs.

It was held that the local authority owed a duty under s 298 of the Education Act 1993 (now s 19 of the Education Act 1996) to make arrangements for the provision of suitable full-time or part-time education. 'Suitable education' in relation to a child means efficient education suitable to his (or her) age, ability and aptitude and to any special needs he may have. That was a statutory duty owed to each sick child individually and not to sick children as a class. A statutory duty could not be downgraded to a statutory power.

Further, it was held that the council had, as a matter of strict legality, the resources to perform its statutory duty under s 298. Whilst it did not wish to bleed its other functions of resources so as to enable it to perform the statutory duty under s 298, it could, if it wished, divert money from other educational applications which were merely discretionary so as to apply such diverted money to discharge the statutory duty. In other words, the argument was not one of insufficient resources to discharge the duty but of a preference for using the money for other purposes.

It was also held that the court would not second-guess the authority in the way in which it spent its limited resources, provided it satisfied statutory duties before satisfying statutory discretions.

The main importance of the *Tandy* case will be in disputes between parents and/or pupils and local education authorities. It will be necessary to decide whether the breach of duty arises out of a statutory duty or a statutory power or discretion which falls short of being a duty. The decision may also be of some relevance to independent schools with pupils who have special needs that are not being adequately supported by the local education authority.

### 12.4.3   Social aspects of learning difficulties

During 1995, the *Daily Telegraph* printed an article written by Jon Westling (then President-Elect of Austin University in Massachusetts) concerning the labelling of students as 'learning disabled'.

He referred to a letter he had received from the University's Office of Disability Services explaining that 'Samantha had a learning disability "in the area of auditory processing" and would need the following accommodations: time-and-a-half on all tests and examinations; double-time on any mid-term or final examinations; examinations in a room separate from other students; copies of lecture notes; and a seat at the front of the class'. The letter also explained that Samantha might fall asleep in class and would need to be filled in on any material she missed while dozing.

Westling went on to state that 15% of school children in Massachusetts were then officially diagnosed as 'learning disabled'; and in Britain, 20% of pupils were said to have 'special needs'.

In his article, Westling emphasised his strong support for the principle that students with specific disabilities deserve an education that helps them achieve their fullest intellectual potential and that the existence of genuine learning disabilities should not be ignored. However, he referred to the 'learning disability movement' as having betrayed this goal. He wrote:

– Finding a subject difficult is not, in itself, evidence of a disability.
– Needing to read at a pace of 40 words per minute to achieve a high level of comprehension may not be an asset but it is not necessarily a disability either.
– Difficulty in grasping mathematical abstractions is not a disability – it is the norm.
– It is obvious that there are disparities – sometimes dramatic ones – in the speed with which people learn, the levels of skill they can attain in solving problems, and in their general acumen.

Westling was critical of standardised tests which identify the learning disabled as those individuals who in some subjects perform significantly below average for their age group. He said: 'There is an odour of tautology in that approach: how do we know that a low score, or even a series of low scores, implies an underlying lack of ability and not, for example, a lack of interest or motivation?'

In the diagnosis of dyslexia, he emphasised the strong distinction to be made between diagnoses that rest on clear, specific criteria and corroborating medical evidence, and the vast penumbra of unspecific and only vaguely diagnosable complaints which include such so-called diseases as 'dyscalculia', 'foreign language learning disability' and 'dysrationalia', which is defined as 'the inability to think and behave rationally despite adequate intelligence'. Westling described 'attention deficit disorder' sometimes referred to as 'attention deficit hyperactivity disorder' as a fugitive disorder with no standard test and a lack of grounding in careful medical or scientific inquiry.

He concluded that the underlying motivation for at least some diagnoses is 'an ideology of extreme egalitarianism that denies the reality of the unequal distribution of intellectual talents'. Contemporary learning disability advocates speak not about children in need, but about societies that label and oppress. Inappropriate diagnoses of 'learning disability' wreak educational havoc from kindergarten to university. Students who have genuine learning disabilities, lumped together with sufferers of imaginary complaints, are denied the education they deserve. Understanding that a subject is difficult but worth pursuing is a dimension of self-understanding.

### 12.4.4   Policy on learning difficulties

An independent school is not required to draw up its policy in relation to learning difficulties but may be strongly advised to do so none the less for these reasons in particular:

–   to reinforce the responsibility of parents to disclose a history of learning difficulties within the family;
–   to ensure that parents do not abandon to the school the parents' share of responsibility for their child's educational development;
–   to explain to parents the type and level of difficulty that the school can or cannot cater for;
–   to establish a regime of routine testing, ie screening of all pupils and a mechanism for communicating the results to parents and deciding on what (if any) further referral or other action is needed.

Subject to the continuing availability of legal aid for claims by pupils, undetected or misdiagnosed learning difficulties are set to become a significant source of litigation. Whilst it is in no one's interest for schools to adopt defensive attitudes in this area, a policy will form the basis of good practice as well as affording a defence to claims that are ill-founded 'boutique disorders' of the kind described by Jon Westling at **12.4.3** above.

A school may decide it should seek professional advice on the final drafting of its policy on learning difficulties. Every policy document should be dated with a review date indicated. Its legal status should be described as contractual or non-contractual and its intended circulation should be indicated.

An important aspect of routine testing for learning difficulties is that the standardised tests currently available to schools are 'screening' and not diagnostic tests. At best, they will reveal the need for a formal assessment to be carried out by a specialist adviser or an educational psychologist. Screening tests are not infallible and it is therefore a sound policy to re-test at the appropriate level every 2 or 3 years or at an earlier stage if cause for concern has been expressed.

It is equally important to ensure that the outcome of screening tests is reported to parents by letter. The letter will inform parents that a learning difficulty is or is not suspected.

The practice in mainstream independent schools of charging parents for remedial teaching has come under question. The dictum of Lord Browne-Wilkinson in *X (Minors)* (above) that 'a school which accepts a pupil assumes responsibility not only for his physical well being but also for his educational needs' suggests that a reasonable amount of remedial teaching – one or two sessions per week perhaps – should be regarded as part of the normal curriculum for children who are in any event normally withdrawn from a lesson in a non-core subject.

There is, in principle, no reason in contract law why schools should not stipulate that additional or remedial tuition is an 'extra' and on present statistical evidence there is no reason to suppose that making a charge would give rise to a claim of indirect discrimination on grounds of sex or race. However, independent schools have in many cases had to make a transition from simply not recognising learning difficulties to detecting and providing for them, and it has been suggested that to charge for such tuition is a form of moral, if not legal, discrimination and at odds with the ethos of a school community.

## 12.5    TEACHING STANDARDS

### 12.5.1    National Curriculum

The National Curriculum introduced under the Education Reform Act 1988 is not compulsory for independent schools although they customarily take notice of it and seek to exceed its requirements.

In April 1993, the Secretary of State asked Sir Ron Dearing as Chairman of the Schools' Curriculum and Assessment Authority (SCAA) to carry out a review of all the statutory curriculum orders and the framework for assessing pupils' progress in England, with a parallel review for Wales. Dearing's final recommendations were accepted in full by the government and, after a subsequent review by SCAA, they formed the basis of new Orders which were published in January 1995.

The revised version of the National Curriculum was generally thought to represent a significant improvement on its predecessor and included a 5-year moratorium in order to provide a period of stability after years of turmoil.

The National Curriculum includes the 'Key Stages' in the course of a pupil's progress through compulsory education, a prescribed syllabus as contained in the individual Subject Orders, and assessment arrangements.

The four main Key Stages are:

- Key Stage 1        Pupil ages 5–7        Years 1 and 2
- Key Stage 2        Pupil ages 7–11        Years 3, 4, 5 and 6
- Key Stage 3        Pupil ages 11–14        Years 7, 8 and 9
- Key Stage 4        Pupil ages 14–16        Years 10 and 11

Years 7 and 8 for pupils aged 11–13 are often regarded as the best time for pupils at preparatory schools. It is a time when they reach the top of the school and can make the best use of all the facilities and activities on offer. By then, they have acquired their basic skills and are ready to accept the full quality and range of the teaching in class, games and sports, often from specialists, that is available in many of these schools. The cut-off at age 11 under Key Stage 2 is a matter that is therefore regretted by many preparatory schools, although in the case of girls, it has for many years been normal to transfer schools at 11.

## 12.5.2   Curriculum policies

The curriculum outline, timetable and rationale will be based on a number of policies drawn up or approved by the head and governors. Many schools have academic governors, often heads of other schools, who will advise as needed. It is important that all the staff are inducted and receive training on the curriculum policies that are to be followed.

One that can be controversial, particularly with certain ethnic and religious groups, is sex education which by definition includes education about AIDS, HIV and other sexually transmitted diseases but is otherwise non-specific.

Parents in the maintained sector have the right to request that a pupil be wholly or partly excused from receiving sex education at the school except insofar as such education is specified in the National Curriculum. There is a statutory obligation to deliver sex education in a manner that encourages pupils to have due regard to moral considerations and the value of family life. Guidance on this was given in DFE Circular 5/94 *Sex Education in Schools*. Particular difficulties arise over teaching pupils about contraception and homosexuality, and there needs to be a policy which draws a clear distinction between education and personal advice.

Religious education (RE) does not form part of the National Curriculum for maintained schools but enjoys a special status in the basic curriculum and is normally taught at independent schools.

The curriculum policies adopted at independent schools might include those relating to:

- Schemes of work.
- Internal examinations and testing and external examinations.
- Homework, marking and various aspects of presentation.
- Information technology across the curriculum and computer misuse.
- Special need and gifted children.
- Health education, including sex, drugs and substances.
- Monitoring academic progress and reporting to parents.
- Social policies such as equal opportunities, including race, gender, multi-culture, disability and citizenship.
- Careers and citizenship.

There may be many other policies in addition.

### 12.5.3   Substandard teaching

The clearest evidence of substandard teaching will be when:

–   there has been a failure to notice a material change in the syllabus; or
–   the wrong syllabus is taught; or
–   a design technology teacher carries out too much of the pupil's practical work.

In any of these cases, the pupil is likely to be marked down in a public examination. That may be a matter of considerable disappointment but it will not necessarily cause economic loss unless success in the particular subject is of crucial importance to the next stage of the pupil's education, training or work. In this case, he (or she) may have to resit the year and will lose at least his first year's earnings on the assumption he would have obtained employment.

During a resit year, the pupil may be paying his own tuition fees. If they are paid by his parents, they will be entitled to recover the cost under the contract for educational services. At present there seems to be no direct authority for suggesting that the pupil might be entitled to general damages for disappointment and inconvenience.

### 12.5.4   Examination disappointment

Disappointment in public examinations without some additional evidence of negligence is unlikely to be sufficient for a claim of professional negligence. It has been explained at **12.2.1** that professional people – and teachers are no exception – do not in general guarantee their product, nor can they do so. There is no guarantee that tried and tested teaching techniques will benefit every pupil and there may be a number of influences at work in the background including home circumstances, natural ability and also the application of the pupil concerned.

In the *Keating* case discussed earlier, Sir Thomas Bingham MR said at p 670 of the report:

> 'The question which does arise is whether a teacher ... owes a duty of skill and care in relation to the child's education which goes beyond the duty to safeguard his or her physical and, I would add, mental well-being. Suppose that there was no allegation of dyslexia or some other equivalent dysfunction in the present case, but merely an allegation that the child with better teaching could have achieved higher academic standards, or improved examination results, or a more highly paid career. Could it be held that the teacher, if he had failed to teach with reasonable skill and care, and the authority as his employer, was liable in damages in such a case? My provisional view is that the answer must be "No", because the plaintiff in such an action could not show any measurable injury other than economic loss, and it is established by the judgments in *Van Oppen* that no case lies in negligence in respect of such loss.'

### 12.5.5   Changes of teacher

A difficult case is where, by reason of maternity leave or sickness, there are two or three changes of teacher at critical times during the GCSE or A-level course. In theory, a change of teacher should make no difference and *Mount v Oldham Corporation* [1973] 1 QB 309, CA, is authority for suggesting that a teacher's absence for 6 months with a serious illness would not necessarily frustrate the contract. In practice, it is a very unsatisfactory situation for the pupil and the parents and one that is recognised as such by every school. It is submitted, however, that these are in the nature of life events that often cannot reasonably be provided for in advance and are therefore unlikely to amount to a breach of the professional duty to use reasonable skill and care.

### 12.5.6   Inability to keep order

There may or may not be professional liability in the case of a teacher who is substandard in the sense that he (or she) is unable to keep reasonable order and discipline in the classroom, fails to inspire his (or her) pupils and generally delivers a second-rate product. Each case will turn on its facts. Evidence will include the response of the school to any complaints or concerns expressed. Such cases are unlikely to lead to damages for professional negligence because of the difficulty of identifying a quantifiable loss. It is more likely that parents could sustain a small set-off against fees as a contractual remedy in such a case.

## 12.6   WITHHOLDING EXAMINATION RESULTS

Independent schools which have had their contracts with parents professionally drafted will normally have provided a condition to the effect that the school is entitled to withhold information and property at any time when fees are unpaid.

In *Grenar v The Royal School, Hindhead* (1997, unreported), parents owed some £8,000 to the school and refused to reach any form of agreement for payment by instalments. When the pupil completed her GCSE examinations, the governors warned that they would withhold her examination results and certificates, her National Record of Achievement and her portfolio of artwork unless the parents entered an instalment arrangement which would allow them to pay over more than 6 years. The parents made no allegations of complaint against the school but still refused. The results were initially withheld.

The pupil issued proceedings alleging she had been caused personal injury as a result of the distress she had suffered. She disclosed a psychiatric report purporting to show that she had suffered an 'adjustment disorder'. On that basis, she obtained an interlocutory injunction ordering a release of her GCSE results.

The governors' application to strike out the pupil's action on the grounds that it was scandalous, vexatious and an abuse of process was successful. It was held, inter alia, that:

– the contract for educational services came to an end when the pupil left the school after her GCSEs;
– once she had left school no continuing duty of care was owed to her;
– it would not in any event be just and reasonable to impose a duty of care towards the pupil in circumstances which would have the effect of defeating a valid condition in the contract allowing the school to withhold information and property at any time when fees were unpaid;

– the examination contract was made between the school and the examining board, and the pupil had no right of intellectual property in the examination results.

The cause of action in this case was alleged psychological injury caused by negligence rather than economic loss caused by professional negligence, but it appears that the judge's findings would have been sufficient to dismiss either cause of action.

## 12.7   WRONGFUL EXPULSION

Expulsion and the requirement to leave are considered at Chapter 16. The point that arises under the heading of professional negligence is a requirement to leave that is based on an inadequate investigation or unfair procedures or which is a disproportionate sanction having regard to the nature of the breach of school discipline.

In *R v Cobham Hall School ex parte S* [1998] ELR 389, QBD, the head wrote to parents explaining that their daughter's assisted place was being 'reallocated' because the pupil's academic work and behaviour had not been to the required standard. The head's evidence was that she dealt with the matter in this way rather than stigmatise the girl by an expulsion. The case involved a judicial review of the head's decision in which the pupil sought a declaration that the school had acted unlawfully and also an order of mandamus directing the school to reinstate her. Dyson J stated *obiter* at p 401 to the effect that if the school acts unlawfully over an expulsion, the court has jurisdiction to require the school to reinstate the pupil on a non-paying basis if necessary, for example if an assisted place is no longer available. In the *Cobham Hall* case, the school was not ordered to reinstate the pupil.

The position of a private, self-regulating community such as an independent school will be subject to review by the courts under the Human Rights Act 1998. Both the school and the pupil will acquire rights under the Act in any case in which the school is found to have been carrying out a public function. In any event, the 'human rights overlay' will increase the importance of there being fair procedures when expulsion or a requirement to leave is being considered.

Undoubtedly, some cases of wrongful expulsion can give rise to economic loss but whether the action of a parent or a pupil will succeed will depend on balancing the human rights of the pupil with the rights of the school community having regard to the particular circumstances of each case. The numbers of these cases may depend on the continuing availability of legal aid for money claims.

## 12.8   PARENTS' CLAIMS

In a case of undetected or misdiagnosed special needs, parents may have a cause of action for breach of their contract with the school but they will only be able to claim in respect of *their* losses rather than those of the pupil. The parents' losses may include the cost of remedial teaching and/or of the pupil repeating a year and maintenance of the pupil during that year when he (or she) might otherwise have been earning his own living, and certain heads of special damage. Parents may in addition be entitled to claim repayment of fees for earlier terms if the facts show that the school was in fundamental breach of its obligations during those terms.

In an unreported case in 1996, parents had entered their son as a boarder in the lower sixth form of an independent school. At the end of his fifth term, the boy was assessed by an educational psychologist appointed by his parents as having a 'semantic processing difficulty' which arose out of his slow thought-processing. The school applied for and obtained additional time for the pupil in his A-level examinations. The parents, however, alleged that the school was at fault for having failed to detect and refer the processing difficulty. The parents sought repayment of past fees and release from outstanding fees. In the event, the pupil obtained the A-level grades that were expected and the parents settled the school's claim and withdrew their defence and counterclaim.

## 12.9   SPORTS

The growth in importance of professional sport may in due course produce claims of professional negligence against schools although none have been reported to date. The schools that are most vulnerable will be those which set out to attract pupils of exceptional aptitude and ability in a particular sport and then fail to teach the techniques or provide the opportunities reasonably to be expected of a school offering that level of specialist service. There would be formidable obstacles in such cases, not least in proving loss and damage of a kind that the law recognises.

## 12.10   PSYCHOLOGICAL INJURY

Leaving aside cases based on undetected or misdiagnosed learning difficulties or other special needs, the complexity and uncertainty of a pupil's remedy for an alleged breach of professional duty in tort has led practitioners to find another hook on which to hang a claim for damages for economic loss. This hook is psychological injury. The *Grenar* case, discussed at **12.6** above, was an example.

Claims based on psychological injury have a number of hurdles to overcome. The plaintiff will need to satisfy the conditions for proving a psychological injury which are:

- that the plaintiff has sustained a recognisable psychiatric illness which has been diagnosed; and
- that a person of reasonable fortitude would be likely to experience shock in the circumstances of the case; and
- that the condition would not have been suffered *but for* the acts or omissions complained of.

The plaintiff will also need to prove causation between the act or omission and the injury. That can be very difficult in cases of psychological injury when the real cause may have more to do with family circumstances and the temperament, lifestyle, general intelligence and application of the pupil than with the act or omission complained of.

The numbers of cases that are brought will to some extent depend on the continuing availability of legal aid which at the time of writing is set to be abolished for most money claims.

## 12.11  NEGLIGENT REFERENCE

A confidential reference or record may be the cause of a pupil failing to gain admission to a school, college or university of choice or suffering some other disadvantage. In those cases, it may be difficult for the pupil to show that he (or she) has suffered quantifiable loss. A clearer case would be the negligent reference that prevents getting a training contract or job.

In *Spring v Guardian Assurance plc* [1995] 2 AC 296, where the negligent reference was described by the judge at first instance as 'the kiss of death to the plaintiff's career in the insurance industry' it was held that the former employer owed a duty to give a reference that was fair and balanced and that if the person giving the reference was not in possession of all the facts he must use reasonable care and skill to find out the facts. The plaintiff was entitled to bring his action for a breach of a professional duty in tort or contract, although contract should be used where a contractual relationship existed.

## 12.12  LIMITATION PERIODS

A legal action will be time-barred unless commenced within the period prescribed by the Limitation Act 1980. Time runs from the date when the cause of action accrued but that date is not always free from doubt. In the case of a person under 18, the limitation period starts to run on his (or her) eighteenth birthday. The complex rules governing limitation of actions are set out in the standard text books and are outside the scope of this chapter, but brief reference is made to them below.

–    For an action in tort or contract not involving personal injuries or death, the limitation period is 6 years.

–    The limitation period for actions for trespass to the person such as assault and false imprisonment is 6 years even where personal injury is the consequence.

–    For other cases involving death or personal injury the limitation period is 3 years but this is subject to special rules that apply under Limitation Act 1980, ss 11–14 and 33.

–    The Latent Damage Act 1986 inserted a new s 14A into the Limitation Act 1980 which applies to claims in negligence other than those involving death or personal injuries. Section 14A provides an alternative limitation period of 3 years from the 'starting date' (see below). There is a 15-year long-stop from the last of the dates on which an act or omission occurred which constituted negligence to which the damage claimed is attributable.

–    It appears that s 14A of the Limitation Act 1980 applies only to actions for the tort of negligence and not to claims framed in contract (see *Société Commerciale de Reassurance v Eras (International) Limited* [1992] 2 All ER 82, CA.

– Section 14A(5) inserted into the Limitation Act 1980 by the Latent Damage Act 1986 provides that the 'starting date' is: 'The earliest date on which the plaintiff or any person in whom the cause of action was vested before him first had both the knowledge required for bringing an action for damages in respect of the relevant damage and a right to bring such an action'.

– 'Knowledge' for these purposes means knowledge of 'the material facts about the damage', that is, such facts as could lead a reasonable person to consider the damage sufficiently serious to justify instituting proceedings. It also means 'knowledge' that the damage was attributable in whole or in part to the act or omission complained of, and knowledge of the defendant's identity or the identity of any other person whose act or omission constitutes the alleged negligence.

## 12.13  PROFESSIONALISM

### 12.13.1  Meaning of 'professional person'

The authors of *Jackson and Powell on Professional Negligence* (Sweet & Maxwell) identify four characteristics of the occupations which are regarded as professions.

### *(1)  The nature of the work*

The features identified are: the work is skilled and specialised; a substantial part of it is mental rather than manual; and a period of theoretical and practical training is usually required before the work can be adequately performed.

### *(2)  The moral aspect*

A professional person is expected to be committed to certain moral principles which go beyond the general duty of honesty. He (or she) is expected to provide a high standard of service for its own sake and to be particularly concerned about the duty of confidentiality. He (or she) may also owe a wider duty to the community (in the context of a school, the school community) which may on occasions transcend the duty to the individual (the particular pupil).

### *(3)  Collective organisation*

The person usually belongs to a professional association which regulates admission and seeks to uphold standards. Such associations commonly set examinations to test competence and issue professional codes on matters of conduct and ethics.

### *(4)  Status*

Most professions have a high status in the community although public opinion of a particular profession will vary from time to time, often depending on the treatment of that profession in the media. It is well known that teachers widely regard their salary levels as undermining the value in which they are held in the minds of the public.

## 12.13.2    Case-law

Traditionally, the word 'profession' was confined to the three learned professions, the Church, medicine and law, but the categories have expanded during the twentieth century.

In *Commissioners of Inland Revenue v Maxse* [1919] 1 KB 647, Scrutton LJ said:

> '... a profession in the present use of language involves the idea of an occupation requiring either purely intellectual skill, or a manual skill controlled, as in painting and sculpture or surgery, by the intellectual skill of the operator, as distinguished from an occupation which is substantially the production or sale or arrangements for the production or sale of commodities.'

In *Carr v Inland Revenue Commissioners* [1944] 2 All ER 163, Du Parcq LJ stated, when upholding a finding that an optician was carrying on a profession:

> '... I think that everybody would agree that, before one can say that a man is carrying on a profession, one must see that he has some special skill or ability or some special qualifications derived from training or experience ... ultimately one has to ask this question: Would the ordinary man, the ordinary reasonable man ... say now, in the time in which we live, of any particular occupation, that it is properly described as a profession? Times have changed ... the work of the surgeon used to be carried on by a barber, whom nobody would have considered a professional man. The profession of the chartered accountant has grown up in comparatively recent times, and other trades or vocations ... may in future years acquire the status of professions.'

Most of the cases about professional negligence during the last 50 years have involved architects, engineers, quantity surveyors, property surveyors, solicitors, barristers, medical practitioners, insurance brokers, accountants and auditors and, most recently, members and managing agents at Lloyd's. The teaching profession has hardly featured in the development of the law relating to professional negligence.

## 12.13.3    Implications for teachers

The practical implications for teachers of being subject to the professional duty to use reasonable skill and care appropriate to the particular circumstances, may be described, broadly, in four categories.

### (1)    Reputation and integrity

A teacher's position depends on personal integrity, good reputation and a willingness when necessary to prefer the interests of others to the teacher's own interests. There is a statutory requirement that teachers who are dismissed or who resign in circumstances of misconduct are reported to DfEE under reg 7 of the Education (Particulars of Independent Schools) Regulations 1997. 'Misconduct' means misconduct of any kind and does not require a criminal conviction.

### (2)    Competence and skills

Qualified teachers undergo professional training at the start of their careers and are required to undertake continuing training and education in the form of INSET days. They are expected to develop wide-ranging skills, not only in their specialist subjects but often in ancillary subjects, games, sports and the many aspects of pastoral care. A teacher is expected to accept an ethos of life-long learning and to demonstrate leadership skills and of increasing importance, to accept appraisals. A failure to keep up-to-date may mean that a teacher and, vicariously, the governors or school, are subject to professional liability if injury or damage has been caused.

## *(3) Responsibility and judgement*

Much of a teacher's working life is concerned with the exercise of judgement. Those who earn a living by the exercise of judgement will, from time to time, be subjected to criticism and a requirement of accountability. As a profession, teachers tend to deal less well than many other professionals with criticism of their actions or methods. However, in an increasingly litigious age, they are likely more often to face allegations of professional negligence and to be required to attend court and give evidence. However unwelcome, that is necessarily to be regarded as part of the job when it arises, and it may in due course become a suitable area for training. Moreover, teachers are subject to a range of policies in operation at a school which often amount to a code of conduct and ethics. Within certain limits, teachers are expected to maintain those standards in their private lives and, in that sense, they are never free from the responsibilities of their position or office.

## *(4) Planning and motivation*

As important as any of the other characteristics of a 'professional', a teacher needs to be a 'self-starter' with the ability to prepare, plan and organise his (or her) work and career, but also to make time for recreation to avoid stress and staleness. There must be an ability to motivate children and colleagues, which in turn requires technical competence, self-esteem and confidence.

These are some of the qualities and standards that are, to an increasing extent, demanded of teachers both by employers and indirectly by the law.

# Chapter 13

## PASTORAL CARE

### 13.1  INTRODUCTION

This chapter is concerned with some of the legal and practical – rather than sociological – aspects of the pastoral care of children at independent day and boarding schools. The closely related matters of behaviour, discipline and bullying are considered at Chapter 15.

Pastoral care helps pupils to succeed in their learning tasks and fosters their personal maturity. It is a thread that runs throughout life at school from classroom to games and from organised activities and outings to the less formal structure of the day or boarding house. The underlying ethic of pastoral care is to give pupils good experience so that they develop self-respect and acquire skills for coping with life. The main thrust of pastoral care is towards the happiness, safety and welfare of each pupil and the integrity of the house and school community.

### 13.2  LEGAL ASPECTS

The legal context of pastoral care is a combination of statute, regulation, contract, tort and case law and also guidance issued by Department of Health under s 7 of the Local Authority and Social Services Act 1970, and the procedures of natural justice.

#### 13.2.1  Statute and regulation

The main statutory provisions are by now familiar.

Section 3(1) of the Health and Safety at Work etc Act 1974 imposes a duty to conduct the school in such a way as to ensure so far as reasonably practicable that persons *not* in the school's employment are *not* exposed to risks to their health or safety.

Section 2(9) of the Children Act 1989 has the effect of allowing parents to delegate parental responsibility for their children although the parents do not under s 2(9) surrender or transfer it. At school, the head is the person to whom responsibility is delegated, and he or she is entitled to delegate onwards to teachers and other responsible members of the staff.

Section 3(5) of the Children Act 1989 provides that a person who has the care of a child may, subject to other provisions of the Act, 'do what is reasonable in all the circumstances for the purpose of safeguarding or promoting the child's welfare'. This section provides wide powers and authority when properly directed.

Pastoral care can only be delivered efficiently when premises and systems for ensuring the welfare of staff and children are reasonably safe. Thus, compliance with regulations that have a bearing on health and safety have to be considered in this context also.

Section 13 of the Supply of Goods and Services Act 1982 provides:

> 'In a contract for the supply of a service where the supplier is acting in the course of a business [which includes an independent school], there is an implied term that the supplier will carry out the service with reasonable care and skill.'

When the Human Rights Act 1998 comes into force it will require that all existing legislation must be interpreted so as to be compatible with the rights contained in the European Convention on Human Rights 1950, to the extent enacted. It will become unlawful for a public authority (including courts and tribunals) to act in a way which is incompatible with those rights. It remains to be seen what effect the Act will have on the policies of the governors, the duties they owe to parents under contract and the duty of care they owe to pupils in tort.

### 13.2.2   Contract

It is to be taken as an implied term of the contract between school and parents that the school will provide pastoral care to the extent reasonably necessary for a particular child in particular circumstances. The contractual aspects are probably limited to those which have been expressly promised and those that are reasonably necessary to the safety and welfare of the child. The remaining parts are to be treated as 'value-added'.

There can be no guarantee that a child will be happy at school. In *Mount v Oldham Corporation* [1973] 1 QB 309, CA, Lord Denning MR said:

> 'After a boy goes to school, he may be very unhappy. The school may not suit him. Other boys may be unkind to him. The staff may change for the worse, and so forth. The parent may be quite reasonable in withdrawing the boy; but he must still give a term's notice or pay a term's fees in lieu of notice.'

Much will depend on the reasons for the pupil's unhappiness. If the cause is repeated bullying by staff or pupils or undetected learning difficulties or some other serious failure on the part of the school such as to destroy the basis of confidence in the provision of good care and a successful education, the parents will be entitled to withdraw the pupil immediately and without liability for payment of fees in lieu of notice.

### 13.2.3   Tort

Normally, the pupil has no contractual relationship with the school. Instead, the school owes a duty of care to the pupil which, since the Children Act 1989, amounts to a duty to take reasonable care to safeguard and promote the child's welfare. A child who suffers physical or psychological injury or damage to property in consequence of a breach of that duty will be entitled to bring an action for damages for injuries and other loss and damage including financial loss. The complexities of these cases have been considered in Chapters 11 and 12.

### 13.2.4    Case-law

Most of the cases about pastoral care arise in response to a claim for unpaid fees or fees in lieu of notice, or else out of alleged bullying or undetected dyslexia. Few of them reach the law reports.

*Taunton School v Wright* (1997) 4 EPLI 67 was a case about parents who withdrew a pupil without notice from a large independent school because they were dissatisfied with the headmaster's unwillingness to deal personally with a particular complaint. It was held that it is a feature of many independent schools in the UK that housemasters are the first point of contact with parents. Only if the housemaster has failed to satisfy the parents' enquiries would direct access to the head be expected. It would be impossible for the head to run a large school properly if he dealt with every enquiry from a parent.

In *Re B (Minors)* (1994) *The Times*, 12 May, CA, Butler-Sloss LJ said in the context of a dispute between parents over schooling:

> '... children are suffering if they are not given the space and peace that they require to get on with their own affairs at school. And their affairs at school are more important than either of their parents'. School has to be a haven. School has to be a place where children get on and do their work in order that they may be successful grown-ups ...'

### 13.2.5    Guidance

The Department of Health has issued guidance under s 7 of the Local Authority and Social Services Act 1970. Volume 5 of that guidance ('The Blue Book') is addressed to independent schools and local authorities who exercise social services functions towards independent schools.

### 13.2.6    Fair procedures

Since *R v Fernhill Manor School ex parte A* [1994] ELR 67, it is to be taken as an implied term of the contract between school and parents that there will be procedural rules designed to ensure that parents receive fair treatment in accordance with the principles of natural justice in the case of an expulsion or a requirement for the pupil to leave permanently. In response to this, many schools have instituted a system of a governors' review of decisions that will affect the pupil's future by which parents or pupils may be aggrieved.

## 13.3    COMMUNITY ASPECTS

The quality of pastoral care will be dictated by the attitudes, behaviour, perception and training of each member of the staff as a role model. The community aspects are expressed in the culture of the school, that is to say: its aims and objectives; its customs and traditions; its standards and values; the behaviour and attitudes of its members; and the policies, principles, rules and procedures laid down by the governors.

The community aspects of pastoral care regularly feature as a counterclaim in litigation over unpaid fees and fees in lieu of notice. The vast majority of such cases are resolved in favour of the school. These are mainly unreported cases arbitrated or tried in county courts up and down the country. The points that arise include the following:

### (a)  Classroom

Inadequate or too much homework/prep; criticisms over marking; 'bawling-out' and humiliation by the teacher of the pupil in front of other pupils; complaints about facilities for exam preparation; alleged insufficient help with catching up after illness; teachers who leave the class unattended for a long time; teachers refusing to listen; inconsistent behaviour by teachers, and favouritism.

### (b)  Discipline

Unjust or inappropriate punishment; failure by staff to deal with disruptive pupils; 'borrowing' or theft of clothing or equipment; insufficient information given to parents about the behaviour of their children.

### (c)  Social and routine

Insufficient help from the staff over friendship difficulties and bullying and over missing clothes and equipment; insufficient supervision at meal times leading to pupils 'skiving' meals; allegations that a pupil has been 'forced' to eat unattractive or unsatisfactory food; alleged assaults on a pupil's dignity and privacy; the pupil being made to 'look stupid' through not knowing what to do next because of insufficiently clear instructions; favouritism in selection for performance or participation in drama and other cultural activities; in particular, allegedly favouring the children of teachers.

### (d)  Sport

Inequality of access to sports and games; favouring the best and sidelining the less skilful; lack of encouragement; favouritism shown to children of employed staff; 'bawling-out' of pupils in front of their friends and their friends' parents.

### (e)  Boarders

Insufficient supervision to detect bullying, homesickness and family worries; accessibility of drugs and alcohol; insufficient information to parents.


## 13.4  HEALTH AND MEDICATION

### 13.4.1  Legal duties

Parents, the health authority and the pupil's medical practitioners each owe duties of various kinds:

### (a)  Parents

The main carers of a child are the parents. They are responsible for ensuring that a child under school-leaving age attends school if well enough. In the case of a boarder, parents delegate their duties under s 2(9) of the Children Act 1989 to the head during term time.

### (b)  Health authority

The health authority has legal responsibility for the health of residents in its area. This will include assisting the school with training and support in relation to the medical needs of pupils.

### (c)  Medical practitioners

A pupil's medical practitioners including his (or her) GP and dentist must in general treat the pupil in a manner consistent with a responsible body of medical opinion and recognised medical practices. The school doctor and school dentist are not employees of the school. They advise and treat in their professional capacities as medical practitioners and are therefore subject to the same general duty. Day-pupils will probably remain registered with their own GPs and dentists. Boarding pupils at an independent school are normally required to register with the school doctor.

### (d)  School

The school has several areas of power, responsibility and duty:

– at common law, to act as would a reasonably prudent parent and, where appropriate, as would a professional teacher;

– under the Children Act 1989, to do what is reasonable, for example in an emergency, for the purpose of safeguarding or promoting the pupil's welfare;

– under the health and safety legislation, to have a health and safety management policy and to implement it through training and procedures. The Infection Control Guidelines issued by Department of Health are guidelines intended to reduce the risk of transmission of diseases such as HIV/AIDS and hepatitis and should be followed;

– in relation to special educational needs, to have adequately trained staff who will detect learning difficulties, notify parents and refer them to sources of remedial help;

– under the Education (School Premises) Regulations 1996, to provide accommodation for medical or dental examination or treatment.

### 13.4.2  Practical approach

The combination of these duties and the trend towards viewing medical needs as requiring support rather than separation of the pupil means that the school:

– may need to draw up an individual *health care plan* for pupils with long term medical needs;

– may need to draw on outside training resources and support, for example from the health authority;

- will need to *assess risk* for pupils with medical needs especially in the case of out-of-school trips, sports activities and work experience, and if necessary allocate additional support;

- have adequate policies and procedures, both generally and for individual pupils, which are communicated to all staff (including supply and visiting teachers) and parent helpers.

As in most areas of health and safety compliance, it will be a question of achieving a balance between, on the one hand:

- bureaucracy which impedes the school's ability to function at all or might at worst lead to refusal of places to pupils with medical needs; and, on the other hand,

- inactivity that exposes children to risk.

### 13.4.3   Information and records

Custom and practice is to adopt a common sense approach to confidentiality. In the interests of safety and welfare, information about the pupil's medical needs must be made available as necessary:

- it may be made a condition of admission that parents disclose health information about their children and that they and pupils of sufficient age and understanding authorise the proper use of that information;

- staff must be briefed in appropriate circumstances;

- the school medical officer is entitled in proper circumstances to override confidentiality in the case of a pupil under 16. For a pupil aged 16 or over, consent to override confidentiality in appropriate circumstances should be made a condition of the pupil's attendance at school.

The main considerations in relation to documents and records are:

- Each school should consider formulating and publishing its policy concerning confidential information and HIV/AIDS and hepatitis.

- Pupils of sufficient age and understanding or their parents are able to gain access to medical records under the Access to Health Records Act 1990 and/or the Data Protection Acts 1984 and 1998, subject to withholding on grounds that disclosure might be harmful to the patient.

- Notes held by the school form part of the pupil's general file and belong to the school. They may have to be produced to the court at the discovery stage of litigation if the notes are relevant. In an unreported case in 1996, an estranged father engineered litigation over unpaid school fees with the object of obtaining disclosure of his daughter's medical records but was unsuccessful in that instance.

### 13.4.4   Medication

A school may be held liable if injury is caused as a result of:

- the wrong medicine being administered; or

- the right medicine being administered, but in the wrong quantity; or
- the right medicine being given in the right quantity but in the wrong way; or
- a failure properly to supervise possession of medicine.

Parents of day-pupils are primarily responsible for obtaining supplies and administering medicines that have been prescribed for the pupil. School staff who agree to take on this task do so under s 2(9) of the Children Act 1989 (delegated parental responsibility). The school must ensure that staff taking on this role have been adequately trained and that insurance will meet any resulting liability. Ideally, medicines should be self-administered by the pupil, if sufficiently mature, with staff supervision. If pupils need to carry their own medication, for example inhalers for asthma, then this should be monitored so that the health of other pupils is not endangered.

The school should have a written and publicised policy on giving out non-prescription medication such as analgesics and make certain that insurers have been notified of the policy and accept the risk. The school must have a safe system for storing, recording and accessing medicines. Parents should be asked to dispose of any medicines which are unused. There should be a clearly written system which staff understand and are trained to use with proper records and careful scrutiny of instructions. Medication should be a checklist item for out-of-school visits and tours.

There was anecdotal evidence in 1997 of insurers imposing unreasonable conditions on staff who administered non-prescriptive medication. Schools need to adopt a firm stance in these cases so as to ensure that their ability to serve the needs of the children is not compromised. Professional advice should be taken where necessary.

### 13.4.5   Emergency treatment

The Children Act 1989, s 3(5) (doing what is reasonable in all the circumstances) provides sufficient authority to heads and teachers *in loco parentis* to authorise emergency medical treatment. Even so, it is usual for the standard terms and conditions of the parent contract and also for forms of parental consent to include an express authority on the part of parents. These are, in general, matters of common sense, and specific authorities are needed as much to give comfort to doctors and insurers as to parents.

### 13.4.6   Late X-ray

Disputes have arisen, particularly in the case of boarders, over the treatment of pupils who sustain an injury at school. In relation to possible bone injuries, there seem to be two bodies of responsible medical opinion:

- those who take the 'wait and see' approach, avoiding X-rays where possible on grounds of potential damage to the patient; and

- those who take the view that immediate diagnosis is preferable, that the risk from one X-ray is very small, that people have many more routine X-rays at the dentist and when they pass through airport security, and that a person needs 40 or 50 X-rays before real cause for concern arises.

If, within sensible limits, both of these views are regarded as responsible in the case of a pupil under 16, it is for the parents to decide on the basis of advice from the doctor which course they prefer. No doubt, the parents will take account of the views of a child of sufficient maturity and understanding, and cost should not be a material factor in these circumstances. Provided the fees list and standard terms and conditions are well drafted, there will be an express if not implied authority for the school to incur and charge costs as necessary.

The problem has arisen in cases where the initial symptoms suggested there was no fracture but the pupil continued for some days to experience a greater than expected amount of pain and discomfort and a later X-ray showed there was a fracture. Problems of this nature are often just an aspect of communication with parents. Most parents in the case of a possible fracture would want to be advised:

–   whether there is a risk of complications or significant additional pain and distress if the injury is observed for 2 or 3 days before a decision is taken about X-rays;
–   how weight-bearing or other use will be tested and whether there is a risk of the fracture becoming extended as a result;
–   the pros and cons of a single X-ray, bearing in mind all other exposure in the modern world;
–   what the indications are at present and what kind of injury it is likely to be if not a fracture.

It is likely there will be as many different opinions among parents as there are among doctors, and the schools which are, after all, *in loco parentis*, will not want to trouble parents unnecessarily following every small bump and strain. It is suggested here, however, that parents should be informed in every case of need for a judgement whether or not to X-ray. That is particularly so in a case of a musician or games player who has suffered an injury that might affect specific activities.

## 13.5   BOARDERS

### 13.5.1   Nature of boarding

An editorial comment in the *Daily Telegraph* for 23 March 1998 gave this robust view of boarding:

> 'The attraction of boarding is surely that unique mixture of quality and toughness. The boarding experience inherent in such an education is diluted when all adverse circumstances are removed. Like fighting men, boarders are a breed apart because of what they have been through. Remove that element and they might as well stay at home ... as Thomas Hughes' and Enid Blyton's novels illustrated, the public school tradition proved a wonderful stimulus for "creativity" – that most hallowed of qualities in contemporary education.'

This view of boarding seems to straddle two quite different cultures: boarding as it was 50 or more years ago in sometimes harsh and threadbare conditions; and as it is now, in a great many schools that provide a quality environment with a range of opportunities and a training in the ups and downs of community life.

## 13.5.2 Structure

The Children Act 1989, s 63 has been amended so as to require that a boarding school need only register as a children's home if more than three pupils are accommodated for more than 295 days in any two consecutive years.

A school's responsibilities of pastoral care in relation to boarders are, of their nature, more extensive than those for day-pupils because care is for 24 hours of the day and often for seven days a week during term time, and also encompasses full catering, tuck, medical expenses, toiletries and pocket money. If boarders are organised in houses, their care is normally structured through some or all of the following: a housemaster or housemistress, house tutor, senior matron (qualified SRN) and an assistant matron and house mother, most or all of whom will be resident. The head has overall responsibility and there may be gap-year assistants in addition. The school chaplain will have a specific moral and spiritual role as pastor and there may also be a school counsellor.

The organisation of a boarding house requires careful line management, communication and duty rotas so that there is never an hiatus. In some of the larger schools, boarding is organised in such a way that all meals and social activities take place in the house and are, for all practical purposes, the sole responsibility of the housemaster or housemistress who must negotiate budgets and facilities direct with the bursar.

## 13.5.3 Conduct of boarding house

Each boarding house is its own community and will tend to develop a unique character and ethos. It is likely to have its own rules and regime and additional points of discipline, sanctions and rewards. There will be systems for detecting signs of unhappiness, despondency or abuse and for dealing with complaints and worries. Nowadays, the arrangements for pastoral care of boarders will seek to involve the parents to a far greater extent than formerly.

## 13.5.4 Legal compliance

### (a) Standard of accommodation

The Education (School Premises) Regulations 1981, among other things, deal with space in dormitories, washing and sanitary accommodation, provision of meals, day room space and sick rooms.

### (b) Children Act 1989

Section 87 of the Act makes the proprietor of an independent school responsible for taking reasonable steps to safeguard and promote the welfare of children. Section 87 also provides for inspection by the local authority. This responsibility is invariably delegated to the social services department.

There have been reports of some unsatisfactory inspection procedures by Children Act inspectors. In some cases, the inspectors appeared to be untrained. In other cases, they were felt to have acted oppressively, making demands, for example, that all staff, however long-serving, should be made the subject of List 99 and criminal background checks. In other cases again, there were reports of inspectors causing concern among 12-year-old pupils that they should have made more complaints against the school.

Whilst inspections can be and usually are completed satisfactorily by co-operation, the housemaster or housemistress in any case of concern should not hesitate to ask for the 'chapter and verse' relied on by the inspector as the basis for a particular request and, if necessary, be prepared to take legal advice or refer the matter to the inspector's senior manager.

### (c)   Health and safety

A housemaster or housemistress will normally have responsibility for health and safety delegated to him or her by the head and should therefore carry out a risk assessment of the boarding house and ensure that appropriate measures are taken to minimise or prevent risks and that staff employed at the house are adequately trained.

Particular attention is needed to be given to: roofs and attics (and access to them); windows, doors and floors; stairways; gas and electrical systems; facilities such as toilets and changing rooms; cleanliness of premises; and generally maintaining plant, equipment and systems in efficient working order and good repair.

### (d)   Fire precautions

At present, school boarding houses do not require a certificate issued by the fire authority under the Fire Precautions Act 1971 but there is a general requirement of law to take adequate fire precautions. These will include:

–   fire doors, fire escapes, detection and alarm systems and extinguishers, all regularly inspected and maintained;
–   evacuation procedures tested regularly by fire drills;
–   systems for safe storage, regular collection and disposal of waste;
–   furniture which is made of materials which comply with the Upholstered Furniture (Safety) Regulations 1980.

### (e)   Catering

The Food Safety Act 1990 and Food Hygiene (Amendment) Regulations 1990 (amending the 1970 general regulations) apply to school boarding houses that are concerned in the preparation of food. They address the premises, cleanliness, handling of food, training of food handlers and measures needed to protect food from the risk of contamination.

### (f)   Other compliance

Chapter 21 makes reference to other areas of legal compliance that may also apply to a school boarding house.

### 13.5.5   Contracts made by pupils

The Minors' Contracts Act 1987 provides to the effect that contracts made by a person under the age of 18 will not be legally binding on that person unless the contract was for a 'necessary' or 'of benefit' to the minor. The other contracting party, if over 18, will, in general, be bound by his (or her) part of the contract.

A pupil who buys goods which are not of 'satisfactory quality' will have his (or her) rights as a consumer and in addition his rights under the 1987 Act if the goods were not 'necessaries' or of 'benefit'. 'Necessaries' means goods that are suitable to the condition in life of the minor and suitable to his actual requirements at the time of sale and delivery.

### 13.5.6   Change from boarding

The contract with the parents normally requires a term's written notice before a pupil changes from boarding to day status and, in default, a term's difference in fees will be payable in lieu. In some cases, the contract provides that change can only take place at the start of a school year so that there is minimal disruption to the boarding house community.

The contract normally provides also that pupils who do not settle to life in a boarding house or to boarding generally or who are a disrupting influence may be required to leave boarding temporarily or permanently and become a day-pupil. In a case where parents live at some distance, this may be tantamount to requiring the pupil to leave the school, and regard should be had to all the circumstances before such a requirement is imposed.

### 13.5.7   Boarders from overseas

Additional considerations arise for boarders from overseas who will need a holiday guardian in the UK to attend school premises in the case of emergency, to attend parents' evenings, to liaise with the overseas parents and to take or communicate decisions. The UK guardian should also be willing to attend the pupil's special days such as prize giving, matches, concerts and similar events as a caring parent would, and to make travel arrangements as necessary and receive the pupil at home if too unwell for school or if suspended or required to leave.

The legal issues that arise over the care of overseas boarders during school holidays are considered at Chapter 14. Particular care is needed to detect any signs of unhappiness in a group of overseas pupils who socialise together and communicate in their own language.

## 13.6   CHILD PROTECTION

Child protection is concerned with support for the child abused away from school and prevention of abuse while the child is in the care of the school. Closely allied to these is the training of staff to recognise and deal appropriately with signs of abuse, and detection of staff who may be abusers; and also the protection of staff who are wrongly accused.

These matters involve consideration of the Rehabilitation of Offenders Act 1974, and its exceptions, the checks that must now be made when employing staff, misconduct reports, and the official guidance that has been issued by DfEE. Also considered are some of the areas in which the concerns of the authorities come into conflict with those of parents and school when all are seeking to work in the best interests of the child.

### 13.6.1   Rehabilitation of offenders

The Rehabilitation of Offenders Act 1974 was designed to allow those who had been convicted of all but the most serious criminal offences to shed their past provided they did not re-offend during the rehabilitation period applicable to the conviction. In essence, a person whose conviction was 'spent' under the Act would, in most circumstances, be entitled to lie if asked about it.

The main rehabilitation periods are:

– for an absolute discharge: *6 months*;
– for a conditional discharge, binding-over and probation: *one year*;
– for a custodial sentence of less than 6 months: *7 years*;
– for a custodial sentence of 6 to 30 months: *10 years*.

It was, however, recognised that there would need to be some exceptions to the Act for the protection of children. Article 14 of the Rehabilitation of Offenders Act 1974 (Exceptions) Order 1975, SI 1975/1023, as substituted in 1986, requires disclosure of spent convictions on the part of those who are concerned with children. It applies to:

'Any office or employment concerned with the provision to persons aged under 18 of accommodation, care, leisure and recreational facilities, schooling, social services, supervisions or training, being an office or employment of such a kind as to enable the holder to have access in the course of his normal duties to such persons, and any other office or employment the normal duties of which are carried out wholly or partly on the premises where such provision takes place.'

This article is wide enough to include governors, non-teaching staff and holiday guardians as well as teachers. An applicant for a job which falls within art 14 is not entitled to lie about previous convictions.

### 13.6.2   Barring for misconduct

The Education (Teachers) (Amendment) (No 2) Regulations 1995, SI 1995/259, which amend the Education (Teachers) Regulations 1993, SI 1993/543, provided the basis for the Secretary of State's power to bar people on grounds of misconduct from teaching.

The Education Act 1996, s 473(2) provides that:

'A person is guilty of an offence if he –

(a)   acts as the proprietor of an independent school, or
(b)   accepts or endeavours to obtain employment as a teacher or other employee in any school,

while he is disqualified from so acting or from being so employed by virtue of an order made under section 470 or 471.'

DfEE Circular 11/95, *Misconduct of Teachers and Workers with Children and Young Persons*, explains the powers of the Secretary of State to bar people, on grounds of misconduct, from teaching and other employment in schools. It gives details of the Secretary of State's powers to bar automatically those convicted of child sex offences, to request medical evidence and to lift the bar on teachers' employment.

Circular 10/95, *Protecting Children From Abuse: The Role of the Education Service*, is also of general relevance in this context.

### 13.6.3  Checking background

Although there is no mandatory requirement on the part of a school to check the criminal background and DfEE status of a job applicant, it is an offence to employ a person who is subject to a ban or restriction. The following checks are available.

### (a)  List 99

List 99 is maintained by the DfEE and made available to associations such as HMC, GSA, IAPS and ISA, among others. The list contains the name, date of birth and teacher reference number of individuals barred from employment in education or any work providing access to educational institutions. A person may be barred for many different reasons, including bringing the profession into disrepute (for example by absconding with the money for a school trip), or for having an illness which is considered to be dangerous to others, or for having committed a sexual offence, or for having a record of violent behaviour. The DfEE does not make List 99 available to private organisations, but it passes on the list to the Department of Health and can access further information from the Department of Health and the police as outlined below.

### (b)  DoH Adverse Report List

This list, complied by the Department of Health (DoH), is far more comprehensive than List 99. It includes anyone whose disposition, condition or record of misconduct (social or professional) may be considered to be a threat to the well-being of children were they to be employed or engaged in work or activities in any way related to children. The Adverse Report List comprises not just teachers but people from all walks of life, and in some cases whole families or households. For instance, if social services conduct an inquiry into a case of child abuse and are unable to determine the culprit, every member of the household may be entered on the Adverse Report List. The DoH consultancy service will conduct checks on behalf of private organisations.

### (c)  Criminal background check

Schools are expected to make a criminal background check with the police before employing a member of staff. It is not unknown for 'similar name' errors to be made.

### 13.6.4  Misconduct reports

Regulation 7 of the Education (Particulars of Independent Schools) Regulations 1997 (replacing those of 1982 and 1994) provides:

'(1)  Where a person employed at a registered school ceases to be so employed by reason of his misconduct, the proprietor shall report the facts of the case to the Registrar in writing within one month following the date on which that person ceases to be employed at the school.

(2)   Paragraph (1) applies whether or not that person –

(a)   is convicted of a criminal offence in relation to the misconduct concerned, or
(b)   (where he has a contract of employment) is dismissed by his employer or would have been so dismissed or considered for dismissal but for his resignation.'

Regulation 8 provides:

'(1)   If the Secretary of State is satisfied that the proprietor of a school has failed to comply with any requirement specified in Regulation 5, 6 or 7 ("a Part II requirement") he may, subject to paragraphs (2) and (3), order the deletion from the Register of the name of that school.'

Regulation 8(2) and (3) provides to the effect that the proprietor shall be given 2 months' notice before the school is deleted from the Register of Independent Schools and if he complies with the Part II requirement within that period the school shall not be deleted.

Regulation 7 is sufficiently wide to cover misconduct of any kind, sexual or otherwise. It is far from clear in a number of other respects, for example:

–   where the alleged misconduct has led to dismissal even though the dismissal would be found by a tribunal to be unfair; or
–   where the misconduct occurred in a previous employment; or
–   where there has been sexual misconduct of a kind that was an offence when committed but is not an offence at the time when it is discovered, for example consensuary acts of sodomy.

In its present form, reg 7 can cause serious concerns to a school that wishes to be fair both to the school community and to the teacher concerned. In one case, a teacher volunteered that he had been convicted of two offences of gross indecency with another consenting adult 15 years earlier. These were offences that were only criminal because they had taken place in a public park but in all other respects they were lawful expressions of sexual orientation. The teacher concerned had never been the subject of rumour, gossip or complaint and there was no reason to consider him a danger to children. Whilst the school decided to accept his resignation, reg 7 left in doubt whether the school would be in default if it failed to make a misconduct report.

### 13.6.5   Guidance for staff

The National Association of Head Teachers (NAHT) has produced guidelines for use when an allegation of impropriety is made against a member of staff.

### 13.6.6   Social services

Against the background that the safety and welfare of the child is paramount, it will not always be easy for a school to decide how best to deal with an incident that has occurred outside the school or is alleged to have occurred in school. The contractual relationship with parents and the duties owed to the pupil add an important dimension that is not present to the same extent in the maintained sector.

Social services and the police have their own legitimate interest in discovering allegations of abuse. This sometimes leads to a suggestion being made by Children Act inspectors that the school is under a legal obligation to inform the social services department of every allegation of improper behaviour towards children. That, it is submitted, is not the law; nor will it always serve the interests of the child to make a report in disregard of the honestly held wishes of a child of sufficient maturity and understanding and the wishes of his (or her) parents. Some relevant considerations are set out below.

## (a) Concerns of social services

Social services departments say there has been a significant increase in the number of complaints of child abuse at schools of all kinds, and, generally, since 1995, and that there are established and growing paedophile networks, comprising mainly but not entirely men. Social services say they need all the intelligence information they can gather. Perhaps the member of staff concerned will leave the school but resurface in an environment with children where police checks do not have to be carried out. Dismissal of a teacher and a report made to the DfEE will not necessarily result in information being given to social services.

A separate area of concern is that when there are signs of abuse against one pupil there may be others who have not made complaints. Perhaps some of those pupils will be struggling to cope with the effects and will need counselling.

For these reasons, social services want to be informed of every incident or suspicion. So far as they are concerned, it is not enough that the parties directly involved have dealt with the matter. Social services say they have a duty to protect the wider community, that they are experts and that the investigation will be carried out in strict confidence and sensitively. In most cases, they will lead the investigation and will keep the police informed, but the police will take over if criminal proceedings are contemplated.

## (b) Concerns of the police

The Association of Chief Police Officers and other organisations share the concerns of social services and are critical of what is seen to be a reluctance to call in the child protection agencies either early enough or at all. The interest of the police is to preserve evidence while it is fresh. That includes the taking of statements and ensuring that the prospects of a conviction are not prejudiced.

## (c) Concerns of the parents

The parents' view of what best serves the safety and welfare of their own children may be at variance with the view of social services and the police. Parents may feel that an incident which appears to be minor in nature is best forgotten and not rehearsed in endless statement taking, counselling sessions and, at worst, proceedings at court.

Sometimes they may be unsure of the confidentiality of social services or the police and they may lack confidence in the authorities' ability to avoid making matters worse. They may, for example, decide that they do not want to do anything which places their son or daughter at risk of having to give evidence at court.

There may also be general unhappiness and embarrassment at having to raise the matter. There may be a concern not to place unfair pressure on someone they see as a good teacher and quite possibly innocent, and there may also be an element of anxiety that the family's relationship with the school will be changed. Moreover, children who are about to transfer to another school in any event or who are approaching public examinations will not want the distractions of an investigation by social services or the police. The quality of 'counselling' can also be variable.

The problem has been highlighted by cases of alleged indecent 'shirt tucking' or touching at the top of the thigh or behind. A charge of indecent assault follows, which is then dismissed by magistrates or transferred to the Crown Court before it is withdrawn or the defendant is acquitted following a jury trial. Even allowing for video evidence, the ordeal through which the pupil is put (not to mention the defendant, who may be innocent) may be thought disproportionate to the allegations and, at the end of it all, the pupil may feel that he (or she) has been disbelieved. It is cases of this kind that are considered in the remarks made above, which may lead parents to suggest that such allegations are often best dealt with privately and internally rather than by involvement of social services, the police and criminal proceedings. More serious cases should, however, be reported, after advice.

### (d) Concerns of the school

The school owes a duty to exercise reasonable care and skill to ensure the safety and welfare of all its pupils. When a complaint is made against a teacher, there is always the risk that the teacher may turn out to be an abuser, but there is also the possibility of malice by a pupil against a member of staff. There may be concern about leaks to the media and unnecessary damage being caused to the reputation of the school community as a whole. Legal advice may be that there is, in most cases, no *statutory obligation* to report suspicions or even to report clear evidence of abuse whatever may be good, or best, practice.

A factor that is important at independent schools is the relationship of trust and confidence that arises out of the contract between parents and the school. Contractual obligations are unlikely, in most circumstances, to take precedence over a statutory duty to safeguard and promote the welfare of a child. Even so, parents may consider that, in the absence of a statutory requirement, schools should not involve child protection agencies without prior consultation with the family. Parents may be satisfied that they can deal with problems of this nature as a family matter. To a certain extent, this will depend on the age, sex and known record of the child, and the nature of the allegations and all the other circumstances.

Schools may have in memory some of the hard cases, which have occurred over the years, of allegations against members of staff that, after one or 2 years of criminal investigation, suspension, waiting, trial and exposure in the press and on television, turned out to be unsupported by credible evidence.

### (e) Generally

These cases are always very difficult. Each interested party may have cogent and child-centred reasons for its views. No doubt the child protection agencies take care not to create an incorrect impression that there is a duty to notify every suspicion and an unfettered right on their part to investigate but experience has not always borne that out.

Heads are entitled to take into account the fact that they are *in loco parentis*. They are in charge of the closed community for which they are responsible. They are entitled under s 3(5) of the Children Act 1989 to do what is reasonable in all the circumstances for the purpose of safeguarding or promoting the child's welfare. That will often be a matter of professional judgement exercised in consultation with parents and a child who is of sufficient age and understanding.

Every case needs to be considered on its merits and, where necessary, specialist legal advice should be sought.

### 13.6.7   Worries and complaints procedure

Since the Children Act 1989, schools have been expected to institute procedures for ensuring that pupils have someone with whom they can discuss worries or complaints. In general, they are encouraged to turn to close friends or an older pupil or their form teacher, housemaster/housemistress, deputy head, house tutor or matron.

If they feel unable to talk to a member of staff, pupils are encouraged to speak to their parents or are given the means of contacting the school doctor, or an independent listener, a member of the local social services department or the telephone number of Childline (0800 1111 (freephone)).

## 13.7   COUNSELLING

The growing practice among independent schools of providing a counselling facility is consistent with the underlying principles of the Children Act 1989, but the issues that arise are far from straightforward and are considered below.

### 13.7.1   The 'Blue Book'

Volume 5 of the 'Blue Book', issued in 1991 by the Department of Health under s 7 of the Local Authority and Social Services Act 1970 is addressed to independent schools and local authorities who exercise social services functions in relation to independent schools.

The term 'counselling' is not used in Volume 5, but the following statements appear:

'Boarders need to be able to have access to appropriate staff in private' (para 3.4.2(e)).

'An effective means by which children's concerns or complaints can be heard ... provision for contact with an adult outside the school's structure including telephone Help Lines where appropriate for those situations where an additional element of confidentiality or independence is needed' (para 3.11.1).

'Arrangements for children to register complaints in confidence to a person not on the staff of the school ... sometimes the school doctor or chaplain may be able to fulfil this role very well ...' (para 3.11.7).

Some schools meet the spirit of this guidance by means of the school doctor and chaplain and senior members of staff who are authorised to use their discretion over breaches of school discipline told to them in confidence. Invariably, the policy under this system is to make an early medical referral if there are concerns.

In other cases, schools establish an in-house counselling service provided by a member of staff who may have many years of practical experience as a counsellor, with or without formal qualifications. Others again use the services of a retained self-employed counsellor who attends school premises or to whom pupils are referred externally.

The practical problems in these cases revolve around legal compliance, confidentiality and record keeping, and the competence of the counsellor. These are examined in turn.

### 13.7.2   Legal compliance

The head must comply with (among others) the following legal duties:

–   Under Children Act 1989, s 87, the head and governors owe a legal duty 'to safeguard and promote the welfare of each child'.

–   The head must comply with the duty of care he (or she) owes to the pupil in tort and the duties owed to parents by virtue of his (or her) delegated parental responsibility under s 2(9) of the Children Act 1989.

–   The head must also comply with the contractual duties that exist between the school and the parents. When those come into conflict with duties owed to the pupil, the contractual duties will normally give way.

–   The head's duty under the *Gillick* principle (cf *Gillick v West Norfolk and Wisbech Area Health Authority and Another* [1986] 1 FLR 224) is to preserve the confidentiality of a person under 16 of sufficient maturity and understanding, a person over 16 being entitled to full confidentiality.

–   The head owes a duty under s 3(1) of the Health and Safety at Work etc Act 1974 to conduct the school in such a way as to ensure, so far as reasonably practicable, that persons *not* in the school's employment are *not* exposed to risks to their health or safety.

–   The head is also responsible to the governors under his or her contract of employment to conduct the school in a proper manner so as to ensure its stability and its compliance with the law.

–   The head must discharge the governors' duty under s 8 of the Misuse of Drugs Act 1971 not to allow school premises to be used for purposes in connection with controlled drugs.

Section 3(5) of the Children Act 1989 provides that a person (such as a head) who has care of a child 'may do what is reasonable in all the circumstances for the purpose of safeguarding or promoting the child's welfare'. This section can be overridden by other provisions of law, but in some circumstances, s 3(5) taken with s 87 can be relied on to override certain of the duties of confidentiality under the *Gillick* principle, mentioned above.

If an in-house counsellor is permitted to operate with complete confidentiality, there is a risk of a sub-culture arising in the school about which the head knows nothing. That is an untenable position. It could mean that:

–   the head is disabled from carrying out the legal duties summarised above; and

–   a pupil could be hospitalised having taken an overdose and the first the head knows of it is when an anxious parent telephones asking why the child is in hospital (this has in fact happened).

There is also a contingent risk of legal liability. For example, a 14-year-old girl might undergo one or 2 years of confidential counselling by the in-house counsellor. Then, at the age of 20, she develops anorexia, bulimia or some other psychological disorder. She obtains expert evidence to the effect that negligent counselling prevented timely and proper treatment in earlier years. In a case like this, the school would be wholly unable to answer these allegations if the counsellor had left employment and had disappeared leaving no records of any kind.

### 13.7.3   Confidentiality

#### (a)   *Health professional*

Most, if not all, categories of health professional would consider themselves bound by the same rules of confidentiality that bind qualified medical practitioners ('doctors'). In general:

–   a patient has a right to expect that his (or her) doctor will not pass on any personal information which he (or she) learns in the course of his professional duties, unless the patient gives permission;

–   when the patient consents to disclosure of information, the doctor must make sure that the patient understands the extent of, and the reasons for and the likely consequences of disclosure;

–   the doctor must make sure that patients know when information about them is likely to be disclosed to others and that they have the opportunity to withhold permission;

–   a patient's request for confidentiality can be overridden *in exceptional circumstances* where the health or safety of others would otherwise be put at serious risk. Then, only so much information as is necessary for the purpose should be released, and the doctor must make sure that the recipients of information understand that it is given in confidence. The doctor must be prepared to explain and justify his (or her) decision;

–   A doctor can be compelled to disclose in court information covered by medical confidentiality but he may seek the protection of the court which may, at its discretion, allow him to decline to answer or give the information in confidence to the judge without necessarily having to disclose it to opponents.

## (b)   Catholic priests and chaplains

A Catholic priest acting in accordance with his vows must be prepared to die before he reveals the secrets of the confessional. However, this practice only relates to secrets told to him in the circumstances of the confessional. In other circumstances, his position is little different from that of a chaplain belonging to another church, such as the Church of England, who will observe confidences unless there is very good reason to override confidentiality in exceptional circumstances.

## (c)   Counsellors

'Counselling' covers a very wide gamut of largely unregulated activity, ranging from the highly competent to the dangerously incompetent. The problem that is likely to arise in a school turns on the degree of confidentiality that has been assured to the pupil. A counsellor employed by the school should not be authorised to assure absolute confidentiality, as that makes it impossible for the head to discharge a number of important legal duties that he (or she) owes to the pupil, the parents, the governors, the staff and not least to the counsellor.

## (d)   Rights of the pupil

A person aged 16 or over is entitled to full confidentiality subject to other provisions of law, for example, those relating to illegality.

A pupil under 16 of sufficient maturity and understanding is entitled to confidentiality by virtue of the *Gillick* principle.

It is important that the necessary limits of confidentiality should be explained to the pupil at the outset or as soon as a difficulty starts to arise. The pupil should be encouraged to involve his (or her) parents and certain of the staff in resolving problems. In some cases, however, the family circumstances will be at the root of the problem and the pupil may wish to withhold from parents the fact that he (or she) is being counselled. That wish should be respected if the pupil is '*Gillick* competent'.

## (e)   Limits to confidentiality

The law of confidence does not protect illegality. If a pupil admits to having possessed, used, supplied or sold controlled drugs, that information is not confidential at law. The same applies to information about other criminal offences, for example those to do with firearms, theft, fraud, computer hacking, sexual assault, aiding and abetting actual or attempted suicide, etc.

A counsellor has no *legal* obligation to inform the police of any such matter, although there may be a moral obligation to do so, which will usually be in conflict with the counsellor's ethical obligations. There are no hard and fast solutions other than to adopt a pragmatic approach under which:

–    the pupil is not deceived;

– the counsellor imparts the information that is necessary to protect the pupil or others from serious harm and imparts it only to those who need to know and on a confidential and restricted basis. Thus, it may not be necessary to inform the police of a particular matter.

### 13.7.4 Practical considerations

If the school appoints an external, self-employed counsellor, reasonable care should be taken to check his (or her) credentials and background and establish the limits of the counsellor's authority. If this is done, negligence on the part of the counsellor will not be that of the school. Care should also be taken to check the professional indemnity insurance arrangements and to make certain that all material facts have been disclosed to insurers.

If the counsellor is employed by the school, however skilled, experienced and qualified the counsellor may be, it is suggested here that his (or her) role should be seen as very limited in scope. Unless the subject matter consists of isolated problems, there should be an early referral to a qualified medical practitioner. In other words, the role of the counsellor should be seen as no greater than that of the wise and caring parent or teacher who has the time to listen and to give practical advice and to pick up any sign which may indicate the need for a medical referral.

It is also suggested that a member of the senior management team with no responsibility for discipline should be informed whenever counselling has continued for longer than, say, a term or whenever there is cause for serious concern. Other considerations apart, it may be necessary to inform class or sports teachers about a pupil who is particularly vulnerable.

In-house counsellors will themselves need a regime of support and training to ensure that they remain professionally detached and able to fulfil the role competently. They will need to be able to talk over problems with other suitably qualified professionals. For example, there should be a regular supervision meeting with (perhaps) a medically qualified governor and (perhaps) the chaplain and/or others. Membership of an accredited professional body is desirable.

### 13.7.5 Credentials

Prior to engagement of an in-house counsellor, satisfactory references should be obtained together with clearance under List 99 (if available), a criminal background check and an enquiry made of the Department of Health. Membership of the British Association for Counselling may or may not be considered a prerequisite but the counsellor should be required to agree to the school's code of confidentiality and accountability.

### 13.7.6 Records

It is suggested also that the counsellor should be required to maintain adequate notes of each consultation, the advice given and the name of anyone to whom information is imparted. The contents of those notes should be and remain confidential, the confidence to be overridden only in the most exceptional circumstances. They should remain at school premises if the counsellor leaves employment. The notes should, however, be sufficiently full to enable the counsellor to justify his (or her) conduct at each stage. In other words, the counsellor must be accountable in general terms within the normally permitted limits of confidentiality.

# Chapter 14

## CARE OF PUPILS FROM OVERSEAS

### 14.1  INTRODUCTION

Boarding pupils at independent schools in the UK may need care and accommodation provided by a 'UK guardian' during exeats, half terms and holidays, and for a variety of other purposes. In this chapter we consider the meaning of 'UK guardian' and some of its legal implications. The terms 'UK guardian' and 'holiday guardian' are used interchangeably.

### 14.2  OVERVIEW

The UK guardian will normally be:

−   a person chosen by the overseas parents; or
−   a person chosen by the school; or
−   a person chosen by an agency or a guardianship practice appointed by the parents or the school.

The expression 'guardian' to describe these arrangements is misleading, since, by s 5 of the Children Act 1989, a guardian is a person appointed by the court or a testamentary guardian under the will of a person who has died.

None the less, independent schools still use 'guardian' to mean a person who provides care and accommodation for a pupil in the circumstances mentioned above. There is no harm in this, provided it is understood that the legal powers and procedures of guardianship do not apply to these arrangements. Moreover, the adjective 'legal' adds nothing to 'guardian' and can be misleading when applied to holiday arrangements.

The legal character of holiday guardianship depends on the circumstances, but is far more complex than may be apparent at first sight. The legal mechanisms and other considerations may include:

−   *Multi-party contracts* involving the pupil, the overseas parents, the school, the agency or guardianship practice and the guardian family with whom the pupil will be living.

−   *Private fostering* within the meaning of s 66 of the Children Act 1989, subject to the prohibitions in s 69 and the provisions in Sch 8, para 9 to that Act.

−   *Duty of care in tort*, which has been described in Chapter 11.

−   *Delegated parental responsibility* under s 2(9) of the Children Act 1989.

– *Privacy and confidentiality* and the extent to which they can and should be overridden in certain circumstances.

– *The rights of the child*, having regard to age and disabilities.

– *Child protection.*

– *Immigration matters*, including visas.

– *Health and safety* and risk assessment where necessary.

– *Agency*, since in varying circumstances each party may be the agent of one or more others.

– *Insurance of potential liabilities*, and the provision of personal accident insurance.

– *Jurisdiction*, ie which system of law regulates the arrangements.

The rest of this chapter is concerned with a consideration of the legal areas identified above, and a number of the cultural and practical aspects of holiday guardianship arrangements.

## 14.3   ROLE OF THE UK GUARDIAN

The school will wish to be satisfied that there is a suitable adult in the UK who is fully authorised to take decisions for the pupil and who has undertaken as appropriate to:

– attend school premises in case of emergency;

– attend a parents' evening, liaise with the overseas parents and take or communicate decisions concerning the child's education, pastoral care and other needs;

– attend the pupil's special days such as prize giving, matches, concerts and similar events as a caring parent would;

– make travel arrangements as necessary;

– receive the pupil at home if too unwell for school, or if suspended, rusticated or required to leave.

Although the school's responsibility for the overseas pupils ceases when the pupil goes to the UK guardian, the school would normally wish to be satisfied that the guardian is a fit and proper person who can provide suitable caring accommodation and an appropriate level of protection and supervision. Some schools want to interview the proposed UK guardian, others do not.

The UK guardian may be the agent of the overseas parents in dealings with the school and must act in accordance with the express or implied authority conferred on him (or her) by the overseas parents or by the applicable provisions of UK law. As agent, the UK guardian will not be personally liable to pay the fees or fees in lieu of notice, unless he has expressly undertaken with the school that he will do so. Sometimes, the UK guardian collects payment of the fees in the foreign currency and remits them to the school in pounds sterling. Once again, the UK guardian is acting as agent not as principal unless there is express agreement to the contrary.

There should be a high degree of co-operation between the UK guardian and the school. On occasions, it will be necessary and appropriate for the school or the UK guardian to override the confidentiality to which a pupil is legally entitled. That aspect is considered later on.

## 14.4 CONTRACTUAL ASPECTS

### 14.4.1 Generally

One, and sometimes several, contractual relationships will be running concurrently to regulate matters of payment and the main powers and duties. If a conflict of interests arises, certain of the contractual terms must give way, to the extent that they are inconsistent with the welfare of the child. An element of flexibility should be built in to any formal contractual documents by which these arrangements are established. Contractual documents will not have much meaning to overseas parents who neither speak nor read English, and so translation of the essential parts at least should be considered. Direct enforcement of any payment provisions may prove difficult unless payment has been obtained in advance.

### 14.4.2 The school

The school will not normally be a contracting party in the guardianship arrangement, but if it is involved in introducing the overseas parent to a guardian family, there will be a contract of agency with one or both of those parties and, in addition, the school will come under a duty of care to the pupil and overseas parents.

In its contract with the overseas parents, a school will normally insist on a UK guardian being appointed in order to carry out the role described above. However, in some cases, the overseas parents will be unable to make a suitable appointment and will ask the school to do so. In the absence of an agreement to the contrary, the school is not obliged to undertake this responsibility but if it does, there are broadly the following choices of appointment:

- a teacher at the school premises or at the teacher's home;

- a family known to the school which is willing to undertake private fostering responsibilities; or

- an agency or guardianship practice which will nominate, appoint and delegate to a guardian family.

Each of these carries different legal implications for the school which are discussed as they arise.

The school will not be a party to or in any way responsible for an appointment made directly between the overseas parent and the UK guardian. But the school will or may come under a duty of care if it is involved in the selection of agent, guardianship practice or guardian family.

### 14.4.3 The pupil/student

It is unlikely that there will be any contractual arrangement between the pupil/student or any other party under 18. The arrangement is one made for the care and welfare of the pupil rather than by him or her. That is the theory, at least. While in the UK and under school-leaving age, the pupil is required as a matter of law to attend school during term time. At other times, those who have primary or delegated parental responsibility have a duty to provide satisfactory accommodation, care and maintenance for the pupil. There may be a visa condition requiring any change of address to be notified to the Home Office.

School-leaving age will soon be extended to the end of the academic year in which the pupil reaches the age of 16. Whether or not the pupil is at school (but subject to any immigration restrictions), he (or she) is free to live where he wishes without sanction under the law. However, the school will invariably require the UK guardianship arrangements to continue and if so, the pupil must abide by that rule if he intends to remain at the school.

The pupil is unlikely to have a contractual relationship in respect of his (or her) care.

### 14.4.4 The overseas parents

The legal position of the overseas parents is that by sending the child to school in England or Wales, they have delegated their parental responsibility in accordance with s 2(9) of the Children Act 1989. Delegation in that sense is a delegation of tasks and not of responsibility. The overseas parents should be expected to remain in contact with the school by telephone and fax and should be able to communicate in English directly or through an intermediary.

With the easy availability of flights to and from most parts of the world, the overseas parents will not normally be more than 24 hours' travel time away from the school should the need for their presence arise, although this assumption may be distorted by difficulties over passports, travel visas and other practical considerations. The overseas parents must be ready to make an alternative appointment of UK guardian, or authorise the school to do so, should the need arise.

Other than the obligations mentioned above, the main obligation of the overseas parents relates to payment of fees directly or indirectly to the school, the fees payable to a guardianship practice, and the payments to be made to the holiday guardian for his (or her) time and trouble and for the pupil's maintenance when not at school.

The legal relationship between the overseas parents and the school will be primarily regulated by the contract for educational services. In addition, the overseas parent may be in contract with a directly appointed guardian family and/or with an agency or guardianship practice.

### 14.4.5   The guardianship practice

There may be a distinction between:

(a)  *a guardianship practice* – the proprietors of which personally accept the responsibilities of UK guardianship and delegate certain of them to an approved guardian family; and

(b)  *a guardianship agency* – which does not accept those responsibilities but merely acts as a commercial intermediary in finding a suitable guardian family.

There is probably little difference between the responsibilities of an agency and those of a 'practice' in relation to the selection of a guardian family. The real difference will be one of relationships, ie who is the person that carries out the role of UK guardian in communication with the school, attendance at special days, making travel arrangements and at times of crisis if the pupil absconds or is expelled or required to leave.

### 14.4.6   The guardian family

The guardian family will almost certainly have a contractual relationship with the overseas parents. Depending on the circumstances, the guardian family may also have a contractual relationship with the school, or with an agency or practice. Its duties to the pupil/student will be owed under the duty of care in tort rather than by contract.

The involvement of an agency will have the legal effect of introducing the overseas parent to the guardian family – even though they may never meet – and also the effect of bringing about a contractual arrangement akin to private fostering under which duties will be owed in both directions. Normally, payments to the guardian family will be made via the agent or practice.

In other cases, the school may be an agent introducing the two parties, and then it is likely that payment arrangements will be made direct between the overseas parent and the guardian family.

In each case, there should be a satisfactory form of contract which sets out the rights and duties of the parties.

## 14.5   PRIVATE FOSTERING

Under Part IX of the Children Act 1989, a child is a 'privately fostered child' if he (or she) is:

–    under 16 (under 18 if disabled); and

–    cared for and provided with accommodation by (broadly) someone other than a parent or relative,

and the accommodation is (or will be) provided:

–    for 28 days or more; or

–    for more than 2 weeks if the child is accommodated at an independent school during school holidays.

Section 66(2) of the Act states:

> 'A child is not a privately fostered child if the person caring for and accommodating him –
>
> (a)  has done so for a period of less than 28 days; and
> (b)  does not intend to do so for any longer period.'

This wording creates uncertainty about whether a person is engaged in private fostering if he (or she) intends to accommodate the child during exeats, half terms and sickness periods, in addition to school holidays. Usually the autumn and spring holidays will each be shorter than 28 days, but, if the shorter periods are added together, the arrangement will last for 28 days or more.

It is submitted that, in the absence of wording in the Act to the effect of '28 days in any period of 12 months', the meaning is 'continuous period'. If this is right, then each period of care, whether it be school holidays or half term, is treated as separate and distinct, and the arrangement is unlikely to be one of private fostering. In any event, it is not private fostering if the carer is a parent or relative.

In cases where the continuous period is 28 days or more (or more than 2 weeks at an independent school) the main statutory provisions are:

–     Children Act 1989, s 67, which imposes a duty on every local authority 'to satisfy themselves that the welfare of children who are privately fostered within their area is being satisfactorily safeguarded and promoted and to secure that such advice is given to those caring for them as appears to the authority to be needed'. The UK guardian must notify the local authority not less than 2 weeks before fostering is to begin;

–     the Children (Private Arrangements for Fostering) Regulations 1991, which contain detailed provisions on which the local authority will advise; and

–     Children Act 1989, s 70, which makes it an offence if a person fails without reasonable excuse to give any required notice or information to the local authority. Various other offences are also created which are punishable by a fine and/or imprisonment.

The main purpose of this legislation was to bring to the attention of the local authority private fostering businesses being run in overcrowded and unsuitable accommodation, sometimes little better than a doss-house or even a brothel. Independent schools have, on the whole, a very good record of helping to ensure that holiday accommodation for overseas pupils is satisfactory. They and the guardian families they use are, none the less, potentially brought into the regulatory framework described above.

## 14.6   DUTY OF CARE IN TORT

The meaning of 'duty of care' and of legal negligence was discussed in Chapter 11 and the principles are not repeated here.

### 14.6.1 The holiday guardian

The UK guardian will be found to owe the duty of care of the ordinary careful parent in relation to the pupil or student. The extent of the duty will depend on the age and other attributes of the pupil. For example, and as explained above, a person over the age of 16 is free to leave home and is, therefore, free to leave the home of a guardian family and live elsewhere, or even disappear, subject to immigration restrictions or the requirement to attend school, if under school-leaving age. This may be difficult for overseas parents from some cultures to understand, and care should be taken to explain the legal position to them under UK law. There is little that can be done directly to prevent the pupil walking out if he (or she) is financially independent, although the school is entitled to require the pupil to leave if arrangements for holiday care are not satisfactory.

### 14.6.2 The school

#### (a) The school's duty

A common law duty of care will arise if the school acts at the request of overseas parents or others or on its own initiative in making arrangements for the pupil's accommodation and care. The school must take reasonable care over the appointment of an agency or guardianship practice. The school should satisfy itself that the family circumstances and arrangements are appropriate and may be liable for failing to do so if that failure is the foreseeable cause of injury or damage. The duty owed by the school is both to the pupil and to the guardian family.

#### (b) Selecting a guardian family

Schools that maintain a panel of families willing to act as holiday guardians should take the following prudent steps:

– meet the holiday guardian at his (or her) home;

– ensure that the normal child protection checks are carried out. These are discussed in more detail below;

– ensure that the guardian is given a written summary of his rights and responsibilities;

– ensure that the guardian family knows everything material concerning the pupil (including any medication he may need) and any particular problems to be anticipated;

– be satisfied that the guardian and the pupil have adequate public liability insurance and that insurers have been notified of the financial and other arrangements. House contents insurers should also be notified (if different);

– carry out a rough and ready risk assessment and be satisfied that there are no unacceptable or abnormal risks.

A checklist of some of the points that might be covered in a risk assessment is set out in Figure 1 below.

***Figure 1.*** Risk assessment checklist.

| The Risk | Points out of 5 (0 = no risk) |
|---|---|
| What is the risk of minor accidental injury (eg dog bite) to the child? | |
| What is the risk of major accidental injury to the child? | |
| Is the child likely to be exposed to drugs, solvents or pornography? | |
| Is there a risk of the child being bullied or physically assaulted, sexually assaulted or neglected? | |
| What are the risks of loss or damage to the child's personal belongings? | |
| Is there a risk of cultural or religious incompatibility? | |
| What are the risks to the child in the event of sudden illness of the child or others? Has the holiday guardian sufficient experience to cope? | |
| What are the risks of the child causing personal injury or damage to property of the holiday guardian or the family? | |
| What is the known conduct and general behaviour of the child? Is he (or she) likely to be involved in drugs, alcohol, smoking, substance abuse or other criminal activity or unacceptable mischief? | |
| What are the risks of the child absconding or of being snatched by an estranged parent? | |
| Is there anything in the past experience of the guardian family or the child that gives cause for concern? | |

If any of these risks scores more than 2 points, a system should be devised for avoiding or minimising the risk and giving advice and warnings to the holiday guardian. High-scoring risks should be a cause for reconsideration of suitability.

An exercise of this nature need not go overboard, nor should it be made a condition of insurance cover. But it is a sign that the school has taken its responsibility seriously and it also provides a record of the care that has been taken in finding an appropriate placement.

If the child is then injured by negligence or by deliberate act of the holiday guardian family, that will *not* be the fault of the school, and the school should not be held legally liable. That does not mean the school cannot be sued, but, if sued, there should be indemnity from the liability insurers, provided all proper disclosures have been made. Accordingly, the school's legal costs would be covered and there should be no award of damages; but if damages were awarded they would be paid by the insurers.

The school should only recommend an agency to overseas parents if it is satisfied that the agency is reputable and experienced in providing care and accommodation for pupils. If the school is going to state its belief or opinion that an agency is reputable it should make sure that there is a reasonable basis for that belief or opinion. Otherwise the school should make it clear to the overseas parents that the parents will be contracting directly with the agency and must satisfy themselves of the quality of the service being offered.

### (c)   Teachers as holiday guardians

It has been quite common for overseas pupils to stay at schools in the care of a teacher during exeat weekends and half terms and, sometimes, during school holidays. The school will normally compensate the teacher for this extra responsibility and add a charge to the pupil's account. Experience varies as to how well these arrangements work, but it has been observed that children sometimes feel it is second best to be left at school or in the care of a teacher while their peers go home to families. The local authority must be informed of any such arrangement at school premises lasting, or intended to last, longer than 12 days.

An alternative arrangement is where the teacher takes the pupil into his home environment and again is compensated for the cost and responsibility. However, these arrangements create a potential conflict of interests and are generally disapproved by social services. Peer group suggestions of favouritism may be made. It is altogether more difficult if a pupil makes an allegation, malicious or otherwise, of impropriety against the teacher or another member of the teacher's family. The school may then be faced with investigating the matter or involving the police and ultimately with losing both a good teacher and a pupil who is withdrawn.

None the less, there may sometimes be little alternative if care arrangements have to be made at short notice and the overseas parents have not authorised the cost of using the services of a guardianship agency or practice.

### 14.6.3   Guardianship practice

The guardianship agency or practice is also under a duty to use reasonable care over the selection of the guardian family and the communication of important matters that have a bearing on the child's safety and welfare.

The extent of the duty is unclear where, for example, a pupil over school-leaving age absconds. The overseas parents and school should of course be informed immediately. A joint decision should be taken, on professional advice if necessary, about whether there is an obligation to inform the immigration authorities and whether help from the police might be anticipated. Unless there is reason to believe that the pupil's safety and welfare are in danger, the police are unlikely to become involved in a straightforward case of a person exercising his (or her) legal right to choose where to live.

## 14.7   DELEGATED PARENTAL RESPONSIBILITY

Children Act 1989, s 2(9) provides:

> 'A person who has parental responsibility for a child may not surrender or transfer any part of that responsibility to another but may arrange for some or all of it to be met by one or more persons acting on his behalf.'

In an arrangement whereby care and accommodation for the child is provided away from school premises for less than 28 days, the legal relationship is likely to be one of *delegated parental responsibility*. However, it is important to understand that 'delegation' means a delegation of tasks and not a surrender, transfer or shedding of responsibility by the parents. Even so, in practical terms, the holiday guardian will carry full day-to-day responsibility.

## 14.8   PRIVACY AND CONFIDENTIALITY

The pupil will be entitled to the rights of privacy and confidentiality discussed in Chapters 13 and 22 subject to those rights being overridden in limited circumstances where necessary to avert the risk of serious harm or to avoid illegality. Sometimes, there can be undue anxiety about the extent to which the school, the guardianship practice and the guardian family are entitled to exchange confidential information about the pupil.

It is submitted that, wherever the welfare of children is concerned, the best guide is common sense. Those who are charged with the care of children will need all relevant information if they are to discharge their duties. This is easy enough to state but there may be circumstances in which a pupil has spoken to the school counsellor in confidence and on the specific condition that information is withheld from the guardian family lest it is relayed to the overseas parents.

Each of these cases will turn on its own facts. The circumstances may be such that the school decides to withhold detail from the guardian family but care should be taken not to place the guardian family in an unfair or untenable position.

## 14.9   CHILD PROTECTION

The checks that can and should be made of those who will have the care of a child were discussed at Chapter 13 and are:

–   the DfEE's List 99;

–   criminal background check;

–   the Department of Health's Adverse Report List.

The Disqualification for Caring for Children Regulations 1991 specify a number of offences, conviction for which disqualify a person from privately fostering children.

## 14.10   RACE RELATIONS

Race Relations Act 1976, s 36 provides:

> 'Nothing in Parts II to IV shall render unlawful any act done by a person for the benefit of persons not ordinarily resident in Great Britain in affording them access to facilities for

education or training or any ancillary benefits, where it appears to him that the persons in question do not intend to remain in Great Britain after their period of education or training there.'

Part II of the Act relates to discrimination in the employment field by employers, partnerships, trade unions, qualifying bodies, vocational training bodies, employment agencies and the Manpower Services Commission.

Part IV of the Act relates to 'other unlawful acts' including discriminatory practices, discriminatory advertisements, instructions to discriminate, pressure to discriminate, liability of employers and principals, and aiding unlawful acts.

## 14.11   JURISDICTION

The various legal contracts that arise in a guardianship arrangement should be expressed to be subject to the exclusive jurisdiction of English law and the courts in the district where the school is situated. Provided the arrangement is subject to the jurisdiction of English law, an action for money unpaid under the contract can be brought in England and judgment obtained here, provided procedural rules about the service of proceedings are followed. Enforcement may be costly and difficult but the chances of making a recovery are greater if the litigation is controlled in the UK and not under a foreign jurisdiction.

Moreover, it is important that the overseas parents and pupils understand that, while in the UK, the pupil is subject to the legal system applicable in the relevant part of the UK, which also includes some aspects of European law ('Community law').

Disputes have arisen where a pupil comes from a legal jurisdiction which accords far fewer rights to a person under 21 than are given under UK law, for example the right to leave school or to leave home or to have sexual intercourse. The parents in these cases need to be told that neither the school nor the guardian family has any right to exercise jurisdiction over the pupil in the UK that is not provided by law. Taking steps to restrain the movements of a person over 16 could amount to false imprisonment or some other trespass to the person.

## 14.12   SCOPE OF HOLIDAY GUARDIANSHIP

### 14.12.1   Periods of care and accommodation

Arrangements may be needed for the three main school holiday periods (with transport arrangements); the three half-term periods (with travel arrangements); exeat weekends (with travel arrangements); and when the school is closed due to illness or bad weather, or when the child is required to leave, is suspended for disciplinary reasons or is excluded for non-payment of fees.

### 14.12.2   Consent of the overseas parents

The general categories of matters for which parental consent is needed include medical treatment; treatment of minor ailments; travel by public transport; swimming and other medium- to high-risk sports and activities, and going out alone or with others.

A child aged 14 or over can, as a matter of law, go in to a bar with an adult, but may not buy drink or alcohol there; can be employed on a weekday as a street trader by parents; (if male) can be convicted of various sexual assaults; can possess a shotgun, air weapon or ammunition; and can be given a custodial sentence. Parental consent ought therefore to be obtained if the child is to go out accompanied during daylight hours in the local area; to go away from the local area during daylight hours with other young people and friends, and to travel unaccompanied on local transport.

Children aged 16 or over are, in general, subject to few practical restrictions. They can leave school; take part in public performances; leave home without the consent of those with parental responsibility; record a change of name; (if female) consent to sexual intercourse; obtain certain social security benefits; apply for their own passport; choose their doctor; buy cigarettes, tobacco and cigarette papers; buy beer, cider or wine; buy fireworks; be a street trader; and enter or live in a brothel. At the time of writing, it has been proposed to reduce the age of consent for homosexual activities from 18 to 16, although proposed legislation has been deferred. None the less, the consent of overseas parents should be sought if the holiday guardian intends to allow the child to travel freely out of the local area or go out in the evening with friends or alone.

### 14.12.3   Insurance

It is advisable that a child in the care of a holiday guardian has the following benefits and liability insurance:

–   personal accident benefits for the child;

–   cover against loss of or damage to the child's personal belongings;

–   cover for health and hospital expenses relating to the child;

–   public liability cover in respect of the child's negligent acts or omissions.

### 14.12.4   Information and confidentiality

The holiday guardian may be appointed by the overseas parents, by the school or by an agency. Whoever is in the chain of responsibility should ensure that all material information including confidential information is given to the holiday guardian to enable that person to discharge such duties as are owed. As a matter of law, it is not a breach of confidence at law when acting in good faith to pass information concerning the pupil where to do so averts a risk of serious harm to a child's health and safety or to pass on information relating to illegality, gross immorality or conduct contrary to public policy.

### 14.12.5   Vetting

The holiday guardian should be asked to consent to enquiries being made of the police and others for the purposes of vetting the suitability of the holiday guardian to provide care and accommodation for a child. The statutory basis for vetting is the

Disqualification for Caring for Children Regulations 1991 which specify a number of offences, conviction for which disqualify a person from privately fostering children.

## 14.13 THE MAIN OBLIGATIONS OF A HOLIDAY GUARDIAN

The obligations and the extent of the duty depend on the age of the child, the specific instructions that have been given to and accepted by the holiday guardian, the general law and all the circumstances. Examples are given below.

### 14.13.1 Responsibility and welfare

The holiday guardian will take full responsibility for the child, subject to age, in the manner specified. In particular, the holiday guardian would be expected to provide appropriate meals and reasonable entertainment and to maintain contact with the child, the school and the parent both in term time and in the holidays. The general standard of the responsible and caring parent applies. So far as possible, the child should be assimilated into the holiday guardian's family. The privacy, rights, religion and customs of the child must be respected.

### 14.13.2 Passing information

The holiday guardian should ensure that the overseas parent and, where appropriate, the school and agency receive all necessary information about the child and about arrangements to be made for the child in relation to school, travel, health, diet, religion, security and all other matters affecting welfare.

### 14.13.3 General discipline and good order

The holiday guardian will be expected to act with reasonable care so as to ensure that the child maintains appropriate standards of hygiene, behaviour, good manners and language; and, so far as possible, to see that the child obeys the law and to enforce any rules laid down by the parent or the school, especially those concerning smoking, alcohol, drugs, solvents, pornography, and other unauthorised or unlawful activities; and to protect the child from exposure to dangers of that nature both within and outside the home. Corporal punishment without prior consent from the overseas parent and rough handling should be prohibited, but physical coercion or restraint to an extent that is reasonable and lawful may be permitted.

### 14.13.4 Supervision of the child

The holiday guardian should observe the reasonable wishes of the parent and of the school and set rules as to when the child may be alone in the house for short periods; may go out with friends or with the holiday guardian's children; or may go out in the immediate area or may travel long distances unaccompanied.

### 14.13.5 Absence and delegation of duties

If the holiday guardian is to be absent for any part of the day or night not contemplated above, he (or she) must appoint a responsible person to be in charge of the child.

Overseas parents and/or school or agency should be informed in advance if the holiday guardian will be away from home with or without the child for more than 48 hours.

### 14.13.6 Accommodation and privacy

The child should have his (or her) own room unless shared accommodation has been requested or consented to. The reasonable privacy of the child must be respected by all members of the holiday guardian's family.

### 14.13.7 Contact with the parent and the school

The holiday guardian must allow reasonable contact with the overseas parent by telephone and fax (if available). The child must be able to receive visits from the parent upon reasonable notice. The holiday guardian must keep the school informed of matters which the school ought to be told concerning the child.

### 14.13.8 Dangerous sports and activities

The prior consent of the overseas parents should be obtained before the child is allowed to take part in unduly hazardous or dangerous sports and activities. The holiday guardian must ensure that all necessary training, safety equipment and supervision are provided and precautions are taken in relation to any such activities that are permitted or undertaken.

### 14.13.9 Emergencies

The holiday guardian will be expected to notify the parent, agency or school as appropriate immediately in the event of any accident or emergency giving rise to a serious injury or the requirement for emergency medical treatment of the child or any unpleasant or potentially damaging incident affecting the child or the holiday guardian. If contact cannot be made as above, the holiday guardian should be fully authorised in writing to act *in loco parentis* in accordance with responsible advice given by appropriately qualified professional advisers.

### 14.13.10 General approach

The holiday guardian should be expected to maintain a friendly, helpful and co-operative approach with the overseas parent, agency or school as the case may be and all others in all dealings in relation to the child.

### 14.13.11 Termination of the arrangement

The holiday guardian should be required to give appropriate notice to terminate the agreement under normal circumstances. Four weeks' notice expiring at least 2 weeks before the next exeat, half-term or holiday period would be normal. If short notice is necessary in the best interests of the child or because the relationship has broken down, there must be an adequate mechanism for ensuring appropriate care and accommodation for the child in any interim period.

## 14.13.12  Payment of the holiday guardian

Payment will vary in accordance with the type of arrangement. At its simplest there may be a daily rate plus expenses within agreed parameters, for example, the cost of essential clothing and travel and reasonable entertainment and pocket money. Arrangements that involve the school or an agency as intermediary are more complex, and there is the problem of ensuring that payments are made in advance in pounds sterling.

## 14.13.13  Legal liability and insurances

The holiday guardian should be advised to check that all material disclosures have been made to their household and liability insurers. Motor insurers should be informed in case they were minded to take the unworthy point that the child was being carried 'for hire or reward'. Those who make the guardianship arrangement may wish to satisfy themselves that insurances are in place. Among the risks to be contemplated are that the child might cause personal injury or damage to property at the holiday guardian's home or to third parties. Equally to be contemplated is the risk that the holiday guardian's family may cause personal injury to the child or loss or damage to his (or her) property.

## 14.13.14  Jurisdiction

An agreement concerning holiday guardianship should express the place at which the agreement was made (being a place in the United Kingdom) and that it is subject to the exclusive jurisdiction of English law.

## 14.14  SOME PRACTICAL PROBLEMS

The following is a short anecdotal list of problems that have arisen during holiday guardianship arrangements and have given rise to the need for third party intervention:

– serious homesickness or general unhappiness of the child, not the fault of the holiday guardian;

– the school withholding from the holiday guardian information that a girl had developed a propensity to cut herself at school;

– a boy bringing drink, drugs and cigarettes to the holiday guardian's home;

– a boy caught shoplifting whilst in the care, but out of the supervision, of the holiday guardian;

– a boy who brought pornographic magazines and videos to the holiday guardian's home and showed them to younger children of the family;

– concerns about a sexual assault by a boy on a female member of the guardian family and vice versa;

- a 17-year-old girl absconding without any trace; she was later found to be safe, living in a flat in London, but had not communicated with the school, holiday guardian or her parents;

- unprofessional, tactless and mercenary behaviour by a particular holiday guardian who refused to take the child on family outings because 'we are not being paid to do that'.

These instances illustrate the level of openness, care and communication that is needed between all those who undertake some part of the holiday responsibility for an overseas pupil.

## 14.15   FORMS OF LEGAL AGREEMENT

Holiday accommodation is primarily a matter for the good sense of those who are experienced in the care of children. Even so, there should be satisfactory forms of legal agreement in each case. The forms need not be over-complex, provided there is a sufficiently detailed code of practice to which those working in the field generally subscribe. Discussions about a code of practice have been taking place between people working in the field notably through an organisation known as AEGIS which was launched in November 1997 and has set out to become a professional and qualifying body for guardianship practices.

The main headings of a legal agreement concerning guardianship are: formal details and signatures; fees and other payments; the contractual structure of the arrangement; the nature and purposes of the arrangement; vetting; the main obligations of the parties and general conditions. The formal details should contain a list of contact numbers including emergency contacts.

# Chapter 15

## BEHAVIOUR AND DISCIPLINE

### 15.1 INTRODUCTION

This chapter is concerned with matters of policy on behaviour and discipline, together with the attitudes (and their legal consequences) of staff, parents and pupils to each other. Attitudes are perhaps the defining aspect of a school's culture. If violence, bullying, other forms of unkindness, or drugs and pornography are tolerated at school or in the home, it will become almost impossible to operate an effective policy on behaviour and discipline.

Corporal punishment is another aspect of behaviour and discipline. Formal corporal punishment has all but disappeared from schools, and Parliament voted finally to abolish its use at independent schools when the Schools Standards and Framework Bill received its third reading in March 1998. However, there remains a thin dividing line between some aspects of *lawful restraint* (which is not within the legal definition of corporal punishment) and *rough handling* and *physical abuse*, which are. Accordingly, some of the legal principles, statute and case-law about corporal punishment will continue to be relevant and are considered.

### 15.2 POLICY

A policy about behaviour and discipline has four distinct elements: the aims and authorities provided by the policy; the behaviour protocol; the school rules and sanctions; and the procedures, such as for investigation of complaints and rumours and review of a decision to expel or to require a pupil's removal from the school.

Every policy has a legal status, either contractual or non-contractual, and it is better for that to be defined in the first place by the school, rather than left to the court in the event of a dispute.

Authority for the school's policies derives from the governors, although in practice, policy is normally set by the head and ratified by the governors. That is appropriate, because the head is responsible for good order and discipline at the school, and also for its culture and ethos. He (or she) has the responsibility of ensuring that policies reflect the intended culture of the school community and are implemented.

## 15.3   BULLYING

Bullying is intolerable because it is a cruel, repeated and unjustified oppression by the powerful over the powerless. It is a complex process with legal implications and no easy answers. Until the early 1990s, it was a field that many schools had neglected and sociologists and criminologists had made their own.

By 1985, the social legislation of the 1970s had started to change attitudes in the workplace. The process was assisted by substantial awards of compensation in cases of victimisation and harassment and also by a new awareness of the principles of 'quality' described in various improvement initiatives such as BS5750/ISO9000 and *Investors In People*. In relation to schools, following the Eltham Report in 1989, the DFE funded the Sheffield Bullying Research Project 1991–93 which led to publication of the DFE book entitled *Bullying: Don't Suffer in Silence*.

### 15.3.1   Meaning of 'bullying'

The DFE book, at Part 1/8, describes the features of bullying as:

- deliberately hurtful behaviour
- repeated often, over a period of time
- when it is difficult for those being bullied to defend themselves.

Part 1/8 also states that bullying can take many forms, but three main types are:

- physical bullying – hitting, kicking, taking belongings;
- verbal bullying – name calling, insulting, racist remarks;
- indirect bullying – spreading nasty stories about someone, excluding someone from social groups.

In a strictly legal sense, bullying of a kind for which the school might be held liable in negligence is behaviour of the kind described above:

- which has an element of concerted behaviour or persistence;
- about which the school authorities knew or should have known; and where
- the school did not respond appropriately; and where
- the pupil has suffered physical or psychological injury as a result.

In his book, *Bullying in Schools* (Jessica Kingsley Publishers, 1996), Ken Rigby distinguishes between:

- Malign bullying, which is the deliberate exploitation of a power differential involving an initial desire to hurt which is expressed in action, directed by a more powerful person or group against someone less powerful. The action is without justification. Typically, it is repeated and enjoyed by the bully and someone is hurt as a result.

- Non-malign bullying where the bully does not appear to be hostile at all and may even be good-natured, balanced and likeable. Such people see their hurtful conduct as 'teasing' or 'a game' and do not know the harm they are doing.

– Educational bullying where, through intellectual arrogance, one person finds fault after fault with the work of another, exposing 'inferiority', whether it be in the classroom or in sport, music or other activities, and does so on the pretext that it is 'for the good' of the other person.

A bully, whether a boy or girl, is often an intelligent, accomplished and manipulative person who is capable of turning a peer group against a single individual. Sometimes that individual may have no practical alternative but to leave and seek a fresh start at another school.

Very little is known about victims of bullying. They often come from families that are self-enclosed where the children are over-protected. Moreover, victims and their parents can also be manipulative.

In a more general sense, a single episode in which a stronger aggressor sets out to cause injury, fear, distress or unhappiness to a weaker victim may also be described as bullying, and, depending on the circumstances, the aggressor can be prosecuted for a criminal assault, theft or damage and may also have committed a tort. It is unlikely that the school authority would be held liable in negligence for single episodes that it could not reasonably have known about or prevented, and which lacked the necessary element of concerted behaviour or persistence by those responsible.

One has to accept that an element of unkindness is endemic among the staff and pupils at virtually all schools and in other communities. It is not realistic to think it can ever be completely eradicated; nor would a child who had never been exposed to such behaviour learn to cope in the outside world. The real legal questions are about degree, persistence and the way the culture of the school operates to reduce the incidence of bullying and also how effectively episodes that are noticed or reported are handled.

The school authority is not expected to know or apply psychological techniques, but it must nowadays put satisfactory systems in place for identifying and dealing pragmatically with the problem of bullying, at risk of legal liability in default. It is not sufficient simply to have a system. The system must operate and be driven.

### 15.3.2 Reported cases

In 1997, a number of reports appeared in the press to the effect that about 10 school children each year commit suicide and a number more attempt suicide by hanging, overdose or other means. Many more again harm themselves in other ways, for example, by cutting, body piercing and tattoos, and some develop eating disorders such as anorexia nervosa and bulimia. Although many of these cases may have reference to family and other psychological problems, a significant number are thought to be a child's response to being bullied at or on the way to and from school.

*Sebastian Sharp* (unreported, 1996) concerned a reported out-of-court settlement of £30,000 in a case where a pupil alleged that constant bullying at school had affected his education and left him traumatised. He had alleged that he was regularly kicked, punched and assaulted from the age of 11, when he started at school, until he ran away at 15.

*Hamad v Dame Allen's School* (1997) *Daily Telegraph*, 14 May, concerned a pupil aged 18 at the date of settlement, who was reported to have received £4,000 in compensation following months of daily racist abuse and physical injuries at the hands of seven A-level students. The action was supported by the Commission for Racial Equality, although the basis of the settlement has been the subject of some controversy.

In *R v McBratney and Murray* (1997) *Daily Telegraph*, 28 May, two girls aged 17 and 16, attending a State school, were convicted, and one was given a custodial sentence for repeated bullying of a classmate. The classmate had died following an overdose after receiving a telephone warning that she would be beaten again and have her head shaved if she did well in her examinations.

There were also newspaper reports on 27 May 1997 that three 14-year-old girls attending Keith Grammar School in Banffshire had tried to commit suicide after bullying, and there have been numerous further articles in the press concerning the number of cases against schools that are being prepared for trial and involve physical and psychological injuries caused by bullying.

### 15.3.3   Approaches to bullying

Rigby (mentioned earlier at **15.3.1**) suggests that there are three quite distinct approaches to dealing with bullies.

#### *(a)   Moralistic approach*

The mechanism of this approach is to explain to the bully the values underlying the school policy about bullying and the importance of showing respect and tolerance for others. The bully is required to write an essay explaining that what he (or she) has done is contrary to the school's explicit values and requirements and also to write an apology to the person who was bullied. The position is then explained to the parents.

This method is unlikely to be successful with a bully who is motivated by malice and who will cynically acquiesce and bully again in ways which are harder to detect.

#### *(b)   Legalistic approach*

The mechanism here is to impose a penalty or sanction ranging from school chores, withdrawal of privileges and time-out, to detention, suspension, or the requirement to leave.

The legalistic approach has a number of advantages. It is quick. It sends a clear message to others. It can provide a sense of 'justice'. It may involve 'naming and shaming'. On the other hand, this approach requires the precise facts of the case to be established if injustice is to be avoided and it is unlikely to lead to a genuine reconciliation between the bully and victim.

#### *(c)   Humanistic approach*

This is based on a sincere belief on the part of the teacher that the bully is 'an OK person' whose behaviour needs to be changed and the belief also that bullying is normal human behaviour. 'No blame' and 'non-judgemental' are expressions that are likely to arise in this context.

The 'no blame' approach has become common in both State-funded and independent schools. Instead of punishing a bully or 'naming and shaming', the children themselves are expected to work out a solution under the guidance of their teachers. The system has proved controversial. Some heads claim it is successful. Others describe it as 'psycho-babble'. Kidscape, the anti-bullying charity, is reported as saying that the 'no blame' approach will produce a generation of lager louts and muggers who take no responsibility for the consequences of their actions. One feature of the 'no blame' approach is that parents are rarely informed of incidents until the problem has become quite serious. That is seen as reducing the likelihood of parents punishing their children which would, in the perception of the school, undermine the school's humanistic policy.

## 15.3.4 Alternative approach

It is perhaps trite to point out that bullying is the antithesis of kindness and that bullies have always thrived in environments where they have been tolerated. Perhaps it follows that the only effective way of eradicating the worst kinds of bullying is a two-pronged attack:

- intolerance of bullying;
- attitudes and practices that constantly drive a culture of kindness throughout every aspect of the school. ('Kindness' is a very potent 'selling message' with most parents.)

The driving of this culture needs to be unremitting and aimed at everyone: staff, pupils and parents. It is tough-minded and it allows for aspects of each approach described by Rigby – moral, legal and humanist – in the right way and at the right time.

The greatest practical problem in driving the culture of kindness will arise with children of dysfunctional families where the dysfunctions include:

- cynical attitudes to human relations;
- failure by parents to accept the child for what he (or she) is, or to consider the child's feelings;
- acrimonious or violent relationships between the parents;
- violence, sarcasm and ridicule against the child, or sexual misconduct;
- failure to develop positive social values, such as honesty, consideration and respect for the needs of others;
- lack of co-operation between family members, for example, rarely eating together and not solving family problems together;
- misguided pride of parents (who may see themselves as loving and caring) in admiring and cultivating their children's aggressiveness, toughness and dominance;
- over-indulgence by parents who, although kind and caring, may themselves be coerced or bullied by their children and are unable adequately to cope with them.

It is more likely than not that a child bringing these attitudes and behaviour into school will very soon find a like-minded group and/or a victim for his (or her) unkind words or actions.

The so-called moralistic and humanistic approaches to these children may be effective in dealing with cases at the less serious or less persistent end of the spectrum, but it is suggested here that they are unlikely to be effective in changing the behaviour of a dysfunctional person who is intent on causing harm, or is motivated by his (or her) own ability to abuse power. A school community can only withstand these individuals for a limited period of time. If they and their families cannot respond appropriately to a range of advice and sanctions it will serve neither the pupil nor the school for that pupil to remain a member. Another school may be able to help. Ultimately the pupil may be assessed as having special needs that are outside the provision that a particular school can make.

This view may be seen as unfashionable in some quarters but the success of a school, not to mention the safety and welfare of its staff and pupils, depends on every member of the school sharing and contributing to a common set of aims and a common culture. A school which retains a bully after it has exhausted its options for dealing with that person will lay itself open to legal liability.

The practice of some members of staff of 'bawling-out' children and humiliating them in the classroom or on the games field can cause serious damage to the school's culture and is a matter for legitimate complaint on every occasion. It is also conduct that can fortify the pupil-bully and may be a disciplinary offence for the member of staff concerned.

### 15.3.5  School's duty

In *X (Minors) v Bedfordshire County Council* [1995] 3 WLR 152, Lord Browne-Wilkinson stated:

> 'In my judgment, a school which accepts a pupil assumes responsibility not only for his physical well-being but also for his educational needs ...'

This dovetails with s 3(5) and s 87(1) of the Children Act 1989, which confer powers and duties on those who have the care of children to safeguard and promote their welfare.

The obligations described above are proactive in nature and the duties imposed by law, in practice, amount to these:

– to establish a policy that will reduce the incidence and promote the detection of bullying;
– to use reasonable care and skill to ensure that the policy operates satisfactorily and continuously;
– to ensure that the policy is in accord with a responsible body of opinion about bullying;
– to ensure that episodes of bullying which are detected are dealt with appropriately;
– to keep parents informed of antisocial behaviour that is or should be part of the pupil's permanent disciplinary record or is evidence of a deteriorating trend.

The 'responsible body of opinion' aspect gives rise to difficulties. Many will argue that the humanistic 'no blame' or 'shared concerns' approach is irresponsible *simpliciter*. Others will say that to follow it becomes irresponsible when it is seen not to be working. It is submitted that a school will be vulnerable if it has exclusively followed the 'no blame' approach, where expert evidence shows that it could not reasonably have been expected to work in the particular circumstances.

## 15.3.6 Legal proceedings

A victim of bullying who, through the negligence of a school, has suffered physical or psychological injury may be entitled:

– to bring an action in negligence against the school;
– to make a complaint to the police of assault or some other criminal offence against the bully;
– to bring a civil action against the bully, although any policy of insurance covering the third-party liability of the bully would be unlikely to cover deliberate criminal acts;
– to bring a civil action against the bully's parents if, in rare circumstances, they had in some way acquiesced in the circumstances that led to the injury.

Under the present law, a pupil will be entitled to legal aid in his own right, irrespective of his parents' means, although at the time of writing the Lord Chancellor has proposed abolition of legal aid for money claims.

The limitation period for a civil claim in negligence against the school or the bully (ie the period within which the pupil must begin his claim) will start on the pupil's eighteenth birthday and run for 3 years. Thus, the pupil can start an action at any time before the age of 21 and in rare cases that time-limit can be extended.

These claims against the school are unlikely to be straightforward, particularly if based on psychological injury. A plaintiff would, in practice, have to show among others:

– that there had been frequent expressions of concern by the parent and/or the pupil; or
– that members of staff had witnessed the bullying or had become aware of it or should have become aware of it and that the school did not respond appropriately; and
– that bullying was the sole cause of the injury and damage or contributed materially to it.

## 15.3.7 Settlement of claims

Claims for personal injury involving persons under 18 cannot be settled in a way that binds the pupil unless the court has formally approved the settlement, having seen an affidavit which sets out the facts and exhibits a medical report.

Personal injury claims are sometimes settled on the basis of a parents' indemnity. This means that, if the pupil were to sue the school in the future, the parents would be legally bound to indemnify the school or its insurers. The parents' indemnity mechanism would normally be confined to a relatively small claims in which the child is not thought to have suffered any long term damage. The child is not bound by the settlement and the case could resurface in the future.

## 15.3.8   Records

By the time a bullying case reaches litigation, it is likely that a number of witnesses (teachers, matrons, pupils and perhaps the head) will have left the school. If the school is to answer a claim effectively, it must have records which explain the school's anti-bullying policy, the measures taken to promote it, the procedures for identifying, investigating and dealing with bullying incidents and the training given to staff. Frequently, a school's anti-bullying policy is underpinned by regular bulletins to parents which form part of the records.

## 15.4   DISCIPLINE AND SANCTIONS

## 15.4.1   Background

Good order and discipline are as much a matter of culture as of regime and they are the responsibility of the head. Surveys commissioned by the Independent Schools Information Service since 1990 have consistently shown discipline to be one of the top-rated attractions of independent schools over the State-funded sector.

Formal corporal punishment (as distinct from rough handling and physical abuse) was still in regular use in independent schools throughout the 1960s but gradually diminished during the years leading up to the Education (No 2) Act 1986. Section 47 of that Act had the practical (if not legal) effect of removing corporal punishment as an option at State-funded schools and also for pupils with assisted places or otherwise paid for out of public funds at independent schools. Thereafter, with some notable exceptions, corporate punishment has largely disappeared, and Parliament voted for its final abolition in March 1998. Abolition remains controversial, but more so in society at large than in schools themselves.

The remainder of this chapter is concerned with the legal rights of teachers, parents and pupils in relation to school discipline and sanctions.

## 15.4.2   Teacher's authority

Matters have moved on since *Cleary v Booth* [1893] 1 QB 465 in which it was held that the teacher's disciplinary authority derived only from the *in loco parentis* principle. The modern position is that the authority of a teacher at an independent school to discipline the children in his (or her) care arises out of a number of overlapping principles and authorities conferred by:

- statute law;
- the common law;
- the *in loco parentis* rule;
- the office of teacher;
- the teacher's contract of employment;
- the policies of the governors.

### 15.4.3 Statutory provisions

A number of statutory provisions have a bearing on school discipline and sanctions. In addition, reference is made below to:

– European Convention on Human Rights 1950 (ECHR);
– United Nations Convention on Human Rights 1950 (UNCHR); and
– United Nations Convention on the Rights of the Child 1989 (UNCRC).

The three Conventions have not been ratified by the UK Parliament but respect is paid to their provisions and to the decisions of the European Court of Human Rights. Parts of the Conventions are comprised in the Human Rights Act 1998, which has now received Royal Assent although its provisions have not yet been brought into force.

### (a) Children Act 1989

Section 2(9) provides:

> 'A person who has parental responsibility for a child may not surrender or transfer any part of that responsibility to another but may arrange for some or all of it to be met by one or more persons acting on his behalf.'

Section 3(1) provides:

> 'In this Act "parental responsibility" means all the rights, duties, powers, responsibilities and authority which by law a parent of a child has in relation to the child and his property.'

Section 3(5) provides:

> 'A person who ... does not have parental responsibility ... but has care of the child, may (subject to the provisions of this Act) do what is reasonable in all the circumstances of the case for the purpose of safeguarding or promoting the child's welfare.'

Section 87(1) provides:

> 'It shall be the duty of: (a) the proprietor of any independent school which provides accommodation for any child; and (b) a person who is not the proprietor of such a school but who is responsible for conducting it, to safeguard and promote the child's welfare.'

### (b) Education Act 1996

Section 9 provides:

> 'Children are to be educated in accordance with the wishes of their parents so far as that is compatible with the provision of efficient instruction and training and the avoidance of unreasonable public expenditure.'

It was held in *Campbell and Cosans v United Kingdom* [1982] 4 EHRR 293, a case concerning corporal punishment, that education includes discipline.

### (c) Human Rights Conventions

The main provisions of the Conventions are due to be introduced into UK law under the Human Rights Act 1998.

Article 8 of the First Protocol to ECHR states that public authorities should not interfere with the individual's private and family life.

Article 2 of the First Protocol to UNCHR, in the context of the right to education, calls upon States to uphold the religious and philosophical convictions of parents.

In *Campbell and Cosans* (above), Scottish parents had kept their children away from a school that used corporal punishment because of their religious or philosophical opposition to that form of punishment. Their views were upheld under Article 2.

Article 28 of UNCRC provides that:

> 'Parties shall take all appropriate measures to ensure that school discipline is administered in a manner consistent with the child's human dignity and in conformity with the present Convention.'

### 15.4.4   Corporal punishment

Although corporal punishment has now been finally abolished in all schools in the UK, the statutory and regulatory provisions of the UK Parliament and also the Convention principles and case-law continue to have relevance to all sanctions and also to rough handling and physical abuse. The main provisions are as follows.

### (a)   Education (No 2) Act 1986

Section 47(1) provided in relation to corporal punishment:

> '... giving the punishment cannot be justified on the ground that it was done in pursuance of a right exerciseable by the member of staff by virtue of his position as such.'

It is to be noted that this section did not apply to independent schools other than for pupils with assisted places or paid for out of public funds.

Section 47(4) provided:

> 'A person does not commit an offence by reason of any conduct relating to a pupil which would, apart from this section, be justified on the ground that it is done in pursuance of a right exerciseable by a member of the staff by virtue of his position as such.'

### (b)   Education Act 1993

Section 293(2) amended the 1986 Act by adding s 47(1)(a):

> 'Where, in any proceedings, it is shown that corporal punishment has been given to a pupil by or on the authority of a member of staff, giving the punishment cannot be justified if the punishment was inhuman or degrading.'

In addition, a new s 47(1)(b) was added to the 1986 Act to the effect that in determining whether or not such punishment is inhuman or degrading:

> 'Regard shall be had to all the circumstances of the case, including the reason for giving it, its nature, the manner and circumstances in which it is given, the persons involved and its mental and physical effects.'

This section echoed Article 3 of the First Protocol to ECHR.

Regulations in 1987 (amended in 1989) prohibited the use of corporal punishment in respect of holders of assisted places and those whose education was publicly funded.

Further regulations in 1989 prescribed certain categories of pupils at independent schools on whom corporal punishment may not be administered.

### (c)　DES Circular 7/87

This Circular, being guidance rather than law, defined corporal punishment as:

> '... an intentional application of force as punishment: this includes not only the use of the cane or the tawse, but also other forms of physical chastisement such as slapping, throwing missiles such as chalk, and rough handling.'

### (d)　Education Act 1996

Section 548 replaced s 47 of the 1986 Act and s 292(3) of the 1993 Act in broadly similar terms.

Section 549(1) defined 'corporal punishment' as:

> '... doing anything for the purpose of punishing the pupil concerned (whether or not there are also other reasons for doing it) which, apart from any justification, would constitute battery.'

Section 549(2) provided:

> 'A person is not to be taken for the purpose of s 548 as giving corporal punishment by virtue of anything done for reasons that include averting an immediate danger of personal injury to or an immediate danger to the property of, any person (including the pupil concerned).'

Section 550 provides (in the case of a State-funded school) to the effect that it would be unlawful to refuse admission or to suspend or exclude a pupil because the pupil or parents do not consent to corporal punishment, but this provision was altered in the Education Act 1997 which is discussed at **15.4.6** below.

### (e)　Case-law

In *Costello-Roberts v United Kingdom* [1994] ELR 1, a head had administered three strikes on the bottom of a 7-year-old through his shorts with a rubber-soled gym shoe. The European Court of Human Rights reviewed the authorities and concluded that whether or not there was a breach of Article 3 of ECHR 1950 depended on such factors as the nature and extent of the punishment, the manner and method of its execution, its duration, its physical and mental effects, and in some instances, the sex, age and state of health of the victim. The court held on a majority of five to four that the punishment had not been sufficiently severe to constitute a breach of Article 3. Moreover, the treatment did not entail the kinds of adverse effect on physical or moral integrity as would bring it within the scope of Article 8 (the right to a private life). The court indicated that in some cases Article 8 might afford greater protection than Article 3. The court also decided unanimously that the applicant had an adequate route to a remedy under domestic law (as required by Article 13). Finally, in this case the court observed that:

> 'The sending of a child to school necessarily involves some degree of interference with his or her private life.'

## 15.4.5 Rough handling and physical abuse

In *R v Hopley* [1860] F & F 202, Cockburn CJ said that all punishment given to pupils must be 'reasonable', not 'for the gratification of passion or rage' or overly protracted or too severe.

In *Mansell v Griffin* [1908] 1 KB 947, Phillimore J said:

'It is enough for a teacher to be able to say, "The punishment which I administered was moderate, it was not dictated by bad motives, it was such as is usual in the school, and such as the parent of the child would expect that the child would receive if it did wrong".'

In *Scorgie v Lawrie* (1883) 10 RCSR 610, it was held that if punishment is reasonable, the teacher is not liable for accidental injury to the pupil.

These cases remain good authority for the rule that every punishment must be a moderate and reasonable response to the relevant behaviour. Teachers who lose control and make any form of physical attack on pupils are likely to be disciplined and may very well face dismissal on grounds of misconduct. A school dismissing an employee in these circumstances is bound to make a misconduct report to DfEE under reg 7 of the Education (Particulars of Independent Schools) Regulations 1997.

Rough handling is a form of physical abuse and includes pulling, pushing, shaking, hair-pulling, punching, kicking, prodding and actions of that nature, whether or not the intention is punishment. Throwing chalk and other missiles comes into the same category. Other than in the most exceptional circumstances, these measures are not a legitimate form of physical contact with pupils whether in State-funded or independent schools. They can give rise to a criminal charge of assault and a civil action in battery. (But see also the draft guidance from DfEE on s 550A of the Education Act 1996, discussed at **15.4.6** below.)

DES Circular 7/87, which is guidance rather than law, added this category of physical contact to the definition of 'corporal punishment'.

There is anecdotal evidence of a serious deterioration in school discipline in many parts of the State-funded sector since Education (No 2) Act 1986 removed the defence of 'lawful chastisement', which, in practice, had the effect of ending the use of corporal punishment in State-funded schools.

## 15.4.6 Lawful restraint

Teachers have always been entitled to use physical coercion to avert an immediate danger of personal injury or damage to property, but were, throughout the 1980s, warned repeatedly that physical coercion for any other reason which resulted in a complaint would lead to an investigation and might result in disciplinary proceedings, dismissal, prosecution for assault and a civil action in damages. Teachers in the independent sector also became concerned about these risks and sought guidance on the meaning and limits of 'lawful restraint'.

A classic hypothetical question was put. Suppose a 14-year-old pupil in class stands by the window and repeatedly disobeys an instruction to return to his place. He is disrupting the class and undermining the authority of the teacher but he is not yet causing a danger to himself or others. Is the teacher legally entitled to take him firmly by the arm and lead him back to his place? Perhaps there would be no consequences if the pupil co-operated, but if he resisted, at what point must the teacher disengage? Moreover, if the pupil sustained a small bruise on his arm, whether or not it turns out to have been caused by the teacher, would there be a prima facie case of an assault occasioning actual bodily harm, witnessed by a class of pupils?

Section 4 of the Education Act 1997 (which does not apply directly to independent schools but which provides guidance that those schools can follow) inserts a new s 550A in the Education Act 1996 (mentioned above) which provides:

> 'A member of the staff of a school may use, in relation to any pupil at the school, such force as is reasonably necessary in the circumstances for the purpose of preventing the pupil from doing (or continuing to do) any of the following, namely –
>
> (a) committing any offence,
> (b) causing personal injury to, or damage to the property of, any person (including the pupil himself), or
> (c) *engaging in any behaviour prejudicial to the maintenance of good order and discipline at the school or among any of its pupils, whether that behaviour occurs during a teaching session or otherwise*' (emphasis added).

Section 550A came into force on 1 September 1998 at the same time as the provisions of the Act relating to behaviour and discipline took effect. Draft guidance was issued by DfEE in February 1998 which discussed the meaning of 'reasonable force', the circumstances in which physical intervention might be necessary or appropriate, and the kind of factors staff should bear in mind when deciding whether to intervene. The guidance also stressed the importance of schools having a clear policy about the use of force, logging incidents and making sure that parents were informed both about the school policy, and any incident involving their child. Neither s 550A nor the draft guidance, authorised the use of any form of corporal punishment. The guidance offered no advice about specific techniques of restraint.

Situations identified in the guidance in which physical intervention might be appropriate or necessary include, but are not limited to:

– pupils who are fighting;

– a pupil who is engaged in, or is on the verge of, committing deliberate damage or vandalism to property;

– a pupil who is causing, or at risk of causing, injury or damage by accident, by rough play, or by misuse of dangerous materials or objects;

– a pupil who is running in a corridor or on a stairway in a way in which he (or she) might have or cause an accident likely to injure himself or others;

– a pupil who persistently refuses to obey an order to leave a classroom;

– a pupil who is behaving in a way that is seriously disrupting a lesson;

– a pupil who absconds from a class or tries to leave school (but note that this will only apply if a pupil could be at risk if not kept in the classroom or at school).

The guidance runs to five pages and provides examples of 'reasonable force' which include 'touching, holding, pushing, pulling, leading a pupil by the arm, or shepherding a pupil away by placing a hand in the centre of the back.'

A teacher should not, 'except in the most exceptional circumstances where there is no alternative':

–   hold a pupil around the neck, or by the collar, or in any other way that might restrict the pupil's ability to breath;
–   slap, punch or kick a pupil;
–   twist or force limbs against a joint;
–   trip up a pupil;
–   hold or pull a pupil by the hair.

Teachers are reminded also that they should always avoid touching or holding a pupil in a way that might be considered indecent.

Finally, the guidance emphasises the need to use other strategies before using force and to adopt a calm and measured approach to a situation. There should be a detailed, contemporaneous, written report of any occasion where force is used, and the school should keep an up-to-date record, preferably in an 'incident book' of all incidents in which force is used by a member of staff to control or restrain a pupil. Immediately after such an incident there should be an oral report to the head or a senior member of staff and a written report should be provided as soon as possible afterwards.

### 15.4.7   Investigations

Because an independent school is a private self-regulating community, all but the most serious criminal offences are likely to be dealt with internally as breaches of school discipline. The outcome may be serious, for example expulsion or a requirement to leave, and it follows that there must be a proper investigation.

In *Secretary of State for Education and Science v Tameside Metropolitan Borough Council* [1977] AC 1014, HL, Lord Diplock said, in the context of carrying out an investigation: 'The obligation of the decision-maker is to ask the right question and to take reasonable steps to acquaint himself with the relevant information to enable him to answer that question correctly'.

In *R v London Borough of Camden and The Governors of Hampstead School ex parte H* [1996] ELR 360, CA, Kennedy LJ said, in the context of an educational appeal: 'Having decided what factual issue or issues they had to resolve and what enquiries they could reasonably make in order to resolve them, the governors and the LEA had to make sure that the enquiries proposed were reasonably thorough'.

In *R v Roman Catholic Schools ex parte S* [1998] ELR 304, a pupil had been seriously assaulted. The identity of one of the assailants was in dispute. Moses J held that the appeal committee had failed to probe fully into the circumstances of the child's identification and quashed the exclusion decision. Moses J confirmed that in cases of this nature there could be no objection in principle to reliance on hearsay evidence but he also identified three principles of importance:

(1) 'Those conducting an inquiry must decide what critical issues of fact they should resolve and what inquiries could reasonably be made to resolve those issues.'

(2) 'They must give careful and even-handed consideration to all the available evidence in relation to those issues.'

(3) 'Those conducting an inquiry do not need, on every occasion, to carry out searching inquiries involving the calling of bodies of oral evidence.'

The judge, however, said that when a question of identification arose, it would normally be necessary to hear oral evidence from the identifying witness.

Traditionally, the procedures of natural justice were not thought to apply to private communities in which the parties expressly or by implication contracted out of such procedures. However, in *R v Fernhill Manor School ex parte A* [1993] 1 FLR 620, Brooke J stated to the effect that those responsible for governing independent schools should have procedural rules designed to ensure that parents receive fair treatment in accordance with the principles of natural justice in the case of an expulsion. Since then, if not before, it is to be taken as an implied term of the contract for educational services that the procedures of natural justice will apply at an independent school.

In *DPP v G (Duty to Investigate)* (1997) *The Times*, 24 November, QBD, Gage J was satisfied that the headteacher of a State-funded school was not a person charged with investigating offences and incidents for the purposes of the Police and Criminal Evidence Act 1984. However, Brooke LJ was more cautious and said that 'each case would depend on its particular facts' as to whether the headteacher is charged with investigating an offence.

That case was decided in the context of a State-funded school. It is not part of the normal custom and practice at independent schools to operate the procedures which might be encountered in a police station, such as administering a caution or tape-recording interviews.

However, care should be taken to keep accurate records of each stage of an investigation noting the date and time, who was present and what was said and done. Regard must be had to the age and vulnerability of the pupil who is under investigation. It is good practice and in some cases necessary to inform parents and to ensure that a member of staff of the appropriate gender accompanies and helps the pupil.

The police should be involved as early as possible if the matter has serious criminal implications. Parents should be informed in such cases and all evidence must be preserved.

### 15.4.8 Suspension and expulsion

Suspension (also referred to as 'exclusion' in the State-funded sector) may arise in two distinct circumstances:

(1) a fixed-term sanction in its own right, recorded on the pupil's permanent disciplinary record; or

(2)  as a means of removing the pupil from school, pending investigation of a rumour or complaint concerning the pupil. This is a neutral rather than a disciplinary measure and should not be recorded on the pupil's permanent disciplinary record, although it may at the conclusion of the investigation lead to a sanction which is so recorded.

It is not appropriate to offer a governors' review of a decision to suspend a pupil for either reason. A parent's request for a review in those circumstances is normally refused.

Suspension, the requirement to leave and expulsion are substantial topics in their own right and are considered in Chapter 16.

### 15.4.9   Detention

There are two distinct kinds of detention. One is a punishment in its own right. The other is the process of segregating a pupil, pending investigation of a rumour or complaint.

### *(a)   Punishment*

The behaviour and discipline policy of an independent school will normally allow for rules that authorise detention for the purpose of a task such as writing an essay or doing chores. Another form of detention common in boarding schools is 'gating'. It is good practice to ensure that every detention is properly recorded. For practical reasons, the detention should be carried out as soon as possible, but allowance should be made for a pupil who has a pending examination or some other significant commitment. Parents of a day-pupil should be informed if the detention is to take place at the end of a school day and may cause inconvenience or anxiety over travel arrangements.

Detention is a lawful form of punishment of pupils if used reasonably and in moderation. The principle in *R v Hopley* [1816] F & F 202 (mentioned above) remains a sound guide to teachers. The duration and other circumstances of detention will vary according to the age of the pupil.

In *Terrington v Lancashire County Council* (unreported, 1986), it was suggested that the detention of a whole class where there is known to be only one culprit may be unlawful.

### *(b)   Segregation*

Segregation is often necessary for the purpose of carrying out a proper investigation into a rumour or complaint, for example, after a find of drugs or their paraphernalia, airgun pellets or ammunition, pornography (printed or electronic), examination cribs or some other illegal or possibly stolen property. The pupil who is segregated should not be locked in and should be made as comfortable as possible and visited regularly by a 'neutral' teacher of the appropriate gender. Care should be taken to ensure that the pupil has access to the telephone and adequate food and drink and that he (or she) does not become unnecessarily distressed and is not placed in fear.

In at least one case, legal aid has been granted to a pupil who alleged that he had been falsely imprisoned by virtue of being segregated for the purposes of an investigation. In the absence of misconduct on the part of the school, such a claim is very unlikely to succeed but if the segregation is to continue for more than an hour it is good practice to inform the parents of the circumstances in the case of a pupil under the age of 16.

## 15.4.10   Search

Section 3(5) of the Children Act 1989 states:

> 'A person who ... does not have parental responsibility ... but has care of the child, may ... do what is reasonable in all the circumstances of a case for the purpose of safeguarding or promoting the child's welfare.'

This section, together with rules and procedures made under the school's behaviour and discipline policy, will normally provide sufficient authority for a school to carry out a search of a pupil's space and belongings where there is reasonable cause to do so.

Reasonable cause would include a rumour or complaint that the pupil is in possession of articles or substances contrary to school discipline, of a kind identified in the previous section. It is not part of a school's role to become a miniature police State, but the law must be upheld and, for example, it would be an offence on the part of the school under s 8 of the Misuse of Drugs Act 1971 knowingly to permit the illegal use of controlled drugs on school premises. A number of pretexts for searches are used, such as a fire drill. It is then lawful to carry out a reasonable search of a pupil's property and space, provided there are reasonable grounds for suspicion.

It is also lawful in these circumstances to require a pupil to turn out the contents of pockets or a bag. Clothing should not be searched until it has been removed from the wearer and care should be taken to ensure the pupil's privacy and dignity so far as possible, girls being supervised by a woman. There should be no element of intimate search or of physical compulsion in removing clothing. If necessary, the police should be called.

Members of staff may need to be on their guard against allegations by pupils, parents and their lawyers that an item has been 'planted', or an allegation that a teacher has stolen an item or used drugs that have been seized. As a protection, every searching procedure should be witnessed and recorded in writing. Video and audio tape-recording is unlikely to assist with these procedures. The rule is 'keep it simple', but use procedures that are both appropriate and fair, and keep records. Ensure that notes are dated and signed and that they record who was present, what was done and also the time of day.

## 15.4.11   Confiscation of property

Confiscation is not unlawful and, in some cases, is necessary, for example if a pupil has a dangerous object, such as a weapon, or drugs and other substances which may be abused. Certain items, for example a firearm, should be handed to the police. In most cases, a teacher is not entitled to destroy an item that has been confiscated. Nor must he (or she) retain it for their own use; in most cases, the item should be returned to the parents as soon as practicable. There have been cases of pupils in possession of harmless substances intended to resemble drugs. These too should be confiscated.

## 15.4.12   Punishments generally

DFE Circular 8/94 lists a number of punishments and procedures that are acceptable in the State-funded sector, including isolating the pupil (although not locking them in a restricted space), support from senior staff, contacting parents, making the pupil complete work, reducing break or lunch time, detention, withholding privileges, and carrying out tasks.

The Circular also identifies rewards including public commendation, merit marks, letters home, entries in homework or exercise books and displays of pupils' work.

## 15.4.13   Extent of jurisdiction

In *R v Newport (Salop) Justices ex parte Wright* [1929] 2 KB 416, it was held that a teacher's disciplinary authority extends to a pupil's misbehaviour outside school, for example where a pupil was smoking in a public place contrary to school discipline or hitting another pupil on the way to or from school.

The school's behaviour and discipline policy should make it clear that the school's jurisdiction extends to pupils who are outside the care of the school and away from school premises if their conduct is such as to cause serious damage to the reputation of the school, or injury or other loss to members of the school community. In one case, a number of pupils were required to leave following a 'car-walking' incident during the holidays, when they caused serious damage by walking and jumping along the roofs and bonnets of a line of parked cars.

## 15.4.14   Appeals against disciplinary sanctions

A governors' review should be offered to parents following a decision to expel or require removal of the pupil. This is also considered in Chapter 16. As noted earlier, a governors' review should not be offered or permitted following any lesser sanction, such as suspension, gating or detention.

On occasions, however, a sanction will be imposed that is unjust. The 'take your medicine like a man' approach of earlier years is less appropriate nowadays and some independent schools provide in their behaviour and discipline policy that a pupil who is aggrieved by a decision may ask for it to be reviewed by his tutor or another senior member of staff. There is no mandatory requirement for such a system.

## 15.5   DRUGS AND SUBSTANCES

In general, parents expect that, whatever their children may do at weekends, an independent school will be an environment that is free of controlled drugs and the paraphernalia, culture and temptation to use drugs and other harmful substances. This may seem more aspirational than realistic at a time when some children under the age of 12 have tried illegal drugs and nearly half of all 15–16-year-olds and most sixth formers admit to having done so. Smoking, drinking and drug use have become an ordinary part of so-called 'youth culture' and non-injected heroin use is increasing. None the less, the aspiration of being a drug-free environment is one to which independent schools generally hold firm. Until the mid-1990s, pupils caught in possession were usually required to leave or expelled. While the policy remains firm, there has generally been, since 1995, a more flexible response.

### 15.5.1 Education issue

In its 'Drugs Guidelines' paper in 1995, an HMC working group accepted the principle referred to in DFE Circular 4/95 'Drug Proof' that 'drug misuse is an educational issue'. That acceptance carries two implications:

(1) that schools should provide education to pupils and parents about drugs, and training for their staff; and
(2) that involvement in drugs should be met by an educational response.

### 15.5.2 Criminal law

The possession and use of controlled drugs remains a criminal offence but offences are now so common that very few cases of use and social supply are even investigated by the police, let alone prosecuted. The police have placed these offences in the category 'trivial'.

This, whilst it may be pragmatic, none the less has a domino effect on school discipline. The argument may go as follows:

– if the offence is 'trivial' it should be dealt with as such;
– requiring a pupil to leave following possession or a social supply of drugs is a *disproportionate* sanction unless the same sanction would be applied to a trivial assault or theft;
– imposing a disproportionate sanction is a breach of contract and may be a breach of the parent's *legitimate expectation* that the pupil will be able to complete the GCSE or A-level course.

No doubt arguments of these and other kinds will also be advanced under the Human Rights Act 1998.

### 15.5.3 Independent schools

An independent school is entitled to take the tangential view that:

– it is a private, self-regulating community which is free to operate the policies of the governors so long as they are consistent with the general law of the land;
– the governors' policies are bound to respond to the wishes of the vast majority of responsible parents, otherwise the justification for the school's existence disappears;
– the governors are bound to comply with s 8 of the Misuse of Drugs Act 1971 so as to ensure they do not commit an offence by permitting controlled drugs on school premises;
– the governors owe statutory and common law duties to safeguard and promote the welfare of each child;
– involvement in drugs will tend to harm a pupil's integrity, independence, opportunities and respect for the law.

### 15.5.4　Policy on drugs

A modern policy on drugs and substances will typically address the following subjects.

#### (a)　Detection

The greatest deterrent to pupils coming into school under the influence of drugs or bringing drugs into school for sale or consumption is likely to be certainty of detection. On the other hand, it is not part of the school's role to become a mini police State. From the mid-1980s, independent schools have gradually adopted a policy of requiring pupils to provide a sample for urine testing where reasonable grounds for suspicion exist. The hair test is not yet in widespread use.

#### (b)　Educational aspects

The policy will contemplate training about drugs and substances for all members of staff so that they can respond appropriately to pupils seeking individual advice and help, and so that teachers are alert to the warning signs of drug misuse.

Pupils will also receive education about drugs and substances, usually through the school's health education programme and the extra-curricular involvement of outside agencies, and, in addition, by dealing appropriately with questions about drugs in whatever context they might arise. The policy might also contemplate the education of parents.

#### (c)　Advisory aspects

The policy may encourage pupils to discuss their anxieties about drugs or substances in confidence with a member of staff or some other responsible adult. Likewise, parents may be asked to inform the head if they have any reason to think that their child may have been involved with drugs or other substances at home or at school.

If this system is to work, there must be the necessary degree of trust and confidence and an understanding that information given and matters brought into counselling *in circumstances that are genuine* will not result in disciplinary sanctions or adverse record. This can be achieved, for example, by the head who has been approached in this way warning the whole school that every rumour will be investigated, no matter how near to public examinations, that a pupil under suspicion will be asked to give a sample for testing and that a positive sample or a refusal to give a sample is likely to result in the pupil being required to leave.

This approach levels the playing field for the whole school, including the pupil about whom information has been given, and allows for the normal disciplinary sanctions to be applied to pupils who then infringe.

#### (d)　Disciplinary aspects

The disciplinary aspects of a policy on drugs and substances will include investigation, testing and sanctions.

Since the HMC paper, a number of schools have tried using a 'supportive regime' under which a pupil whose guilt has been established agrees to a regime under which he or she may be asked to give a sample for testing without there necessarily being any grounds for suspicion. Samples would be destroyed following a negative test. Tests of this nature do not form part of the pupil's permanent medical record.

The normal sanctions for smoking and use of alcohol in breach of school discipline tend to be less severe nowadays than 20 years ago, but the dangers, particularly with alcohol, are ever-present and were highlighted following the tragic death of a 14-year-old pupil at Millfield in June 1998.

# Chapter 16

## EXPULSION AND REVIEW

### 16.1 INTRODUCTION

This chapter is concerned with expulsions in the traditional and modern sense and also the need for proper investigation, fair procedures, proportionality of sanction and the opportunity for a governors' review.

Expulsion, in the traditional sense, means immediate dismissal in disgrace from an independent school or some other community. Expulsion is capable of stigmatising a person for the rest of his (or her) life. Yet many dismissals that are still characterised as 'expulsions' are for adolescent errors rather than offences motivated by malice or evil. For these reasons and as the education stakes become ever higher and the world becomes more litigation-minded, every expulsion, so-called, is likely to be made the subject of a legal review by parents and their lawyers.

State-funded schools use 'exclusion' instead of 'expulsion'. In the independent sector, 'exclusion' is the normal expression when a pupil is not allowed to return to school while fees are unpaid, and the word therefore has no disciplinary connotation for the pupil.

### 16.2 LEGAL ASPECTS

#### 16.2.1 Overview

As noted earlier, the legal relationship between the school and parents arises out of the contract for educational services. An implied, if not express, term of that contract is that parents warrant the attendance and good behaviour of the pupil and the pupil is the agent of the parents so far as these matters are concerned. The school's legal relationship with the pupil arises out of a duty of care which the school owes in tort to the pupil.

The disciplinary rules that apply to the pupil will be those authorised by the behaviour and discipline (or equivalent) policy published by the governors of which the rules and sanctions will be a part.

Nowadays, top grades are needed at GCSE and A-level in order to compete for the best employment or further education opportunities. Public examinations are becoming modular and work involving projects increases the importance of continuity of education. Parents may, under the Human Rights Act 1998, have a legitimate expectation that, in consideration of the fees they are paying to independent schools, the pupil will not be required to leave early other than in accordance with contract or for grave cause which is adequately substantiated.

## 16.2.2 Contract

*Fitzgerald v Nothcote* (1865) 4 F & F 656 established the rule that the school would no longer be bound by its implied contract with the parents to provide an education for the child if the child misbehaved in such a way as to justify his (or her) expulsion.

The factors that may justify expulsion will vary with the mores of the time. The former public school environment commonly tolerated violent bullying, excessive corporal punishment and many other kinds of harshness. The psychological and developmental needs of children and adolescents were little understood at that time. But the old public school system would not tolerate conduct which dishonoured the school, homosexual activity, theft, smoking, drinking, breaking bounds and running away. In general, drugs and pornography were not an issue in earlier times.

Nowadays, the mores are different. Expulsion, or a requirement to leave, is likely to be imposed for bullying and violence, sexual misconduct, bringing drugs into school and vandalising school property.

In *Price v Wilkins* (1888) 58 LT 680, it was held that an unjustifiable expulsion of a child from school could constitute a breach of the contract between the school and the parents.

It is also to be taken as an implied term of the contract that sanctions will be proportionate to the breach of school discipline and that, where expulsion is a disproportionate sanction, it may be remedied by an injunction ordering temporary reinstatement of the pupil pending a full hearing of the merits.

The decision to expel or require removal of a pupil on less than a term's notice will be a breach of the school's contract with the parents unless the decision was:

– taken in good faith for a breach of discipline or offence that was sufficiently serious according to the authorised and published policies, principles and rules, or under the criminal law; and

– on the basis of guilt that has been reasonably well established by means of procedures that ensured fair treatment of the pupil and parents, including a review of the head's decision if required, and reasons given or clearly understood. It is submitted that 'reasonably well established' means the same as 'proved on the balance of probabilities', ie with 51% or greater certainty.

A *prima facie* wrongful expulsion without a satisfactory governors' review will entitle parents to issue proceedings for breach of contract and to seek a mandatory injunction ordering temporary reinstatement of the pupil pending a full hearing and other remedies. At present, judicial review is only available against an independent school if the case involves an element of public funding (see the *Fernhill Manor School* and *Cobham Hall School* cases, discussed at **16.2.4** below), but even then, contractual remedies are likely to be quicker than judicial review and the contractual remedy is not restricted to reviewing procedures. The merits of the case can also receive fuller consideration.

Schools are well advised to check that their legal expenses and/or professional indemnity insurances cover the legal costs of defending judicial review proceedings. There is evidence of insurers having sought to deny cover.

It has been suggested that the expulsion of a pupil frustrates the contract and thus brings about a termination of the contract by operation of law with the financial consequences described at Chapter 5. The reasoning behind this argument is that expulsion makes it impossible to perform the contract since the pupil is no longer at school. The fault is that of the pupil and not of the contracting parties, namely the school or the parents. This argument will probably be overcome if the school's standard terms and conditions expressly provide for expulsion or required removal of the pupil in a case of a serious breach of school discipline. It is probably also an implied if not express term of the contract that the parents warrant the attendance and good behaviour of the pupil and that the pupil is the agent of the parents.

### 16.2.3 Tort

In *Hunt v Damon* (1930) 46 TLR 575, it was held that an unjustified expulsion was not an actionable tort on which the pupil could sue. The action had to be brought by the parents in contract.

However, following *X (Minors) v Bedfordshire County Council* [1995] 2 WLR 152, HL, in which Lord Browne-Wilkinson stated, '... a school which accepts a pupil assumes responsibility not only for his physical well-being but also for his educational needs ...', it seems far more likely that a pupil would in fact be able to bring an action in tort (in addition to the parents' action in contract) for a wrongful expulsion if:

–   the pupil could show that he (or she) had thereby suffered physical or psychological injury or damage to his education by reason of the wrongful expulsion; or
–   (if the pupil had suffered economic loss alone) could show there was a special relationship between himself and the school within the parameters of *Hedley Byrne* (discussed in Chapter 12).

The discussion about whether, following an alleged wrongful expulsion, a pupil would have a right to seek damages and an injunction in tort is more than academic. At present, and until abolished, a pupil is entitled to legal aid in his own right irrespective of the financial circumstances of his parents. A party with legal aid against whom a 'loser's costs order' is made is unlikely in practice to have to pay those costs, since the order must be expressed in terms to the effect that it shall not be enforced without leave of the court. Leave would only be granted if the pupil came into a substantial sum of money. Moreover, a party seeking an injunction is normally required to give a cross-undertaking in damages which is unlikely, in practice, to bite against a pupil with legal aid but would bite against parents funding the action privately.

### 16.2.4 Fair procedures

The first element of fair procedures is to hold a sufficient investigation of the circumstances, as to which see **15.4.7** above.

Until 1993, the assumption was that expulsions from an independent school were not subject to judicial review. Because an independent school is a private self-regulating community, a contractual term which gave the head absolute jurisdiction over admissions and expulsions could not be challenged other than as a breach of contract (*Price v Wilkins* above). The rules and procedures of natural justice were not thought to apply to investigations and procedures leading to expulsion from a private community.

In *R v Fernhill Manor School ex parte A* [1993] 1 FLR 620, QBD, a girl was expelled from an independent school for alleged bullying and had not been given an opportunity to state her side of the case. An application for judicial review failed on the grounds that the legal relationship with the parents was regulated by private contract and was not subject to judicial review. However, Brooke J expressed the hope that those responsible for governing independent schools would design procedural rules to ensure that parents received fair treatment in accordance with the principles of natural justice in the case of an expulsion.

From then on, it was widely assumed by lawyers advising independent schools that a requirement for fair procedures in these circumstances was to be treated as an implied term of the contract for educational services.

*R v Cobham Hall School ex parte S* [1998] ELR 389, QBD, was the first case in which the High Court accepted jurisdiction to review a decision of an independent school although there had been a judicial review of a City Technology College (see *R v Governors of Haberdashers' Aske's Hatcham College Trust ex parte T* [1995] ELR 350 (Dyson J)).

In the *Cobham Hall* case, a pupil who held an assisted place was informed that her place would be withdrawn because she was making insufficient progress. This was intended to be a kind way of ensuring that she left the school because her conduct and attitudes were inconsistent with continuing membership of the school community. It was held that, because the case involved an element of public funding, namely an assisted place, the court had jurisdiction to review the decision of the headmistress. In the event, the pupil lost her case for other reasons.

Most independent schools are registered charities. It has been suggested that a charitable school should be justiciable by reason of its being a charity and holding its property and assets on trust for the public good. That proposition has not been tested in the context of an expulsion.

Independent schools are not immune from developments in the law relating to fair procedures emerging from the State-funded sector.

In *R v Board of Governors of the London Oratory School ex parte R* (1988) *The Times*, 17 February, McCullough J said:

> 'It must be right that [a pupil] facing possible expulsion should know the nature of the accusation made against him, that he should have an opportunity to answer, and he should appear before a tribunal that acts in good faith.'

It is, however, possible for defective procedures to be cured at a later appeal.

In *R v Governors of St Gregory's RC Aided High School and Appeals Committee ex parte M* [1995] ELR 290, it was alleged that a pupil at a maintained school had used the 'f-word' in the presence of a teacher. The governors did not allow the pupil to present his side of the story and 'indefinite exclusion' was ordered. The exclusion was later upheld at a properly conducted appeal. On judicial review, Turner J held that the procedures adopted at the appeal cured the defect at the original hearing and that even though the appeal committee did not give full reasons for his decision, 'indefinite exclusion' for this offence was not unreasonable. The court was satisfied that all concerned knew the basis of the decision.

In *R v Stoke Newington School ex parte M* [1994] ELR 131, the panel which decided to exclude a pupil included a teacher who was known to be in dispute with that pupil. At judicial review, the court said that this should not have happened but it was not prepared in the circumstances to quash the decision to exclude.

### 16.2.5 Human rights

The Human Rights Act 1998, when it comes into force, is expected to result in parties to litigation seeking to reopen settled points of law. Only time will tell how successful they may be, but it is expected that arguments about 'legitimate expectation' that a certain state of affairs will continue will erode still further the head's authority to expel pupils or require them to leave other than for grave cause.

### 16.2.6 Proportionality of sanction

As noted earlier, proportionality of sanction has started to feature in the law relating to expulsions. There appear to be no reported cases from the independent sector, but those from the State sector are very likely to carry influence.

On judicial review, the court's function is to review procedures and the rationality and legality of decisions, rather than the merits of the case. There is, however, some evidence of that distinction being eroded in the light of two cases in which the court treated proportionality of sanction as justiciable.

In *R v London Borough of Newham ex parte X* [1995] ELR 303, a boy had been excluded from a State school in his GCSE year for an incident off school premises when he was not in school uniform. The disciplinary procedures laid down had not been followed. The court ordered that the pupil be reinstated and accepted the European Convention concept of *proportionality* implicit in DFE Circular 10/94 'Exclusions from School' in the context of a child who was in his GCSE year.

In *R v Staffordshire County Council ex parte A* (1996) *The Times*, 18 October, three boys deflated a tyre on a teacher's car as an April Fool joke. The only pupil to be excluded was A, who was present during the prank but did not directly take part in it. A had a history of bad behaviour which influenced the decision to exclude him. The pupil argued that exclusion was disproportionate to the offence. Turner J decided, in effect, that the court had power to decide the issue of proportionality, although in this case the appeal was disallowed because there were other relevant factors including the disruption to the everyday life of the school and the effect of misbehaviour on other pupils.

### 16.2.7 Conduct of parents

In the maintained sector, misconduct by parents may justify exclusion of the pupil.

In *R v Neale and Another ex parte S* [1995] ELR 198, the pupil was initially suspended for an indefinite period because of disruptive behaviour. His mother, accompanied by a representative from the African People's Education Group, came to the school and placed the child in a classroom. She left the premises only after being threatened with arrest by the police. The headteacher decided that the parent's action had undermined the authority of the school governors and imposed permanent exclusion. At the subsequent judicial review, Dyson J took the view that a parent's attitude towards a headteacher or school governors, expressed through defiant conduct, could be a relevant consideration in permanent exclusion, as education at school involved a partnership between the pupil, the school and the child's parents.

In the independent sector, it is to be taken as an implied, if not express, term of the contract that serious or persistent misconduct by parents will justify the head in requiring the removal of the pupil.

### 16.2.8 Reinstatement of the pupil

It seems that the court, on judicial review of an exclusion from a State-funded school, will be prepared to consider reinstatement of a pupil if the issues relate to procedural matters or proportionality rather than educational factors.

In *R v The Board of Governors of Stoke Newington School and Others ex parte M* [1994] ELR 131, Potts J said:

> 'The question whether an excluded child should be reinstated is essentially for those who are concerned with the administration of the school and the education of [the] child. Educational factors will have to be taken into account, which are outside the province of this court.'

That dictum is consistent with the decision that was reached in *Cobham Hall School* (see **16.2.4**), in which the court accepted jurisdiction to review a decision of an independent school but dismissed the application for educational reasons.

In *R v London Borough of Camden and the Governors of Hampstead School ex parte H* [1996] ELR 360, the Court of Appeal was prepared to say, in conflict with Circular 10/94, that the headteacher of a maintained school is entitled to take into account the effect that reinstatement of an excluded pupil would have on the school as a whole. The facts were that the pupils, who were alleged bullies, had shot H with an airgun. The headteacher excluded the pupils, but the governors reinstated them. The victim, H, applied to the court, saying that he had a right to intervene and that his interests should be considered. It was held that the governors' decision to reinstate was flawed. There had been insufficient regard to the effect that restoring the bullies to the school would have on the victim and the school as a whole. The governors were required to reconsider.

### 16.2.9 Guidance from the DfEE

DFE Circular 10/94 'Exclusions from School' provides guidance to headteachers and governing bodies in the State-funded sector. Although the Circular has no direct application to independent schools, a court considering an expulsion or required removal from an independent school may be asked to take its terms into account, so far as relevant.

In *R v London Borough of Islington ex parte Rixon* [1997] ELR 66, QBD, Sedley J distinguished between statutory and non-statutory guidance to maintained schools, saying in relation to DfEE Circulars that they 'must be conscientiously taken into account'. That means that they should be considered with care, not necessarily followed, but departed from only when it is reasonable to do so.

Paragraph 21 of the Circular lists ten preliminary factors which 'the head teacher should in all cases first consider' in relation to the behaviour. They are:

−   the age and state of health of the pupil;

−   the pupil's previous record at that school;

−   any particular circumstances unique to the pupil which might sensibly be taken into account in connection with the behaviour, eg strained or traumatic domestic situations;

−   the extent to which parental, peer or other pressure may have contributed to the behaviour;

−   the degree of severity of the behaviour, the frequency of its occurrence and the likelihood of it recurring;

−   whether or not the behaviour impaired or will impair the normal functioning of the pupil or other pupils in the school;

−   whether or not the behaviour occurred on school premises or when the pupil was otherwise in the charge of school staff or when the pupil was on the way to or from school. An important consideration in cases of doubt is the extent to which behaviour away from the school had a serious impact on the life of the school;

−   the degree to which the behaviour was a violation of one or more rules contained in the school's policy on behaviour, and the relative importance of the rule(s);

−   whether the incident was perpetrated by the pupil on his (or her) own or as part of a group (using one pupil as a scapegoat should always be avoided); and

−   whether consideration has been giving to seeking the support of other agencies, such as the Education Welfare Service or Educational Psychology Service.

It will be observed that only three of these preliminary factors are 'school-centred'. That, arguably has the effect of shifting the balance between the individual and the community in favour of the pupil and making it far more difficult for the headteacher to safeguard the community. As noted earlier, the list of preliminary factors does not apply directly to independent schools but it would none the less be wise to take them into account.

## 16.2.10   Exclusion from State-funded schools

The Education Act 1996, ss 154–160 set out the current statutory basis of the head's responsibilities and powers in matters of discipline and exclusion from State schools.

Section 156(2) permits fixed-period exclusions for up to 15 school days in any one term. That can be 30 consecutive days covering the end of one term and the beginning of the next, ignoring the holidays. Section 156(2) also abolished 'indefinite exclusion', but permitted 'permanent exclusion'.

These provisions were amended by the Education Act 1997, ss 6 and 7 of which amended 'fifteen school days in any one term' to 'forty-five school days in any one school year'. This applies both to maintained and grant-maintained schools. Section 7 of the 1997 Act altered the rules about appeals.

There is a formal appeals system in the State-funded sector which has made litigation over permanent exclusions from State schools a significant growth area for education lawyers. Appeals under the statutory system which then go on to judicial review and further appeal can take up to 2 years or more to conclude. The main focus of the cases has been on fair procedures, proportionality of sanction, the conduct of parents and reinstatement of an excluded pupil.

## 16.3    CUSTOM AND PRACTICE

At an independent school, the head's traditional right to expel a pupil with little risk of being called to account was a powerful symbol of the authority vested in the head by the governors. That authority remains intact, as it must if the community is to function efficiently. But the head is far more likely nowadays to be called to account for his (or her) decision and the fairness of the investigation and procedures.

'Expulsion' continues to send a strong signal to parents and pupils but use of that expression can also lead to misunderstandings and unnecessary risks of litigation when applied to adolescent errors for which, in reality, parents are being asked to 'withdraw' the pupil, or the pupil is being 'asked' or 'required' to leave and will be helped to find a fresh start at another good school.

Heads have not always appreciated the importance of the distinction between expulsion (proper) and the requirement to leave. Nor have they always appreciated the reasons why the parents and pupil should be entitled to a governors' review of the decision.

### 16.3.1    Meaning of expulsion

In its traditional sense, expulsion from a public school involved some or all of the following consequences:

- The pupil was banished forthwith from the school community. His (or her) belongings were sent on afterwards. There was unlikely to be a realistic prospect of placement in another good school. There was no right to a governors' review.

- A formal letter of expulsion was written to the parents. Notices stating the fact and reason for expulsion would be posted on the main notice board and the staff room.

- The fact and reason for expulsion would be stated in reply to any enquiry about the pupil at any time in the future.

– The pupil would not be shown as a leaver in the normal way and for all practical purposes, any record of the pupil having been a member of the school was expunged from the roll. The pupil would not in the future be entitled to claim any connection with the school or to return.

– The event was used as an example '*pour encourager les autres*'.

– Fees due and unpaid up to and during the term of expulsion were payable in full together with any extras or disbursements. Fees in lieu of notice were not payable. The deposit would be retained by the school.

Expulsion in this sense was likely to have a very serious effect on the life of the pupil and his (or her) self-esteem, family relationships, and also younger siblings at the school, and his (or her) examination performance, future employment and career. It might also be the event which, happening at a critical moment, was decisive in the pupil 'going off the rails'. There was a contrary view, however, that, in some cases, expulsion had a galvanising effect. The person 'pulled himself together' and sometimes went on to redeem his reputation in war service.

Expulsion with these consequences was commonly used several times a year as a response to matters that would nowadays be considered trivial or even normal breaches of school discipline, for example, smoking, visiting the local pub, minor sexual contact between boys, or boys and girls, at boarding school and breaking bounds or running away.

### 16.3.2   Changing mores

From the 1960s onwards, family and social breakdown and the influence of the media and pop culture were on the increase. It was noticed that children were reaching puberty at an earlier age. There was greater sexual freedom and by the mid-1970s there were drugs in city-centre schools, a matter openly acknowledged by Dr John Rae, the Headmaster of Westminster (1971–86).

Most boarding schools started to make supervised bar facilities available for older pupils on school premises. Smoking, although (with some exceptions) still forbidden, was more likely to be dealt with by sanctions other than expulsion. In most schools, minor theft was no longer a matter for immediate expulsion but repeated theft or premeditated shoplifting remained so.

By the 1990s, the education stakes had become very much higher than before. Pupils needed top grades in public examinations to stand any chance of competing successfully for the best jobs or further education opportunities. At the same time, schools became better able to appreciate the effect of social breakdown, youth culture and media influences. Discipline became regarded more as a matter of pastoral care and assumed a far more constructive ethos. The Children Act 1989 had introduced a duty to safeguard and promote the welfare of the child and in-school counselling of pupils was also introduced. Corporal punishment had been all but discontinued.

Even though some of these changes made the job of heads much more difficult, many came to understand that breaches of school discipline were better treated as 'adolescent errors' and 'education issues' than as expulsion offences. Perhaps the need to protect the fee base had something to do with this, since many schools could not withstand the financial cost of expelling 10 or 15 pupils following a drugs find (although bringing drugs into school was still regarded as an expulsion matter). More important, however, was a greater understanding of the influences at work during the adolescent years.

### 16.3.3    Expulsion

There will still be cases in which expulsion (proper) is the appropriate response to the event that has occurred. Examples will include shooting, stabbing, rape and attempted rape, arson, serious commercial drug dealing and systematic hacking of the school's computers. Even in these cases, however, parents should be offered a governors' review, although it may be unlikely they would wish to take up the offer.

### 16.3.4    Asking the parents to withdraw the pupil

For breaches of school discipline that do not justify expulsion, but, in the opinion of the head, require that the pupil must leave permanently, there should be consultation with the parents and also the pupil who is of sufficient age and maturity.

The purpose of the consultation is to help the parents to understand why the pupil cannot remain, and to discuss the leaving status (discussed at **16.3.6**) that will be accorded to the pupil and the help that will be given in finding a fresh start at another school. There will still be a difficulty if the pupil holds an assisted place, which is not transferable, or if the pupil is engaged on an A-level course that cannot be adequately replaced at another institution, but all of these matters need to be considered and discussed.

If the parents accede to the head's request that they withdraw the pupil, there should not, in these circumstances, be a charge to fees in lieu of notice, although all fees and extras up to and including the present term will normally be payable without remission for the weeks of term unexpired. (State-funded schools are not permitted to ask parents to withdraw a pupil in this way.)

If, following consultation, the head remains satisfied that the pupil must leave, but the parents refuse to withdraw him (or her), the head is entitled to suspend or continue the pupil's suspension from school and inform the parents that consideration will now be given to formally requiring the pupil's removal, and the head will notify his (or her) decision to the parents within, say, three days. This ensures that the head will have a sufficient opportunity to check the facts, consult with the chairman of governors and colleagues and take legal advice, if necessary, so that the case has received every proper consideration.

### 16.3.5    Required removal

The head should explain to parents that if he (or she) comes to the conclusion that the pupil must be removed, the parents will be entitled to a governors' review, but, depending on the findings of the governors, if the decision is upheld, the pupil may be accorded a different leaving status (discussed below). The head is less likely to be able to offer the same level of help in finding a fresh start and there may be different financial consequences for the parents in that the deposit will not be returnable.

When requiring removal, the head should state the facts he has found, the reasons for his decision, the pupil's leaving status and the financial position. An application form for a governors' review together with a copy of the review procedures should be sent at the same time.

### 16.3.6 Leaving status

The head's decision to ask parents to withdraw or to require the removal of a pupil will often come as a shock and a grave blow to the parents and perhaps the pupil too. In modern times, this is not an occasion for flexing muscles. It is an unhappy event to be worked out with kindness and understanding on both sides. When the parents understand and accept that the pupil will be leaving, their main concern is likely to be the future effect. Experience shows that if matters of leaving status can be resolved, the parents are far more likely to accept the head's decision. Some points of leaving status and associated arrangements are considered below.

#### (a) Future prejudice

Will the pupil be able to continue his (or her) course somewhere else? What will happen in the case of a pupil who is studying three or four A-levels in minority subjects that are not offered at any nearby college accessible to the pupil? What help can the school offer a pupil who is due to sit GCSEs or A-levels this year or this term?

#### (b) Announcements

What (if any) announcement will be made of the fact and/or reasons for the pupil leaving at this stage? How, where and in what terms will the announcement be made? If the circumstances have attracted publicity in the press, or may do so, what (if any) statement will be made to the press?

#### (c) The pupil's file

What record will be entered in the pupil's file as to the reason for his (or her) leaving? For how long will the files containing that record be retained?

#### (d) References

How will the school respond to enquiries for a reference about the pupil? A reference may be requested in a standard form, but how will an open reference be given? It is known that some schools and other educational establishments, notably certain 'crammers', will not accept pupils who have been required to leave their previous school because of involvement with drugs. On the other hand, whenever a reference is supplied, there is a requirement of law that the giver of the reference exercises reasonable care and skill. Failure to do so may attract damages (see *Spring v Guardian Assurance plc* [1995] 2 AC 296, HL).

#### (e) Fresh start

What assistance are the head and staff able or willing to give the family in finding a fresh start for the pupil at another school?

## (f)  Course and project work

What steps will be taken immediately to identify and collect up all the pupil's work to be returned to the parents or transferred to another school? What (if any) help can and will be given with continuity? Which members of staff should be consulted?

## (g)  Financial aspects

What sums will be payable by the parents to the school or credited by the school to the parents' account if a deposit is held? What can be done with the pupil's uniform?

## (h)  As a leaver

Will the pupil's name be shown as a pupil in the ordinary way in the school magazine? Will he (or she) be shown as a leaver in mid-year or simply at the end of the year? Will the pupil be permitted to attend the leavers' ball or similar event? May the pupil play for alumni teams? Under what circumstances may the pupil attend school premises in the future? From what date? Will the pupil be eligible to join the school's association? From what date?

## 16.4  GOVERNORS' REVIEW

A head who investigates a complaint or rumour is likely to find himself (or herself) in the position of investigator, prosecutor, jury as to the facts and judge as to the sentence, as well as being expected to balance the interests of the school community as a whole with those of the pupil and his (or her) parents. That is the nature of headship in a private self-regulating community, but it is none the less a difficult cocktail of duties to discharge in accordance with natural justice.

In a large school, the head may very well delegate the investigation, but, even so, an aggrieved parent is likely to suggest that there have been procedural irregularities of a kind that render the expulsion unfair and wrongful. It is therefore to be treated as an implied, if not express, term of the contract that parents will be offered a governors' review of the head's decision to expel.

### 16.4.1  Head's authority

There is a tendency among heads to consider that a review procedure will undermine their authority, both because their decision will be questioned and because the governors might substitute a different decision.

Parents may feel genuinely aggrieved, because they do not know all the facts, they have not been involved in the investigation and they do not believe their offspring to be capable of what has been alleged. Perhaps they have heard a different version from the pupil, or believe that the investigation was oppressive and that the pupil made untruthful statements or admissions out of fear. The parents may be aware of other cases that were treated differently and may feel that the sanction in this instance is disproportionate and they would like to discuss the possibility of reinstatement. Perhaps they only want to clarify the pupil's leaving status.

All of these concerns should be discussed with the head in the first place, but if agreement cannot be reached, it is reasonable and in accord with the principles of natural justice that there should be a review or appeal mechanism. Parents who are refused a governors' review will be entitled to apply to the court in any event.

A further reason for offering a governors' review is that parents would be very unlikely to succeed in an application for a mandatory injunction requiring temporary reinstatement of the pupil if the judge is informed that a review procedure has been offered but not taken up. Moreover, recent experience has been that once parents have been offered a governors' review and have considered the way in which they would put their case, they will normally decide in favour of dealing informally with the head and not going through with a full review.

### 16.4.2 Appeals – rehearing and review

There are, broadly, two quite distinct types of appeal mechanism:

(1) *appeal by way of rehearing* which is concerned with the merits of the case, is adversarial in nature, wide in scope, often with legal representatives for both sides, where evidence is formally presented and cross-examined and a decision is given; and

(2) *appeal by way of review*, which is concerned with the fairness of the investigation and sanction, and is informal in nature, limited in scope and more likely than not to lead to an agreed solution.

At an independent school, a review is usually preferable to a rehearing.

### 16.4.3 Formalities

A request form and a copy of the review procedure should, if possible, be handed or sent to the parents at the time when the decision to expel or require removal is communicated. The request form initiates the appeal by way of review and the parents should be asked to state the matters that they would like reviewed. Perhaps there is no dispute over the facts or the procedures used but the parents want to discuss the sanction. In this way, the clerk to the governors will know what papers to prepare.

The document containing the procedure should describe the format of the meeting, who is entitled to be present, the way in which the meeting will be conducted and the matters that will be taken into account. Where practicable, the review should be held within 7 days of request and sooner if possible. The pupil will be under suspension during that period.

### 16.4.4 Procedures

In *R v Governors of St Gregory's RC Aided High School* (referred to above), Turner J held that procedures adopted at the appeal cured defects in the procedures at the original hearing. The same is capable of applying at an appeal by way of review.

The normal procedural features of a review are as follows.

## (a)   Composition of review panel

The review panel may reasonably comprise three governors who have not, to date, been involved in the case. The panel should not include the chairman of governors who will have been kept informed by the head. In the case of a girl pupil, there should be at least one female panel member. The chairman of the panel should be appointed before the meeting and should liaise with the clerk as to the contents of the bundle of documents (see *(d)* below). The panel should be convened by the clerk to the governors who will be in attendance to take notes and advise as to procedure.

## (b)   Purpose of review

Unlike a rehearing, the purpose of a review is to look again at the procedures that have been used, the rationality of the decision and the proportionality of the sanction. This is analogous to the role of the judge conducting a judicial review. It is not for the panel to substitute its own view of the case in place of the head's view unless matters have gone very far wrong. At the end of the meeting (whether at the meeting itself or the following day) the panel's decision should normally be either:

–   to uphold the head's decision; or

–   to refer the matter back to the head for further consideration of matters that have been canvassed during the review.

The panel may wish to give its own opinion of the way certain issues should be viewed. However, it is not the role of the panel to overrule the head, and thereby undermine his (or her) authority unless it is necessary to do so in order to avoid injustice.

## (c)   Those present

The following should normally be present throughout the review meeting:

–   the panel members and the clerk to the governors;

–   the head and any other senior member of the staff who has been involved in the investigation;

–   the parents, who should not be legally represented. Parents should be permitted to be accompanied by a friend, and perhaps the friend will be a lawyer, but he (or she) should not be someone whom the parents have instructed, or intend to instruct, in legal proceedings;

–   the pupil, if of sufficient age and understanding, together with (if required) a teacher chosen by the pupil who is willing to speak on his (or her) behalf. A teacher should be reassured that his (or her) position as an employee will not be compromised by speaking up for the pupil or questioning the evidence.

If factual issues are in dispute, witnesses who may be required to give a first-hand account of the events should be asked to wait in an adjoining room. Other pupils should not normally be asked to take part in the review meeting and certainly not without prior consultation and the consent of their parents.

## (d)  Documents

Before the appeal hearing, the clerk should prepare a bundle of documents, consisting of written statements that have been given, relevant correspondence and a summary of the pupil's disciplinary record and school log. If practicable, a copy of the bundle should be provided to each member of the review panel, the head and the parents prior to the meeting. Additional documents may be indicated by the circumstances of the case but, in general, documents should be kept to a minimum. There may be good reason not to identify pupils who have given statements. That is a matter for the discretion of the chairman.

## (e)  Style of meeting

Everyone is likely to be anxious. Cabinet rather than court-style seating and an informal atmosphere are preferable. The meeting room should be neither too imposing nor too confined. Paper and pens should be provided at each place. The ethos should be that of seeking a solution so that there is no sense of there being a winner or a loser.

## (f)  Legal status of meeting

The chairman should indicate the intended legal status of the meeting as 'open', in the sense that its proceedings may be referred to in the event of there being subsequent legal proceedings, but in other respects the meeting is 'confidential', as between those present and so, for example, its proceedings must not be discussed with the press.

## (g)  Conduct of the meeting

The meeting should be conducted by the panel chairman, who will be advised by the clerk. It may be helpful for the chairman to explain to all present how he (or she) intends to conduct the meeting, and identify the scope of the discussion as it appears from the parents' review form. The sheet of procedures, which the parents have already received, should be explained, and the chairman should explain again that, although this review meeting cannot oust the jurisdiction of the court in the event that it is conducted unfairly or a decision is reached that is irrational, it is the intention of the governors that the outcome of this meeting will be a full and final resolution of the matter. It is a useful check for the chairman to enquire at appropriate moments during the meeting whether the parties are satisfied with the way in which it is being conducted and to note their response.

The clerk should take notes of everything that is said and those speaking should be asked to slow down if necessary. It is probably not appropriate to tape record a review meeting but that is a matter for the chairman's discretion.

## (h)  Burden of proof

The decision to expel, or to require removal, is a civil, not a criminal, matter. The normal burden of proof is the *balance of probabilities*, ie 51% certainty. In other words, the head should have reached his (or her) decision on the basis of guilt that was reasonably well established. The review panel should adopt the same burden of proof in its own deliberations.

### (i)    Outcome of review meeting

The panel may decide that it would like the head to give further consideration to some of the matters discussed at the review. It may be that the head has arrived independently at the same conclusion. There is then every prospect of a solution being reached at the meeting or subsequently, together with confirmation of the pupil's leaving status if he (or she) is not to be reinstated.

### (j)    Decision and subsequent appeal

If the matter has not been resolved by the end of the meeting, it is for the head to consider the observations of the review panel and notify his (or her) decision to the parents and to the chairman as soon as possible thereafter. If the review meeting has been properly conducted and the subsequent decision is neither irrational nor disproportionate, the parents will have no legal justification for beginning a legal action and would run the risk of having to pay the costs of an unsuccessful action. Experience of review procedures in operation is that they are very rarely followed by litigation.

## 16.5    CONCLUSION

A decision to expel or require a pupil to leave an independent school should be one of great concern to all those who are involved. It should not be characterised as 'expulsion' other than in the gravest case. Doing so can give rise to misunderstandings, unnecessary litigation and a less favourable 'leaving status' than is merited in the circumstances.

The head should offer a review procedure in every case of expulsion or required removal, but not following a suspension or other sanction. If no review procedure is offered, it is likely that aggrieved parents will either contact the chairman of governors direct or consult solicitors and be advised to commence legal proceedings where there are grounds. Nowadays, heads are more likely to be held accountable in these cases than they were 20 years ago. It is not being held to account that undermines the head's authority, but being found to have acted improperly or unfairly.

# PART 3

# ASPECTS OF GOVERNANCE AND MANAGEMENT

# Chapter 17

## CHARITABLE TRUSTS AND EDUCATIONAL CHARITIES

### 17.1  INTRODUCTION

Independent schools, unless privately owned are invariably *charitable trusts*, that is, a public trust for the benefit of the community. Some private schools are owned by *private trusts* which are not charitable.

Those who have the management and control of the administration of a charity are called *charity trustees*. In the case of an educational charity, the charity trustees are normally the governors of the school, by whatever name the governing body is known.

The powers and duties of a charity trustee and the degree of personal responsibility that accompanies them are central to the role of a governor. He (or she) will therefore need to have a broad understanding of those powers and duties and also of what is meant by a trust, a charitable trust, an educational charity and charitable status. These matters are considered in turn below.

### 17.2  PRIVATE TRUSTS

#### 17.2.1.  Meaning of 'trust'

A trust exists where a person known as a *trustee* has money, property or rights which he (or she) is bound to hold or exercise for or on behalf of another, known as a *beneficiary*; or for the accomplishment of some particular purpose/s known as an *object* or *purpose*.

One of the original purposes of a trust was the private purpose of protecting accumulated family wealth from being dissipated by young or sometimes not-so-young inheritors, by creating a split between the management of property and its beneficial interest. From the 1500s, trusts became increasingly complex and are now sophisticated devices of law used for many different purposes.

#### 17.2.2  Development of trusts

Trusts presented a problem to the system of common law that was slowly being developed by judges in the fifteenth century. They were essentially a private affair that depended on the honesty and prudence and sometimes secrecy of trustees, particularly after the death of the person who set up the trust. At a time when there were few books or records in private hands and the printing press had barely been invented, a dispute over the existence or administration of a trust did not fall readily into any of the categories of common law precedent of the time. The rough and ready systems of the common law had not the means of investigating abuses and, for a while, the judges administering the common law refused to recognise or enforce trusts. That approach was eventually seen to be unfair or 'inequitable' to those who had been defrauded by dishonest trustees, yet found themselves without a remedy.

Gradually, a section of the judiciary came to recognise that it was their function to do justice or *equity* in disputes relating to trusts and the Court of Chancery evolved a system of duties and powers of trustees, rights of beneficiaries, principles or maxims describing the standards of conduct expected and, finally, remedies which the Court of Chancery would enforce. Thus a system of equity grew up alongside the common law and, to a limited extent, the two systems remain separate today, with some courts having chancery jurisdiction and others not.

From about 1535 onwards, 'equity' recognised two types of trust: *private trusts* for the benefit of individuals and *public trusts* for the benefit of the community. It is convenient to regard these as overlapping circles with more similarities than differences.

As the law of trusts developed, the device became increasingly sophisticated. A trust could be secret or half-secret as a means of benefiting, for example, an illegitimate child or mistress, whilst concealing their existence. Trustees could be given discretion as to when and to whom, within a certain class of beneficiaries, they distributed income or advanced capital. During the last 150 years, express trusts have been used for such purposes as the lawful avoidance of tax and keeping trust property out of the hands of creditors.

Other concepts have evolved, notably the *resulting trust* and also the *constructive trust*, the latter being a useful device for imposing obligations on those who have come into possession of money or property to which they are not entitled. Equity (meaning justice and fairness) imposes a duty on such persons to behave in relation to that money or property as though they were trustees.

Trusts will not be enforceable if they offend against morality or public policy or the provisions of any statute, or if a private trust has the effect of tying up capital or accumulating income for too long a period. Any such trust is held to be *illegal*, or *unenforceable*.

## 17.2.3   Trustees generally

A trustee holds money or property in a *fiduciary capacity*. That means broadly that he must exercise his powers in good faith and for the purposes for which they were conferred on him. A trustee, other than a constructive trustee must be aged 18 or over. A trustee may be an individual, a *corporation sole*, such as a bishop, or a *corporation aggregate*, such as a municipal corporation. There are also *trust corporations*, for example the Public Trustee, the Treasury Solicitor, the Official Solicitor and certain other charitable or public corporations appointed by the Lord Chancellor.

Complex rules govern the appointment, retirement and removal of trustees and the vesting of trust property. In general, these matters are regulated by the trust deed itself and by the provisions of the Trustee Act 1925 and the Trusts of Land and Appointment of Trustees Act 1996.

### 17.2.4  Duties of trustees

For most practical purposes, the core duties of a trustee are to act prudently and carry out the terms of the trust. The law expects a trustee to use the same degree of care in discharging his trusteeship as would a prudent man of business in supervising his own affairs.

The other main duties, namely the duty to act honestly and in good faith, not to profit personally from the trust and not to get into a conflict of interests are, in essence, a gloss on the duty to act with prudence.

It has been said that trusteeship is the highest duty known to the law and there is no doubt that the duties of a trustee are extremely onerous. They have to be carried out with the utmost diligence, otherwise the trustee is personally liable to replace trust assets that have been lost through his (or her) default.

The duties and also the powers of private trustees are broadly similar to those of charity trustees and are described later, with some differences of detail, under 'charitable trusts'.

### 17.2.5  Breach of trust

In *Re Vickery* [1931] 1 Ch 572, Maugham J said that a trustee will be guilty of a breach of trust if 'he knows that he is committing and intends to commit a breach of duty, or is recklessly careless in the sense of not caring whether his act or omission is or is not a breach of his duty'. It has also been held that 'wilful default' does not necessarily involve conscious wrongdoing.

In general terms, a trustee can be personally liable both for acts of *commission* and of *omission*, that is:

− acts which he (or she) commits that are in breach of his duties or in excess of his powers; and

− acts that he should have done but failed to do in accordance with his duties and powers.

A trustee will only be liable for breaches of trust by a *co-trustee* where he (or she) is personally at fault, for example because he has left trust income in the hands of a co-trustee for too long without making proper enquiries; or he has concealed a breach committed by his fellow trustees; or he has stood by while, to his knowledge, a breach of trust was being committed.

### 17.2.6  Consequences of breach

#### (a)  Injunction

A beneficiary, or the Attorney-General in the case of a charitable trust, may obtain an injunction to restrain a threatened breach of trust.

### (b)   Account of profits

If a trustee improperly uses trust money or property, for example, by acting outside his (or her) powers (*ultra vires*) or by deliberate wrongdoing, he is liable personally to replace the money used. In addition, if he made a profit from its use he must pay over the full profit. Moreover, the trustee can be charged with the amount of interest on the capital which the court considers he ought to have received. Alternatively, at the beneficiary's option, he can be required to pay compound interest at 1% above the clearing banks' base rate on the amount of the trust property improperly employed.

### (c)   Tracing

Equity allows a beneficiary to 'trace', ie follow funds that have been misappropriated. Often those funds will have become mixed with the trustee's own funds or with the funds of an innocent party. There are complex rules for ensuring as fair a result as possible having regard to the interests of all parties. The burden of proof rests with the trustee.

### (d)   Personal action against the trustee

A beneficiary may sue the trustee personally and will not, in general, be bound by the normal rules concerning delay and acquiescence that can be a bar to common law actions. Under s 61 of the Trustee Act 1925, the court is entitled to relieve a trustee wholly or partially from personal liability if it appears that he (or she) has acted honestly and reasonably and ought fairly to be excused for the breach or for omitting to obtain the directions of the court. However, the burden is on the trustee to prove that he acted honestly and reasonably. That will always be a question of fact depending on the circumstances of the case.

### (e)   Criminal aspects

A trustee who dishonestly appropriates property belonging to another with the intention of permanently depriving the other of it is guilty of theft under s 1(1) of the Theft Act 1968. It follows that, in certain circumstances, an intention to defeat the trust can be regarded as theft and prosecuted as a criminal offence.

### (f)   Payment of costs

A trustee will normally be ordered to pay the costs of proceedings made necessary by a breach of his (or her) duty as trustee where he has committed a direct breach of trust or where he has refused or neglected to do his duty as trustee. The costs of an innocent co-trustee who has been made a co-defendant in proceedings for breach of trust may be ordered to be paid by the trustee who actually committed the breach.

### 17.2.7   Exemptions and reliefs for trustees

There are the following reliefs and limitations to the liability of a trustee:

–     By s 30(1) of the Trustee Act 1925 he is answerable and accountable only for his (or her) own acts, receipts, neglects or defaults, and not for those of any other trustee or agent, unless the loss has happened through his own wilful default.

– A beneficiary who actively concurred or specifically acquiesced in a breach of trust can obtain no relief against the trustee in respect of it if the beneficiary was of full age, under no incapacity, not under undue influence and was fully informed of the circumstances.

– A trustee may be granted relief by the court under s 61 of the Trustee Act 1925, which has been referred to at **17.2.6(d)** above.

– Trustees who act together in breach of trust are jointly and severally liable. A trustee will generally be entitled to an indemnity or contribution from co-trustees who acted in breach of trust. Where one of the trustees is a solicitor controlling the administration of the trust and the other trustees are swayed by his advice to acquiesce in a breach of trust, the solicitor must indemnify his co-trustees against all the loss.

– A trustee may be entitled to an indemnity from a beneficiary if the trustee committed a breach of trust at the instigation or request or with the consent in writing of the beneficiary.

– Some relief may be obtained from trustee indemnity insurance. Such policies, however, must exclude claims arising from dishonesty, fraud or malicious conduct and the insurance will not pay fines or penalties.

## 17.3 CHARITABLE TRUSTS

### 17.3.1 Development of charitable trusts

Since the Statute of Uses in 1535, and earlier, the law has accepted that express trusts could be created to dedicate property for purposes beneficial to one or another sector of the community. These are public trusts, which have much in common with private trusts, the main differences being in relation to the purposes or objects of the trust, supervision of the way they are conducted and availability of information about them.

The growth of *general charitable uses*, ie charitable purposes, became frequent after 1535 and during the next 350 years the word 'charity' acquired a much wider technical meaning at law than in popular speech. In the words of Lord Ashbourne in *Re Cranston* [1898] 1 IrR 431, it is a word which is 'wide, elastic'. There has, in fact, never been a statutory definition of those purposes which are charitable, except for the very limited definition in s 1 of the Recreational Charities Act 1958. In the White Paper of 1989, *Charities: A Framework for the Future*, it was said that any attempt to enact a statutory definition was fraught with difficulty and would put at risk the flexibility of the present law which was its greatest and most valuable feature.

It is, however, accepted that there are three conditions for recognition of a charity. They are that:

– the purposes of the institution must be within the spirit of the preamble to the Statute of Charitable Uses 1601; and

– the institution must exist for the benefit of the public; and

– it must be exclusively charitable.

## 17.3.2    The 1601 preamble

The Statute of 1601 set out in the preamble a list of charitable objects, the best summary of which was given by Lord Macnaughtan in *Income Tax Special Purposes Commissioners v Pemsel* [1891] AC 531. He divided charities into four categories, set out below.

### (a)    Trusts for the relief of poverty

'Poverty' does not mean destitution. It has a wide and indefinite meaning of persons who have to 'go short' in the ordinary sense of that term, having regard to their status in life. However, the essence of the gift must be one for relief of the elderly or poor. A gift will not be for the relief of poverty if it can benefit the rich as well as the poor. Moreover, there must be an element of public benefit.

### (b)    Trusts for the advancement of education

An educational trust, to be charitable, must exist for the benefit of the community, but no element of poverty need be shown for a gift or trust for the advancement of education to be held charitable. Educational trusts are considered in more detail at **17.6** below.

### (c)    Trusts for the advancement of religion

Once again there must be a sufficient element of public benefit. 'Religion' is not restricted to Christianity, but, to qualify as charitable, it must contain elements of faith and worship. In *Gilmour v Coats* [1949] AC 426, HL, a gift to an enclosed contemplative order of nuns failed. The nuns prayed for the world, but the court held that prayer is 'manifestly not susceptible of proof'. However, a gift for masses for the dead was held in *Gibbs v McDonnell* [1990] Ch 1 to have sufficient public benefit because the mass is part of a public ritual.

### (d)    Other purposes beneficial to the community

This category covers matters within the spirit of the 1601 statute. Included as charities have been a gift for a fire brigade, a gift for the increased efficiency or morale of the army, gifts for the promotion of industry, commerce and art, and trusts for orphans and orphanages, among many others.

Gifts which have not been upheld as charitable have included gifts for sport (unless they are for sport within schools or the army), trusts for specific animals which are not charitable (although trusts for animals generally will be upheld if they promote and encourage human kindness). Amnesty International was held non-charitable in a case in 1982 because of its political element which was found to be more than incidental.

The Recreational Charities Act 1958 allows as charitable the provision, or assistance in the provision of, facilities for recreation or other leisure-time occupation, if the facilities are provided in the interests of social welfare. Social welfare is satisfied if the facilities are provided with the object of improving the conditions of life for the persons for whom the facilities are primarily intended and either: (a) persons have need of these facilities by reason of youth, age, infirmity, disablement, poverty or social and economic circumstances; or (b) the facilities are to be made available to the members or female members of the public at large. The element of public benefit is necessary even under the 1958 Act.

### 17.3.3  Meaning of 'charitable status'

The essential elements of charitable status are the three conditions mentioned above: that the institution falls within one of the four purposes described by Lord Macnaughton; that the institution exists for the benefit of the public; and that it is exclusively charitable. Once these conditions are present, an institution has charitable status as a matter of law and must be registered in accordance with s 3 of the Charities Act 1993. It is subject to the restrictions imposed on charities but it is also entitled to enjoy the privileges that the law accords to charities as of right.

During the 1990s and at other times, references have appeared in the media to the possible 'abolition of charitable status' for independent schools. There are a number of possible interpretations of that expression, but the most likely seems to be the removal of fiscal privileges from educational charities which cannot demonstrate the relief of poverty, in the sense of persons who have to 'go short', having regard to their status in life, or which cannot demonstrate some other benefit to the community.

There appear to be no proposals to alter three other aspects of charitable status, namely that:

– a charity is not subject to the rule against inalienability so that capital may be tied up indefinitely; and that

– a gift which has vested in a charity within the perpetuity period can be the subject of a gift over to another charity outside that period; and that

– charities themselves do not fail for uncertainty of objects.

### 17.3.4  Objects of a charitable trust

In the law of private or non-charitable trusts, the gift has to be made to a person, company or corporation. A gift made to a purpose or an object which cannot sue is not an enforceable trust.

The opposite applies to a charitable gift. Because it is exclusively charitable and benefits a sector of the community, the Attorney-General, representing the Crown can sue to enforce it and insist on the trust being carried out if necessary by a scheme *cy-près* (explained below). For these reasons, a charitable gift can never fail absolutely for uncertainty of objects.

### 17.3.5  *Cy-près* doctrine

If the object of a charitable trust fails then, unlike a private trust, the trust property can be applied for another charitable purpose as close as possible to the original trust. This is known as the doctrine of *cy-près*.

The rules about applying charitable property *cy-près* are now set out in Part IV of the Charities Act 1993. The current rules represent a considerable relaxation of the position before the Charities Act 1960 and allow application of property *cy-près* in a variety of circumstances where, for example, the original purposes of the gift have been fulfilled or cannot be carried out or only provide a use for part of the property; also where the original purposes have been adequately provided for by other means or have ceased to be, at law, charitable or have ceased in any other way to provide a suitable and effective method of using the property. Regard must be had to the original spirit of the gift in any consideration of an application *cy-près*.

### 17.3.6   The Charity Commissioners

The Charity Commissioners were first established by the Charitable Trusts Act 1858 following Lord Brougham's investigations under the Royal Commission of 1819. The constitution of the Commissioners is now governed by the Charities Act 1993 ('the Act').

The general function of the Commissioners set out in s 1(3) of the Act is the promotion of the effective use of charitable resources by encouraging the development of better methods of administration, by giving charity trustees information or advice on any matter affecting the charity and by investigating and checking abuses.

The general object of the Commissioners at s 1(4) of the Act is to act in the case of any charity (unless it is a matter of altering its purposes) as best to promote and make effective its work in meeting the needs designated by its trusts.

The Charity Commissioners are not permitted to act in the administration of a charity but they have considerable monitoring and supervisory powers, which include the keeping of the register, the receipt of annual accounts, powers to obtain information, and the temporary, remedial, permanent and protective powers exerciseable following an inquiry.

By s 29 of the Act, their powers also include the giving of advice to charities. Advice may be given, for example, as to whether a proposed action is within the objects of the charity, but the Commissioners will not advise on policy matters or on legal questions concerning rights of those outside the charity. A charity trustee who acts in accordance with the opinion or advice of the Commissioners is deemed to have acted in accordance with the trust, unless he knows or has reasonable cause to suspect that the opinion or advice was given in ignorance of material facts. An appeal against an opinion or advice of the Commissioners given under s 29 of the Act must be brought before the court as charity proceedings under s 33 of the Act. It has, however, been held in *Mills v Winchester Diocesan Board* [1989] 2 All ER 317 that the Commissioners do not owe a duty of care to the potential objects of a charity.

The Charity Commissioners have the same powers as the Attorney-General acting *ex officio* to take legal proceedings with reference to charities or the property or affairs of charities, or to compromise claims with a view to avoiding or ending such proceedings. These powers may only be exercised with the agreement of the Attorney-General.

The Commissioners also have powers to sanction acts that would otherwise be beyond the powers of a charity (s 26 of the Act).

In carrying out their functions and objects, the Commissioners have jurisdiction and powers concurrent with those of the High Court for certain purposes (s 16 of the Act).

### 17.3.7 Registration of charities

By s 3(7) of the Charities Act 1993, it is the duty of the trustees of any charity to apply for it to be registered unless:

– it is *excepted* by order or regulations. Charities in this category include the Boy Scouts;

– it is an *exempt* charity within the list in Sch 2 to the Act. The list includes the colleges of Winchester and Eton, certain universities and all grant-maintained schools. The general law of charity declared in the Act applies to exempt charities. They are subject to the jurisdiction of the court but exempt from all the supervisory and restrictive powers of the Commissioners under the Act;

– the charity is one which has neither any *permanent endowment* nor the use or occupation of any land and its income from all sources does not amount in total to more than £1,000 per year.

Further, no charity is required to be registered in respect of any registered place of worship.

It follows under these rules that an association of 'Friends' or the parents' association of a school which operates under a constitution and collects more than £1,000 net per year for a charitable purpose is required to register as a charity, but this would not apply to an ad hoc group of individuals engaged in occasional voluntary fund-raising activities.

Registration as a charity confers only a *status*. It does not, of itself, create a legal entity that can hold property or sue and be sued in its corporate name. A corporate structure, or a certificate of incorporation of the trustees as a body corporate, is needed for this purpose under s 50 of the Charities Act 1993. Even with a certificate, the trustees do not acquire limited liability in respect of their contract, torts and non-compliance. Further, it is provided by s 54 of the Act:

> 'After a certificate of incorporation has been granted under this part of this Act all trustees of the charity, notwithstanding their incorporation, shall be chargeable for such property as shall come into their hands, and *shall be answerable and accountable for their own acts, receipts, neglects, and defaults*, and for the due administration of the charity and its property, in the same manner and to the same extent as if no such incorporation had been effected' (emphasis added).

Once registered, a charity with a gross income of at least £5,000 in its last financial year must state that it is so registered on all of its official documents and, regardless of its gross income, it will be entitled to relief from taxes and rates.

The Commissioners are obliged to remove from the register any institution which no longer appears to them to be a charity because, for example, it has changed its objects to non-charitable or it has exercised a power of revocation.

There is no body in Scotland equivalent to the Charity Commissioners and there is no register of Scottish charities. However, Part I of the Law Reform (Miscellaneous Provisions) (Scotland) Act 1990, provides that a body established under Scottish law or managed or controlled mainly in or from Scotland ('a recognised body') which applies its income for charitable purposes only, may be accepted by the Inland

Revenue Commissioners as entitled to tax relief under s 505 of the Income and Corporation Taxes Act 1988.

A recognised body in Scotland is subject to the supervision of the Lord Advocate and the Court of Session. Charities Act 1993, s 80 none the less gives the Charity Commissioners a degree of jurisdiction in the case of a recognised body in Scotland, which is controlled or managed by a person in England or Wales, and vice versa.

### 17.3.8   Permanent endowment

Permanent endowment is a concept of charitable law which has reference to non-expendable property.

The concept can be a problem when (inter alia) the school needs to sell property in order to repay liabilities, or is undertaking 'incorporation', or if the school has to close in deficit.

Surprisingly little has been written about permanent endowment. The underlying principle is that if property is permanent endowment it must not be used up as if it were income, for example to make payments or grants or to pay creditors. Permanent endowment is described at s 96(3) of the Charities Act 1993 as follows:

> 'A charity shall be deemed for the purposes of this Act to have permanent endowment unless all property held for the purposes of the charity may be expended for those purposes without distinction between capital and income, and in this Act "permanent endowment" means, in relation to any charity, property held subject to a restriction on its being expended for the purposes of the charity.'

Thus, s 96(3) has two limbs:

–   there is deemed to be permanent endowment unless all the property of the charity is expendable; and

–   'permanent endowment' means property held subject to a *restriction* on its being expended for the purposes of the charity.

Section 96(3) leaves unanswered the question of whether 'restriction' means an express restriction or whether it only means the absence of an express power to use up the proceeds of sale of the property.

Nor is that resolved at para 7 of Appendix 3 to the *Statement of Recommended Practice* (SORP) of October 1995, which describes permanent endowment in the following way:

> 'A capital fund where there is no power to convert the capital into income is known as a permanent endowment fund, which must generally be held indefinitely.
>
> This concept of "permanence" does not however necessarily mean that the assets held in the endowment fund cannot be exchanged (though in some cases the trusts will require the retention of a specific asset for actual use, eg a historic building).
>
> What is does mean is that the permanent endowment fund cannot be used as if it were income, ie to make payments or grants to others.
>
> Where assets held in a permanent endowment fund are exchanged, their place in the fund must be taken by the assets received in exchange – "exchange" here may simply mean a

change of investment, but it may also, for example, mean the application of the proceeds of sale of permanent endowment land and buildings in the purchases or improvement of other property.'

The central point is as to the meaning of 'no power to convert the capital into income'. There may be no express power but charity trustees owe a duty to carry out the objects of the trust in accordance with its terms, and they have very wide powers at law enabling them to do so. At its simplest, the very nature of a charity is to collect from the rich and give to the poor although, of course, the concept has become far more complex than this.

For understandable reasons, the stance adopted by the Charity Commission in relation to endowments is initially restrictive in each case. Often, the assumption is made that charitable property is permanent endowment unless the contrary can be shown. That has resulted, for charitable schools at least, in many schemes of administration which contain clauses restricting the power of the charity trustees to spend capital whereas the creating instrument frequently contained no such restriction.

Examples of clauses in a creating instrument that plainly establish permanent endowment in relation to particular land or a particular fund include:

–   'the clear proceeds of sale shall be invested in trust for the charity', accompanied by a clause that provides for the application of income but does not provide for the expenditure of capital;

–   a requirement in a deed that the property must be held for the purposes of the charity *only*, and for no other purpose; or

–   a similar requirement that property must be held *only* as a source of income for the charity.

In *Edwards v Hall* (1855) 6 De GM & G 74, Lord Cranworth LC said at p 87:

'By the endowment of a school, an hospital or a chapel, is commonly understood, not the building or purchasing of a site for a school, an hospital or a chapel but the providing of a fixed revenue for the support of those institutions.'

It is submitted that, in the absence of a clear statement or inference as to the donor's intention, the absence of an express restriction means that charity trustees have power to spend capital as if it were income but this is by no means a consistent policy of the Commisioners.

The practical importance of ensuring that charitable property is not wrongly treated as permanent endowment can be seen in a case where a school may have two choices: to sell some of its land in order to pay off debts, or to close. It must be assumed that the founder who originally endowed the school did not intend that the school should close unless the contrary was expressed in or to be inferred from the creating instrument. In practice, the Commissioners have on occasions permitted charity trustees to sell property that has been deemed to be permanent endowment (whether or not on a true construction it is such), subject to the terms of a recoupment order under which the property will be replaced on a pound for pound basis over 30 years or more. A recoupment order of this kind takes no account of income or inflation and is therefore a halfway house between the rigors of the permanent endowment rule and the freedom of charity trustees to serve the objects of the charity. None the less it can be unsatisfactory.

Another practical issue is whether permanently endowed property can be transferred to a company limited by guarantee when a charity is undergoing 'incorporation'. Until recently, the Commissioners considered this could not be done since a limited company is the beneficial owner of its assets which will therefore be available to creditors in a winding up. To help overcome that problem, the Commissioners have authorised schemes under which permanent endowment was transferred to a corporate trustee which, under s 35 of the Charities Act 1993 conferred the status of trust corporation. This tends to be an artificial and over-complex mechanism for a school. An alternative which is gaining recognition is to provide in the memorandum and articles of 'Newco' a power for the company to hold assets as trustee and thus ring-fence them from creditors. A further alternative is to leave the permanently endowed assets in the hands of the existing trustees who will grant a long lease of them to Newco subject to forfeiture of the lease in the event of the school closing.

## 17.3.9   Charity trustees

Section 97(1) of the Charities Act 1993 states for the purposes of the law of England and Wales:

> ' "Charity Trustees" means the persons having the general control and management of the administration of a charity.'

Charity trustees will normally be appointed under the terms of the charitable scheme. In the case of a charitable school, the governors (by whatever name known) will normally be the charity trustees since they are the persons having the general control and management of the administration.

A corporation sole and a company limited by guarantee is often a charity trustee in its own right.

The statutory powers as to the appointment of new and additional trustees contained in ss 36, 37 and 40–56 of the Trustee Act 1925 apply also to charitable trusts, but better procedures are now set out in s 83 of the Charities Act 1993.

Trustees who are expressly appointed, and company directors, must be over the age of 18, although a person under the age of 18 can become a *constructive trustee* if he comes into possession of property for which he should account or of which he should make restitution. Accordingly, it is not appropriate to appoint a person under 18, for example a pupil, as a governor of a charitable school. Odd though it may seem, this question has actually arisen.

## 17.3.10   Directors of a charitable company

The directors of a charitable company, such as a corporate school, come within the definition of 'charity trustees', even though at law they are not trustees but are fiduciaries (*Re City Equitable Fire Insurance Co Ltd* [1925] Ch 407, at 426). The powers and duties of the directors will be set out in the memorandum and articles of association. In general, the directors will be given power to do whatever is lawful and necessary to achieve the objects of the charity.

Directors will be personally liable to the charitable company for any loss occurring as a result of acting beyond their powers.

In addition to the duties of charity trustees described earlier, the directors of a charitable company are subject to the statutory obligations imposed by the Companies Act 1985 in the same way as the directors of any other registered company. The companies legislation creates over 200 separate offences of non-compliance, but in practice these present little risk to trustees who act prudently and in accordance with competent professional advice.

The appointment and removal of directors is largely governed by ss 303 and 304 of the Companies Act 1985 and also by the Company Directors Disqualification Act 1986 and the terms of the particular memorandum and articles of association.

As fiduciaries, the directors are under a duty to exercise their powers for the purposes for which they were conferred and to do so in good faith for the benefit of the company and not to put themselves in a position in which their duties to the company and their personal interests conflict. They must exercise their powers in furtherance of the charitable objects of the company and not in the interests of some section of the company. The directors of a charitable company are obliged to act gratuitously and it appears from *Re French Protestant Hospital* [1951] 1 Ch 567 that the degree of care and skill expected of the director of a charitable company is greater than for a director of a non-charitable company.

## 17.4 DUTIES OF CHARITY TRUSTEES

As noted earlier, the main duties of a charity trustee are broadly the same as those of a private trustee. These, together with certain differences where they occur, are now considered below. For these purposes, unless the context otherwise suggests, 'trustee' includes 'charity trustee'.

### 17.4.1 Immediately on appointment

When a trustee accepts a trust he (or she) should acquaint himself with the terms of the trust and the contents of any documents handed to him as trustee and the assets of the trust. He must take possession of the trust property and ensure that it has been vested in accordance with the trust deed. He must consider the investments and if necessary, he must institute legal proceedings to safeguard or recover the trust property. It is prudent also to enquire whether there have been past breaches of trust for which he might be jointly liable. To any reasonable extent that the trustee requires professional advice in relation to any of these matters, that is properly an expense of the trust or charity provided the trust deed or governing instrument contains appropriate powers.

### 17.4.2 Comply with the terms of the trust

A trustee or charity trustee must carry out the trust in accordance with its terms as set out in the trust instrument or Scheme drawn up by the Commissioners. He (or she) must exercise his powers and carry out his duties irrespective of the fact that he is an unpaid volunteer and it causes him loss or inconvenience to do so.

### 17.4.3   Fidelity and prudence

A trustee must not connive at or knowingly facilitate a breach of trust. He (or she) must not cause loss or risk to the trust property or get into a conflict of interests. He must strictly carry out the terms of the trust and do so with prudence and reasonable diligence. In cases of doubt or difficulty, a trustee may take legal advice and other expert advice. If the advice is wrong but it was reasonable for the trustee to have relied and acted on it, he may be relieved from responsibility. If a point is not clear, then, as a rule, the trustee should obtain the direction of the court, or in the case of charity trustees, the advice of the Commissioners.

### 17.4.4   Act personally

A trustee is personally responsible for the exercise of his (or her) judgement and for the performance of his duties. He can delegate tasks but he cannot surrender, transfer or shed responsibility for the way those tasks are carried out. It is submitted, by analogy to a company case *Norman v Theodore Goddard* [1991] VCLC 1028, that a trustee, in the same way as a company director, is entitled to trust persons in positions of responsibility until there is reason to distrust them. However, he must exercise reasonable supervision and ask questions that should be asked. He must not 'close his eyes' to possible wrongdoing, or he will be personally liable for loss that results.

The decisions of trustees must be taken unanimously in the case of a private trust. In trusts of a public or charitable nature, however, the majority may, as a rule, bind the minority.

### 17.4.5   Impartiality between beneficiaries

The general rule is that a trustee must look to the interests of all beneficiaries and must not be partisan. This is of particular importance if a trustee is also a beneficiary of a private trust. Moreover, the terms of a private and charitable trust may require a certain class of beneficiary to be given preference and a private trustee may be required to exercise his discretion. In all such cases the trustee must act impartially, honestly and in accordance with the terms of the trust.

### 17.4.6   Keep accounts and give information

A trustee must keep an accurate account of the trust property. He (or she) must always be ready to give information to persons entitled to have it. He is entitled to be paid the costs of furnishing accounts and information in compliance with his duty. If he neglects or fails in this duty, he will be personally liable for the costs of legal proceedings to compel production of the information or accounts.

### 17.4.7   Investment

A trustee must invest trust property wisely, acting as a prudent man making investments. Trustees must obtain the best rate of return available and diversify risks, even where that may be contrary to the political, social or moral views of some of the beneficiaries. Charity trustees are, however, permitted greater discretion. They may exclude certain types of investment such as, for example, armaments; although they are not entitled to pursue a policy of ethical investment which would be financially detrimental to the trust funds (*Harris v Church Commissioner for England* [1992] 2 All ER 300).

Investment by non-charitable trustees must be within the terms of the Trustee Investments Act 1961 unless the trust deed or governing instrument otherwise permits. Charity trustees have greater powers under the Charities Act 1993. Section 70 of the Act enables the Secretary of State, by order, to allow charities that are restricted under the 1961 Act to invest more than 50% of their funds in equities. Section 26 of the Act enables the Charity Commissioners to make an order specifically authorising charity trustees to enter into *discretionary investment management agreements* in the absence of an express power of delegation in the governing instrument. The Charity Commissioners have indicated that they will make such an order if delegation can be justified because of the value of the investments and the frequency of transaction.

The Trusts of Land and Appointment of Trustees Act 1996 provides trustees with power to purchase land in England and Wales but not in other countries unless the trust instrument so authorises.

### 17.4.8 Compliance with the Charities Act 1993

The Act imposes some duties on charity trustees that either do not apply or are found elsewhere in relation to private trustees. They are:

– the duty under s 3(7) to register the charity;

– the duty under s 41 to keep accounts;

– the duties under ss 42 and 43 to have accounts audited or independently examined;

– the duties under ss 45 and 47 to make an annual report and an annual return to the Charity Commissioners.

### 17.4.9 Apply for a scheme

If charity trustees wish to depart from their trust they should first approach the Charity Commissioners for a scheme to alter the purposes of the charity. Further, s 29 of the Charities Act 1993 gives power to the Charity Commissioners to advise charity trustees, although s 1(4) provides that the Commissioners shall not themselves have power to act in the administration of a charity.

### 17.4.10 Act gratuitously

Neither a private trustee nor a charity trustee is entitled to be paid a salary or charge fees for his time, unless permitted by the terms of the trust. A professional charging clause is common under a private trust but the position is different for charitable trusts.

The Charity Commissioners' starting-point is that remuneration of a charity trustee is not essential for the carrying out of the charity's objects. The Commissioners have, however, indicated that they will authorise remuneration where it can be shown to be necessary and reasonable in the interests of the charity.

A charity with a remuneration clause for trustees will therefore be accepted for registration if the clause limits the remuneration to a reasonable sum for services undertaken as a trustee. However, the courts have also indicated in *Steel v Wellcome Custodian Trustees Ltd* [1988] 1 WLR 167 at 174, that they are reluctant to relieve paid trustees of liability for breach of trust.

The Commissioners will take into account the size of the charity, the nature of its activities, the degree of involvement required of the trustees, the specialist nature of the skills required and the cost of obtaining those skills by employing others. The same principles will apply to requests for the authorisation of one-off payments to trustees for specific work undertaken for the charity.

An employee, such as the head or bursar of a charitable school, cannot be appointed as a trustee unless there is a specific authority allowing him to be so appointed, and he (or she) must not attend meetings when the terms of his (or her) appointment are considered.

### 17.4.11   Not to make a personal profit from the trust

The duty of a trustee not to profit from his trust is closely connected with the duty to act gratuitously. Neither a private trustee nor a charity trustee is entitled to use trust property for his own purposes, nor, as a rule, to receive any direct or indirect benefit such as payment, at the cost of the charity, to himself or his firm for supplying goods or services to the charity. In the case of a charitable trust, a clause to this effect is usually contained in schemes made by the Commissioners.

The governing body of a charitable school often includes people in the professions or business such as a solicitor, accountant, financial adviser, computer or marketing consultant or builder who would stand to gain personally if their firm became a supplier of services or goods to the charity.

It is reported at para 92 of *Decisions of the Charity Commisioners* (1970), and is now the practice, that the Commissioners will permit a form of clause which provides that a person who supplies goods or services to a charity may be appointed a charity trustee, provided that he absents himself from any meeting at which any transaction in which he is interested is discussed and provided also that the other trustees are satisfied that any transaction is advantageous to the charity.

It is submitted that this clause is not without its difficulties. It does not sufficiently address the difference between large and small transactions. Nor does it address the difference between a supplier of many years who then becomes a trustee as distinct from a trustee of many years who starts making supplies to the charity. It is also submitted that the proviso that the transaction must be advantageous to the charity needs further qualification in terms of the method of selection of the supplier.

An example of the practical difficulties that may arise is where charity trustees, influenced by a solicitor co-trustee acting in good faith, decide to commence costly litigation over a building dispute using that solicitor's firm. Thereafter, the solicitor must absent himself from all discussions about the quality of the firm's advice in litigation. The trustees are thus deprived of his contribution and advice which may not be in the best interests of the charity. Moreover, the trustees may find it embarrassing to criticise the way in which the solicitor's firm has conducted the action or to ask questions about other matters such as the level of charging.

Another example is the extent to which a trustee with a personal interest can, perhaps unconsciously, influence the trustees to direct work to his own firm when that firm may not be sufficiently specialist to deal with the work competently.

There is anecdotal evidence of solicitor governors forgoing their share of the profit of their firm to the extent that it is attributable to work done for the charity. It is submitted, however, that that is irrelevant to the practical concerns which these situations raise, and irrelevant also to the cash flow value of the fees to the firm.

The duties of a trustee to act gratuitously, not to make a personal profit and not to get into a conflict of interests remain important safeguards of trust and charitable property and should not be side-stepped without substantial justification and authority.

## 17.5 THE POWERS OF CHARITY TRUSTEES

Charity trustees have generally greater powers than private trustees. Both categories may (and sometimes must) exercise the lawful powers that are set out in the documents creating the trust or given by statute. They must exercise those powers reasonably and in good faith and for the purposes for which they were created. Every new trustee has the same powers, authorities and discretions as an original trustee.

Both categories of trustee also have some limited powers of delegation under s 23(1) of the Trustee Act 1925 and a private trustee may delegate his functions to beneficiaries of full age by virtue of s 9 of the Trusts of Land and Appointment of Trustees Act 1996.

Both categories of trustee also have powers to invest and to insure trust property.

There are, however, the following differences between an ordinary trustee and a charity trustee:

–   A charity trustee does not have the powers given by s 16 of the Trustee Act 1925 to non-charitable trustees to raise money by sale or mortgage for purposes authorised by the trust instrument.

–   Charitable land can be held by more than four charity trustees, whereas s 34(3)(a) of the Trustee Act 1925 limits the number to four, in the case of ordinary trustees.

–   Charity trustees are given additional powers under the Charities Act 1993 to co-operate with local authorities and other charities and they are given the power to delegate, generally or specifically, the execution of documents to at least two of their number.

–    Sections 36–40 of the Charities Act 1993 restrict the circumstances in which charity trustees can exercise their power of sale or otherwise deal with charity property.

–    Charity trustees can take their decisions by a majority. Ordinary trustees must be unanimous.

–    Charity trustees may exclude certain types of investment, as was seen earlier.

In addition to these, charity trustees have the following powers.

### 17.5.1    Power to sell etc

Charity trustees have always had a general power at law to sell, lease or mortgage charity land, whether expressly authorised by the governing instrument or not.

There are also statutory provisions which may have the effect of regulating the common law power described above. The main statutory power to deal with charity land is in s 29 of the Settled Land Act 1925, as amended by the Trusts of Land and Appointment of Trustees Act 1996. This confers on charity trustees all the powers of a tenant for life of settled land and of the trustees of the settlement. Accordingly, charity trustees can sell, exchange, lease, mortgage and grant options subject to the usual restrictions:

–    sale must be for the best consideration in money that can be reasonably obtained;

–    leases must comply with the conditions laid down in ss 41 and 42 of the Act;

–    mortgages may only be created for the purposes specified in s 71;

–    options must comply with the statutory conditions in s 51.

None of these powers, however, confer on trustees the power to dispose of land in breach of any trust, covenant or agreement binding on them, or in breach of the restrictions contained in s 36 of the Charities Act 1993. Accordingly, permanent endowment, where it exists, remains non-expendable capital, subject to the power of the Commissioners to make a recoupment order (see also **17.3.8** on permanent endowment).

Sections 36–40 of the Charities Act 1993 contain restrictions to which charity trustees must have regard when they sell, mortgage, lease or otherwise dispose of land including land which is permanently endowed. They may, however, sell, lease or otherwise dispose of land without an order of the court or the Charity Commissioners if they have complied with certain conditions, broadly:

–    the disposition must not be to a connected person or a trustee or nominee for a connected person as listed in Sch 5 to the Act;

–    before entering the agreement for sale, lease or other disposition of the land, the charity trustees must:

    –    consider a report from a qualified surveyor instructed by the trustees and acting exclusively for the charity; and
    –    advertise the proposed disposition (or not) as the surveyor has advised; and

– decide that they are satisfied that the terms of the disposition are the *best that can reasonably be obtained* for the charity.

Less onerous conditions apply to the grant of a lease by a charity to an unconnected person for a term ending not more than seven years after it is granted. Then, the charity trustees must obtain and consider the advice of a person whom they reasonably believe to have the requisite ability and practical experience to provide them with competent *advice* about the proposed disposition; and decide that they are *satisfied*, having considered that person's advice that the terms of the disposition are the *best that can reasonably be obtained* for the charity.

It is submitted that the grant of a licence is not a 'disposition' of land since a licence is a permission and not an interest in the land.

Charity trustees may obtain an order from the Charity Commissioners permitting them to deal with charity property in a way beneficial to the trust where they would otherwise have no power to carry out the particular transaction.

### 17.5.2 Power to borrow money

Charity trustees may borrow money and, subject to the restrictions at s 38 of the Charities Act 1993 they may charge charity property to secure the loan. The trustees remain personally liable to repay the loan, although they are entitled to be repaid out of the charity property if it is available and sufficient for that purpose.

Before mortgaging charity land, the trustees must, under s 38 of the Charities Act 1993, obtain and consider proper advice given to them in writing concerning:

– whether the proposed loan is necessary in order for the charity trustees to be able to pursue the particular course of action in connection with which the loan is sought by them;

– whether the terms of the proposed loan are reasonable having regard to the charity as a prospective borrower; and

– the ability of the charity to repay on those terms the sum proposed to be borrowed.

'Proper advice' is the advice of a person 'who is reasonably believed by the charity trustees to be qualified by his (or her) ability in and practical experience of financial matters; and who has no financial interest in the making of the loan in question'.

### 17.5.3 Power to insure

Charity trustees have the statutory power under s 19 of the Trustee Act 1925 to insure the charity property up to three-quarters of its value. The Charity Commissioners, however, stated in 1972 that they regard it as the duty of charity trustees to keep the property insured up to its full value.

A charity is now permitted by the Commissioners to pay the premiums for insurance for a policy to cover trustees against personal liability from acts, either properly undertaken in the administration of a charity, or undertaken in breach of trust, but under an honest mistake. It should be noted, however, that such insurance will not indemnify trustees for the consequences of the contracts which they make with employees, parents, the bank, landlords, professional advisers and other suppliers. Moreover, the quality and scope of cover of these policies is variable, and the terms of cover and claims should be carefully checked in advance. Consent of the Commissioners is needed if the trust instrument does not contain the power to effect this kind of insurance.

### 17.5.4 Power to make ex gratia payments

Charity trustees have, with the consent of the Charity Commissioners or the Attorney-General, power to make *ex gratia payments*, for example to discharge a moral obligation but this power is not to be exercised lightly or on slender grounds.

### 17.5.5 Power to waive entitlement to property

The Charity Commissioners have the same power as the Attorney-General to authorise charity trustees to waive a charity's entitlement to receive property where the trustees regard themselves as being under a moral obligation to do so.

It is submitted that governors of a charitable school do not need consent to waive school fees or fees in lieu of notice at the normal levels up to, say £20,000 for one family in particular cases of hardship or where there is some other good reason.

## 17.6  EDUCATIONAL CHARITIES

### 17.6.1  Education as a charitable purpose

It was held in *R v Income Tax Special Commissioners* (1909) 78 LJKB 576, at 578, that there is no need for any element of poverty in a gift or trust for the advancement of education. To be charitable at law and in equity, it must:

– be for an educational purpose which the law regards as charitable; and

– fall within the letter or spirit of the Statute of Charitable Uses 1601; and

– provide education which is beneficial or of value to the community; and

– provide benefits that are available to the public or to a sufficiently important section of the community.

A great many cases have come before the courts for a decision as to whether they were within the category of 'education' and were therefore charitable. 'Education' has been given a wide meaning. A few examples of gifts that have been held charitable because they are for the advancement of education are: gifts for the establishment and support of colleges, professorships, fellowships, lectureships, scholarships and prizes; a trust in favour of a student union, provided the union exists to support the college to which it is attached; the provision of care of school children in sickness; promotion and encouragement of the physical development of children and young persons; and the provision of fives courts or squash courts at a school.

Also held to be for the advancement of education have been the promotion of commercial education, Christian healing, ethical principles, economic and sanitary science, and the education of boys of all ages in the principles of discipline, loyalty and good citizenship, the Boy Scouts and the game of chess.

'Education' is even wider than this and extends to trusts to establish and support museums and art galleries as well as research directed towards confirming a pre-existing theory rather than challenging and validating the theory. There are, however, limits. The gift must be of some educational value. The trust must not be political or propagandist and it must not have the purpose of changing the law but it can have an incidental non-charitable purpose.

A trust for the advancement of education must provide benefits that will be available to the community or to a sufficiently important section of the community. The following gifts among others have been upheld as charitable: a gift for women and girls who are not self-supporting, a gift to the daughters of missionaries, and a gift to persons professing particular religious doctrines.

A trust directing that preference be given to certain individuals can attain charitable status but it may not always be given relief from income tax if too high a proportion of its income is paid to the preferred individuals.

## 17.6.2 Trading activities of charitable schools

Educational charities of all kinds often seek to increase their income by licensing the use of their land, buildings, plant and facilities during holiday periods. This also enables them to serve the community within the spirit of charitable law.

If the activity is educational, such as a summer school, the provision of educational services is charitable as is the provision of services incidental to the main activity. However, services that are not incidental will be treated as commercial. Commercial activities, if significant, are normally conducted through a trading company, which will usually need to be registered for value added tax. Its profits will be covenanted up to the school. Care must, however, be taken to ensure that commercial use of the assets does not create excessive wear and tear, that the charity receives a fair return for the use of its facilities and that the nature and extent of commercial activity is not such as to be out of balance or inconsistent with the charitable purposes.

## 17.6.3 Discrimination provisions

Certain trust deeds contain provisions that restrict the benefits available to persons of one sex rather than another. In the case of a school, perhaps the charitable objects provide for the education of boys only. Or there may be a scholarship donation that is restricted to one set to the exclusion of the other.

Section 78(2) of the Sex Discrimination Act 1975 addresses these matters in relation to independent schools and other educational establishments, but not special schools. The section allows the governors to apply to the Secretary of State for the removal or modification of the restriction. If the Secretary of State is satisfied that removal or modification would conduce to the advancement of education without sex discrimination, he may by order make such modifications of the instrument as appear to him expedient.

If the trust was created by gift or bequest, no such order may be made until 25 years after the date on which the gift or bequest took effect, unless the donor or his personal representatives, or the personal representatives of the testator, have consented in writing to the making of the application for the order.

## 17.7  TAXATION OF EDUCATIONAL CHARITIES

The privileged tax status of charities goes back to 1842, when income tax was first introduced. There is no general exemption from taxation for charities, but there are specific provisions relieving charities from liability for individual taxes. If all the conditions for a particular exemption are not complied with, tax will be payable. Similarly, tax will be payable if there is no specific exemption, for example, income arising under Schedule E.

The law has also allowed tax incentives to individuals and companies who make donations to charities. Relief for individuals and/or companies is available from income tax, corporation tax, capital gains tax and inheritance tax. The main reliefs are considered below.

### 17.7.1  Income tax

Section 505(1) of the Income and Corporation Taxes Act 1988 sets out the income tax exemptions for charities, but there are conditions of the exemption. The main condition is that the income must be applied for charitable purposes only and the condition will not be satisfied if part of the income is applied for non-charitable objects. In *IRC v Educational Grants Association* [1967] Ch 993, trustees of an educational trust made grants to children of employees of the founder of the trust. These were held not exempt from income tax.

The following is a summary of the exemptions:

–   Section 505(1)(a) contains what may be the only reference anywhere in statute law to a 'public school', but the term is not defined. The subsection provides that the rent and profits of land belonging to a public school, among others, or vested in trustees for charitable purposes is exempt from income tax under *Schedule A* and *Schedule D*.

–   *Schedule C6*, in respect of any interest, annuities, dividends, or shares of annuities.

–   *Schedule D*, in respect of any yearly interest or other annual payment.

–   *Schedule F*, in respect of any distribution, where, in any such case, the income in question forms part of the income of a charity, or is, according to the rules or regulations established by Act of Parliament, charter, decree, deed of trust or will, applicable to charitable purposes only.

–   *Schedule C*, in respect of any interest, annuities, dividends, or shares of annuities which are in the name of trustees and are applicable solely towards the repairs of, inter alia, any college or chapel, or of any building used solely for the purposes of divine worship, so far as the same are applied to those purposes.

–  *Schedule D*, in respect of the profits of any trade carried on by a charity, if the profits are applied solely to the purposes of the charity and either the trade is exercised in the course of the actual carrying out of a primary purpose of the charity or the work in connection with the trade is mainly carried out by beneficiaries of the charity.

The trading activities of a charity will be subject to income tax under Schedule D, Case I, unless exempt, as a result of:

–  the trade being exercised in the course of the actual carrying out of the primary purpose of the charity; or

–  the trade being mainly carried out by beneficiaries of the charity.

Charities are also allowed to undertake certain fund-raising activities which will be exempt from income tax, provided:

–  the charity is not regularly trading;

–  the trading is not in competition with other traders;

–  the activities are supported substantially because the public are aware that any profits will be devoted to charity;

–  the profits are transferred to charities or are otherwise applied for charitable purposes.

The type of activity contemplated here for independent schools would be such as a craft fair or gymkhana.

Independent schools often use a trading company as a vehicle for the school's trading activities which are not taxable if the company's profits have been covenanted up to the charity or paid by a gift aid. It is desirable to ensure that control of the trading company is in different hands from the control of the charity.

## 17.7.2  Corporation tax

Section 832(1) of the Income and Corporation Taxes Act 1988 defines 'company' as including 'unincorporated association'. Charitable schools and other charities of either type are exempt from corporation tax on the same basis as described above for income tax.

## 17.7.3  Capital gains tax

A charity is exempt from capital gains tax on gains accruing to the charity and applied for charitable purposes (s 256(1) of the Taxation of Chargeable Gains Act 1992). The Finance Act 1986 contains provisions designed to prevent misuse of charitable status when it appears to the Inland Revenue that two or more charities are acting in concert with the aim of avoiding income tax, corporation tax or capital gains tax.

## 17.7.4　Value Added Tax

### (a)　General description

There is no general exemption for charities from VAT, but, in practice, many charities do not have to charge *output tax* on what they supply because it is an *exempt supply* listed in Sch 9 to the Value Added Tax Act 1994. However, they have to bear *input tax* on what they buy in order to make the exempt supply, which cannot be set off against outputs if the charity is not registered for VAT.

The provision of education or vocational training by a school, university or college is exempt from VAT by virtue of Sch 9, Group 6, Item 1 of the Act. The provision of goods and services or instruction supplemental to the provision of education is also exempt, for example the provision of meals to students attending a course (see Sch 9, Group 6, Items 4 and 5).

Some goods and services are *zero-rated* in accordance with the list set out at Sch 8 to the Act. Zero-rating can benefit a charity in two ways:

– the charity does not pay input tax on any zero-rated supply that it is buying; and

– it need not charge output tax on zero-rated supplies it makes, for example, books and journals and food other than hot food and food in the course of catering which are at standard rate.

The VAT legislation in the United Kingdom is subject to the Sixth Council Directive on VAT which has direct effect in the United Kingdom. It is unlikely that the UK Parliament can impose VAT on educational supplies without there first being a change to the Sixth Council Directive.

### (b)　Registration for VAT

As from 1 December 1997, a school must generally register for VAT if the value of standard-rated and zero-rated supplies made by the school exceeds £49,000 in any 12-month period; or will exceed £49,000 in the next 30 days.

Alternatively, a school may register for VAT on a voluntary basis in order to make an input tax recovery, that is, to recover part of the tax it has incurred on its purchases.

### (c)　Supplies that are normally exempt

The following supplies made by an independent school will normally be exempt from VAT. Exemption means that the supply and its value is ignored for the purposes of calculating the registration threshold.

– Educational and vocational training do not bear VAT where the supply is provided by an 'eligible body', such as an independent school.

– Catering does not bear VAT if it is for the direct use of pupils receiving education that is exempt. Even sales of crisps and fizzy drinks can be exempt if they are part of, and less than, the value of the usual main meal.

– Sales to pupils of equipment and stationery that is 'closely related' to education which is exempt do not bear VAT.

- Examination fees charged to pupils or their parents are exempt.

- Room hire is exempt, unless the option to tax has been taken, or services and facilities such as catering are also provided.

- School trips are exempt, although travel may be subject to the VAT Tour Operators Margin Scheme provisions in certain cases.

### (d) Supplies that are normally standard-rated

Catering which does not fall within the exemption described above is standard-rated. Its value is included when calculating the VAT registration threshold. Examples are charges made for catering to teachers, parents, governors or other visitors, which will be standard-rated unless such meals are provided in a dining hall which caters mainly for pupils and the school cannot readily identify the value of sales to non-pupils; and catering at dances, concerts and similar events. Other examples of standard-rated supplies are:

- School uniforms that do not fall within the rules for zero rating described below.

- Income from the hire of sports facilities, unless 'long let' provisions apply.

- Income from vending machines, unless they are to be regarded as part of exempt catering.

- Income from pay phones and photocopying.

- Income from shop sales and school photographs.

- Admission charges to concerts, sports events, etc, unless exempt as a 'one-off' fund raising activity undertaken by a charity where other relevant provisions are met.

- Advertising, unless zero-rated because it falls within the 'charitable' exceptions.

- Income from car parking spaces.

### (e) Supplies that are normally zero-rated

Zero-rated supplies are added to standard-rated supplies for the purposes of calculating whether a school must register for VAT. Examples of supplies that are normally zero-rated are:

- School uniforms and games kit, if they are regarded as children's and not adults'. Clothes which bear a prominent logo or badge identifying them as part of the official school uniform can, by concession for schools which cater solely for pupils under the age of 14, be zero-rated, irrespective of size.

- Books.

- Advertising which qualifies under the 'charitable' exceptions.

### (f)   Recovery of input tax

Input tax is the tax which the school pays when it buys goods or services for internal use or resale. There are three categories of input tax and different rules about recovery relate to each:

–   Input tax cannot be recovered when it relates wholly and exclusively to the making of exempt supplies, such as the purchase of equipment that will be used solely for the provision of education.

–   Input tax can be recovered in full if it relates wholly and exclusively to the making of taxable supplies such as goods sold through a school shop.

–   'Residual input tax' can only be recovered in part if it does not relate wholly and exclusively to either of the other categories. Residual input tax is associated with items such as legal and accountancy costs and also with equipment that may be used partly for the provision of education and partly for a taxable purpose such as hiring out to third parties. The 'partial exemption' rules are then applied to determine how much of the input tax can be reclaimed.

### (g)   Generally

VAT is a complex tax and VAT liability will often depend on very subtle distinctions between one set of circumstances and another. There is also reported experience of schools that received expert professional advice being able to make substantial VAT recoveries that would otherwise have been overlooked.

### 17.7.5   Stamp duty

It is provided by s 129 of the Finance Act 1982 that no stamp duty is payable on conveyances or transfers on sale, voluntary dispositions or leases to charities, but s 129(2) requires such instruments to be adjudicated.

### 17.7.6   Rates

Section 43(6) of the Local Government Finance Act 1988 provides rating relief for charities in respect of financial years beginning on or after 1 April 1990, where:

–   the ratepayers are a charity or the trustees for a charity; and

–   the hereditament (property) is wholly or mainly used for charitable purposes (whether of that charity or of that and other charities).

The non-domestic rate will automatically be reduced by 80% or, in the case of unoccupied hereditaments, by 100%.

## 17.8   TAXATION OF CHARITABLE GIFTS

Government policy from the 1980s onwards was to increase the tax incentives to individuals and companies to make donations to charities. These are considered in turn.

### 17.8.1 Income tax

#### (a) Payment to a charity under deed of covenant

A donor may make a deed of covenant, capable of lasting more than three years, in favour of a charity. Sums paid to the charity under the deed of covenant will be regarded as the income of the charity, provided it is a gift in the real sense and not made in exchange for some consideration. The tax arrangements are then as follows:

- the donor may deduct basic rate income tax from the annual sums before paying to the charity; and

- the charity can recover basic rate tax from the Inland Revenue; and

- in addition, the donor will normally obtain relief from higher rate tax on the covenant payments.

#### (b) Gift-aid

Tax relief can also be obtained for a donation that has not been made under a deed of covenant. This is commonly known as gift-aid and was introduced by the Finance Act 1990. The gift must be a minimum of £250 and it must be unconditional and without any associated benefit to the donor. The tax relief arrangements work in a similar way as for covenants.

#### (c) Sponsorship

An individual who is taxed under Schedule D, Case I or II may be able to obtain tax relief for payments he makes for charitable purposes such as small donations to local charities and also sponsorship of charitable activities.

### 17.8.2 Corporation tax

Covenanted donations to charity by a company are relieved from corporation tax on a similar basis to that set out above for individuals who pay income tax and there are also analogous provisions for non-covenanted donations.

### 17.8.3 Capital gains tax

An individual or company may give (ie dispose of) an asset to a charity on the basis that no gain or loss is deemed to arise from the disposal. The donor will not be assessed to capital gains tax and the unrealised gains passed to the charity which will probably be exempt from tax on a later disposal.

### 17.8.4 Inheritance tax

An outright gift to a charity is exempt from inheritance tax by virtue of s 23(1) of the Inheritance Tax Act 1984. However, it must be an outright gift so that the money or property cannot be reclaimed and the donor reserves no interest to himself unless for full consideration.

# Chapter 18

## LEGAL STRUCTURES

### 18.1 INTRODUCTION

This chapter is concerned with the legal structures by which independent schools are constituted and regulated. A significant number of schools have connections with the Crown, or with the established Church, municipal corporations, livery companies, universities, commercial interests and charities for the poor. Some schools are structured as *corporations* by Royal Charter or special Act of Parliament. Some are *limited companies* formed under the Companies Acts and others are *unincorporated associations,* or *unincorporated trusts.* Yet others are non-charitable, privately owned as trusts, companies, partnerships or sole traders.

Matters of *structure* (meaning legal entity) and *status* (meaning whether charitable or non-charitable) dictate the form and contents of the documents by which a school is constituted, regulated and governed and also the personal liabilities of those who direct or govern it. It follows that the governors of an independent school need to have some understanding of these matters if they are to govern effectively and avoid incurring individual personal liability.

### 18.2 PUBLIC CORPORATIONS

#### 18.2.1 Meaning of 'corporation'

The main differences between a public corporation and a private or public limited company are that a corporation is not regulated by the Companies Act 1985 (unless also registered under the Act) and that it exists to serve the public interest. A limited company may, if not charitable, serve purely private interests. Major companies such as utilities which are owned by shareholders, but on which the public are to some extent dependent are treated as 'quasi-corporations'.

The essential characteristics of a corporation are that it is formed by a special Act of Parliament or Royal Charter for public, although not necessarily charitable, purposes. A corporation has its own name and a corporate identity, separate from that of its members. The corporation can sue and be sued in its own right and can hold property. Its signature is normally made by means of its common seal impressed with the required formalities. A corporation has perpetual succession the effect of which is that its original member/s and their successors are one. It holds its general property beneficially, not in trust although it may accept specific property on charitable trusts. The members of a corporation enjoy limited liability unless the Act or Charter creating it provides otherwise.

## 18.2.2   Different kinds of corporation

Corporations, as distinct from limited companies, are divided into two areas.

### (a)   Ecclesiastical corporations

These exist for the furtherance of religion and for perpetuating the rights of the church. An ecclesiastical corporation is not within the definition of 'charity' in s 96(2) of the Charities Act 1993.

### (b)   Lay corporations

These are sub-divided as follows:

–   *Eleemosynary corporations*, which are constituted for the perpetual distribution of free alms and bounty of the founder to such persons as he has directed. They are generally hospitals or colleges. 'Hospital', in this sense, has its original meaning of a charitable institution for reception and education of the needy young (and also the old and destitute). They include certain corporate schools and they hold their corporate property upon charitable trusts. The word 'eleemosynary' comes from the Greek *eleos* meaning 'pity' and eleemosyne meaning 'alms'.

–   *Civil corporations* which exist for temporal purposes and include the Sovereign herself, certain ministers of the Crown, local government authorities, public bodies exercising administrative or advisory functions or controlling public industries and services (many having been privatised by the 1990s), and livery companies and institutions for the advancement of arts, science, professional and trade associations and other purposes.

## 18.2.3   Corporations sole and aggregate

A *corporation sole* is the incorporation of an individual office, such as a bishop or vicar. Other examples are the Sovereign, certain ministers of the Crown, government officers by statute and the Public Trustee. The colleges of Winchester and Eton are structured as corporations sole. The person who holds office is a body politic, having perpetual succession. He also has double capacity both as a corporation and as an individual. He does not require a seal but has powers to use a seal.

A *corporation aggregate* is a collection of individuals (which can include another corporation or company) united into one body, having perpetual succession under an artificial form. A corporation aggregate has no individual capacity but only its capacity as a corporation. It is separate from the members of which it is composed. Most corporations are aggregate rather than sole.

## 18.2.4   Establishing a corporation

There are only three methods in English law for the incorporation of a body of persons so as to form a legal entity separate from its individual members.

## (a)  Royal Charter

A Royal Charter is the exercise of the Royal prerogative of the Sovereign. A number of independent schools including Winchester, Eton and, more recently, Radley and The Cheltenham Ladies College, among others, are incorporated by Royal Charter. Edward VI (1547–1553) granted more Royal Charters to schools than any other Sovereign. A number of them use the Tudor Royal Arms as their badge. Most such use has not been formally authorised by the College of Arms but is not usually prohibited. Use of the 'full achievement' is, however, regarded as 'over the top'.

## (b)  Statute

A number of schools are corporations, constituted by special Act of Parliament such as that which incorporated Epsom College, among many others.

## (c)  Companies Acts

Many schools which decided in the nineteenth century or later to adopt the structure of a limited company would not, at the time, have satisfied the criteria for a special Act of Parliament. They, instead, used the mechanisms provided by the Companies Act 1862, which introduced companies limited by guarantee, or subsequent companies legislation, the most recent substantive Act being the Companies Act 1985. To the extent that the objects of these schools are exclusively charitable, their purposes are public and they have charitable status. However, their constitution and regulatory framework differs from that of a corporation in a number of respects, which are considered below.

## 18.2.5   Part VII of the Charities Act 1993

Sections 50–62 of the Charities Act 1993 now make it possible for the trustees of an unincorporated charitable school (and other charities) to apply to the Charity Commissioners under s 50 for a 'Certificate of Incorporation of the Trustees as a body corporate'. A certificate does not, however, confer limited liability on the trustees or the governors of the school. It merely enables them to sue and be sued in their corporate name and to hold property. This structure is considered in more detail under the heading 'Incorporation of the Trustees' at **18.3** below.

## 18.2.6   Schools established by Royal Charter

### (a)  Royal Charters generally

The expression 'Royal Charter of incorporation' means any grant by virtue of the Royal Prerogative, whether the instrument of grant is called a grant, a warrant or a charter. Schools established by Royal Charter usually existed as charities under another legal structure, for example, as an unincorporated association, which then petitioned for a Royal Charter. As noted above, a Royal Charter is the exercise of the Royal Prerogative of the Sovereign. A Royal Charter prescribes the objects, powers and constitution of the organisation to which it is granted. So complete is its corporate autonomy that the ultra vires rule does not affect its members under the Charter, although in their capacity as charity trustees, they are bound by it at risk of personal liability in default.

In modern times, incorporation by Royal Charter has generally been confined to professional, charitable, scientific, educational or learned non-profit-making institutions or societies. There have also been occasional grants to livery companies. It is most unlikely nowadays that a concern trading for profit would become incorporated in this way.

An applicant for a Royal Charter must prepare a petition, accompanied by a copy of the draft charter which is sent to the Privy Council Office. The Privy Council determines whether or not to make a recommendation to Her Majesty in Council. The prospects for a successful petition would not normally be strong unless there is a clear public interest to be served, the organisation has been of national standing for a number of years, it is and will remain financially sound, its objects are suitable for recognition by Royal Charter (ie, they serve the public interest), the organisation is fully representative of the interests it purports to serve, and it can be said to be pre-eminent in its own field.

### (b)    Charter of incorporation

The charter of incorporation responds to the petition and is given under letters patent (so called because the document was traditionally written on open sheets of parchment. A patent is an exclusive right or privilege). The charter recites words to the effect: 'We, having taken the said petition into Our Royal Consideration, have been pleased, by virtue of Our Prerogative Royal and of Our especial grace, certain knowledge and mere motion, to grant and declare . . . for Us, Our Heirs and Successors . . . as follows . . .'.

The charter will then provide to the effect that the members of the petitioning organisation shall become members of the 'body corporate hereby constituted', which shall 'forever hereafter be one body corporate and politic by the name of [XYZ] and by the same name shall continue to have perpetual succession and a common seal .. and by the same name shall and may sue and be sued in all courts . . . and shall have power to do all other matters and things incidental or appertaining to a body corporate'.

The charter will set out the powers of the corporation and will normally provide that there shall be a Patron, a President and Vice-Presidents. The affairs of the corporation shall be controlled by a council constituted in accordance with the byelaws (or 'wholesome statutes and ordinances') set out in the Schedule to the charter. There may be different classes of corporate and non-corporate members of the corporation as the byelaws shall prescribe. The charter will normally provide also that the byelaws may be altered by a resolution of two-thirds of the members present provided that alterations which are contrary to the purposes of the charter would require a certificate from the Privy Council.

### (c)    Alterations to the charter

Once a corporation has been created by charter, the charter itself can only be amended or altered by the grant of a Supplemental Charter or by Order in Council, if the original charter allows for that. An eleemosynary corporation, established by charter from the Crown (as distinct from one established by special Act of Parliament) is subject to no further control by the Crown other than that reserved to it by the charter.

The Charity Commissioners may not make a Scheme inconsistent with a charter although they may probably make a Scheme to regulate matters not provided for in the charter.

### 18.2.7 Livery companies

A number of livery companies, most notably the Mercers, Merchant Taylors and Haberdashers, but a number of others also, established famous schools, among them St Paul's and St Paul's Girls (Mercers), and others such as Merchant Taylors' and Haberdashers', carrying the name of their livery companies; and also Colfe's (Leathersellers).

Livery companies are of themselves non-charitable. Their origins were in mediaeval fraternities which were religious and social in nature, and craft guilds which were concerned with trade regulation and monopoly. In 1884, there were said to be 12 great City livery companies and another 62 minor companies. In general, they began as voluntary associations, but became recognised as City companies and were later incorporated by Royal Charter. Some were not incorporated until modern times.

The first charters of incorporation were granted by Edward III (1327–1377) and Richard II (1377–1399) and contained wide powers to control the trade of the company and set the limits of its jurisdiction within so many miles of the City of London. New livery companies can be created at any time, but a company seeking a grant of livery should, except in very special circumstances, be a City company of at least five years' standing. In general, a livery company has three grades of members: freemen, liverymen and assistants, the latter being members of the court or governing body.

An educational charity established by a livery company will often be an unincorporated trust whose trustees are charity trustees. An example is Haberdashers' Aske's, founded by the livery company in 1690 with a legacy from Robert Aske.

### 18.2.8 Schools established by special Act of Parliament

Many of the proprietary schools founded from 1830 onwards were originally the property of a body of shareholders, but later transformed into charitable institutions. A number of these were later constituted under special Acts of Parliament giving them the legal structure of a corporation aggregate, classed as eleemosynary. A corporation established by special Act is regulated by statutes which are the equivalent of byelaws under a Royal Charter. The Sovereign is constituted by law the visitor of all civil corporations, including schools incorporated by special Act.

The general rule is that a civil corporation holds its property beneficially and not subject to trust. However, a corporation such as a school that accepts and holds property, not for its own corporate purposes, but upon special charitable trusts connected with those purposes is subject to the jurisdiction of the court and of the Charity Commissioners. Insofar as their property is applied for the advancement of education or another charitable purpose, the school enjoys the fiscal relief granted to charity.

### 18.2.9   Schools incorporated under the Companies Acts

#### (a)   Separate personality

Companies limited by guarantee have become a common legal structure for charities of all kinds since they were first permitted under the Companies Act 1862. A large number of preparatory schools are structured in this way, as are an increasing number of independent secondary and all-age charitable schools. A privately owned school is more likely to be structured as a company limited by shares, or as a sole trader or partnership, but some are private trusts.

A limited company is, like a corporation, a legal person in its own right. It is said to have its own legal personality, separate from that of its individual members and directors. It makes its own contracts and is therefore the employer of its staff. It can commit torts and be vicariously liable for the torts of its employees. It can commit criminal offences under common law and by non-compliance with statute.

However, a company cannot shield directors from personal liability for certain contracts, torts and crimes where the common law and statute so provide. A well-known instance of this was the prosecution that followed the Lyme Bay Canoeing Disaster in 1993 when a company, OLL Limited (The St Alban's Centre), became the first company in English legal history to be convicted of corporate manslaughter (death resulting from gross negligence) and the company was fined £60,000. Its director, Peter Kite, also became the first director of a company (in that capacity) to be given an immediate custodial sentence for manslaughter.

#### (b)   Companies limited by guarantee

Commercial companies will normally be limited by shares as a means of regulating voting rights and the distribution of profits. However, charitable companies do not make distributable profit and are expected to use the structure of a company limited by guarantee. A guarantee company is formed under s 2(4) of the Companies Act 1985. Its memorandum of association states that the liability of its members is limited to such amount as the members may respectively undertake to contribute to the assets of the company in the event of its being wound up. The sum is typically £10 per member.

The memorandum and articles should be in the form set out in Table C or Table D of the Companies Regulations 1995. In practice, however, the form and content can vary widely to take account of individual circumstances. There is no provision for a company limited by guarantee that a model set of articles will apply unless excluded.

#### (c)   Omitting 'Limited' from the name

Section 30 of the Companies Act 1985 allows the word 'limited' to be omitted from the company's name if (inter alia) the objects are charitable, if its surplus must be applied in promoting its objects and if its assets on a winding-up would be transferred to another body with similar objects. The exemption can be obtained by filing a statutory declaration in Form 30(5)(a). A charitable company which does not have the word 'charity' or 'charitable' in its name must state the fact that the company is a charity in legible characters in all its business documents, including cheques, orders for money or goods, conveyances of land, invoices and receipts.

A charitable company must also comply with s 349(1) of the Companies Act 1985 and s 67 of the Charities Act 1993 and publish its name on the same documents (but not conveyances of land) even if it is exempted from using the word 'limited'. A failure to comply with these provisions is a criminal offence under ss 349(2)–(4) of the 1985 Act and s 68(3) of the 1993 Act.

### (d) Members and directors

It is common for a limited company that incorporates a school to have a small number of members/guarantors, each of whom is also a director, but the Charity Commissioners are always concerned to ensure that there is real and substantial accountability.

Persons acting in the capacity of a member have limited powers and can only exercise those powers in general meeting. The statutory powers of a member, which cannot be taken away from them include the power under s 303 of the Companies Act 1985 to dismiss directors. There is also power to petition for a compulsory liquidation. Power reverts to members if, for some reason, the directors are unable or unwilling to exercise their powers of management, or if no board of directors exists or the board cannot act because its meetings are inquorate.

The rights of the members/guarantors are, in most respects, set out in the articles of association. Members are entitled to have an annual general meeting and the articles would normally provide, at the very least, that they are entitled to consider the accounts and balance sheet and reports, and that they may elect the directors, appoint auditors and fix their remuneration and pass special resolutions of which proper notice has been given.

As noted earlier, persons acting as directors of a school company are often the same individuals as those who are the members, but the function of directors is quite different from that of members. In the case of a school, directors are normally referred to as 'governors' or 'trustees'. They are responsible for the running of the school and will usually be charity trustees within the meaning of s 97(1) of the Charities Act 1993. The business and procedures will be regulated by the articles of association.

The company, rather than the directors or members, will be the employer of the head, bursar and all the staff. It is the company rather than the directors or members who will be the contracting party with parents, the landlord, the bank, professional advisers and other suppliers. On occasions, individual director/governors may be asked by the school's bank to give a personal guarantee in respect of borrowings. Professional advice would normally be against doing so.

### 18.2.10 Friendly societies and industrial and provident societies

A charitable mutual assurance association which restricts its members to those who are poor may apply under the Friendly Societies Act 1992 for registration as a friendly society. A registered friendly society has corporate status and can hold property. This structure is not appropriate for a charitable school.

A charity which is established for the purpose of carrying on an industry, trade or business intended to be conducted for the benefit of the community may adopt the legal structure of an industrial and provident society (IPS) under the Industrial and Provident Societies Act 1965.

Both kinds of society are listed at Sch 2 of the Charities Act 1993 as exempt charities and are therefore outside the scope of the Act and the jurisdiction of the Charity Commissioners. It has been suggested that an industrial and provident society might be an appropriate structure for a new charitable school or one that is unincorporated and established but seeks limited liability.

Although a charitable school is to be regarded as a 'business' for these purposes, it is submitted, at first sight, that an IPS is unlikely to be an appropriate structure for the following reasons:

– The control of the society is vested in the members equally and the principle of one vote per member would apply. Unless the school were to become a co-operative of parents and pupils, membership would have to be restricted to governors. However, the business of the society has to be conducted for the mutual benefit of the members which suggests a requirement of parents and pupils being members in addition to governors. Furthermore, there must be no artificial restriction of membership that offends the co-operative principle.

– There is a requirement that special reasons are shown why the society should be registered under the Act rather than as a company under the Companies Act 1985.

Since 1996, the Charity Law Association has been in discussions with the Charity Commission with a view to finding a structure that provides limited liability for the trustees in relation to third-party transactions, but is simpler than the current memorandum and articles of association of a company. The result may therefore be something closer to an industrial and provident society.

## 18.3   INCORPORATION OF THE TRUSTEES

It is possible for the trustees of an unincorporated school to apply to the Commissioners under s 50 of the Charities Act 1993 for a 'certificate of incorporation of the trustees as a body corporate'. A certificate does not, however, confer limited liability on the trustees or governors of a school. It merely enables them to sue and be sued in their corporate name and hold property. Gifts made to the charity before incorporation which have not actually taken effect, and gifts made subsequently will take effect as if they had been made in favour of the incorporated body.

Section 54 of the Charities Act 1993 emphasises the position on liability as follows:

'After a certificate of incorporation has been granted under this Part of the Act all trustees of the charity, notwithstanding their incorporation, shall be chargeable for such property as shall come in to their hands, and shall be answerable and accountable for their own acts, receipts, neglects and defaults, and for the due administration of the charity and its property, and in the same manner and to the same extent as if no such incorporation had been effected.'

The certificate procedure also eliminates a number of statutory requirements that apply to limited companies over the publication of their name, registered office and place of registration. The procedure is open to schools that are prevented from transferring their undertaking to a company limited by guarantee because they have permanent endowment. However, in terms of the protection of governors from personal liability, this procedure is very much second-best.

The Charity Commission is unwilling to incorporate trustees without being satisfied of the need. If a charity vests property in the Official Custodian and either invests in common investment funds, where the holding is in the name of the charity or in the name of a nominee company, the Charity Commission will generally reject an application for incorporation. It is likely that ss 50–62 of the Act will be as little used as the Charitable Trustees Incorporation Act 1872, which was mainly for religious charities reluctant to vest property in the Official Custodian.

Incorporation of the trustees under these provisions is a hybrid designed for administrative efficiency. As a classification it has more in common with unincorporated charitable schools than with full incorporation.

## 18.4  CORPORATE TRUSTEE

'Trust corporation' is defined at s 117 (xxx) of the Settled Land Act 1925 and in other parts of the 1925 property legislation as:

'the Public Trustee or a corporation either appointed by the court [or the Charity Commissioners] in any particular case to be a trustee or entitled by rules made under s 4(3) Public Trustee Act 1906 to act as a custodian trustee.'

A corporate trustee is, of its nature, non-charitable, because it does not meet the three conditions for recognition of a charity, discussed in Chapter 17. However, when a corporate trustee is appointed by the Charity Commissioners, the effect under s 35 of the Charities Act 1993 is to confer the status of a trust corporation on the corporate trustee.

A corporate trustee may be appointed for a charity:

– pursuant to powers in the charity's governing instrument; or

– by an Order or Scheme of the Charity Commission.

Following appointment, it is the corporate trustee, rather than individuals, in whom the land or investments of the charity will be vested. The corporate trustee of a charitable school is likely to have the governors as its directors. The corporate trustee has limited liability and will make contracts and will sue and be sued in its own name.

The Charity Commissioners seem to have made more use of this structure than of a certificate of incorporation of the trustees as a body corporate under s 50 of the

Charities Act 1993, discussed in the last section. It provides a device that can afford limited liability to the governors of a school whose property is permanently endowed.

None the less, it is an artificial and unwieldy structure for an independent school. It results in over complex documents namely:

– the memorandum and association of the non-charitable corporate trustee;

– a separate charitable scheme detailing the object and the powers and duties of the corporate trustee;

– separate articles of government of the school.

In effect, the governors 'disappear' into the corporate trustee and the scheme document makes scant reference to the governors or the school. That is unsatisfactory, since the governors of a charitable school are the visible managers of the assets and also the people to whom and by whom accountability is delivered.

Moreover, the corporate trustee becomes the contracting party yet produces accounts with a nil balance which is potentially confusing for those who deal with the school. The directors of the corporate trustee remain charity trustees within the meaning of s 97(1) of the Charities Act 1993. Their position becomes unnecessarily complicated by being subject to the regimes of a trust corporation, a company and a charity. There is an additional dimension of difficulty when considering the application of the Transfer of Undertakings (Protection of Employment) Regulations 1981 (TUPE), as amended by the 1995 regulations.

It is submitted that a better and simpler system of incorporation for a school whose property is not sufficiently affected by permanent endowment is to transfer the assets and the undertaking of the school to a charitable company limited by guarantee whose members and directors are the governors and whose documents describe the charity and the school as they are.

## 18.5   UNINCORPORATED CHARITABLE SCHOOLS

Whether a school is incorporated or unincorporated will make no difference to the personal liability of governors who act in breach of trust, or in wilful default, or who cause loss to the assets of the charity by acting beyond the powers provided to them in the governing instrument. They will be personally liable in these circumstances.

These matters apart, there are very important differences between incorporated and unincorporated status so far as individual governors are concerned. These are discussed below.

### 18.5.1   Unincorporated trusts generally

An unincorporated trust has no legal personality or entity. It exists only by its trustees and its purposes, although, as we have seen above, the trustees of an unincorporated charitable trust can now obtain a certificate of incorporation under Part VII of the Charities Act 1993 enabling them to sue and be sued and also to hold land in their corporate name.

By about the year 1500, it had become common to dedicate property on express trust for various charitable purposes, including the foundation of schools. An example from a nineteenth century case is *Attorney-General v Dean and Canons of Christ Church* (1821) Jac 474 in which property was devised to the Dean and Canons of Christ Church, Oxford, in trust to constitute and support a grammar school at Portsmouth, to appoint a master and usher, and pay them a salary.

Most charities for the advancement of education began as trusts and were recognised as charitable after the time of the Statute of Uses in 1535. However, after the Companies Act 1862, many of them preferred to adopt the structure of a company and an increasing number are now registered as companies limited by guarantee.

The duties and powers of charity trustees were considered at **17.4** and **17.5** respectively. However, the obverse is the extent to which the individual governors and trustees of an unincorporated school may be exposed to the risk of personal liability if the school has to close whether in surplus or deficit or if there is a major uninsured liability in excess of the realisable value of the charity's assets.

## 18.5.2  Personal liability

In this section, references to a trustee or governor and his (or her) potential liability mean a trustee or governor who is actively involved in controlling the assets of the charity.

It has been seen earlier that an unincorporated trust exists only by its trustees and its purposes. It has no corporate personality. All its acts and omissions are those of the trustees personally. This position carries a number of implications for those who are considering governance of an unincorporated charitable school or other trust. Some of these are now considered below.

### *(a)  Contracts made by the governors*

The contracts made by a school are, in general, contracts with employees, with parents, with a landlord, or bank or other mortgagee, with other financial institutions for the supply of equipment for catering and energy services, with a construction company, and contracts with professional advisers such as solicitors, accountants, computer and public relations consultants.

The legal position is that each serving governor of an unincorporated school is, in effect, *personally* the contracting party in each of these cases. If the school closes in surplus, the governor will be entitled to be indemnified from the assets of the charity when realised. If the school closes in deficit, however, the governor will be liable to pay or contribute to the liability of himself (or herself) and his co-trustees to satisfy all enforceable debts and other liabilities.

As employer of the head, bursar and each member of the teaching and non-teaching staff, each governor is *vicariously liable* for breaches of contract, tort and non-compliance in the workplace. Thus, in the event of an employee being guilty of direct or indirect discrimination on grounds of sex, race or disability, or being guilty of harassment or victimisation, or wrongful dismissal, and a significant uninsured award being made in the industrial tribunal or at court, that will be the personal liability of the governors if the assets of the charity are insufficient, whether or not they knew or had reason to suspect the misconduct. Whether or not they would have rights of recovery against the member of staff who incurred the liability would depend on the terms of the person's employment contract and the insurances maintained by the school. These are matters on which it is prudent for governors to take specialist legal advice.

The consequences of most contracts are uninsured.

## (b)    *Torts and insurance*

The consequences of most torts will be covered by the school's insurances against employers' liability, public liability, professional indemnity and trustee indemnity insurance. To this extent, torts are of less concern than contracts, in terms of personal liability, to a governor of an unincorporated school.

Torts are such matters as negligence, occupiers liability, breach of statutory duty, trespass to the person, interference with service and family rights, fraud, malicious prosecution, defamation, malicious falsehood, wrongful interference with goods, trespass to land, nuisance, infringement of intellectual property rights, and breaches of statutory duty.

As noted in relation to contracts, a governor will be liable (subject to indemnity from insurance and the assets of the charity, if sufficient) for unintentional torts committed by himself, his co-governors in relation to school affairs, and those committed by the school's employees during the time he was serving as a governor. The limitation date for bringing actions in tort varies between three and six years and can in some cases be longer. Governors should make certain that trustee indemnity insurance provides cover for governors who have retired.

It was held in *T v North Yorkshire County Council* (1998) *The Times*, September 10, CA, that a school authority was not vicariously liable for the acts of a deputy head who sexually assaulted a mentally handicapped pupil on a school trip. Serious sexual misconduct to a pupil was not an authorised act carried out in an unauthorised way. It was an independent act outside the course of employment.

Insurers are, in some circumstances, entitled to avoid a policy if there has been non-disclosure of a material fact or a misrepresentation. Moreover, they may be entitled to refuse payment of a claim where the nature of the risk has changed during the course of the insurance year or claims conditions have not been met. There may also be problems of under-insurance or an area of risk not covered at all or if, by an oversight, the premium has not been paid.

An insurance broker will, in many circumstances, be the agent of the governors and not the agent of the insurer. This means that a material fact stated to a broker but not passed on to insurers may, none the less, entitle insurers to avoid the policy or deny a claim. For these reasons, the utmost care is needed to see that insurance advisers are of substance, competent and efficient and also that they have the degree of specialist knowledge needed to arrange adequate and enforceable cover of risks within schools, and that they are insured in respect of their own negligent acts and omissions.

## (c) Legal compliance

Many statutes, and the regulations made pursuant to them, contain legal duties, the breach of which may have criminal or civil consequences. The Companies Act 1985 alone contains more than 200 offences and other consequences of non-compliance and there are many hundreds more under other aspects of legislation relating, for example, to charities, employment, discrimination, data protection, health and safety, registration of schools, money laundering, consumer credit, school transport, town and country planning, and construction regulations.

In practice, a school that is well managed and acts on the basis of competent professional advice is likely to find that it is already acting in compliance with those areas of the law that affect it. From time to time, however, there may be a failure of compliance and, in rare cases, a school may be prosecuted. That happened in the early 1990s in an unreported case when governors were convicted and fined for a 'bald tyre' offence in relation to the school minibus.

Prosecution of an incorporated school would normally be against the limited company alone. Only in extreme cases, analogous to the Lyme Bay Canoeing Disaster, mentioned earlier, would governors be prosecuted personally. At an unincorporated school, however, the governors and/or a member of staff are the only available target for prosecution.

## (d) Suing and being sued

An unincorporated school, unless granted a certificate of incorporation under s 50 of the Charities Act 1993, cannot sue or be sued in its corporate name. The only parties with capacity are likely to be the governors or trustees, who will be named in the proceedings. A writ issued out of the Central Office in London is a public document which is open to inspection by the media and others, and carries a risk of unwanted publicity, particularly for a governor who is a public figure.

Moreover, a judgment obtained against an unincorporated school would be a judgment against the governors personally. If a pupil brings a claim for damages for personal injuries against the governors, a year or more may elapse between the pupil obtaining judgment and damages being assessed and paid. The defence of the claim will be conducted by the school's insurers, giving the governors little control. It is quite possible, moreover, that the fact of an unsatisfied county court judgment will be registered against the names of individual governors and entered on the lists of credit reference agencies. Such, in turn, may adversely affect a governor's ability to re-mortgage his home or refinance his business. It also renders a solicitor governor subject to the requirements of s 12 of the Solicitors Act 1974 and other professionals may be similarly affected.

Governors of an incorporated school are unlikely to be affected in this way, since it is the school that would be sued and not the governors personally.

## (e) Legal and administrative procedures

On occasions, it becomes necessary for the governors of an unincorporated school to secure or enforce the rights of the school by means of a legal charge or charging order.

Then, the application for registration at HM Land Registry has to be made in the name of each individual governor, which may cause delay, loss of priority and prejudice to the security, and, therefore, to the assets, of the charity. This can be a particular problem during the summer months, when a number of the governors may be abroad on holiday. By contrast, in the case of an incorporated school, all registrations are made in the name of the company.

### (f) Aggressive creditors

Unsatisfied judgments of £750 or more against the governors of an unincorporated school can be enforced by obtaining a charging order over a governor's home, or alternatively by garnishee proceedings, or by serving a statutory demand and then petitioning for the governor's bankruptcy. For a variety of reasons it is highly unlikely that these procedures would go beyond the initial stages, but if they are threatened or commenced, they are likely to cause serious concern and anxiety to a governor.

Any school which is incorporated is not entirely free of such threats, except that action would be taken against the company and not against individual governors and there is also a risk of a winding-up petition being advertised.

### (g) Resignation and retirement

The extent to which a governor can shed his personal liabilities by resigning or retiring will depend on a number of factors. In the case of banking arrangements, which are reviewed annually, it is likely that the retiring governor will be released from his liabilities if banking facilities are renewed after the bank has received notice of the retirement.

There may be a novation of certain liabilities. Novation takes place when two contracting parties agree that a third shall replace one of them. Then there is a new contract. Novation will not normally be inferred from acts and conduct alone without some distinct request and a novation cannot be forced on a new party without his agreement.

Accordingly, it is submitted that a governor of an unincorporated school will not, by his retirement alone, be released from liabilities that arose under contracts made or current while he was in post. It is also submitted that a new governor will not be fixed by liabilities that arose before he accepted trusteeship, but he will be bound, as a trustee, to safeguard the assets of the charity and act as described in **19.5.2**.

### (h) Attracting and retaining governors

The function of governance is fundamental to the successful operation of a charitable school. A school which is incorporated, whether a corporation or a limited company, has perpetual succession. An unincorporated school has not. If governors resign, and new governors of adequate calibre cannot be attracted, an unincorporated school is unlikely to thrive and may fail in its present form.

Even a flourishing school can very easily face a reversal of fortune through no fault of management, as a result of matters such as political intervention. An example of this was the Education (Schools) Act 1997, which phased out assisted places over seven years. Other examples have been increased competition through the introduction of free sixth-form colleges and grant-maintained schools and also the effect of the so-called 'peace dividend' in the early 1990s, which resulted in a reduction in the demand for boarding places. These, together with warnings about possible fiscal measures against educational charities have caused many schools to revise their development plans and those who are unincorporated, to consider applying for a limited liability structure.

### 18.5.3 Other practical considerations

#### (a) Commercial decisions

The charity trustees of a school may be required to take decisions of strategic importance to the school involving substantial borrowings and expenditure. Examples of this include moving the location of the school or entering a contract for construction of a new building or major refurbishment, or acquiring new computer systems. The governor of an unincorporated school taking such decisions may be influenced in favour of excessive caution by the fact that a major commercial decision which goes wrong could result in financial disaster for himself and his family. A corporate structure, on the other hand, avoids inhibiting factors of this nature but does not affect the duty which applies to both kinds of governors to carry out the terms of the trust and act prudently.

#### (b) The governing instrument

Governing instruments for both structures need updating from time to time. A school, whose objects are directed at giving a classical education to children of one gender but which is now co-educational with a nursery and pre-prep, will need to ask the Charity Commissioners to write a new Scheme. Some of the older Schemes contain provisions as to the appointment and dismissal of staff, particularly the head, which, if implemented, would incur the charity a significant liability for compensation under the supervening employment legislation. Professional advice may be needed to identify the extent of the amendments necessary and, unless professional advisers are being instructed to deal with 'incorporation', the Commissioners should be asked to write a new Scheme.

### 18.5.4 Remaining unincorporated

There are some apparent advantages to a charitable school in remaining unincorporated but these are more illusory than real.

#### (a) Freedom from the Companies Acts

An unincorporated charity is not regulated by the Companies Act 1985 in relation to the duties of directors and the annual accounting formalities. In practice, however, the Act adds relatively little to the duties and responsibilities that are imposed in any event by the Charities Act 1993, regulations made pursuant to it and the Statement of Recommended Practice (SORP) of October 1995.

## *(b)* *Freedom from proceedings under the Company Directors Disqualification Act 1986*

Unincorporated trustees are outside the scope of the Act.

## *(c)* *Privacy of accounting information*

The accounts of an unincorporated charity are not available to the public from Companies House in the way that company accounts are. However, the philosophy behind the Charities Act 1992, which was largely replaced in the 1993 Act, was said to be that charities should be accountable to the public, who have put their money in the public domain.

Section 47 of the 1993 Act provides that any annual report or other document kept by the Commissioners in pursuance of s 45(6) '. . . shall be open to public inspection at all reasonable times . . .'. Section 45(6) refers to an 'annual report' containing such a report by the trustees on the activities of the charity during that year and such other information relating to the charity or to its trustees or officer as may be described by regulations made by the Secretary of State. Most educational charities have an annual income above £100,000 and are required to provide the Commissioners with a full statement of accounts which has been audited and will be available to the public.

## 18.6  UNINCORPORATED ASSOCIATIONS

The final legal structure for consideration is that of the unincorporated association, which has no legal personality and therefore no legal existence separate from its members.

In essence, an unincorporated association is a contract between the members. It is an association of persons bound together by a common purpose having identifiable rules and an identifiable membership.

This is not a common legal structure for a school which is more likely to be an unincorporated trust, a company limited by guarantee or a corporation by statute or royal charter, or else privately owned.

However, many schools have an organisation of 'friends' and/or a parents' association who undertake fund-raising activities for the benefit of the school. Such organisations that operate under a constitution, do so as unincorporated associations. Insofar as their purpose is exclusively charitable they are subject to the registration requirements of s 3 of the Charities Act 1993 if their income from all sources amounts to more than £1,000 per year, unless they are exempt or excepted by order or regulations from being registered.

Those who deal with an unincorporated association need to establish with whom they are contracting and who they would sue if necessary, that is, an individual, the officers or the committee members. Equally, the officers of an unincorporated association need to be satisfied that contracts which they enter are within the powers given to them by the constitution, if there is one, or that they have been authorised directly or indirectly by the membership. Otherwise, an individual officer may find that he has incurred personal liabilities without right of indemnity or contribution from the other members.

Separate trustees may be appointed to hold the property (if any) of an unincorporated association.

## 18.7  PROPRIETARY SCHOOLS

The proprietors of a privately owned school will be either a sole trader, two or more persons in partnership with each other, a limited company, or the trustees of a private trust.

Proprietor-owned schools are not subject to the Charities Act 1993 or the jurisdiction of the Charity Commissioners in any way, but nor do they have the privileges of charitable status, and in particular, the fiscal benefits, other than general exemption from value added tax for educational services. They are subject to the same regime as charitable schools as respects provisional and final registration of the school under Part VII of the Education Act 1996 and the regulations pursuant to that Act, in particular, the Education (Particulars of Independent Schools) Regulations 1997.

Sole traders and partners will be personally liable in respect of contracts, torts and non-compliance in exactly the same way as the governors of a charitable school that is unincorporated. A privately owned school that is incorporated will have for its directors the same protections as the governors of a charitable school that is incorporated. The trustees of a private trust will have the powers, duties and liabilities of a private trustee as described in Chapter 17.

A proprietor-owned school will not be able to take advantage of s 30 of the Companies Act 1985, which allows omission of the word 'limited' from its name, because it is very unlikely that the requirements of s 30 can be complied with in the case of a privately owned school. However, the school can trade by means of a business name which does not include the word 'limited', provided there is compliance with ss 348–351 of the Companies Act 1985 in the case of a limited company and/or s 4 of the Business Names Act 1985 in relation to an individual, partnership and company.

# Chapter 19

## THE GOVERNING BODY

### 19.1  INTRODUCTION

This chapter is about governors of independent schools and their role as charity trustees and managers of the charitable assets. As part-time, unpaid, non-executives, they must, at risk of personal liability in default, ensure that they carry out the terms of the trust and do not act in excess of the powers given by the trust instrument or by statute.

Governors receive little enough in the way of appreciation or thanks. They may come in for criticism from the head and bursar and also from parents at times of change or crisis. Often they are accused of being 'out of touch' or of not knowing the school or the staff well enough or failing to turn up at show-piece events and governors' meetings. Much of this criticism shows a misunderstanding of their role and contribution.

The governing body is an essential structure at a charitable school. The head is accountable to the governing body. Governors in turn are accountable in a number of ways that are discussed below. Every school that is doing well owes a significant part of its success to the governing body.

### 19.2  CLASSES OF GOVERNOR

A person may become the governor of an independent charitable school in, broadly, one of five ways: as a life governor, an ex-officio governor, a representative governor, a nominated governor, or a co-opted governor.

#### 19.2.1  Life governors

Some schools founded after about 1830 awarded governorship to those who contributed a substantial sum of capital to the school: in those days, anything from £10–£20, worth the equivalent today of £5,000–£10,000. Even now, it is not unusual to encounter a scheme based on a trust deed of that time which provides for the trust to be carried on under the 'general superintendence' of a governing body, called 'governors' or 'life governors', consisting broadly of:

– anyone, whether connected with the school or not, who contributed £20 or more to the school's capital fund;

– former pupils contributing £10;

– ministers of certain churches contributing £10;

- former pupils who had taken a degree at a British university – no financial contribution required;

- individuals nominated by certain churches – no financial contribution required;

- representative educationalists – no financial contribution required.

Commonly, the deed provided that this body of governors or life governors would appoint an executive council of between 15 and 30 governors called 'council members' who would manage the trust. Over the following 150 years, some of these large governing bodies have grown to as many as 300 or 400 members, of whom perhaps only 20 or 30 turn up to the annual general meeting. Often these governing bodies are benign, but in some instances they form factions which seek to influence or 'second-guess' the business of the executive council. Their one-off financial contribution of £10 or £20 is no longer of consequence to the development of the school and, although these bodies sometimes include individuals who make a real contribution in other ways, they are not 'governors' in the modern sense. Such power as they have is exercised at the annual general meeting where their business, as prescribed by the scheme, is normally:

- to choose a chairman for the meeting;

- to elect from a nominated list new members of the executive council to replace those retiring;

- to elect additional life governors, a president, a treasurer, an auditor and stock trustees when necessary;

- to consider the annual report of the council and the balance sheet of the trust for the preceding year;

- to consider any proposals (of which notice has been given) affecting the management of the trust.

Normally, the meeting has no real *locus standi* to criticise the executive council or to remove council members before their normal rotation date or, indeed, to pass a vote of censure or demand further accountability. Nor is it easy to see who such a meeting genuinely represents or what modern purpose it has if it is attended by only 10% of the membership, and if those who attend do not serve on the executive council and have no other current knowledge of the school or connection with the main part of the school community.

For these reasons, a degree of consultation has taken place in recent years in some schools and with the Charity Commission with a view to rationalising and modernising governing bodies of this kind, in some cases to dissolve and in other cases to reduce their size.

## 19.2.2   Ex-officio governors

'*Ex officio*' means appointed by virtue of office. Thus, the holder of the office is appointed directly or imposed on the governing body. The appointment is perpetual. Common appointments ex officio are the Lord Lieutenant of the County, and the Bishop or the Dean who presides over the chapter of a cathedral or a collegiate church.

By virtue of their office, ex-officio governors do not rotate other than through death or loss of office. An ex officio governor is entitled to a place on the governing body, but cannot be compelled to take it up. If he (or she) does so, he assumes all the legal responsibilities of a governor, or of a director in the case of a school incorporated as a company limited by guarantee.

### 19.2.3   Representative governors

A representative governor is one whose appointment is required under the scheme and again is imposed on the governing body to represent an external interest such as that of a church or a political, judicial or academic interest.

Older schemes do not provide for an election or an approval mechanism. The appointment will be made direct by the Master of an Oxford College or as the case may be.

There is an alternative, but probably incorrect, meaning of 'representative'. In some schemes there is provision for a governor who has been elected by the governing body to 'represent' a section of interest, such as the staff. In that case, the representative is imposed on the staff rather than on the governing body, but in practice the function is more one of liaison than representation, particularly if the staff have not been consulted.

Many schools report that it is becoming more difficult to persuade representative bodies to make an appointment at all and, moreover, that representative governors have sometimes accepted their appointment reluctantly and do not play a full part in the governance of the school. For these reasons, there is a trend, when schemes are being revised, to reduce the number of representative governors, after consultation.

Representative governors are commonly appointed for a period of three to seven years and are sometimes, but not always, re-eligible.

### 19.2.4   Nominative governors

A nominative, or nominated, governor is also one whose appointment is required under the scheme and who is imposed on the governing body normally, but not always, to represent certain internal interests of the school, such as a body of life governors, the school association of former pupils, the staff or the parents and friends.

Unlike the normal arrangement with representative governors, there may be an election mechanism for nominative governors. Some schemes provide that any number of governors may be nominated and there will then be an election. More modern schemes provide that the governors may decide not to approve a nomination and shall, in that case, request further names, of whom one shall be appointed. Other schemes again provide that nominations are made by the executive council for the approval of the nominating body.

Across the various kinds of scheme, the expressions 'nominative' and 'representative' are sometimes used interchangeably but, for the reasons given above relating both to interests and mechanisms of appointment, it is probably better to regard these appointments as serving quite distinct purposes.

As with representative governors, schools increasingly report difficulties in persuading nominating bodies to nominate or nominated governors to play a full part in governance. Therefore, upon scheme revision and following consultation, it is becoming usual to reduce the number of outside nominating bodies.

Nominative governors are commonly appointed for a period of three to five years and are not necessarily re-eligible.

Nominative governors remain a useful way of maintaining, and even improving, the accountability of a governing council in schools that are considering a reduction in the size of the governing body or dissolving or repositioning the life governors.

### 19.2.5   Co-optative governors

Co-opted, or 'co-optative' or 'elected', governors are normally elected by a majority of the executive council. Often the co-opted governors will be in the majority and they will provide the specific skills and gender balance that the governing body requires. Usually, they will be co-opted because of their ability to make a special contribution and give time to the affairs of the school. Usually, co-opted governors will rotate every three or five years and be re-eligible subject to an overall limit and an age limit of 70. This is to encourage the influx of new people and fresh ideas.

## 19.3   GOVERNANCE STRUCTURES

There are broadly four models of governance, with a number of variations for each model.

### 19.3.1   Three-tier

The three-tier system is the model used for an unincorporated school if there are life governors. It consists of:

–   A body of governors that is potentially unlimited in size and may have 300 to 400 members of whom usually only about 10% are active. This kind of body is more akin to the members of a company limited by guarantee – but with fewer powers – and it has no real governance function.

–   An executive council of between 15 and 30 members who are the governors and charity trustees within the meaning of s 97(1) of the Charities Act 1993. Section 97(1) defines charity trustees as 'the persons having the general control and management of the administration of a charity'.

–   Five to 15 stock trustees, who hold the land and investments but who are not charity trustees within the meaning of s 97(1) because they are directed under the scheme to act in all respects in accordance with the instructions of the executive council. Often, the scheme or a subsequent order of the Commissioners, has required the stock trustees to vest the charity's land in the Official Custodian.

A three-tier system tends to appear in large schools that are unincorporated and were founded from about 1830 onwards. It is also common in schools that are incorporated under Royal Charter or by special Act of Parliament. As indicated earlier, the three-tier structure can be faction-prone and costly to administer. It is sometimes regarded as too cumbersome for the needs of modern governance, where the trends, subject to safeguards, are towards slimming down to the smallest effective unit. A number of schools, however, report that the structure continues to work satisfactorily because the life governors (or their equivalent) leave the entire running of the school to a small executive council.

## 19.3.2 Two-tier

The two-tier system, common in religious foundations, normally consists of:

–  A body of trustees who hold the land and investments and retain many of the decision-making powers in relation to the school. They are the charity trustees within the meaning of s 97(1) of the Act.

–  A body of administrative governors, who are nominally the governors of the school, but the extent of whose powers is often uncertain. In particular, it is far from clear whether they are charity trustees.

This model is also common in unincorporated schools set up under trust deeds by municipal charities and livery companies, although there are a number of variations of the model in each case.

For example, some religious foundations consist of a community, one part of which is composed of those members who are 'finally professed'. They are referred to as the Chapter. The head of the community is the Abbot, Dean, Prior or Prioress who is appointed by the Chapter. The trust deed gives the trustees power to appoint administrative trustees who act as a board of governors comprising ex-officio governors, chapter governors, co-opted governors and external governors (who are neither a chapter governor nor a co-opted governor).

This degree of complexity is designed to obtain the best of both worlds, the spiritual and temporal, but it leaves open to doubt who is the proper body to sue or be sued, who are the charity trustees and who may exercise the various powers of a charity trustee. A structure of this nature creates an overlap between charity law and the even more arcane area of ecclesiastical law. It seems, although the matter is not free from doubt, that in a number of these communities the appropriate party to sue and be sued is the head of the community, who, in most cases, would be subject to a vow of poverty!

A variation of the two-tier model for religious communities is the Dean and Chapter, in which the governing instrument may provide that the Dean will be chairman and will nominate some members of the Chapter. They elect the other governors.

There is some evidence of a trend for change among religious institutions in the two-tier model. No longer is the school realistically to be seen as a training ground for novices entering the community and religious schools have become more secular, many of them having appointed lay heads and staff during the last decade. There has been greater recognition of the need for religious communities to let go of their schools.

Sometimes, this has been done by means of a leasehold arrangement, under which the school's land and buildings have been leased to a company limited by guarantee, the leases being subject to break clauses and a forfeiture clause in the event of the school closing or ceasing to be charitable. That kind of arrangement has sometimes proved unsatisfactory because of the inherent insecurity caused by break clauses. Building development is inhibited, because new buildings will, in due course, revert to the landlord. Fund raising by appeals is difficult when no assurance can be given about the future of the school. It may be best to regard the leasehold arrangement as an interim measure and work towards releasing the school altogether, with its assets, if an appropriate consideration can be agreed.

The need for 'livery company' schools to be released in this way is less apparent at present, although, in some cases, it may exist. A conflict of interests can arise if appointees of the livery company form a majority of the governors and the livery company also owns the site.

The two-tier structure also applies to a number of schools that are incorporated as companies limited by guarantee which have a separate membership from the directors, who are the board of governors and charity trustees. The 'separate membership' model can tend to work in the same way as a body of life governors, sometimes benign, but on occasions faction-prone.

### 19.3.3   Single-tier: large governing body

The third model is common in unincorporated schools which may have a governing body of between 15 and 30 members, being a mixture of ex-officio, representative or nominated and co-opted. This model is seen in schools which were originally founded under Royal Charter in the sixteenth century but whose charter was 'repealed and abrogated' and their corporation dissolved pursuant to the Endowed Schools Acts 1869–1873. These schools were reconstituted as unincorporated trusts or else were allowed to remain corporate, but without limited liability, under a Scheme of the Endowed Schools Commission.

The schemes of many of these schools are long overdue for modernisation, not least to ensure that the governors have sufficient powers to run a school in the next millennium. There is also a discernible trend towards slimming down the governing body by reduction in numbers and also by reconstituting the system of nominations to make it more relevant to modern needs. At the same time, governors are expressing greater interest in becoming incorporated so that the school can more easily be run under modern systems of management, and also to afford greater protection to governors against the risk of personal liability in contract, tort and legal compliance and particularly in the event of sudden closure.

### 19.3.4   Single-tier: small governing body

This model, with a governing body of usually between eight and 15 members, is the norm for an incorporated school or the result of a recent merger that will lead to incorporation. It is common in preparatory schools of which an IAPS Bursars survey in 1992 estimated that about 80% were incorporated – far more than any other category of independent school.

This size of governing body is consistent with the '*all members are directors*' model of company. Questions can arise about accountability and whether so small a governing body will become a self-perpetuating oligarchy. However, provided there is sufficient rotation of governors and, in appropriate cases, provision for nomination, there will be sufficient accountability in the day-to-day dealings with staff and parents and also in the audit process and the annual formalities with the Charity Commissioners and Companies House. This model is potentially the most efficient of all.

## 19.4   CHAIRMAN AND OFFICERS

### 19.4.1   Chairman

A surprising feature of many charitable schemes is that the chairman is an annual appointment, although re-eligible. This is not the case with the 'Dean and Chapter' model in which the Dean is likely to be chairman *ex officio*. Nor will it be the case under a modern set of memorandum and articles for an incorporated school.

The role of chairman is crucial in a number of ways. First, a chairman of governors may at the best of times find that he (or she) spends at least one day a week during term time on school business. At times of crisis, the chairmanship can become a full-time job for a while, always undertaken voluntarily and without payment, but with expenses reimbursed.

Secondly, in a successful school there will need to be close co-operation between the chairman and the head and bursar. If the relationships are successful, it would be unsatisfactory for the chairmanship to rotate every year.

Thirdly, and very important, the chairman must fulfil a leadership role. Leadership implies sharing the head's plan and vision, which will often span three to five years. That, in turn, will need budgetary and other support. Annual rotation of the chairmanship would inevitably cause uncertainty and perhaps damage continuity of development.

The concept of annual rotation can imply an element of 'Buggins's turn' if that is the way things happen in practice. There is also the question of continuity so far as staff and parents are concerned. It is suggested here that the chairman should be appointed for four years and be re-eligible for a further four years subject to an age limit of 70 or, in exceptional cases, 75. The scheme normally provides that the chairman shall have a second and casting vote in meetings.

### 19.4.2   Officers

It is often convenient to appoint one or two vice-chairmen to preside over meetings in the temporary absence of the chairman and to take over should the chairman die, retire or resign suddenly.

The Treasurer, if such an office exists, will often be the chairman of the finance committee. Sometimes, there will be a separate Treasurer as an additional check on the activities of the finance committee. How well that works in practice will depend on the personalities. Under modern schemes of management, the office of Treasurer tends to disappear.

The Secretary will be the company secretary of an incorporated school. Often, that person will be the bursar. In an unincorporated school, the Secretary is normally referred to as the Clerk to the Governors who is likely to be the bursar or a partner in the firm of solicitors which normally advises the school.

Usually, there are no other officers.

## 19.5   NEW GOVERNORS

### 19.5.1   Prior to appointment

A person who has indicated willingness to serve as a governor should, prior to appointment, be provided with information about the school, the obligations of a trustee and a governor and what, specifically will be expected of him (or her). It is suggested here that the information should include:

–   *The school* – a profile of the school giving a short account of its history, structure, staff roll, pupil roll and a copy of the school calendar, a copy of the school's year book or hand book and its entry in the Independent Schools Year Book, the prospectus and parent contract documents.

–   *Legal structure* – an account of the legal structure and charitable status of the school, with profiles of the governors and executives and a diagram showing the management structure, a copy of the governing instrument, an explanation of whether or not the liability of governors is limited and in what respects, and the insurances, including trustee indemnity insurance.

–   *Financial information* – a copy of the last financial statements and a summary of the current financial position of the school.

–   *Progress and plans* – a copy of the last Inspection Report and a summary of the business, development and marketing plans.

–   *Duties of charity trustees* – a copy of the Charity Commissioners' booklet *Responsibilities of Charity Trustees*, and references to or extracts from other published texts and the Governing Bodies Association's *Guidelines for Governors*.

–   *Executive summary* – if practicable, a two-page summary of factual information from this list and a statement of the intended role of the governor and the likely commitment of time required, setting out the objective and aim of the school and a description of its ethos and culture.

Documents of this nature should be supplied and received subject to the strictest confidence and should be returned uncopied if the appointment is not accepted. A person who is considering becoming a governor should be given an opportunity to meet the school solicitor and/or accountant in order to discuss any concerns arising from the documents. Subject to the powers in the governing instrument and advice from the Commissioners, if necessary, it is submitted that the charity is entitled to bear the reasonable costs of professional advice for a person who is asked to become a governor.

## 19.5.2 On appointment

A new governor who becomes a charity trustee is under a legal duty to acquaint himself or herself with the terms of the trust, the contents of any documents handed to him (or her) as trustee and the assets of the trust. He (or she) must take possession of the trust property and ensure that it has been vested in accordance with the trust deed. He must consider the investments and, if necessary, he must insist that legal proceedings are instituted to safeguard or recover trust property. It is prudent also to enquire whether there have been past breaches of trust for which he might be jointly liable.

On a practical level, a new governor should try to find out as much as possible about the school and the way in which it is run. One way of doing this is to spend a whole day there or different parts of several days, by arrangement, taking meals with the staff and pupils and listening to the current issues and picking up nuances of culture.

Some governing bodies organise themselves into special focus groups covering the whole school, the task of each group being to understand the way things work in that area. The governing body will thus, collectively, gain first-hand knowledge of the whole school and be better able to understand proposals, recommendations and the traditions and terminology of the school.

## 19.6 COMPOSITION OF GOVERNING BODY

In most cases, the governors will be charity trustees within the meaning of s 97(1) of the Charities Act 1993. Whether or not incorporated, they accept personal liability in the event of a breach of trust or other wilful default or in the event of loss being caused to the charity by acting beyond the powers given to them in the governing instrument.

If unincorporated, they also accept that they personally will sue and be sued and will hold the land and investments (unless the land is held by the Official Custodian or stock trustees). They will also be personally liable and vicariously liable (subject to indemnity from the assets of the charity, if sufficient) for all contracts, torts and offences of non-compliance by the governors and in their name. Moreover, a charity trustee may not benefit or have a personal or other financial interest in the affairs of the trust beyond that permitted by the scheme.

All of these factors may have a bearing on the composition of the governing body.

### 19.6.1 Requirements of scheme

The governing instrument will prescribe the various classes of governor, for example ex-officio, representative, nominative, co-optative and life governor. If those requirements cannot be met, the charity trustees must apply to the Commissioners for a new scheme.

## 19.6.2  The head

It used to be fairly common for the proprietor and head, and sometimes his (or her) spouse, of a private school which then opted for charitable status to be appointed a governor subject to a requirement that he (or she) took no part in any discussion or decision relating to any matter in which they had a personal interest. A few larger schools adopted this practice also, but it is submitted that the practice is inherently unsound.

The role of governors is to protect and manage the assets and to set or ratify policies. The role of the head is to run the school and account to the governors – two quite different roles.

The head needs to be free to manage the school within the governors' constraints of plan, policy and budget. The head should know and understand the school's financial position, but his advice to the governors should not be coloured by considerations of personal liability that fall outside his role as manager, head and leader.

In practice, many governing instruments provide – and should provide – that the head has a right to be present at meetings of the governors, subject to being asked to withdraw in certain circumstances. The head's role, when present, is to advise but not to vote.

## 19.6.3  The bursar

The bursar is also an employee of the governors (or of the corporate entity) and for reasons similar to those given for the head, the bursar should not be appointed a governor. The bursar will be asked to attend part or all of a governors' meeting in an advisory capacity. Often, also, the bursar is clerk to the governors of an unincorporated school or company secretary to an incorporated school, and in either case will attend meetings ex officio, but not as a governor.

## 19.6.4  Current parents

The tradition of public and, later, independent schools has been against having a current parent elected to the governing body, although, in practice, a number of governors elected for other reasons are current parents. The practice in some smaller independent schools is different and is required to be different in State-funded schools.

There is a conceptual difference between an elected 'parent-governor' on the one hand and a governor who happens to be a parent on the other. Elected parent-governors may not initially understand the extent of the duties and liabilities they will be undertaking as charity trustees and also the duties of confidentiality to which they will be subject. The elected parent-governor is likely to come under very considerable pressure from sectional interests in the school and, in some cases, may have his (or her) own agenda.

A parent-governor – and equally a governor who happens to be a parent – may be caused embarrassment in a variety of circumstances if their child is awarded a scholarship, bursary or some other form of financial allowance or if the parent supplies goods or services to the school, possibly in exchange for a reduction in fees, but otherwise within an express power in the governing instrument; or if the pupil is regularly seen to be given more positions of responsibility, such as school head, house prefect, captain of a team or leading performer in dramatic and other events; or if the pupil is regarded as a bully who is not being adequately dealt with. There is great potential for conflict of this kind which can only damage the internal culture of the school as a whole.

Nowadays, parents take a far greater interest than formerly in the way the school runs. If it is decided to have parent representatives on the governing body, the mechanism to be preferred, particularly in a school with a large proportion of day-pupils, is that of nomination by parents of a governor who is not a current parent, but who may be a former parent, and who is acceptable to the majority of the governing body; alternatively, a person elected by the parents out of a list nominated by the governors. The issue of accountability is covered in more detail at **19.8** below.

### 19.6.5   Teachers

Many of the problems that affect parent-governors apply also to teacher-governors with the additional problem that teachers are employees. Unlike in the State-funded sector, the independent sector has, in general, avoided making Scheme provision for teacher-governors.

The mechanism discussed under 'Nominated governors' at **19.2.4** above may prove to be an effective means of achieving accountability. Some governing bodies with the whole-hearted agreement of the head, invite teacher representatives to attend parts of some governors' meetings to discuss particular matters of interest within the school but this should never be a forum for criticism of the head or for undermining the head's authority in any other way.

### 19.6.6   Solicitors

There may be one or more members of the governing body who are practising solicitors. One may be a partner in the firm of solicitors that advises the school. Their position has been discussed earlier at **17.4.11** in the context of trustees not making a personal profit from the trust, save to the extent that there is power in the governing instrument. In one unreported case, the firm of which a solicitor-governor was a partner, charged fees for work done for the school. The governing instrument contained no power in that behalf. Following an investigation by the Charity Commissioners, the solicitor was required to repay the fees that had been charged.

The traditional formula for overcoming this kind of problem has been for a solicitor to act as clerk to the governors or as company secretary. Then, the governing body has the benefit of the solicitor's advice and is able to instruct that solicitor's firm in legal matters in which the firm is sufficiently expert, without being in breach of the terms of the trust.

A solicitor-governor whose firm is not likely to be concerned in the provision of legal services to the school should not be expected to carry out professional work free of charge. His (or her) role is essentially that of identifying legal issues or problems that may arise and recommending to the governors that those matters are referred for specialist advice. A solicitor advising in his (or her) capacity as a governor may not have insurance cover for negligent advice because he is almost certainly acting in a private capacity and not within the course of his practice. Moreover, much of the advice required by independent schools, particularly in relation to legal compliance, is in a discrete area of expertise in which the solicitor may not be a specialist.

### 19.6.7  Suppliers

In the nature of things, a governor may be a senior manager in a firm which, sooner or later, is asked to supply goods or services to the school, for example, financial or accounting services, information technology or marketing services, energy, food, drink and so on. The rule about not making a personal profit from the trust, discussed at **19.6.6** under 'Solicitors', will apply here also.

### 19.6.8  Skills

The ex-officio, representative and nominative governors are likely to supply a range of the relevant skills needed by the governing body. The remaining skills will be supplied by co-optative governors and may perhaps include those of an accountant, doctor, lawyer (judge, barrister, solicitor or academic), member of the clergy and one or two heads of other schools or representatives of higher education.

In the modern age, and depending on the emphasis of the school, it may be helpful to include representatives of business and industry (banking, transport, construction and so on), the armed forces and the worlds of the arts and culture, property (architect, surveyor or developer), computer technology, advertising and public relations, and financial services.

In marketing terms, there is much to be said for recruiting a high profile governor whose skills, for example as a musician, athlete or dancer, will help to promote a relevant focus area of the school.

### 19.6.9  Relevance

The governing instrument may have been last revised at a time when the school was a boarding school for boys aged 13–18 with a robust ethos and an all-male governing body. For many of those schools, times have changed. They may now be an all age school (2–18), co-educational and with a separate international studies centre.

The composition of the board needs to reflect every aspect of the school, including age and gender. Even in an all-boys school, efforts should be made to ensure there is a sufficient number of women governors who have relevant skills and experience. An important function of the governors is to form panels that will be able to hear disciplinary appeals from staff and pupils. It is desirable and, in some cases, necessary to constitute these panels with men and women.

### 19.6.10  Communication

To parents and outsiders, the governing body can seem arcane and mysterious. There is a common misunderstanding that governors are paid for their services and although the governing body is sometimes perceived as powerful, there is little understanding of their role and proceedings.

The back pocket of the prospectus may contain a sheet listing the names of the governors. Better still is a short profile of each governor, accompanied by a brief narrative of the constitution and role of the governing body. This is suggested because questions about these matters so often arise in the course of discussion by parents both during and outside set-piece events.

## 19.7 FUNCTIONS OF THE GOVERNING BODY

Most of the business of the governing body is carried out by committees, often composed of two or three governors advised by the head, bursar and others as necessary. Typically, when all is running smoothly, those committees meet once per month in term time. The full governing body may only meet between one and five times per year. Although the governors are responsible for every aspect of the school, most of their tasks (but few of their responsibilities) can and should be delegated in particular to the head who must run and manage the school with the bursar (if any) and such other executives as are available to the head.

### 19.7.1 Committee structure

The most detailed business of the governors will be carried out by one or more committees of the governors and the Scheme should provide authority for this to happen. Committees, however constituted, will need to cover the following:

- finance and general purposes;
- curriculum and pastoral care;
- human resources;
- policy, quality and marketing;
- property and estates;
- nominations (if applicable).

Schools differ in the number of committees that are constituted, but most will need to use ad-hoc working groups for special purposes and projects and the governors will need to be able to convene an unbiased panel to deal with disciplinary appeals from staff, parents and pupils.

Each committee will need a simple structure with terms of reference such as the following:

- its composition;
- who will chair the committee;
- those who will attend to advise;
- frequency of meetings;
- remit, in accordance with terms of reference.

The success of committees will depend largely on the energy, enthusiasm and commitment of the individuals who serve on them and the setting of deadlines.

## 19.7.2   General functions

The governors are required by virtue of their office to:

- ensure that all the functions of the school are authorised by the powers provided in the governing instrument and by charity law;

- appoint the head and bursar;

- settle the division of responsibilities between the head and bursar and other key members of the management team and also the lines of reporting;

- set the policies by which the school will be run and which will dictate the school's resulting culture – in practice it will be the task of the head and senior management team to originate and formulate matters of policy for the approval and ratification of governors;

- approve the development plan proposed by the head and senior management team;

- control finance by setting realistic budgets and approving systems and safeguards;

- understand the extent of legal compliance duties and be satisfied that there is a rolling programme for meeting them;

- deal with the school's bankers when necessary;

- deal with the regulatory authorities when necessary, including the Charity Commission, the Department for Education and Employment, Inland Revenue, HM Customs and Excise, the Trading Standards Department, and the local authority social services and environmental health departments;

- be satisfied that the sale or purchase of land is authorised by the governing instrument and conducted in accordance with ss 36–38 of the Charities Act 1993;

- ensure that redundancies and other crises are sufficiently anticipated, avoided where possible and managed when they happen;

- ensure that competent professional advice has been budgeted for and taken when necessary.

## 19.7.3   Relationships

It is very important that the governors support the head and ensure he or she is not undermined. If the head is plainly wrong on any point the matter needs to be dealt with, but sensitively.

The governors' relationships with the head, bursar and staff are discussed in the GBA–GBGSA booklet entitled *Guidelines for Governors* and are not duplicated here, but there are some additional points to be made:

### (a)  Crisis management

Governors have an important role at times of crisis in taking some of the pressure away from the head who has to continue running the school and also in dealing with professional advisers, the media, the staff and the parents.

### (b)  Accountability

This is considered in more detail at **19.8** below.

### (c)  Supporting the head

Headship can be a lonely position and the governors' interest and support, without interference, is likely to matter very much to the head. In the context of high-profile departures both in politics and schools of recent years a gratuitous and unnecessary 'expression of confidence' can be more likely to unsettle than encourage. The support role is better provided through a combination of clear thinking, wise advice, good communication and consultation, and appraisals.

### (d)  Appraisals

Although many heads have resisted the introduction of appraisal systems, particularly at senior management level, an annual appraisal when past successes (and areas of difficulty) are reviewed and future goals are set is, or should be, an invaluable way of letting the head know how well he (or she) is doing. The importance of appraisals cannot be over-emphasised.

### (e)  Parents and staff

Parents and staff do expect to see and meet well briefed governors at show-piece events and consultative meetings. These events can provide valuable feedback from the market place and give early warning of problems as well as confirmation that the school is delivering.

### (f)  Training

Although the Governing Bodies Association provides a handful of courses for governors each year and some schools make their own arrangements for governor training internally, it is thought that few more than 5% of governors of independent schools receive a sufficient level of training in the legal, accountancy, educational and social issues that affect their schools. This can be disheartening for heads and bursars who may feel on occasions that they have an uphill battle, unnecessarily, in persuading governors to their point of view and then communicating the decisions of governors to the staff.

## 19.8  ACCOUNTABILITY

The practical meaning of 'accountability' is to do with having to explain a course of action to a person who is entitled to know and who is in a position to insist that matters are put right.

Parents often have little understanding of the extent and limits of the governors' accountability. Whenever a charitable Scheme is being revised, the Charity Commissioners are quite properly concerned to know what the accountability arrangements will be so that the management of the charity does not end up in the hands of an unanswerable and self-perpetuating oligarchy. Some of these issues are considered below.

### 19.8.1    Governors' position

Governors are charged with managing the assets of the charity, considering reports from the head and discharging the many functions described at **19.7.2**. Management of the assets goes far beyond considerations of investment and spending. The assets of a school include the land and investments, the school itself and its ability to function and develop and the confidence of the staff and parents. The assets also include the intellectual property and other confidential information relating to finance, name, goodwill, budgets and development plans. The school may be in a parlous financial position, although the governors have realistic plans for recovery over several years. Information of that kind, other than as required annually, is commercially sensitive and must normally be kept confidential by governors so as not to destabilise the school and detract from its work.

The governors are also responsible for keeping private information concerning parents, pupils and staff confidential other than to the extent that disclosure is required or permitted by law.

Parents and staff are entitled to know, in general terms, why a particular state of affairs exists, but they are not entitled to know the detail of private discussions and deliberations that have taken place behind closed doors at a governors' meeting. No more would a customer or shareholder of ICI be entitled to the same information from the board of directors of that company, although the director/shareholder comparison is not exact.

The matters discussed at a governors' meeting will necessarily include a whole range of confidences from the private business of parents and pupils to the financial position and plans for the school, and, sometimes, the performance of the head and other senior executives or teachers. There may be a number of serious worries at any one time but these are, and must remain, within the head's and governors' circle of confidentiality. Great care is needed to avoid adverse rumour and gossip that could so easily destabilise and undermine the school's position with its competitors. There is a whole range of issues about which parents and even staff should never know and are not entitled to know. The difficulty, sometimes, is deciding on which side of the line a particular question may fall.

### 19.8.2    Parents' position

In *Price v Dennis* (1988) LEXIS (see **10.3.3(b)** above) one of the issues concerned the parents' liability to pay a term's fees in lieu of notice when they withdrew the pupil following the summary dismissal of the head by the owner of a private school. The Court of Appeal decided against the parents and on this issue, Glidewell LJ said:

'I do not accept that her [the proprietor's] power to [dismiss Mr Cassidy] can, as a matter of law, be cut down by requiring her to consider the effect that it would have on other members of staff and on the parents . . . any intelligent person would realise that dismissal of the headmaster was bound to have repercussions. But that as a matter of contract she could be restrained in some way from dismissing him because of those considerations, I do not accept.'

This is a practical illustration of where the dividing line falls between the responsibilities of the school authority (whether a proprietor or charitable) and accountability to staff and parents.

Parents are customers, but they are customers with a difference. They are not buying a one-off commodity or a fortnight in an hotel. They are buying into a set of relationships which may last from one school term or for up to 15 years. In their perception, they are buying into a vision for the future of their children and many want to play an active part in managing that.

Thus, there is an inevitable tension between the right, the need and the wish to know. It will often take considerable political skill and firmness on the part of the governors to regulate the relationships. In the words of Glidewell LJ in *Price v Dennis*, the governors must 'take reasonable steps to retain the confidence of *parents who themselves act reasonably*' (emphasis added).

When the governing instrument provides for nomination of a governor by the parents and/or teachers there is much to be said for drawing up a protocol which regulates the matters that may or may not be reported, so as to save embarrassment or misunderstanding later on.

### 19.8.3   Confidence in the head

This issue is discussed in more detail at **20.5**.

When the governors' confidence in the head is under question, great care must be taken to ensure their concerns are not leaked outside private meetings, otherwise the head may be fatally undermined in this and any future post. Soundings can be taken in a variety of ways that do not create leaks.

If the head departs under a compromise agreement, the agreement may contain a clause to the effect that the fact and contents of the agreement shall remain confidential between the parties. Then, there is a contractual limit to the information the governors may disseminate. In the period between confidence being lost and the compromise agreement being signed it is quite possible for parents and staff to exert so much pressure on the governors that there is a risk of forcing the governors to publicise the fact and some of the reasons for their loss of confidence, even where there has been no misconduct. This only serves to emphasise how important it is for staff and parents to act responsibly and to place their own confidence in the judgement of the governors. If the school has been successful in other ways and the experience of the parents and pupils is generally good, there will be no reason to do otherwise.

### 19.8.4   Accountability generally

The over-complex structures of governance from 100 or more years ago were necessary partly to provide for the funding of independent schools, but also to ensure that there were safeguards at a time when there was little in the way of regulation or management systems, and difficulties over transport and illness were more likely than now to prevent governors attending meetings.

Nowadays, there is scope for much greater accountability in the real sense:

–   by means of nominative or representative governors;

–   by regular rotation of governors and invitations to outsiders to seek nomination and election to the governing body;

–   at private meetings between governors and parent or staff committees;

–   to former pupils and friends organisations who frequently take a close interest in the school's development;

–   at show-piece events such as speech day and through the annual report of the chairman and head;

–   to the Charity Commissioners, through annual formalities and under their substantial powers under the Charities Act 1993 to protect the public interest and to whom parents can refer their concerns in grave circumstances;

–   to Companies House, in the case of schools that are incorporated;

–   to the Department for Education and Employment and other authorities if there are concerns about the efficiency of education or about matters of child protection or any of the matters listed at s 469 of the Education Act 1996;

–   by school inspections conducted by Ofsted as to regulatory and other matters and on behalf of the Independent Schools Council for affiliated schools;

–   by virtue of the media to whom the governors are not in any sense accountable but by whom their decisions may be influenced in certain cases.

The ultimate power lies in the hands of parents, who can withdraw their children, and staff, who are free to find other employment before they resign. But those who have power must exercise it responsibly and for the benefit of the community, respecting the responsibilities and the legal and moral constraints under which the governors are bound to conduct the business of the charity and the school.

## 19.9   RETIREMENT AND DISQUALIFICATION

### 19.9.1   Retirement

Even though appointed for a period of years, governors are normally free to retire from office forthwith at any time. As a matter of courtesy and good management, as much notice as possible should be given and at least one month. Some governing instruments specify a period of notice.

Resignation of influential governors because of a deterioration in the financial position or concerns about personal liability in the case of an incorporated school can tend to destabilise the board and may trigger other resignations. This is less likely to happen in a case of a school that is incorporated and offers governors the protections they are entitled to have in the conduct of their own business affairs. It is usual for a modern governing instrument to prescribe retirement at the age of 70 and also in accordance with rotation periods, subject to continuing eligibility.

### 19.9.2 Disqualification

Section 72 of the Charities Act 1993 provides to the effect that a person shall be disqualified for being a charity trustee or trustee for a charity if:

(a) he has been convicted of any offence involving dishonesty or deception;

(b) he has been adjudged bankrupt or sequestration of his estate has been awarded and (in either case) he has not been discharged;

(c) he has made a composition or arrangement with, or granted a trust deed for, his creditors and has not been discharged in respect of it;

(d) he has been removed from the office of charity trustee or trustee for a charity by an order made by the Commissioners or by the High Court on the grounds of any misconduct or mismanagement in the administration of the charity for which he was responsible or to which he was privy, or which he by his conduct contributed to or facilitated;

(e) he has been removed, under s 7 of the Law Reform (Miscellaneous Provisions) (Scotland) Act 1990 (powers of Court of Session to deal with management of charities), from being concerned in the management or control of any body;

(f) he is subject to a disqualification order under the Company Directors Disqualification Act 1986 or to an order under s 429(2)(b) of the Insolvency Act 1986 (failure to pay under county court administration order).

Section 72 contains additional provisions concerning disqualification. Section 73 of the Act provides the penalties of a fine and/or imprisonment for offences in a case of a person acting as a charity trustee or trustee for a charity while he is disqualified for being such a trustee by virtue of s 72.

### 19.9.3 Removal

Schemes normally provide a number of circumstances in which a charity trustee or governor may be removed, but in general they are covered by the provisions of s 72, above. Reflecting s 303 of the Companies Act 1985, however, it may be desirable to provide that a governor may be removed by a majority vote upon special notice. Such a provision can be invoked in a case of a governor who is deliberately obstructive or indiscreet or whose conduct is in some other way prejudicial to the proper governance of the school.

It is usual also to include a provision that a governor who, without acceptable explanation, is absent from all meetings of the governors during a period of one year shall automatically cease to be a governor.

## 19.10    THE GOVERNOR AS MEMBER OF A COMPANY

The governors of an incorporated school may be both directors of the company and also its members. The following is a summary of their powers and duties in their capacity as members of a company limited by guarantee.

The only time members can lawfully exercise any control over the affairs of the company is at a general meeting. Otherwise the company is run by the directors and the members are not entitled to interfere or 'second-guess' the decisions of the directors.

The Companies Act 1985 provides the following powers of members of a company limited by guarantee, subject to the provisions of the memorandum and articles:

–    alter the objects of the company (s 4 – special resolution required);

–    alter the company's articles of association (s 9(1) – special resolution required);

–    alter any condition in the company's memorandum which could have been contained in its articles (s 17(1) – special resolution required);

–    change the company's name (s 28(1) – special resolution required);

–    alter the company's memorandum so as to impose unlimited liability on directors, managers or any managing director (s 307(1) – special resolution required);

–    approve the assignment by a director or manager of his office to another person (s 308 – special resolution required);

–    resolve that the company be wound up voluntarily (Insolvency Act 1986, s 84(1)).

Members also have certain statutory powers which cannot be taken away from them and may be important in controlling the directors. These include:

–    power to dismiss directors (Companies Act 1985, s 303);

–    power to petition for a compulsory liquidation (Insolvency Act 1986, s 122(1)(a) special resolution required);

–    power to insist on a resolution of members holding 5% of the total voting rights being put on the agenda of an AGM (s 376);

–    power to requisition an EGM by members holding 10% of the votes (s 368).

Furthermore, power to control the company reverts to the members in limited circumstances as follows:

–    if for some reason the directors are unable or unwilling to exercise their powers of management, for example if no board of directors exists;

–    if the board of directors cannot act because its meetings are inquorate, power reverts to the general meeting of the members. The members are then agents of the company.

Members have limited rights in addition to their powers. The most common rights (some of them being statutory duties) are:

- to have an annual meeting within 15 months of the last (s 366);

- to pass elective resolutions, electing to dispense with an AGM (s 366A); or dispense with the laying of accounts and reports (Companies Act 1989, s 16) and then the accounts must be sent to each member; or electing to dispense with the obligation to elect auditors annually – then there is annual reappointment until the appointment is terminated by resolution under s 393;

- to conduct the business of the AGM in accordance with the terms of the articles. For a guarantee company, the usual agenda would be: consideration of the accounts, balance sheets and reports; election of directors; appointment of auditors and fixing their remuneration; any special resolutions required;

- members may reject the reports of the directors; however, this operates only as a vote of censure on the directors but has no other immediate effect. A committee of inspection can be appointed;

- members may inspect the minutes and have a copy for which they pay (s 382).

It will be apparent from the above that members, in general, have no legal right to exercise any control over the affairs of the company. They are not privy to the discussions and decisions of the board of directors. They are not entitled to second-guess those decisions or obstruct the running of the company. They may only act at a general meeting which can be the AGM or an EGM.

## 19.11 THE GOVERNOR AS COMPANY DIRECTOR

This section applies only to schools which are incorporated as limited companies (normally limited by guarantee) under the Companies Acts. References to 'the Act' are references to the Companies Act 1985, unless otherwise stated.

The duties owed by a director are owed principally to the company, which is a legal person in its own right. The interests of creditors are protected under s 214 of the Insolvency Act 1986. The duties owed by a director to the company are, in most instances, replicated or exceeded by those that apply to a charity trustee. Detailed discussion is therefore unnecessary here, but the following points are worthy of note.

### 19.11.1 Fiduciary duties.

Technically, a company director is a *fiduciary* and not a trustee. The fiduciary duties of a director are to act in good faith and to exercise his or her powers for proper purposes. Section 310 of the Act renders void any attempt to exclude the liability of a director for negligence, default, breach of duty or breach of trust in relation to the company. However, s 310 does not prevent the operation of s 137 of the Companies Act 1989, which allows the company to change its memorandum and articles of association so as to enable it to purchase and maintain for its officers insurance against any of these liabilities. The policy must not indemnify trustees in relation to wilful or criminal acts, but can indemnify against actual or alleged breach of duty; breach of trust; negligent acts; error or omission; misstatements; misleading statements; breach of warranty of authority or other act done or wrongly attempted.

## 19.11.2   Breach of fiduciary duty

The company has the following remedies against a director who has acted in breach of his or her fiduciary duties: a right to recover company property that has been misappropriated; a right to avoid a contract made by a director who had a personal interest in it; a right to an account of unauthorised profits; a right to recover company property from a party who knowingly assisted in a fraudulent breach of trust; a right to require a defaulting trustee to restore trust property; and a claim in damages for loss caused to the company by the direct entering into of an ultra vires transaction.

## 19.11.3   Contracts with third parties

Section 349(4) of the Act provides that where a director signs or authorises a cheque or order for money or goods (and certain other transactions) in which the company's name is not mentioned, the director is personally liable on such signature.

## 19.11.4   Vicarious liability

A director who knowingly, deliberately or recklessly commits a tort or directs a tort to be committed by the company in such a way as to indicate that it was his own act or conduct and not that of the company can be held personally liable in respect of that tort. Moreover, it was held in *Wallersteiner v Moir* [1974] 1 WLR 991 and *Adams v Cape Industries* [1990] 2 AC 433 that a director can be held liable for the acts of the company under general principles of law whenever it is necessary to do so in order to achieve justice. This rule would be applied only in exceptional cases so as not to infringe the more fundamental principle that directors and members of a company are quite separate from and not generally liable for the acts of the company.

## 19.11.5   Statutory liability

Section 306 of the Act provides that a company's memorandum can provide that its directors will have unlimited liability. In addition, there are a number of provisions in the Companies Acts which impose personal liability on directors.

## 19.11.6   Criminal liability

Under the Companies Acts there are more than 200 offences which a director can commit and which give rise to criminal liability of a director either as a principal offender; as a joint principal with the company; as a party who has aided, abetted, counselled or procured the offence; for incitement; for conspiracy and for attempt. A company director can be criminally liable in the same way as anyone else for offences such as fraud and arising out of gross negligence causing death or personal injury.

## 19.11.7   Liability for the acts of co-directors

A director may be liable for the acts and omissions of co-directors if grounds for suspicion existed but the director was negligent or wilfully closed his eyes and failed to investigate or supervise. Section 727 of the Act allows the court to relieve a director from liability if he can show that he acted honestly and reasonably and ought in all the circumstances fairly to be excused.

### 19.11.8   Insolvency

Company insolvency is regulated principally by the Insolvency Act 1986 and the Company Directors' Disqualification Act 1986. The test of whether a company is solvent is set out in s 123 of the Insolvency Act 1986 which defines insolvency as '... unable to pay its debts as they fall due or ... the value of the company's assets is less than the amount of its liabilities taking into account its contingent and prospective liabilities'. A detailed examination of the insolvency provisions is outside the scope of this chapter.

### 19.11.9   Wrongful trading

Under s 214 of the Insolvency Act 1986 there may be personal liability for continuing to operate the company when the director knew or ought to have concluded that there was no reasonable prospect that the company would avoid going into insolvent liquidation. Insolvent liquidation is an unlikely contingency for a school that has a substantial asset base because of the realisable value of its land and buildings; although redundant school buildings are not always easy to sell.

### 19.11.10   Environmental issues

Section 157 of the Environment Protection Act 1990 provides that, where the company commits an offence under any provision of the Act, and it is proved that the offence was committed with the consent or connivance of a director or other officer, that person as well as the company shall be guilty of the offence. Prosecutions under this legislation are rare. Even so, governors may wish to consider commissioning an environment 'audit', particularly if there is reason to think any of the school's land is contaminated.

### 19.11.11   Shadow directors

A shadow director is also the subject of duties and obligations. Section 741(2) of the Act defines a shadow director as a person 'in accordance with whose directions or instructions the directors of a company are accustomed to act'. Under normal circumstances, a professional adviser who customarily attends meetings of governors in order to advise does not run the risk of being deemed a shadow director any more than if the governors were to visit that adviser at his or her office premises. Acting on the basis of professional advice is a wholly different concept from acting in accordance with a person's directions or instructions. The point has occasionally caused unnecessary concern.

# Chapter 20

## HEADSHIP

### 20.1 OVERVIEW

This chapter is mainly concerned with the appointment and dismissal of heads of independent schools.

Headship of an independent school of whatever size is a unique and dual role. It is that of chief executive and head teacher on the one hand and the head of a self-regulating closed community on the other. The head's tenure of office will, in general, depend on the confidence of the governors in his (or her) leadership of the school community.

The following passages, taken from John Rae's Foreword to his book *Delusions of Grandeur*, published in 1993 by HarperCollins, provide a typically idiosyncratic view of the role of an independent school head. Dr Rae was the Headmaster of Westminster School between 1971 and 1986 and Chairman of the Headmasters Conference (as it then was) in 1977. Dr Rae states:

> 'The English public schools, or independent schools as they prefer to be called, are like little kingdoms. Most of them are wholly or partly residential communities. They are self-governing. They have proud histories and entrenched traditions. To the outsider, their ancient buildings and rituals and their apparent detachment from the world may suggest Ruritania or Lilliput rather than a real country, but to the insiders the analogy of a kingdom is accurate enough.

> The public school headmaster exercises personal power to a greater degree than many people in positions of authority. It is neither absolute nor unfettered power: a headmaster can be dismissed by the governing body that appointed him and his plans may be frustrated by his senior colleagues who, like medieval barons, combine against him. But a determined headmaster who is politically astute is difficult to dislodge and dangerous to oppose.

> In recent times the arbitrary, even tyrannical, nature of the headmaster's power has been played down. Today's public school headmaster wishes to be seen as a chief executive not as an autocrat, but it is a change of style not of substance.'

Until very recently, little or no training was available for newly appointed heads. They were expected to move from teaching, deputy headship or running a house into a full management role. It is not uncommon for a newly appointed headmaster to say that after holding his first assembly, he returned to his study, closed the door and wondered what he should be doing next.

## 20.2   THE HEAD'S JOB

The following passages from Dr Rae's book give a first-hand, personal and often controversial account of life as head of an independent school. (The headings have been added.)

### 20.2.1   Survival

'How I was going to make an impact on Westminster, I did not know. My immediate concern was survival. Those who have not done the job are surprised to learn that public school headmasters worry about being sacked. It doesn't show. But even when I was well established at Westminster, I feared that I might be given notice to quit. In my first term, I treated every problem as a test of my fitness for the task.'

### 20.2.2   Early dealings

'I could not railroad the governors and masters ... I had to learn the art of institutional politics: how to persuade, manipulate, intrigue and out-manoeuvre. The autocrat in me chafed at the slowness of it all. I had to submit to governors' recommendations when I did not think that they were qualified to judge the issues involved; I felt obliged to set up committees of masters to consider questions to which I already knew the answer. Why could they not see that Westminster had to change if it was to compete successfully with its rivals?'

### 20.2.3   Winning the confidence of others

'A distinctive feature of the headmaster's job is that he has to convince different audiences – the pupils and the teachers (not to mention the parents and the governors) – that he has a magic touch and a special authority. It is not enough for him to be good with the pupils and bad with the staff, or vice versa. Failure to convince one audience undermines his credibility with the other. If the pupils see the headmaster defeated by the staff or the staff see the pupils defy the headmaster with impunity, the circumstances exist in which "charisma can turn to catastrophe". Then, like a medicine-man whose bluff has been called, the headmaster must seek another tribe or a different job.'

### 20.2.4   Effecting change

It is relatively common for an independent school head to say that it will be difficult to effect change until he (or she) has appointed more than half of the members of the Common Room. That concern was echoed by Dr Rae in this passage:

'In a public school, the leaders of the old guard are usually the senior housemasters. They may be good at their job but a new headmaster is never fully convinced that they are loyal to him. He sees them as the natural opponents of the reforms that he wishes to introduce. The problem is that he cannot change them, at least not quickly ... it took a long time to create a team of housemasters who had all been chosen by me. Only when that team was at last assembled did I feel that I was working with colleagues who shared my view of what was required to make Westminster a successful school. Unlike a chief executive in industry, a headmaster cannot put his own men and women into key positions within a few weeks of taking over; he may have to work for years with housemasters and heads of academic departments he would not have chosen.'

## 20.2.5 The 'old guard'

'Discipline was their topic because it was the issue on which all headmasters were vulnerable and on which it was easy to imply with impunity a failure of firm leadership. They enjoyed needling the headmaster, too; perhaps they resented seeing a younger man occupying a position to which they had once aspired . . .

Every headmaster has his enemies on the staff, though enemies is too strong a word since most of the time they are no more than what the Duke of Wellington called "croakers" – those who find fault with every decision. As long as the croakers confined themselves to croaking and moaning below decks I could ignore them. But if their disaffection was translated into intrigue they would be dangerous.'

## 20.2.6 Relations with the governors

'. . . they were men of the world who had seen too much in public life to panic at the first unfavourable reference to the school in the newspapers. Their worldliness made my life easier. But it was also a weather vane of their attitude to me; when worldly men started to worry about boys' shirt-tails not being tucked in, I knew it was time to look for another job.

Public school headmasters enjoy an independence that most heads of State schools are denied. The latter have to accept that governors have the right to be involved in the appointment of members of staff, a degree of interference that would have been totally alien to most of Westminster's governors. The traditional independence of public school headmasters owed much to Dr Arnold who had refused to take over the headmastership of Rugby in 1828 unless the governors gave him an assurance that they would not interfere in the administration of the school . . .

One of a headmaster's most difficult tasks is to explain the governors' decisions to the Common Room, particularly when he has argued against those decisions himself . . .

Most headmasters could tell similar stories about what are politely called "misunderstandings" between governors and teaching staff. The pupils did not give a hoot who the governors were or what they did, but it mattered to the teaching staff, who found it frustrating that people with so little knowledge of running an independent school should have the final say in decisions that would make or mar the school's future.

The longer I remained a headmaster, the more critical I became of the role of the public school governing body but I could see no alternative. The headmaster had to be accountable to somebody.'

An old aphorism is that 'more people know Tom Fool than Tom Fool knows'. That is never more the case than for the head of an independent school. He or she is ex officio a public figure. Whereas the managing director of a commercial enterprise may be more or less anonymous if he chooses, that will not usually be an option for the head of an independent school. One of the most powerful marketing signals from a school is that there is 'a very good new head'. A school, other than one that is distinguished by its brand name, is likely to be known more by its head than by any other single element of its reputation except perhaps any short-lived burst of adverse publicity.

These then are some of the reasons why the issue of confidence is so fundamental to the head's success and survival in office. Confidence is of course equally crucial to the governors. A wrong appointment may be an expensive error which sets the development of the school back for two or more years and, if mishandled by a divided governing body, can in turn shake the confidence of staff and parents.

The remainder of this chapter is concerned with the selection and appointment of a head; settling the head's contractual terms; relationships between the governing body and the head, and the whole issue of confidence – when and why confidence may be lost and the consequences.

## 20.3   THE ASPIRING HEAD

This section, which is non-legal in nature, has been distilled from informal comments of senior and preparatory school heads.

A number of them said that their decision to apply for a headship was part of a career plan but the majority, in their mid to late thirties acted out of a sense of challenge on seeing a position advertised. Most, on looking back, felt they had been unprepared for the tasks of management and counted themselves fortunate to have landed on their feet and been able to learn quickly. A commonly shared view in retrospect was that preparation for headship should have begun some years before the first job application form was completed. The remainder of this section summarises the advice and comments of those heads.

### 20.3.1   Model of school

Headship of a small day school carries many of the same responsibilities but quite different tasks from headship of a large boarding school organised in semi-autonomous houses.

In a small day-school there will be a high degree of personal contact between the head and each member of the staff, parents and pupils. The head is likely to teach some classes and take games. It may be difficult to find enough time and energy for management and administration, yet often the head will have to manage without a bursar. The financial position will often be more volatile and there may be limited scope for investment, development and expansion.

By contrast, in a large boarding school the occasions for personal contact with the head will be far fewer. The danger will be that the head remains in his (or her) study and becomes invisible unless time is specially allocated for walking the job. Visibility and communication were thought to be a crucially important factor in gaining the confidence of governors, staff and parents at either model of school.

### 20.3.2   Preparation for headship

It was thought that an aspiring head should aim to build a curriculum vitae which described in particular any executive functions undertaken at previous schools, articles published and relevant skills and interests developed.

It was also thought that training should be undertaken particularly in the areas of: business and financial management; marketing and public relations; financial accounting and budgeting; information technology; the law relating to contracts, torts, employment, children, compliance and educational charities; public speaking; and the history and structure of independent schools with particular reference to the role of governors.

A knowledge of current educational and relevant political issues was thought to be essential together with an understanding or at least a view of the likely impact of science and technology on school and national life during the next five years.

### 20.3.3 Personal objectives

A candidate and his (or her) spouse need to consider their personal and career objectives very carefully – practical matters such as accommodation, financial package, spouse's career, a need to be near other members of the family and so on.

Is the candidate really looking for a leadership role and a whole new way of life rather than simply another job? Will this job involve too much that is new, for example: first experience of headship; boarding; co-education; senior school; independent school? How many new challenges can the candidate realistically hope to get to grips with quickly?

### 20.3.4 Interview

How well could the candidate tackle the kind of questions that are likely to arise at interview? An indication may be obtained from the specimen questions listed in Table 4 at the end of this chapter. Would it improve or damage the candidate's chances of appointment if the governors decided to visit the candidate's present school by arrangement for a first-hand account of his (or her) track record there?

### 20.3.5 Information required to make an informed decision

Candidates were also advised to find out as much as possible about the school to which they are applying. Taking over a highly successful school brings its own problems and challenges. A new head would be expected to improve matters and not preside over a decline in the school's fortunes. On the other hand, taking over a school that is at a low ebb, although more attractive, may be unwise if viability is in doubt and closure is looking likely. The main points to consider were set out below.

### (a) The present head

Who will the candidate be succeeding? A successful head? A failed head? A demi-god? A folk-hero? An exciting role-model? A quiet academic? Will the candidate be able to place an early stamp of authority on his (or her) tenure of office?

### (b) Quality of leadership

What has been the quality of the leadership at the school? What is the quality of leadership from the governing body? Are they united? Is there a synergy? Or are the governors a motley collection of individuals? Have the governors been working to a clear vision and plan? Has it been successful? Is it attractive to the candidate and is it one that the candidate will want to build on or change? Is the school happy and motivated? Is it moving forward or stagnating? How are its ethos and culture described? What is the governors' attitude towards legal compliance?

### (c)   Time scale

Will the candidate be given sufficient time to drive and develop his (or her) plans or is the school already in a parlous state with only a limited time for survival?

### (d)   Marketing culture

Is there a strong marketing culture running through the school? Are there good relationships with feeder and senior schools? What is the image and reputation of the school both in the community and within the professional associations? What is the school *famous* for? What can it be made famous for? How realistic are the fee levels? Where is the competition from both independent and State sectors? How has the school fared on inspection?

### (e)   Resources

Are there effective financial controls? Are there adequate resources, including human resources? Is there a capable bursar, or will the bursar's work fall on the head? Is there sound budgeting? Will the head's plans receive sufficient financial backing?

### (f)   Presentation

What impression does the corporate identity and livery of the school convey? When were the prospectus and the corporate identity last revised? Is there a modern form of contract between school and parents (parent contract)? What are the special points of terminology and tradition?

### (g)   Job description

How specific is the head's job description? What will be the division of responsibilities with the bursar and the lines of reporting to the governors? What (if any) is the role contemplated for the candidate's spouse or family? If accommodation will be provided, is it suitable?

### (h)   Obtaining information

Information of a formal nature can be gathered from a number of publications including the official ISIS guide, *Choosing Your Independent School*, the *Independent Schools Year Book*, the school's prospectus and the other information disseminated to candidates by the governors. However, an understanding of the less tangible matters is likely to come mainly from visiting the school and, depending on the circumstances, from meeting the retiring head and the bursar (if any).

Ultimately, the decision taken by the candidate on an issue involving personal relationships will normally be taken on the basis of instinct or 'gut-feeling'. The candidate may form an initial view of five or ten objectives during a five-year tenure. These views may change once the candidate is in post. The decision taken by the candidate will be about whether he (or she) would be likely to have confidence in the governors and win their confidence and be given the resources necessary to turn those objectives into reality.

## 20.4 APPOINTMENT OF A HEAD

Under ideal circumstances, a head will be able to give the governors at least 18 months' notice of his (or her) intention to retire or make a career move to another headship and will be of considerable assistance both in the appointment of a successor and in effecting a smooth hand-over. In a case of illness or loss of confidence, however, the governors may have less time to prepare, and the task of making the right appointment will become correspondingly more difficult.

### 20.4.1 Search committee

The governors may decide to form a 'search committee', which will, in appropriate circumstances, be advised by the retiring head. The role of the search committee will be broadly:

– To decide whether to place a public advertisement and/or whether to use a firm of executive recruitment consultants ('head hunters'). The articles of government of some schools require:

'... the head shall be appointed by the governors after due public advertisement and shall be a graduate of some university or possess a qualification of equivalent status.'

The governors would be acting *ultra vires*, ie outside their powers, if they made an appointment in contravention of such an article and if the appointment proved bad and resulted in loss to the assets of the charity, the governors could be required to replace the loss personally subject to any right of recourse to insurers or waiver by the Charity Commissioners.

– To set the timetable and agenda in consultation with the head and under a strict regime of confidentiality.

– To prepare a *person specification*, setting out the personal qualities required and the skills that will be needed to do the job (see Table 1 at the end of this chapter).

– To prepare an outline *job description* to be sent out with letters offering an interview (see Table 2 at the end of this chapter).

– To prepare in consultation with the school's legal advisers an outline of the *main terms of employment* to be sent to the successful candidate when the position is offered. A specimen of the main terms is set out at Table 3 and this, subject to amendment as necessary, will form the basic template for preparation of the full employment contract – a very much larger and more complex document – in due course.

– To prepare an *advertisement* and *application form* which complies with the laws against discrimination on grounds of sex, race and disability and provides any consents that will be required to comply with the Data Protection Acts 1984 and

1998. Applicants should be informed if, as will normally be the case, that the appointment will be subject to a satisfactory medical report. Applicants should also be asked to consent to the normal *checks* being made via the police, DfEE List 99 and the Department of Health. Legal advice may be needed as to the circumstances in which gender or religion is a *'genuine occupational qualification'* for the particular school having regard to its charitable objects and current structure.

– To prepare a model *letter of response* to an application offering an interview and an alternative model letter of courteous rejection.

– To prepare a *'candidate record sheet'*.

Although head-hunters may be able to advise as to the form and content of the documents referred to above, there is much to be said for the search committee clarifying its own ideas in consultation with the remainder of the governors by preparing their own first drafts.

Smaller schools may feel that they cannot justify the cost of head-hunters or they may do their own head-hunting or have a specific appointment in mind.

In his book entitled *Letters to Parents* (HarperCollins, 1998) John Rae sounds this warning:

'Governors do not always have a clear idea of how the school should develop and so are unable to match the candidate to the task. They may have a bee in their bonnet about what qualities a head should have, regardless of the school's needs at the time. Their chances of making the right decision are further decreased by the practice of allowing all the governors to have a say in the final selection. "Plenary selection" means the head may be chosen as a result of the votes of governors who seldom attend meetings and know little about the real needs of the school.

This amateur approach, characteristic of independent schools, does not preclude the possibility of making a good appointment, but it has resulted in some well-known disasters. Executive recruitment companies cannot guarantee a perfect match but, by being much more thorough in drawing up the short list, they increase not only the chances of the best available people applying but also of a successful outcome. Or to put it another way, executive recruiting turns the process of identifying and selecting candidates who match the school's requirements from an amateur into a professional operation.

If I were you, I would be biased in favour of a school that had used an executive recruitment company. At the moment they are few and far between ... a professional approach is vital in the independent sector where the number of good candidates for headships is falling and the number of heads leaving early is rising.'

Another reason for forming a small search committee is to improve the chances of the search being kept confidential for as long as possible unless the plans of the retiring head have been announced. It is vital not to undermine the head's position by taking action behind his or her back where this can be avoided.

## 20.4.2   The 'person specification'

The starting point is to decide on the personal qualities required and the skills that will be needed to do the job. The first task of a search committee is therefore to draw up a person specification, which serves the following purposes:

–   Informing the literature with which head-hunters are to communicate the nature of the job to potential applicants.

–   Informing the 'sift criteria' which will be adopted by the search committee in settling any long list or short list. Sift criteria are those qualities or attributes that will be decisive in the final assessment of a candidate.

–   Ascertaining as far as possible that the person appointed will be compatible with the major parts of the job description.

–   For each member of the search committee to have in mind when meeting candidates.

The person specification is a tool of selection only. It will not become part of the job description or the employment contract. It is the responsibility of the search committee to choose the person who best matches the specification, however, the specification is unlikely to be matched in all respects.

## 20.4.3   Job description

The job description given in Table 2 at the end of this chapter is a specimen only and will need to be tailored when the particular skills of the successful applicant are known.

The job description of a head should never be considered without reference to that of other executives and, in particular, the bursar (by whatever title known). At many schools, the head is regarded as the chief executive, and the bursar is the finance director, with responsibility for financial management and for the non-academic functions, such as catering and building maintenance. Whilst this seems to be a clear division of responsibilities, often in practice it is unclear how far the bursar comes under the head's authority. This lack of clarity can give rise to significant tensions, sometimes reaching the point at which one or other executive has to leave.

Part of the problem is the wide range of ability and experience of individuals who are called bursars. Some are highly capable and come from an armed forces and/or accountancy or business background. Others may be accounts clerks who have been promoted and may lack the wider experience needed for an executive post. In some larger schools there may be a finance bursar, a domestic bursar and an estates bursar, each with administrative support.

It is therefore unwise to try and generalise about what the division of responsibilities between head and bursar should be. Suffice to say that the Independent Schools Bursars Association, representing the bursars of some 600 of the top independent schools, considers it vital that a bursar should have clearly defined responsibilities and, whilst working closely and consulting regularly with the head, should have direct access to an executive committee of the governors and if necessary the whole governing body.

There is some merit in this view because it is a rare head who has equal strength, interests and ability in academic matters, finance, administration and marketing. Nor, it might be said, should the head's energies be diverted into the detail of finance and administration. The likelihood of serious tension is increased if a bursar is required to report only to the head on matters of finance and administration when the head may have little aptitude or interest in those areas. Plainly, however, a high degree of consultation in both directions between head and bursar is desirable, necessary and an aspect of good management practice.

## 20.4.4   Dealing with applications

For a medium-size or large school in a city area, it is not uncommon to hear that there have been 150 or more responses to headship advertisements in the national and education press.

Governors may wish to consider how many new challenges an applicant will be undertaking if successful, for example: first headship; moving from state sector to independent sector or from preparatory to senior/all-age; or first experience of boarding or co-education. It has been suggested that a new head may be successful in gaining the confidence of governors, staff and parents sufficiently quickly in one or two new areas but not more.

## 20.4.5   Interview

Detailed advice about the selection process is given in the GBA–GBGSA publication entitled *Guidelines for Governors*. The procedures might include:

–   A tour of the school, with or without the candidate's spouse, but including a view of the accommodation which the applicant would be required to occupy, if appointed. It is not unusual for tours of this nature to be conducted by the present head and for there to be a small number of casual encounters with members of staff and pupils.

–   Either one or two formal interviews. A list of specimen interview questions is given in Table 4 at the end of the chapter. It is unlikely that time will allow for detailed discussion of each of those questions. Some will be seen as more important than others but the list indicates the level of preparation that a serious applicant needs to undertake.

–   A social gathering which the candidate and perhaps his (or her) spouse may be asked to attend, such as a dinner ('death by dining') with a number of the governors. The candidate, having had adequate notice, might be asked to give a short presentation at that event.

–   A visit to the candidate's present school by arrangement so as to find out at first hand how successful he (or she) has been whilst there. This is likely to flush out anything adverse.

## 20.4.6   References

Mention was made at **12.3.2** of the House of Lords decision in *Spring v Guardian Assurance plc* [1995] 2 AC 296. In that case, a former employer of a self-employed insurance agent gave a negligent reference in respect of the plaintiff. The reference was described by the judge at first instance as 'the kiss of death to his career in the insurance industry'. The plaintiff's claim for damages was eventually successful when the House of Lords decided that the former employers owed a professional duty to use reasonable skill and care in giving a reference that was fair and balanced. If the person giving the reference did not have sufficient knowledge he (or she) must find out the required information at first hand.

A negligent reference can rebound in two ways. First, the former employee can recover damages in contract if a reference given negligently has caused him economic or other loss and damage. Secondly, the new employer may bring a claim based on the *Hedley Byrne* rule for a sufficiently careless misstatement about the employee that has misled and caused loss to the new employer.

These rules give rise to a difficulty when the applicant for a headship has left his previous employment under the terms of a compromise agreement under the terms of s 203 of the Employment Rights Act 1996. It may be that the applicant resigned from his post at the previous school because the governors had lost confidence, and there is an agreed set of restrictions about what will and will not be said by way of reference. These matters are considered in more detail later in this chapter. However, the onus in each case will be on those who are seeking the reference to be satisfied with the answers to the questions they have asked and, if necessary, to visit the applicant's present school. Equally, the person giving the reference must say nothing that tends to mislead.

### 20.4.7   Salary

The initial annual salary will, in some cases, be fixed by reference to minima set by the school associations and the appropriate scale point number on the Pay Spine for Heads as defined by the School Teachers' Pay and Conditions Document, produced annually by the Department for Education and Employment. Usually, there will be provision for an annual review, the review to be completed by an agreed date each year and the increments to take effect from a later agreed date.

It is normally provided that the head's salary, accrues from day to day during both term and holiday periods. For purposes of calculation of salary, the school terms begin on 1 September, 1 January and 1 May respectively and end on 31 December, 30 April, and 31 August. It is normally provided that the annual salary is paid by 12 equal monthly instalments in arrears.

The employment contract should set out the provisions that will apply in the event of absence owing to illness, injury or other disability.

### 20.4.8   Pension provision

The head's service may be pensionable under the Teachers' Superannuation (Consolidation) Regulations 1988, as amended, or under a separate pension scheme. When the employment contract is drafted it should state whether or not a contracting out certificate is in force in respect of the pension contributions.

## 20.4.9   Expenses

Upon production of vouchers or other evidence of payment, the head should be entitled to reimbursement of the cost of any reasonable travelling, hotel, entertainment or other out-of-pocket expenses properly incurred in the course of the head's employment. Expenses in the proper sense are not benefits in kind.

Course fees are also a tax-free expense, provided the course leads to the acquisition of knowledge or skills which are either necessary for the duties of the employment or are directly related to increasing the effectiveness of the employee in the performance of his (or her) present or prospective duties. The course need not lead to the employee obtaining any qualification.

## 20.4.10   Benefits in kind

The benefits listed below are those most commonly considered, although not always agreed.

The law in respect of benefits, emoluments and allowable business expenses is complex and contains grey areas. In general terms, '*emoluments*' means money or *money's worth*. Once it has been decided that an item provided for an employee constitutes a taxable emolument, its *taxable value* will vary in accordance with specific legislation.

## 20.4.11   Professional subscriptions

The governors should expect to pay the annual cost of membership of the head's professional association. Where it can be shown that membership of the body by the head employee is required *wholly, exclusively and necessarily* in the performance of the head's duties, payment by the employer should be an allowable and therefore non-taxed expense.

## 20.4.12   Private medical insurance

The provision of private medical insurance and for medical check-ups is a common benefit provided to employees and a usual benefit paid in respect of a head, the head's spouse and dependent children. It will, however, result in a benefit-in-kind charge equal to the cost of providing the benefit.

## 20.4.13   Education of the head's children

Guidance issued by the Inland Revenue, after the decision of the House of Lords in *Pepper v Hart* [1993] AC 593, confirms that school fees, where teachers pay at least 15% of normal fees, are not a taxable benefit. Accordingly, it is normal for the head's children to be educated free of charge or at a reduced percentage of the fees, to be negotiated between the governors and the head. The basis of this rule is the long-established practice of independent schools to regard the real cost of educating teachers' children on the *marginal additional cost* basis incurred by the school in taking on those extra pupils.

## 20.4.14 Provision of a car

It is normal for a head to provide his or her own car and to be reimbursed for business mileage, which will be tax-free provided it does not contain any profit element. Travel from home to work and other private mileage is not classified as business use.

The tax-free mileage rates allowed by Inland Revenue in 1997/98 were:

| *Motor Vehicle Engine Size* | *Up to 4,000 miles pa* | *Over 4,000 miles pa* |
| --- | --- | --- |
| Up to 1,000 cc | 28p | 17p |
| to 1,500 cc | 35p | 20p |
| to 2,000 cc | 45p | 25p |
| Over 2,000 cc | 63p | 36p |

Provision of road tax, motor insurance, maintenance and repairs are taxable benefits.

As an alternative, use of a 'pool' car will not lead to a tax liability as a benefit in kind, subject to four conditions which are directed to the general availability of the car, excluding purely private use and ensuring that the pool car is not normally kept overnight on residential premises.

## 20.4.15 Mobile telephone

Mobile telephones may have been a luxury in the early 1990s but latterly they have been regarded not only as a normal business tool, but as an essential aspect of school security. From 6 April 1991 a flat-rate benefit in kind charge of £200 was assessed in respect of mobile telephones provided to employees which they might use in part for personal purposes, and the same for mobile telephones installed in company cars provided to employees. The charge could be avoided if there was no private usage or the employee reimbursed the employer for the full cost of private usage and the appropriate proportion of running costs.

## 20.4.16 Relocation costs

The statutory regime provided at s 76 of and Sch 5 to the Finance Act 1993 provides an upper limit of £8,000 on the tax-free element of employee relocation packages. The following expenses fall within the £8,000 tax-free limit:

–   house sale expenses (legal fees, mortgage loan redemption penalties, agents' fees, advertising costs, utility disconnection charges, insurance and security costs while the premises are empty and rent payable whilst the premises are empty);

–   purchase expenses (legal fees, mortgage loan procurement charges, survey fees, Land Registry fees, stamp duty charges and utility connection charges);

–   abortive purchase expenses;

–   costs of transportation of household belongings (including packing and unpacking costs, temporary storage charges, costs of detaching and re-attaching household fittings);

– travel and subsistence expenses when house hunting, including employees' travel costs between old home and new place of work, etc;

– bridging loan expenses;

– duplicate expenses (domestic goods purchased to replace those that were used at the old home but are not suitable for use at the new home).

### 20.4.17 Staff accommodation

On 8 May 1951, a memorandum was agreed between the Association of Governing Bodies of Public Schools (GBA) and the Board of the Inland Revenue covering taxation of staff accommodation. Following discussions in 1996, the Independent Schools Joint Council (ISJC) (now ISC) has agreed with the Inland Revenue that the 1951 Memorandum should remain in force as the basis for all settlements up to and including the financial year 1996/97. New guidance was issued for exemptions for 1997/98 and subsequent years. The guidance is briefly as follows.

Living accommodation will be exempt from tax:

– where it is *necessary* for the *proper performance* of the employee's duties that he (or she) should reside in the accommodation; or

– where the accommodation is provided for the *better performance* of the duties of that employment *and* it is one of the kinds of employment in the case of which it is *customary* for employers to provide living accommodation for employees (emphasis added).

In a school with boarders, it will invariably be a condition of the head's employment that he (or she) occupies accommodation at school premises and the contract should so provide. Moreover, it should be a condition that the head is not entitled to sub-let the accommodation. In other words, the accommodation should have no 'money's worth' to the head.

The position is less clear in the case of day-schools. The criteria are '*better performance*' and '*customary*'. It is a moot point whether 'customary' means customary in independent schools or whether it necessarily means customary in day-schools of all types, both maintained and independent. ISJC advised in February 1997 that it may carry the latter meaning.

This interpretation, if correct, is capable of operating to the detriment of the charity. There is widespread and well-founded concern about school security and vandalism. It is submitted that it would be wrong to penalise the conscientious head of a day-school who has opted to live in a flat at school premises with the object not only of being able to work late into the evening but also to carry out a caretaker role and perhaps save on the costs of employing a caretaker. It is also submitted that the position may be different as between a day preparatory school that is part of a senior school with boarding provision, and a day-school pure and simple that has a long established history of separate caretaking arrangements.

*Better performance* involves there being an explicit description of the duties. There must be a requirement that the head is on call outside his (or her) normal hours and evidence that the head is in fact frequently called out.

ISJC has also drawn the attention of schools to the fact that the exemption from tax relates solely to accommodation provided by the school. There is no exemption for additional salary paid in compensation for living out rather than living in.

## 20.4.18  Employment contract

Table 3 at the end of this chapter contains an outline of the main terms of employment, but the employment contract itself, if professionally drafted, will be a very much longer and more complex document, which incorporates a number of other documents such as the policies of the governors where these are written and the School Handbook.

There are a number of forms of employment contract for heads in circulation. Some of them have been prepared by or on behalf of the various organisations representing heads of independent schools. Others have been prepared by specialist employment lawyers. There are also some inept adaptations of earlier forms which have been rendered a positive danger by more recent legislation and case-law.

The employment contract for a head should not be regarded as a standard form. The contract itself should:

- comply with the law as most recently amended;

- comply with the charitable objects and the articles of government, in the case of a charitable school;

- satisfy the objectives of the governors and head and be approved by the head's professional association.

For these reasons, it is prudent good practice for governors to ensure that specialist legal advice is obtained. There are a number of pitfalls for the unwary and an ineptly drafted contract may prove very costly for the school if the appointment is unsuccessful.

The correct legal personality of the employer must be identified. In the case of an incorporated school, the employer is generally the company or corporation. In the case of an unincorporated school the employer may be the governors of the school personally or the trustees of a trust. Some charitable schemes, particularly those of religious foundations, authorise a single person such as 'the Abbot' to be the employer. Alternatively, if the trustees have been incorporated by certificate under Part VII of the Charities Act 1993, the name of the employer will be the same as the corporate name of the trustees.

The address of the employer should be correctly stated. It may be the address of the school or may be the address of the registered office of a company at, or remote from, the school.

The school's articles of government may provide that the head's employment contract shall contain a minimum period of notice such as 'two terms' [one term's] notice in writing taking effect at the end of a term . . .'. If there is a conflict between the Articles and the contract, it should be taken that the provision which is more favourable to the head prevails. The remaining terms and conditions of the contract, and the documents normally incorporated into it, are outside the scope of this book.

## 20.5   CONFIDENCE ISSUES

### 20.5.1   Confidence generally

Reference has been made at **20.2** above to the sense of insecurity experienced by a great many heads of independent schools. The responsibilities of the job are immense. The head is accountable to governors who, however knowledgeable and conscientious, are essentially unpaid, part-time, non-executives. At times when the pupil roll is growing with full fee payers, when the school is showing well in the league tables, when the show-piece events have passed off successfully and the financial statements show a surplus, there may be a moment for the head to relax and enjoy the fruits of his or her work. But most of the time, success creates its own anxiety about any signs of slipping backwards, or a lack of new ideas for taking the school forward.

A sense of insecurity can give a positive stimulus, but equally it can be destructive if the reason for it is a failure on the part of the governors and senior staff to tell the head how they think s/he is doing and where matters might be improved.

This is one of the essential roles of 'appraisal', so long resisted in the independent sector. There is a world of difference between grunts of support and encouragement at governors' meetings, which may mean anything from very little to nothing at all, on the one hand and a detailed examination of achievements and realistic goals and targets and the resource, training and other support needed. A good appraisal system is at the very core of communication between the head and the governors and there is every reason to think that some departures following loss of confidence might have been unnecessary had this level of communication existed.

An example is that of governors who, in a particular school, may be essentially reactive and have left it to the head to drive the school in the direction he (or she) thinks fit. There are then some adverse reports in the press or from parents or senior staff which unsettle the governors, and relationships go downhill from there. Equally, there are cases in which the head needs some additional support which is not forthcoming in order to form the vision or plan for the school. There can also be a problem with governors who are too proactive and who second-guess every decision that the head makes. The right balance may be difficult to achieve.

Lack of communication is not always the fault of governors. Sometimes, it will be the head who, for whatever reason, has not been able to formulate a clear vision and list of problems to be addressed and a method of solving them and to put them to the governors for approval or advice. Sometimes governors will be heard to say that they 'do not know what the head is doing' and 'cannot find out'.

Leaving aside clear cases of misconduct and incapability, the confidence of governors is largely intangible. In a school community it can be built or destroyed by small groups of governors, staff or parents. One thing is clear, however: once confidence has been irretrievably lost the head will have to go, irrespective of where the fault lies. It can all happen very quickly and suddenly. Cases have been reported of heads who thought they were doing well only to be told that they did not command the support of the community, and that they must leave.

It will be apparent that the head's relationship with the chairman of the goverors is crucial and needs to be maintained with mutual trust and frankness. A new head, particularly, must be given time and support. Governors need to take care not to talk themselves into a position of no confidence, if that can be avoided.

Cases of loss of confidence are known to cause great concern to the heads' professional bodies, in particular HMC, to whom it may seem that the head's job is, in effect, at the pleasure of the governing body. No governing body, however, welcomes the unplanned and unbudgeted departure of the head. Every effort will be made to repair relationships where possible. But, if the school is failing, or staff and parents no longer accept the head, or if the governors and head can no longer find a basis of mutual trust and confidence, then, as with any other high profile appointment, the head must go. The head is not bound to accept the compromise agreement that may be offered but will usually understand the sound reasons for doing so.

### 20.5.2   Basis of confidence

The legal and factual relationship between governors and head is based on mutual trust and confidence in the head's ability:

−   to articulate a vision or plan for the school and the means by which it will be carried out and to agree those matters with the governors;

−   to meet agreed goals and targets, and run the school;

−   to gain the trust and confidence of the staff and in particular the senior management team and in particular to create and not destroy existing teams and to manage the people for whom the head is responsible. This is part of 'leadership' by a different name;

−   to be visible to staff, parents and pupils and to establish good personal relationships consistent always with the need to stand back and give decisions when required;

−   to perform effectively at show-piece events and assemblies;

−   to understand the market place and formulate and manage a marketing strategy;

−   to understand the trends in the market place that will most affect the pupil roll and the parents' ability to pay fees;

−   to identify and address priorities before peripherals and to be well-organised;

−   to be frank and open with the governors and not be found to have misled them;

−   to be financially aware and accountable for expenditure and to act in accordance with budgets that have been set;

−   to deal promptly and competently with problems so as to avoid undue recourse by parents and others directly to the governors;

−   to act with propriety in his (or her) private life.

In the absence of misconduct, loss of confidence is generally based on shortcomings in several of the areas listed above.

For a new head, there is relatively little time to establish himself (or herself) with the staff and parents. Particularly at a day school, news of the new head will travel fast and can easily turn into gossip and rumour until parents have seen some evidence of performance and direction. During the early days, in public at least, the head will need to be long on vision and short on detail – the other way round will tend to cause confusion and a sense that there is no plan.

### 20.5.3   The governing instrument

The governing instrument – and also the employment contract – should be checked before any steps are taken to suspend or remove a head who has lost the confidence of the governors. It is not uncommon for articles of government made pursuant to a charitable scheme to provide clauses such as the following:

*'Suspension of the Head*

The governors may by resolution passed by not less than two-thirds of those present at a meeting and voting on the question suspend the head from duty for misconduct or any [other] good and urgent cause.

*Dismissal*

Where the determination of the head's contract of employment or his or her dismissal without notice for misconduct or other good and urgent cause is to be considered at a meeting of the governors:

  (a) not less than ten clear days' written notice (which shall include a statement of the grounds for the determination or the dismissal, as the case shall be) of the meeting shall be given to the head; and

  (b) the head shall be entitled to appear and be heard at the meeting and to be accompanied by a friend or be represented by a legally qualified person.

A resolution by the governors to determine the head's contract by notice, or to dismiss without notice for misconduct or any other good and urgent cause, shall not take effect until it has been confirmed at a second meeting of the governors at which not less than two-thirds of their number are present and held not less than fourteen days after the date of the meeting at which it was passed.'

There may be a useful purpose in these articles in so far as they prevent a minority of the governors holding a special meeting at short notice to oust the head but it is difficult to see how the meeting at paragraph (a) can serve any purpose of natural justice.

It is inevitable that before the governors hold the first meeting to consider the head's dismissal the majority if not all of the governors will have discussed the matter privately and decided that for whatever reason the head has lost their confidence to the point that dismissal must be considered. Thus, the first meeting is before a tribunal which, almost by definition, is unanimously biased against the head. When matters reach that point there would be little prospect of the head persuading the governors to change their minds since relationships would already be shattered.

None the less, it seems that the meeting must be held unless both parties agree that it is unnecessary. A dismissal in contravention of this article would be *ultra vires* because it is unconstitutional and it is likely that dismissal in these circumstances could be restrained by injunction.

### 20.5.4   Practical aspects

Governors who believe that the head has lost their confidence will not necessarily have an opportunity of explaining their decision to others who may criticise them. Therefore, it is suggested here that unless there has been misconduct or serious incapability, governors should avoid taking a vote of no confidence unless they are already sure that it would be supported by a substantial body of staff, parents, and senior pupils.

The governors also need to be clear as to the procedures they must follow in accordance with the governing instrument and the head's contract of employment.

Timing can be very important if public examinations are about to start or the school photograph, an open day, a prize-giving, a VIP visit or an inspection is about to take place.

Other important considerations will include: the compensation and legal costs of dismissing the head and whether there are insurers of the legal expenses who must first be notified; the terms under which the head occupies his (or her) accommodation and who else is in occupation; the likely interest of the local or national press; and the question of who will succeed the head on a temporary basis and whether that person will be acceptable to the staff and parents.

It is not unknown for a third party, with or without the tacit support of the head, to take up the head's cause and involve members of the staff and influential parents in a campaign for the head's reinstatement and the resignation of some or all of the governors. Conduct of that kind creates a risk of damage to the school and particularly to the head and can cause serious prejudice to discussions that might otherwise have resulted in a compromise agreement that would be of benefit to the head.

In the event of legal proceedings, minutes of the governors' meetings would have to be disclosed and would reveal any changes of mind or other inconsistencies and splits. Legal costs, not all of which will be insured, may run to considerable sums. Quite apart from the distress and anxiety of the head, the governors will find the aftermath time consuming and stressful. It is also likely to amount to a serious distraction from the development of the school.

From the head's point of view, it is as well to recognise immediately that once confidence is lost, his (or her) future is best served by going quickly (unless it is a case of early retirement). At the time of writing, it is apparently unprecedented for a case of this kind to be resolved in an employment tribunal and such a course would make it very difficult for the head to gain another similar appointment in the independent sector.

On any view, the time scale for settlement and announcement is likely to be a matter of days before control of the situation is taken by outsiders and the head's reputation is damaged.

## 20.5.5   'Without prejudice' meeting

For the reasons given above, it is the custom and practice of independent schools to try and deal privately with issues of loss of confidence so as to ensure that:

– the head's contractual terms are honoured, no unnecessary damage is caused to his (or her) reputation and he (or she) is placed in the best position in the circumstances to obtain future employment; and that

– the governors retain the confidence of the staff, parents and pupils; and the reputation of the school is not harmed in the media.

The head is the most vulnerable party at this stage and will be depending on the governors to provide a fair hearing, a fair and balanced reference (including the parameters of an oral reference) and an agreed and fair formula for the announcements that must be made.

A 'without prejudice' meeting between two of the governors, duly authorised by the board, and the head can be a useful mechanism for explaining the governors' loss of confidence and the reasons for it. If the announcement is a complete surprise to the head he (or she) is unlikely to be in a position to make representations at that meeting and will wish first to obtain advice from his (or her) professional association or legal advisers in any event. The procedure from there forward will depend to some extent on whether the governors require the head to leave immediately or whether it is proposed that the head should see out the rest of the term and leave then, with or without a formal event and presentation.

## 20.5.6   Suspension etc

At the early stage of discussions, confidentiality is of the utmost importance both to the head and to the school. However, a head who feels a sense of injustice and determination to fight for his (or her) survival may be inclined to try and curry support from members of the staff and even some parents. Then, news of the discussions will tend to get out within a matter of hours and very quickly turn into gossip, rumour and enquiries from staff, parents and the local press. In most cases therefore it will be desirable from both points of view that the head stays away from school premises. The legal mechanisms for this, subject always to the contractual position and the charitable Scheme, may be:

– *Agreed absence*: whereby the head agrees, at the request of the governors, to take a few days away from school.

– *Suspension*: if the head will not agree to take time off and give an assurance of confidentiality, the governors may have no alternative, subject to the provisions of the governing instrument and the head's employment contract, but to suspend. However, suspension necessarily implies writing to parents and it must be assumed that every circular letter to parents will very quickly find its way to the press. It may be necessary for the governors to pass a resolution pursuant to the articles of government before suspension can be imposed. Moreover, suspension often (wrongly) suggests to third parties that there has been misconduct and care will be needed not to give misleading signals.

– *Garden leave*: this is a mechanism requiring an employee who is under notice of dismissal, where the contract so provides, to remain in the vicinity of his or her home and subject to many of the duties under the employment contract, and not to take alternative employment.

In a case of suspected misconduct, the head should be warned of the effect of reg 7 of the Education (Particulars of Independent Schools) Regulations 1997. Regulation 7 requires the school authority to notify the DfEE if any employee has been dismissed for misconduct or has resigned to avoid dismissal for misconduct.

## 20.5.7   Staff and parents

Reference has been made above to the likely reaction of staff, parents and press to the unexplained absence of the head. It is very important that staff and parents understand that the information which governors can provide to them will, in most circumstances, be very limited and utmost restraint by all is necessary otherwise there is a risk of destabilising the school.

In *Price v Dennis* (1988) LEXIS, CA, the owner of a private school summarily dismissed the head. One of the issues in the case was whether certain parents, who because of that event had withdrawn their child without a term's notice, were liable to pay a term's fees in lieu of notice. On that point, Glidewell LJ stated:

> 'I do not accept that her [the proprietor's] power to [dismiss Mr Cassidy] can, as a matter of law, be cut down by requiring her to consider the effect that it would have on other members of staff and on the parents ... any intelligent person would realise that dismissal of the headmaster was bound to have repercussions. But that as a matter of contract she could be restrained in some way from dismissing him because of those considerations, I do not accept.'

Nor, it is submitted, in the case of a charitable school, are the staff and parents entitled to insist on detailed information about the developing situation other than in the most general terms. Glidewell LJ also stated in *Price v Dennis* that one of the duties of the proprietor of a school (which includes the governors of a charitable school) is: 'to take reasonable steps to retain the confidence of parents *who themselves act reasonably*' (emphasis added).

## 20.5.8   Dismissal

In the absence of a compromise agreement, the governors may given written notice of dismissal in accordance with the terms of the head's contract but subject in each case to the provisions of the articles of government. During the period of notice, garden leave may be imposed if provided for in the contract and many of the other provisions of the contract will remain in force. The contract apart, the head may still be entitled to make an application to an employment tribunal for compensation for unfair dismissal.

In a case of gross misconduct, following investigation in accordance with normal procedures and also in accordance with the articles of government, the head may be summarily dismissed, possibly having first been suspended, and will not be entitled to a notice payment or salary and benefits in lieu thereof, other than as provided by contract.

## 20.5.9    Confidentiality

Except in cases of misconduct, whether or not publicised in the media, custom and practice is for the parties to agree the terms of any announcement and reference. The practical effect is to operate as a 'gag' on both the school and the head. There are good reasons for this. If everyone were free to give their own version of why the head was leaving, there would in no time be dozens of stories in circulation. Such is the nature of a closed community. That may, to some extent, happen in any event but a confidentiality agreement gives the parties greater control over what is essentially a private matter, even though it directly affects others. But a confidentiality agreement cannot prevent a party making disclosures that are required by law, such as those made by a witness in legal proceedings or to the tax authorities or to respective professional advisers.

There is, however, some strength in the opposite view that, in some cases, a confidentiality agreement can prevent the school from putting right misleading or ill-informed statements or opinions that may surface 6 or 12 months after the event. Furthermore, if the head delays in reaching agreement and rumours are circulating, the governors may decide that they have no alternative but to make a public announcement that the head has lost their confidence and give such further elaboration of that as they see fit, consistent with the contractual duty of 'mutual trust and confidence'.

Which course is taken will be a matter of judgement in every case. However, employment lawyers have suggested that the principle in *Malik v BCCI* [1997] 3 WLR 95 may be extended to cover employees who have been stigmatised by the treatment they have received at the hands of their employers. As yet there is no authority to support that proposition in the context now under discussion but specialist legal advice should be taken in every case before the governors decide to publicise the reasons for the head's departure.

## 20.5.10    Compromise agreement

A compromise agreement under s 203 of the Employment Rights Act 1996 should be drafted by a specialist employment lawyer and should take account of tax exemptions, school accommodation, confidentiality and public announcement among other considerations. The employee must receive independent legal advice.

## 20.6    HEADSHIP GENERALLY

Dr John Rae in his book *Letters to Parents* (HarperCollins, 1998) (referred to at **20.4.1** above) answered the question 'How much does the head matter?' in this way:

> 'The head does not need to be autocratic any more, but he does have to be convincing to an unusual community made up of young people and adults. I doubt whether it is easy for him to achieve this if too many of the important decisions are made by someone else, yet the trend in recent years has been to limit the head's authority ...

> For good or ill ... the head does make all the difference, a factor which worries some critics. They argue that the tradition of solo leadership in schools is out of date and that

decisions should be arrived at via a democratic process in which all the teachers participate. But who in this participating democracy will ultimately take the hard decisions, and who will stand up at morning assembly and explain to the school why the decisions had to be taken? Perhaps more than any other organisation, this community of adolescents and adults needs a leader it can identify and focus upon.

A good head will consult senior colleagues on the staff and carry the governing body with him even if that entails some compromise. But the initiative is his. The governors modify his plans, not vice versa. The senior staff may modify his plans too; he cannot push through an unpopular change if all hands are against him. But he sets the agenda and day by day makes all the important decisions as well as many trivial ones that could be made by others ...

Some governing bodies now say they need a head who can market the school, but when pupils are asked, the quality most frequently mentioned is approachability. What makes a successful head is not his marketing skills, or his ease of manner, but his ability to persuade the school to believe in him. In that sense, the ultimate source of his authority is charismatic. He has got what it takes to inspire others.

You won't find that on his curriculum vitae. You might recognise it when you meet him, although don't forget you have to look through the eyes of the pupils and the teachers ...'

Increasingly, the school associations such as the Independent Association of Preparatory Schools (IAPS) and the Girls' Schools Association (GSA) have introduced and developed induction courses for new heads. A national professional qualification for heads is being introduced and it appears that at last and long overdue, headship is being accorded the level of professional training and induction that is plainly necessary.

A handful of training days for governors are provided each year by the associations of governing bodies (GBA and GBGSA). Individual schools are more likely now than before to arrange training events for their governors or for staff to which governors are invited but overall, the level of training for governors of independent schools remains wholly inadequate for the complexities of modern governance.

***Table 1.***    Specimen 'person specification' for a head.

---

### The Personal Qualities and Skills Needed

- *Academic Record* – a person [male or female] with a good academic background, a good employment record and sound references.

- *Career Record* – a person with impeccable background and integrity.

- *Personality* – a strong, not dominant, personality; able to be diplomatic and tactful; cool in a crisis; willing to consult; a team player who can also stand back and command respect; eager to improve his/her own professional skills through personal development training.

- *Leadership Qualities* – a person with the authority and ability to inspire confidence in governors and other colleagues and parents; a person who is hardworking and leads from the front and will be visible; a person able to convince individuals and meetings of a point of view and carry them with him/her.

- *Presentation and Health* – a person who is of conventional appearance and dress; who is and appears physically fit and energetic; [a non-smoker]; a person who is articulate, 'customer-driven' and appears willing to 'go the extra mile'.

- *Strategic Skills* – a person who has developed an understanding of the main education trends and issues and can develop a vision and plan that will be consouant and relevant; a person who is politically aware.

- *Management Skills* – an effective communicator with a modern approach to matters of quality, team work and appraisals; a person with a track record of identifying priorities, getting things done effectively, efficiently and without fuss; able to manage change for better performance of the objective and aim of the school; a person who understands how to handle and shape matters of ethos and culture within a school.

- *Market Orientation* – a person who is aware of the market place and who understands the marketing methods that are appropriate to schools; a person who is commercially aware.

- *Previous Experience* – a person who has specific experience at the level required for example previously a head, deputy head, director of studies, housemaster or housemistress in a boarding and/or day school environment.

---

***Table 2.*** Specimen job description for a head.

---

## Job Description

---

### 1. Consultation

'Consultation' where used in this Job Description, means the reasonable discussion of issues and the opportunity to make oral or written representations as to those issues.

The Head shall have direct access to the Governors and shall consult:

- with the Governors on all matters affecting the duties of the Head;
- with the Bursar on all matters affecting the duties of the Bursar;
- with the [senior management team] on all matters of actual or proposed policy and other matters of which the [senior management team] should be aware.

The Head is entitled to be present at interviews for the appointment of a Bursar and to be consulted before an appointment is made.

The Bursar shall, save in exceptional circumstances, be entitled to be present at any consultation between the Head and the Governors concerning the performance or conduct of the Bursar.

---

### 2. Leadership and Management

The Head is responsible for:

- the leadership and management of the School as a whole and in particular of the pupils, the teaching staff and the parents;
- planning the development of the school;
- implementing the policies, procedures, instructions and decisions of the Governors from time to time;
- maintaining high standards of management (including middle-management), teaching and pastoral care throughout the School.

The Head shall (where appropriate):

- establish a satisfactory structure of middle management among the teaching staff and review the operation of middle management;
- manage improvement and change throughout the School subject always to budgetary restrictions.

The Head shall ensure that the [senior management team] meets at least once each [week] [calendar month]. The Head shall be entitled to chair each meeting and shall ensure that a brief minute of each decision is kept.

---

### 3. Strategic and Policy Matters

The Head is required to initiate matters of strategy and policy for consideration of the Governors and to act in accordance with the budgets, policies, procedures, instructions and decisions of the Governors from time to time.

The Governors are entitled, following consultation with the Head and for good reason to alter the powers, duties, responsibilities and restrictions delegated to the Head upon giving written reasons for any such decisions if so requested.

---

***Table 2.***    Specimen job description for a head *(cont)*.

---

**4.    The Teaching and Matronal Staff**

The Head is responsible, in relation to the teaching and matronal staff, for:

- their selection, appointment, obtaining of references and checks, job specifications and deployment and their dismissal or suspension in accordance with the disciplinary procedures from time to time laid down;
- the terms of their employment including any benefits such as staff accommodation and staff discounts;
- their management, supervision, performance and professional standards;
- their appraisals, personal development plans, motivation and confidence in the management of the School.

The Head shall, within the prescribed budgetary limits take advice from external professional advisers approved by the Governors and shall consult with the Governors about any employment dispute or issue which might give rise to unbudgeted expenditure.

The Head shall consult with the Governors before appointing a [Deputy Head], a [Director of Studies] or a [School Chaplain].

---

**5.    The Curriculum and Pastoral Care**

The Head is responsible for setting the academic, games/sports and activities curriculum in accordance with the best modern education practice and the aims and objectives set by the Governors and for preparing and resourcing a programme of extra-curricular and cultural activities for pupils and, where appropriate, for parents.

The Head is responsible to determine measures to be taken with a view to promoting, among the pupils:

- self-discipline and proper regard for authority;
- good behaviour of the pupils; and
- good order and discipline at all times when pupils are present on the school premises and whenever the pupils are engaged in authorised school activities, whether on school premises or elsewhere.

The Head shall comply at all times with the Governors' policy as to the discipline, suspension, rustication, removal or expulsion of pupils provided that no pupil shall be expelled by the Head without prior consultation with the Chairman of the Governors (or with the Deputy Chairman if the Chairman is not available) and in any event shall act fairly and in accordance with the principles and procedures of natural justice.

The Head shall [shall not] be bound to teach [no fewer than ( ) periods per week]

---

**6.    Communication and Relations with Parents**

The Head shall use utmost endeavours to ensure that the School:

- is conducted in a manner that is parent and pupil friendly;
- operates efficiently and, within reasonable limits, in a manner convenient to parents and pupils;
- communicates clearly and promptly with parents and pupils;
- satisfactorily manages the expectations of parents and pupils;

***Table 2.*** Specimen job description for a head *(cont).*

---

6. **Communication and Relations with Parents** *(cont).*

- has and operates satisfactory procedures for prompt handling of complaints or queries;
- manages the relationship with parents effectively and retains the confidence of parents and pupils.

---

7. **Marketing and Public Relations**

The Head is responsible for representing the School in the community by:

- ensuring that the School has adequate promotional literature presented to an appropriate high standard;
- ensuring that the desired image and reputation of the School are adequately reflected in the quality of all printed materials going out of the School;
- establishing and maintaining a visible presence in the 'market place' of the School and at school premises;
- maintaining good relations and frequent contact with [feeder schools];
- bringing an appropriate 'marketing culture' to the School so that each member of staff and of the Governing Body is aware of the contribution s/he can make to the promotion of the School;
- maintaining good relations with parents, prospective parents, the authorities and the media;
- recruitment of pupils with the object of keeping the School full consistent always with the standards set by the Governors;
- drawing up, in consultation with the Executive Committee, and presenting to the Governors and implementing a sound and appropriate Marketing Plan.

---

8. **Quality**

The Head is responsible for driving 'quality' at the School so as to ensure that each employee:

- receives a proper induction and is well motivated;
- is 'parent and pupil driven';
- knows the aims of the School and has a Personal Development Plan setting out general and specific goals and targets agreed with his/her manager;
- knows the contribution expected of him/her and has agreed success measures which are reviewed in the course of regular appraisals;
- is provided with a training programme in relation to relevant academic and pastoral matters and relevant aspects of marketing and relations with parents;
- is able to achieve his/her full potential.

---

9. **Professional Development**

The Head shall:

- undertake at least 20 hours of formal training per year in relevant disciplines including academic and pastoral matters, management, marketing and public relations, technology and legal and accounting updates and where appropriate video training for presentations and such other training as may be necessary for the better performance of the Head's duties;

---

***Table 2.*** Specimen job description for a head *(cont).*

---

**9. Professional Development** *(cont).*

- maintain a Professional Development Plan;
- be appraised once per year or more frequently by a Governor and one external appraiser, both selected by the Head subject to the approval of the Governors.

---

**10. Advising the Governors**

The Head is responsible for and shall in relation to any Meeting of the Governors or of any committee or group [including the Executive Committee] established by the Governors:

- advise the Governors in the exercise of their functions;
- attend each such meeting;
- submit items for the agenda of all meetings.

The Head shall have the right to speak at meetings but may on being given reasonable notice be required to withdraw from a Meeting of the Governors for such good reason as they may decide.

---

***Table 3.*** Outline of the main terms of employment for a head.

---

## Summary of the Main Terms of Employment

---

The successful applicant will be required to enter into a formal contract of employment with [state the correct name of the party who will be contracting as employer]. A summary of the main terms and conditions of the contract is given below, but this document does not constitute an offer of employment.

---

1. **Commencement date and duration** – it is expected that the employment will begin on [state date] and continue until terminated by written notice of [one term] expiring at the end of a term. For these purposes, a school term expires on 31 December, 30 April or 31 August.

---

2. **Responsibilities and duties** – please refer to the attached job description which will be subject to such variations as are agreed before contracts are signed.

---

3. **Hours of work** – the Head's hours of work will not be restricted to normal school hours and shall be such hours as are necessary properly to discharge the responsibilities and duties of the head.

---

4. **Paid holidays** – the Head will be entitled to reasonable holidays away from the school during normal school holidays, subject to compliance or lawful agreement under the Working Time Regulations 1998.

---

5. **Remuneration** – an initial annual salary in accordance with [scale point number] on the Pay Spine for Heads as defined by the annual School Teachers' Pay and Conditions Document issued by the DFEE. There will be an annual review taking into account such facts as the governors consider relevant. The annual salary is payable by 12 equal monthly instalments in arrears. In addition, the head shall be entitled to:

    (a) payment of the annual subscription to [professional association];
    (b) membership for the head and the head's spouse and independent children of a private medical insurance scheme arranged and paid for by the school; and
    (c) [free] education of the Head's children up to the normal school leaving age.

---

6. **Pension arrangements** – the Head's service is pensionable in accordance with [state brief details of the pension scheme].

---

7. **Accommodation** – [family accommodation is provided at school premises which the Head will be required to occupy].

---

8. **Expenses** – reasonable travel, hotel and subsistence expenses will be reimbursed upon production of vouchers or other evidence of payment.

---

9. **Car** – the head will be expected to provide his/her own motor car. The governors will pay a mileage allowance for business use in accordance with Inland Revenue guidelines.

---

10. **Notice** – the appointment will be terminable on [one term's] [two terms'] notice expiring at the end of a term.

---

*Table 3.*    Outline of the main terms of employment for a head *(cont).*

---

11. **Medical examination** – the Head shall be required to undergo a medical examination prior to confirmation of his/her appointment and may be required to undergo examinations at the governors' expense during the course of his/her employment.

---

12. **Place of work** – the Head will be required to work at school premises and at such other places in the United Kingdom and abroad as shall be required for the performance of the Head's duties. The Head shall not be required to work outside the United Kingdom for more than 21 days in a calendar year.

---

13. **Responsibilities of the Head's spouse** – the spouse shall be expected to assist the Head in the proper performance of the Head's duties. Job description, salary and pension benefits to be agreed.

---

14. **Tax** – the Head will bear any tax payable in respect of benefits in kind.

---

In addition to the terms and conditions summarised above the employment contract will include a full statement of terms and conditions relating to responsibilities and duties, maternity allowances, redundancy allowances, health and safety, confidential information and documents, grievance and disciplinary procedures, suspension, summary termination and definitions and interpretations

In other respects, the Head's employment will be in accordance with the school's existing customs and policies as amended from time to time.

***Table 4.*** Specimen interview questionnaire for headship candidates.

| Specimen Interview Questions |
| --- |

**1. The candidate's perception of the school**

- What have you heard or read about the school? What is your impression of us from the outside?

- What do you think of our prospectus and entry forms and general presentation?

- What, at this stage, do you see as our strengths or weaknesses?

- What is your vision for a school like this?

**2. Management skills**

- How would you describe your style of management?

- What kind of decisions will be difficult for you?

- What kind of people do you find it difficult to work with?

- What do you feel about appraisal systems generally? Would you wish, as head, to have an appraisal?

- How would you deal with a long standing member of staff resistant to change?

- How about one whose performance was unsatisfactory?

- What do you see as the ideal management team within the school?

- Where do competent part-time staff fit in – if at all?

- To what extent do you think you might require the help of external legal advisers or other external advisers?

- Have you had any part in the preparation of a development plan for a school such as this? What do you regard as the areas in which a school like this can develop?

- Have you ever been involved in introducing an appraisal system or a quality management programme into a school? How would you set about it?

- What importance do you attach to in-service training of staff?

**3. Parents and pupils**

- How soon after appointment would you wish to meet the parents? What sort of things would you want to say to them at that early stage?

- How would you run the reception process for prospective parents?

- How would you deal with awkward or complaining parents?

- How will you organise parent year group evenings?

- How will you get to know each child personally?

- Bullying is liable to occur in any school. How will you deal with it?

- What experience have you had in handling public relations disasters such as pregnancy or death, or incidents of theft, drink and drugs?

***Table 4.***    Specimen interview questionnaire for headship candidates *(cont)*.

---

**3.   Parents and pupils** *(cont)*.

- What are your views concerning expulsion as distinct from the required removal of a pupil for lack of progress or on disciplinary grounds?

---

**4.   Curriculum and technology**

- What has been your involvement in a major curriculum project?

- Are you familiar with the National Curriculum?

- What is your approach to constructing the timetable? Would you continue to do so? If not, how would you delegate?

- What do you think about our present curriculum structure and the length of classroom periods?

- How would you extend the application of computers for use within the school?

- To what extent do you think that classroom activity will be computer dependent in 10 years time?

- How many classroom periods would you wish to teach yourself? At what level?

- What are your views about Britain as a member of the European Community? How would your views influence the curriculum?

- How much importance do you attach to extra curricula activities and school trips?

- To what extent do you regard science and industry as having any relevance to life at this school?

- What is your approach to special educational needs?

---

**5.   Pastoral matters**

- How do you think a child's progress should be monitored throughout the school?

- What is the length of a realistic day for children in this school?

- How would you ensure high standards in things like discipline and behaviour?

---

**6.   Public relations and marketing**

- To what extent would you wish to gain a high profile in the local community? How would you set about doing that?

- Would you plan to write educational articles or produce educational features for the local newspapers?

- Would you be willing to be interviewed about education issues on local radio and television?

---

**7.   Personal and family circumstances**

- What are your family circumstances?

---

***Table 4.*** Specimen interview questionnaire for headship candidates *(cont)*.

---

**7. Personal and family circumstances** *(cont)*.

- How does your [spouse] feel about this post?

- What effect would the move have on your children and their education?

- How would you describe your personal qualities and style of leadership?

- Clearly you have many strengths. What are your weaknesses?

- Other than annual leave, do you regard school holidays as 'time off'?

- How important is leisure to you? How many hours a week would you expect to work in term time?

---

**8. Professional development**

- What training would you require for your own professional development? How many hours a year? How would you set about getting it?

- In what other ways would you plan for your own professional development?

---

**9. The governing body**

- What do you see as the function of the governing body?

- What questions have you for us?

---

# Chapter 21

## THE BURSAR

### 21.1 INTRODUCTION

This chapter describes the scope of a bursar's role at an independent school and goes on to consider some of the areas of legal compliance which are normally the bursar's responsibility.

The literal meaning of *bursar* is 'one who keeps the purse'. In a modern independent school the bursar's role goes far beyond that. He or she normally occupies an executive post and is the business manager by whatever title known, for example director of finance and administration. Many bursars are also appointed clerk to the governors or company secretary.

The Independent Schools Bursars' Association (ISBA), founded in 1927, is the professional body which represents the bursars of about 600 of the top independent schools in England, Scotland and Wales, as well as overseas. Membership of ISBA is extended to the school rather than the individual bursar. Preparatory school bursars receive support from the Independent Association of Preparatory Schools (IAPS).

### 21.2 ROLE OF THE BURSAR

#### 21.2.1 Bursars generally

There is a great variance in the range of a bursar's skills and responsibilities. In a small school, the bursar may be a part-time accounts clerk or accountant, the remainder of the administration responsibilities being undertaken by the head. In a large school, with an annual turnover of some millions of pounds and with a large estate to manage, the bursar may preside over a department of significant size. The duties may be allocated between a finance bursar, a domestic bursar and an estate bursar, each responsible for a team of employees.

Bursars come from a variety of backgrounds such as the armed forces, accountancy, banking, and education, and bursaring is usually, therefore, a second or third career. There is no defined profession of bursar and, as yet, there are no formal professional qualifications, but many bursars are none the less highly skilled professionals.

The specimen job description in Table 1 at the end of this chapter indicates the extraordinary scope of a bursar's duties in a large school, but competence in these areas is only part of the job. A capable bursar needs good 'people' skills and has to be able to say 'no' to budgetary and other requests without demotivating those concerned. A bursar must also be able to delegate and must know when expert professional advice is needed.

## 21.2.2   Division of responsibilities

In her address to the Annual Conference of the ISBA in 1994, Mrs Joan Clanchy, then headmistress of North London Collegiate School, said:

> 'You may feel "added value" is not properly bursar's business. Of course it is bursar's business and I think costs are head's business. If heads and bursars do not make the whole of a school, its priorities, direction and aims their joint business, the misfortunes that await such a school will be deserved. Heads and bursars have to move like Torvill and Dean because we both face the music.'

Two very important aspects of the relationship between head and bursar are their respective division of responsibilities and their lines of reporting to governors. Tensions in these two areas will very easily lead to a breakdown of working relationships and the resignation of one or other.

Conventionally, and by analogy to a corporate structure, the head is regarded as chief executive and marketing director, whilst the bursar is regarded as director of finance and administration. Those labels give an indication of roles but little more than that.

In practice, Mrs Clanchy's analysis is better and the most effective senior management team is likely to be one in which the head, bursar and other senior members of the teaching and administrative staff meet regularly and respect each other's sphere of responsibility. Provided that team is co-operating closely, it will normally make sense for the bursar to have direct access to the executive committee of the governors without having to report through the head on each occasion. It is unlikely that a capable executive bursar would agree to any other arrangement although there are heads who find this difficult to accept.

A typically idiosyncratic view was given by John Rae in his book *Delusions of Grandeur* (HarperCollins, 1993), when he stated:

> 'At Westminster, the Headmaster was the chief executive and the Bursar was the finance director, with responsibility for financial management and for the non-academic functions such as catering and building maintenance. It looked like a clear division of responsibility but, in practice, it was nothing of the sort. The Bursar reported to the governing body; how far he came under the Headmaster's authority was never made clear. I could complain to the Bursar about the revolting chicken but I could not insist that he sacked the chef or spent more money on school food.
>
> The Bursar was also Clerk to the Governors. Close contact with the most influential members of the governing body encouraged him to adopt, like Malvolio, a more distant attitude to members of the teaching staff. Since bursars tended to be former officers of the armed services who were used to working in a clearly defined hierarchy and teachers were often sensitive to any suggestion that their status was inferior, the potential for conflict was considerable.'

## 21.2.3   Preparatory schools

The status of preparatory school bursars was addressed in a paper prepared by the Bursars' Committee of the IAPS and presented at the Annual Conference of the IAPS

Bursars in February 1993. The paper was based on a survey sent to all 531 IAPS schools in the UK to which there were 280 replies.

Bursars were asked to say where they felt they fitted into the hierarchy of their schools. Their perceptions were:

- equal with head                          11%
- below head, above deputy head            31%
- equal with deputy head                   33%
- below deputy head                        25%

When asked to say where they felt they ought to fit into the school hierarchy the responses were:

- equal with head                          14%
- below head, above deputy head            41%
- equal with deputy head                   33%
- below deputy head                        12%

It was noted in the same paper that, in 96% of cases, the bursar had direct access to the chairman of governors on school matters. In 67% of cases, the bursar was clerk to the governors, and in 81% of cases in which the school was incorporated, the bursar was company secretary.

An alternative view is that although, with very few exceptions, there will be a differential in the head's favour over salary and benefits, it is misleading in other respects to try and draw a comparison between the bursar and academic staff.

### 21.2.4   Clerk to the governors

The bursar's role as clerk to the governors will be to convene meetings of the governors and their committees, to advise when called upon to do so and to keep minutes.

The bursar will also be responsible for convening a panel of governors to review disciplinary decisions in relation to staff or pupils. Being clerk to the governors implies additional responsibilities.

In some schools, the clerk to the governors is a partner in the firm of solicitors that normally advises the school. That is a traditional device which overcomes the rule in the law of trusts and charities that a trustee shall not derive a personal interest or benefit from his position. If this device is used it is desirable that the bursar should be invited to attend meetings of governors in an advisory capacity unless some matter is being considered that affects him (or her) personally.

### 21.2.5   Secretary

If the school is incorporated, the bursar will often be appointed the secretary which, in the case of incorporation under the Companies Acts will mean the company secretary. This role again involves additional responsibilities of legal compliance there being some 200 possible criminal offences of non-compliance provided in the Companies Act 1985 and a further 13 in the Charities Act 1993. In practice, the risk of offences of non-compliance will normally be avoided if the bursar relies on specialist advice from accountants and lawyers and other professionals when necessary.

### 21.2.6   Fees disputes

Unpaid school fees can be an area of difficulty between head and bursar, particularly when a decision is taken to exclude a pupil because the fees are unpaid. It is important for the head and bursar to work out their division of responsibility in this respect.

The head's first consideration is the welfare of the child and he or she may be disposed to accept assurances from parents which, on any commercial view, a capable bursar would not accept. It can be particularly difficult for a head who knows the family personally. It should be remembered that the governors are trustees of the assets which include fees receivable and any authorisation to waive fees should derive from an authority given by the governors. Therefore, the head and bursar need to be clear as between themselves:

– who is authorised to threaten exclusion and in what circumstances?
– who is authorised actually to exclude and who will write the exclusion letter?
– who is authorised to waive fees or agree to an instalment arrangement?

Financial control is the responsibility of the bursar who must be as tough as necessary. But when a pupil has been withdrawn suddenly amid concerns over an aspect of teaching or pastoral care, the bursar should make efforts to establish the background and discuss the parents' complaints or concerns with the head or housemaster/ mistress before pursuing a claim for fees in lieu of notice. Specialist legal advice may be needed if the circumstances indicate that a claim for fees will be met by a defence and counterclaim alleging professional negligence. In general, although not in every case, the sudden withdrawal of a pupil during term time by parents whose fees are up to date will indicate that there is a problem that needs investigation.

### 21.3   LEGAL COMPLIANCE

A full account of the legal compliance obligations of an independent school is outside the scope of this chapter.

'Compliance' is a lawyer's expression which covers the duty to comply with the Acts of Parliament, regulations and case-law of the United Kingdom, and also the Directives, regulations and decisions and case-law of the European Community, in addition to compliance with the school's charitable Scheme and articles of government and any regulations made under them.

The weight and volume of legal compliance is vast, and many statutes and regulations provide for criminal sanctions (ie fine and/or imprisonment) and/or civil penalties.

Alarming though this may sound, particularly for the governors of a school that is unincorporated, there are practical safeguards. Schools that rely on specialist professional advice are less likely to commit offences in those areas. In addition to professional advice, considerable assistance is available from departments of local government and other regulatory authorities and in some instances from the school's professional organisation. In general, the authorities do not go out of their way to prosecute where advice or a warning would suffice and would be heeded.

Even so, there have been cases in which governors or the school company have been prosecuted, including, during the 1990s, a school company fined £30,000 following a criminal conviction arising out the sudden death of a pupil in the school's swimming pool, and governors who were fined £3,000 following conviction for a 'bald tyre' offence in respect of the school minibus. Cases such as these serve to emphasise the importance to every unincorporated school of seeking incorporation. If there is no 'corporate buffer' between the prosecuting authority and the governors, the only target for a prosecution will be the individual governors personally.

Independent schools have sometimes been reluctant to accept the expense and additional workload of dealing with their compliance obligations, but the majority have done their best to comply with the health and safety legislation. In general, the 'no gain without pain' principle applies. An organisation that attends to legal compliance will be a better organisation at the end of it. Having complied, the cost and effort of doing so will soon become historic. Compliance is now an aspect of inspections carried out on behalf of the Independent Schools Council (formerly ISJC).

The main legal compliance headings for an independent school are given below.

### 21.3.1 Companies

Many charities are constituted as companies limited by guarantee incorporated under the Companies Acts. The most recent substantive Act is the Companies Act 1985 arranged in 747 sections and 25 schedules. It has been amended by subsequent statutes and supplemented by regulations. The Act contains a great many compliance duties affecting companies, their members and directors. The criminal penalties for default are authorised by s 730 and set out in Sch 24.

A detailed discussion of the Act is outside the scope of this book. Particular points to note are:

– s 30, which exempts a private company limited by guarantee from using 'limited' as part of its name in certain circumstances;

– ss 348–351, which specify the information about the company that must appear in, broadly, all printed material, cheques, invoices and receipts. There are fines for being in default.

Related legislation includes:

– the Business Names Act 1985, which applies to a person (such as the governors of an unincorporated school) who uses a 'business name' ie broadly, a name other than his own;

– the Company Directors Disqualification Act 1986, which, inter alia, requires the court to make a disqualification order against a company director where the company has at any time become insolvent and the directors' conduct makes him unfit to be concerned in the management of a company;

–   the Insolvency Act 1986, which regulates individual and corporate insolvency. The Act is arranged in 444 sections and 14 Schedules and creates a number of criminal and civil offences. Of particular importance are s 213 (fraudulent trading), s 214 (wrongful trading), and s 217 (personal liability for debts).

### 21.3.2   Consumer credit

The Consumer Credit Act 1974 is discussed at **9.8.19** and has been supplemented by a number of regulations including the Consumer Credit (Exempt Agreements) Order, SI 1989/869, and the Consumer Credit (Agreements) Regulations, SI 1983/1553.

### 21.3.3   Contract for educational services

Although there is no requirement of statute or regulation that a school should produce its contract with parents in written form, there are a number of statutory provisions that do, or may, apply to the contract in any event. They arise in the areas of trade descriptions, consumer credit, supply of goods and services, unfair contract terms, data protection, copyright, design and patents, the Children Act 1989, money laundering, misrepresentation, and deposits under the Banking Act 1987.

It is at the very least good practice to ensure that contractual terms are clearly stated in writing, and that the Independent Schools Council has informed its Inspectors that this is an area of advisory compliance.

### 21.3.4   Copyright

The Copyright Designs and Patents Act 1988 came into force on 1 August 1989. The Act protects literary works (including tables, compilations and computer pro-grammes); dramatic works, musical works; artistic works; sound recordings, film including video; broadcasts; cable programmes and published editions. There are a number of concessions available to schools in the use of copyright work.

### 21.3.5   Data protection

The Data Protection Acts 1984 and 1998 are explained at Chapter 23.

There are a number of other statutes and regulations that have a bearing on data protection, including those relating to:

–   computer misuse;
–   health records, access to health records and medical information and control of such access.

### 21.3.6   Educational charities

The Charities Act 1993 consolidates most, but not all, of the earlier legislation regulating charities. Section 3(7) imposes a duty on charity trustees to apply for registration of a charity and to supply the documents and information required in s 3(6). The Charities (Accounts and Reports) Regulations 1995, which came into force on 1 March 1996, have been supplemented by the Statement of Recommended Practice (SORP), and have considerably altered the presentation and content of accounts by all schools which are charities. Schools will need to rely on their professional advisers to ensure compliance.

The Charities Act 1993 is arranged in 100 sections and 8 Schedules. Its detailed provisions are outside the scope of this chapter, but of particular relevance are:

–   the requirements of s 5 in relation to the information to be stated on broadly all printed material, correspondence, cheques, invoices and receipts – there are fines for being in default;

–   the restrictions on dispositions and mortgages of land contained respectively in ss 36 and 38 of the Act.

### 21.3.7   Employment contracts and procedures

The Employment Rights Act 1996 came into force on 22 August 1996 and consolidates most, but not all, of the earlier employment legislation, the detail of which is outside the scope of this section. In addition to the 1996 Act, there are statutes and regulations governing the following:

–   discrimination on grounds of sex, race and disability; these categories can include indirect discrimination on grounds of age or religion;

–   transfer of undertakings and collective redundancies;

–   equal pay;

–   part-time employees;

–   compensation for redundancy and premature retirement of teachers;

–   rehabilitation of offenders and checks with the DfEE, Department of Health and the police; and relating also to barring persons who are unfit to have contact with children.

Council Directive 93/104/EC, known as the Working Time Directive, has been implemented in the Working Time Regulations 1998 which contain provisions for a 48-hour week for most employees, and daily and weekly rest periods with special provisions for night working, and minimum holidays.

*Fairness at Work*, a White Paper due to be implemented by October 1999, contains proposals for union recognition and to reduce to one year the qualifying period for unfair dismissals. It is also proposed to remove the compensation cap on claims for unfair dismissal. The paper covers the Parental Leave Directive under which employees will, in due course, be entitled to maternity and paternity leave and reasonable time off work for reasonable family reasons, such as the ill health of a child.

At the time of writing, some amendments to the law relating to collective redundancies and transfer of undertakings have also been proposed.

### 21.3.8   Health and safety

The Health and Safety at Work etc Act 1974 is in 85 sections and 10 Schedules. It sets out the general duties of employers to employees and others and makes provision for health and safety regulations, approved codes of practice and enforcement. Offences are dealt with at ss 34–42. A great many regulations have been made pursuant to the Act and EC Directives including:

-   The Health and Safety 'Six Pack' 1992, being six sets of regulations covering management of health and safety at work; personal protective equipment at work; display screen equipment; work equipment; manual handling operations; and health, safety and welfare in the workplace. These regulations took effect on 1 January 1993.

-   The Control of Substances Hazardous to Health Regulations 1994 (COSHH) which consolidated the amendments to the 1988 COSHH regulations.

-   Regulations covering various aspects of education including work experience, school premises, activity centres and the medical needs of pupils in school.

-   Regulations about training, consultation of employees and reporting injuries, diseases and dangerous occurrences.

-   Statutes and regulations concerning fire precautions, fire safety and safety of places of sport; and fire safety conditions attached to licenses for public entertainment at school premises.

-   Food hygiene and safety including a requirement to register school kitchens.

-   Regulations relating to noise at work.

-   Regulations covering electrical systems and services, equipment and every work activity which involves electricity. The regulations also cover portable electrical equipment.

-   The Construction (Design and Management) Regulations 1994, SI 1994/3140, which came into force on 31 March 1995 and are known as the CONDAM regulations. They implement part of the EC Directive 92/57/EC of 24 June 1992 and apply to everyone associated with construction projects. They impose specific duties on five key parties: the client; the designer; the planning supervisor; the principal contractor; and contractors and the self-employed.

-   Regulations to do with first aid, the requirement to maintain an accident book and record details of accidents, safety signs and signals, miscellaneous provisions about entering school premises and statutes relating to occupier's liability.

The health and safety regime introduced a statutory obligation to make risk assessments and to keep records of various kinds.

### 21.3.9   Liability insurance

Section 1(1) of the Employers' Liability (Compulsory Insurance) Act 1969 requires an employer (for example, the governors or the school) to be insured for their own liability to an employee. A certificate of insurance must be displayed at every place where persons are employed. The position of a parent helper at school premises or on a school trip should be considered in this context.

Motor vehicle insurance is also a requirement of law, pursuant to the Road Traffic Acts. Other liability insurances such as public liability, professional indemnity and trustee indemnity are not a statutory requirement but should be regarded as necessary.

## 21.3.10   Licensing

Several statutes and regulations create a requirement to obtain a licence for the use of premises. The licensing requirements relate mainly to:

– safety standards at functions to which the general public are admitted;

– premises used for the public performance of a play;

– occasional sales of intoxicating liquor at a function during a period not exceeding 24 hours;

– small lotteries, private lotteries and society lotteries;

– use of premises for polling purposes in an election.

## 21.3.11   Money laundering

EC Directive 91/308/EEC requires satisfactory evidence to be obtained of the identity of a client/customer where a single sum or a number of small sums totalling £10,000 or more is paid in cash.

There are a number of statutes regulating the reporting requirements and procedures to be used to help detect those who change the identity of illegally obtained money so that it appears to have originated from a legitimate source. They include the Proceeds of Crime Act 1985, the Drug Trafficking Offences Act 1986, which was amended by the Drug Trafficking Act 1994, and the Criminal Justice Act 1988.

## 21.3.12   Registration of independent schools

Part VII of the Education Act 1996 contains the registration provisions and offences in relation to the registration of independent schools. Other statutory provisions and regulations in this area include:

– the Education (Particulars of Independent Schools) Regulations 1997, which came into force on 1 January 1998 and replaced the earlier regulations of 1982 and 1994 (schools should note in particular reg 7 regarding mandatory reports of misconduct by employees);

– statutory provisions concerning special educational needs and approval of independent schools that admit statemented pupils;

– various other registration requirements in relation to school kitchens, educational charities, the Data Protection Acts 1984 and 1998, and pupil registers.

Part VIII of and Sch 6 to the Children Act 1989 deal with registration of children's homes, the welfare of children in those homes and persons who are disqualified from carrying on or being employed in children's homes. Section 87 of the Act applies to children accommodated at independent schools, most of which are now outside the definition of children's homes.

## 21.3.13   School transport

The Transport Acts 1962 to 1985 contain the law relating to the school minibus and small bus permits under s 19 of the 1985 Act. Also of application to a school minibus are the Road Vehicles (Construction and Use) (Amendment) (No 2) Regulations 1996, SI 1996/163, which came into force on 10 February 1997, in relation to seat-belts.

## 21.3.14   Town and country planning

The Town and Country Planning Acts 1990 consist of four statutes and numerous regulations, circulars and policy guidance. They principally address the construction and use of property. In addition, there are building regulations and fire regulations associated with construction, and provisions relating to tree preservation orders, listed buildings, buildings within conservation areas, temporary buildings, and special events.

A matter of particular relevance to a boarding school is when there is an intended change of use of a boarding house into provision for day education. There may be a requirement to seek planning permission if the change will lead to greater traffic intensity and/or parking difficulty in a residential area. Each case will turn on its own facts.

The Environmental Protection Act 1990 and associated Code of Practice lay down requirements for proper arrangements for the disposal of waste and a duty of care to ensure that the school deals with reputable contractors.

These areas of legal compliance should not be regarded as by any means exhaustive. New statutes and regulations are appearing all the time and the Labour Government of May 1997 has promised a substantial legislative programme.

## 21.4   COMMUNITY LAW

Until 1964, the Parliament of the UK was, at law, supreme. All its legislation, of whatever kind, was binding on whomsoever it addressed. There could be no effective appeal beyond the judicial committee of the House of Lords or the Privy Council.

Erosion of that supremacy began in 1964 when the European Court of Justice stated that Community Law has primacy over all conflicting national law of whatever kind. Gradually, over time, that position has come to be recognised by the Parliament and courts of the UK, although its effects can cause complexities in some situations. None the less, matters of legal compliance must now, in every case, be considered against the background of Community law and, to a growing extent, the European Convention on Human Rights 1950, parts of which are, at the time of writing, set to pass into domestic legislation.

The following is a brief explanation of the main concepts and points of terminology under Community law:

- The Treaty of Rome 1957 brought the EEC (now called the EC) into being. The Treaty of Rome is arranged in Articles and has been amended several times. It lays down general principles and objectives and provides for secondary legislation to be passed to further these.

- The Treaty of European Union 1993 ('the Maastricht Treaty') brought the European Union (EU) into being. The European Union encompasses the EC.

- These Treaties, together with the Treaty of Paris 1951, the Euratom Treaty 1958 and the European Economic Area Agreement 1994, are known as the Founding Treaties. They are both *constitutional documents* and *primary legislation*. All other legislation is secondary.

- The secondary legislation, which is passed further to the Treaty of Rome, is of three types: Regulations, Directives and Decisions.

- Regulations are of general application, binding in their entirety and directly applicable in all Member States. They do not require implementation by the Member States.

- Directives are binding only on the Member States to which they are addressed and only as to the result to be achieved. They require implementation but they leave it to the Member States to choose the form and method of implementation. In certain circumstances, Directives which a Member State fails to implement or does not implement properly may nevertheless be enforced in national courts by affected individuals.

- Decisions are addressed to particular persons or companies and are the means by which the Community authorities apply Community law in specific situations.

- The European Court of Justice (ECJ) sits at Luxembourg (and is not to be confused with the European Court of Human Rights, which deals with the European Convention on Human Rights and sits in Strasbourg). It gives authoritative rulings on the interpretation, application and effect of Community law. It has a first tier court, the Court of First Instance (CFI).

- The European Commission is the executive arm of the EU. It also plays a part in the legislative process by which Regulations, Directives and Decisions are adopted by the Community institutions. On some matters it can legislate alone, usually by way of powers delegated to it by the Council of Ministers.

- The UK Parliament passes primary legislation applicable in the UK and approves secondary legislation.

The UK courts give primacy to directly effective Community law where it conflicts with national law (unless they were to hold that the conflict was deliberately intended by Parliament – a finding which has never yet been made). Where a question as to the interpretation of Community law or of the validity of a piece of secondary legislation arises in a national court, the latter may refer it to the ECJ for a ruling (Article 177) and the House of Lords, as the final court of appeal, *must* refer it, other than in exceptional circumstances.

***Table 1.*** Specimen job description for a bursar.

---

## Job Description

---

### 1. Consultation

'Consultation', where used in this Job Description, means the reasonable discussion of issues and the opportunity to make oral and written representations on those issues.

The Bursar shall have direct access to the Governors and shall consult:

- with the Governors on all matters affecting the duties of the Bursar;
- with the Head on all matters affecting the duties of the Head;
- with the Executive Committee on all matters of actual or proposed policy and other matters of which the Executive Committee should be aware;

[The Bursar is entitled to be consulted concerning the appointment of a Head.]

The Head shall, save in exceptional circumstances, be entitled to be present at any consultation between the Bursar and the Governors concerning the performance or conduct of the Head.

---

### 2. Professional Duties

The Bursar's professional duties shall be carried out in accordance with and subject to such as may be applicable of the following: the Trust Deed; the Articles of Association; the Scheme or Order of the Charity Commissioners; every other governing instrument; the rules, regulations, policies, directions, restrictions and instructions made or given by the Governors; and the terms of the Bursar's employment.

---

### 3. Finance and Administration

The Bursar is responsible for:

3.1 In consultation with the Executive Committee, preparing the School's Business Plans and presenting them to the Governors; working with the Head to implement the plan when it has been approved by the Governors;

3.2 In consultation with the Head:

- allocating, controlling and accounting for the financial and material resources of the School in accordance with the policies of the Governors;
- arranging for the safety and security and effective maintenance of the assets of the School in accordance with the requirements of the Governors and, where applicable, the Charity Commissioners;
- ensuring that proper books of account (including income and expenditure accounts and balance sheets) are kept and that reports of the material and financial affairs of the School are produced to the Governors in accordance with their requirements and with the requirements of the law including [*insert as necessary*].

3.3 The Bursar is further responsible for:

- advising the Governors on general financial policy;
- preparing annual estimates of income and expenditure;
- preparing annual budgets for departments within the school;
- monitoring income and expenditure in relation to budget and presenting regular management reports on them;

---

***Table 1.*** Specimen job description for a bursar *(cont)*.

3. **Finance and Administration** *(cont)*.

- advising on investments;
- preparing the pupils' bills and collecting all fees and other dues;
- the payment of all salaries and wages, including PAYE, Superannuation and National Insurance;
- scrutinising and passing for payment all invoices and statements of account;
- organising Special Appeals for Capital Funds;
- keeping analyses of costs and other statistical records;
- preparing long-term assessments of future financial performance of the school;
- preparing financial appraisals of particular projects;
- advising on taxation, including Income and Corporation Tax, Capital Gains Tax, Inheritance Tax, Value Added Tax and any other relevant tax;
- advising on the financial implications of the Charitable Status of the school;
- dealing with the school's income tax and rating assessments;
- administering pension schemes for teaching and other staff;
- operation of a Composition Fees Scheme;
- administering the Government Assisted Places Scheme within the school;
- managing Bursary and Scholarship Funds;
- in consultation with the Executive Committee, formulating, implementing and complying with and ensuring the compliance of all members of the non-teaching staff with the rules of the School and any legislation for the time being in respect of employment protection, discipline, data protection, equal opportunities, sexual harassment, and health and safety at work;
- having regard to any matters affecting or pertaining to the legal position duties or liabilities of the School (except those regarding the education of pupils);
[● acting as Clerk to the Governors or Company Secretary and as Secretary to the Governors' Committee and the School's Trusts];
- supervising the School's insurance in all forms;
- buying – either directly or indirectly – the principal commodities for consumption or use;
- acting as Correspondent for the DfEE and being responsible for the records and returns required;
- maintaining contact with the Statutory Authorities and with other organisations;
[● acting as Registrar].

4. **School Buildings, Grounds and General Duties**

The Bursar is responsible for:

- maintenance of school buildings;
- security of school buildings;
- the installation and maintenance of equipment for protection against and escape from fire;
- the maintenance and efficiency of the installations and plant for electric supply, heating, domestic hot water, cooking, water-softening, etc;
- the supervision of the lighting and ventilation of school buildings;
- drawing up outline specifications for new buildings, obtaining tenders, planning permission, liaison with school architects;

*Table 1.*    Specimen job description for a bursar *(cont)*.

---

**4.   School Buildings, Grounds and General Duties** *(cont)*.

- upkeep of playing fields, gardens, all-weather surfaces, running tracks and tennis courts;
- land drainage;
- maintenance of boundaries, footpaths, roads, rights of way;
- supervising catering, the swimming pool and its plant, the school shop, the laundry, sports equipment and facilities, minibuses and transport;
- arranging for staff accommodation and dealing with the letting of property to school employees and third parties;
- letting of premises to outside organisations.

---

**5.   Non-Teaching Staff**

The Bursar is responsible for:

- the selection and appointment of the non-teaching staff of the School [except      ] (where the selection and appointment of any member of staff has been delegated to the Bursar by the Governors then any such selection or appointment shall be on such terms and such remuneration as from time to time may be laid down by the Governors);
- deploying and managing all non-teaching staff of the School and allocating particular duties to them;
- dismissing or suspending non-teaching staff in accordance with the School's disciplinary procedures from time to time laid down by the Governors for different categories of staff;
- supervising and participating in the arrangements made by the Governors regarding the appraisal of the performance of non-teaching staff; participating in arrangements made for the appraisal of the performance of the Bursar, participating in the identification of areas in which the Bursar would benefit from further training and undergoing such training;
- ensuring that all non-teaching staff in the School have access to advice and training appropriate to their needs, in accordance with the policies of the Governors;
- providing information about the work and performance of the non-teaching staff employed at the School where this is relevant to their future employment.

---

# Chapter 22

## PRIVACY AND CONFIDENTIAL INFORMATION

### 22.1  INTRODUCTION

This chapter is concerned with the rights and obligations of an independent school and its community in relation to matters of privacy and confidential information.

English law does not yet recognise a general right to privacy. Instead, it provides some disparate causes of action at common law, a number of statutory protections and the right in equity (ie based on the equitable principle of 'fairness') to bring an action for breach of confidence in certain circumstances.

This chapter needs to be read in the context of the Human Rights Act 1998, which received Royal Assent on 9 November 1998 and will be in force by the millennium. A brief introduction to the Act is given at Chapter 25.

### 22.2  INTERESTS TO BE PROTECTED

The individuals and areas of life at an independent school most likely to be affected by matters of confidence and privacy come under the following headings.

#### 22.2.1  Pupils

The following matters raise issues of confidence in relation to pupils: their medical records; non-medical records; general health; reports and references; access to data about themselves; their private correspondence; aspects of their pastoral care, conduct and discipline; their sexual orientation; information told in confidence to a doctor, chaplain or counsellor; exploitation of their achievements, and use of photographs. Some additional issues arise in relation to privacy rather than confidence on such matters as personal property, space, search and detention, and intellectual property rights.

#### 22.2.2  Parents

Issues of confidence relating to parents might include: confidentiality of details of family and financial circumstances; access to data about themselves; communication with other schools about the family and about unpaid fees; any special terms and conditions of the contract for educational services; concerns about the child stated in confidence.

### 22.2.3   Staff

Issues of confidence might cover information provided to members of staff in confidence by parents and pupils; details of their contracts of employment, salary and benefits; their performance and discipline record; health and medical information; photographs of themselves; information about their sexual orientation; their intellectual property rights; access to data about themselves.

The privacy rights of staff may relate to their personal property and space; their intellectual property; or the results of a DfEE List 99 check, criminal background check or Department of Health or Social Services check.

### 22.2.4   Governors

Governors are in a different category from pupils, parents and staff. There is less likely to be confidential information concerning them save for the results of a List 99 or Department of Health or criminal background check.

### 22.2.5   The school

The school (however constituted) has intellectual property which includes: its name, badge and designs; its database; its business, financial, development and marketing plans, and its general know-how and trade secrets.

In addition, there is a large amount of confidential information concerning a number of those matters and also relating to staff, pupils and their parents. Discussions in closed meetings of the governors, and the advice they receive from professional advisers including the lawyers and from the school doctor, chaplain and counsellor, will be confidential as, normally, will information given to and received from regulatory authorities.

The Data Protection Act 1998 has been described as a new law of privacy in its own right. Whether or not this will turn out to be true, it will for the first time apply to certain manual records and is likely to alter the nature and presentation of certain information that is kept by a school.

It should be remembered that governors (who are normally the charity trustees) owe a personal duty to take possession of, safeguard or recover trust property of every kind, including the intellectual property of the charity. Thus if, as could happen, there is a wrongful use of the school's database by a body of staff or parents, the governors may be bound to take legal action to protect and recover the property of the charity.

## 22.3   CONFIDENTIAL INFORMATION

'Confidence' protects the *substance* of expression. This is in contrast to copyright which protects the *form* of expression. Obligations of confidence can also protect certain personal and fiduciary relationships, such as those between doctor and patient and solicitor and client, and also matrimonial and family confidences, inventions, trade secrets and goodwill, and the internal workings of central and local government, as well as those of public or private companies and organisations such as a school.

In *Seager v Copydex Ltd* [1967] 1 WLR 923, Lord Denning stated at p 931:

> 'The law on this subject does not depend on any implied contract. It depends on the broad principle of equity that he who has received information in confidence shall not take unfair advantage of it.'

Anyone claiming a breach of confidence must be able to show:

– that the information possessed the necessary quality of confidence about it;

– that it was imparted in circumstances which conveyed an obligation of confidence; and

– that there was unauthorised use of that information.

An unauthorised use of confidential information or material is a breach of confidence which is actionable and can be restrained, but the law of confidence will not protect illegality, gross immorality or conduct contrary to public policy. Examples of information that will not be protected are:

– past and contemplated crime;

– torts that are contemplated;

– health risks to the public, and

– a well-founded suspicion of misconduct.

To these must be added, in the case of children under the age of 16 and in some cases over 16, serious concerns over the safety and welfare of the child which will, in appropriate circumstances, override legal obligations of confidence.

## 22.4 PRIVACY

Privacy rights may be considered under the three category headings set out below.

### 22.4.1 Civil liberties

Civil liberties are, broadly, those aspects of the European Convention on Human Rights 1950 which have been recognised by the English court. Most of those Convention rights have now been introduced into English law by the Human Rights Act 1998, which is discussed in Chapter 25.

The main rights to privacy that arise out of the Convention are those relating to: the right to be left alone; the right to communicate privately; the right not to have personal information published; the right to a private life and the right to have access to personal information.

In practice, the exercise of these rights is greatly reduced and, at times, eliminated by conflicting rights such as freedom of expression, freedom to take photographs and legislation that authorises 'bugging' in the public interest. Moreover, the culture of English law in this area is generally reactive so that often a person must already have suffered quite serious damage before the law will intervene. This was expressed by Sir John Donaldson MR in *Attorney-General v Guardian Newspapers Limited (No 2)* [1988] 3 All ER 545 at 596, when he stated:

'The starting point of our domestic law is that every citizen has a right to do what he likes, unless restrained by the common law or by statute.'

Civil liberties are therefore a residual concept. They are what is left behind after legal limits have been defined.

## 22.4.2   Common law rights

'Common law' is the expression used to describe legal principles evolved by senior judges in the higher courts as distinct from those established by European Directive or by statute law or regulation in the UK. The main common law causes of action that protect privacy are:

–   *Action for breach of confidence*, as described in **22.3** above.

–   *Action to prevent breaches of intellectual property rights*, such as copyright, design, patent, trademark and service mark, and also the 'passing off' action, where one trader wrongfully uses the name or get-up of another.

–   *Action for defamation*, ie libel or slander.

–   *Action for malicious falsehood*, sometimes known as 'injurious falsehood', which includes slander of title and slander of goods, and false statements about a person and his property made with malice, which deceive another person and cause loss.

–   *Action in nuisance*, where there is a breach of duty owed between neighbouring occupiers of premises. Nuisance is in the nature of a continuing wrong, maintaining some state of affairs, such as the repeated escape of noise, smells, fluids, cricket balls, animals and so on. Nuisance is a tort that is designed to protect an occupier's right to the enjoyment of his (or her) land and is thus an aspect of privacy. A person is taken to have suffered harm if his right to enjoyment is impaired. An action in private nuisance can only be brought by a person who has a proprietary interest in land. A licensee has no such proprietary interest (*Hunter and Others v Canary Wharf Ltd* [1997] AC 655, HL).

–   *Action in trespass to the person*, which is a generic term covering assault, battery, false imprisonment, abduction or kidnapping. An assault is the act of putting another person in fear of attack. A battery is the actual attack. False imprisonment involves preventing a person without lawful justification from exercising his (or her) right to leave the place in which he (or she) is. This cause of action serves the principle of privacy that a person has the right to be left alone.

–   *Action for trespass to property*, which is a tort involving entering upon land in the possession of another, remaining there or placing or projecting any object upon it without lawful justification. A person who is lawfully on land, but is then lawfully required to leave, becomes a trespasser if he (or she) does not leave within a reasonable time. Statute has derogated from this in the case of tenants and licensees of property.

–   *Wardship* under the inherent jurisdiction of the court. Wardship is an aspect of privacy, because restrictions are imposed on the right of the media to identify a person who is a ward of court. However, wardship may not be used as a means of 'gagging' the press (*R v Central Independent Television plc* [1994] 3 All ER 641, CA).

## 22.4.3 Statute

There are a number of statutory provisions that protect privacy by creating rights, sometimes protected by criminal sanctions, for example:

- s 40 of the Administration of Justice Act 1970 (as amended), which protects debtors from harassment;

- ss 61–80 of the Criminal Justice and Public Order Act 1994, which create offences of criminal trespass and, in particular, aggravated trespass;

- s 1 of the Interception of Communications Act 1985, which makes it an offence to intercept a communication in the course of its transmission by post or by a public telecommunications system, except where one of the parties to the communication has consented to the interception or where it has been authorised under a warrant given by the Secretary of State;

- s 58(1) of the Post Office Act 1953, which gives a right of interception of communications if done in obedience to a warrant from the Secretary of State. The power of interception is exercised mainly by the Metropolitan Police, Customs and Excise and the security services;

- s 8 of the Rehabilitation of Offenders Act 1974, which, subject to certain exceptions, entitles a person to lie about the existence of criminal convictions that are 'spent'. This is discussed in more detail at **22.6.3**. Certain of the provisions do not apply to those who work with children;

- the Protection from Harassment Act 1997, which has been used successfully to restrain and prosecute stalkers;

- the Data Protection Act 1984, which, by October 2001, will be replaced by the Data Protection Act 1998. The 1984 Act requires individuals who obtain, hold or use data about living individuals to obtain a registration and comply with seven principles. The Act also provides certain rights to individuals who are the subject of information held about them. The 1998 Act adds an eighth principle and widens the scope of protection to include certain manual records. It also entitles 'data subjects' to be told how information was obtained, why it is being processed and to whom it may be disclosed. It provides injunctive relief and rights to compensation in wider circumstances than before. The 1998 Act is considered in more detail in Chapter 23.

There are also statutory provisions relating to reporting restrictions, health and safety and medical reports and records which are considered later in this chapter, together with those statutory provisions which expressly permit invasions of privacy and publication of confidential information.

## 22.4.4 Where the law does not give protection

### (a) Unauthorised photographs

Photographs are also considered at **22.7.1** below. In *Hellewell v Chief Constable of Derbyshire* [1995] 4 All ER 473, the plaintiff claimed breach of confidence for distribution of a photograph taken of him by the police to help in the prevention of crime. Although his claim was struck out, the judge suggested that if someone with a telephoto lens were to take, from a distance and without authority, a picture of another person engaged in some private act, his subsequent disclosure of the photograph would amount to a breach of confidence.

It is not tortious to take unauthorised aerial photographs of property and to use the photographs for advertising unless by virtue of an agreement which is subsequently breached.

### (b)  Publishing information

Publishing a true but private fact about a well-known public figure, for example, that he keeps paedophile material, is not of itself tortious, but the *Hellewell* case may have some application if there is an element of persecution.

### (c)  The right to be left alone

This right is not protected as such, but the torts of trespass to the person and trespass to property can be used when they arise. Moreover, following the success of the Protection from Harassment Act 1997, it is quite possible that a tort of harassment will be developed by the courts before long in order to deal with stalkers who, for whatever reason, have not been prosecuted and whose conduct has caused personal injury or other loss.

## 22.5  INTELLECTUAL PROPERTY

'Intellectual property' is a generic term covering work products generated by human intellect and having certain characteristics, including innovation, novelty and inventiveness. The intellectual property of an independent school includes: its name, badge and designs; its database; its business, financial, development and marketing plans; and its general know-how and trade secrets.

The main intellectual property rights are:

- rights under the law of confidence, which protects the *substance* of expression;
- copyright, which protects the *form* of expression of an idea;
- design registration, which protects the appearance of an article;
- patent, which protects the physical embodiment of an invention;
- trademark, which is a mark applied by a trader to denote origin.

These are now considered in turn.

### 22.5.1  Obligation of confidence

There may be an obligation of confidence in relation to an idea that has not been reduced into material form and which, therefore, is not protected by copyright or in any other way. An example would be if a pupil who has an original idea for a piece of music or some other work, hums or recites it to another person such as a member of staff in confidential circumstances. The originator would be entitled to prevent that information being used without his (or her) consent.

Merely humming or reciting the piece is not sufficient to create an obligation of confidence. It must be imparted in circumstances which convey that obligation to a recipient who accepts it as an obligation or who is bound to do so because of the nature of the legal relationship between them.

Obligations of confidence are also important in the context of a patent. A person cannot claim patent protection for any information which is already in the public domain anywhere in the world. However, a confidential communication of an invention does not necessarily destroy its novelty or the right to patent protection.

## 22.5.2 Copyright

Contrary to popular belief, there is no system of registering copyright. It either subsists or it does not. If it subsists it can be enforced by action. Section 1 of the Copyright, Designs and Patents Act 1988 describes the categories of original work in which copyright may subsist.

### (a) Literary, dramatic, musical or artistic works

This category will include designs, sketches, paintings, prints, engravings, sculptures, diagrams, maps, photographic films, graphics, computer programs, musical scores, perforated rolls for reproducing sound, labels, advertising literature, directories, lists, charts, brochures, architectural designs and works of 'artistic craftsmanship'.

### (b) Sound recordings, films, broadcasts or cable programmes

This category includes films on video cassette or magnetic video disk, cartoon films, home videos, television broadcasts, radio programmes, cable programmes, transmissions of computer program information in electronic form, cinema film soundtracks and recorded concerts.

### (c) The typographical arrangement of published editions

This category creates an additional copyright in the typography of published editions of literary, dramatic or musical works which is quite distinct from the copyright in the works themselves. The purpose of this right is to protect the publishers of new editions of work (where copyright in the original work has expired) from the photocopy pirate. Its protection will extend to the unauthorised copying of material such as an article in a newspaper or magazine.

## 22.5.3 Registered designs

A design, in this context, means the appearance of an article, as distinct from a drawing which may be separately protected by copyright. In order to be registrable, a design must be 'new' within the United Kingdom, even though it need not be new elsewhere.

The Registered Designs Act 1949 confers protection against unauthorised copying of a registered design for up to 25 years, although the registration must be renewed every 5 years. A person does not become the owner of a registered design until an application for a registration has been made and a registration has been granted.

The protectable features of a design refer to its shape, configuration, pattern or ornament applied to an article by any industrial process. Examples would include moulded plastic furniture, etched patterns on cut-crystal glasses and sculptured lamp stands.

Registered designs are sometimes used to overcome the rule that there can be no copyright protection of a name. If the name is comprised in a novel design such as a logo, that design may be registered which confers additional rights to those provided by the common law action of *passing-off*.

### 22.5.4    Patent

A patent protects the physical embodiment of an invention which is:

– *Novel* – the test of 'novelty' is that the invention has not been made available to the public in any way, anywhere in the world. In other words, secrecy is vital because public disclosure destroys novelty. The precondition for a patent is that there is an 'invention'. Section 3 of the Patents Act 1977 states that a patentable invention must involve an 'inventive step' which will be established only if it is not obvious to a person skilled in the art, having regard to any matter which forms part of the state of the art.

– *Capable of industrial application* – this requirement means that it must have some useful application or advantage in a practical sense and it must result in a changed physical state of affairs.

– *Not excluded by statute from patentability* – s 1(2) of the Patents Act 1977 creates a presumption that the following inventions are unpatentable: a discovery; a scientific theory; a literary work; a method of doing business; a computer program; and the presentation of information. Other examples are also given but the presumption of unpatentability can be rebutted. For example, a computer program is not of itself patentable but a program which controls a new technological process may be.

Patent law is immensely complex and a more detailed account of it is outside the scope of this chapter. Anyone with an invention which ought to be protected should, as a first step, seek the advice of a reputable patent agent.

### 22.6    PRIVACY RIGHTS OF TEACHERS

#### 22.6.1    Intellectual property rights

In the nature of the job they do, teachers may create a great deal of intellectual property both related to and quite separate from their employment. Non-curriculum work may include external lectures, delivered and published; books and articles; musical compositions and arrangements; paintings and graphics; and computer programmes, inventions and other processes. Ideally, the ownership of such work will be established as a matter of school policy and in the teacher's contract or other terms of employment, but these matters are often overlooked.

Section 11(2) of the Copyright, Designs and Patents Act 1988 provides:

'Where a literary, dramatic, musical or artistic work is made by an employee in the course of his employment, his employer is the first owner of any copyright in the work subject to any agreement to the contrary.'

Most important here is the meaning of the words 'in the course of his employment'. Plainly, work done during the employer's time (normal working hours) and using the employer's facilities will belong to the employer. But what of work done by the employee in his own time using his own facilities and know-how? And what of the cases that fall in between?

Each case will turn on its own particular facts but some of the following factors may be relevant:

- whether the contract of employment required the employee to produce work of this kind;

- the extent to which the employee used the employer's secretarial services or technical facilities;

- the extent to which the work was based on work carried out for the employer during normal hours;

- whether the employer had installed facilities in the employee's home for continuity of work of the kind in question;

- whether the employee was paid to complete outstanding work at home;

- the extent to which the work was supervised by the employer;

- the general practice of the employer of treating the copyright in employees' work as belonging to the employee author.

In *Noah v Shuba* [1991] FSR 14, an employee was expected to research and contribute to scientific journals in his spare time 'in addition to official duties'. The employee wrote a book in his spare time specifically related to his employer's business and using his employer's official notepaper when communicating with outside sources as well as using available secretarial services. The book was published by the employer. It was held that copyright belonged to the employee, as it had not been written in the course of his employment. He had not been contractually bound to write the book.

It is good practice for the author of work in which he (or she) asserts copyright to mark each page of the original work with the conventional copyright statement '©' followed by the author's name and date and to ensure that the genesis of the first copy can be proved, perhaps by depositing it with a solicitor in a sealed envelope. In the case of a patentable invention, care must be taken to preserve secrecy and to ensure that any private discussion of the matter is impressed with an obligation of confidence.

### 22.6.2 Waiver of privacy

There are various circumstances under which teachers are required to waive certain of their rights of privacy and confidentiality, and others in which their rights have been removed by statute. These include:

-   An implied, if not express, duty under the contract of employment to make material disclosures that may affect the validity or enforceability of insurance policies maintained by the school, for example disclosures about health that may be material to motor insurers.

-   Consent to the school processing (ie obtaining, holding and using) data about the teacher.

-   Disclosure that the teacher suffers from a notifiable disease (which does not, currently, include AIDS or HIV).

-   Disclosure of other information lawfully requested on a job application form or in other circumstances. At the time of writing, it does not appear to be unlawful discrimination for a school to ask an applicant for employment about matters of sexual orientation, although this position may change very shortly. Other disclosures might arise out of questions about smoking, drinking and use of drugs, and about health matters.

-   Disclosure of spent convictions by those who are concerned with the provision of certain facilities to persons under 18.

### 22.6.3   Statutory provisions

#### *Spent convictions*

On this last point, the general rule under the Rehabilitation of Offenders Act 1974 is to the effect that a person is entitled to lie about the existence of spent convictions. The rehabilitation periods after which a conviction is 'spent' are:

-   for an absolute discharge, *six months*;
-   for a conditional discharge, binding over and probation, *one year*;
-   for a custodial sentence of less than six months, *seven years*; and
-   for a custodial sentence of six to 30 months, *ten years*.

Prison sentences exceeding 30 months are not subject to rehabilitation.

One of the exceptions to this general rule is contained in art 14 of the Rehabilitation of Offenders Act 1974 (Exceptions) Order 1975, SI 1975/1023 (as amended). Article 14, which was substituted in 1986, is a wide provision requiring disclosure of spent convictions on the part of those who are concerned with children. The article is wide enough to include governors, non-teaching staff and holiday guardians. Article 14 applies the disclosure requirement to a person intending to work in:

> 'Any office or employment concerned with the provision to persons aged under 18 of accommodation, care, leisure and recreational facilities, schooling, social services, supervision or training, being an office or employment of such a kind as to enable the holder to have access in the course of his normal duties to such persons, any other office or employment the normal duties of which are carried out wholly or partly on the premises where such provision takes place.'

#### *Medical reports*

The Access to Medical Reports Act 1988 established a right of access by individuals to reports relating to themselves prepared by medical practitioners for employment or insurance purposes. Section 7(1) of the Act provides that a medical practitioner shall not be obliged to give an individual access to any part of a medical report whose disclosure would, in the opinion of the practitioner, be likely to cause serious harm to the physical or mental health of the individual or others or would indicate the intentions of the practitioner in respect of the individual.

## 22.7 PRIVACY RIGHTS OF PUPILS

A number of commonly occurring situations that have a bearing on privacy, confidential information and the intellectual property of a pupil are considered below. They must also be considered in the context that membership of a private, self-regulating community such as an independent school necessarily involves an element of reduction or curtailment of a person's civil liberties and other rights.

### 22.7.1 Photographs

It is custom and practice for a variety of photographs to be taken of pupils at school. These range from the set-piece photographs of the school, house, class, team and theatre cast to individual portraits and snapshots of activities, groups and individuals. Some schools record year groups on a video film which is edited and made available for sale to parents. These are community activities undertaken in appropriate circumstances for which the express permission of parents and pupils would rarely, if ever, be sought.

Moreover, it is the custom and practice of independent schools to regard parents and pupils as being among the most effective means of marketing the school, with the object of replacing those pupils who leave in the ordinary way and thus ensuring the continuity of the school. It is quite rare for a parent to object to the allegedly unauthorised use of a pupil's photograph in the prospectus or at an exhibition, but it does occasionally happen.

It is to be taken as an implied term of the contract for educational services that photographs of pupils will not be taken or used for purposes contrary to normal custom and practice or express agreement. It would almost certainly be a breach of contract with the parents and a breach of an implied obligation of confidence owed to the pupil to exploit a pupil's photograph by using it without consent outside the normal context of the school. In any such case, it would be good practice, as well as a usual courtesy, to seek the consent of a pupil of sufficient age (probably 13 and over) and, where appropriate, the consent of parents. This point may arise, for example, in the case of a former pupil who has become a supermodel or pop singer who may be caused embarrassment or even financial loss by the unauthorised publication of a photograph from his (or her) school days.

Subject to this, there is no general right of privacy that restricts the taking of photographs. Nor, within the constraints mentioned above, does an obligation of confidence arise. The general rule, as above, is that the photograph may be published and used for any purpose and the use cannot be restrained (*Pollard v Photographic Co* (1888) 40 ChD 345). However, if a photograph is taken in accordance with an agreement whose terms are subsequently breached, that would be a breach of contract which can be restrained and compensation can also be awarded.

Different rules apply to the use of high-powered telephoto lenses with the object of obtaining photographs of people in confidential circumstances. Such photographs may well be subject to an obligation of confidence.

### 22.7.2   Personal space

Arrangements should exist at a school for the degree of privacy that is appropriate to the community and the pupil, having regard to the community's religious, moral and ethical beliefs and those of its pupils. Each child should be provided with appropriate space for the storage of personal belongings that he or she is authorised to bring into school premises. It is submitted that, from the age of 8 onwards, this should be lockable space, but with safeguards to allow for lost keys and appropriate inspections of lockers if there is any suspicion of them containing offensive or illegal material or a problem of hygiene or of defacement.

### 22.7.3   Search and detention

A balance has to be maintained between keeping discipline and good order on the one hand and running a mini-police state on the other. On occasions, it will be necessary and reasonable to search a pupil's desk, locker and other space if there are grounds for suspecting that they may contain illegal drugs, the paraphernalia of drugs, substances for abuse, pornography, firearms, ammunition, stolen property or other items contrary to school discipline and generally to ensure health, safety, hygiene and good order.

Searches should be carried out in a manner that, so far as possible, respects the privacy and other rights of the pupil and maintains appropriate confidentiality. Staff engaged in searches and checks of this nature need to protect their own position. It is not unknown for allegations of 'planting' or theft to be made, or allegations that drugs, when found, were taken and used by staff.

Care should be taken in the matter of searching a pupil's person or clothing. As general guidance, a pupil may be asked to turn out his (or her) pockets or bag. Pockets should not be searched until the clothing has been removed in appropriate circumstances. If there are grounds for requiring any further search, the police should be called and the pupil should be segregated and supervised until the police arrive. Occasionally, allegations of false imprisonment are made in these circumstances. Attention should be given to the pupil's need for food and refreshment and to use a telephone and toilet. Care must be taken not to cause any unnecessary distress.

### 22.7.4   Correspondence

An obligation of confidence arises in relation to letters written by a pupil to his (or her) parents and vice versa (*Thompson v Stanhope* (1774) Amb 737). It is probable that this principle would extend to confidences arising out of correspondence between others in a family relationship to the pupil, and to all correspondence in the case of a person over the age of 16. Offensive or illegal correspondence would fall to be dealt with as a matter of school discipline after the event.

Section 1 of the Interception of Communications Act 1985 makes it an offence to intercept a communication in the course of its transmission by post or by a public telecommunication system except where one of the parties to the communication has consented to the interception or where it has been authorised under a warrant given by the Secretary of State.

Section 58(1) of the Post Office Act 1953 gives a right of interception of communications if done in obedience to a warrant from the Secretary of State. The power of interception is exercised mainly by the Metropolitan Police, Customs and Excise and the security services.

Notwithstanding these provisions, in one advisory case, a headmaster received information that a 13-year-old pupil had formed an attachment with a teacher at her previous school, possibly in circumstances of sexual abuse. It was thought possible that the teacher would write to her at her present school. The head arranged for her post in and out to be intercepted. Notwithstanding the legislation referred to above, the head considered that he was entitled by virtue of s 3(5) of the Children Act 1989 to open a letter identified as coming from that source. One such letter was opened and passed by the head to the community police officer for further action. The head was not prosecuted, nor did any such question arise.

## 22.7.5 Sexual orientation

At the time of writing, there is a proposal to reduce the age of consent for homosexual activities to 16. This is likely to increase the pressure on gay people to 'out' themselves or be 'outed'.

At present, there is no express rule of law which brings matters of sexual orientation within the provisions of the Sex Discrimination Act 1975, and in February 1998, the European Court of Justice in *Grant v South West Trains* [1998] 1 FCR 377 rejected a claim of discrimination over its refusal to provide an employee's lesbian partner with a travel pass which would have been provided to a spouse. That decision has postponed (but probably only temporarily) a formal acceptance that 'orientation' is a discrimination issue.

Traditionally, in boarding schools, homosexual activity between pupils was dealt with as a matter of school discipline and often resulted in immediate expulsion. To the extent that such activity remains a criminal offence in respect of a person under the age of 18, it is not protected by an obligation of confidence. The position may change when the age of consent reduces to 16 and the Human Rights Act 1998 comes into force.

## 22.7.6 Progress reports

It is an implied, if not express, term of the contract for educational services that regular progress reports about the pupil will be supplied to those who have parental responsibility. This is a justifiable infringement of the pupil's right of privacy in respect of a pupil under the age of 16. By custom and practice, it is submitted that there is an implied consent on the part of pupils, aged 16 and over, that their progress will be reported to their parents. Pupils of that age who wish expressly to withdraw consent are likely to place themselves in opposition to the governors' policies and if the matter could not be resolved they would almost certainly have to leave.

Questions often arise about duplicate reporting following a separation or divorce. The absent parent continues to have parental responsibility unless removed by the court or by adoption. The law actively encourages the full involvement of both parents so far as is practicable in the welfare and upbringing of the child. It is consistent with this that the absent parent, even though he (or she) may not be a contracting party with the school, should receive reports. Reporting in these circumstances is a justifiable infringement of the pupil's privacy unless there are compelling reasons to the contrary. In that event, the matter would normally be referred to the court.

### 22.7.7   Counselling

Confidential counselling gives rise to a number of difficult issues which were discussed earlier at **13.7**.

### 22.7.8   Secrets

Teachers are sometimes placed in a difficult position if a pupil imparts a 'secret' which has serious implications for the safety and welfare of that pupil or someone else. It might be information about the use of drugs or substances or a risk of suicide or about serious bullying. It may be information given to a teacher in the home environment by his (or her) son or daughter who is a pupil at the school and who will be identified as the source of the information should action subsequently be taken.

As noted earlier, the law of confidence does not protect illegality, gross immorality or conduct contrary to public policy. The obligation can also be overridden when there is reason to be concerned about serious harm being caused to a pupil.

A teacher who is off duty and at home is still subject to an implied, if not express, duty of mutual trust and confidence under his (or her) contract of employment. The teacher is bound to take such limited action as is necessary to avert a risk of serious harm, whether information about that risk comes to him at home or during normal hours and regardless of who is the source of the information. In such cases, the teacher will discharge his duty if he arranges for the information to be passed via one or two intermediaries, to be followed by action which ensures the source is not identified.

### 22.7.9   The *Gillick* principle

A landmark case about confidentiality between a doctor and a child patient was *Gillick v West Norfolk and Wisbech Area Health Authority and DHSS* [1986] AC 112, HL. In that case, a general practitioner prescribed a contraceptive pill for a girl under the age of 16 without consulting her parents. It should be noted that sexual intercourse with a girl under the age of 16 was then, and remains, a criminal offence on the part of the male but not the female.

It was held that a patient under the age of 16 who none the less has sufficient maturity and understanding to appreciate what is involved in a medical treatment or procedure is entitled to confidentiality. The doctor may only inform the parents or guardian if he (or she) is *not* satisfied that the patient has sufficient maturity and understanding and provided he informs the patient that this is being done. (Of course, full confidentiality applies to persons of 16 and over.)

A practical example of how the *Gillick* case can operate would be if a 14- or 15-year-old girl boarder, of sufficient maturity and understanding, has under-age sex. Fearing that she is pregnant, she confides in a member of staff with strict instructions that her parents and family doctor are not to be told. The staff make arrangements for her to receive advice from a reputable family planning clinic. Two members of staff drive the pupil to the clinic and wait while she is seen, but take no part in the consultation. The girl is given a 'morning-after' pill and is unwell for some days thereafter. The parents find out what has happened and allege that the school has acted negligently and in breach of a term of the parents' contract with the school. It is submitted here that the staff have acted in a proper manner in accordance with the *Gillick* principle, but each such case must be taken on its merits and the pupil should be strongly encouraged to involve her parents.

## 22.7.10 HIV, AIDS, and hepatitis

A pupil is entitled to such confidentiality as can be assured in these cases consistent with taking proper precautions in accordance with the Department of Health Infection Control Guidelines. There is no proposition of law that entitles the parent body as a whole to know whether any pupil at the school is affected by one of these conditions.

## 22.7.11 Pupils' health generally

It would not be an actionable breach of confidence for information about a pupil's health (including HIV, AIDS or hepatitis) to be passed between members of staff who need to have that information in the interests of the welfare of the pupil and the safety of staff and other pupils. Care must, however, be taken to use all such information in a proper manner. Details about a pupil's health must not be made generally available via the school's computer system to those who have no need to know of it.

## 22.7.12 Data protection

The Data Protection Acts 1984 and 1998 are considered in some detail in Chapter 23. The right of access to data is that of the *data subject*. A pupil, if of sufficient age and understanding, is the data subject in respect of medical records. The pupil is also the data subject in respect of the pupil's file, references and reports but the school's data protection registration will presumably authorise processing (ie obtaining, holding and using) of that data for purposes of communication with parents. It is submitted that a request for access to data made by a child may be denied unless it can be established that he (or she) is capable of understanding the nature of the application and it is deemed to be in his (or her) best interests to gain such access. The same applies to a consent given by a child in favour of a parent or guardian to procure records on the child's behalf.

## 22.7.13 School medical officer

A boarding pupil will normally be required to transfer to the National Health Service list of the school medical officer. A day-pupil normally will not. The school medical officer is likely to be retained, but not employed, by the school. The contractual position makes no difference to the doctor's obligation of confidence to the patient. The instances will be rare in which a doctor finds that he (or she) must override confidentiality in the interests of the pupil's safety. An example might be if he has to refer the pupil to hospital or for psychiatric treatment because of a serious eating disorder or episodes of self-harm, where the matter is going to come out. It is submitted that the head, *in loco parentis*, ought to be given the minimum information necessary to enable the head to discharge his (or her) legal duties and every effort should be made to obtain the pupil's agreement to involve the parents.

## 22.7.14 Medical records

There are a number of statutory provisions that cover a person's right of access to medical records and also the right for access to be refused:

- The Data Protection (Subject Access Modification) (Health) Order, SI 1987/1903 provided that a data subject (eg a pupil) may be refused access to computerised information held on his (or her) health only when to supply that data would be likely to cause 'serious harm' to the physical or mental health to the person concerned or lead to the identification of another person.

- The Access to Medical Reports Act 1988 established a right of access by individuals to reports relating to themselves prepared by medical practitioners for employment or insurance purposes. Section 7(1) provides that a medical practitioner shall not be obliged to give an individual access to any part of a medical report whose disclosure would, in the opinion of the practitioner be likely to cause serious harm to the physical or mental health of the individual or others or would indicate the intentions of the practitioner in respect of the individual.

- The Access to Health Records Act 1990 established a right of access to health records by the individuals to whom they relate and other persons to provide for the correction of inaccurate health records and for the avoidance of certain contractual obligations and for connected purposes. The Act gives *access to* manually held health records, which were not covered by the Data Protection Act 1984. A child will be denied access unless it can be established that he (or she) is 'capable of understanding the nature of the application'. A parent or guardian is not entitled to procure the records on a patient's behalf unless the patient consents or is seen to be incapable of understanding the nature of the application but it is deemed to be in his (or her) best interests to gain such access.

- The Access to Health Records (Control of Access) Regulations 1993, SI 1993/746, were made pursuant to the 1990 Act.

## 22.7.15 Special educational needs

The Data Protection (Miscellaneous Subject Access Exemptions) Order 1987, SI 1987/1906, provided that a statement of a child's special educational needs made in accordance with regulations under the Education Act 1981 (as amended by Education Act 1996) need only be disclosed to those specified in these regulations.

## 22.7.16 Confidential references

Schedule 7, para 1 to the Data Protection Act 1998 deals with confidential references given by the data controller in relation to education, training or employment. The Acts of 1984 and 1998 apply to the processing of confidential references, but there is an exemption to the effect that the data subject has no right of access to see the reference itself. It is necessary to ensure that any document created or processed as a confidential reference is clearly marked to that effect. The 1984 Act will be repealed when the 1998 Act is fully in force, by October 2001.

### 22.7.17   Waiver of privacy

Certain of the privacy and confidentiality rights of pupils and their parents may be waived in the following circumstances:

–   by express consent provided in the school's standard terms and conditions, or otherwise;

–   by operation of law in circumstances such as those described above;

–   in the course of litigation.

It was held in *Kershaw v Whelan* [1996] 1 WLR 358 that a client who sues his (or her) solicitor waives his privilege of confidentiality. That means, in general terms, that confidential documents, so far as they are relevant, will come into the domain of all those who are concerned in the litigation.

Although there have been no reported cases on the point, the situation of a parent or pupil suing the school may be analogous. The point has arisen in the context of sanatorium records, where a parent defended and counterclaimed in an action over unpaid fees, saying that medical care of his daughter had been sub-standard. As a matter of law, the confidentiality of the sanatorium records is that of the pupil and not the parents, in a case which falls within the *Gillick* principle (mentioned above). If a pupil of sufficient age and understanding supports the parents' counterclaim in such a case, it is arguable that the pupil waives his (or her) right of confidentiality. If, however, there is a conflict between the parent and pupil on this issue, the matter of confidentiality will have to be decided by the court.

## 22.8   PRIVACY RIGHTS OF PARENTS

Parents are entitled to expect that the school will take all due care of confidential information about parents and their family and financial circumstances. Parents are 'data subjects' for the purposes of the Data Protection Acts 1984 and 1998, and data must only be processed in accordance with the school's registration and the eight data protection principles. Parents are entitled to exercise their statutory rights of access to data including, in due course, manual records.

Consideration is given below to two distinct situations that can involve considerations of the parents' rights to privacy and confidence.

### 22.8.1   Unpaid fees

When a pupil is set to transfer from one school to another, either at a natural break-point or at some other time, it is customary for information to be exchanged about payment of fees. There is a long-standing custom between certain groups of independent schools that a pupil will not be admitted to the new school if fees are unpaid at the previous school.

One justification for this practice is that charity trustees are required to exercise prudence and not unnecessarily to expose the charity to the risk of financial loss. Although checks could be made with a credit reference agency, the most direct indication in many cases is likely to be the parents' previous track record. Another reason is that it does not serve the best interests of the child to be admitted, only to be excluded soon afterwards because the fees are unpaid. Of course, there may be a bona fide dispute over the fees or fees in lieu of notice at the previous school and such circumstances will be taken into account.

Under the Data Protection Acts 1984 and 1998, information about unpaid fees held in machine-readable form or produced in hard copy from a computer is *data* which must be processed in accordance with the seven principles under the 1984 Act. Depending on the terms of the school's registration, the release of such information is a potential breach of the Act. The 1998 Act will extend those provisions to certain manual records.

The most straightforward way of overcoming this problem is to require parents, at the time they are accepting the offer of a place, to confirm that all fees and other sums payable to the previous school have been, or will be, paid before entry to the new school and to provide consent to an exchange of information about fees with the previous school.

The Data Protection Act apart, it is submitted that the fact and amount of a debt is not of itself confidential information or subject to an obligation of confidence implied in the contract with parents. After all, the school is entitled to sue and obtain a judgment and the matter then becomes one of public record on the Register of County Court Judgments.

The *reason* for the debt may very well be protected by an obligation of confidence. If, for example, a parent has informed the bursar that he (or she) is about to be made redundant or that his business is failing or he is undergoing divorce, it is submitted that he is entitled to expect that information to be kept confidential in relation to any discussion about fees.

## 22.8.2   School file

The school file about a pupil will often be a combination of hand-written and word-processed documents. There may be a disciplinary file or a house file separate from the school file. The documents may comprise a combination of factual statements, opinion and intentions. They may concern either or both of the parents and the pupil, and also third parties.

It is all potentially 'data' within the meaning of the Data Protection Acts 1984 and 1998. To the extent that the parents are the data subject, they are entitled under the 1984 Act to have access to those parts of the files as relate to them and are, broadly, processed by computer. Under the 1998 Act, they will, in due course, be entitled to have access to certain manual records as well. A number of the records will be covered by various of the statutory exemptions but specific legal advice will be needed in cases of particular difficulty.

A question arises whether the data controller (normally the school) is entitled to alter the data in any way before granting access pursuant to a request. The legislation does not appear to be specific on this point. One view is that data 'freezes' at the date when a request for access is made. An alternative view is that it is a matter for interpretation in accordance with the First Data Protection Principle: that personal data shall be processed fairly and lawfully and shall not be processed unless one of the conditions in Sch 2 or Sch 3 to the 1998 Act is met. Again, this is a matter for specialist legal advice should the question arise.

## 22.9   REPORTING RESTRICTIONS

Schools of all kinds are caught up in the conflict that exists between the interests of justice, the freedom of the press, the rights of a private self-regulating community and the rights of individual members of staff, parents and pupils. Independent schools may be more exposed than others to prurient interest from some elements of the media who consider it in the public interest to penetrate and publish information about a school community whenever the opportunity presents itself. There have been cases of a newspaper reporter posing as a prospective parent on the telephone in order to get a story from the head.

The main occasions for publicity about a school arise in the context of:

– a major disaster, such as at Dunblane;

– tragic accidents or events, such as a road accident, or death, or attempted suicide;

– a police inquiry, or allegations to do with drugs, sexual impropriety, pornography or some other alleged criminal offence or arrest;

– an arrest or a criminal trial of a person connected with the school;

– the 'child of famous father' syndrome;

– allegations relating to maladministration, bullying or undetected learning difficulties;

– a disaffected pupil walking out of school and seeking to cause damage to the school's reputation;

– disaffected parents who are dissatisfied with a decision of the head or of a court of law.

Quite apart from direct interest from the media, an investigation that involves social services and the police will almost always result in information being provided to the press, either by way of leaks or because the practice of some police forces is to issue their own press releases.

Not all publicity is unwelcome. Some heads have taken the view that a robust statement to the press about the way in which the school has handled a drugs incident helps to reinforce the school's policy on that matter. But, in other instances, such as an isolated case of alleged sexual impropriety by a member of staff, the intensity, level and style of reporting can cause immense damage and have the effect of stigmatising the whole school, undermining the confidence of parents and adding immeasurably to the governors' task of managing events. There have been numerous cases in recent years in which newspaper reports about school-related incidents and about individuals went far beyond the requirements of legitimate public interest.

The remainder of this chapter is concerned with the statutory and other protections that may be available to schools and individuals in these cases.

### 22.9.1  Family proceedings

Section 97 of the Children Act 1989 provides for privacy for children involved in certain proceedings. In particular, s 97(2) states that no person shall publish any material which is intended, or likely to identify:

– any child as being involved in any proceedings before a magistrates' court in which any power under the Children Act may be exercised by the court with respect to that or any other child; or

– an address or school as being that of a child involved in any such proceedings.

This section confers privacy for children in all proceedings in the family court.

For these purposes, to 'publish' includes to broadcast by radio, television or cable television; or to 'cause to be published'. 'Material' includes any picture or representation.

### 22.9.2  Sexual crime

There is very wide protection to the alleged victims of sexual crime, although restrictions on reporting victims' names can be lifted. The legislation applies not only to victims who will be witnesses in a particular case but also to victims who are no more than innocent third parties in sexual cases.

### 22.9.3  Any proceedings – any court

Section 39 of the Children and Young Persons Act 1933 gave the court power to direct in relation to *any proceedings* in *any court* that:

'(a) no newspaper report of the proceedings shall reveal the name, address or school, or include any particulars calculated to lead to the identification, of any child or young person concerned in the proceedings, either as being the person by or against or in respect of whom the proceedings are taken, or as being a witness therein;

(b) no picture shall be published in any newspaper as being or including a picture of any child or young person so concerned in the proceedings as aforesaid;

except in so far (if at all) as may be permitted by the direction of the court.'

A breach of s 39 is an offence subject to a fine not exceeding level 5 on the standard scale. The power of the Crown Court to give a direction under s 39 is subject to judicial review (*R v Leicester Crown Court ex parte S* (1991) 155 JP 405).

As noted above, s 39 applies to any proceedings in any court. It appears that a direction under s 39 need not have a time limit attached.

Section 39 applies once proceedings have started. However, a question arises about press releases and reports issued before that date. Plainly, a report prior to proceedings which identifies the school by name or by means of a photograph or identifies any member of the school community will remove the protection afforded by s 39 and contravene its purpose and spirit, but may not be an offence.

For these purposes, *a child* is a person under the age of 14 and a *young person* is a person who is 14, 15 or 16 (see s 70(1) of the CYPA 1969). However, s 68 of the Criminal Justice Act 1991 provides that persons aged 17 are to be treated as 'young persons' for certain purposes.

## 22.9.4   Youth courts

Juvenile courts were renamed 'youth courts' and juvenile court panels were renamed 'youth court panels' by s 70 of the Criminal Justice Act 1991 as from 1 October 1992.

Section 49 of the Children and Young Persons Act 1933 is concerned with newspaper reports of proceedings in a youth court. Its terms are similar to s 39 but with the addition of:

> '... provided that the court or the Secretary of State may in any case, if satisfied that it is appropriate to do so for the purpose of avoiding injustice to a child or young person, by order dispense with the requirements of this section in relation to him to such extent as may be specified in the order.'

As with s 39, publishing any matter in contravention of s 49 is an offence punishable by a fine not exceeding level 5 on the standard scale.

The limitations of ss 39 and 49 were exposed at the end of 1997 in the case of *William Straw,* the then 17-year-old son of the Home Secretary, Jack Straw. William Straw was accused of selling cannabis. He had been identified in newspapers in Scotland, Ireland and France, and information about the case, together with Straw's identity was readily available on the Internet. None the less, the Attorney-General, John Morris, applied for an injunction to restrain the press in England and Wales from identifying the accused.

Moses J decided that an injunction could be granted under s 2(2) of the Contempt of Court Act 1981 (see **22.9.6** below) because publication prior to proceedings would create a substantial risk that the course of justice in the proceedings in question would be seriously impeded or prejudiced. An injunction would help to maintain the purpose of s 49.

The injunction was, however, lifted by Toulson J on the grounds that William Straw's identity was widely known. It was held that merely publishing the identity of Jack Straw and his son would not have impeded a fair trial. Toulson J relied on an earlier dictum of Sir Nicolas Browne-Wilkinson in the *Spycatcher* case in 1987:

> 'In the contemporary world of electronics and Jumbo Jets, news anywhere is news everywhere.'

## 22.9.5 Committal proceedings

Section 8(1) of the Magistrates' Courts Act 1980 provides that in committal proceedings, the media may report the defendants' names, the charge, the plea and the outcome. They are not entitled to report evidence unless reporting restrictions have been lifted at the instance of *all* defendants. This is a change from earlier years when one defendant could lift restrictions for all.

## 22.9.6 The course of justice

The Contempt of Court Act 1981 contains provisions that allow the court, before proceedings start, to postpone or prohibit publication. However, it is clear from the *William Straw* case that these provisions are aimed at preventing pre-trial publication of a person's criminal record or other material which clearly could prejudice a fair trial. They are not aimed at protecting the privacy of individuals or organisations.

Section 2(2) of the Contempt of Court Act 1981 prohibits the publication of material which 'creates a substantial risk that the course of justice in the proceedings in question will be seriously impeded or prejudiced'.

Section 4(2) of the Act allows a court to order postponement of publication where it appears to be necessary for avoiding a substantial risk of prejudice to the administration of justice in those proceedings or in any other proceedings pending or imminent.

Section 11 of the Act provides that where a court has already prohibited publication earlier in the case, for example under s 4(2), it may later make a longer-lasting or even permanent prohibition, provided this is necessary for the reasons that originally applied under s 4(2).

## 22.9.7 Hearings in chambers

In a first instance decision, *Forbes v Smith and Another* (1998) *The Times*, 14 January, it was held by Jacob J that a judgment or order made in chambers is *not* a secret document and can be published (see also s 12(12) of the Administration of Justice Act 1960).

This decision appears to contradict an earlier first instance judgment in *Alliance Perpetual Building Society v Belrum Investments* [1957] 1 WLR 720 at 724, when Harman J held that to publish an account of matters proceeding in chambers was a contempt of court and there was no right to give any account of them while the action was pending and had not been adjourned into court. That judgment, in turn, was based on a speech of Lord Loreburn LC in *Scott v Scott* [1913] AC 417 at 445, who said that a judge may allow reports of such proceedings to be published if to do so illustrates some point of principle. In rare cases such as a trade secrets action, the court will have express power to restrict publication of a judgment or order given in chambers.

## 22.9.8 Press Complaints Commission

The Press Complaints Commission Code of Practice dated January 1998 states (inter alia):

### 'Privacy

i. Everyone is entitled to respect for his or her private and family life, home, health and correspondence. A publication will be expected to justify intrusions into any individual's private life without consent.

ii. The use of long-lens photography to take pictures of people in private places without their consent is unacceptable. Note – private places are public or private property where there is a reasonable expectation of privacy.

### Children

i. Young people should be free to complete their time at school without unnecessary intrusion.

ii. Journalists must not interview or photograph children under the age of 16 on subjects involving the welfare of the child or of any other child, in the absence of or without the consent of a parent or other adult who is responsible for the child.

iii. Pupils must not be approached or photographed while at school without the permission of the school authorities.

iv. There must be no payment to minors for material involving the welfare of children nor payment to parents or guardians for material about their children or wards unless it is demonstrably in the child's interest.

v. Where material about the private life of a child is published there must be justification for publication other than the fame, notoriety or position of his or her parents or guardian.'

It is not tortious to take unauthorised aerial photographs of property provided that doing so does not involve trespassing on land. This point sometimes arises when a school attracts media interest and reporters are refused permission to enter school premises in order to take photographs. There appears to be no basis on which photographers and film crews may be prevented from taking or publishing photographs from adjacent property (with permission) or the public highway or footpath provided no obstruction is caused.

## 22.9.9   Employment tribunals

Rule 14(1) of Sch 1 to the Employment Tribunals (Constitution and Rules Procedure) Regulations 1993, SI 1993/2687, gives an employment tribunal power to make restricted reporting orders.

However, it was held by the Court of Appeal in *X v Z Limited* (1997) *The Times*, 18 April that this power was not to be exercised automatically at the request of one or both parties, but after considering whether it is in the public interest that the press should be deprived of the right to communicate information to the public if it becomes available. The case concerned alleged sexual misconduct.

In *Scott v Scott* [1913] AC 417, it was held that when both sides consent to an order prohibiting publication, that is exactly the moment when the court should examine with particular care whether such an order should be made.

## 22.9.10   Duty of counsel

Paragraph 610 of the Bar Code of Conduct provides that counsel must, if possible, avoid naming in open court any third party whose character would thereby be impugned. The judge also has a duty to restrain unnecessary cross-examination.

## 22.10   OTHER PROTECTIONS

The general principle set out in *Scott v Scott* [1913] AC 417 is that justice should be openly administered. However, at common law there is a power to restrict access to hearings concerning patents, breach of confidence or other causes where publicity would frustrate the purpose of the action. Blackmail victims are often referred to by letters and disclosure of their identity has been held to be contempt (*R v Socialist Worker Printers and Publishers Ltd ex parte Att-Gen* [1975] 1 All ER 142, DC). The Law Lords in *Scott v Scott* were divided on whether there was a more general power to take evidence in private in the interests of justice. In *R v Hove Justices, ex parte Gibbons* (1981) *The Times*, 19 June, magistrates had held that prosecution witnesses on charges of procuring obscene publications should remain anonymous. Gibson J refused to quash their order.

Schools are always vulnerable when there is a trial of an alleged criminal offence by a present or former teacher, parent or pupil to which the school is an innocent third party. It is a matter for the discretion of the judge whether to hear counsel briefed on behalf of the school to make representations as to why publication of the school's name should be restricted. It will be apparent from the discussion above that the grounds on which a judge may make such an order are limited. Legal argument about these matters will take place in the absence of the jury but members of the public, including the press, are entitled to be present. Matters stated in argument may be published at the conclusion of the trial unless a further restriction is imposed.

In a much publicised case in 1996, parents whose daughter had left a school some ten years earlier had alleged sexual impropriety on the part of a teacher from that time and had allegedly threatened to kill him. At the ensuing criminal trial in the Crown Court, one parent used the witness box as a forum to make wide-ranging allegations, unsupported by any credible evidence, about the school and, apparently, having little relevance to the charge against her. The judge, having heard counsel on behalf of the school, still declined to impose a reporting restriction or to intervene to any material extent in her evidence. As a result, the school was subjected to allegations, widely published in the press, which it was given no opportunity to answer to disprove. The pupil was by then an adult and so s 39 of the Children and Young Persons Act 1933 did not apply, and s 2(2) of the Contempt of Court Act 1981 did not address the privacy of the school or its community.

It will be easier for a sympathetic judge to direct a reporting restriction under the Children and Young Persons Act 1933, s 39 in a case in which a party or a witness is a person under the age of 17 and at school. It is submitted that in any case in which there is a reasonable prospect of a direction, the press should be expected to exercise restraint during the period before the proceedings commence.

# Chapter 23

## DATA PROTECTION

### 23.1 INTRODUCTION

Nowadays, personal information is a traded commodity. Data protection is about personal privacy and in particular, protecting individuals from being caused damage by the unfair use of personal data about themselves. The law recognises that information which is entered wrongly, is out of date or is confused with information about someone else can cause problems. It may mean that a person is unfairly refused jobs, benefits, housing, credit or a place at college or at an independent school. It could mean that a person is overcharged for goods or services or even arrested in error.

The Data Protection Act 1984, and the various sets of regulations made under the Act, established the statutory framework for protection and enabled the United Kingdom to ratify the Council of Europe Convention on Data Protection, allowing data to flow freely between the United Kingdom and other European countries with similar laws. The Act covered *personal data* where that data was *automatically processed*. The Act gave individuals certain rights whilst requiring those who recorded and used personal information on computer to be open about that use and to follow proper practices.

The 1984 Act will be repealed and replaced by a new Data Protection Act 1998, which implements a European Directive that set the standard for data protection throughout the countries of the European Union. Section 69 of the 1998 Act provides that the only provisions which will come into effect on the day the Act is passed are the definition sections and those provisions enabling subordinate legislation to be brought in. Schedule 8 of the Act includes some important transitional provisions. A new raft of regulations is to be expected in addition to the Act.

This chapter examines the main provisions and some of the ways in which the 1998 Act will affect independent schools.

### 23.2 OVERVIEW

#### 23.2.1 Main points

The Data Protection Registrar, whom the Act renames the 'Commissioner', has indicated that those who currently comply with the provisions of the 1984 Act have already achieved approximately 80 per cent compliance with the new Act. From October 1998 onwards, the main data protection points are:

- those who hold information about living individuals have to obtain a data protection registration and comply with eight (formerly seven) data protection principles;

- *personal data* about living individuals must not be 'processed' (ie obtained, held or used) unless one of six conditions in Sch 2 to the Act is complied with;

- *sensitive personal data* may not be processed (ie obtained, held or used) unless one of nine conditions in Sch 3 is also complied with;

- some *manual data* is now covered by the Act, whereas the 1984 Act applied only to data held on computer;

- individuals have certain rights of access and other rights in relation to data held about them;

- non-compliance with the Act is an offence and may additionally result in an injunction being granted (s 9) and compensation being awarded (s 11).

### 23.2.2  Terminology

The main terminology under the Act is as follows:

- *Personal data* means 'any information relating to an identified or identifiable natural person'.

- *Data subject* means an identified or identifiable natural person. 'Identifiable' means one who can be identified, directly or indirectly, in particular by reference to an identification number or to one or more factors specific to physical, physiological, mental, economic, cultural or social identity. We are all 'data subjects'.

- *Data controller* means a natural or legal person, public authority, agency or other body which alone or jointly with others determines the purposes and means of the processing of personal data. The concept is one of 'control'. In the context of a school, the controller would be the school authority.

- *Data processor* means the person who actually does the processing, for example the bursar in a school.

- *Subject access* means the right of a subject to have access to data about himself or herself. A person writes a 'subject access' letter to apply for access.

- *Processing* means obtaining, holding or using personal data. Once a data controller is registered under the Act, he will be free to process personal data within the terms of the registration and provided none of the data protection principles is contravened.

- *Sensitive personal data* means information as to racial or ethnic origin, political opinions, religious beliefs, trade union membership, physical/mental health or condition, sexual life, criminal offences and sentences imposed.

### 23.2.3   The data protection principles

The eight data protection principles are (paraphrased) as follows:

(i)      Personal data shall be processed (ie obtained, held or used) lawfully.

(ii)     It shall be obtained only for specified and lawful purposes and shall not be processed for other incompatible purposes.

(iii)    Personal data shall be adequate and relevant but not excessive.

(iv)     Personal data shall be accurate and kept up to date.

(v)      Personal data shall not be kept for longer than is necessary for its lawful purpose.

(vi)     Personal data shall be processed in accordance with the rights of data subjects.

(vii)    Appropriate measures shall be taken to prevent unauthorised or unlawful processing or accidental loss or destruction of or damage to personal data.

(viii)   Personal data shall not be transferred outside the European Economic Area (EEA) unless to a country that ensures an adequate level of protection for the rights and freedoms of data subjects.

### 23.2.4   Relevance to independent schools

A school will hold personal data of many different kinds including: details of its governors; the files of its employees; the names and addresses of parents and pupils; information about its suppliers and pupils' files.

Furthermore, the school will hold examination scripts, examination results, confidential references, disciplinary and academic reports on pupils, medical and other health records, the accident book, the admissions register, the attendance register and countless other items of written information of this nature. Under the new Act, all these are potentially, or may contain, personal data, whether held on computer or as manual records.

### 23.2.5   Exemptions

Sections 26–38 of, and Sch 7 to, the 1998 Act contain a large number of exemptions. Of particular importance to independent schools, *confidential references* given by the data controller in education, training or employment are exempt under Sch 7, para 1, but only to the extent that the data subject does not have the right of access to see the reference. From now on, it will be important to ensure that a confidential reference is clearly marked as 'confidential'.

Examination marks and scripts are exempt under Sch 7, paras 7 and 8. In effect, this simply means that the candidate is not entitled to see the results of examinations or any other information until the results are communicated to him (or her) and he is not entitled to information recorded by him during an examination. Also of relevance to a school is an exemption in relation to management forecasts and negotiations.

Other new exemptions include: journalism, literature and art (s 31); research, history and statistics (s 32); armed forces; Crown employment and Crown or ministerial appointments; self-incrimination; and information about human embryos.

Other exemptions that were provided by the 1984 Act and will continue to apply include: national security; crime; taxation; health and social work; regulatory activity; judicial appointments; legal professional privilege; domestic purposes; and disclosures required by law or court order.

## 23.3   REGISTRATION

The current registration system will be replaced with a similar, though simplified system. Detailed regulations will be brought in, but at the time of writing, the Act specifies only that applications for registration must include the following information:

–   the data controller's name and address;

–   a description of the personal data being or to be processed by or on behalf of the data controller;

–   a description of the purpose or purposes for which the data are being or are to be processed;

–   a description of any recipient or recipients to whom the data controller intends or may wish to disclose the data;

–   the name and address of any representative of the data controller who is nominated for purposes of the Act;

–   the category or categories of data subject to which the personal data to be processed relates;

–   the names or descriptions of any countries or territories outside the European Economic Area (EEA) to which the data controller transfers, intends or may wish directly or indirectly to transfer the data (the EEA consists of all 15 EU States and in addition Norway, Iceland and Liechtenstein);

–   a description of measures to be taken for the purposes of complying with the Seventh Data Protection Principle;

The last four of these registration requirements were not required under the 1984 Act.

## 23.4   THE FIRST DATA PROTECTION PRINCIPLE

### 23.4.1   The Principle

Personal data shall be processed fairly and lawfully and, in particular, shall not be processed unless:

–   at least one of the conditions in Sch 2 is met; and

– in the case of sensitive personal data, at least one of the conditions in Sch 3 is also met.

## 23.4.2 Schedule 2

Schedule 2 includes six separate conditions, one of which must be complied with when 'processing' (ie obtaining, holding or using) 'personal data'. The conditions are that:

(1) *the data subject has consented to the processing* (emphasis added);

(2) the processing is necessary for the performance of a contract with the individual;

(3) the processing is required under a legal obligation;

(4) the processing is necessary to protect the vital interests of the data subject;

(5) the processing is necessary for the administration of justice;

(6) the processing is necessary for the purpose of legitimate interests pursued by the data controller or third party to whom the data is disclosed, except where the processing is unwarranted in that it would prejudice the rights and freedoms or legitimate interests of the data subject.

It may be helpful to recap at this point. Assume that the school is a registered data controller. It is free to hold or use personal information for the purposes for which it has been obtained. However, the information must be used or held fairly and lawfully and in accordance with at least one of the conditions listed above.

A common situation is one where the pupil is transferring to another school at a time when fees are unpaid at the present school. It is the custom and practice of independent schools to exchange information about unpaid fees. One reason for doing this is to reduce the likelihood of a pupil being admitted to a new school and then being excluded at half term because his parents have not paid the fees. That serves neither the interests of the pupil whose education is disrupted nor those of the school which may be unable to fill the place in mid-year. It makes sense for the school to include an express condition in its standard terms and conditions that the parent consents to information of this kind being exchanged. Consent can be of a general kind as distinct from the *explicit consent* required under Sch 3 (below).

A number of other problems surrounding disclosure of information about a pupil or his parents in proper circumstances can be resolved by reference to the conditions listed above.

## 23.4.3 Schedule 3

As noted earlier, 'sensitive personal data' is information as to racial or ethnic origin, political opinions, religious beliefs, trade union membership, physical/mental health or condition, sexual life, criminal offences and sentences imposed. Schedule 3 includes nine separate conditions, one of which must be complied with when 'processing' (ie obtaining, holding or using) 'sensitive personal data'. These conditions are more strict than those in Sch 2. They are:

– the data subject has given his 'explicit consent' to the processing;

- the processing is necessary for the purposes of exercising or performing any right or obligation conferred or imposed by law on the data controller in connection with employment;

- the processing is necessary to protect the vital interests of the data subject or another person if consent cannot be given by or on behalf of the data subject;

- *the processing is carried out by [broadly] charitable organisations* (emphasis added);

- the information has already been made public by the data subject;

- processing is related to legal advice or proceedings;

- processing is necessary for the administration of justice;

- *processing is necessary for 'medical purposes' and is undertaken by a health professional or a person who owes a duty of confidentiality equivalent to that which would arise if that person were a health professional* (emphasis added);

- the processing is specified in a statutory document.

The effect is that sensitive information may only be held or used if one of the conditions listed above is satisfied, and also if the data controller is registered in accordance with the Act and regulations to be made. It should be remembered also that the new legislation applies to manual records save those covered by the exemptions discussed earlier.

### 23.4.4   Interpretation

Interpretation of the First Principle goes further than under the 1984 Act because it states that data will not be treated as processed fairly unless (in summary) the data subject is given the following information:

- the identity of the data controller and his representative;

- the purpose for which the data is intended to be processed; and

- further information which is necessary to enable processing to be fair.

There are certain exemptions to this, but in general terms, these provisions amount to a significant new burden on data controllers.

These provisions about interpretation will come into force on 24 October 2001.


### 23.5   THE OTHER PRINCIPLES

### 23.5.1   The Second Principle

Personal data shall be obtained only for one or more specified and lawful purposes, and shall not be further processed in any manner incompatible with that purpose or those purposes.

The purpose for which personal data is obtained must either be specified in the notice given to the data subject or in the notification to the Commissioner. Regard must also be had to the purpose for which the data is intended to be processed by any person to whom it is to be disclosed.

### 23.5.2   The Third Principle

Personal data shall be adequate, relevant and not excessive in relation to the purpose or purposes for which they are processed.

### 23.5.3   The Fourth Principle

Personal data shall be accurate and, where necessary, kept up to date.

Guidance on the Fourth Principle states that data is inaccurate if incorrect or misleading as to any matter of fact. If the subject has notified the data controller that the data is inaccurate, the data should indicate that fact.

### 23.5.4   The Fifth Principle

Personal data processed for any purpose or purposes shall not be kept for longer than is necessary for that purpose or those purposes.

### 23.5.5   The Sixth Principle

Personal data shall be processed in accordance with the rights of data subjects under this Act.

### 23.5.6   The Seventh Principle

Appropriate technical and organisational measures shall be taken against unauthorised or unlawful processing of personal data and against accidental loss or destruction of, or damage to, personal data.

Guidance on the Seventh Principle is potentially far-reaching. Security measures must be appropriate to the harm that might result if the data is not secure, given its nature. The data controller must take reasonable steps to ensure the reliability of any staff who have access to the personal data. Perhaps most importantly, where the processing is carried out by a data processor on behalf of a data controller (any person other than an employee of the data controller) that data processor must have sufficient written guarantees in respect of security measures and the data controller must take reasonable steps to ensure compliance with those measures.

### 23.5.7   The Eighth Principle

Personal data shall not be transferred to a country or territory outside the European Economic Area unless that country or territory ensures an adequate level of protection for the rights and freedoms of data subjects in relation to the processing of personal data.

Schedule 4 of the Act sets out nine cases where this Eighth Principle does not apply (s 4(3)) – for example, where the data subject has given his consent to the transfer.

The Eighth Principle will come into force on 24 October 2001.

## 23.6   RIGHTS OF DATA SUBJECTS

### 23.6.1   Making an enquiry

The rights of individuals ('data subjects') to have access to information about themselves have greatly increased under the 1998 Act.

In order to make an enquiry, a person should write a '*subject access*' letter asking for a copy of all the information held about that person to which the Data Protection Act 1998 applies. The Commissioner advises that a subject access letter is best sent by recorded delivery and that a copy be kept of it.

The data controller is entitled to ask the data subject to fill in an application form or to provide more details to help to establish his (or her) identity and to help the data controller find the information. In addition, the data controller is entitled to require the data subject to pay a fee not exceeding £10 per register entry. There are however, special conditions for requests made on behalf of children.

### 23.6.2   Subject access rights

A data subject is entitled to have:

– a copy of the data that is being processed (ie held or used) by the data controller;

– a description of the data;

– a description of the purposes for which it is being processed;

– a description of the recipients and information as to its source.

### 23.6.3   Automatic processing

Nowadays, fully automated decision making is becoming increasingly common particularly in the areas of credit checks and psychometric testing for employment purposes, creditworthiness or to assess reliability or conduct.

Sections 7(1)(d) and 13 of the 1998 Act provide the following new rights:

– an individual is entitled to be informed of the logic involved in decisions that have been made by a computer unless it is a trade secret;

– an individual may notify a data controller that he (or she) should ensure that no decision which significantly affects the individual is based on automatic processing;

– *the data controller must inform individuals if decisions are made on an automated basis and the individual has the right to require that the decision is reconsidered* (emphasis added).

Certain types of decision, for example a decision whether or not to enter a contract, are exempt from the effects of this section.

These provisions will come into force on 24 October 2001.

### 23.6.4  Direct marketing

The years since the 1984 Act have seen a huge increase in various forms of direct marketing such as telesales and mailshots. Highly sophisticated lists of names and addresses sorted by socio-economic or some other grouping are regularly bought and sold, often by organisations that exist for that purpose. The result is a huge proliferation in the amount of 'junk mail' or 'cold calling' that many people receive.

Section 10 of the 1998 Act gives data subjects a new right to require a data controller to stop, or not to begin, processing personal data for the purpose of direct marketing. Direct marketing is defined to mean the communication of advertising or marketing material directed to particular individuals. This right is backed up by giving the court the power to order compliance.

Section 10 will come into force on 24 October 2001.

### 23.6.5  Injunction

The 1984 Act and regulations allowed the data subject to claim compensation if he has suffered damage or distress.

Section 9 of the 1998 Act provides a new right whereby data subjects may require a data controller to cease or not to begin the processing of material which is or is likely to cause substantial damage or substantial distress which, in either case, is unwarranted.

As stated earlier, 'processing' includes the obtaining of information. This section may therefore be invoked by a potential data subject to prevent information being collected and/or obtained about him (or her). However, the section does not apply where any condition in paras 1–4 of Sch 2 is met.

Section 9 will take effect on 24 October 2001.

### 23.6.6  Compensation

Under the 1984 Act, compensation was only available for damage and distress caused by inaccuracies of data or destruction of data or by the disclosure of data to a person not cited in the register as a 'disclosee' for the data unless the data subject consented to the disclosure.

Section 11 of the 1998 Act provides that an individual who suffers damage due to contravention by a data controller of any of the requirements of the Act is entitled to compensation. Contravention resulting in distress can also lead to compensation when:

−   damage has also been caused; or

−   the contravention relates to the processing of personal data for 'special purposes' (journalism, artistic or literary purposes).

It will, however, be a defence for a data controller to prove that he (or she) took such care as in all circumstances was reasonably required.

Section 11 comes into effect on 24 October 1998 insofar as it mirrors the 1984 Act, but the new provisions about compensation will not come into effect until 24 October 2001.

### 23.6.7   Correction

In addition to ordering compensation, a court may, as before, order a data controller to rectify, block, erase or destroy inaccurate data. Section 12 came into force on 24 October 1998.

## 23.7   TRANSITIONAL PROVISIONS

### 23.7.1   Commencement

Section 69 provides that the definitions and those provisions enabling subordinate legislation to be brought in came into force on the date the Act was passed (24 October 1998). Most of the other provisions will not be in force until 24 October 2001.

### 23.7.2   Exemptions

The following exemptions are available with effect from 24 October 2001:

–   Manual data which was being processed (ie held or used) before 24 October 1998. A question arises over corrections and additions to manual data. If, for example, a pupil's file is held by a school on 24 October 1998 and the following day an address is updated and a new report added, it appears that the new material is not covered by this exemption although it may be exempt by virtue of some other provision of the Act.

–   Computer data held before 24 October 1998 where the processing is other than by reference to the data subject.

–   Payrolls and accounts.

–   Automated data processed by unincorporated members clubs and mailing lists.

–   Back-up data.

–   The conditions in Schs 2 and 3 to the Act (discussed above in connection with the First Data Protection Principle).

–   The obligation in Sch 1, Part II, para 2 to the Act to give information to the data subject as to the identity of the data controller, his representative, the purpose for which the data is intended to be processed and other relevant information.

–   The obligation to have a written contract between the data processor and the data controller under para 13 of Part II of Sch 1.

–   The rights of data subjects contained in s 7(1)(b), (c)(ii), and (d).

–   Sections 9–11 which cover injunctive relief, processing for the purpose of direct marketing and compensation (in part).

–   The data subject's rights under s 13 in relation to automated decision making.

### 23.7.3  Manual data

Manual data held immediately before 24 October 1998 is exempt from the First Data Protection Principle other than with respect to giving information about the identity of the data controller and the purposes for which the data will be processed etc in accordance with Sch 1, Part II, para 2.

Manual data held immediately before 24 October 1998 is not exempt from the Second, Third, Fourth and Fifth Data Protection Principles or from s 12 which relates to correction.

These exemptions are available until 24 October 2001.

## 23.8  COMPLIANCE SUMMARY

This chapter has set out to provide a working summary of new and very complex legislation but it does not replace the need for specialist legal advice on specific problems. The Data Protection Act 1998 will be supplemented by several sets of regulations and orders introduced between October 1998 and October 2001.

In the meantime, every school will need to carry out a thorough review of the personal data which it holds and the steps that it needs to take to amend its forms so as to provide the information to data subjects that is required under the Act and also to obtain a correct registration and the consents required under Sch 2 and any 'explicit consent' required under Sch 3 of the Act.

The Act, excluding the regulations to follow, appears to give rise to no fewer than 25 points of preparation and compliance, which will in turn require a combination of review, new systems, checklists, consents and alterations to existing forms.

# Chapter 24

## MARKETING AND QUALITY

### 24.1 INTRODUCTION

This chapter aims to provide a practical introduction to the thought and planning which underlies the marketing strategy of an independent school. It has been written primarily for those who have no previous knowledge or background in this area and whose schools lack the resources to pay a development director or professional firm. The basic premise of this chapter is that marketing is an activity of management. Almost every management decision will have marketing and quality implications. Where possible, the text has been written in point style and jargon is avoided. Detailed strategies are outside the scope of this chapter.

### 24.2 OVERVIEW

'Marketing' is about becoming famous and being seen as desirable or even indispensible to the customer. In practical terms, it is about finding and retaining customers, selling a defined product to them and delivering to consistently high standards. For an independent school as for any other business, there are two main aspects to be considered:

– satisfying the existing customers;

– finding new customers.

Advice to independent schools about marketing tends to be formulaic: a combination of 'strengths and weaknesses' analysis, market research and questionnaires, acronyms, plans and promotional initiatives. These are important tools, but if not used in the right way, they can swamp the real purpose of the exercise. Putting this another way, 'if it isn't simple, it won't work'!

The marketing of services, and, in particular, education services, is about raising awareness of and selling an *environment with opportunities* whose key elements are:

– a 'strong' *internal culture* maintained within the school;

– a confident and expansive *external culture* projected to the market place;

– a culture that builds relationships with visitors, customers and intermediaries, such as feeder schools;

– a defined *product* and brand image for which the school is, or will become, *famous*;

- *consistent service delivery* to a high standard;

- opportunity and potential converted into *reality*;

- high standards of *presentation*.

These elements are fundamental. Without them, no amount of market research, segmentation, planning or promotion will produce customers or retain them.


## 24.3   INTERNAL CULTURE

The *attitudes, performance and behaviour* of the employees and governors are the defining features of a school's internal culture. If the culture is strong, matters of internal dissent or frustration will *never* be discussed with customers or outside the school. This needs virtually to be an absolute rule.

Parents, pupils and the wider community should not normally become aware of the internal culture as such. Instead, they should see what it produces. The internal culture will be dictated mainly by matters such as:

- vision, objectives, aims and quality of leadership, together with ethos, which is made up broadly of attitudes and behaviour, custom and tradition, standards and values, policies, principles, rules and procedures;

- the quality of induction and training given to staff and governors, the quality of management and the practical organisation of the school's output.

The main features of a strong internal culture are:

- *Leadership and teamwork*, consistency and self-discipline, supported by a positive appraisal system.

- *Discretion and loyalty* avoiding the generation of adverse rumour and gossip.

- An *ethos of improvement* which supports those who are genuinely trying to maintain and improve standards, but is intolerant of those who are not. Regular (ie annual) appraisals of everyone from the head and bursar downwards are of key importance.

- *'Can-doism'*, which implies professionalism, motivation, energy and resource-fulness at each level throughout the school. Implied in this is the need for leadership and discipline which foster the professionalism, self-confidence, personal qualities, skills, careers and aspirations of every employee.

- *Management of change*: anticipating, initiating and responding to change, since without change there is stagnation, the antithesis of education. Every employee needs to understand his or her role in the constant evolution of the school.

- *Legal compliance*: understanding that organisations which aim positively to comply with the many regulations that have appeared in the last 20 years will tend to be in better shape than those which do not.

- *Customer focus*, which implies a greater understanding of parents and pupils and their needs and why on occasions they appear dissatisfied, demanding or lacking in trust and confidence.
- *Corporate identity*: a unity of purpose expressed in tangible form.
- A readiness to follow up, monitor and evaluate.

All these features of internal culture are also aspects of quality management and need to be worked on continuously. They are the bedrock of the marketing effort in a modern business.

## 24.4   EXTERNAL CULTURE

The school's external culture is the part that is seen and experienced by parents and pupils and further afield by the community and feeder schools. The external culture needs to be confident and expansive, recognising that:

- the only justification for a service is that it satisfies a market demand;
- customers are a key ingredient in the success of the operation;
- it is the present customers who are the attraction to others;
- selling services is about selling benefits, promises and memories.

It is everyone's job – governors, executives, teachers and non-teachers – to project the external culture and give out the success messages about their school, day by day and week by week. In time, those messages will be picked up by others and promoted further, but it all starts from within the school.

The external culture also needs to assume that the present and prospective customer is looking for most, if not all, of the following:

- firm and friendly leadership and management of the relationship between head, staff and customers;
- good experience, which the customer will equate with value for money;
- benefits rather than features; and in particular:
    - acquisition benefits, such as kudos and a sense of value;
    - functional benefits, such as a happy child, achievements and other results;
    - relationship benefits, under which the customer sees the school identifying and responding positively to his or her needs;
- consistent service delivery;
- a 'level playing field' and real access to that which has been promised;
- competent and customer-oriented handling of questions, anxieties and complaints.

Much of this is summarised in the expressions 'customer-driven' and 'customer-focused'. Far from being a submissive approach, as is sometimes thought, a culture that is actively looking for ways to improve the service is confident and tough-minded. It also knows where the line has to be drawn.

Signs of a strong external culture (not listed in order of importance) include:

–   well-presented buildings and grounds;

–   the site looking busy, so that visitors will take positive images and sounds away with them;

–   good-quality promotional material;

–   news circulating that registrations are on the increase and those who have registered their children are being brought into the culture of the school;

–   a friendly and efficient response from the telephonist and receptionist onwards;

–   induction for new parents and children, explaining the geography, terminology and routine so that they are not made to feel at a disadvantage or uncomfortable;

–   the school's key messages (nobody else's) being repeated and discussed at dinner parties and other social occasions in the catchment area;

–   people saying 'it is a kind school' – no bullying;

–   a head who is visible and accessible and known and respected in the community; staff who welcome interaction and are not thought to be incompetent, lazy or demotivated;

–   active bodies of former pupils and 'friends' who raise funds;

–   parents receiving one-page letters reporting new ideas;

–   there is a well-organised and wide-ranging choice of extra-curricular activities which really are delivered;

–   somebody famous has joined the governing body or has registered his (or her) child at the school;

–   existing and prospective parents visit the site; there is touch-line support for events such as matches and plays;

–   new scholarships, exhibitions and bursaries have become available;

–   parents are enquiring about making lump-sum prepayments;

–   the site is also made available to the local community;

–   things happen on time; parents are not kept waiting;

–   academic standards are high; discipline is effective; the children are friendly and well-mannered;

–   new things are happening – improvements (however small and inexpensive), new subjects in the curriculum, and so on;

–   the school makes on-site provision for children with mild learning difficulties;

- there are strong relationships with feeder schools;

- financial management is seen to be efficient; fees are paid on time; there is seen to be no waste.

An important aspect to understand about the school's external culture is that the school, its head and teachers will be exhaustively discussed in the catchment area and perhaps further afield. Exactly what is discussed and in what way will depend almost entirely on people's experience and the way that experience is managed by the school. Therefore, the governors and head need to decide their key messages and promote them for all they are worth. Equally important is to test the features of external culture (as applicable) with both the current and prospective parents. If the insufficient attention is paid to the current parents they will very soon disappear 'out of the back door', unnoticed until it is too late.

## 24.5 THE PRODUCT

Independent schools compete with each other in the market place to design, package, price, sell and deliver a service or product that parents will be happy to buy year after year. It follows that the *marketing strategy* must have reference to *product*, and vice versa. Both of them need to respond to the most fundamental principle of marketing, stated earlier:

> 'The only justification for a service is that it satisfies a market demand.'

Business failures of all kinds in the last 25 years have had much to do with the product or service failing to connect with the demands of the marketplace. A school may offer the finest teaching of Sanskrit and Arabic in the nation, but if nobody wants to buy it, there is no business.

### 24.5.1 The buyer

From the parents' point of view, the education product is essentially *aspirational*. A good education is seen as the key to life's opportunities. The earlier the start, the better. For many parents, the cost is well worth the trade-off that means a smaller house, an older car and fewer holidays – always provided that delivery matches expectation.

The old idea of offering what the organisation wanted to offer instead of what the customers wished to buy is no longer a tenable strategy for a service provider, if it ever was. The product has to be grounded in the known demands and values of the marketplace and strongly differentiated from that which is offered by competitors. Some market research is unavoidable but for a school it may be best achieved in small internal focus groups.

### 24.5.2 Product analysis

There will be no common view of what makes up the product of an independent school for a particular child. Various ideas have been suggested, for example that the product is:

- the whole service which the school provides to pupils and parents;

- the measured difference between the child who enters the school and the child who leaves some years later;

- the measurable extent to which the school has enabled the child to achieve to his or her full potential;

- the final achievements and destination of the child.

The difficulty with all of these is that they are mainly retrospective measures, whereas the task considered here is how to design, package and promote a service product that will attract parents and lead them to make the *buying decision*.

The lists and suggestions offered below represent one means of arriving at a definition of the school's product. There may be other ways, for example by analysing the different stages that lead up to the buying decision. The lists suggested below apply equally to existing customers who regularly each term will reaffirm or remake their decision (or not, as the case may be) to buy the school's services in preference to transferring the pupil to another school.

The 'product' is the range of opportunities that arise out of the environment offered and the services and benefits that the school sells and the parents buy. Its real character is defined by the customer's perception of it. For present purposes, the product is analysed in three elements: services; tangibles and intangibles.

## (a)   Service element

- High academic ability, mixed ability or below average ability?
- Provision for special education needs on the premises? Off the premises? Not at all?
- Provision and ethos of sports and games?
- Provision for music and drama and other cultural activities?
- The extent of extra curricular activity, trips and tours?
- Discipline, pastoral care and the tutorial system?
- Boarding or day provision?
- Length of day – short or extended?
- Length of week – 5-day, 6-day or 7-day (fully boarding)?
- Leave weekends or exeats?
- Provision for boys only, girls only or co-education?
- Age range?
- Size of school?
- Class sizes; teacher–pupil ratio?
- Religious affiliation (if any)?
- Attitudes and behaviour of governors, head and staff?

## (b)   Tangible element

- The school site.
- The teaching facilities: specialist teaching rooms; laboratories; workshops; information technology and library.

- The sports facilities: sports pitches; sports hall; gymnasium; swimming pool; tennis courts, squash, fives court, astroturf, etc.
- Telephone and reception arrangements.
- Position in the league tables.
- Materials, including promotional literature.
- Visible systems and productions such as the *pupil profile*; and the *invitation to respond* to the school report. Pupils' work.
- The house system.
- The corporate identity, school uniform and badge.
- Performances of music and drama, art displays.

## (c) Intangible element

- The parents' perception of the image and reputation of the school and their response to the head and staff.
- The idea, belief and aspiration of parents of how the school will serve them.
- The parents' priorities.
- The perception that *this school* and no other, to the same extent, will satisfy the parents' need.
- The perceived benefits: acquisition, functional and personal relationships.
- The opportunities offered and the likelihood that they will be converted week by week for the benefit of the child, to the reasonable satisfaction of the parents.
- The ethos as seen during a conducted tour or as known by reputation.
- The parents' response to the school uniform/dress code.
- The perceived positive (or negative) influence of former pupils, the parents' association and the friends.
- The parents' perception of the cost and of the value for money they will obtain.
- Sentiment; good experience in the past; convenience.

It is from these lists, with the addition of any other features and benefits that apply, that the governors and head need to fashion a product:

- for which the school is or will become famous, and by which it is differentiated from the product of other schools;
- which the school will promote through all segments of the market;
- which will probably be appropriate to some families and not others (for example, an academic school will not be suitable for some children);
- which can be adapted to the needs of each pupil for whom the school is appropriate;
- which will satisfy a market demand and give good experience to parents and pupil;
- which will be talked about in favourable terms throughout the catchment area.

It has been noted earlier that if the school does not define and communicate its product, the marketplace will form its own perception.

MORI surveys carried out on behalf of the Independent Schools Information Service during the 1990s show that over 70% of 'buying decisions' are taken following a visit to the school site. Less clear is whether the buying decision is made on the basis of the tangible and service elements which provide the packaging or whether it is most influenced by the intangible elements which will tend to inform the real decision maker – 'gut-feeling'. Cost will often be one of the major considerations, particularly for a family with two or more children to educate.

### 24.5.3   Branding

The brand is both a name and an image. The image can add to or detract from the name and is far more resilient than the name.

Some of the most famous schools are considered to be 'brand names' in the sense that, at the point of sale, parents will recognise the name, the buildings and the reputation as a mark of consistent quality more regularly than they will recognise the individuals who provide the service. The branding of a complex and mainly intangible service is far less straightforward than the branding of goods.

A problem of confused branding can arise when the *persona* of the head is greater than the public image of the school. Some parents will be able to see no further than the persona of the head. Their satisfaction will rest entirely on his (or her) presence and performance. Others will consider they are 'buying' the school rather than the head. A dichotomy of this kind creates a severe weakness in the ability to *define the product* and market it effectively. There will also be longer-term difficulties in bringing about change. A school needs a clearly defined identity that is greater than that of the head.

## 24.6   MARKETING STRATEGY

The school's aim and values (ie its direction) must not dictate its marketing objectives (ie its intended destination). The means of getting to the destination is the strategy.

Perhaps the most famous statement of strategy in modern times was that of the American General Norman Schwarzkopf during the Gulf War in 1991. When asked at a press conference about his strategy for winning the war he replied:

> 'We're gonna cut 'em off, then we're gonna kill 'em.'

'Strategy' is used here to mean an overall plan, the details and implementation of which remain to be worked out. A strategy needs to be based on thorough groundwork and preparation.

In this section, marketing is treated as an aspect of management which must inform almost every management decision. As a general rule, there is little purpose in a management decision which does not serve the product. A decision taken on compassionate grounds may very well have positive implications for the product. There is a narrow range of exceptions to this rule, for example when the school accepts a child suffering from HIV or AIDS in the knowledge or belief that doing so may damage the confidence of some parents.

### 24.6.1   Explanation of strategy

Robert Horton, Chairman of Railtrack, in his keynote speech to the Independent Schools Bursars' Association in 1994 gave this explanation of strategy:

'It is fundamental to any business to have a strategy. Some of your governors may not like the school to be thought of solely as a business and in a sense they are right. There are over-arching objectives of producing good citizens and, in religious foundations, turning out pupils who have received some specific grounding. But, nonetheless, if the business fails everything fails.

Strategy is not simply a spread-sheet of the cash flows for the next few years. It is a carefully worked through description and analysis of the options open, the likely market response to those options and a well thought out and logical way ahead. By definition it is tough-minded. In a business, strategy cannot exist without consideration of structure and organisation. All great businesses became so because they got their organisation right; and many a downfall – GM, IBM, Kodak in our time – because they failed to adapt their structure to today's circumstances.'

Implicit in any marketing strategy is the understanding that it will affect and be affected by everything that happens in the organisation. It is everybody's job. If marketing is treated as an activity of management, those who are responsible for marketing should also be part of the management team.

The following methodology may be found helpful as a means of working a marketing culture into all aspects of the strategy.

### 24.6.2 Assessment of present position

The starting-point is the question: 'Where are we now?'. Draw up a profile of the school which sets out in short bullet points the most basic information, of the kind each governor should have in any event:

– *The school:* State its name and address; describe its location; the kind of school it is; the current pupil roll; its foundation and brief history; its present objectives and aims.

– *The site and tenure:* Describe the site, its acreage, the tenure of its land, its main buildings and playing fields and its most marketable attributes.

– *Governance:* Describe the constitution, the legal status and governing instrument; list the officers and governors, the skills they represent and the committees through which they work.

– *Structure and management:* Describe the organisational divisions of the school by age or house system and the way it is managed.

– *Style, ethos and culture:* Describe these aspects of the school as they would be seen externally. Describe the internal and external culture, along the lines discussed at **24.3** and **24.4**.

– *Financial information:* List the main sources of income and the net surplus of the last three years.

– *Staff analysis:* List the executives and full- and part-time teaching staff and peripatetics. Identify particular roles and pupil–teacher ratios.

- *Analysis of pupil roll:* Set out as a table the current pupil roll by year group and category with last year's numbers for comparison. Describe the entry points, examination and scholarship and bursary system; identify the parts of the school that are full and those that are not, and why not.

- *Interactions and relationships:* Assess the points of interaction with parents and prospective customers? How well do they work? What is the record of complaints? How are they handled?

- *Market features and competitor analysis:* Identify and anaylse the catchment area and wider marketplace; feeder schools; performance in the league tables; competitors; and fee structure. Describe the corporate identity by reference to school stationery, promotional literature, uniform, livery and badge and as it would be perceived externally.

- *Key advisers and service providers:* List the school bankers, legal advisers, accountants, other financial advisers, property advisers, insurance brokers, marketing and public relations advisers, pupil recruitment agencies, and all those who contribute to the school's image and reputation. Consider their overall contribution to the success of the school.

- *Fund raising:* Describe the school association; the 'Friends' organisation; school shops; fund raisers and also the activities that raise funds; and the trading company/ies. Again, evaluate their contribution.

Having profiled the school in this way, identify the strengths and weaknesses, the parts that seem good and those that may need to change. In particular, list any problems and suggest how they may be solved. (See Table 1 at the end of this chapter.)

### 24.6.3    The quality markers and product

Assess the present quality markers for each area of the school and for governors, executives, staff, pupils and parents. Look at such matters as vision and the way it is communicated; induction of new staff and pupils; the systems for ensuring that everyone knows what is expected of them; appraisals; career development, induction and training of staff; care of equipment; relationships; product knowledge; the system for reviewing targets and success measures; and complaints handling.

Describe the core product and how it is delivered, and how the core product is augmented by add-ons, packaging, display at point of sale, pricing and brand image.

### 24.6.4    Market segments

Make a complete analysis of the market segments currently being served by reference to the factors indicated at **24.8.3**.

### 24.6.5    Vision, objective, aim and market focus

Consider the following questions: '*What are we famous for?* What, realistically, do we want to be famous for?' This is the route into a consideration of the practical options that are open. Perhaps the school has a unique strength that will attract a particular kind of pupil or governor. Consider what can be developed, what market need it will serve and by what means it may be promoted.

## 24.6.6 Financial review

The quality and reliability of the management information should be reviewed. There will be areas for cutting cost and eliminating waste. Closely allied to spreadsheets are matters such as the state of the customer and past pupil database and how efficiently it is worked.

Consider also whether the management systems have got to grips with the real cost of boarding and whether it is paying its way or being subsidised by day-pupils. That exercise can produce surprising results. Is there a computer programme that enables reliable performance improvement targets to be set? Can some administrative costs be 'unbundled' with the administrative function being carried out externally? Is the school getting the right professional advice? Would it cost less to employ maintenance contractors on the payroll instead of sub-contracting? Is the money in the bank working as hard as it might? Is the fee structure right or wrong? Are there avenues for additional fund raising or even an appeal?

## 24.6.7 Short-term needs and options

A full analysis of the kind described above is likely to identify a number of short-term needs and options around which a plan can be constructed. Perhaps it makes sense to downsize or else invest heavily in particular parts of the school to pursue a certain focus. Perhaps some specific promotional initiatives will be needed immediately in order just to stand still. Almost certainly a lick of paint will be needed somewhere. It is so often matters of detail when worked together which can lift the customers' perceptions and bring a renewed sense of success and forward movement.

## 24.7 DRAWING UP A PLAN

A short, clearly focused plan, regularly reviewed and adjusted, is likely to be more useful than one consisting of endless tables and narrative. There are many possible formats. One that has been found useful is the '*what* and *how*?' approach, ie '*What* are the problems? *How* will they be solved?' A full plan would take into account such matters as: objectives; focus and product; marketplace, competitors and differentiation; finance and costs; site and facilities; staff; parents and pupils, and governors. The plan would start with a short statement of where the school is at present. An abbreviated example of the '*what* and *how*' model of plan is provided in Table 1 at the end of this chapter.

This methodology does not make the traditional distinctions between a business plan, development plan and marketing plan. That is the necessary consequence of treating marketing as an integral part of every aspect of management. Even so, when the details of implementation are worked out in the form of action plans, the traditional divisions will probably reappear and there is no harm in that. The essence of this is to try and keep matters of detail from strangling the formulation of strategy.

## 24.8   IMPLEMENTATION

Implementing strategy is difficult. It takes energy, time and resource. It needs to be continuous. It needs to be based on a confident understanding, without complacency, of the internal culture, the external culture, the product and the market segments. The importance of this cannot be over-emphasised.

### 24.8.1   Marketing budget

Many of the measures suggested in this chapter have little or no cost implication. Even so, an effective marketing programme will include elements that involve expenditure. Typically, independent schools budget about 1% of gross fee income which is, in general, much less than any other type of business. If a development director or marketing director is employed, the budget will need to be very much higher.

### 24.8.2   Management

The school's marketing will need to be managed and co-ordinated, if not by a development director then by the head or admissions registrar or a governor or marketing consultant or specialist. It is likely the governors will set up a marketing committee which will need to work closely with the senior management team.

### 24.8.3   Segmenting the market

The market segments of a school are likely to be selected from:

–   the age groups and gender groups being targeted;
–   the boarding or day market;
–   the existing customers;
–   the local and regional catchment areas;
–   feeder schools;
–   the international dimension;
–   special interest groups, eg disabled, learning difficulties, gifted children;
–   institutions – religious, military, commercial, sports and others;
–   government departments and agencies;
–   former pupils, parents' association and friends.

There are likely to be differences in the frequency and method of approach to each segment.

### 24.8.4   Database

The quality of the marketing database will be of first importance in mounting any successful marketing campaign. The database needs to be organised in accordance with the market segments. The data itself will constitute 'data' about living individuals and must therefore comply with the eight (formerly seven) Data Protection Principles described in the Data Protection Acts 1984 and 1998 and discussed in Chapter 23. A data protection registration will be required.

### 24.8.5   Management of fund-raising groups

'Friends' can have a huge, positive marketing impact, particularly amongst day-pupils' parents and can fund-raise as well as promote through a dinner party network. An appropriate constitution should be drawn up. If the objects of the group are charitable and their income exceeds £1,000 per annum, the friends will be required to register as a charity under s 3(7) of the Charities Act 1993. A properly constituted body undertaking fund-raising should obtain public liability insurance.

Former pupils may also be a source of funds, and an element of management by the school will increase their awareness of how they can help.

### 24.8.6   'Front of mind'

The initial aim must be to bring the school, its product and its benefits to the attention of every customer in each market segment. That means getting 'front of mind' and:

–   ensuring that the school is well-known rather than a well-kept secret;
–   continuing to promote its image and reputation however successful it may be – Rolls Royce still advertise;
–   achieving several points of contact with those in each segment of the market;
–   adopting a mainly strategic rather than saturation approach (rifle, not shotgun);
–   ensuring that everyone is talking and giving positive signals about the school.

A number of methods have been used to get 'front of mind', some colourful and in dubious taste, but memorable none the less; others more conventional. The conventional methods include:

–   open days advertised locally: these are the most powerful selling device because they bring potential customers to site where, or following which, the buying decision is often made;
–   use of the school site for other activities (but not so as to conflict with charity law);
–   publication of education features in the press;
–   other use of the media to report pupils' work in the community, centenary celebrations and so on;
–   advertisements of scholarships and bursaries;
–   reports of a new head or new governors with a high profile or new 'sons of famous fathers', particularly from overseas;
–   direct mailing and leaflet drops;
–   exhibition stands at education and county shows;
–   a foreign tour to attract overseas pupils.

These initiatives can help create awareness but are best used to reinforce an existing profile. The overriding aim is to bring people to site. It is at this point (or soon after) when decisions are made.

### 24.8.7   Direct mailing

Direct mailing can be controversial and may generate complaints as well as interest. Leaflet drops are less likely to generate complaints. Both methods are saturation rather than strategic techniques but they can be useful as a form of advertising a specific event and raising the school's profile at the same time.

A mailshot might typically comprise: a flyer which describes the event being promoted; a carefully drafted single-page letter about the activities and successes of the school and the benefits of education there; a sheet with well-chosen pictures and personal endorsements to illustrate the statements in the letter, and a reply card.

The objective of the mailshot will be to bring the event and the school to the attention of a relevant segment of the marketplace and so to bring people to the site. The likely response rate is no greater than about 1% and the commercial databases are rarely up to date or accurate. A mailshot can be used to promote a school generally or for a more specific purpose such as to publicise a summer activities programme or to make the school and its facilities more accessible to the community at large in accordance with its general charitable purposes. That can bring its own longer-term benefits by virtue of the reply cards returned and the level of interest generated. The cost of direct mailing to 10,000 addresses including postage is likely to be £4,000–£5,000 plus VAT at today's rates.

### 24.8.8　Communications audit

It can be a useful expression of the internal and external culture of the school to set up a communications audit:

– internally so as to obtain unattributed feedback from the staff about how well the management team is doing and the issues that need to be addressed; and

– externally to obtain the views of parents.

Questionnaires are available from the Independent Schools Information Service and some of the other associations. The questionnaire needs to be in a form that is capable of accurate analysis and response. Those who have taken the trouble to complete a questionnaire will expect follow-up action and report. A school that lacks the resources to deal with the follow-up stage should probably not embark on a communications audit of this kind.

### 24.8.9　Use of school premises

Many schools maximise the use of their premises by additional charitable use, such as arranging summer schools for students and certain kinds of holiday activities for children. There is also a wide variety of commercial uses that may be carried out under a suitable trading company structure provided the arrangement between the charity and the company is made at arms-length and excessive wear and tear is not caused to the assets of the charity; and provided the profits of the commercial activity are covenanted to the charity. These include the following.

#### (a)　Charitable use

– Religious and educational groups. Retreats and other religious events.
– Foreign students and exchanges. Adult education and evening classes. Summer schools.

- Music, choral and orchestral societies.

### (b) Commercial use

- Ballooning.
- Use for filming and advertisements.
- Car parking and vehicle storage.
- Music festivals and concerts.
- Antique/craft fairs.
- Testing new products, for example toys.
- Conference centre.
- Weddings and parties.
- Family weeks/weekends. Creches.

The facilities that are commonly used include:

- *Teaching and residential accommodation* – classrooms and halls, laboratories, refectory, dormitories, music rooms, chapel.
- *Sports facilities* – sports complex, sports pitches, swimming pool, rifle range, riding school, river, golf course.
- *Miscellaneous facilities* – additional land, catering facilities and catering staff, licensed bar, theatre/cinema/recording facilities, laundry, computer facilities.

Even a small school with few facilities may be able to derive financial or at least marketing benefit and also serve the community by arranging activity weeks or holiday study groups which are advertised in the local press.

### 24.8.10   Overseas visits by head

The reputation of independent education in the United Kingdom is such that there is a constant demand from abroad for places at good schools. Schools that recruit from overseas sometimes ask their heads to make an annual visit, not only for purposes of recruitment, but also to meet parents. Good quality printed material and a short promotional video are useful in creating strong visual images of the school and its opportunities.

### 24.8.11   Promotional material

The quality of the school's promotional material is very important. The material will include: the prospectus, records of examination success and success in scholarships and places won at schools and universities, flyers and personal endorsements. The corporate identity may need a facelift to get a sharper, more modern image using colours that are in fashion and papers with modern textures. Perhaps it is time to simplify and modernise the school uniform.

### 24.8.12   Kerb appeal

The site, and particularly the access to it, must look as attractive as possible, consistent with the requirements of security. Even a lick of paint or a minor refurbishment can send success messages to existing customers as well as first-time visitors.

### 24.8.13   Changes to the curriculum and school hours

One measure that may be indicated for a day-school with a six-day week, and one that has significant marketing implications, is to reduce either to a five-day week or else to a five-day curriculum with enhancement workshops or activities on Saturdays. That kind of change will need very careful consultation with parents and staff over an extended period.

There will be several different areas of concern, for example that:

–   this kind of change will amount to a fundamental alteration in the product;
–   it will mean extending the length of school terms and losing the benefits of breaking up before, and going back after, the State schools;
–   it will cause difficulties for parents at weekends and it may place a greater burden on staff;
–   it may spell the end of games and sports in their present form;
–   it will lead to the 12- and 13-year-old pupils in years 7 and 8 moving prematurely to senior schools and perhaps turn a preparatory school into a primary school;
–   it will involve dropping Latin or some other subject from the curriculum;
–   it will spoil the atmosphere of the school for boarders.

The planning and consultation for this kind of change may need to envisage a timescale of one or two years and gradual introduction in order to take the parents along with the changes.

### 24.8.14   Fees

Schools that appear expensive compared with their competitors may need to consider reducing the level of fees if they can afford to do so against the expectation of more pupils coming in. A more difficult route is to segment the product and make certain elements of expense optional. That can cause parental resistance if they feel it will lead to a division in the community between those parents who can afford all the options and those who cannot.

Schools have traditionally enjoyed the cash-flow benefit of having three pay days per year, namely first day of each term. Parents, however, tend to have 12 pay days in every year and many welcome the option of paying fees by monthly instalments. Instalment arrangements need to be carefully structured so as to comply with the consumer credit legislation (discussed at **9.8.19**). Schools vary between those that levy a surcharge on parents who wish to pay by instalments and those who do not. There are also instalment schemes run by commercial operations which enable the school to receive payment in full at the start of each term and parents to pay by instalments, although these arrangements may be subject to a clawback in the event of parents defaulting.

There is growing recognition also that many parents who cannot afford private education for *all* their children will feel it unfair to favour one or two only and they may then opt for the maintained sector. Schools have long recognised the principle known as the *marginal rate of cost* that applies to each additional pupil beyond a certain number in the school. It may be that a school which is well resourced and not full can afford to give generous allowances for second and subsequent children where the parents' financial circumstances indicate.

### 24.8.15  New scholarships and bursaries

Scholarships, exhibitions and bursaries can be an excellent means both of promoting a school and raising academic standards. Scholarship examinations will attract bright children and high standards tend to attract good staff. Some governing instruments contemplate that a substantial number, as many as 5%, of places will be offered with full or partial fee exemption to bright children as well as to those who may have a particular need.

## 24.9  TIMES OF ADVERSITY

### 24.9.1  Complaints

Every complaint should be viewed as a marketing opportunity. A genuine complaint or concern that is well handled and has a satisfactory outcome is more likely to enhance than to damage the reputation of the school in the longer term.

### 24.9.2  Adverse publicity

Schools need to put in place crisis management procedures that will enable them to handle unforeseen events, tragedy or adverse publicity in a positive way that sends strong signals about the school's ethos of caring and kindness, both for those families directly affected and for the rest of the school community.

### 24.9.3  Falling pupil rolls

No quick fix or simple solution has been found to the problem of pupil rolls that have fallen to a critical point where closure has to be considered. For this to happen suggests either that a segment of the market has suddenly disappeared or that there is over-capacity or that the school has not been driven by a marketing culture.

A sudden cost-cutting exercise may lead to cost savings that the school cannot, in reality, afford. This may turn into to the familiar quality trap: internal inefficiency; deterioration of service quality; dissatisfied customers; a deteriorating atmosphere; a deteriorating service; a last-ditch promotional initiative; further customer dissatisfaction; a further deteriorating situation; and further financial difficulties.

A school that has been round this circle once and immediately embarks on it for a second time is very likely to face closure in the absence of a sudden cash injection or a last minute improvement in the roll. If it can keep going it will need to begin again rebuilding its marketing culture from the bottom up. That is almost certain to need fundamental changes in staff attitudes and in particular a willingness to attend meetings and work together to develop from the key ideas.

## 24.10    FUND-RAISING AND APPEALS

Fund-raising is an integral part of a marketing strategy and may consist of a one-off appeal for a project that is clearly defined or else a continuous fund-raising strategy, for example to provide bursaries.

A one-off appeal for funds is a valuable form of profile-raising, in addition to fund-raising, because it sends signals that the school is committed, enthusiastic and forward-looking, and planning new facilities and improvements in its product.

There are a number of rules of thumb about appeals:

– They cannot be done satisfactorily on the cheap.

– They cannot be 'bolted on' to the role of a development director. They need to be separately funded, led and resourced.

– An appeal needs realistic ambitions and target figures.

– A 'unique reason for giving' needs to be identified for each individual or group of prospective donees.

– Obtaining substantial donations is likely to depend on 'person-to-person' contact and on the quality of the relationships that are built.

– The division of labour will be approximately 90% research and 10% asking for donations.

– About 80% of donations will come from 20% or fewer of the donors.

### 24.10.1    Legal aspects

For a large appeal, a school is likely to engage the services of a professional fund-raiser. Part II of the Charities Act 1992 defines a professional fund-raiser as any person (apart from a charitable institution or a connected company) who carries on a fund-raising business, or any other person who, for reward, solicits money or other property for the benefit of a charitable institution, unless this is done in the capacity of an agent of a person carrying on a fund-raising venture.

This definition is aimed at bringing into regulation those who run fund-raising businesses that profit from the appeals and campaigns they organise for charitable institutions. It does not apply to volunteers who receive only out-of-pocket expenses, since they would not be acting for reward.

Charity trustees will need to check their governing instrument to ensure they have power to employ and pay fund-raisers, since it is far from clear that s 23(1) of the Trustee Act 1925 allows charities to employ agents in order to raise funds.

The Institute of Charity Fund-raising Managers (ICFM), which was set up in 1984 to provide professional support to fund-raisers, has drawn up a detailed Code of Practice relating to fund-raising in schools.

## 24.10.2   Preparation

The first step will be to develop a database which might be segmented as follows:

– former parents going back ten years;
– former pupils;
– donors to an earlier appeal;
– current parents;
– other known well-wishers.

The appeal director will need to put together a team comprising:

– a professional fund-raiser whose initial contract should be shorter rather than longer;
– an appeal president and appeal chairman, both of whom will probably be distinguished former pupils;
– an appeal committee composed of people who will be able to devote quality-time to fund-raising;
– there will need to be a suitably staffed appeal office.

In practice, fund-raising from the major donors will be most effective if carried out person to person by the appeal director, rather than by committee members.

Detailed discussion of the phases of an appeal are outside the ambit of this chapter but typically they will include:

– the 'major donor' phase, involving a specially prepared document and a personal visit from the Appeal Director;
– a major campaign directed to all former UK pupils, inviting them to regional meetings and following up with letter contact and a leaflet;
– the official launch of the appeal, with a glossy appeal brochure;
– a campaign directed to the parents, sending them the glossy brochure;
– a campaign directed to potential donors overseas, including personal visits.

The effect of taking initiatives before the official launch is to raise or obtain promises of substantial funds, possibly one-third or one-half of the target figure, to act as a springboard for the main campaign with parents. Further discussion of appeals and fund-raising is outside the scope of this book.

## 24.11   SUGGESTED READING

David Pardey's book *Marketing for Schools* (Kogan Page, 1991) provides a clear and useful account of the way in which marketing principles and techniques can be applied in schools.

***Table 1.***    Abbreviated example of a 'what' and 'how' model.

**Date when last revised:**

*Note:* Timetable and individual responsibilities should also be identified.

| WHAT? | HOW? | COST £ |
|---|---|---|
| 1.   We need to strengthen our internal culture so as to ensure that our staff understand and can communicate the plan and vision for this school. | • *Staff briefings.*<br>• *Redraft our parent contract documents.*<br>• *Modernise and improve the Staff Handbook.*<br>• *Consult internally by questionnaire and respond positively.*<br>• *Identify other means of improving staff motivation and enjoyment of their work.*<br>• *Provide an INSET Day that will explain their role in marketing; regular follow-up.*<br>• *Etc.* | *£x* |
| 2.   We need to shed our drab, old-fashioned corporate identity and appear more modern and forward-looking. | • *New prospectus.*<br>• *Updated logo and letterhead*<br>• *Simpler and brighter uniform*<br>• *Paint the front elevation and tidy up the driveway*<br>• *Etc.* | *£x*<br>*£y*<br>*£z*<br>*£a* |
| 3.   Our product needs some adjustment and a sharper focus. In particular we want to be, and be seen as:<br><br>• Very strong academically.<br>• With particular strengths in music, art and open air activities where our competitors are weak.<br>• Etc. | • *Introduce a scholarship worth 50% of fees.*<br>• *Introduce five exhibitions worth £500 pa.*<br>• *Target and publicise appointment of new staff.*<br>• *Etc.* | *£x+*<br><br>*£y+*<br><br>*£z* |

**Table 1.** Abbreviated example of a 'what' and 'how' model (*cont*).

| WHAT? | HOW? | COST £ |
|---|---|---|
| 4. We need to become better known within a fifteen mile radius. | • *Attract two high profile governors.* <br> • *Publish educational features in press.* <br> • *Offer and advertise a new scholarship and exhibitions (as above).* <br> • *Sponsor the seasonal flower display on a busy roundabout.* <br> • *Take exhibition stand at County Show and advertise it by a leaflet drop.* <br> • *Etc.* | *No cost* <br> *No cost* <br><br><br> *£y* <br><br> *£z* |
| 5. We need to bring people to the school site. | • *Plan and advertise an Open Day for 2 June.* <br> • *Host a quiz competition for children, advertised by mailshot with a famous personality presenting the prizes.* <br> • *Scholarship examinations (as above).* <br> • *Etc.* | *£z* |
| 6. We need to increase the fees by 9% which is 5% more than economic conditions would normally justify. | • *Careful presentation to parents before 25 March.* <br> • *Offer the following additional benefits:* <br> • *Offer a standing order scheme.* <br> • *Offer a discount for early payment; a lump sum prepayment scheme; improved discounts for siblings.* <br> • *Etc.* | |
| 7. For our parents, we need to begin a new process of consultation aimed at discovering their wishes and needs and harmonising those with our vision for the school. | • *Arrange focus groups.* <br> • *A set piece event chaired by a television professional (who happens to be a parent).* <br> • *Follow up with an attractively presented summary of our plans and proposals for the school.* | |
| Additional Items | | |

# Chapter 25

## HUMAN RIGHTS

### 25.1   INTRODUCTION

This chapter provides a brief introduction to the Human Rights Act 1998 and the ways in which the Act may in future affect the rights and fundamental freedoms of an independent charitable school, its staff, parents and pupils.

The Act, which is arranged in 22 sections and 4 Schedules, received Royal Assent on 9 November 1998 and will come into force at or before the millennium, the purpose of the delay being to allow enough time for the training of judges and officials. In practice, its principles are already being applied.

The Act will result in the development of a new British regime of human rights based on those set out in the European Convention on Human Rights 1950. Thus, the Act will have constitutional effect. Its preamble gives a clear indication of its aim:

> 'An Act to give further effect to rights and freedoms guaranteed under the European Convention on Human Rights; to make provision with respect to holders of certain judicial offices who become judges of the European Court of Human Rights; and for connected purposes'

Many of the rights and fundamental freedoms guaranteed by the Act are aspirational rather than absolute. It has been suggested that Convention rights point to Magnetic North and all other rights will have to be turned in that direction. They will require interpretation in the light of case-law on human rights since the 1950 Convention was established, but the courts will not be bound to treat that body of case-law as binding precedent.

A constant theme running throughout the law on human rights is that a fair balance needs to be found between:

- the demands of the general interest of the community; and
- the requirements of protecting the fundamental rights of individuals.

The balance will differ from one nation to another and from one decade to another. To begin with, at least, very little will be cast in stone. The general aim is to maintain and promote the ideals and values of a democratic society. Those values are said to include pluralism, tolerance, broadmindedness, the rule of law with access to the courts, and freedom of expression, with freedom of political debate being at the very core of the concept of a democratic society.

English law has, in general, paid respect to many of the Convention rights since 1950 but, until now, those rights have not been directly accessible via the courts of the United Kingdom but only by way of the European Court of Human Rights in

Strasbourg. That will now change. The various arms of the State will be required to act in a way which is compatible with Convention rights and, equally, the courts of the United Kingdom will be required to interpret those rights in the cultural and social context in which they arise, and to enforce them. In essence, Convention rights will overlay and blend with all settled principles of law applicable in the United Kingdom.

## 25.2   SCOPE OF THE ACT

The new law is all about the protection of individuals (corporations as well as humans) from violations of their Convention rights by the State and public authorities, but it will go very much further than that, in practice. Courts and tribunals are 'public authorities' under s 6(3) of the Act and s 6(1) states: 'It is unlawful for a public authority to act in a way which is incompatible with a Convention right'. Thus, the court and other tribunals will also be required to apply Convention rights when resolving disputes between parties to litigation.

By s 6(3), a 'public authority' also includes any person certain of whose functions are functions of a *public nature*. Plainly, a local education authority (LEA) is a 'public authority' and therefore amenable to judicial review. On the face of it, an independent school – which is a private, self-regulating community – is not a public authority, although the point is not free from doubt, and it may, in any event, be a private authority some or all of whose functions are of a *public nature* within the meaning of s 6(3).

In *R v Haberdashers' Aske's Hatcham College Trust ex parte T* [1995] ELR 350, Dyson J held that a City Technology College was an independent school operating its admissions policy within a statutory regime which provided for State-funded education and was therefore performing a *public function* and was amenable to judicial review.

In *R v Cobham Hall School ex parte S* [1998] ELR 389, QBD, Dyson J held on judicial review that an independent school was a private law body exercising a *public function* when it re-allocated a pupil's assisted place as an alternative to requiring the pupil to leave the school on grounds of her attitude and behaviour.

Those cases may be authority, albeit at first instance only, for saying that an independent school falls within the definition of a 'public authority' or a 'person certain of whose functions are functions of a public nature'. Questions will arise whether an independent school established under Royal Charter or special Act of Parliament will be treated as a public authority by virtue of that fact alone or whether independent charitable schools generally should be treated as public authorities because they hold their property and investments on trust for the public benefit. It is submitted, however, that there is a distinction to be drawn between:

-   matters of constitution and the vesting of property in a charitable body, on the one hand, which are matters of public accountability; and
-   the functions performed by that body, some of which may be public and others of which are undoubtedly *private in nature*.

Section 6(5) of the Act provides that, in relation to a particular act, a person is not a public authority by virtue only of s 6(3)(b) if the *nature of the act is private*. It remains to be seen how this will be interpreted in cases that involve the day-to-day activities of independent schools.

Whether or not an independent school will be treated as a public authority for the purposes of the Act, a court or tribunal deciding disputes is a public authority under s 6(1) of the Act and must not act in a way which is incompatible with a Convention right. It seems to follow that Convention rights will apply in disputes between a school, its employees, parents and pupils when such disputes come before the court or before an employment tribunal or the Independent Schools Tribunal.

The 'public authority' point is relevant in this context to whether pupils backed by legal aid and in dispute with independent schools will be able to use judicial review instead of having to rely on tort and breach of statutory duty, or their parents suing in contract.

In practice, the substantive law of the United Kingdom is already consistent with Convention rights in most of the areas that have day-to-day application to a school. Even so, the particular focus of the Act for independent schools is likely to be:

–   of *general application*: ensuring natural justice and fair procedures; pro-portionality of sanction; meeting the legitimate expectations of staff, parents and pupils; and considering matters of privacy and freedom of expression;
–   of *minority application*: questions of sexual orientation and sexuality generally; and all kinds of discrimination on grounds including age, religion, political or other opinion, property, birth or other status.

A trigger of the Act will be any *unjustified* interference with a guaranteed right or fundamental freedom. Examples of 'interference' (by no means always unjustified) might include: denying a permission or a licence; removing the means of enjoyment of a right; removing property; imposing a tax; imposing excessive damages; imposing a statutory ban; criminalisation of an act; abuse of the libel law; and prior restraint orders such as injunctions.

Thus, the main short-term application of the Act to an independent school will probably be over matters of procedural fairness, but the Act is also likely to be invoked by those who seek to push out boundaries and assert freedoms in a new way with the object of changing the disciplines, traditional standards and values of schools.

It is too early to predict the practical effect of the Act during the next decade. It has been suggested that it will mean a fundamental difference of approach on the part of judges when deciding cases. The traditional approach was to decide the merits of a case, putting social and cultural issues to one side. In future, judges will have to consider social and cultural issues because they have become constitutional rights. There will be an increased emphasis on principles and morals, but not necessarily so as to preserve those that are traditional.

## 25.3 THE ARTICLES

Section 1(3) of the Act introduces those of the Articles of the 1950 Convention which are now comprised within the Human Rights Act 1998. Following the numbering given in the Convention, their headings in Sch 1 to the Act (but without their text) are:

- Article 2 – Right to Life
- Article 3 – Prohibition of Torture
- Article 4 – Prohibition of Slavery and Forced Labour
- Article 5 – Right to Liberty and Security
- Article 6 – Right to a Fair Trial
- Article 7 – No Punishment Without Law
- Article 8 – Right to Respect for Private and Family Life
- Article 9 – Freedom of Thought, Conscience and Religion
- Article 10 – Freedom of Expression
- Article 11 – Freedom of Assembly and Association
- Article 12 – Right to Marry
- Article 14 – Prohibition of Discrimination
- Article 16 – Restrictions on Political Activity of Aliens
- Article 17 – Prohibition of Abuse of Rights
- Article 18 – Limitation on Use of Restrictions on Rights

Schedule 1, Part 2 also introduces the following Articles from the First Protocol to the Convention:

- Article 1, First Protocol – Protection of Property
- Article 2, First Protocol – Right to Education
- Article 3, First Protocol – Right to Free Elections

Part 3 of Sch 1 introduces the following Articles from the Sixth Protocol to the Convention:

- Article 1, Sixth Protocol – Abolition of the Death Penalty
- Article 2, Sixth Protocol – Death Penalty in Time of War

Section 1(2) of the Act provides that these Articles are to have effect for the purposes of the Act 'subject to any designated derogation or reservation' (as to which see ss 14 and 15). This is a reference to those provisions of the Convention to which the United Kingdom has not yet agreed and which are outside the scope of this chapter.

## 25.4 OPERATION AND INTERPRETATION

The Act will apply at two quite distinct levels:

(1) *vertically*, between the State and the individual. Section 4 provides that if the court is satisfied that a provision of primary legislation is incompatible with a Convention right it may make a Declaration of Incompatibility;

(2) *horizontally*: the court will be required to apply Convention rights, where necessary, between the parties to a dispute before a court or tribunal. That will not give rise to a Declaration of Incompatibility.

For present purposes, it is unnecessary to give detailed consideration to the principles of interpretation that will apply under the Act, but the main requirements are as follows.

– The court must have regard to the language used in any particular statute.

– The court must interpret a statute in good faith by reference both to the wording and to the object and purpose of the statute and the practice since the statute was introduced.

– Interpretation should be dynamic, in the light of evolving conditions.

– The aim is to maintain and promote the ideals and values of a democratic society (considered at **25.1** above).

– The rules are designed to be 'practical and effective' and to secure a fair balance between the demands of the general interest of the community and the rights of the individual.

– Any restriction on a freedom guaranteed by the Convention must be 'proportionate to the legitimate aim pursued'. There must be a 'reasonable relationship of proportionality between the means employed and the legitimate objects pursued by the contested limitations'.

– The burden of proof will be on the complainant unless the right is subject to exception when the burden of proof will be on the respondent to show that there is a justification for a prima facie breach.

– Courts and tribunals must seek to ensure compatibility with the Convention.

## 25.5 PRACTICAL APPLICATION OF THE ACT

### 25.5.1 Public authorities exercising a public function

Public authorities must be taken as including: government departments such as the DfEE; local authorities and licensing authorities; regulatory authorities such as IMRO; those who control immigration; Inland Revenue and Customs & Excise; the police and Serious Fraud Office; the prison authorities; broadcasting authorities and those who control human fertilisation. Local education authorities who control State schools are public authorities, but not independent schools, with the possible exception of schools constituted by Royal Charter or under a special Act of Parliament.

Acts of public authorities in relation to education and children that might become the subject of Convention claims by way of judicial review may include:

– decisions of an LEA with respect to special schools (First Protocol, Article 2);
– decisions of an LEA which funds places at independent schools (First Protocol, Article 2);
– decisions of the Special Educational Needs Tribunal (First Protocol, Article 2);
– applications for foundation school status by minority races or religions (Article 14 and First Protocol, Article 2);

- decisions by social services departments which have the effect of separating children from their parents (Article 8);
- adoption of children (Article 12).

## 25.5.2   Private authorities exercising a public function

Private authorities within this category might include: professional bodies such as The Law Society and the General Medical Council constituted under statute and entitled to hold trials that determine civil rights; the Stock Exchange; sports associations such as the Football Association and the various Olympic and athletics authorities; the Jockey Club and the Gaming Board; and, possibly, independent charitable schools.

Since the *Hatcham College* and *Cobham Hall* cases, referred to at **25.2** above, it seems that independent schools are capable of exercising a public function to the extent that their admissions policy is regulated by a statutory regime or a pupil is publicly funded by means of an assisted place or otherwise.

Examples of possible Convention claims involving independent charitable schools may include:

- denial of a Convention right in relation to a contract (First Protocol, Article 1);
- disputes over admissions (Article 14) and expulsion from or the requirement to leave a school (Article 6 and First Protocol, Article 2);
- disputes with the press over privacy (Article 8);
- disputes about discrimination on grounds of age, religion and sexual orientation, not so far directly covered in the discrimination laws (Article 14);
- employment disputes which might arise principally under Articles 6, 8, 9, 10 and 14, considered at **25.5.3** below;
- disputes about: sexual orientation and sexual freedom from the age of 16 upwards; rights for smokers and drug users; cults and pseudo-religions; punishments and other sanctions.

## 25.5.3   Employment disputes

There are already very detailed employment protection laws in the United Kingdom that have been supplemented by the Working Time Regulations 1998 and the Public Interest Disclosure Act 1998, which provides protection for 'whistle-blowers'. Further proposed measures are contained in the White Paper entitled 'Fairness at Work' to be implemented by October 1999. These leave less scope than might be expected for Convention claims in the workplace. None the less, whether the dispute concerns a public authority or a private authority, employment tribunals will be required to have regard to Convention rights, although they will not be entitled to make a Declaration of Incompatibility.

Examples of possible claims arising out of employment include:

- disputes about respect for family life in cases where executives are expected to undertake excessive travel (Article 8);
- respect for a person's correspondence such as e-mails, diaries and other kinds of record (Article 8);

- disputes based on the anti-discriminatory provisions and requirements for equal treatment and the rights of homosexuals and transsexuals (Article 14);
- disputes about rights to free speech in the workplace and the need for confidentiality (Article 10);
- dismissal for unacceptable or incompatible beliefs: for example, an employer may be prevented from refusing employment or dismissing a person who is in breach of a 'clean living' requirement in an employment contract.

It appears there are some categories of social and economic rights for employees that are not guaranteed by the Convention, for example there is no right to work and, while provisions for 'garden leave' are permitted, a person has no countervailing right to exercise his (or her) skills.

## 25.6   MAINTAINING A BALANCE

It has been suggested that the culture which arises under the Human Rights Act 1998 is rights-based and may be insufficiently balanced by responsibilities. That is a balance which the courts will be expected to find and maintain by applying the rules of interpretation indicated above at **25.4**.

In addition, some of the Articles contain some balancing qualifications of their own.

For example, Article 10 (Freedom of Expression) contains the following qualification at para 2:

> 'The exercise of these freedoms, since it carries with it duties and responsibilities, may be subject to such formalities, conditions, restrictions or penalties as are prescribed by law and are necessary in a democratic society, in the interests of national security, territorial integrity or public safety, for the prevention of disorder or crime, for the protection of health or morals, for the protection of the reputation or rights of others, for preventing the disclosure of information received in confidence, or for maintaining the authority and impartiality of the judiciary.'

A number of the other Articles also contain qualifications in similar or slightly different terms as appropriate. They are: Article 8 (Right to Respect for Private and Family Life); Article 9 (Freedom of Thought, Conscience and Religion); and Article 11 (Freedom of Assembly and Association).

## 25.7   INDEPENDENT SCHOOLS

An independent school, if charitable, is governed and regulated by its governing instrument and by the policies of the governors and the practices and procedures that are adopted under contract or otherwise. Those in turn need to be properly authorised by the governing instrument whether that is a trust deed and charitable scheme or whether it is a Royal Charter, special Act of Parliament or memorandum and articles of a company limited by guarantee.

In order to comply with the spirit and intent of the Human Rights Act 1998, schools of all kinds need to ensure that they always meet the requirements of natural justice, that sanctions are always proportionate to the legitimate aim that the sanction seeks to achieve, and that the legitimate expectations of parents and pupils are respected. The law does not recognise any difference of standard in practices and procedures between independent schools and State schools.

However, the Human Rights Act must be set in its proper context. It does not create new rights or take away any existing rights of either the school community or individual members of staff or the parents or pupils. The Act will provide easier access to rights which already exist. One of the rights of an independent school is to be a private, self-regulating community, largely outside the control of the State but subject always to the general law of the land.

Independent schools and those who use them are always vulnerable to political interference, the most recent example of this being the phasing out of assisted places. Perhaps the Human Rights Act will help to underpin the right of the independent sector to regulate itself, but that in turn may depend to some extent on the sector's response to the Act. If its policies and procedures are not consonant with the Act, it is very likely, over time, that statute will intervene in particular areas, for example, over admissions and disciplinary appeals.

Because the Act will overlay and blend with every settled principle of law, it must be expected that those who wish to push out the boundaries and change culture will, on occasions, seek to use – and on occasions, misuse or abuse – the Act. Then it will be a matter for the good sense of the judiciary to set limits having regard to the needs of the parties before the court and/or the wider communities who will be affected.

Beyond this, it is impossible to predict the changes that the Act will bring about, or their time scale. It has been suggested by Lord Lester of Herne Hill QC who, over many years, led the campaign for incorporation of Convention rights into the law of the United Kingdom, that it will take 30 years to understand the implications of the Act, but that it will bring about a major cultural revolution in the United Kingdom.

# Bibliography

Davies, Michael, *The Public Schools 1939 to 1945*
GBA–GBGSA, *Guidelines for Governors*
*Halsbury's Laws of England*
ISIS, *Choosing your Independent School*
ISIS, *Independent Schools Year Book*
*Jackson and Powell on Professional Negligence* (Sweet & Maxwell, 1997)
Pardey, D, *Marketing for Schools* (Kogan Page, 1991)
Rae, Dr John, *Delusions of Grandeur* (HarperCollins, 1993)
Rae, Dr John, *Letters to Parents* (HarperCollins, 1998)
Rigby, Ken, *Bullying in Schools* (Jessica Kingsley Publishers, 1996)
Stewart, WAC, *The Educational Innovators*

# Index

**Roman references are to paragraphs, italic references to page numbers.**

Absence
head, on loss of confidence    20.5.6,
  20.5.7
pupil
  attendance register    7.8.6
  authorised/unauthorised    7.8.3,
    7.8.6, 7.8.7
Abuse    13.6
Adverse Report List (DoH)    13.6.3,
  14.9, 22.2.3, 22.2.4
punishment, when is    15.4.5
social services involvement    13.6.6
Academy
meaning    2.1.4
Acceptance form    6.4.5, 9.4, *see also*
  Admission form
Accident
book    21.3.8
liability, *see* Negligence
publicity aspects    22.9
Accommodation (pupil)
*see also* Boarding
complaint on    8.4.14
overseas pupil, holiday etc
  14.1 *et seq*, 14.13.6
Accommodation (staff)    20.4.17
Accountant    19.5.1, 19.6.8
Accounts    18.5.4
data protection exemption    23.7.2
Act of Parliament
establishment by    18.2.8
Admission    7.1 *et seq*
charitable objects, effect on    7.2
discretion of head as to    7.2, 8.2.2,
  8.3.4
discrimination    7.2, 7.3, 7.4, 7.5.2
  cases    7.4.2
  legislation    7.4.1
form
  acceptance    6.4.5, 9.4
  contents    6.4.5
  one parent only signing    6.3.3
  prospectus, in    6.4.2

signature on    6.4.1, 6.4.5
HIV/AIDS, and    7.5.3
lists    7.6
meaning    7.1
offer of place, *see* Place
policy    7.2, 7.5
problems over    7.7
procedures    7.6
register    7.8.4
  corrections    7.8.4
  deletions    7.8.5
  inspection    7.8.8
selection of pupils    7.3, 7.5.1–7.5.3,
  8.3.5
Adverse Report List, *see* Abuse
Advertising
VAT    17.7.4
Advice, professional
*see also* Accountant; Solicitor governor
legal compliance, and    19.7.2, 21.2.5,
  21.3
Age
compulsory school    7.8.1
leaving, *see* Leaving age
supervision ratios, and    11.9.8
Agency    5.5.2, 5.8.2
child ordering goods etc, position of
  parent    5.5.2
AIDS/HIV    7.5.3
confidentiality    22.7.10, 22.7.11
education on    12.5.2
reducing risk of    13.4.1
Alcohol    15.5.4, 16.3.2, *see also* Drugs;
  Expulsion
Allergy    6.4.5, *see also* Health
Annual return    17.4.8, 18.5.4
Appeal (disciplinary)
expulsion decision, of    16.4.2,
  *see also* Expulsion: governors'
  review
Appeal (financial)    24.6.6, 24.10,
  *see also* Fund-raising
Appraisal    19.7.3, 20.5.1
Arnold, Dr T    1.2, 2.2.5, 20.2.6

Assault
  common law action        22.4.2
  disciplinary measure as        15.4.6,
    15.4.7
  indecent        13.6.6
  limitation period for action        12.12
Assets
  *see also* Intellectual property rights; Land;
    Premises
  management by governors        19.8.1
Assisted places scheme        4.2.2, 6.4.4
  contractual position of parents        6.4.4,
    12.4.2(d)
  phasing out of        4.2.2, 8.2.1, 18.5.2
Asthma
  attack,        teacher's duty        11.3.2(b)
  inhalers        13.4.4
Athletic        11.9.9
Attendance
  by-laws for (C19)        3.1
  implied term        16.2.1
  legal compliance        7.8
    failure to attend        7.8.3
  register        7.8.6
    inspection        7.8.8


Beale, D        1.3
Bedales        1.3, 1.4, 4.2.1
Behaviour        15.1 *et seq*
  *see also* Bullying; Discipline; Pupil;
    Rules
  implied term as to        16.2.1
  outside school        15.4.13
  parent, of, *see* Parent
  parent support        8.4.2
  protocol        8.3.6, 15.2
  teacher, of, *see* Teacher
Benenden
  foundation        1.3
Board school        3.1
Boarding        13.5–13.5.7
  change to day-pupil
    contract terms        13.5.6
    planning regulation        21.3.14
  community characteristics        8.2.2
  cost of        9.8.4, *see also* Fees
  decline in numbers        4.2.3
  delegated parental responsibility
    8.3.2, 13.4.1
  factors for and against        4.2.3
  feature of public school        2.2.2

fire precautions        13.5.4
health aspects        13.4, 13.5.4
homesickness, etc        13.3
houses, *see* House system
meals        13.5.4
origins/early schools        1.1, 1.2
  girls'        1.3
overseas pupils, *see* Overseas pupil
parental involvement        13.5.3
pastoral care aspects        13.3, 13.5,
  13.7.1
registration (children's home)        13.5.2,
  21.3.12
reputation of British schools        4.2.3
sex discrimination exception        7.4.1
statistics        4.2.3, 4.2.4
welfare of child        13.5.4
Books
  copyright        22.5.2
    employment, made during        22.6.1
  VAT zero-rated        17.7.4
Boys
  *see also* Origins
  public school 'all boys' characteristic
    2.2.4
Breach of contract, *see* Parent contract
Bryce Commission        1.3, 3.2
Bullying        15.3
  DFE book        15.3
  dealing with, practicalities        15.3.3,
    15.3.4
  early schools, in        1.2
  injury from, action for        15.3.6
    parents' indemnity        15.3.6
    settlement        15.3.7
  meaning, types and degree of        15.3.1
  pastoral care aspects        13.3
  policy on        6.4.8, 15.2, 15.3.5, 15.3.7
    expulsion for, case        8.2.2
  present day        4.2.3
  preview weekend, at, and place
    cancellation        5.11.4
  psychological illness, causing        11.7.2
  records on        15.3.7
  statistics and case examples        15.3.2
  welfare of child, and        15.3.5
  withdrawal of child for        10.14.16
Bursar        10.3.1, 13.5.2, 17.4.10, 19.6.3,
  21.1 *et seq*
  appointment        19.7.2
  chairman of governors, co-operation
    with        19.4.1, 21.2.3

Bursar *cont*
  Clerk to governors    19.6.3, 21.2.2,
    21.2.4
  company secretary, as    19.4.2, 19.6.3,
    21.2.5
  duties    21.2.1
  employee of governors/company etc
    19.6.3
  fees, unpaid, and    21.2.6
  governors meetings, attendance at
    19.6.3, 21.2.4
  head
    relations with    20.4.3, 21.2.2
    role in choice of    20.4.3, *398*
  job description, specimen    *398–400*
  legal compliance aspects    21.3–
    21.3.14
  meaning    21.1
  motor insurance, check on    11.9.6
  professional bodies for    21.1
  qualifications and skills    20.4.3,
    21.2.1
  role    21.1, 21.2
  responsibility division with head
    21.2.2, 21.2.6
  school not having    20.3.1, 20.3.5
  secretary, as    21.2.5, *see also*
    'company secretary' *above*
  status    21.2.3
Bursary    6.4.4, 7.6, 24.8.15
Buss, F    1.3
Butler's Education Act 1944    3.3.3


Cancellation of place    9.4.1, 9.4.2,
    10.12, 10.14.1
  preview weekend, after    5.11.4
Canoeing    11.9.9, 18.2.9
Capital gains tax    17.7.3, 17.8.3
Car
  *see also* Insurance; Transport
  head, for    24.4.14
Care and supervision    11.1 *et seq*
  after school hours    11.9.4
  before start of school    11.9.2
  breach of statutory duty    11.2.1, 11.10
  duty of school, examples    11.9
  negligence liability    11.2 *et seq*,
    *see also* Negligence
  standard of supervision
    helper    11.9.7
    teacher    11.4, 11.9.7

    teacher:pupil ratios    11.9.8
Catering, *see* Meals
Chairman of governors    19.4.1, 20.5.1
Chapel    17.7.1
Chaplain    13.5.2, 13.7.3, 13.7.4
Charge, *see* Mortgage/charge
Charitable company, *see* Charity, school as
Charity Commissioners
  consent of    17.5.4, 17.5.5
  corporate trustee, appointment of
    18.4
  jurisdiction    18.2.8
  order empowering trustees    17.5.1,
    17.5.3
  powers and functions    17.3.6
  scheme    17.4.9, 18.2.6, 18.5.3, 19.6.1
Charity, school as    6.3.2, 17.1, 17.3
  *et seq*
  accounts    18.5.4, 21.3.6
  advice to, or to trustees    17.3.6,
    17.4.3, 17.5.2
  annual return    17.4.8, 18.5.4
  beneficiaries, impartiality as to    17.4.5
  charitable company    18.2.4
    directors of    17.3.10, 18.2.9, 19.10
    governing body, structure    19.3.4
    governing instrument    18.5.3
    limited by guarantee    18.2.9, 18.3,
    18.4, 19.3.2
    members of    18.2.9
    omission of 'limited'    18.2.9
    tax exemption    17.7.2
  'charitable status'    17.3.3
  charitable trust, legal issues    17.3,
    17.4
    scheme to alter    17.4.9
  'charity trustee'    17.3.9, 17.3.10,
    19.3.1, 19.3.2
    accounts, etc    17.4.6, 17.4.8
    borrowing    17.5.2
    breach of trust    17.4.10, 19.6
    decisions    17.5
    differences from private trustee
    17.5
    duties    17.4–17.4.11
    employee not to be    17.4.10
    ex gratia payments    17.5.4
    insurance by    17.5, 17.5.3
    investment powers    17.4.7, 17.5
    limited liability, structure for
    18.2.10, 18.4
    new    19.5.2

Charity, school as *cont*
  'charity trustee' *cont*
    no personal profit   17.4.11
    personal liability   19.6
    personal responsibility   17.4.4
    powers   17.5–17.5.5
    removal of   19.9.2, 19.9.3
    remuneration   17.4.10
    registration duty, *see* 'registration'
      *below*
    supplier of goods or services to charity
      as   17.4.11
    waiver of fees, etc   17.5.5
    *see also* Incorporated body of trustees
  corporate trustee   18.4
  cy-près doctrine   17.3.5
  exempt   17.3.7, 18.2.10, 18.6
  gift to, *see* Gift
  land
    holding   17.5
    rent and profits from   17.7.1
    trustee powers as to   17.5.1
  objects   7.2, 7.5.1, 17.3.1, 17.3.2,
    17.3.4
    education   17.3.2, 17.6
    uncertain   17.3.3, 17.3.4
  permanent endowment   17.3.8, 17.5.1,
    18.3, 18.4
  registration   17.3.7, 17.4.8, 21.3.6
  Scotland   17.3.7
  stationery, etc, information on   21.3.6
  tax reliefs   8.2.1, 17.3.7, 17.6.1, 17.7
    capital gains tax   17.7.3
    corporation tax   17.7.2
    donation to charity, on   17.7, 17.8
    income applied for charitable purposes,
      condition   17.7.1
    income tax, list   17.7.1
    rates   17.7.6
    stamp duty   17.7.5
    value added tax   17.7.4
  trading activities   17.6.2, 17.7.1
  trust instrument   17.4.1, 17.4.2
  unincorporated, *see* Unincorporated trust
Cheque
  director's liability   19.11.3
  dishonoured, from third party   5.5.1
  information on
    charities   21.3.6
    companies   21.3.1
Child, *see* Pupil

Child protection   13.6
  *see also* Welfare
  checks on staff   13.6.3
  criminal conviction, disclosure   22.6.3
  guidance for heads   13.6.5
  overseas pupil   14.6.2, 14.9
Children's home
  registration and regulation   13.5.2,
    21.3.12
Christ's Hospital   1.1.1, 1.1.2, 2.2.1
Church school   3.1
Civil liberties   8.2.2, 8.2.4, 22.4.1,
  *see also* Human rights
Clarendon Commission   1.2, 2.1.3, 3.2
Class size
  early schools   1.2
  policy on   6.4.8
Clubs   8.3.5
Co-education   4.2.1
  school changing to
    discrimination exemption   7.4.1
    governing instrument amendments
      18.5.3
Collateral contract   5.5.3
College/collegiate
  meaning   2.1.4
Community   6.4.6, 8.1 *et seq*
  *see also* Pastoral care
  closed, concept of   2.1.5, 8.2.2, 8.4.2
  effect   8.2.2
  ethos, maintenance of   8.2.1, 8.3.7
  head, position in, *see* Head (teacher)
  inter-dependence   8.2.2
  life, training in   2.2.10
  mutual trust and confidence   8.4.2,
    13.6.6
  parental involvement   8.4.4, 8.4.5
  self-regulation,   2.1.5, 6.4.1, 8.2.2
Company, *see* Charity, school as;
  Corporation/company; Guarantee,
  company limited by
Complaint   8.4.14, 10.14.4, 10.14.6–
  10.14.9
  handling, and reputation of school
    24.9
  pupil adviser   13.6.7, 13.7
  situations giving rise to   13.3
    alleged abuse of pupil   13.6.6
Composition fees   5.8.3, 5.11.1, 6.4.7
  contingency events   6.4.7
Comprehensive education   4.1.3, 4.2.1
Compromise agreement   20.5.10

Confidence (belief in another)
head, loss of    20.5
confidentiality agreement    20.5.9
mutual trust and    8.4.2, 13.6.6
head and governors    20.5.2
Confidence (privacy)    22.1 *et seq*
age and maturity, and right to    *see*
Gillick principle
breach, action for    22.3, 22.4.4
complaint, registering in    13.7.2,
13.7.3
correspondence/ phone calls    22.7.4
data, *see* Data protection
governors' duty    19.8.1
health professional    13.7.3, 22.3,
22.5.1, 22.7.9
illegality, immorality, etc and    13.7.3,
27.7.8
information, protection of    22.3, 22.7
obligation, circumstances for    22.5.1
overriding of rights    22.3
parents/family matters    22.2.2, 22.2.3,
22.8
unpaid fees    22.8.1
photo, use of    22.7.1
police/social services, in case alleged
abuse    13.6.6
pupil, rights, *see* Overseas pupil; Pupil
school, rights    22.2.5
staff, rights    22.2.3, 22.6
waiver, circumstances for    22.6.2,
22.7.17
Confiscation    15.4.11
Constitution    18.1 *et seq*
*see also* Charity, school as; Corporation
forms of    6.3.2, 18.1
Construction projects
health and safety regulation    21.3.8
planning aspects    21.3.14
Consumer credit legislation    21.3.2
Contract
action for breach    12.3.1, 12.3.2
discipline failure    12.5.6
educational psychologist, against
12.4.2(d)
negligent reference    12.11
wrongful expulsion    16.2.2, 16.2.3
illegal    5.4.5, 5.8.1
limited company, with    18.2.9
director, position of    19.11.3
minor, with    13.5.5
school and parent, between, *see* Parent
contract

unincorporated trust, by governors of
18.5.2
Contractor
liability for injury to    11.10.2
reputable, dealing with    21.3.14
Contributory negligence, *see* Negligence
Copyright, *see* Intellectual property rights
Corporal punishment    8.2.4, 15.1,
15.4.1, 15.4.4
case-law    15.4.4
flogging, early schools    1.2
regulatory provision in UK    15.4.4
Corporation/company
Act of Parliament, established by
18.2.8
charitable company, *see* Charity, school
as
civil corporation    18.2.2
corporate manslaughter    18.2.9
corporate trustee    18.4
corporation aggregate    6.3.2, 18.2.3
corporation sole    6.3.2, 17.2.3, 17.3.9,
18.2.3
eleemosynary corporation    18.2.2,
18.2.6, 18.2.8
friendly society    18.2.10
gift to charity by    17.8.2
incorporation, methods for    18.2.4
limited company    6.3.2, 18.2.1,
18.2.4, 18.2.9
charitable, *see* Charity, school as
company secretary    19.4.2, 19.6.6,
21.2.5
directors, *see* Governors
employer of staff    18.2.9
governing body    19.3.4
legal structure and liability 18.2.9
limited by guarantee, *see* Guarantee,
company limited by
omission of 'limited'    18.2.9
proprietary school as    18.7
unincorporated school compared
18.5.2
livery company    18.2.7, 19.3.2
meaning of 'corporation'    18.2.1
public corporation    18.2
ecclesiastical and lay    18.2.2
Royal Charter    18.2.4, 18.2.6, 18.2.7
applicant, petition by    18.2.6
charter of incorporation    18.2.6
supplemental charter    18.2.6
statutory corporation    6.3.2, 18.2.4

Corporation/company *cont*
  trustees as body corporate   17.2.3,
    17.3.7, *see also* Incorporated body of
    trustees
  trading company   17.6.2, 17.7.1
Corporation tax   17.7.2, 17.8.2
Correspondence   22.7.4
Counselling   13.7
  accountability of counsellor   13.7.6
  Blue Book   13.7.1
  confidentiality   13.7.2, 13.7.3
  credentials and clearance   13.7.5
  in-house or self-employed   13.7.4
  legal compliance issues   13.7.2
  negligence   13.7.4
  records   13.7.6
  referral to doctor   13.7.4
Court, *see* Legal proceedings
Criminal conviction
  governor   19.9.2
  staff   13.6.1, 22.6.2, 22.6.3
    check on   13.6.3
    report after   13.6.4
Criminal prosecution   18.2.9, 18.5.2
  *see also* Legal proceedings; Sex offence/
    misconduct
  alleged abuse, for   13.6.6
  director, of   19.11.6
  governors/company, of   21.3
  privacy protection, relating to   22.4.3
  reporting restrictions   22.10
    sexual offence victim   22.9.2
Crowther Report   4.1.1
Curriculum   8.3.5, 12.5.2
  *see also* National Curriculum
  changes to, considerations   24.8.13
  policies in independent school   12.5.2
Custom and practice   6.4.9, 8.2.2
  expulsion of pupil   16.3
  fee payment   9.4.1, 9.4.2, 9.8.19
    deposit   9.4
    time for   5.11.1, 5.11.3, 9.8.1
  law on independent schools informed
    by   5.11.3
  notice rule   10.2
  term implied by   5.3.1


Damage
  property, to   11.2.1, 11.7.2
  pupil causing   9.8.2
  pupil suffering   11.7.2, *see also*
    Negligence

Damages, *see* Negligence; Parent contract
Dartington Hall   1.4
Data protection   21.3.5, 22.4.3, 22.7.14,
    22.8.1, 22.8.2, 23.1 *et seq*
  accuracy of data   23.2.3, 23.5.3
    correction etc of inaccurate   23.6.7
  basics of   23.2.1
  consent of subject to disclosure, etc
    23.4.2, 23.4.3
  contravention of provisions   23.6.6
  data held by school, scope/
    compliance   23.2.4, 23.8
    references   23.2.4, 23.2.5
  definitions   23.2.2
  EEC, transfer of data out of   23.5.7
  exemptions   23.2.5, 23.7.2
  keeping data   23.5.4
  lawful holding and using   23.2.3,
    23.4.1–23.4.4
    conditions   23.4.2
    information to subject, new provisions
      23.4.4
  lawful purposes   23.5.1
  manual data   23.2.1, 23.4.3, 23.7.2,
    23.7.3
  principles   23.2.3, 23.4, 23.5
    first   23.2.3, 23.4
    others   23.5
  registration (new system)   23.3
  security measures   23.5.6
  sensitive personal data   23.2.1, 23.2.2
    conditions for use   23.4.3
  subject rights   23.4.2, 23.4.3, 23.4.4,
    23.5.5, 23.6
    access   23.6.1, 23.6.3
    automatic processing, as to   23.6.3
    compensation   23.6.5, 23.6.6
    correction or erasure   23.6.7
    direct marketing, and   23.6.4
    injunction to prevent processing
      23.6.5
  new, commencement   23.7.2
  transitional provisions   23.7
  unpaid fees on school transfer, relevance
    to   23.4.2
Database   22.2.5
  fund-raising, for   24.10.2
  marketing, for   24.8.4
Day education
  change to, from boarding, *see* Boarding
  headship   20.3.1, 20.4.17
  rise of numbers   4.2.3

Day education *cont*
  rise of numbers *cont*
    factors for     4.2.3
Dearing report     12.5.1
Death, *see* Limitation period; Pupil
Debt
  school fees as     5.11.1
Defamation
  allegation of     10.14.18
Dentist     13.4.1
Deposit     5.8.3, 5.9, 6.4.5, 6.4.7, 7.6
  acceptance     9.4
  additional     9.5
  cancellation of place     9.4.1, 9.4.2
  discounted place, and     9.7
  elements in     7.6, 9.4
  meaning     9.2
  overseas pupil, for     9.6
  requirement to leave, and     16.3.5,
    16.3.6
Detention     15.4.9, 22.7.3
Developments (education, of)
  *see also* Origins
  1860–1944     3.2
Direct grant school     3.3.3, 4.2.1
Direct mailing     24.8.7
Directive (EC)     21.4
Director, *see* Charity, school as: charitable
    company; Guarantee, company limited
    by
Disability     7.4.1, 7.5.1, 8.3.4
Discipline     15.4
  abuse, constituting     15.4.5
  acceptable punishments     15.4.12
  appeal     15.4.14, 19.6.9
  bullying, *see* Bullying
  changes in society, and     8.2.1
  confiscation     15.4.11
  corporal punishment, *see* Corporal
    punishment
  detention     15.4.9, 22.7.3
  expulsion, *see* Expulsion
  fairness, *see* Natural justice
  inappropriate     13.3
  incident book     15.4.6
  investigation procedure     15.4.7
  lawful restraint     15.4.6
    guidance     15.4.6
  physical intervention
    report of     15.4.6
    situations for     15.4.6
  records     15.4.6, 15.4.7, 15.4.9,
    15.4.10

  review, *see* Expulsion
  search     15.4.10, 22.7.3
  school policy on     6.4.8, 15.2, 15.4.2
  suspension     15.4.8
  teacher, by     15.4
    authority     15.4.2, 15.4.3, 15.4.13
    behaviour outside school     15.4.13
    failure in     12.5.6, 13.3
    force, use of     15.4.6
    reasonableness     15.4.5
Disclaimer
  negligence liability, efficacy     11.6.3
  prospectus, in     6.4.2
Discount     6.4.7, 9.8.18
  deposit, and     9.7
Discrimination     7.2, 7.3, 7.4
  charity/trust, provisions which are
    7.4, 17.6.3
    removal of     17.6.3
  larger deposit for overseas pupils     9.6
  sex and race     7.4–7.4.3, 7.5.2, 17.6.3
    employment contract, and 21.3.7
    overseas pupil     14.10
  transitional exemption order     7.4.1
Dismissal
  head, of, *see* Head (teacher)
  unfair, qualifying period     21.3.7
Disqualification
  director, of     19.11.8, 21.3.1
  governor, of     19.9.2
  teacher, *see* Teacher: barred
Dividends/distribution
  tax relief     17.7.1
Doctor     13.4.1
  confidentiality     13.7.3, 22.3, 22.5.1,
    22.7.13
    data protection     23.4.3
    Gillick principle     22.7.9
  co-optative governor     19.6.8
  examination by     8.3.10
  retained by school     22.7.13
Drugs     15.5
  criminal offences     15.5.2
  disciplinary issues     15.5.2
    15.5.4
  education on misuse     15.5.1, 15.5.4
  legal compliance     13.7.2, 13.7.3,
    15.4.10, 15.5.3
  policy on     6.4.8, 7.3, 15.5.3, 15.5.4
    elements of     15.5.4
  publicity to school from     22.9
  search for     15.4.10

Drugs *cont*
  segregation on discovery      15.4.9
  urine test      15.5.4
  welfare of child, and      15.5.3
Dyslexia, *see* Learning difficulty


Education
  *see also* Comprehensive education;
        Elementary school
  charitable object      17.3.2, 17.6
    case-law on scope      17.6.1
    gifts/benefits      17.6.1
    *see also* Charity, school as
  developments in 1860–1944      3.1–3.3
  girls, for, *see* Girls
  parental duty      7.8.2
  public school, type in      2.2.5
  standard, *see* Examination; Teacher
  state, *see* Maintained school
Educational psychologist
  duty of care to dyslexic child
        12.4.2(d)
Educational services contract, *see* Parent
        contract; Services, contract for
Electrical safety      21.3.8
Elementary school      3.1, 3.2, 3.3.2
  11-plus      4.1.3
    abolition      4.2.1
Emergency medical treatment      13.4.5,
        13.4.6
  overseas pupil      14.13.9
Employee, *see* Employment contract; Staff
Employer      6.3.1, 6.3.5
  *see also* Health and safety; Staff;
        Vicarious liability
  address of      20.4.18
  contract of employment, *see* Employment
        contract
  governors/trustees of unincorporated trust
        as      18.5.2, 20.4.18
  liability insurance      21.3.9
  limited company/incorporated school
        as      18.2.9, 20.4.18
Employment contract
  discrimination, *see* Discrimination
  dismissal      21.3.7, 25.5.3
  employer to be named      20.4.18
  head's      20.4.1, 20.4.7, 20.4.8, 20.4.18
  notice period      20.4.18
  human rights issues      25.5.3

Employment tribunal
  human rights, and      25.5.3
  reporting restrictions      22.9.9
Endowed school      1.2, 2.1.4, 2.2.1,
        17.3.8
  *see also* Charity, school as
  government control      3.2
  grammar      3.2
  Scheme of the Endowed Schools
        Commission      19.3.3
Entry
  *see also* Admission
  exam      7.5.1, 7.6
  fee      9.4
  form, *see* Admission form
  meaning      7.1
Equal opportunities legislation      7.2, 7.4
Equipment
  use of
    injury from      11.9.9
    supervision of child      11.5.1
    *see also* Games; Negligence
Eton
  inspection      3.2
  legal and charitable status      6.3.2,
        17.3.7
  origins etc      1.1.1, 1.1.2, 1.2, 2.1.3
  resources      2.2.1
European Court of Justice      21.4
European law
  concepts/terminology      21.4
  primacy      21.4
Examination
  entry, *see* Entry
  fees, VAT exemption      17.7.4
  importance of      16.2.1
  results, data protection      23.2.4
  results, withholding of      8.4.12, 11.3.3,
        12.6
    GCSEs      11.3.3, 12.6
  teaching standards, and      12.5.3, 12.5.4
    poor results      12.5.4
Exclusion
  independent school use of term      16.1
  maintained school, from      8.2.2, 8.2.3,
        15.4.8, 16.1, 16.2.10
    'appeal'      16.2.10
    fixed period      16.2.10
    guidance      16.2.9
    misconduct of parents      16.2.7
    proportionality principle      16.2.6
    reinstatement      16.2.8

Exhibition    6.4.4, *see also* Scholarship
Expulsion    16.1 *et seq*
  appeals    16.4.2, 16.4.4
  considerations prior to decision
    16.2.9
  contract issues    16.2.2, 16.2.4
    breach of contract, *see* 'wrongful'
      *below*
  custom and practice    16.3
  discretion of head    8.2.2
  fairness    12.7, 13.2.6, 16.2.4, 16.4
  fee non-payment, for    9.8.7
  fees on    5.11.3, 16.3.1
  fixed period    16.2.10
  governors' review    16.3.5, 16.4, 16.5
    attendance at    16.4.4
    chairman    16.4.4
    composition of panel    16.4.4
    formalities    16.4.3, 16.4.4
    procedure    16.4.4
    result    16.4.4
  grounds for    16.2.2, 16.3.3
    recent social changes, effect of
      16.3.2
    traditional    16.3.1
  guidance for maintained school, account
    of    16.2.9
  human rights    16.2.5
  leaving status    16.3.6, 16.5
  legal review of    16.1, 16.2.2, 16.2.8,
    16.4.1
    judicial review    16.2.2, 16.2.4
  parental misconduct, for    16.2.7
  policy on    6.4.8, 16.2.1
  professional negligence issues    12.7
  proportionality    16.2.6, 16.4.4
  rehearing    16.4.2
  reinstatement    16.2.8
  requirement to leave    16.3, 16.3.5,
    16.3.6
    financial consequences    16.3.5
    status of pupil    16.3.6
  withdrawal of pupil on request
    16.3.4, 16.3.6
    financial consequences    16.3.4
  wrongful    12.7, 16.2.2, 16.2.3
    damages for    5.11.4

Fagging    2.2.7
  origins    1.2
Fairness
  *see also* Natural justice

contract terms, *see* Parent contract;
  Unfair contract terms
expulsion, of, *see* Expulsion
False imprisonment    15.4.9, 22.4.2,
  22.7.3
Fees    2.2.1, 6.4.7, 9.1 *et seq*
  accord and satisfaction    9.8.16
  boarding and tuition elements    9.8.4
  composition, *see* Composition fees
  court order to pay    9.8.12
  day school and public school
    compared    2.1.3
  deposit, *see* Deposit
  dishonoured cheque from third party
    5.5.1
  employer paying    6.3.5
  expulsion, effect on    5.11.3
  extras, charges and disbursements
    9.8.2
  factor in day school places rise    4.2.3
  forms    6.4.7
  frustration of contract, effect on    5.8.3
  guarantor    9.8.14
  head's authority    8.3.12
  in lieu of notice, *see* Notice
  increase/change in    5.10, 6.4.5, 6.4.6,
    6.4.7, 9.8.10
    notice of    9.8.10, 10.14.21
    'reasonable'    9.8.10
  instalments    6.4.7, 9.8.19, 24.8.14
    Consumer Credit Act regulation
      9.8.19
  interest and legal/administration costs
    9.8.15
  late    8.4.7, 9.8.6, 9.8.15
  list    6.4.7, 9.8.1
  meaning    9.2
  no tuition week(s), cases    5.11.3
  non-payment, action by school    5.11,
    8.4.7, 8.4.12, 9.8.7
    confidentiality issues    22.8.1,
      23.4.2
    counterclaim by parent    22.7.17
    county court claim    9.8.15
    withholding exam results    8.4.12,
      11.3.3
  notice, and, *see* Notice
  obligation    6.3.3, 8.4.7, 9.8.11, 9.8.12
    arising    6.4.9
    both parents    9.8.12
    divorced parents    9.8.12
    third party    9.8.12, 9.8.13

Fees *cont*
  overseas pupil        6.3.5, 9.8.13, 14.3
  payment record/ability to pay        6.4.5,
    7.5.1, 7.5.2
  place not taken up        6.4.5 *see also*
    Place
  prepayment        9.8.18, *see also* Discount
  privity of contract, and action for        5.5
  quantum meruit claim        5.11.3, 9.8.5
  reduction        24.8.14, 24.8.15, *see also*
    Scholarship
  refund and waiver        9.8.8
  registration, *see* Registration fee
  short payment        9.8.16
  siblings        24.8.14
  standard term for        9.8.10, 9.8.11,
    9.8.16
  third party paying        6.3.5, 6.4.7,
    9.8.12, 9.8.13
  time for payment        5.11.1, 5.11.3,
    9.8.1, 9.8.6, *see also* 'instalments'
    *above*
  value for money element        24.5.2,
    24.8.14
  waiver        17.5.5
  withdrawal of child, and, *see* Notice;
    Withdrawal of pupil
Financial management
  *see also* Marketing
  responsibility, day-to-day, *see* Bursar
Fire precautions        13.5.4, 21.3.8
First aid        21.3.8
Fleming Committee        2.1.3, 3.3.3
  report        3.3.3
Flogging
  C18/C19        1.2
Forster, WE        3.1
Fostering, *see* Overseas pupil
Foundation
  meaning        2.1.4
Friendly society        18.2.10
Frustration of contract        5.8, 9.8.9,
    10.14.8
  expulsion of pupil        16.2.2
Fund-raising        24.10
  *see also* Trading activities
  appeal, by        24.10
  charity, body as        24.8.5
  contribution evaluation        24.6.2, 24.6.6
  database for        24.10.2
  parents' association/'friends', by
    18.6, 24.8.5
  professional fund-raiser, use of
    24.10.1, 24.10.2
  tax exemption        17.7.1

Games        2.2.8, 4.2.3
  *see also* Negligence
  equal access, favouritism etc        13.3
  player's duty to others        11.4.4
  professional negligence claims        12.9
  referee negligent        7.4.3, 11.9.9
  risks to player, and negligence
    11.3.1, 11.5.1
    different sports        11.9.9
    injury sustained        11.9.9
  sex discrimination issues        7.4.3
General Certificate of Education        4.1.2
General Certificate of Secondary Education,
    *see* Examination
Gift
  school to, tax incentives        17.8
    capital gains tax relief        17.8.3
    company, corporation tax relief
      17.8.2
    covenants        17.8.1
    income tax relief        17.8.1
    inheritance tax        17.8.4
    sponsorship        17.8.1
Gift aid        17.8.1
Gillick principle        13.7.2, 13.7.3, 22.7.9
Girls
  all-girls schools, success of        1.3
  boarding, origins        1.3
  co-education        4.2.1
  education for, background        1.1.1,
    1.1.2, 3.2
  nunnery schools        1.3
  origins/role public schools        1.3, 2.2.4
  pioneers of education for (C19)        1.3
  sports, discrimination issues        7.4.3
Girls' Schools Association        1.3
Girls' Public Day School Trust        1.3
Goodwill        19.8.1
  *see also* Intellectual property rights
  head, importance of        20.2.6
Gordonstoun        1.4
Governing Bodies of Girls' Public Schools,
    Association of        1.3, 2.1.3
Governing Bodies of Public Schools,
    Association of        1.3, 2.1.3
  staff accommodation memorandum
    20.4.17
  training courses        19.7.3

Governing body, *see* Governors
Governing instrument     18.5.3, 19.6,
    20.5.3
    *see also* Charity, school as: charitable
        company; Corporation/company;
        Unincorporated trust
    admissions, and     7.2
    anti-discrimination modifications
        7.4.1
    co-educational, change to, and     18.5.3
    head, and
        authority stems from     8.3.1
        dismissal, check on provisions
            20.5.3, 20.5.4, 20.5.8
Governor(s)     19.1 *et seq*
    accountability of     19.8, 19.8.4
    accountability of head to     8.2.5, 19.1
    administrative     19.3.2
    bursar is not     19.6.3
    chairman     19.4.1
        appointment     19.4.1
        death     19.4.2
        vice-chairmen     19.4.2
    charity trustees     8.2.2, 17.4, 17.5,
        18.2.9, 19.1, 19.5.2, 19.6
        three-tier system, in executive
            council     19.3.1
        two-tier system, in     19.3.2
        *see also* Charity, school as
    classes of     19.2
        governing instrument prescribes
            19.6
    clergy     19.6.8
    Clerk to     19.4.2, 19.6.3
    committees     19.7.1
    confidence
        duty of     19.8.1–19.8.3
        right to     22.2.4
    contracting party     6.3.1, 6.3.2
    co-optative governor     19.2.5, 19.3.3,
        19.6.8
    Dean and Chapter model     19.3.2,
        19.4.1
    delegation to head     19.7
    directors as     18.2.9, 19.2.2, 19.3.4,
        19.11
        duties     19.11, 19.11.1
        member's position vis a vis     19.10
        shadow director     19.11.11
        *see also* Guarantee, company limited
            by
    disciplinary review by     16.4, 19.6.9,
        *see also* Expulsion

disqualification     19.9.2
ex officio governor     19.2.2, 19.3.3,
    19.6.8
financial certainty, need for     10.3.1
functions     19.7.2, 19.8.1
guarantee, company limited by, as
    members of     19.10
Guidelines for     19.7.3, 20.4.5
head
    as/or presence at meetings     19.6.2
    choosing     20.4.5
    dismissal     20.5.3, 20.5.4–20.5.10
    relations with     19.7.3, 19.8.3,
        20.2.6
lawyer     19.6.8, *see also* Solicitor
    governor
life governor     19.2.1, 19.3.1
marketing approach     24.4, *see also*
    Marketing
meetings     19.8.1
    absence from     19.9.3
misconduct     19.9.2
new     19.5
    appointment     19.5.2
    information to     19.5.1
nominative/nominated governor
    19.2.4, 19.3.3, 19.6.5, 19.6.8
officers     19.4.2
parent     8.4.4, 19.6.4
parents as 'customers'     19.8.2
personal liability     8.2.2, 10.3.1, 18.5,
    19.6, *see also* Trustee;
    Unincorporated trust
policy-makers     8.2.2, 8.3.1
profit from trust     17.4.11, 19.6.6,
    19.6.7
representative governor     19.2.3,
    19.3.3, 19.6.8
retirement     19.9.1
review of decisions by     13.2.6, 16.4
secretary     19.4.2
skills mix     19.6.8, 19.6.9
solicitor, *see* Solicitor governor
structures for governance     19.3
    single-tier     19.3.3, 19.3.4
    three-tier     19.3.1
    two-tier     19.3.2
supplier, as     19.6.7
teacher     19.6.5
training     19.3.7, 19.7.2
treasurer     19.4.2
voluntary     19.4.1, 19.6.10

Grammar school      1.2, 1.3, 4.1.3
  collegiate    2.1.4
  decline in late C17/early C18      1.2
  endowed      3.2
  entry to      4.1.3
  national secondary system, and      3.2
  origins in/of      1.1.1, 1.1.2
Grandparent
  paying fees      6.4.7, *see also* Fees: third
    party paying
Grounds
  *see also* Playground
  responsibility for      *400*
Guarantee, company limited by      18.2.9,
  18.3, 18.4
  director      19.11
    breach of trust      19.11.1, 19.11.2
    contracts/cheques      19.11.3
    criminal act      19.11.1, 19.11.6
    disqualification      19.11.8, 21.3.1
    environmental offence by company,
      position      19.11.10
    fiduciary duties      19.11.1
    negligence etc liability      19.11.2,
      19.11.4, 19.11.7
    personal liability      19.11.5, 19.11.7
    vicarious liability      19.11.4
    wrongful trading      19.11.9
  governance structure      19.3.2
  insolvency      19.11.8, 19.11.9, 21.3.1
  legal regulation and compliance
    21.3.1
  members' powers      19.10
  name      18.2.9, 21.3.1
  shadow director      19.11.11
  unincorporated trust becoming      18.5.1
  winding up      19.10
Guarantor
  fees, for      9.8.14
  limited company, for      18.2.9
Guardian      6.3.5, 6.4.5
  overseas pupil, for, *see* Overseas pupil
Gymnastics      11.9.9


HIV/AIDS      7.5.3, 13.4
  confidentiality      22.7.10, 22.7.11
  education on      12.5.2
Haberdashers      18.2.7
Hadow reports      3.3.2
Haemophilia      7.5.3
Harassment, protection from      22.4.3,
  22.4.4

Hazards/hazardous pursuits, *see* Health and
  safety; Games; Out-of-school
  activities; Premises
Head (teacher)
  absence of, effect      5.8.1, 10.3.3,
    20.5.6
  accommodation      20.4.17, 20.5.4
  accountability      8.2.5, 19.1
  admissions discretion      7.2, 8.2.2,
    8.3.4
  appointment      19.7.2, 20.1, 20.4
    notice      20.4, 20.5.8
    search committee      20.4.1
    *see also* 'job (vacancy)' *below*
  appraisal of      19.7.3, 20.5.1
  authority of      8.2.3–8.2.5, 8.3–8.3.16
    acts outside      8.2.4
    expulsion decision review, and
      16.4.1, 16.5
    sources      8.3.1
    support of governors      19.7.3
    support of parents      8.4.3
  bursar, and
    none, position where      20.3.1, 20.3.5
    relations with      20.4.3
  chairman of governors, co-operation
    with      19.4.1, 20.5.1
  change in, and reputation of school
    24.5.3
  child of, school fees      20.4.13
  confidence issues      8.3.11, 20.2.6, 20.5
    loss of confidence of governors, *see*
      'dismissal/departure' *below*
  day-school      20.3.1
  delegation by      8.3.13
  delegation to      19.7
  dismissal/departure      19.8.2, 19.8.3,
    20.1, 20.5.3–20.5.10
    compromise agreement      19.8.3,
      20.4.6, 20.5.10
    confidentiality      20.5.9
    garden leave/agreed absence
      20.5.6
    governing instrument provisions, check
      on      20.5.3, 20.5.4, 20.5.8
    meetings prior to      20.5.3, 20.5.5
    practical issues      20.5.4
    proprietor, by      20.5.7
    summary      20.5.8
    written notice      20.5.8
  duties      8.3–8.3.16
  duty of care      11.4.3, 11.6.1 (deputy),
    *see also* Negligence

Head (teacher) *cont*
  expenses, reimbursement for    20.4.9,
    20.4.10
  expression    8.1
  expulsion of pupil
    considerations for decision on
      16.2.9
    custom and usage, right by    16.3
    governors' review of    16.4
  governor, as    19.6.2
  governors
    meetings, attendance    19.6.2
    relations with    19.7.3, 19.8.3,
      20.2.6, 20.5
  in loco parentis    8.3.1, 8.3.2, 8.3.9,
    *see also* Parental responsibility
  induction course    20.6
  job (vacancy)
    advertisement    20.4.1
    applicants    20.4.4–20.4.6
    description    20.4.1, 20.4.3, *377–80*
    elements of    20.2–20.2.6, 20.3
    employment contract    20.4.1,
      20.4.7, 20.4.8, 20.4.18, *381–2*
    information on    20.3.5
    interview    20.3.4, 20.4.5, *383–5*
    person specification, sample    *376*
    personal objectives, and    20.3.3,
      20.4.4
    potential candidate for    20.3
    recruitment    20.4.1
    reference    20.4.6
    relocation costs    20.4.16
  marketing approach    24.4, *see also*
    Marketing
  medical insurance    20.4.12
  misconduct    20.5.3, 20.5.6
    gross    20.5.8
  overseas promotional visit    24.8.10
  parents, and    8.4.4, 8.4.5
  pension    20.4.8
  qualifications needed    20.3.2, 20.4.1,
    20.4.2, *376*
  Rae, Dr J, on headship    20.1, 20.2,
    20.4.1, 20.6
  references, *see* Reference
  role    19.6.2, 19.7.2, 20.2, 20.3
  salary/benefits and tax    20.4.7–
    20.4.17
    benefits in kind    20.4.10, 20.4.13,
      20.4.14, 20.4.17
    mobile phone    20.4.15

    reduced school fees    20.4.13
    subscriptions    20.4.11
    tax-free mileage    20.4.14
  staff, and    8.3.12, 13.6.5
  suspension    20.5.3, 20.5.6
  training    20.3.2, 20.4.9, 20.6
  welfare of child, duty to safeguard
    8.3.1, 8.3.2, 8.3.9
Headmasters' Conference    2.1.3
Headmistresses, Association of    1.3
Health
  *see also* Health declaration; Illness
    (pupil); Medical examination;
    Medical records
  confidentiality issues    22.7.11,
    *see also* Doctor
  data protection, and    23.4.3
  health authority role    13.4.1, 13.4.2
  health care plan    13.4.2
  legal duties, who has    13.4.1
  medication by school    13.4.4
Health and safety    8.3.3, 8.3.6, 13.4.1
  boarders    13.5.4
  employers' duty    21.3.8
  negligence action, and    11.5.1, 11.9.5,
    11.9.7, *see also* Negligence
  risk avoidance, duty    13.2.1, 13.7.2
  school premises    21.3.8
Health declaration    6.4.5, 7.6, 13.4.3
Health, Department of, *see* Abuse
Helper    11.9.7
Hepatitis    7.5.3, 22.7.10
Holiday
  guardian, *see* Overseas pupil
  use of school, *see* Premises
House system    2.2.6, 2.2.8, 13.5.2
  housemaster
    head, relations with    20.2.4, 20.2.5
    parental first point of contact
      13.2.4
    pupil able to talk to    13.6.7
Human rights    7.4.1, 8.2.2, 12.7, 13.2.1,
    25.1–25.7
  Act
    background, scope and effect
      25.1–25.3, 25.7
    interpretation    25.4
    balance, theme of    25.1, 25.6
    compliance by school    25.7
    Convention (European)    22.4.1, 25.1
      articles incorporated in Act    25.3
      compatibility with    25.4
    UK law, consistency with    25.2

Human rights *cont*
    declaration of incompatibility    25.4,
        25.5.3
    discipline and sanctions    15.4.3,
        15.4.4, 16.2.5
    employment issues    25.5.3
    European Court    21.4
    interference with freedoms, as trigger
        25.2
    proportionality    25.4
    'public authority'    25.2
        education issues    25.5.1
        independent school, whether is
        25.2
        public function, exercising    25.5.2

Illness (pupil)
    *see also* Disability
    absence for    7.8.3, 7.8.7
        persistent/frequent, case on
        12.4.2(f)
    asthma attack at school    11.3.2(b)
    fee payment    9.8.1, 9.8.8, 10.14.8
    health declaration    6.4.5, 7.6, 13.4.3
    HIV/AIDS, hepatitis B, child with
        7.5.3
    home tuition    12.4.2(f)
    long-term    5.8.1, 12.4.2(f)
    morning-after pill causing    10.14.22
    provisional notice to withdraw for
        10.11
Illness (teacher)    12.5.4, 12.5.5
Income
    tax reliefs    17.7, *see also* Charity,
        school as; Gift
Incorporated body of trustees    6.3.2,
    17.3.7, 18.3
    certificate of incorporation    18.2.5
        effect of    18.3
    Charity Commissioners' approach
        18.3
    legal nature    18.3
    liability of trustees    18.3
    transfer of permanently endowed property
        to    17.3.8
Incorporation, *see* Corporation/company
Indemnity
    governor, for    18.5.2
    insurance for trustees    17.2.7, 18.5.2,
        19.11.1
    parents'    15.3.7

Independent school
    *Choosing*, ISIS guide    20.3.5
    definition    2.1.2, 3.3.3, 4.1.2
    developments 1960s onwards    4.2
    future of    4.2.4
    MORI surveys    24.5.2
    *Year Book*    20.3.5
Independent Schools Tribunal    8.4.14
Industrial and provident society    18.2.10
Industrial Revolution    1.2
Information, *see* Data protection;
    Prospectus; Records; Report
Inheritance tax    17.8.4
Injury
    negligent act or omission causing
        11.2.1, 11.7.2
        types of injury    11.7.2
Inspection
    boarding schools    13.5.4
    premises (safety)    11.10
    school, of    3.2, 19.8.4, 21.3
Instalments, *see* Fees
Insurance    9.8.1, 18.5.2
    *see also* Indemnity
    charity trustees, by, *see* Charity, school as
    employers' liability    21.3.9
    legal expenses    20.5.4
    medical, for head    20.4.12
    motor    11.9.6, 21.3.9
    overseas pupil, for    14.12.3
Intellectual property rights    8.4.10,
    11.7.2, 19.8.1, 22.5
    *see also* Confidence (privacy)
    breach, action to prevent    22.4.2
        access to hearing, restricting    22.10
    copyright    21.3.4, 22.5, 22.5.2, 22.6.1
    employee, work etc made by    22.6.1
    governors' duty 22.2.5
    patent    22.5.4, 22.6.1
    registered design    22.5.3
    school, of    19.8.1, 22.2.5
        database    22.2.5
    teacher, of    22.6.1
Interest    9.8.15
    guarantor, payment of    9.8.14
    tax relief    17.7.1
Interview
    head    20.3.4, 20.4.5, *383–5*
    pupil    7.5.1
Investigation    15.4.7

Judicial review    16.2.2, 16.2.4

Land
   charity trustees' powers    17.5.1,
      19.3.2
   environmental audit   19.11.10
   governors' role   19.7.2
   holiday income from   17.6.2
   rent etc, tax relief   17.7.1
   trespasser   11.10.2, 22.4.2
Learning difficulty   12.4
admissions   7.5.1
   attention deficit hyperactivity
      disorder   12.4.1, 12.4.3
   dyslexia   12.4
     case-law   12.4.2
     meaning   12.4.1
     nature of   12.4.2
     personal injury or congenital
       condition   12.4.2
   independent school duty   12.4.2
   causation and quantum issues
      12.4.2(d), 12.4.2(e)
   'reasonable skills'   12.4.2
   special relationship between teacher/
      child   12.3.3
   local education authority duty
      12.4.2(d), 12.4.2(f)
   refusal/failure to recognise   5.11.4,
      12.4.2, 12.4.4
     claims   12.4.2
     negligence   12.4.2
   policy on   6.4.8, 8.2.2, 12.4.4
   psychological illness, causing   11.7.2
   remedial tuition
     claimable loss, as   12.8
     'extra', as   12.4.4
   screening tests   12.4.4
   social aspects and diagnosis   12.4.3
   special educational needs   12.4.1,
     12.4.2
     disclosure of statement   22.7.15
     regulatory provisions   21.3.12
     statistics   12.4.3
     statemented pupil   21.3.12, 22.7.15
     teacher's duty   8.4.1, 12.3.3, 12.4.2

Lease
   charity trustees' power   17.5.1
Leaving age
   historical   3.2, 3.3.2
     raising to 15   3.3.3
   pupil reaching, and fees in lieu of
     notice   10.14.23

Legislation
   social and consumer, effect of   2.1.5
Legal aid   15.4.9, 16.2.3, *see also*
   Negligence
Legal proceedings   22.9
   access restrictions   22.10
   counsel's duty in   22.9.10
   intellectual property/confidence, restricted
     access to   22.10
   reporting restrictions   22.9.22.10
     any court   22.9.3
     chambers hearing   22.9.7
     committal proceedings   22.9.5
     employment tribunal   22.9.9
     family court   22.9.1
     risk of impeding course of justice
      22.9.6
     sexual offence victim   22.9.2
     youth court   22.9.4
Licence
   letting   17.5.1, 17.6.2
   regulatory for events, liquor etc
     21.3.10
Limitation period   12.12, 15.3.6
List 99   13.6.3, 13.7.5, 14.9, 22.2.3,
     22.2.4
Livery company   18.2.7, 19.3.2
Local education authority   3.1, 3.3.2
   dyslexia, etc, duty/vicarious liability
     12.4.2(d), 12.4.2(f)
   Human Rights Act, and   25.2
   preference of parents, obligation as
     to   7.2
   secondary schooling plans   4.1.3
Location   2.2.3
Logo   22.5.3
Lottery, licence for   21.3.10

Maintained school   3.3.3, 4.2.2
   admissions policy   7.2
   collective worship   8.3.14
   dyslexia undetected, cases   12.4.2
   exclusion from, *see* Exclusion
   guidance for heads   8.2.3
   home/school agreement   8.2.3
   parent, misconduct by   16.2.7
   pupil records   8.3.16
   secondary, *see* Secondary school (State)
   sex education   12.5.2
   teacher-governor   19.6.5

Management
  financial, *see* Bursar
  firm and friendly, aim      24.4
  forecast, data protection exemption
      23.2.5
  marketing aspects, *see* Marketing
Marketing      24.1 *et seq*
  competitors, identifying      24.6.2
  complaints handling      24.9.1
  database      24.8.4
  demand, meeting      24.4, 24.5.1
  essence of      24.2
  fees, value for money, convenience
      etc      24.5.2, 24.8.14, 24.8.15
  finances      24.6.6, 24.8.1, 24.8.5, 24.10,
      *see also* Fund-raising
  head's *persona*      24.5.3
  management of      24.8.2
  methods      24.8
    adverts      24.8.6
    communications audit      24.8.8
    curriculum and hours      24.8.13
    direct mailing      24.8.7
    open days, activities      24.8.6
    premises, use of      24.8.6, 24.8.9,
      24.8.12
  parents' views      24.4, 24.5.1, 24.5.2,
      457
  plan      24.7
    implementation      24.8–24.8.15
  'product'      24.5.2
    image and reputation      24.5.2,
      24.8.6
    name and branding      24.5.3
    services, site and facilities      24.5.2
  publicity, dealing with adverse      24.9
  pupil roll, maintaining      24.9.3
  reference book      24.11
  school culture, and
    external      24.4
    internal      24.3
  strategy      24.4, 24.5.1, 24.6
    analysis of market segments
      24.6.4, 24.8.3
    explanation to governors, staff etc
      24.6.1
    financial elements      24.6.6
    profile of present status      24.6.2
    quality markers      24.6.3
    short-term plan      24.6.7
  targeting      24.8.3

Marlborough College      1.2
  admission of girls      4.2.1
Meals
  bursar, catering responsibility      20.4.3
  hygiene      21.3.8
  kitchens, regulation of      21.3.12
  legal compliance      13.5.4
  supervision, standard of food etc      13.3
  VAT      17.7.4
Medical examination      8.3.10, 13.4.1
Medical officer, school, *see* Doctor
Medical records      13.4.3
  access of pupil/parent to to      22.7.12,
      22.7.14
  data protection regulation      21.3.5,
      22.7.12
Medical report
  access of employee etc to      22.6.3
Medical treatment
  emergency      13.4.5
  X-rays      13.4.6
Medication      13.4.4
Merchant Taylors      18.2.7
Middle Ages      1.1.1
Military career
  preparation for      2.2.9
Minibus/small bus permit      21.3.13,
      *see also* Transport
Minor
  *see also* Pupil
  contract with      13.5.5
  damages      11.8.2
Misconduct
  head, of      20.5.3, 20.5.5
  parent, of      8.3.8, 16.2.7
  pupil, of, *see* Discipline
  teacher, of, *see* Teacher
Misleading statement
  *see also* Misrepresentation
  prospectus, in      6.4.2
Misrepresentation
  parent contract, in, meaning and
      remedies      5.4.2
Money laundering      21.3.10
Montessori, M      3.3.2
Mortgage/charge
  charity trustees' power      17.5.1, 17.5.2
  governor of unincorporated school,
      by      18.5.2


Name of school
  asset, as      19.8.1

Name of school *cont*
  business, regulation of   21.3.1
  changing, company limited by
    guarantee   19.10
  intellectual property right   22.2.5,
    22.5.3
  'limited', dropping   18.2.9, 21.3.1
  marketing aspects   24.5.3
National Curriculum   2.1.5, 4.2.2, 8.3.5,
  12.5.1
  independent school position   2.1.5,
    12.5.1
  key stages   12.5.1
  policies   12.5.2
National Secondary System
  effect on public schools   3.2
  origins and evolution   3.2
Natural justice   8.2.2, 8.2.5, 8.4.1
  fairness of procedures   13.2.6, 15.4.7,
    16.2.4
Negligence   11.2
  *see also* Professional liability
  bullying, liability for   15.3.1, 15.3.6
  causation   11.7, 12.10
    aspects of   11.7.1
  child
    age of, relevance   11.9.8
    contributory negligence   11.5.2,
      11.6.6, 11.8.2
    injuring another child   11.5.2
    minimising risk to   11.5.1
    playing, risks   11.5.1, 11.5.2,
      11.9.2, 11.9.9
    standard of care of   11.4.4
    very young   11.9.1, 11.9.4, 11.10.1
    warnings   11.5.1, 11.6.3
  damage   11.7, 11.7.2
    knowledge of, and limitation
      period   12.12
    psychological injury   11.7.2, 12.10
    types of   11.7.2
  damages   11.8
    compensation as purpose   11.8.1
    economic/financial loss   11.7.2,
      11.8.2, 12.10
    minor, for   11.8.2
    mitigation   11.8.1
    pain and suffering   11.8.2
    types of   11.8.1
  defences   11.6.1–11.6.7
  duty of care   11.2.1, 11.2.2, 11.3
    breach   11.6

    contractual situation, in   11.3.3
    examples of foreseeable risks at
      school   11.3.1
    foreseeability   11.2.2, 11.3.1
    guardian of overseas pupil   14.2,
      14.6
    'reasonable and just'   11.3.3, 11.5.1
    standard of, *see* 'standard of care'
      *below*
  examples of school situations   11.9
    after school hours   11.9.4
    before school starts   11.9.2
    breaks and lunch times   11.9.3,
      11.9.7
    leaving school during day   11.9.7
    out-of-school activities   11.9.5
    split-site schools   11.9.7
    transport   11.9.6, 11.9.7
    wandering child   11.9.1, 11.9.4
  games and sports
    player's duty of care   11.4.4
    risks   11.3.1
  governor of unincorporated school,
    and   18.5.2
  learning difficulty undetected   12.4.2
  legal aid   12.10, 15.3.6
  legal proximity/neighourhood   11.3.2
    off-duty teacher   11.3.2(b)
    principle   11.3.2(a)
    rescuer, teacher as   11.3.2(b)
  limitation period   12.12, 15.3.6
  personal injury/damage to property,
    restricted to   11.2.1, 11.7.2
  preconditions for liability, list   11.2.1
  professional   6.3.4
  proving   11.2.2, 11.3
  psychological injury   12.6, 12.10
  reference, in giving, *see* Reference
  sports referee, of   7.4.3
  standard of care   11.4
    cases   11.4.3, 11.4.4
    child, of   11.4.4
    objective test   11.4.4
    parent, of   11.4.1
    teacher, of   11.4.2, 11.4.3, 11.4.4
  teacher:pupil ratios   11.9.8
  vicarious liability   11.6.1
Nominative governor, *see* Governors
Northern Ireland   1.1.2
Notice
  extra tuition, for   10.8, 10.14.11
  fees increase   9.8.10, 10.14.21
  head's employment contract, in
    20.4.18

Notice *cont*
  school giving to parent, of major
      change    5.10, 6.4.6
    curriculum, to    8.3.5
    fees increase    9.8.10
  term's, fees in lieu    8.4.8, 10.1 *et seq*
    assisted place pupil    6.4.4
    cancellation after acceptance    9.4.1,
      9.4.2, 10.12, 10.14.1
    case authorities    10.3.3
    consumables    10.5
    dismissal of head, withdrawal on
      20.5.7
    disputes over, examples    10.14
    dissatisfaction/complaint, and
      10.14.4
    fair and reasonable operation of
      rule    10.10
    illegality as defence    5.4.5
    implied into contract    5.3.1, 10.2
    legal nature    10.3.3
    liquidated damages, fees as    5.11.2
    necessity for    10.3.2
    obligation arising    6.4.9, 10.2
    rate    10.5, 10.14.12
    reasons for    10.3, 10.4
    rule set out    10.2
    scholarship, etc, pupil    6.4.4, 10.5,
      10.14.12
    short notice    5.11.2, 10.6
    term for, efficiency of    10.14.12
    time for payment    10.6
    unfair contract term, challenge as
      10.4
    whole term    10.14.2
  termination of contact, for    8.4.8, 10.7
    form of    10.7
    provisional    10.11
    'term's notice', meaning    10.7
    time for    10.10
    *see also* 'term's, fees in lieu' *above*
  withdrawal without    5.9, 10.6
    circumstances when no breach
      9.8.10, 10.2
Nuisance 22.4.2
Nursery    4.2.2
  Voucher Scheme    4.2.2


Occupiers' liability    11.10.2
Offer of place, *see* Place

Origins    1.1–1.4
  boys' schools from 1600    1.2
  elementary schools    3.1, 3.2
  girls' schools from 1650    1.3
Out-of-school activities    8.3.5, 9.8.1
  health care    13.4.2
  supervision    11.9.5
Overseas pupil    4.2.3, 6.3.5, 13.5.7,
    14.1 *et seq*
  *see also* Discrimination
  age of 16, reaching    14.4.3, 14.11,
    14.12.2, 14.14
  attracting, promotional visit    24.8.10
  child protection checks    14.6.2, 14.9,
    14.12.5
  confidence and privacy rights    14.8,
    14.12.4, 14.13.6, *see also* Pupil
  deposit for    9.6
  emergencies    14.13.9
  fee payment    6.3.5, 9.8.13, 14.3,
    14.4.1
  fostering    14.2, 14.4.2, 14.5, 14.9,
    14.12.5
    guardianship as    14.5
    regulatory framework    14.5
  guardian in UK    6.3.1, 13.5.7, 14.1,
    14.2, 14.3
    agency finding    14.2, 14.4.5,
      14.4.6, 14.6.2
    agent, as    14.3, 14.4.2
    appointment    14.2, 14.4.2, 14.6.2,
      14.12.4
    contractual issues    14.4, 14.11,
      14.13.11–14.13.14, 14.15
    delegation of duties if absent
      14.13.5
    discipline and supervision    14.13.3,
      14.13.4
    duty of care    14.6, 14.13.1, *see also*
      Negligence
    family    14.4.6
    fees, position as to    14.3
    friendly approach    14.13.10
    insurance issues    14.12.3, 14.13.13
    legal complexities    14.2
    meaning    14.2
    obligations    14.13
    payment    14.13.12
    'practice' finding    14.2, 14.4.5,
      14.6.3
    problems, examples    14.14
    risk assessment checklist    14.6.2

Overseas pupil *cont*
  guardian in UK *cont*
    role and suitability     14.3, 14.6.2,
      14.12.5
    school involvement and liability
      14.3, 14.4.2, 14.6.2
    scope     14.12
    teacher as     14.4.2, 14.6.2
    termination notice     14.13.11
  hazardous activities     14.12.2, 14.13.8
  holiday arrangements     14.2 *et seq*,
    14.12, 14.13.6
  jurisdictional issues     14.11, 14.13.14
  parent contract     14.4.2, 14.4.4
  parents     14.2, 14.11
    child's contact with     14.13.7
    consent of, situations for     14.12.2,
      14.13.8
    delegation of responsibility     14.4.4,
      14.7
    information on child to     14.13.2
  race discrimination prohibition     14.10
  visa     14.4.3


Parent
  absence from home     8.4.11
  association of parents     18.6, *see also*
    Fund-raising
  confidentiality issues     22.8
  consent to child's activities     14.12.2
  consultation with/account of views, *see*
    Marketing
  expectations     8.4.9
  fee paying issues, *see* Fees
  governor     8.4.4, 19.6.4
  head's authority over     8.2.3, 8.3.8
  home circumstances/upbringing of
    child     8.4.11, 15.3.4
  improper conduct/misconduct     8.3.8,
    16.2.7
  involvement (with school)     4.2.3,
    6.4.6, 8.4.4, 8.4.5
  moving home     10.14.5
  party to contract     6.3.1, 6.3.3
    fee payment     9.8.11, 9.8.12
    *see also* Parent contract
  requirement to act reasonably     5.1.1,
    5.6, 5.9, 6.4.6, 8.4.2
    breach of, effect     16.2.7
    governors, and     19.8.2
  rights and duties     8.4, 10.3.2

support expected
  for child     6.4.6, 8.4.11
  for school/head's authority     8.4.3,
    8.4.9, 10.3.2
Parent contract     5.1 *et seq*, 6.1 *et seq*
  acceptance     6.4.5, 6.4.9
  acceptance deposit, *see* Deposit
  agency issues     5.5.2
  alleged defect     10.14.9
  boarding     13.5.6
  breach     5.3, 5.6.1, 5.6.3, 5.7, 5.9
    circumstances     5.9
    failure to pay etc fees     5.11.1–
      5.11.3, 6.4.7
    legal expressions, use of     5.9
    minor     5.9
    remedies     5.11
    withdrawal without notice     5.9,
      10.6
  child, position of     5.5, 5.5.2, 5.5.3
    collateral contract, suing on     5.5.3
    contracting with school direct
      5.4.6, 6.3.1, 6.3.4
    ordering goods on parents' account
      5.5.2
    remedy against school     6.3.4
  collateral contract     5.5.3
  consideration     5.1.1, 5.3.1, 6.3.4,
    *see also* Fees
  construction by court     6.2
  consumer contract, as     5.3.2
  contract for educational services, as
    5.1.1
  damages     5.6.3, 5.9, 5.11
    breach of warranty     5.3
    fraudulent or negligent
      misrepresentation, for     5.4.2
    liquidated     5.11.2
    mental distress/injury to feelings
      5.11.4
    partial performance, for     5.6.2
    special     5.11.4
    unliquidated     5.11.4
  duress/undue influence     5.4.4, 5.9
  educational services     6.4.9
  enforceability     5.2
  fees, *see* Fees
  formalities     5.1.1, 6.4
    entry form, *see* Admission form
    prospectus     6.4.2
  frustration     5.8
    effect of     5.8.3

Parent contract *cont*
  frustration *cont*
    frustrating events        5.8.1, 9.8.9
    non-frustrating events        5.8.2
    illegal        5.4.5, 5.8.1
    'mere puff'        5.3.1, 5.4.2
    misrepresentation        5.4.2, 5.9
    mistake inducing        5.4.3
    nature and elements of        5.2
    non-disclosure        5.4.2
    obligations of parties        5.1.1, 5.6,
      6.4.6, 6.4.9
    offer, *see* Place
    'opportunity and environment'
      concept        5.1.2
    parental rights        8.4.12
    parties        6.3
      identification and scope        6.3.1
      limited company        18.2.9
      parent(s)/guardian        6.3.1, 6.3.2
      pupil        6.3.4
      school        6.3.2
      third party as        6.3.1, 6.3.5
    performance        5.6, 5.7
      discharge from obligation, *see* 'breach'
        *above*
      standard of        5.6.2
      time for        5.6.3
    policies of school, whether
      contractual        6.4.8
    privity        5.2, 5.5
    rescission        5.4.2, 5.9
    specific performance and injunction
      5.11.5
    standard terms and conditions        6.4.5,
      6.4.6, 9.8.1
    statutory regulation        21.3.3
    termination        5.7, 5.8, 8.4.8, 12.6
    terms        5.3, 6.2, 6.4.6, 6.4.9
      basic        5.1.1, 5.3
      change to, by one party        5.10, 6.4.6
      exclusion clause        5.4.1
      express        5.3.1, 5.8.2
      fairness        5.3.2, 5.4.1, 6.4.1, 6.4.6
      implied        5.3.1, 6.4.7, 8.2.5, 10.3.3,
        13.2.2, 16.2.1
      third party        6.3.1, 6.3.5, 9.8.12, 9.8.13
      cheque bouncing        5.1.1
    unfair contract terms unit        5.3.2
    unilateral variation        5.10
    void, circumstances        5.4.2, 5.4.3,
      5.4.5

  writing, need for        6.2, 6.4.1, 21.3.3
Parental leave        21.3.7
Parental responsibility, person with
  consent to child's attendance
    6.4.5
  contracting party        6.3.1, 6.3.3
  delegation        8.3.2, 13.2.1, 14.4.4, 14.7,
    15.4.3
Parents' association        18.6, *see also*
  Fund-raising
Party to contract, *see* Parent contract
Pastoral care        13.1 *et seq*
  cases on        13.2.4
  child protection, *see* Abuse; Child
    protection; Sex offence/misconduct
  class, work and conduct of        13.3
  community of school, and        13.3
  complaints, *see* Complaint
  contract, implied into        13.2.2
  discipline        13.3
  fair procedures        13.2.6
  guidance (The Blue Book)        13.2.4,
    13.7.1
  health and safety aspects, *see* Health and
    safety
  health care        13.4
  tort, duty in        13.2.3
Patent, *see* Intellectual property right
Performance tables        4.2.1, 4.2.2,
  10.14.15
Permanent endowment        17.3.8
Personal injury
  accident book        21.3.8
  bullying, from        15.3.6, 15.3.7
  liability for, to pupil        11.7.2, 12.10,
    15.3.6
  limitation period        12.12
  pupil suffering, *see* Negligence
  visitor/trespasser suffering        11.10.2
Photograph        22.2.3, 22.4.4, 22.7.1
  aerial, of land        22.9.8
  press, by, Code on        22.9.8
  pupil, of, school use of        22.7.1
Place
  acceptance, *see* Admission form
  cancelling/'no show'        5.9, 5.11.2,
    6.4.5, 10.14.1, 10.14.9
  bullying at preview weekend
    5.11.4, 10.12
  fees in lieu of notice        10.12
  offer of        6.4.1–6.4.4, 7.6, 7.7
    error        8.3.4

Place *cont*
  offer of *cont*
    legal position 6.4.3, 6.4.9
    letter, form of   6.4.4
    obligation stemming from
      acceptance   6.4.9
    place filled, effect of   10.14.10
    reservation of   6.4.9
    withdrawal of   8.3.4
Planning   21.3.14
Play
  licence for premises for   21.3.10
Playground
  injury in   11.10.1
    climbing etc apparatus   11.9.9
    safety checks etc   11.10
  supervision, *see* Care and supervision
Police
  involvement with teacher's improper
    behaviour   13.6.6
Policies   6.4.8, 8.2.2
  admissions, on   7.2, 7.5, 8.3.4
  behaviour and discipline   15.2, 15.3.5
  contractual or non-contractual   6.4.8
  curriculum   12.5.2
  learning difficulties, on, *see* Learning
    difficulty
  scope   6.4.8
  selection   7.3
Polling, use of premises for   21.3.10
Prefects, system of   2.2.7
Premises
  access, health and safety   21.3.8
  charity, *see* Charity, school as: land
  closing, head's authority   8.3.8
  commercial use of   17.6.2, 21.3.10,
    24.8.6, 24.8.9
    examples   24.8.9
  complaint on   8.4.14
  condition of, and marketing   24.4,
    24.8.12
  construction/planning, *see* Construction
    projects
  destruction/part destruction   5.8.1
  hazardous activities on   11.9.5,
    11.9.7, 11.10
  holiday use, *see* 'commercial use of'
    *above*
  insurance   17.5.3
  licence for certain uses   21.3.10
  management of   20.4.3
  occupiers' liability   11.10.2

rates   17.7.6
safety   11.10
security   8.3.8
sports facilities, income from   24.8.9
supervision of child on, *see* Care and
  supervision
visit to, *see* Visit
visitor to   11.10.1, 11.10.2
worship, used for, tax relief   17.7.1
Preparatory school
  bursars   21.2.3
  professional body for   21.1, 21.2.3
  legal structure   19.3.4
Press Complaints Commission
  Code of Practice   22.9.8, *see also*
    Legal proceedings
Privacy   22.4
  *see also* Confidence (privacy)
  common law causes of action   22.4.2
  European Convention, rights under
    22.4.1, *see also* Human rights
  family court proceedings   22.9.1
  'publish', meaning   22.9.1
  pupil, of   8.3.9, 13.3, 22.2.1, 22.7–
    22.7.17
  statutory protection   22.4.3
  teacher/staff   22.2.3, 22.6
  victim of sexual crime   22.9.2
Private trust, *see* Trust
Privity of contract   5.2, 5.5, 12.3.2
Professional liability   12.1 *et seq*
  contract action   12.3.1, 12.3.2
    losses   12.8
    who can sue   12.3.2, 12.8
  illness/change of teacher   12.5.4,
    12.5.5
  learning difficulties, dyslexia, etc, *see*
    Learning difficulty
  order and discipline failure   12.5.6
  'profession'   12.13.1
    case-law   12.13.2
  public examinations, and   12.5.3,
    12.5.4
  reasonable skill and care   12.2
    categories   12.13.3
    standard of care   12.2.1
    teacher's duty   12.2.2, 12.3.3,
      12.5.4, 12.13.3
  standards   5.11.4, 8.4.1, 12.5
    curriculum and syllabus   12.5.3
  tort action   12.3.1, 12.3.3, 12.4.2
Progressive schools   1.4

Promotion
  initiatives     24.6.7, 24.8
  promotional material     24.4, 24.8.10,
      24.8.11, *see also* Prospectus
Property
  confiscation     15.4.11
  damage to, negligence claim     11.2.1,
      11.7.2
  missing and 'borrowed'     13.3
  trespass to, action for     22.4.2
  withholding of, by school     8.4.12
Proportionality     8.2.2, 16.2.6
Proprietary schools     1.2, 2.1.2, 2.1.3,
      6.3.2, 18.7
  legal structure     18.2.8, 18.7
  limited company, as     18.7
  proprietor     18.7
    barring of     13.6.2
    dismissal of head     20.5.7
    liability of     18.7
    welfare of child, responsibility
        15.4.3
Proprietor-owned school, *see* Proprietary
      school
Prospectus     6.4.2, 6.4.6, 7.6
  contents, form and legal status of
      6.4.2
  misleading statement in     6.4.2
  photo of pupil, use in     22.7.1
  well-presented, need for     24.4,
      24.8.11
Provisional notice     10.11
Psychological injury, *see* Negligence
Public examination, *see* Examination
Public functions     21.3.8, 21.3.10
Public school
  earliest reference     1.1.1
  education at, 'whole man'     2.2.5
  essential characteristics     2.2
  house system     2.2.6
  income tax exemption, and     2.1.3
  meaning     1.1.1, 2.1.3
  1920s/30s, in     3.3.2
  statutory reference to     17.7.1
Public School Commission     1.2
Publication, *see* Intellectual property rights;
      Privacy
Publicity
  adverse, handling     24.9.2
  preventing, *see* Legal proceedings;
      Privacy
  requirements on stationery, *see* Cheque
  school, *see* Marketing; Prospectus

Punishment, *see* Discipline
Pupil
  attendance     6.4.6, 7.8
  behaviour etc     6.4.6, *see also*
      Discipline
  civil liberties, *see* Civil liberties
  confidential information, *see* 'privacy and
      dignity' *below*
  correspondence     22.7.4
  death     5.8.1, 7.8.5
    corporate manslaughter of     18.2.9
    negligence causing     11.9.9, *see also*
        Games; Negligence
  illness, *see* Illness (pupil)
  medical examination     8.3.10
  medical records, *see* Medical records
  negligence, by or to, *see* Negligence
  parent contract, and, *see* Parent contract:
      child, position of
  personal injury, *see* Negligence
  privacy and dignity     8.3.9, 13.3,
      22.2.1, 22.7–22.7.17
    secret etc confided in teacher
        27.7.8
    space/lockers     22.7.2
  punishment, *see* Discipline
  records     8.3.16, *see also* Records
  refusal to attend     5.8.2, 9.8.9
  report (progress), on     22.7.6
  rights and duties     8.4, *see also* Human
      rights
  segregation     15.4.9
  selection     7.3, 7.5.1
  unhappy     13.2.2, *see also* Bullying;
      Pastoral care
  walking out     9.8.9, 10.13
  welfare of     8.3.1, 8.3.2, 8.3.9, 8.3.16,
      8.4.13, *see also* Pastoral care


Quantum meruit     5.11.3, 9.8.5


Race, *see* Discrimination
Records
  access     22.8.2, *see also* Medical
      records
  counsellor keeping     13.7.6
  data protection regulation     21.3.5,
      22.7.14, 22.8, 23.1 *et seq*, *see also*
      Data protection
  disciplinary, *see* Discipline

Records *cont*
  manual    23.2.1, 23.4.3, 23.7.2, 23.7.3
  medical, *see* Medical records
  pupil    8.3.16
  sanitorium, of    22.7.17
Rae, Dr J    20.1, 20.2, 20.4.1, 21.2.2
Reference    8.3.11
  confidentiality    22.7.16, 23.2.5
  data protection    23.2.4, 23.2.5
  negligence liability    8.3.11, 12.11 ,
    16.3.6, 20.4.6
  required removal after    16.3.6
Register (pupil)
  admissions    7.8.4, 7.8.5
  attendance    7.8.6
  regulation of    21.3.12
Registration
  charity, of, *see* Charity, school as
  children's home, as    13.5.2, 21.3.12
  independent school, of    21.3.12
Registration (by school)
  *see also* Admission; Register (pupil)
  date of, and admission criteria    7.5.1
  fee, *see* Registration fee
  form    6.4.2, 7.6, 9.3
Registration fee    5.8.3, 7.6, 9.3
Rehabilitation of offenders    13.6.1,
  21.3.7, 22.4.3, 22.6.3
Reinstatement of pupil    16.2.8
Religion
  absence for    7.8.3, 7.8.7
  chaplain    13.5.2, 13.7.3
  charitable objects, and    7.5.1, 7.5.2
  church school    3.1
  denominational schools    1.1.2, 2.2.3,
    2.2.11
    Stonyhurst    1.1.2, 2.2.3, 2.2.7
  education, religious    8.3.14, 12.5.2
  governance structure for religious
    body    19.3.2
  non-denominational school    7.5.2
  principle of    2.2.11
    introduction    1.2
  worship    8.3.14
Religious school    19.3.2, *see also*
  Church school
Removal, required    16.3.5, 16.3.6,
  *see also* Expulsion
Renaissance
  development of schools    1.1.2
    girls'    1.3

Report    8.3.11
  medical, access to    22.6.3
  misconduct of teacher, mandatory
    13.6.4, 21.3.12
Report (progress)    22.7.6
Reporting restrictions    22.9, *see also*
  Legal proceedings
Reputation (of school), *see* Marketing;
  Name
Residence, area of    2.2.3, 7.5.2
Restraint    15.4.6
Review
  governors', of expulsion    16.4
Roedean
  foundation    1.3
Rough handling    15.4.5
Royal Charter
  reconstitution as unincorporated trust
    19.3.3
  school established by    18.2.4, 18.2.6
Rugby
  Dr T Arnold's aims    1.2, 20.2.6
  origins    1.1.2, 2.1.3
  revolt in    1.2
Rules    6.4.5, 6.4.6, 15.2
  *see also* Discipline
  breaches    8.2.2, 8.2.4
  compliance    8.4.6
  setting    8.3.6


Safety, *see* Health and safety
Salary    3.2
  trustees' remuneration    17.4.10
Scholarship    3.2, 4.2.4, 6.4.4
  deposit    9.7
  details in prospectus    6.4.2
  fees in lieu of notice, and    6.4.4, 10.5
  new, as marketing plan    24.8.15
  offer
    letter for    6.4.4
    subject to    7.6
  withdrawal or clawback    6.4.4,
    10.14.20
School
  charity, *see* Charity, school as
  community, *see* Community
  constitution, forms of    6.3.2, 18.1,
    *see also* Corporation; Trust;
    Unincorporated association/body;
    Unincorporated trust
  definition    2.1.1

School *cont*
    party to contract     6.3.2
    policies     6.4.8
School Boards     3.1
Scotland     1.1.2, 17.3.7, 19.9.2
Search of pupil/property     15.4.10, 22.7.3
Seat belts, *see* Transport
Secondary school (State)     4.1.3
    comprehensive system     4.1.3, 4.2.1
    post-WWII     4.1
    provision for all (1944)     3.3.3
    types     3.3.2
Security     8.3.8
Selection     7.3, 7.5.1
Self-regulation     2.1.5, 6.4.1, 8.2.2
Services, supply of
    contract for
        charity trustee, with charity
            17.4.11
        educational services, *see* Parent
            contract
        skill and care, implied term     12.3.2,
            13.2.1, *see also* Pastoral care;
            Professional liability
        school 'product', as, marketing of
            24.5.2
    VAT     17.7.4
Sex discrimination, *see* Discrimination
Sex education     12.5.2
Sex offence/misconduct
    teacher, by     13.6.2, 13.6.3, 13.6.4,
        18.5.2
    victim, privacy for     22.9.2
Sexual orientation
    pupil     22.7.5
    staff, of, and privacy     22.2.3, 22.6.2
Sherborne     1.2
    farming programme (WWII)     3.3.3
Single-sex school     1.3, 7.4.1, 7.5.2
Sixth form
    education provision     4.1.1
    offer of place refused, fees     10.14.23
    pupil leaving at end of A levels
        5.11.3
Smoking     15.5.4, 16.3.2, *see also* Drugs;
    Expulsion
Social services
    teacher's improper behaviour,
        involvement     13.6.6
Social worker
    'professional', as     12.4.2

Solicitor governor     17.4.11, 18.5.2,
    19.6.6, 19.6.8
    advising new governors     19.5.1
    Clerk to the governors, as     19.4.2,
        19.6.6, 21.2.4
    company secretary, as     19.6.6
    profit from trust     17.4.11
Special Act of Parliament     18.2.8
Special needs, *see* Learning difficulty
Sports, *see* Games
Staff     10.3.1
    *see also* Bursar; Teacher
    child protection checks     13.6–13.6.7
    employment contract regulation
        21.3.7
    head's authority to engage/dismiss
        8.3.12
    non-teaching, responsibility for     *400*
    part of school community     8.2
    privacy     22.2.3, 22.6
Stamp duty     17.7.6
State
    *see also* Local education authority
    independence from     8.2.2
    school, *see* Maintained school; Secondary
        school (State)
Stationery, *see* Cheque
Statistics     4.2.3, 4.2.4
Statutory duty, breach of     11.2.1, 11.10,
    12.3.1, 18.5.2
Step-parent     6.3.5, 9.8.12
Summerhill     1.4
Supervision, *see* Care and supervision
Suspension
    head, of     20.5.3
    pupil, of     15.4.8, 16.3.4
Swimming
    consent of parent     14.12.2
    injury/death     11.9.9
    supervision ratios     11.9.8

Taunton Commission     1.2, 1.3, 2.1.3,
    3.2
Tax
    fees, payment in kind     6.3.5
    head, position of     20.4.7–20.4.17
    school, position of     6.3.2, 6.4.7, 8.2.1,
        17.7, *see also* Charity, school as
Teacher     12.1 *et seq*
    *see also* Staff
    accommodation, taxation     20.4.7

Teacher *cont*
  assistant master, career prospects   3.2
  bailee, as   11.7.2
  barred   13.6.2, 13.6.3
  care of pupils, *see* Care and supervision
  change of   12.5.5
  check on background   13.6.3, *see also*
    List 99
  complaint about   8.4.14, 10.14.6
  criminal offence, *see* Criminal
    conviction; Sex offence/misconduct
  discipline by, *see* Discipline
  dismissal   13.6.4
  duty of care   8.4.1, 11.3.2, 11.4.2,
    *see also* Negligence; Professional
    liability
  Emergency Training Scheme (post-
    war)   4.1.1
  female, C19 training for   1.3
  guardian to overseas pupil   14.6.2
  head, *see* Head (teacher)
  illness   12.5.4, 12.5.5
  INSET training   12.13.3
  intellectual property rights   22.6.1
  misconduct   12.13.3, 13.6.2, 13.6.3
    allegation of, guidelines   13.6.5
    outside school   13.6.4, 13.6.6
    report on, mandatory   13.6.4,
      21.3.12
  peripatetic   10.8
  qualification   10.14.19
    bogus   10.14.19
    lack, in independent schools   4.1.2
  reasonable skill and professional liability,
    *see* Professional liability
  standards   8.4.1, 12.5, 12.13.3
    damages for low   5.11.4
    *see also* Professional liability
  training   12.13.3
Telephone
  interception of communication
    22.4.3, 22.7.4
  mobile   20.4.15
Theft
  pupil, by   16.3.2
  trustee, by   17.2.6
Third party, *see* Fees; Parent contract
Tort
  *see also* Negligence; Professional
    liability; Statutory duty, breach of
  action in   6.3.4, 11.1 *et seq*, 12.3.3,
    12.11, 13.2.3

  expulsion, for   16.2.3
  limitation period   12.12
  undetected dyslexia   12.4.2,
    12.4.2(d)
  governor of unincorporated school,
    liability   18.5.2
  insurance cover   18.5.2
  meaning   12.3.1
  privacy protection   22.4.2, 22.4.4
Trading activities   17.6.2, 17.7.1, 18.7
Trading company   17.6.2, 17.7.1
Training
  governors   19.3.7, 19.7.2
  heads, *see* Head (teacher)
  health and safety regulation   21.3.8
  quality of, effect   24.3
  teachers, of, *see* Teacher
Transferring school   8.3.11, 8.3.16
  unpaid fees, confidentiality/data
    protection issues   22.8.1, 23.4.2
Transport
  public, parental consent   14.12.2
  school   21.3.13
    seat belts   21.3.13
    supervision on/getting on   11.9.6,
      11.9.7
    withdrawal for lack of   10.14.17
  teacher's private car   11.9.7
Tree-climbing   11.9.9
Trespasser   11.10.2, 22.4.2
Trips
  *see also* Out-of-school activities
  VAT exemption   17.7.4
Trust   6.3.2, 6.3.5
  advance fees   6.4.7
  charitable   17.1, 17.3 *et seq*, *see also*
    Charity, school as
  constructive   17.2.2
  fees, paying   6..5, 9.8.13
  private   17.2, 17.3.4, 17.4.4
    background to   16.2.1, 17.2.2
  public   17.2.2
  resulting   17.2.2
  unincorporated   6.3.2, 18.2.7,
    18.5
Trust corporation
  definition   18.4
Trustees   6.3.2, 8.2.2, 17.2.3–17.2.7
  account of profits and tracing   17.2.6
  asset management   8.4.7
  breach of trust   17.2.5, 17.2.6, 17.2.7,
    18.4

Trustees *cont*
  breach of trust *cont*
    co-trustee, of    17.2.5, 17.2.6, 17.2.7
    injunction to restrain    17.2.6
    charity trustee    17.4, 17.5, *see also*
      Charity, school as; Incorporated
      body of trustees
    contracting party    6.3.2
    corporate    18.4
      appointment by Charity
        Commissioners, effect    18.4
    criminal liability    17.2.6
    decisions of    17.4.4, 17.5
    duties    17.2.4
    fees paid by    6.3.5
    fiduciary capacity    17.2.3
    governors, *see* Governors
    indemnity insurance    17.2.7
    investment powers    17.4.7
    land, purchase of    17.4.7
    personal liability    17.2.4, 17.2.6
      limitations    17.2.7
    *see also* Unincorporated trust
    stock trustees    19.3.1
    who may be    17.2.3
Tudors    1.1.2, 1.2
Tuition, extra
    notice to end    10.8
    remedial teaching    12.4.4


UK guardian, *see* Overseas pupil
Unfair contract term    5.3.2, 10.4
    standard terms, and    6.4.6
Uniform
    requirement    8.2.4
    VAT    17.7.4
Unincorporated association/body    6.3.2,
    18.2.7, 18.6
    holding property    18.6
    legal nature of    18.6
Unincorporated trust    6.3.2, 18.2.7, 18.5
    accounts    18.5.4
    advantages    18.5.4
    company limited by guarantee,
      becoming    18.5.1
    contracts    18.5.2
    criminal prosecution    18.5.2
    disadvantages    18.5.2, 18.5.3
    governance, structures for    19.3.1–
      19.3.3
    governing instrument    18.5.3

incorporation of trustees    18.5.1
    legal charge by    18.5.2
    liability of trustees/governors    18.5.2,
      18.5.3, 19.6
    retirement/new governor, effect of
      18.5.2
    suing/being sued    18.5.2
    tortious liability    18.5.2

Value added tax    17.7.4
    registration    17.7.4
Vicarious liability    11.6.1, 12.4.2(d)
    director, of    19.11.4
    governor, of    18.5.2
Visit
    out-of-school    8.3.5
    to school    7.6, 24.4
      'buying decision' based on    24.5.2
Visitor
    injury to    11.10.1, 11.10.2
    occupiers' liability    11.10.2

Waiting list    9.3
Wales    1.1.2, 1.3
Wardship    22.4.2
Waste disposal    21.3.14
Welfare of child    8.3.1, 8.3.2, 8.4.14,
      13.2.1, *see also* Bullying; Pastoral care
    disciplinary sanctions, and delegated
      responsibility    15.4.3
    professional judgment, matter of
      13.6.6
Westminster
    early days, in    1.1.1, 1.1.2, 1.2
Westonbirt    1.3
Winchester    1.1.1, 1.1.2, 2.1.3
    Great Rebellion    1.2
    legal and charitable status    6.3.2,
      17.3.7
    resources    2.2.1
Withdrawal of pupil    8.4.8, *see also*
      Notice
    deemed, for non-payment    9.8.7
    early in term, and fees    9.8.5
    required by school    16.3.4, 16.3.6
Woodard, N    1.2
Work, Fairness at, White Paper    21.3.7
Work experience    7.8.7, 21.3.8
Working Time Directive    21.3.7
World War I
    effect of    3.3.1

World War II
  effect of   3.3.3
  post-war years   4.1
Worship, *see* Religion

Youth court
  report of proceedings   22.9.4